ROCKDETECTOR

A-Z *of*

DEATH METAL

GARRY SHARPE-YOUNG

www.rockdetector.com

This edition published in Great Britain
in 2001 by Cherry Red Books Ltd.,
3a Long Island House
1-4 Warple Way
London W3 0RG

Reprinted 2004

All you need to know about the author:
Born: Münchengladbach 1964
Raised: On Judas Priest
Status: Decade of wedlock
Raising: Kerr, Krystan, Kjaric
Hair: By Vikernes

Artwork by Axis Europe Plc.
Printed and bound in Great Britain by
Biddles Ltd., King's Lynn, Norfolk
Cover Design by Jim Phelan at Wolf Graphics Tel: 020 8299 2342

Thanks: Iain McNay, Jim Phelan, Sarah Reed, Martin Wickler, Michael
Langbein and to Karl for proof reading.

ISBN 1–901447–35–9

Introduction

Death Metal

Put simply, Death Metal is the leviathan of Heavy Metal taken to its most mind-numbing extreme. During the 80's Thrash Metal had prompted Heavy Metal to take a leap into the unknown. With the floodgates open, even more adventurous souls would fulfill a desire to test the very horizons of Hard Rock.

Even though Death Metal bands operate on the very perimeters of the genre, the scope of musical variety is wide ranging. In general, the style relies on acts pursuing faster more aggressive patterns. Although this is apparent within the ferocity of the guitars and the almost insane pummelling of drums, it is the vocals that personify Death Metal.

Vocalists use their throats as tortured instruments to such an extent that very often the guttural growls, commonly known as 'deathgrunts'- their inception generally attributed to CELTIC FROST's Tom G. Warrior, are completely unintelligible. Over the decade, the vocal range too has varied to accommodate the inclusion of standard Metal 'clean' vocals, ambient whispers and at the opposite end of the spectrum raw animal soundscapes.

Grindcore is the bastard offshoot of Death Metal. It was NAPALM DEATH that lent credence to this burgeoning format, moulding extreme Metal with the harshest of Punk sensibilities. Grindcore acts often push the already frenetic mothership of Death Metal to unparalleled levels of ferocity. It is within the realms of Grindcore that songs are stripped down to mechanized blasts of unrelinquishing power lasting mere seconds, where vocals enter the realms of pure unadulterated rage and where drum machines take over from the limitations of the human body. Melody withers and dies at the merest mention of Grindcore. However, even Grindcore has its operating parameters and bands often tread the almost indivisible boundaries between Metal and Punk with Noisecore, Crustcore and Hardcore.

There are other offshoots such as Doom Death and Gothic Death resulting from the meeting of two disciplines. THERION take this into even more adventurous waters by infusing their albums with symphonic orchestration where strictly no instrument or influence is sacred.

What unites the various factions of Death Metal (and Black Metal) is one word - underground. It is a true minority of bands that achieve a degree of commercial and fiscal success allowing them to survive from their art alone.

The subject matter that feeds this beast is strangely fairly limited. At first the New Wave of Swedish Death Metal pursued the tried and tested formula of fantasy and mythology that had been the core of Metal from the outset. It did not take long for the music to match the content and soon torture, murder and historical extermination became the norm. The Liverpool band CARCASS would exploit the squirm factor of medical horrors, in the process unleashing legions of imitators. CARCASS have directly influenced literally hundreds of international acts intent on squeezing every horrific nuance out of the medical dictionaries with song titles bearing no relation to the actual music.

With surgical gore placed firmly on the menu the taboo denizens of serial murder, necrophilia and sexual psychopaths were ripe for the taking. There are many 'Goregrind' bands who trade exclusively in the perversity and outrage engendered by mass murder. Although pioneering groups such as CANNIBAL CORPSE, IMMOLATION, OBITUARY and MONSTROSITY would develop these fresh meat markets they would soon be outstripped by the hungry pack of international newcomers snapping at their heels.

Naturally much of this material is deemed so repulsive that records - very often split 7" singles - are deliberately extremely limited and rare to find. Goregrind bands will it seems plumb ever newer depths in their quest to outgross their competitors and shock the general public. Album and single covers are often designed solely to offend with the cadaver (whole or in part) in extreme states of physical distress being a staple of the genre. Not content with stretching musical credibility to the very limits, even the product format is tested to destruction, with bands cramming over 50 'songs' onto one side of a vinyl 7" single.

The other extreme on hand to Death Metal was the old age one of pornography. There is a whole gamut of bands operating in this sphere using all manners of sex in order to highlight their extreme nature. What is strikingly obvious about many of these acts, excluding pioneers such as A.C. and THE MEATSHITS who inject a wry irony into their work, is the almost infantile obsession with scatological themes. It is no surprise to find the Japanese entrenched within this operating area. Of course many bands have discovered that the combination of pathology, pornography and psychopathic perversity can hit harder still.

Satan naturally rears his head here. Although the 'Rockdetector A-Z of Black Metal' covers this area of Metal, some acts are included here too as Death Metal provides the perfect vehicle for such outpourings. Bands such as INCANTATION, DISSECTION, MORBID ANGEL and MARDUK straddle the divisions with ease. And, of course, where you find the Devil you will also find his opposite number. Yes, Christian Death Metal is alive and surprisingly well. Rather like life forms surviving in conditions where no life is scientifically thought to exist, bands such as MORTIFICATION and ULTIMATUM defy all the odds and prosper.

Industrial Death is also present with the prevalence of drum machines naturally leading inquiring minds into the fresh malevolence of electronica. The other focus, more prevalent upon the Grindcore borders, is social commentary as personified by AGATHOCLES and CRIPPLE BASTARDS.

Death Metal is also strengthened by its all encompassing spread across the globe. The traditional bastions of Europe and America are bolstered by a profusion of bands from South America, the Mediterranean, Asia, Australasia and Japan. Russia too fosters bands that sell vast quantities of records in their homeland. Also of interest is the classic 'British brain-drain' theory; since NAPALM DEATH and CARCASS kick-started the whole thing the UK has struggled as a minor league player in the Death Metal rankings ever since.

With the birth of Death Metal at the turn of the 90's the degree of ridicule poured upon its originators appeared ready to stifle any prospect of the genre prospering. Now with the millennium behind us the only question is just how extreme can Metal get?

Garry Sharpe-Young

ABHORRENCE
(BRAZIL)
Line-Up: Rangel Arroyo (vocals / bass), Marcello Marzari (bass), Fernando (drums)

Brazilian ultra-Speed Death Metal founded in 1997. ABHORRENCE arrived with the three track 1997 demo 'Ascension' which would later be pressed onto CD in America by the Wild Rags label. The band cut a further demo tape 'Triumph In Blasphemy' prior to signing to nFlorida's Evil Vengeance label for the album 'Evoking The Abomination'. Not only did the album benefit from sleeve artwork courtesy of MOTÖRHEAD artist Joe Petagno but the finished tapes were mastered by MORBID ANGEL man Erik Rutan.
ABHORRENCE also featured on the Relapse 2001 4 way split CD 'Brazilian Assault'. Original bass player Kleber Varnier would later make way for Marcello Marzari.

Singles/EPs:
Reborn To Vengeance / Communication With The Dead / Horde Of The Demons, Seraphic Decay (1998) ('Ascension' EP)

Albums:
EVOKING THE ABOMINATION, Evil Vengeance (1999)
Abattoir / Evoking The Abomination / Sacrificial Offerings / Hellish Annihilation / Storming Warfare / Abhorrer Existence / Reborn To Vengeance / Triumph in Blasphemy

ABHORRENT (AUSTRALIA)

Grindcore act infused with typically base Aussie humour. ABHORRENT's 'The Horror' album included a FILTHY CHRISTIANS cover version. One track on the album eschews vocals in favour of repeated burping!

Albums:
THE HORROR, Dissident (1998)
Santaz Slay / Wally / Underpants / Ultra Mong / Puddle / No 'n' In Funk / Prune Date Ferk / Majestic Sword / Rent A Cop / Love Song / Cool Dude From Beyond The Grave / Blues / Naughty / Filthy / Bastards / War Sux / Ambient

ABHORRENT (BRAZIL)
Line-Up: Robson Blake (vocals), Marcus

Vireoli (guitar), Hudson Andre (guitar), Leandro Soares (bass), Carlos Fibrian (drums)

Thrash-infused Death Metal act ABHORRENT was forged during 1988. However, this original inception of the band would collapse after issuing the 'Horrible Slaughter' demo.
ABHORRENT was reconvened in 1992 for a further session 'Blood On Your Lips'. With guitarist Marcus Vireoli handling bass the band cut album tracks in 1994. Bass player Leandro Soares would be inducted shortly after but these songs would take a full three years to be issued as the 'Rage' album. ABHORRENT did manage to put in a set of European dates to promote the album.
Another tape 'Live In Rage' arrived which included a version of SLAYER's 'Reign In Blood'.

Albums:
RAGE, (1997)
Intro / Let Me Live / Eternal Doubt / Blood On Your Lips / No Chance / Prelude Of The End / The Witch / One Step / Face Of Terror
CAUTION: STRONG IRRITANT, (2000)

ABHOTH (SWEDEN)
Line-Up: Anders Eckmann (vocals), Anfinn Skulevold (guitar), Jörgen Kristensen (guitar), Dag Nesbö (bass), Mats Blyckert (drums)

ABHOTH date back to 1989 when they went under the guise of MORBID SALVATION ARMY. The original line-up included vocalist Jörgen Bröms who departed in 1990 to join AFFLICTED.
It's worth noting that ABHOTH guitarist Jörgen Kristensen and drummer Mats Blyckert have also sessioned for SUFFER in their time.
Following the single release, bassist Dag Nesbö and Blyckert departed, making room for Claes Ramberg on bass and drummer Jens Klovegard.

Singles/EPs:
The Tide / Configuration, Corpse Grinder CGR007 (1993)

ABLAZE MY SORROW (SWEDEN)
Line-Up: Martin Qvist (vocals), Magnus Carlsson (guitar), Roger Johansson (guitar), Anders Brorsson (bass), Alex Bengtsson (drums)

ABLAZE MY SORROW debuted in 1993 with a line-up of vocalist Martin Qvist, guitarist Magnus Carlsson, bassist Anders Brorsson and drummer Fredrik Wenzel and soon issued a demo in early 1994 entitled 'For Bereavement We Cried'. However, Fredrik Wenzel departed in mid 1994 in favour of Alex Bengtsson.

Following recording of the debut album, 'If Emotions Still Burn', guitarist Roger Johansson was substituted by Dennis Linden.

Albums:
IF EMOTIONS STILL BURN, No Fashion NFR015CD (1996)
If Emotions Still Burn / The Rain That Falls / Rise Above The Storming Sea / Denial (The Way Of The Strong) / My Last Journey / As I Face The Eternity / My Revenge To Come
THE PLAGUE, No Fashion NFR026 (1998)
Dusk... / The Truth Is Sold / Into The Land Of Dreams / Mournful Serenade / The Return Of The Mighty Raven / I Will Be Your God / Plague Of Mine / As The Dove Falls Torn Apart / Suicide / ... Dawn

ABNEGATE (ITALY)

Milan's ABNEGATE toured Italy extensively, issuing demos prior to an inclusion on the compilation album 'Nightpieces II'. The band later toured as support to compatriots EXTREMA.

Albums:
INSANE SOULS, Abraxas AX 9406-2 (1995)
Intro - The Sewer / Sewer / Cold life / Crime / Death Without Dying / Christ Can Save Your Soul / Shadowed / Murky Dream / Mental Aggression / Land Of War / No Sleep 'Til Brooklyn

ABOMINANT (KY, USA)

Line-Up: Mike Barnes (vocals), Timmie Ball (guitar), Buck Weidman (guitar), Mike May (bass), Craig Netto (drums)

Founded in 1993 with the union of former EFFIGY members guitarist Buck Weidman and drummer Craig Netto together with erstwhile SARCOMA personnel guitarist Timmie Ball and bass player Mike May.

Songs for a proposed split CD with fellow Kentucky act CATACLYSM were laid down but were duly shelved when their supposed partners split. ABOMINANT issued their tracks as a demo tape regardless.

Weidman would break ranks to join the Air Force leaving ABOMINANT to soldier on as a trio. Before long CATACLYSM singer Mike Barnes was added to the ranks debuting on the late 1994 demo 'Never Truly Dead'. However, the band's second attempt at a commercially released outing was scuppered when label Arctic Circle Records collapsed after ABOMINANT had recorded tracks for a scheduled mini album.

Wild Rags Records signed the band to release this material with fresh songs for the 'Unspeakable Horrors' album.

Founder member Weidman would return to bolster the guitar sound but ABOMINANT once more suffered at the hands of their label when Wild Rags imploded. For the bands fourth album 'Ungodly' ABOMINANT cut a deal with Deathgasm Records.

'Ungodly', which included a version of SACRAFICE's 'Reanimation', featured guest vocals from ESTUARY OF CALAMITY vocalist Ash Thomas.

ABOMINANT included their version of METALLICA's 'Battery' to the tribute album 'Overload 2'.

Albums:
UNSPEAKABLE HORRORS, Wild Rags (1996)
Intentionally Accused / Corruption Morality / Calls From Beyond / Lost / The Ecstasy Of Sufferance / Abominant / Child Of The Sky / Age Of Chaos / Unspeakable Horrors
IN DARKNESS EMBRACE, Wild Rags (1998)
THE WAY AFTER, Wild Rags WRR117 (1999)
UNGODLY, Deathgasm (2000)

ABOMINATION (IL, USA)

Line-Up: Paul Speckmann (vocals / bass / guitar), Dean Chioles (guitar), Aaron Nickeas (drums)

ABOMINATION is another weapon in MASTER vocalist Paul Speckmann's arsenal of Death Metal projects.

Singles/EPs:
Split, Nuclear Blast (1990) (Split 7" single with MASTER)

Albums:
ABOMINATION, Nuclear Blast (1989)
The Choice / Murder, Rape, Pillage And Burn / Reformation / Redeem Deny / Possession / Suicidal Dreams / Life And Death / Victim Of The Future / Tunnel Of Damnation
TRAGEDY STRIKES, Nuclear Blast NB050 (1991)
Blood For Oil / They're Dead / Pull The Plug / Will They Bleed / Industrial Sickness / Soldier / Kill Or Be Killed / Oppression

ABORTED (POLAND)
Line-Up: Gurgloroth Sven (vocals), Niek (guitar), Christophe (guitar), Koen (bass), Frank (drums)

Death Metallers ABORTED, debuting with the demo 'The Necrotorous Chronicles', issued a split album with CHRIST DENIED in 2000 following this with their full length debut 'The Purity Of Perversion'.
The band, forged in 1995 and led by Gurgloroth Sven, also include drummer Steven, bassist Koen ("Bassturbations") and guitarist Niek ("bulging sick string mayhem"). A second guitarist Christophe augmented the band in 1997 and later Steven would relinquish the drum stool to Frank.

Albums:
ABORTED, Soulreaper (2000) (Split CD with CHRIST DENIED)
Eructations Of Carnal Artistry / Sea Of Cartilage / Symposium Of Semiology / Better Impaled Than Crucified / Castration In The Name Of God / The Uncreation
THE PURITY OF PERVERSION, Soulreaper (2000)
Intro / Act Of Supremacy / The Lament Configuration / The Sanctification Of Fornication / Organic Puzzle / Necro-Eroticism / Highway 1-35 / Gurgling Rotten Feces / Wrenched Carnal Ornaments

ABORTION (SLOVAKIA)

Albums:
MURDERED CULTURE, M.A.B. Records (1998)

ABORTUS (AUSTRALIA)

Albums:
JUDGE ME NOT, Battlegod Productions (1999)
Seperatism / Tortured / The Shit That Grits Your Teeth / Soul-Less / Judge Me Not / 2U 4U Fuck You / All That Was / Re-Pray

ABRAMELIN (AUSTRALIA)
Line-Up: Simon Dower (vocals), Mark Schilby (guitar), Tim Aldridge (guitar), Justin Wornes (bass), Ewan Harriott (drums)

Melbourne Death Metal unit initially formed under the title of ACHERON in 1988 by guitarist David Abbot. ACHERON issued the 1991 single 'Deprived Of Afterlife' on French label Corpsegrinder although Abbott departed shortly after together with drummer Jason Dutton. The band pulled in replacements Mark Schilby on guitar and BLOODUSTER drummer Ewan Harriott as the band changed titles to ABRAMELIN in order to avoid confusion with the American ACHERON.
A 1994 mini-album 'Transgression From Acheron' was followed by a full length album 'Abramelin', the latter including a cover version of DEAD CAN DANCE's 'Cantara'. The band travelled to Europe gaining exposure as support to NAPALM DEATH. In 1996 they were backed CATHEDRAL and PARADISE LOST on their Australian dates.
During recording of ABRAMELIN's 'Deadspeak' album during 1998 the band split acrimoniously. Vocalist Simon Dower and guitarist Tim Aldridge regrouped, pulling in DAMAGED drummer Matt Skitz for session work, and re-recorded the album from scratch for a 2000 release.

Albums:
TRANGRESSION FROM ACHERON, Thrust (1994)
Human Abattoir / Humble Abode / Dearly Beloved / Relish The Blood
ABRAMELIN, Thrust (1995)
Misfortune / Grave Ideals (Nekromaniak) / Spiritual Justice / Humble Abode / Stargazer: The Summoning / Stargazer: Stargazer II / Deprived Of Afterlife / Invocation / Cantar
DEADSPEAK, Shock (2000)
Pleasures / Your Casualty / Waste / Bleeding Hearts / The Germ Factory / Fresh Furnace / Plaque

ABSCESS (USA)

ABSCESS included AUTOPSY guitarist Chris Reifert in the ranks. By 2000 Reifert had created THE RAVENOUS band project with Killjoy of NECROPHAGIA and STORMTROOPERS OF DEATH bassist Dan Lilker.
Not to be confused with the contemporary German Industrial act.

Albums:
URINE JUNKIES, Relapse (1995)
Aching Meat / Urine Junkies / Crawled Up From The Sewar / 29th Lobotomy / Horny Hag / Depopulation / Zombification / Blacktooth Beast / The Scent Of Shit / Altar Toy / Suicide Fuck / Raw Sewage / Die Pig Die / Inbred Abomination / Unquenchable Thirst / Abscess / Bloodsucker / Anally Impaled
SEMINAL VAMPIRES AND MAGGOTMEN, Relapse RR 6945 (1996)
Naked Freak Show / Freak Fuck Fest (Naked Freak Show II: Orgy Of The Gaffed) / Patient Zero / Zombie Ward / Mud / Stiff And Ditched / Fatfire / I Don't Give A Fuck / Burn, Die And Fucking Fry / Global Doom / Removing The Leech / Pinworms / Gonna Mow You Down / Disgruntled / Tunnel Of Horrors / Worm Sty Infection / Dirty Little Brats / The Scent Of Shit
TORMENTED, Listenable POSH023 (2000)
Rusted Blood / Filth Chamber / Tormented / Madness And Parasites / Deathscape In Flames / Street Trash / Halo Of Disease / Scratching At The Coffin / Ratbag / Death Runs Red / Wormwind / From Bleeding Skies / Madhouse At The End Of The World

ABSOLUTE ZERO
(Sheboygan Falls, WI, USA)
Line-Up: Frank Rostkowski (vocals / drums), Teddy Rostkowski (guitar), Ben Klemme (bass)

ABSOLUTE ZERO, centred upon the Rostkowski siblings guitarist Teddy and drummer Frank, have issued two demo cassettes. The 'Martyrdom' outing sees Eric Brucker on vocals and Dave Schmidt on bass whilst 'Without Reason' has Brandon Bauer as singer and Jeff Warfield on bass.
Latterly ABSOLUTE ZERO trimmed to a trio with Ben Klemme on bass guitar and Francis Rostkowski assuming the lead vocal position.

ABSONENT CADENCE (CANADA)
Line-Up: Pierre April (vocals), Dominique Simard (guitar), Eric Boily (bass), Dominique Bilodeau (drums)

Albums:
INSIDE-OUT LIFE, (2000)
Dread The Unknown / Salle Justice / Destin / Faux Dieu / Emergence / Father Of Hate / My Enemy Friend / Mind Decadence / Among Them / Jour De Deliverance / Inside-Out Life / Genocide / Nocturnal Cycle / Degenere / Esperence

ABSORBED (HOLLAND)
Line-Up: Jim Klaarmond (vocals), Ferdy Dolserum (guitar), Dennis De Lange (guitar), Jeroen Pomper (bass), Michel Jonker (drums)

A Dutch group heavily inspired by the Swedish Death Metal sound. ABSORBED was founded by former INSOMNIA personnel - guitarist Ferdy Dolsersum and drummer Michel Jonkers, during 1997.

Albums:
SUNSET BLEEDING, Resuscitate RESUS 005 (2000)

ABSTAIN (USA)

An amalgam of Grind and Hardcore bolstered by politically charged commentary. ABSTAIN's 1997 outing 'Defy', which included a brace of DISRUPT cover versions 'Tortured In Entirety' and 'Religion Is A Fraud', came formatted as a 3" CD album.
The band would share a 1998 album 'Live Aboard The M.S. Stubnitz', released by the Australian In League Wit' Satan concern, with Sweden's ARSEDESTROYER. The band would feature on a string of split 7" singles in collusion with NASUM, UNHOLY GRAVE, DENAK and naturally industrious Belgians AGATHOCLES. The 1998 'Dead Generation' split single in union with Spain's DENAK on the Polish Dwie Strony Medalu label included a cover of the AGATHOCLES track 'Senseless Trip'.

Singles/EPs:
Religion Is War, Yellow Dog (1998)
(7" split single with NASUM)

Hate In The Head, (1998) (7" split single with UNHOLY GRAVE)
Self Infliction / The Feeding / Senseless Trip, Dwie Strony Medalu (1999) ('Dead Generation' 7" split single with DENAK)
Fuck Your Values, (1999) (7" split single with AGATHOCLES)

Albums:
DEFY, Relapse (1997)
My Generation / Superiority Complex / Discriminating Nation / Why / The Feeding / No Values / Pseudoscience / Choke / Circle Of Fools / Poetic Justice / Tortured In Entirety - Religion Is A Fraud / House Of Straw
LIVE ABOARD THE M.S. STUBNITZ, In League Wit' Satan (1998) (Split album with ARSEDESTROYER)
Superiority Complex / Mass Action / Discriminating Nation / Choke / My Generation / Our True Nature / No Values / Pseudoscience / Self Infliction / Why / Mediawhore / Burn Down The Mall / Terrorizer

ABSURD EXISTENCE (GERMANY)

Albums:
ANGELWINGS, Force (1995)

ABYSSOS (SWEDEN)
Line-Up: Rehn (vocals / guitar), Meidal (bass), Andreas Söderlund (drums)

ABYSSOS are a Sundsvall based vampiric Black Death Metal band. A demo in 1996 'Wherever Witches Might Fly' marked their arrival and secured a deal with the British Cacophonous label. They issued their debut album during 1997.

Albums:
TOGETHER WE SUMMON THE DARK, Cacophonous (1997)
We Hail Thy Entrance / Misty Autumn Dance / Banquet In The Dark - Black Friday / Lord Of The Sombre Reborn / In Fear They Left The World Unseen / As The Sky Turns Black Again - Love Eternal / Together We Summon The Dark / I've Watched The Moon Grow Old / Through The Gloom And Into The Fire
FHINSTHANIAN NIGHTBREED, Cacophonous NIHIL33 CD (1999)
Masquerade In The Flames / Finally I Kissed The Pale Horse / Where Angels Fear To Tread / She Only Flies At Night / Worthless For Sale? / Finsthanian Nightbreed / Queen Covered In Black / Wherever The Witches Might Fly /

Firebreathing Whore

A.C. (Boston, MA, USA)
Line-Up: Seth Putnam (vocals / guitar), Scott Hull (guitar), Tim Morse (drums)

Dubbed by many as the vilest band on the planet. A.C. (ANAL CUNT) was created by former EXECUTIONER man Seth Putnam in 1988 initially intended as a joke act designed to offend as many people as they could while playing their instruments as badly as possible for an intended life span of a month at the most. Such was the cult the act engendered A.C. are still at it over a decade later delivering a seemingly endless stream of strictly non P.C. abuse. Perversely the band, which has never employed a bass guitarist, has become a major attraction in Japan.
A.C.'s debut line-up comprised Putnam, BRATFACE guitarist Mike Mahan and drummer Tim Morse and as such delivered a hint of what was to come with the '47 Song Demo' tape. The '5643 Song EP' on Stridecore Records was limited to a mere 307 copies of various vinyl colours. Acknowledging the band's already established underground status a bootleg 7" split single with PATARENI was leaked onto the market. A.C. members would also surface on other groups recordings with the singer appearing on the SHIT SCUM 'Manson Is Jesus' 7" single as well as sessioning with POST MORTEM.
With this line-up the band toured Europe but split upon their return. A.C.'s debut full length CD 'Fast Boston H.C' was issued by Ecocentric Records in a plain card cover but confusingly would be reissued the same year retitled 'Greatest Hits Vol. 1' with the same catalogue number.
By 1991 Fred Ordonez was on guitar for an infamous split EP with THE MEATSHITS and a further shared effort with PSYCHO. Putnam would also add guest vocals to the track 'Group Pressure' on PSYCHO's 'Riches And Fame' 10" EP. By the following year John Kozik of TOETAG had taken the position for the 'Morbid Florist' EP.
Between 1993 and '94 A.C. operated with two guitarists with Kozik alongside a returning Ordonez. In this incarnation the band cut an irreverent live cover version of JUDAS PRIEST's 'Breaking The Law' for a 7" single and the album 'Everyone Should Be Killed', released in Europe with new sleeve artwork by British Extreme Metal aficionados Earache

Records. However Ordonez made a rapid exit midway through these recordings.

A.C. garnered further media exposure in 1995 by offering an Oi! Version of the BEE GEES Disco hit 'Stayin' Alive'. This outing saw Paul Kraynak as Kozik's guitar partner.

Mainstream act PANTERA were by now open fans of A.C.'s and it came as no surprise that Putnam was credited with backing vocals on their 'Great Southern Trendkill' opus. A.C. undertook their only proper national tour to date in 1996 with Deathsters INCANTATION. Putnam honoured the event with a track 'Kyle From Incantation Has A Moustache' to which Kyle Severn himself graciously contributed drums. The band by now was down to a trio of Putnam, Morse and guitarist Scott Hull, with Hull also operating in AGORAPHOBIC NOSEBLEED, PIG DESTROYER and JAPANESE COMEDY TORTURE HOUR. The 1998 acoustic 'Picnic Of Love' album was reportedly recorded for a miserly $100.

In true spoofing style Putnam and Martin released two supposedly 'Black Metal' demos credited to IMPALED NORTHERN MOON FOREST. These recordings would later see an official release as a 7" single on M.T.S. Records.

The band comprised of Putnam, guitarist Josh Martin and drummer Nate Lineham for 1999's 'It Just Gets Worse'. PANTERA's Phil Anselmo and Choke of SLAPSHOT also guested on the record. In typical fashion the album ran into trouble before its release with a planned song 'Conor Clapton Committed Suicide Because His Father Sucks' provoking the expected outrage. The song had its title changed for the record. German distributors also rejected the album due to the song 'Hitler Was A Sensitive Man'. Overall A.C. confronted the expected maturity process by delivering a set of songs more extreme than anything they had previously delivered.

By 1999 John Gillis had taken the drum stool as A.C. issued a shared split live album with INSULT. Former drummer Tim Morse later created THE PRETTY FLOWERS and MORSE CODE.

Singles/EPs:
88 Song EP, Wicked Sick (1989) (7" single)
We'll Just Have To, Total Noise TNT 45-05 (1989) (split 7" single with SEVEN MINUTES OF NAUSEA)
5643 Song EP, Stridecore (1989) (7" single)
Another EP, Total Noise TNT 10 (1991) (7" single)
Split, Wicked Sick 4 (1991) (Split 7" single with THE MEATSHITS)
Split, Axction ACT 14 (1991) (Split 7" with PSYCHO)
Unplugged EP, Psychomania 002 (1991) (7" single)
Live EP, Psychomania 003 (1991) (7" single)
Some Songs / Song No. 5 / Chump Change / Slow Song From Split 7" / Unbelievable / Siege / Greatful Dead / I Don't Wanna Dance / Even More Songs / Radio Hit / Some More Songs / Morrisey / Song No. 6 / Guy Lombardo, Relapse RR023 (1993) (7" 'Morbid Florist' EP)
Breaking The Law, Wicked Sick (1993) (7" single)
Stayin' Alive (Oi Version), Earache (1995) (7" single)
In These Black Days, Hydrahead HH666-12 (1997) (Split EP with EYEHATEGOD)
88 Song EP, Fudgeworthy FUDGE 17 (1997)
Split, MTS MTS009 (2000) (Split EP with RAUNCHOUS BROTHERS)

Albums:
GREATEST HITS VOLUME ONE, Ecocentric ER 104CD (1991)
EVERYONE SHOULD BE KILLED, Earache MOSH 101CD (1993)
Some Songs / Some More Songs / Blur Including New HC Song / Even More Songs / Tim / Judge / Spin Cycle / Song / Pavarotti / Unbelievable / Music Sucks / Newest HC Song / Chiff On And Chips / Guy Smiley / Seth / I'm Not Allowed To Like AC Anymore / EX A Blur / GMOTR / I'm Wicked Underground / Blur Including G / Shut Up Mike / Abomination Of Unnecessarily Augmented... / Radio Hit / Loser / When I Think Of The True Punk Rock Bands / Eddy Grant / MTV Is My Source For New Music / Song Titles Are Fucking Stupid / Having To Make Up Song Titles Sucks / Well You Know, Mean Gene / Song / Iron Funeral / Chapel Of Gristle / Hellbent For Leathermen / Alcoholic / Chump Change / Slow Song For Split 7" / Des Bink's Hairstyle / Newset H.C. Song / Greatful Dead / Aging Disgracefully / Brutally Morbid Axe Of Satan / Surfer / You Must Be Wicked Underground If You Own This / Choke Edge / Otis Sistrunk / Russty Knoife / Fred Bash / Guess Which Ten Of These Are Actual Song

6

Titles / Our Band Is Wicked Sick (We Have Flu) / Guy Le Fleur / Song / Empire Sandwich Shop / Morrisey / Selling Out By Having Song Titles / Grindcore Is Very Terrifying / Song / Guy Lombardo

OLD STUFF PART TWO, Devour DEVOUR4 (1994)

TOP 40 HITS, Earache MOSH 129CD (1995)

Some Hits / Some More Hits / Pepe, The Gay Waiter / Even More Hits / MJC / Flower Shop Guy / Living Colour Is My Favourite Black Metal Band / Lenny's In My Neighborhood / Stayin' Alive (Oil Version) / Benchpressing The effects Of Kevin Sharp's Vocals / Josue / Delicious Face Style / No 19 To Go / Stealing Seth's Idea - The New Book By Jon Chang / Morbid Dead Guy / Believe In The King / Don't Call Japanese Hardcore Japcore / Shut Up Mike Part 2 / Hey, Aren't You Gary Spivey? / Breastfeeding J.M.J. / Bullock's Toenail Collection / Foreplay With A Tree Shredder / 2 Down 5 To Go / I Liked Earache Better When Dig Answered The Phone / Brain Dead / Newest AC Song No 3 / The Sultry Ways Of Steve Berger / Escape (The Pina Colada Song) / Lives Ruined By Music / Still A Freshman After All These Years / I'm Still Standing / Art Fag / John / Newest AC Song / Song No 9 (Instrumental) / Cleft Palate / Theme From The A Team / Old Lady Across The Hall With No Life / Shut Up Paul / Lazy Eye (Once A Hank, Always A Hank) / American Woman

40 MORE REASONS TO HATE US, Earache MOSH 149 CD (1996)

Face It, You're A Metal Band / Punching Joe Bonni's Face In / Kill Women / Steroids Guy / Everyone In Allston Should Be Killed / I Noticed That You're Gay / Dead, Gay And Dropped / You Look Divorced / I Hope You Get Deported / Mike Mahan Has Gingivitis / Trapped / You're A Fucking Cunt / Phyllis Is An Old Annoying Cunt / Al Stanku Is Always On The Phone With His Bookie / Bill Scott's Dumb / Harvey Korman Is Gay / You Fucking Freak / Theme From Three's Company / Jeanine Jism Is A Freak / Everyone In Anal Cunt Is Dumb / I Just Saw The Gayest Guy On Earth / Johnny Violent Getting His Ass Kicked By Morrisey / Metamorphosis / I'm Sick Of You / Howard Wulkan's Bald / You're A Trendy Fucking Pussy / Tom Arnold / I Got Athlete's Foot Showering At Mike's / Big Pants, Big Loser / Marc Payson Is A Drunk / Your Family Is Dumb / Furnace /

You're Dumb / Van Full Of Retards / Deche Charge Are A Bunch Of Fucking Losers / Everyone In The Underground Music Scene Is Stupid / Dumb, Fat & Gross / I'm Not Stubborn / Mike Mahan's Sty / 02657 / Gloves Of Metal (Duet With Phillip Anselmo) / Bonus Track

I LIKE IT WHEN YOU DIE, Earache MOSH 169 (1997)

Jack Kevorkian Is Cool / Valujet / You've Got No Friends / You Keep A Diary / You Own A Store / You Got Date Raped / Recycling Is Gay / You're A Cop / You Can't Shut Up / You've Got Cancer / We Just Disagree / Hungry Hungry Hippos / You Are An Interior Decorator / Pottery's Gay / Rich Goyette Is Gay / Branscombe Richmond / You Live In Allston / You Are A Food Critic / Just The Two Of Us / Your Band's In The Cut Out Bin / You're Gay / You Look Adopted / Your Cousin Is George Lynch / You Have Goals / You Drive An IROC / You Play On A Softball Team / Because You're Old / You Sell Cologne / Being A Cobbler Is Dumb / You Live In A Houseboat / Richard Butler / 311 Sucks / Your Kid Is Deformed / You Are An Orphan / You're Old (Fuck You) / You Go To Art School / Your Best Friend Is You / You're In A Coma / Windchimes Are Gay / No We Don't Want To Do A Split 7" With Your Stupid Fucking Band / Rene Auberjonois / The Internet Is Gay / Ha Ha Your Wife Left You / Hootie And The Blowfish / You Went To See Dishwalla And Everclear (You're Gay) / Dropping Drop Dead In McDonalds / Technology's Gay / Your Favourite Band Is Supertramp / I'm In Anal Cunt / You (Fill In The Blank) / Kyle From Incantation Has A Moustache / Bonus Track No. 3

PICNIC OF LOVE, Off The Records 002 (1998)

Picnic Of Love / Greed Is Something We Don't Need / I Wanna Grow Old With You / I'd Love To Have Your Daughter's Hand In Marriage / I Couldn't Afford A Present So I Wrote You This Song Instead / Waterfall Wishes / I'm Not That Kind Of Boy / Saving Ourselves For Marriage / I Respect Your Feelings As A Woman And A Human Being / In My Heart There's A Star Named After You / My Woman, My Lover, My Friend

IT JUST GETS WORSE, Earache MOSH 195 (1999)

I Became A Rape Counsellor So I Could Tell Victims They Asked For It / Easy E Got A.I.D.S. From F. Mercury / I Like Drugs And Child Abuse / Laughing While Lennard Peltier Gets Raped In Prison / I

Convinced You To Beat Your Wife On A Daily Basis / I Sent Concentration Camp Footage To America's Funniest Home Videos / Rancid Sucks (And The Clash Sucked Too) / I Paid J. Howell To Rape You / I Pushed Your Wife In Front Of The Subway / Extreme Noise Terror Are Afraid Of Us / You Rollerblading Faggot / I Sent A Thank You Card To The Guy Who Raped You / I Lit Your Baby On Fire / Body By Auschwitz / I Intentionally Ran Over Your Dog / Sweatshops Are Cool / Women: Nature's Punching Bag / I Snuck A Retard Into A Sperm Bank / Your Kid Committed Suicide Because You Suck / I Ate Your Horse / Hitler Was A Sensitive Man / You Robbed A Sperm Bank Because You're A Cum Guzzling Fag / I Made Your Kid Get A.I.D.S. So You Could Watch It Die / I Fucked Your Wife / Into The Oven / I Gave NAMBLA Pictures Of Your Kid / The Only Reason Men Talk To You Is Because They Want To Get Laid, You Stupid / I Made Fun Of You Because Your Kid Just Died / Domestic Violence Is Really, Really, Really Funny / Dictators Are Cool / Dead Beat Dads Are Cool / I'm Really Excited About The Upcoming David Buskin Concert / Being Ignorant Is Awesome / You're Pregnant, So I Kicked You In The Stomach / Chris Barnes Is A Pussy / Tim Is Gay / BT-AC / I Sold Your Dog To A Chinese Restaurant / I Got An Office Job For The Sole Purpose Of Sexually Harassing Women
LIVE N.Y.C., Wicked Sick 5 (1999) (Split album with INSULT)
Some Songs / Slow Song From Split 7" / Newest HC Song No. 4 / Newset HC Song No. 3 / Some More Songs / Foreplay With A Tree Shredder / Pepe The Gay Waiter / Even More Songs / Don't Call Japanese Hardcore Japcore / G.M.O.T.R. / Flower Shop Guy / Theme From The A Team / Radio Hit / Delicious Face Style / Chump Change / Stayin' Alive / Kill Women / Tom Arnold / Escape (The Pina Colada Song) / Lenny's In The Neighborhood / M.J.C / I'm Still Standing / Art Fag / Guy Lombardo
THE EARLY YEARS 1988-1991, NG Records 751047-2 (2000)

A CANOROUS QUINTET
(SWEDEN)
Line-Up: Marten Hansen (vocals), Linus Nibrant (guitar), Lei Pignon (guitar), Jesper Löfgren (bass), Fredrik Andersson (drums)
Formed in 1991 A CANOROUS

QUINTET, a brutal Death / Black Metal act, released their 'The Time Of Autumn' demo having undergone a multitude of line-up changes up to that point.
Guitarist Leo Pignon later forged a similar Black Metal outfit NIDEN DIV. 187 with members of DAWN and THY PRIMORDIAL releasing two albums 'Towards Judgement' and 'Impergium' on Necropolis Records. Drummer Fredrik Andersson is better known for his role in premier Swedish Black Metal band MARDUK. Andersson also boasts credits with AMON AMARTH and ALLEGIANCE. Vocalist Morten Hansen guested in OCTOBER TIDE's 1999 album 'Grey Dawn'.

Singles/EPs:
Through Endless Illusions / The Joy Of Sorrow / When Happiness Dies / Strangeland, Chaos CD 02 (1994) ('As Tears' EP)

Albums:
SILENCE OF THE WORLD BEYOND, No Fashion NFR 019 (1996)
Silence Of The World Beyond / Naked With Open Eyes / Spellbound / The Orchid's Sleep / The Black Spiral / The Last Journey / In The Twilight Of Fear / Burning, Emotionless / Dream Reality
THE ONLY PURE HATE, No Fashion NFR028 (1998)
Selfdeceiver (The Purest Of Hate) / Embryo Of Lies / Red / The Void / Everbleed / The Complete Emptiness / Retaliation / Realm Of Rain / The Storm / Land Of The Lost

ACCELERATOR (SWITZERLAND)
Line-Up: E. Hofer (guitar), F. Zaugg (guitar), A. Krebs (drums)

ACCELERATOR's 1997 debut album 'The Prophecy' saw guest vocals from Patrick Schaad with female vocals from Esther Hofer. The band had previously made their mark with the 1995 demo session 'The Dark Side'

Albums:
THE PROPHECY, (1997)
The Prophecy / Trapped In Insanity / Wasted / Gone / The End Of Your Time / Loneliness / The Sparrow / Final Journey / In Eternal Bliss

ACCESSORY (GERMANY)
Line-Up: Elmar Keineke (vocals), Matthias Eigner (guitar), Mark

8

Wolzenburg (guitar), Fritz Rogge (bass), Michael Wintzen (drums)

Formed at the close of the 80s amongst a welter of other Death Metal acts, ACCESSORY issued a demo in 1991 and then released the 'Within Your Mind' album in 1994.
The group has since split, with some band members forming COLOUR TRIP.

Albums:
WITHIN YOUR MIND, Toxo TCA/WVR 084-57182 (1994)
Drowning In Tears / Deceptions End / Indifference / Rational Decline / The Fall Of The Wise / Long Forgotten Place / Kissing The Dead / Within Your Mind

ACCIDENTAL SUICIDE (WI, USA)

Albums:
DECEASED, Deaf (1993)
Misery Hunt / The Life I Hate / Morbid Indulgence / Flesh Parade / Unknown / Method Of Murder / Agony Of Rebirth / Homicidal Entrail / My Dangling Corpse / To Eat The Heart

ACCURACY (GERMANY)
Line-Up: Marco B. (vocals / bass), Jacek Dworok (guitar), Roland M. (guitar), Alex Penthin (drums)

A Hardcore Metal band from Munich, the group has recorded a great deal of demo material since its inception and has also toured with the likes of ATROCITY, HEADHUNTER and CHANNEL ZERO.
The band's 1995 EP was produced by Thomas Skogsberg.

Singles/EPs:
Call Us Stupid / Get Fucked / Dude!! / Living Epidemic, Polly POLLY 002-1 (1995)

Albums:
ABSOLUT 100%, Cream 001 (1996)
You Don't Know How It Is / Fallen Deep / Absolut 100% / No Plan At All / Me And Myself / Share Your Pain / Question Of Confidence / Freak Of Confidence / Compendres / Pawn-11-That Ain't Right

ACCURSED (WI, USA)

Albums:
MEDITATIONS AMONG THE TOMBS, Visceral Displeased (1995)
ACELDAMA (MI, USA)

Line-Up: Fred Poole (vocals / bass / keyboards), Amjed Syed (guitar), Doug Julian (drums)

Albums:
BLOOD, Mother Noize (199-)
Blood / Hate / Rapture / Devilworks / Carry Your Cross / Ra / Obey / SYLS / Sin To The Soul / Wings Of Pain / Eternal

ACHERON (AUSTRALIA)
Line-Up: Simon Dower (vocals), David Abbott (guitar), Tim Aldridge (guitar), Justin Wornes (bass), Jason Dutton (drums)

Melbourne Death Metal act forged in 1988 by guitarist David Abbott. The band issued a single in 1991 on French label Corpsegrinder Records prior to Abbott and drummer Jason Dutton leaving.
Pulling in substitute guitarist Mark Schilby and drummer Ewan Harriott the band switched titles to ABRAMELIN in order to avoid confusion with the American ACHERON.
ABRAMELIN bowed in with 1994's 'Transgression From Acheron' mini album.

Singles/EPs:
Deprived Of Afterlife / Death Of Millions, Corpsegrinder (1991)

ACHERON (Chicago, IL, USA)
Line-Up: Wade Laszlos (vocals / guitar), Mark Belliel (bass), Tom Croxton (drums)

Founded in 1986. ACHERON frontman Wade Laszlo would decamp in 1991 following the debut 'Prophecies Unholy' to create THE UNHOLY. Soon ACHERON personnel bassist Mark Belliel and drummer Tom Croxton would jump ship to THE UNHOLY.
Whilst remaining loyal to THE UNHOLY Croxton joined IMPALER in 1998 and has a side project KREPITUS.

Albums:
PROPHECIES UNHOLY, (1990)
THE PAIN DOMINION, (199-)

ACHERON (Tampa, FL, USA)
Line-Up: Vincent Crowley (vocals / guitar), Michael Estes (guitar), Reverend Peter Gilmore (keyboards), Tony Laureano (drums)

Death Metal musically but with clear

Satanic overtones in the lyrics ACHERON are perhaps one of the more genuine of the American exponents of Black Metal. Mentor and frontman Vincent Crowley is the founder of the irreligious underground movement 'Order of the evil eye' whilst renowned Church of Satan priest Reverend Peter Gilmore adds keyboards and contributes lyrically.

Besides their collective musical endeavours ACHERON have made waves in other media forms. One notable event had the band in a televised debate with Christian evangelist Bob Larson. In front of the TV cameras and a congregation of enraged Christians Crowley proceeded not only to debate his point of view but as a finale ripped a bible into shreds showering the pages over the stunned audience. Clearly recognizing valuable publicity Larson invited Crowley back for a series of video discussion forums.

ACHERON, convened in 1988, marked their arrival with the live 1989 demo tape 'Messe Noir'. These recordings would later see a 1995 release on 7" single format by Reaper Records limited suitably to 666 copies. The band's debut album 'Rites Of The Black Mass' swiftly became engendered into underground folklore featuring as it does genuine black mass invocations. Not surprisingly the content of the record provoked an extreme reaction and Crowley was invited onto national television to discuss his views on the 'Entertainment Tonight' show.

ACHERON's next album 'Satanic Victory' was released on Lethal Records although the band were public in their dislike of the finished product. So averse were they to the finished album ACHERON would re-release the record with extra tracks, new packaging and previously unincluded narratives on the Metal Merchant label.

Ex-MORBID ANGEL, INCUBUS and NOCTURNUS drummer Mike Browning has also appeared with ACHERON on their 'Hail Victory' album alongside Crowley and guitarists Tony Blakk and Vincent Breeding.

Ex-ACHERON guitarist Pete Slate would found the Black Death act EQUINOX, later drafting another ACHERON veteran Tony Blakk.

The B side to the 1998 ACHERON single 'Necromanteion Communion' featured a cover version of BATHORY's 'Raise The Dead'.

Guitarist Michael Estes busied himself with a side project act BURNING INSIDE assembled by renowned ICED EARTH, DEMONS & WIZARDS, DEATH and CONTROL DENIED drummer Richard Christy and BLACK WITCHERY guitarist Steve Childers.

Drummer Tony Laureano sessioned for AURORA BOREALIS and MALEVOLENT CREATION. By 2000 he was a member of Dutch act GOD DETHRONED. Another former member, keyboard player Adina Blaze, would join LILITU.

Crowley created WOLFEN SOCIETY with DARK FUNERAL guitarist Lord Ahriman and Jeff Gruslin of VITAL REMAINS in 2000.

Singles/EPs:
Alla Xul / One With Darkness, Gutted (1992) (7" single)
Messe Noir, Reaper (1995) (7" single)
Necromanteion Communion / Raise The Dead, (1998) (7" single)

Albums:
RITES OF THE BLACK MASS, Turbo 007 (1992)
Intro / Prayer Of Hell / Intro / Unholy Praises / Intro / Cursed Nazarene / Intro / The Enochian Key / Intro/ Let Us Depart / Intro / To Thee We Confess/ Intro / Thou Art Lord / Intro / Ave Satanas / Intro / Summoning The Master / Intro / One With Darkness
SATANIC VICTORY, Lethal (1993)
Unholy Praises / Seven Deadly Sins / Satanic Erotica / Prayer Of Hell / 666 / God Is Dead
HAIL VICTORY, Metal Merchant (1994)
Unholy Praises / Seven Deadly Sins / Satanic Erotica / Prayer Of Hell / 666 / God Is Dead / Alla Xul / One With Darkness
LEX TALIONIS, Turbo (1994)
Legions Of Hatred / Enter Thy Coven / Slaughterisation For Satan / Voices Within / Purification Day / Inner Beasts / The Entity / I.N.R.I. (False Prophet) / Lex Talionis March (outro)
ANTI GOD - ANTI CHRIST, Moribund (1997)
Fuck The Ways Of Christ / Shemhamforash (The Ultimate Blasphemy) / Blessed By Damnation / Baptism For Devlyn Alexandra / Total War
LEX TALIONIS - SATANIC VICTORY, Blackened BLACK006CD (1997)
Legions Of Hatred / Enter Thy Coven / Slaughterisation For Satan / Voices Within / Purification Day / Inner Beasts / The Entity / I.N.R.I. (False Prophet) / Lex

Talionis March (outro) / Unholy Praises / Seven Deadly Sins / Satanic Erotica / Prayer Of Hell / 666 / God Is Dead
THOSE WHO HAVE RISEN, Full Moon (1998)

ACID BATH (Louisiana, USA)
Line-Up: Dax Riggs (vocals), Mike Sanchez (guitar), Sammy Duet (guitar), Audrey Petrie (bass), Jimmy Kyle (drums)

ACID BATH's debut album, graced with sleeve artwork entitled 'Skull Clown' from infamous mass murderer John Wayne Gacy, was produced by DIRTY ROTTEN IMBECILES guitarist Spike Cassidy.
Touring America to promote the album ACID BATH guested for CANNIBAL CORPSE and Swedes ENTOMBED.
The 'Edits' mini album is a collection of songs from the second album re-mixed by Cassidy. 'Paegan Terrorist Tactics' once more featured controversial artwork with the painting 'For He Is Raised' executed by the renowned "Suicide assistance" Dr. Jack Kevorkian.
The band suffered a devastating blow in January 1997 when bassist Audrie Pitrie, together with his parents, were killed by a drunk driver.
Vocalist Dax Riggs and guitarist Mike Sanchez founded AGENTS OF OBLIVION. Guitarist Sammy Duet, also a member of heavyweights CROWBAR, forged GOATWHORE in alliance with SOILENT GREEN frontman Ben Falgout II.

Albums:
WHEN THE KITE STRING POPS, Rotten 2095-2 (1994)
The Blue / Tranquilized / Cheap Vodka / Finger Paintings Of The Insane / Jezebel / Scream Of The Butterfly / Dr. Seuss Is Dead / Dope Fiend / Toubabo Koomi / God Machine / The Mortician's Flame / What Color Is Death / The Bones Of Baby Dolls / Cossie Eats Cockroaches
EDITS, Rotten Records (1995)
Venus Blue (with Shit) / Diäb Soulé / Near Death Sensation / Venus Blue (With No Shit) / Bleed Me An Ocean / Dead Girl / Paegan Love Song / New Corpse / Near Death Sensation
PAEGAN TERRORIST TACTICS, Rotten (1996)
Paegan Love Song / Bleed Me An Ocean / Graveflower / Diäb Soulé / Locust Spawning / Old Skin / Near Death Sensation / Venus Blue / 13

Fingers / New Corpse / Dead Girl / The Beautiful / Downgrade

ACID DEATH (GREECE)

An extreme Greek Black / Death Metal band with one album release to their credit.

Singles/EPs:
Apathy Murders Hope, Molonlave Records (1995)

Albums:
RANDOM'S MANIFEST, Black Lotus BLRCD 018 (2000)
PIECES OF MANKIND, (2001)
Lost / While The End Is Coming / Reappearing Freedom / Our Shadows / Frozen Heart / My Destination / Liquid Heaven / Realizing / A-I / The Mirror On The Top Of The World

ACOUSTIC TORMENT (GERMANY)
Line-Up: Sascha Hornberger (vocals / bass), Christian Urff (guitar), Tobias Roller (drums)

Albums:
MY HOPE IS IN YOU, Acoustic Torment (1999)
Intro / Sick World / The First Commandment / Environmental Disaster / Atomic Threat / Total Global Annihilation And… / Indifferent Humanity / My Hope Is In You / Praise The Lord

ACROHOLIA (YUGOSLAVIA)

Singles/EPs:
Split, Abnormal Beer Terrorism (1997) (7" split single with INTESTINAL DISEASE)

ACROSTICHON (HOLLAND)
Line-Up: Corinne (vocals / bass), Richard (guitar), Jos (guitar), Serge (drums)

Formed in 1989 by the trio of Corinne, Richard and Jos, this Dutch Black Metal outfit soon added drummer Serge to the cause and by the end of 1990 could be found opening for CARCASS, followed by gigs with MORBID ANGEL, DEATH and SODOM.
The American independent label Seraphic Decay signed the quartet, although the group's debut album was produced by Colin Richardson against their will.

Singles/EPs:
Lost Remembrance,
Seraphic Decay (1991) (7" single)

Albums:
ENGRAVED IN BLACK, Modern
Primitive PRIM2CD (1993)
Immolation Of The Agnostic / Walker Of
Worlds / Dehumanized / Mentally
Deficient / Lost Remembrance / Zombies
/ Havoc / Relics / Engraved In Black
SENTENCED, (1995)

ADRAMELCH (FINLAND)
Line-Up: Jarkko Rantanen (vocals),
Jani Aho (guitar), Mikko Aarnio (bass),
Seppo Taatila (drums)

Formed by Jani Aho (bass) Jusi Tainio
(drums) and Jarkko Rantanen (vocals /
guitar) in 1991, ADRAMELCH sought out
a vocalist and second guitarist to join the
founding trio and came up with Tuomas
Ala-Nissila and Erik Parviainen
respectively, Rantanen switching to
drums after Tainio departed.
The band recorded the 'Grip Of
Darkness' demo (featuring new bassist
Mikko Aarnio) that led to a deal with the
French Adipocere label.
Following the release of the 'Spring Of
Recovery' single and a show with
DEMILICH, BEHERIT and CRYPT OF
KERBEROS in 1993, Seppo Taatila (ex-
DEMIGOD) joined and contributed to the
recording of 'The Fall' demo. The band
then featured on a compilation released
by the Spanish label Repulse with the
track 'Heroes In Godly Blaze'.
The liaison with the Spaniards led to a
two album deal with Repulse, the first
fruits of which was the commercial
release on CD of 'The Fall' tape.
ADRAMELCH were to lose bassist Aarnio
after the 'Psychotasia' album and also
added the ex-vocalist of DEMIGOD
towards the end of 1996.

Singles/EPs:
Spring Of Recovery, Adipocere (1993)

Albums:
THE FALL,
Repulse RPS 006 MCD (1995)
As The Gods Succumbed / Heroes In
Godly Blaze / Seance Of Shamans / The
Fall Of Tiamat
PSYCHOTASIA, Repulse RPS 015 CD
(1996)
Heroes In Godly Blaze / Psychotasia /
Seance Of Shamans / The Book Of The

Worm / Thoth (Lord Of Holy Words) /
Mythic Descendant / As The Gods
Succumbed / Across The Gray Waters
PURE BLACK DOOM, Severe (2000)

AEON (CROATIA)
Line-Up: Dario Kroznjak (vocals / bass),
Paulo Gavocanov (guitar), Sinisâ Bival
(keyboards), Alexander Puzar (drums)

Initially entitled DISSECTION upon their
formation in 1989. Early on the band,
comprising of vocalist / bassist Dario
Kroznjak, drummer Alexander Puzar and
guitarists Sasa Ristic and Paulo
Gavocanov, performed mainly covers.
Hearing of the high profile Swedish
DISSECTION the band retitled itself
AEON but not before Ristic had quit to
undertake his national military service.
The band plugged the gap with keyboard
player Sinisâ Bival.
The 1995 demo 'Clean Hand Of An
Eternal God' was issued in 1995 followed
by the 1996 effort 'Ephemereal'.

AFFLICTED (SWEDEN)
Line-Up: Joakim Broms (vocals), Jesper
Thorsson (guitar), Joacim Carlsson
(guitar), Fredrik Ling (bass),
Yasin Hillborg (drums)

Previously known as AFFLICTED
CONVULSION and launched in 1988 by
ex-DEFIANCE guitarist Jesper Thorsson,
his guitar partner Joacim Carlsson
previously having been with
DISMEMBER. AFFLICTED released the
first demo in 1990, titled 'Beyond
Redemption'.
The decision to drop the word
'Convulsion' from the band name was
taken once vocalist Joakim Broms had
joined. Further demos followed in 1991
entitled 'The Odious Reflection' and
'Wanderland', prior to the band's first
single ('Viewing The Obscene') on Thrash
Records.
The band suffered a change in
membership when bassist Fredrik Ling
was ousted in favour of Phillip Von
Segebaden following the 'Astray' single in
1992.
During 1993 AFFLICTED recorded the
track 'Seven Gates Of Hell' for the
VENOM tribute album 'Promoters Of The
Third World War' and bass for these
sessions was handled by Mikael Lindevall
of PROBOSCIS.
The 1995 album 'Dawn Of Glory'
witnessed a radical shift in style as Broms

quit to join Deathsters ABHOTH and in came vocalist Michael Van De Graaf. Joacim Carlsson left after the second album's release to join PROBOSCIS then the Roadrunner signed FACEDOWN.

Despite the changes in roster, AFFLICTED have still been able to tour Scandinavia consistently, including shows with ENTOMBED, THERION and DISMEMBER.

Von Segebaden issued the first album from his side project band DEFENDER in 1999 titled 'They Came Over The High Pass'.

Singles/EPs:
Ingrained, Thrash (1991)
Viewing The Obscene / The Empty Word, Thrash THR009 (1991)
Astray / Spirit Spectrum, Relapse 019 (1992)
Rising To The Sun / Ivory Tower, Nuclear Blast ST 45 NB063 (1992)

Albums:
PRODIGAL SUN, Nuclear Blast 77-140032 (1992)
Prodigal Sun / Harbouring The Soul / In Years To Come / Tidings From The Blue Sphere / The Empty Word / Astray / Rising Into The Sun / Spirit Spectrum / The Doomwatcher's Prediction / Consumed In Flames / Ivory Tower
DAWN OF GLORY, Massacre MASS CD055 (1995)
Son Of Earth / Dawn Of Glory / The Oracle / Last Incarnation / Raging Into Battle / Scattered / I Am Vengeance / Cross My Heart / Niflheim

AFTERDEATH (PORTUGAL)

Albums:
BACK WORDS, Guardians Of Metal (1996)

AFTERLIFE (USA)

Albums:
SURREALITY, Grind Core (1993)
Surreality / Eve Of Eclipse / Devine Enlightenment / Dreading The Marrow / Embrace / Shell Of A Being / Dead Lights Glare

AGATHOCLES (BELGIUM)
Line-Up: Matty A.G. Dupont (vocals / guitar), Steve (vocals / guitar), Jan A.G. Frederickx (vocals / bass), Burt A.G. Beyens (drums)

Belgian Grindcore act AGATHOCLES evolved out of the Punk scene in the early 80's. At first a loose collective, AGATHOCLES as a fully fledged band was created in around 1985. They have built a reputation as undisputed leaders of the split 7" single phenomenon.

The self-titled 'Mince-Core' outfit have issued an exhaustive roster of singles, many split efforts with other bands and albums including a split album with Colombians AVERNO in 1995. This is part of a continuing trend as AGATHOCLES have shared vinyl and CD space with the likes of NYCTOPHOBIC, CARCASS GRINDER, SMEGMA, BLOOD and PUTRID OFFAL among many others.

The band has featured on a number of compilation albums in addition to the singles and album listed.

AGATHOCLES' energy seems to know no bounds: by 1996 the band had also performed over 400 gigs. As well as 7" singles AGATHOCLES are not averse to alliances on cassette, and tapes over the years have witnessed unions with DRUDGE, LUNATIC INVASION, BULLSHIT PROPAGANDA, INCONTINENTIA, EXTREME STROKE, IMPEDIGION, MUGGLES, VOLTIFIBIA, SHIT, DEFECATION PURULENTIA and CRIPPLE BASTARDS.

During 1999 AGATHOCLES shared a joint album venture 'Hunt Hunters' on Czech label Obscene Productions, with SUPPOSITORY, the band of erstwhile AGATHOCLES guitarist Matti.

Singles/EPs:
Split EP, (1988) (with RIEK BOOIS)
Split EP, (19--) (With DISGORGE)
Split EP, (19--) (With VIOLENT NOISE ATTACK)
Fascination Of Mutilation EP, (19--)
If This Is Cruel EP, (19--)
Split EP, (19--) (With BLOOD)
Split EP, (19--) (With SMEGMA)
Split EP, (19--) (With PUTRID OFFAL)
Cabbalic Gnosticism EP, (1988)
Split EP, (19--) (With MORBID ORGANS MUTILATION)
Agarchy EP, (19--)
Split EP, (19--) (With PSYCHO)
Split EP, (19--) (With VIOLENT HEADACHE)
Split EP, (19--) (With KOMPOST)
Fascination With Mutilation, Rigid (1990) (7" flexi single. 60 copies)
Traditional Rites, (1991) (Split 7" single with BLOOD)
Sieg Shit / Hatronomous / Hideous

Headchopping / Bigheaded Bastards / Get Off Your Ass / Distrust And Abuse, Boundless Records (1993) ('Distrust And Abuse' EP)

Split EP, (1993) (With NYCTOPHOBIC)

Split EP, (1993) (With PUNISHER)

Split EP, (1993) (With NASUM)

Split EP, (1993) (With MAN IS THE BASTARD)

Split EP, (1993) (With PATARENI)

Split EP, (1993) (With AUDIORREA)

Split EP, (1993) (With SOCIAL GENOCIDE)

Go Fucking / Hatred Is The Cure / No Use... Hatred / An Abstract, Unicorn Records (1993) ('No Use.. Hatred' EP)

Pigs In Blue, Bizarre Leprous (1994) (7" split single with PLASTIC GRAVE)

Wiped From Surface / Debalance Their Policy / Go Fucking Nihilist (Live), Elephant (1994) (7" split single with ROT)

Who Shares The Guilt, Poserslaughter (1995) (Split 7" with NASUM)

Screenfreak, Regurgitated Semen RSR015 (1995) (7" split single with CARCASS GRINDER)

Go Fucking Nihilist / Hatred Is The Cure / No Use… (Hatred) / An Abstract, Boundless (1995) ('No Use…'(Hatred) EP)

Split EP, Morbid 660748 (1996) (With AUTORITAR)

Libidinous Urges / Hate My Mate / A Is For Arrogance / Thy Kingdom Won't Come, Yellow Dog (1996) ('A Is For Arrogance' 7" split single with AUTORITAR)

Big One / The Fog / Teachers / The Accident / Mutilated Regurgitator / Consuming Endoderme Pus / Splattered Brains / Christianity Means Tyranny / Squeeze Anton / Introyy / Threshold To Senility, Morbid 660773 (1996) ('Back To 1987' EP)

No Gain- Just Pain / The Sin I Regret / Insufferable Beings? / Do All The Sick Experience Healing? / L'Ardoise Vierge, MCR Company MCR099 (1996) (7" split single with UNHOLY GRAVE)

Live And Noisy, Bad People BPR009 (1997) (Double 7" single)

Split EP, (199-) (With PREPERATION H)

Split EP, (199-) (With VOMIT FALL) Studio 1988, (199-)

Split EP, (199-) (With EXIT 13) Studio Spain, (199-)

Split EP, Spasmoparapsychotic (1997) (7" split single with KRUSH)

Albums:

SPLIT LP, Deaf (19--) (With DRUDGE)

SPLIT LP, (19--) (With LUNATIC INVASION)

THEATRE SYMBOLISATION OF LIFE, Cyber Music (1992)
Burning Water / Lack Of Personality / Four Walls / Theatric Symbolisation Of Life / Like An Ivy / Suffocation / Kill Your Idols / The Truth Begins Where Man Stops To Think / Train / The Tree / What A Nerve / Alternative - Another Trend / Mutilated Regurgitator / The Accident / Threshold To Senility / Forced Pollutions / Consuming Endoderme Pus / Playing With Lifes / Splattered Brains / Well Of Happiness / Judged By Appearance / Solitary Minded / Trust? Not Me / Lay Off Me / Threshold To Senility / Mutilated Regurgitator / Gorgonised Dorks / Lay Off Me / Consuming Endoderme Pus / Let It Be For What It Is / Theatric Symbolization Of Life / The Tree

CLICHE- LIVE, (199-)

USE YOUR ANGER - LIVE, (199-)

BLACK CLOUDS DETERMINATE, Cyber CYBER10 (1994)
Bastard Breed (Intro) / Scorn Of Humanity / Sentimental Hypocrisy / Megalomanic Stupidity / Hangman's Dance / Black Clouds Determinate / Ubermensch Hilarity / Triple Murder Flesh / Europe's Fairy Tale / Musicianship - Musicianshit / Confront Your Images / Mister Hardcore Syndrome / For White Lies / Technological Boom - Technological Doom / Destroy To Create / Bigheaded Bastard / Hate Birth / Sieg Shit / Well Of Happiness / Birds (Poem) Agarthy / Theatric Symbolization Of Life / Bigheaded Bastard / Lack Of Personality / Squeeze Anton / What Mankind Creates / Distrust And Abuse / Teachers / Hideous Headchopping / Mutilated Regurgitator / Get Off Your Ass / Hate Birth

SPLIT LP, (199-) (With AVERNO)

SPLIT LP, (199-) (With AVERNO)

RAZOR SHARP DAGGERS, Cyber (1996)
A Start At Least / Clean The Scene / A For Arrogance / Thy Kingdom Won't Come / Media Creations / All Gone / Swallow Or Choke / Razor Sharp Daggers / Enough / Throwing Away Crap / Cracking Up Solidarity / Lunatic / Don't Ask / Twisting History / Deserves To Die / Age Of The Mutants / Zero Ego / Gear Wheels / Dear Friends / Hormone Mob / Hash Head, Farmers Death / Dare To Be Aware / Kiss My Ass / All Love Dead / Fear Not / Sieg Shit / Hatronomious / Hideous Headchopping / Bigheaded Bastards / Get Off Your Ass / Distrust And Abuse / Hippie Cult / Provoked

14

Behaviour / Black Ones (Poem): Systemphobic / Anthrodislogical / Labelisation / What Mankind Creates / No! / Rejected Adoption / An Abstract / Faded Novelty / Senseless Trip / Here And Now / Is It Really Mine?
THE LPS - 1989-1991, (199-)
MINCED ALIVE, (199-) (10" Album)
THANKS FOR YOUR HOSTILITY, Morbid MR 03 (1997)
Criminalization Of Strange Behaviour / Life Control / Until It Bleeds / End Of The Line / Doctors Wished Me / Knock Back / Thanks For Your Hostility / Hatred Is The Cure / Be Your God / Distraction / Remember / Cheers Mankind Cheers / Strangulation / Foul / Un Use...Hatred / My Reason / No One's Right / Sheer Neglect / Is There A Place? / Go Fucking Nihilist / Progress Or Stupidity ? / Try! / He Cared / Mankind's Not Kind / Reduced To An Object / Ego-Generosity / ...
SPLIT LP, (1997) (With REIGN OF TERROR)
HUMARROGANCE, Morbid MR 037 CD (1997)
Humarrogance / Because / Model Citizen / Let's Feel Alright / As Years Pass By / It Bothers Me / One Day Fly / White Horse / Ain't I / Beam Me Up, Scotty / Ice Brick / Culture Of Degradation / Closed Down / Alright, Let's Feel / Kneel And Pay / Failure / I Can't Stand / Smelling The Odours Of Death / The Bastards Have Landed / Mince-Core
HUNT HUNTERS, Obscene Productions (1999) (Split album with SUPPOSITORY)
Without A Clue / Careless Wish / Rip The Book / Irreversible Decision / Decimation Of Rights / Slaves To The Beat / Back In Town / Sick Shows Sell / Hunt Foxhunters
MINCE CORE, Controverse (1999)
Threshold To Senility / Consuming Endoderme Pus / Splattered Brains / Forced Pollution / The Accident / Mutilated Regurgitator / Playin' With Lives / Trust Not Me / About A Fascist
ROBOTIZED, (1999) (Split album with DEPRESSION)
Drug Induced Fantasies / Kids For Cash / Get A Life / No Remorse / Robotized / Thanks For Your Hostility / Criminalization Of Strange Behaviour / Is It Really Mine? / Wir Fahren Gegen Nazis

AGGRESSOR (ESTONIA)

Albums:
PROCREATE THE PETRIFICATIONS, EHL Trading (1993)

OF LONG DURATION ANGUISH, Fugata (1994)

AGHORA (USA)
Line-Up: Danishta Dobles (vocals), Santiago Dobles (guitar), Charlie Ekendahl (guitar), Sean Malone (bass), Sean Reinert (drums)

Female fronted Metal band AGHORA include two ex-CYNIC members in their line up in bassist Sean Malone and drummer Sean Reinert. The latter has also been with GORDIAN KNOT.

Albums:
AGHORA, Season Of Mist (2000)
Immortal Bliss / Satya / Transfiguration / Frames / Mind's Reality / Kaliyuga / Jivatma / Existence / Anugraha

AGONY (COLUMBIA)

Albums:
MILLENIUM, Cinismo (1996)

AGONY CONSCIENCE (CZECH REPUBLIC)

Czech Industrially charged Grindcore act AGONY CONSCIENCE are known to have issued a 7" single 'Mass Demented' upfront of the 1997 'Look Into The Silence' album.

Albums:
LOOK INTO THE SILENCE, Sheerjoy (1997)

AGORAPHOBIC NOSEBLEED
(Boston, MA, USA)
Line-Up: Jay Randall (vocals), Scott Hull (guitar)

Grindcore act led by A.C. guitarist Scott Hull. Both Hull and vocalist Jay Randall also busy themselves with other acts as diverse as PIG DESTROYER and JAPANESE COMEDY TORTURE HOUR. Randall also operates THREE RING INFERNO in alliance with Jacob Bannon of CONVERGE.
AGOROPHOBIC NOSEBLEED employed Richard of ENEMY SOIL and Aaron of ULCER on vocals prior to the recruitment of Randall. Although the band employs a drum machine Jason of SUPPURATION handles bass guitar.

Albums:
HONKY REDUCTION, Relapse (1998)

Black Ink On Black Paper / Polished Turd / Filthy Murder Shack / The Withering Of Skin / Empowerment / The House Of Feasting / Die And Get The Fuck Out Of The Way / Insipid Conversations / Vexed / Circus Mutt (Three Ring Inferno) / Lives Ruined Through Sex (For Anita) / Clawhammer And An Ether Bag (For Bill) / NYC Always Reminds Me / Her Despair Reeks Of Alcohol / Chump Slap / Burned Away In Sleep / Grief Is Not Quantifiable / Cloved In Twain / Torn Apart By Dingos / Pagan Territories / Hat Full Of Shit (For Cletus) / McWorld / How Sean Threw His Back Out Sneezing / Bones In One Bag (Organs In Another) / Acute Awareness (For Wood) / Two Shits To The Moon

THE POACHER'S DIARIES, Relapse (1999) (Split album with CONVERGE)
Mantis / Center Of The Hive / Glass Tornado / Landfills Of Extinct Possibility / Pentagram Constellation / Bed Of Flies / Destroyed / Gringo / Infected Womb / Locust Reign / This Is Mine / They Stretch For Miles / My Great Devestator / The Human Shield / Minnesota

AGREGATOR (SWEDEN)
Line-Up: Pierre Richter (vocals / guitar), Christofer Malmström (guitar), Jörgen Löfberg (bass), Peter Wildoer (drums)

Previously known as DEMISE, Helsinborg Death Metallers AGREGATOR scored a deal with German label Crypta, who released the 'Delusions' album and the band also has two tracks, 'Ominous Situation' and 'Dull Reality', on the 1994 compilation album 'Kompakkraft'.

Albums:.
DELUSIONS, Crypta 8211-2 (1994)
Prophecy / Critical Dimensions / Blustering Madness / An Infirm Soul / Pointless Objection / Merciless Living / Human Delay / Internal Severity / Pictures

AGRESSOR (FRANCE)
Line-Up: Alex Colin-Tocquaine (vocals / guitar), Thierry (bass), Laurent (drums)

Antibes Black Thrash Metal trio that recorded their first demo in November 1986, AGRESSOR released a couple more demos and played dates with APOCALYPSE and LIVING DEATH. The band signed to Black Mark for one album, subtly titled 'Satan's Sodomy', graced with an album cover showing the immediate after effects of buggery with the devil!

AGRESSOR's line-up at this juncture was as a trio of vocalist / guitarist Alex Colin-Tocquaine, bassist J.M. Libeer and drummer Jean Luc Falsini. This incarnation recorded the first two demos 'Merciless Onslaught' and 'Satan's Sodomy'.

Things swiftly changed for the group when AGRESSOR added new drummer Thierry and ex-HELLRAISER bassist Laurent in 1988.

The group then signed to Noise, recording 'Neverending Destiny', after which both new men split leaving Alex Colin-Tocquaine to soldier on alone! Thierry joined LOUDBLAST.

Undaunted, Alex put together a brand new line-up of his band, thus the 1992 version of AGRESSOR (which recorded the 'Towards Beyond' album) consisted of Colin-Tocquaine, ex-OUTBURST guitarist Patrick Gibelin, ex-OUTBURST bassist Joël Guigon and ex-DEATHPOWER drummer Stephan Gwegwam.

Gibelin had quit by the time AGRESSOR returned to the studio to cut the ensuing 'Symposium Of Rebirth' album, his place being taken by new guitarist Manu Ragot. The TERRORISER cover track 'After World Obliteration', incidentally, features a guest vocal performance from NAPALM DEATH's Barney Greenaway.

The 2000 incarnation of AGRESSOR saw Colin-Tocquaine and Guigor joined by guitarist Adramelch and drummer Gorgor.

Albums:
LICENSED TO THRASH, New Wave 024 (1987) (Split LP with LOUDBLAST)
Satan's Sodomy / Brainstorm / Bloodfeast / Uncontrolled Desire / Black Church / It's Pandemonium
SATAN'S SODOMY, Black Mark BMCD 36 (1987)
Satan's Sodomy / Brainstorm / Blood Feast / Uncontrolled Desire / Black Church / It's Pandemonium
NEVERENDING DESTINY, Black Mark (1990)
Paralytic Disease / The Unknown Spell / Element Decay / Voices From Below / Blood Feast / Neverending Destiny / Prince Of Fire / Dark Power / The Arrival / Brainstorm / Bloody Corps
TOWARDS BEYOND, Black Mark BMCD 23 (1992)
Intro / Primeval Transubstantiation / The Fortress / Positionic Showering /

Antediluvian / Epileptic Alra / Hyaldid / The Crypt / Future Past - Eldest Things / Turkish March
SYMPOSIUM OF REBIRTH, Black Mark BMCD 55 (1994)
Barabas / Rebirth / Negative Zone / Apocalyptic Prophecies / Erga Meam Salutem / Overloaded / Theology / Civilization / Wheel Of Pain / Abhuman Dreadnought / Torture / Dor Fin-I-Guinar / After World Obliteration
MEDIEVAL RITES, Season Of Mist (2000)
Mediaeval Rites / Bloodshed / The Woodguy Vs. The Black Beast / The Sorcerer / (I Am The) Spirit Of Evil / Wandering Soul / Tye-Melane Helda / God From The Sky / Welcome Home (King Diamond) / On Dolinde / Burial Desecration / Tribal Dance / At Night

ALASTIS (SWITZERLAND)
Line-Up: War D. (vocals / guitar), Nick (guitar), Raff (bass), Graven X (keyboards), Acronoise (drums)

Death Metallers ALASTIS have had a turbulent history since their inception in 1987 with vocalist Zumof, bassist Masmiseim, guitarist War D. and drummer Acronoise. The band was originally titled CRY WAR until 1988 when the 'Black Wedding' demo saw a transition to ALASTIS.
ALASTIS released two demos prior to Masmiseim's departure in 1990 to SAMAEL shortly followed by the departure of Zumof. Endeavouring to keep the ALASTIS spirit alive War. D took over lead vocals for the 1992 album 'The Just Law' before losing bassist Eric.
A new four stringer was found in ex-MISERY man Rotten in 1993. The band added erstwhile OFFERING guitarist Nick in 1995 for their first tour as support to ANATHEMA. Further shows saw ALASTIS on a European package billing with THEATRE OF TRAGEDY and SAVIOUR MACHINE.
For the 1998 album 'Revenge' bass was now in the hands of Raff, ALASTIS also having drafted a keyboard player Graven X.

Albums:
THE JUST LAW, Head Not Found (1992)
The Just Law / Black Wedding / Illusion / Reconversion / Damned For Ever / Nightmare / The City / Faticidal Date / Messenger Of The U.W.
...AND DEATH SMILED, Adipocere

AR029 (1995)
From The UW / Through Your Torpor / Let Me Die / Evil / By Thy Name / Schizophrenia (Mental Suicide) / March For Victory / Your God / Last Wishes / The Psychpath / Messenger Of The U.W. (Second Act)
THE OTHER SIDE, Nuclear Blast 77156-2 (1997)
In Darkness / Never Again / The Other Side / Out Of Time / Through The Chaos / Fight & Win / Slaves Of Rot / Remind / Under The Sign... / End Or Beginning
REVENGE, Century Media 77223-2 (1998)
Just Hate / Burnt Alive / Eternal Cycle / Sacrifice / Ecstasy / Like A Dream / Nemesis / Bring Down / Agony / Revenge
UNITY, Century Media (2001)

ALASTOR (POLAND)
Line-Up: Robert Stankiewicz (vocals), Marius Matuszewski (guitar), Waldemar Osiecki (bass), Slawomir Brylka (drums)

Polish Death Metal band named after the mythological executioner in Hell.

Albums:
SYNDROMS OF THE CITIES, Metal Master (1989)
ZLO, (1994)

ALCHEMIST (AUSTRALIA)
Line-Up: Adam Agius (vocals / guitar), Roy Torkington (guitar), John Lindsey Bray (bass), Rodney Holder (drums)

Although self styled Progressive Death Metal band ALCHEMIST had been created in 1987 they debuted with the track 'Escapism' included on the 1993 Roadrunner 'Redrum' compilation album. European label Lethal Records issued their 'Jar Of Kingdom' album later the same year.
Guitarist Andrew lost his place to Roy Torkington for the second album 'Lunasphere' issued in 1995. ALCHEMIST have opened for numerous European Metal bands in Australia including KREATOR, NAPALM DEATH, CATHEDRAL and PARADISE LOST.
ALCHEMIST recorded a version of 'Eve Of The War' from Jeff Wayne's 'War Of The World's' in 1998.

Singles/EPs:
Eve Of The War, (1998)

JAR OF KINGDOM, Lethal (1993)
Abstraction / Shell / Purple / Jar Of
Kingdom / Wandering And Wondering /
Found / Enhancing Enigma / Whale /
Brumal: A View From Pluto / Worlds
Within Worlds
LUNASPHERE, Thrust - Shock (1995)
Soul Return / Lunation / Unfocused /
Luminous / Clot / Yoni Kunda / My
Animate Truth / Garden Of Eroticism /
Closed Chapter
SPIRITECH, Thrust - Shock (1997)
Chinese Whispers / Road To Ubar /
Staying Conscious / Beyond Genesis /
Spiritechnology / Inertia / Hermaphroditis
/ Dancing To Life / Figments
ORGANASM, (199-)
Austral Spectrum / The Bio Approach /
Rampant Micro Life / Warring Tribes -
Eventual Demise / Single Sided /
Surreality / New Beginning / Tide In,
Mind Out / Eclectic / Escape From The
Black Hole

ALLEGIENCE (SWEDEN)
Line-Up: Bogge Svenson (vocals /
guitar), Pära (guitar), Micke (bass),
Fredrik Andersson (drums)

ALLEGIENCE, a now highly regarded act
founded in 1989, ply old style trad Thrash
on their debut demo 'Sick World'. The
band had got decidedly more brutal by
their second attempt the aptly named
'Eternal Hate'. The band shifted direction
undergoing a radical line up shuffle to
emerge as out and out Black Metal
merchants on their third tape 'Odin Äge
Er Alle'. A fourth stab at the demo scene
with 1994's 'Hafdingadrapa' pursued
more Viking Metal leanings.
Members of ALLEGIENCE also have an
interest in MARDUK sharing drummer
Fredrik Andersson and Bogge Svensson.

Albums:
HYMN TILLHANGAGUD, No Fashion
NFR 014 (1996)
Höfdingadrapa / De Nordiska Lagren /
The Third Raven / Himmelen Rämnar /
Den Krisnes Död / The March Of Warlike
Damned / Stridsärd / Spjutsängen
BLODÖRNSOFFER, No Fashion
NFR021 (1997)
Intag / Med Svärd I Hand / Likbal / En
Svunnen Tid / Heimdal / Yggrasil /
Korpen Skall Leda Oss / Blodörnsoffer /
Blot / Uttag
VREDE, No Fashion NFR028 (1998)
Na Skall Du Do Vite Krist / Sorn Drogens

Hart Med Doden / I Stjarnornas Skugga /
Hrodvittners Rike / Baldersbalet /
Nordens Fader / Hedna Stad Hymn Till
Nordens Hjaltar / Skymning

ALLIGATOR (ITALY)
Line-up: Gianluca Melino (vocals),
Francesco Capasso (guitar), Tiziano
Colombi (guitar), Dario Zanaboni (bass),
Andrea Bellazzi (drums)

Northern Italian Thrash Metallers.

Albums:
CEREBRAL IMPLOSION, Scream
SCREAM003CD (1994)
Cerebral Implosion / Beyond The Reach
Of Fate / The Cage / Decimation / Help /
Lullaby For The Unborn / Skeleton's
Beach / Tarantula / Drinking Milk From My
Knees / Fetching Fear / Natural Dreams

ALTAR (HOLLAND)
Line-Up: Edwin Kelder (vocals),
Bert Huisjes (guitar), Marcel Van Haaff
(guitar), Nils Vos (bass),
Marco Arends (drums)

ALTAR, previously known as
MANTICORE, released a 1992 demo
titled 'And God Created Satan To Blame
For His Mistakes'.
The second album features ex-
MANDATOR guitarist Marcel Verdermen.

Albums:
YOUTH AGAINST CHRIST, Massacre
MASS CD 056 (1994)
Throne Of Fire / Jesus Is Dead! /
Divorced From God / Hypochristianity /
Forced Imprudence / Psycho Damn /
Cross The Bridge Of False Prophecies /
Cauterize The Church Council
EGO ART, Displeased D00046 (1996)
Eidelon / I Take / Ego Art / C.C.C. / Truly
Untrue / Pathetic Priest / Destructive
Selection / Egoverment / Follow Me /
Tonight This Country Will Die
IN THE NAME OF THE FATHER,
Displeased (2000)
Holy Mask / Spunk / God Damn You / In
The Name Of The Father / I Spit Black
Bile On You / Hate Scenario / Pro Jagd /
Walhalla Express / In Our Dominion

ALTAR (SWEDEN)
Line-Up: Magnus Karlsson (vocals /
bass), Jimmy Lundmark (guitar), Fredrik
Johansson (drums)

ALTAR debuted with the demo session

'No Flesh Shall Be Spared'. The bands debut commercial release, a split album 'Ex Oblivione' shared with CARTILAGE, featured EDGE OF SANITY's Dan Swano on keyboards.

ALTAR also had drummer Per Karlsson in the ranks for a period. Karlsson would later join SUFFER then in 1996 SERPENT.

Albums:
EX OBLIVIONE, Drowned Products DC013 (1993)
(Split LP with CARTILAGE)
Nothing Human / Lifeless Passion / Decapitated (New version) / Daymare / A Message From The Grave / Ex Oblivione / Severed On The Attic / No Flesh…

AMAYMON (FRANCE)
Line-Up: Sebastien (vocals / guitar), Christian Bivel (guitar), Vincent (bass), Fred (drums)

AMAYMON is the Thrash Metal band of Adipocere label boss Christian Bivel. The album was a split affair with Canadians PURULENCE.

Albums:
AMAYMON, Adipocere AR016 (1993)
(Split CD with PURULENCE)
Intro / Buried And Forgotten / Evil Prevails / The Rapture / Shemhamphorash / The Goetic Belief

AMBOSS (GERMANY)
Line-Up: Alex Proksch (vocals / guitar / keyboards), Hilti Hammer (guitar), Pete Netta (guitar / psychedelic vocals), Matse Ried (bass), Spike Butcher (drums / classical vocals)

Cologne based Death Metal act.

Albums:
THOSE WHO HAVE LOST THE RIGHT TO EXIST, Crypta DA 8203-2 (1994)
Christian Damnation / Common Sons / Lost... / Maze Of Dreams / Reborn / Reign Of The Moon (Or The Symphonies Of Sarjevo) / Suicidal Overdose / Temples Of Evil

AMETHYST (Spokane, WA, USA)
Line-Up: Marq Allen (vocals / guitar), Bart Stevens (guitar), Gary Rose (bass)

Not only do AMETHYST mark themselves out from the pack by being a Death Metal band with clearly stated Christian beliefs but the band also boasts a full time police officer in the ranks!

The band has weathered an extremely convoluted career enduring many line up shuffles from their inception in Washington during 1985 as Heavy Metal band METALSTORM. The fledgling roster comprised of frontman Marq Allen, guitarist James Peter, bass player Gary Rose and drummer Shannon Corpuz. Peter would break ranks having his position filled by Dave Burdette as the band morphed into FORTRESS. However, discovering a plethora of acts with this title FORTRESS became GENTILE. This title did not stick either and for a matter of months the group went under the name MORDECAI before one of the band members lifted the name AMETHYST whilst reading Revelation in the bible.

Burdette departed for a military career and Bart Stevens took the guitar role. However, AMETHYST suffered a tragic setback when Rose had his hand crushed in an industrial accident. Advised to have at least two fingers removed due to the severity of the injury he reportedly prayed and fasted for another solution. Rose would eventually come through this experience with all fingers intact and allegedly playing better than ever!

Further ructions hit AMETHYST with the decamping of Corpuz and Stevens. The band drafted drummer Doug LeBlanc but found his Catholic upbringing at odds with the rest of the band. The 15 year old John Silver took his place as Robin Skouge was enlisted on guitar. With this line up, and with Bart Stevens guesting, AMETHYST cut their debut eponymous demo. Predictably the group splintered once more with Skouge joining KIDD ROBIN.

New faces for 1990 were guitarist Mark Maye and drummer Charles Heinzerling but in 1992 Allen relocated to Texas. There the singer forged a fresh trio entitled HOLY DEATH in alliance with a rhythm section of bass player Mike Hatcher and drummer Jason Byrd. Before long Allen renamed the band AMETHYST and with a fresh drummer, erstwhile EXHORTATION man William Miller, cut the 1995 demo session 'Inanimate'.

1996 witnessed a return to Washington for Allen and a regrouping of the original AMETHYST with Rose and Stevens, the latter by now a law enforcement officer!

Albums:
THE EARLY YEARS 1986-1996, (2000)

BACK FROM THE DEAD, (2000)

AMON AMARTH (SWEDEN)
Line-Up: Johan (vocals),
Hansson (guitar), Olli (guitar),
Ted (bass), Nico (drums)

Hailing from Tumba, a suburb of
Stockholm, AMON AMARTH trace their
roots back to 1992. The unit's first
available recording was to have been
1993's 'Thor's Rise' demo though this
was withheld and it was to be a full year
before second demo 'The Arrival Of
Fimbul Winter' made it onto the tape
trading scene leading to a deal with
Singapore based label Pulverized
Records.
Following the release of debut 'Sorrow
Throughout The Nine Worlds' drummer
Nico opted out to be replaced by Martin
Lopez.
AMON AMARTH's sophomore release
was produced by HYPOCRISY's Peter
Tägtgren.
AMON AMARTH, supported by
PURGATORY, undertook a tour of
Germany in December 2000.

Singles/EPs:
Burning Creation / The Arrival Of The
Fimbul Winter / Without Fear, (1994)
('The Arrival Of The Fimbul Winter' EP)

Albums:
**SORROW THROUGHOUT THE NINE
WORLDS**, Pulverized ASH001 MCD
(1996)
Sorrow Throughout The Nine Worlds /
The Arrival Of The Fimbul Winter /
Burning Creation / The Mighty Doors Of
The Speargod's Hall / Under The
Graveclouded Winter Sky
**ONCE SENT FROM THE GOLDEN
HALL**, Metal Blade 3984-14133-2 (1998)
Ride For Vengeance / The Dragon's
Flight Across The Waves / Without Fear
/ Victorious March / Friends Of The
Suncross / Abandoned / Amon Amarth /
Once Sent From The Golden Hall
THE AVENGER, Metal Blade (2000)
Bleed For Ancient Gods / The Last With
Pagan Blood / North Sea Storm /
Avenger / God, His Son And Holy Whore
/ Metal Wrath / Legend Of A Banished
Man / Thor Arise
THE CRUSHER, Metal Blade (2001)
Bastards Of A Lying Breed / Masters Of
War / The Sound Of Eight Hooves /
Risen From The Sea 2000 / As Long As
The Raven Flies / A Fury Divine /

Annihilation Of Hammerfest / The Fall
Through Ginnungagap / Releasing
Surtur's Fire

AMORPHIS (FINLAND)
Line-Up: Pasi Koskinen (vocals / guitar),
Esa Holopainen (guitar), Niclas
Etelavuori (bass), Santeru Kallio
(keyboards), Pekka Kasari (drums)

One of Finland's premier acts.
AMORPHIS, whose title derives from the
word 'Amorphous' meaning without
shape or form, have ploughed their own
distinct furrow by combining Death Metal
with elements of 70's inspired
Progressive Rock and even Psychedelia.
Based in Helsinki, AMORPHIS formed in
1990 releasing their first demo, 'Disment
Of Soul', the same year. The band were
picked up by American label Relapse and
recorded six tracks for an intended split
album with INCANTATION, but this never
appeared. However, two songs made it
onto a limited edition 7" single.
The first album, 'The Karellian Isthmus',
received creditable media response and
strong sales, prompting Relapse to
release the previously recorded tracks as
the 'Privilege Of Evil' mini-album.
The next AMORPHIS album, 'Tales From
A Thousand Lakes', is loosely based on
the Finnish national myth of Kalevala.
Toured America in 1994 alongside
ENTOMBED then Europe with TIAMAT.
The 'Tales From A Thousand Lakes'
album features a cover version of THE
DOORS' 'Light My Fire' and features the
first appearance of new keyboard player
Kasper Martenson. Drummer Jan
Rechberger was replaced by Pekka
Kasari in 1995.
Further line-up ructions occurred for the
'Elegy' album with AMORPHIS adding ex-
STONE man Kim Rantala on keyboards
and vocalist Pasi Koskinen.
Holopainen put in an appearance on the
LOVE LIKE BLOOD Gothic Rocker's
'Jubileum' mini album in early 1998.
Laine left the band in 2000 to be replaced
by Niclas Etelavuori. Rantala also made
his exit and was substituted by former
KYYYRIA member Santeri Kallio. The
groundbreaking 'Tuonela' album,
produced by Simon Effemy, would push
AMORPHIS further up the ladder in the
international stakes and provide ample
evidence the band was not content to rest
on its laurels. A loosely conceptualized
outing rooted in Finnish folklore 'Tuonela'
witnessed a strong infusion of
Psychedelia into the bands sound.

AMORPHIS

The 2001 album 'Am Universum', which debuted at number 4 on the Finnish national album charts, also achieved the honour of producing a homeland number one single with 'Alone'. Touring in America would commence with an appearance at the New Jersey Metalfest before Canadian gigs and a short run of headliners in the USA.

Various members of AMORPHIS also bide their time with side projects JAMBOR and ALL HUMANS SUBSTITUTES.

Singles/EPs:
Black Winter Day / Moon And The Sun / Moon And The Sun Part II - North's Son / Folk Of The Moon, Nuclear Blast (1994)
My Kantele / The Brother Slayer / The Lost Son (The Brother Slayer Part II) / Levitation / And I Hear You Call, Nuclear Blast NB 270-2 (1997)
Alone (Radio Edit) / Too Much To See / Alone (Album Version), Nuclear Blast (2001)

Albums:
THE KARELLIAN ISTHMUS, Nuclear Blast NB 72 (1993)
Karelia / The Gathering / Grails Mysteries / Warriors Trial / Black Embrace / Exile Of The Sons Of Uisilu / The Lost Name Of God / The Pilgrimage / Misery Path / Sign From The North Side / Vulgar Necrolatry
PRIVILEGE OF EVIL, Relapse RR6024-2 (1993)
Pilgrimage From Darkness / Black Embrace / Privilege Of Evil / Misery Path / Vulgar Necrolatry / Excursing From Existence
TALES FROM THE THOUSAND LAKES, Nuclear Blast NB 87 (1994)
Thousand Lakes / Into Hiding / The Castaway / First Doom / Black Winter Day / Drowned Maid / In The Beginning / Forgotten Sunrise / To Father's Cabin / Magic And Mayhem / Light My Fire
ELEGY, Nuclear Blast NB 6141-2 (1996)
Better Unborn / Against Widows / The Orphan / On Rich And Poor / My Kantele / Cares / Song Of The Troubled One / Weeper On The Shore / Elegy / Relief/ My Kantele (Acoustic Reprise)
TUONELA, Nuclear Blast NB 110745 (1999)
The Way / Morning Star / Nightfall / Tuonela / Greed / Divinity / Shining / Withered / Rusty Moon / Summer's End
STORIES - TENTH ANNIVERSARY, (2000)

21

Black Winter Day / Against Widows / Tuonela / Grail's Mysteries / Castaway / My Kantele / Way / Brother Slayer / The Orphan / Exile Of The Sons Of Uisliu / On Rich And Poor / Divinity / The Gathering / Drowned Maid / Summer's End / Cares (Live)
AM UNIVERSUM, Nuclear Blast (2001) Alone / Goddess (Of The Sad Man) / The Night Is Over / Shatters Within / Crimson Wave / Drifting Memories / Forever More / Veil Of Sin / Captured State / Grieve Stricken Heart

ANAL BLAST (USA)

ANAL BLAST's 'Vaginal Vempire' album was clad in a witty parody of premier Black Metal act CRADLE OF FILTH's high art album sleeves. The band even willing to morph their logo into 'Anal Of Blast' to complete the effect.

<u>Albums:</u>
VAGINAL VEMPIRE, Nightfall (1998) Smell Your Cunt / Bloody Mary / Nipples, Knees, Ass, Cheeks, Ankles / Pull A Train / Staple Your Pussy Lips Together / Slop Hole / Crimson Smell / Wings Flew Away / Menstral Pancake / Pussy Blood Popsicle / Diaretic Orgasm / Honey / Bloody Hole / Suck Your Shit Off My Dick / Puss Sores / Bloody Brown Mouse / Puss Blood Pentagram (Bloody Cunt Suck Part II) / Spraying Blood - Blood Sprayer / Big Sags / Farm Animal Hammer / Ass Over Snatch / Lubed With Blood / Tampon Tea Bad / Twisted Bonus

ANAL MASSAKER (GERMANY)

Confusingly ANAL MASSAKER's 1998 'Vergewaltiger' album comprised over 70 tracks although only 30 are credited. Cover versions include CARCASS and NAPALM DEATH tracks.
ANAL MASSAKER have forged alliances with acts such as THE MEAT SHITS, MAGGOT SHOES, MEAT PAUNCH MAFIA and BARCASS for split 7" single releases.

<u>Singles/EPs:</u>
Ka Ka EP, (199-)
Bis Wir Schielen, (199-)
(7" split single with THE MEAT SHITS)
Freedom Of Choice, (199-)
(7" split single with MAGGOT SHOES)
C Is For Cookie, (199-)
(7" split single with BARCASS)

Split, Bizarre Leprous (1998) (7" split single with MEAT PAUNCH MAFIA)

<u>Albums:</u>
VERGEWALTIGER, Noise Variations (1998)
Blood Blues / Splattereah / Vaginal Massaker / Don't Abuse / Nation Trust / Carbonized / Vomit Drunk Bart / Clean The Line / Slaughtered Animals / Unclean / Asshole / AZ 70 / Save The Walls / What's The Matter / Know All / A.N.I. / Police Bastards / Doom Dead / Potential Murder / 3 Another A.C. Songs / Grind Bitch / McDonalds / Scum / Instrumental Death / Hegedeath / Getto Kings / Suckers On Dope / Torture / Cruelty To Animals / Deceiver
55 SONGS OF PSYCHEDELIC GRIND NOISE, (199-)

ANARCHUS (USA)

<u>Singles/EPs:</u>
Final Fall Of The Gods, Rigid (199-) (7" single)
Split, Slap A Ham (1992) (Split 7" single with MONASTERY)

ANASARCA (GERMANY)
Line-Up: Michael Dormann (vocals / guitar), Frank (guitar), Chris (bass), Herb (drums)

Bremen based Death Metal group ANASARCA was forged in 1995 with a union of former VOMITING CORPSES personnel vocalist / bassist Michael and drummer Heiner in union with VAE SOLIS men Frank and Chris. Initial fruits of this liaison being the demo tape 'Condemned Truth'.
The 'Godmachine' promotional cassette followed in 1996 which launched the track 'The Weird Ways' appearance on the German compilation album 'Deathphobia 3' and on the Spanish released 'Repulsive Assault 2'. The latter would signal a deal with the Iberian Repulse concern but not before Heiner was replaced by Herb of EYE SEA.
Promoting the debut album 'Godmachine' ANASARCA toured Europe in conjunction with CENTINEX. Second album 'Moribund' was recorded for the Danish Mighty Music label. Guitarist Frank had departed by this juncture.

<u>Albums:</u>
GODMACHINE, Repulse RPS033 (1998) The Way Into The Light / Godmachine /

The Beast (Perverse Penetration) / The Weird Ways / Drowned And Rotten / Like Thorns In My Head / Loss Of Time / Scorn / Corrosive Eclipse / Condemned Truth / Whisper And Cries
MORIBUND, Mighty Music (2001)
Done In Our Name / No More / If Only… / Concrete Tomb / Those Who Have Eyes / 60 Steps / I Will Not Be Broken / A Cloud Of Smoke / I Am / Signs Of Life / Of Life And Death

ANATA (SWEDEN)
Line-Up: Fredrik Schälin (vocals / guitar), Andreas Allenmark (guitar), Henrik Drake (bass), Robert Petersson (drums)

Varberg act ANATA began life as a Thrash / Crossover quartet but soon evolved into a fully fledged lethal Death Metal machine. The band started life in 1993 comprising vocalist / guitarist Fredrik Schälin, guitarist Matthias Svensson, bass player Martin Sjöstrand and drummer Robert Petersson. ANATA released the 1996 demo session 'Bury Forever The Garden Of Lie'.
During 1996 both Svensson and Sjöstrand bade their farewell and new recruits guitarist Andreas Allenmark and bass player Henrik Drake were welcomed into the fold for the 1997 demo 'Vast Lands Of My Infernal Dominion'. ANATA signed with French label Season Of Mist for the debut album 'The Infernal Depths Of Hatred'.
ANATA's second effort formed part of the Seasons Of Mist 'War' series pitching the band up against BETHZAIDA. The band covered BETHZAIDA's 'The Tranquility Of Your Last Breath' and MORBID ANGEL's 'Day Of Suffering' whilst BETHZAIDA reciprocated with their take on ANATA's 'Under Azure Skies'.
ANATA pulled in former ETERNAL LIES drummer Conny Petersson during early 2001.

Albums:
THE INFERNAL DEPTHS OF HATRED, Seasons Of Mist (1998)
Released When You Are Dead / Let The Heavens Hate / Under Azure Skies / Vast Lands Infernal Gates / Slain Upon His Altar / Those Who Lick The Wounds Of Christ / Dethroned The Hypocrites / Aim Not At The Kingdom High
WAR VOLUME III: VS. BETHZAIDA, Seasons Of Mist (1999) (Split album with BETHZAIDA)
Let Me Become Your Fallen Messiah /

With Me You Shall Fall / Day Of Suffering / The Tranquility Of Your Last Breath
DREAMS OF DEATH AND DISMAY, Seasons Of Mist (2001)
Die Laughing / Faith, Hope, Self Deception / God Of Death / Metamorphosis By The Well Of Truth / Dreamon / Can't Kill What's Already Dead / Insurrection / The Enigma Of Number Three / Drain Of Blood / The Temple - Erratic

ANATOMY (AUSTRALIA)
Line-Up: Marty (vocals), Hippyslayer (guitar), Machen (guitar), J.A. (bass), Wazarah (drums)

Australian Black Death Metal band ANATOMY bowed in with the 1991 'Dark Religion' demo following it up with 1992's session 'Those Whose Eyes Are Black'. ANATOMY's 2000 album 'The Witches Of Duthomir' included their take on POSSESSED's 'The Exorcist'. The band would later enroll former BESTIAL WARLUST drummer Markus Hellcunt.

Albums:
TWISTING DEPTHS OF HORROR, Dark Oceans (1994)
For A Darkened Soul / Twisting Depths Of Horror / A Scream Of Seven / Burial Of Armenia / Nucleus Eclipse Torn Abyss / Arrogance Within Humanity
WHERE ANGELS DIE, Destruktïve Kommandöh DSTK7662-2CD (1996)
Last Pleasures For Those Of The Apocalypse Of Hate / Under The Wings / Armagedoom / Forbidden Realms / The Call For Doom / Where Angels Die / The Frozen Darkness
THE WITCHES OF DUTHOMIR, Bleed (2000)

ANCESTROS (COLOMBIA)
Line-Up: Alejandro Garcia (vocals), Mauricio Zuleta (guitar), Carmelo Mendoza (guitar), Julian Palacino (bass), Andrés Zuluaga (drums)

Colombian Deathsters ANCESTROS have issued the demo session 'Colombian Infamy'. Alejandro Garcia replaced original singer Nelson Lara.

ANCIENT CEREMONY (GERMANY)
Line-Up: Christian Anderle (vocals), F.J. Krebs (guitar), Dirk Wirz (guitar), Frank Somin (bass), Stefan Müller (keyboards), Christoph Mertes (drums)

A Melodic Black Death Metal band with Gothic influences. ANCIENT CEREMONY's first recordings resulted in the 1993 demo 'Where Serpents Reign'. The first self-produced mini-CD recorded by the band appeared in 1995, with a full album arriving in 1997.

Singles/EPs:
Forsaken Gardens (Intro) / Cemetery Visions / The God And The Idol / Choir Of Immortal Queens / An Ode To The Moon, Ancient Ceremony (1995) ('Cemetery Visions' EP)

Albums:
UNDER MOONLIGHT WE KISS, Cacophonous (1997)
Eternal Goddess / Her Ivory Slumber / Shadows Of The Undead / Vampyre's Birth / Thy Beauty In Candlelight / Veil Of Desire / Secrets Of Blackened Sky / Dulcet Seduction / Angel's Bloody Tears / New Eden Embraces / Pale Nocturnal Majesty / Under Moonlight We Kiss
FALLEN ANGELS SYMPHONY, Cacophonous NIHIL 32CD (1999)
Death In Desire's Masquerade / Bride's Ghostly Grace / Black Roses On Her Grave / Devil's Paradise / The Tragedy Of Forsaken Angels / Amidst Crimson Stars / Babylon Ascends / Symphoni Satani / Vampyresque Wedding Night
SYNAGOGA DIABOLICA, Alister (2000)

ANCIENT RITES (BELGIUM)
Line-Up: Gunther Theys (vocals / bass), Bart Vandereycken (guitar), Walter Van Cortenberg (drums)

Formed in 1989, ANCIENT RITES, who deal in retro style Death Metal, have fast become one of the leading Belgian Black Metal acts.
The group's initial line-up comprised of vocalist/bassist Gunther Theys, guitarists Johan and Phillip and drummer Stefan. This concoction released the 'Dark Ritual' demo.
A year on, however, and ANCIENT RITES was forced to make changes. Firstly, band roadie Walter Van Cortenberg replaced drummer Stefan and then tragedy struck later in the same year when, in August, guitarist Phillip was killed in a car crash. The band enlisted guitarist Bart Vandereycken but soon after Johan departed leaving ANCIENT RITES as a single guitar band.
In 1992 the outfit recorded the self financed 'Evil Prevails' EP with second

guitarist Pascal. However, Pascal's tenure was brief and soon ANCIENT RITES were a trio once more.
Recording became quite prolific as the band added a track for Tessa Records' 'Detonation' compilation album as well as recording tracks for a Colombian split album on Warmaster Records. ANCIENT RITES also joined forces with Greek act THOU ART LORD for a split 7" single. This activity was followed by intensive gigging across Europe, including dates in Greece with ROTTING CHRIST. A further track was included on a split EP on Molten Lava Records and the band finally released their first full length album, 'The Diabolic Serenades', on After Dark Records in early 1994.
During 1995 ANCIENT RITES toured Europe in with CRADLE OF FILTH and have since cut a split EP with fellow Belgians ENTHRONED.
1998's 'Fatherland' had Theys and Van Cortenberg joined by guitarists Erik Sprooten and Jan 'Orkki' Yrlund.

Singles/EPs:
Götterdammerung / Longing For The Ancient Kingdom / Obscurity Reigns (Fields Of Flanders) / Evil Prevails / Black Plague, Fallen Angel (1992) ('Evil Prevails' EP)
From Beyond The Grave II, Molon Lave (1993) (Split single with THOU ART LORD)
Split, Warmaster (1993) (12" split single with UNCANNY)
Longing For The Ancient Kingdom II, After Dark (1995) (Split single with ENTHRONED)

Albums:
ANCIENT RITES, Warmaster (1992) (Split LP)
THE DIABOLIC SERENADES, Mascot M 7018-2 (1994)
(Intro) Infant Sacrifices To Baalberith / Crucifixion Justified (Roman Supremach) / Satanic Rejoice / Obscurity Reigns (Fields Of Flanders) / Death Messiah / Land Of Frost And Despair / Ussyrian Empire / Longing For The Ancient Kingdom / Morbid Glory (Gilles De Rais 1404-1440) / Ritual Slayings (Goat Worship Pure) / Evil Prevails / Last Rites / Echoes Of Melancholy (Outro) / From Beyond The Grave II
BLASFEMIA ETERNAL, Mascot M7017-2 (1996)
Blasfemia Eternal / Total Misanthropia / Garden Of Delights (Eva) / Quest For

Blood (Le Vampire) / Blood Of Christ (Mohammed Wept) / Epebos Ai Nia / (Het Verdronken Land Van) Sactfinge / Shades Of Eternal Battlefields (Our Empire Fell) / Vae Victis / Fallen Angel
FATHERLAND, Mascot M 7035 2 (1998)
Avondland / Mother Europe / Aris / Fatherland / Season's Change (Solstice) / 13th Of December 1307 / Dying In A Moment Of Splendor / Rise And Fall (Anno Satana) / The Seducer / Cain
THE FIRST DECADE 1989-1999, Mascot (2000)
From Beyond The Grave (1990 demo) / Infant Sacrifices To Baalberith / Death Messiah / Longing For The Ancient Kingdom / Land Of Frost And Despair / Evil Prevails / Last Rites - Echoes Of Melancholy / Total Misanthropia / Blood Of Christ (Mohammed Wept) / Fallen Angel (Outro) / (Het Verdronken Land Van) Sactfinge / Quest For Blood (Le Vampire) / Avondland / Mother Europe / Aris / Seasons Change / Fatherland / Cain

ANCIENT WISDOM (SWEDEN)
Line-Up: Marcus Norman (vocals / guitar), Andreas Nilsson (guitar), Fredrik Jacobsson (bass), Jens Ryden (keyboards)

Previously known simply as ANCIENT the band became ANCIENT WISDOM in 1993. ANCIENT WISDOM's Marcus 'Vargher' Norman also fronts BEWITCHED. Both Norman and bass guitarist Fredrik Jacobsson were previously with THRONE OF AHAZ.
For live work the band added NOCTURNAL RITES drummer Ulf Andersson. Guitarist Andreas Nilsson and Jens Ryden also play in NAGLFAR.
In 2000 Norman founded a Gothic flavoured side project HAYAFOTH in collusion with NAGLFAR's Morgan Hansson.
ANCIENT WISDOM's 2000 album 'And The Physical Shape Of Light Bled' includes a cover of NWoBHM outfit DEMON's 'Day Of The Demon'.

Albums:
FOR THE SNOW COVERED THE NORTHLAND, Avantgarde AV0015 (1996)
A Hymn To The Northern Empire / In The Land Of The Crimson Moon / They Gather Where Snow Falls Forever / Through Rivers Of The Eternal Blackness / The Journey Of The

Ancients / No Tears At His Funeral / Forest Of Summoned Spirits / A Raven's Reflection Of The Ancient Northland
THE CALLING, Avantgarde AV 020 (1997)
The Awakening Of The Ancient Serpents / The Calling Of Nocturnal Demons / As The Twelve Legions Of Angels Died / In The Profane Domain Of The Frostbeast / Spiritual Forces Of Evil In The Heavenly Realms / And To The Depths They Descended / At The Stone Of Ancient Wisdom / Of Darkness Spawned Into eternity / Through The Mist Of Dusk They Arose And Clad The Sky With Fire
AND THE PHYSICAL SHAPE OF LIGHT BLED, Avantgarde (2000)
Preludium Lucifer, Aieth Gadol Leolam / And The Physical Shape Of Light Bled / With His Triumph Came Fire / Interludium The Fall Of Man / As The Morningstar Shineth / The Serpents Blessing / Postludium His Creation Reversed / The Spell

ANESTHESY (BELGIUM)
Line-Up: Frank Liberty (guitar), Werner (guitar), Chris D. (bass), Diego D. (drums)

A Thrash Metal act dating to 1986 and formed by ex-VENDETTA guitarist Frank Liberty, ANESTHESY debuted with their 'Seasons Of The Witch' demo. A further demo tape 'Overdose' (released in 1989) led to a deal with English label C.M.F.T. Unfortunately, after recording their debut album the record label went bust and the tracks remain unreleased.
Undeterred, ANESTHESY re-recorded some of these songs, releasing them as the 'Just Married' EP in 1991.
ANESTHESY have, in their time, supported the likes of NAPALM DEATH, KREATOR, GOREFEST and MORGOTH.

Singles/EPs:
Just Married EP, (1991)

Albums:
EXALTATION OF THE ECLIPSE, Black Mark BMCD 54 (1994)
Primal Exaltation / Beyond Sadness / The Defector / Guardian / Survival Of The Fittest / Intestinal Haemorrahage / The Change / The Ultimate Reincarnatior / Enstrangled Minds / The Sun, The Red, The Blood / Eclipticus Finale Exclinatum

ANGEL DEATH (ITALY)

An Italian Death Black Metal act.

Singles/EPs:
Gore Blood Of War, Hard Blast (1994)
Angeldeath, Hard Blast (1995)

ANGEL NEGRO (COLOMBIA)
Line-Up: Silvia Herrera (vocals), Mauricio Belalcazar (guitar), Andrés Mora (bass), Fabian Aguirre (drums)

ANGEL NEGRO bowed in with the 1994 'Sala 8' cassette. The band had been convened in 1991 with a line up of vocalist / guitarist Mauricio Belalcazar, William Monroy on bass and drummer Alberto Escobar. The following year Silvia Herrera took over the lead vocal role.
With the departure of Escobar and Monroy ANGEL NEGRO welcomed in bassist Andrés Mora and drummer Fabian Aguirre.

Albums:
GUILLAIN BARRE, DMS Producciones (1996)
Intro / Guerros Y Guerreros / Betrayer / Kill My Neighbourhood / Un Mundo En Un Mundo / The End / Sala 8 / Welcome To My Hell / Guillain Barre / Tierra En Decadencia / Autro

ANGELRUST (USA)
Line-Up: Andrew D'Cagna (vocals / guitar), Frank Gordon (bass), Tim Markle (drums)

ANGELRUST was created in October 1999 as a union of MOONTHRONE mentor Andrew D'Cagna and bass player Frank Gordon of Death Metal band MASTICATED ENTRAILS.

Albums:
ARCANE, Frozen Music (2000)

ANGUISH (GERMANY)
Line-Up: Nuno Miguel Férnandes (vocals), Tom Krickl (guitar), Gerd Krieger (guitar), Kalle Bernauer (bass), Mary Nießner (keyboards), Marco Tatomirow (drums)

Albums:
LOST DAYS OF INFANCY, D&S DSR CD 018 (1996)
Swords Of Demokles / Walking Through The Fire / Silent Cry / Lost Days Of Infancy / Civil War / Sad Eyes / Rescue

Me / I Believe / Times Have Changed

ANGUISH (FINLAND)

Singles/EPs:
Ground Absorbs, (199-)

ANTAGONY (Danville, CA, USA)

Californian Grindsters ANTAGONY made their entrance with the 'You Fucking Hippy' demo of 1997. Further cassettes ensued the same year namely 'Loco Shit' and 'Nick Rock'.

Singles/EPs:
The Art Of Hating EP, (1998)

ANTARES

Albums:
SAD HOPE, CCP 100217-2 (2001)

ANTIDEMON (BRAZIL)
Line-Up: Batista (vocals / bass), Kleber (guitar), Eike (drums)

Brazilian Christian Death Metal trio with a female drummer. ANTIDEMON released an eponymous demo upon their inception in 1994 following this with a track included on the 1995 'Refugio De Rock' compilation album. Further promotional cassettes 'Confinamento Eterno' and 1998's 'Antidemon 4 Anos' led to recording of the debut album 'Demonocidio' billed as '27 strikes against Hell'!

Albums:
DEMONOCIDIO, (1999)
Intro / Demonocidio / Suicidio / Usuario / Carnica / Acoite / Libertacäo / Carsas Alcoólicas / Profundo Abismo / Massacre / Holocausto / Ida Sen Volta / Apodrecida / Escravo Do Diablo / Guerra Ad Inferno / Protesto A.M.N. / Mundo Cäo / Terminal Maldicäo / Cadáver / Salário Do Pecado / Cadeias Infernais / Droga / Inferno / Demônios Inatius / Viagern / Libertacäo II / Confinamento Eterno

ANTI SYSTEM (USA)

Albums:
NO LAUGHING MATTER, (199-)

ANTROPOMORPHIA (HOLLAND)
Line-Up: Ferry Damen (vocals / guitar), Vincetit Van Boxtel (guitar), Marc Van

Stiphout (bass), Marco Stubbe (drums)

Although originally a Thrash Death Metal act ANTROPOMORPHIA would evolve into the Nu-Metal band ANTRO. Both bass player Marc Van Stiphout and drummer Marco Stubbe would form part of Death Metal act FLESH MADE SIN convened in 1999 by SAURON vocalist Twan Van Geel and Splatter guitarist Bjorn Van Hamond.

Albums:
NECROMANTIC LOVE SONGS, Blackend (1994)
Crack The Casket / The Carnal Pit / Birth Through Dead / Chunks Of Meat

APOPHIS (GERMANY)
Line-Up: Kristian Hahn (vocals), Roger Kirchner (guitar), Jorg Bartlet (guitar), Christoph Bittner (bass), Erik Stegmaier (drums)

APOPHIS is a German Death Metal act named after the ancient Egyptian mythical serpent that inhabited the underworld devouring lost souls.
The band was called RAISE HELL before 1990 and the first album as APOPHIS, 'Gateway To The Underworld', issued on the band's own label, sold around 2000 copies.

Albums:
GATEWAY TO THE UNDERWORLD, Apophis (1993)
DOWN IN THE VALLEY, Contraption COR010 (1996)
The Sun / Sleep In My Eyes / The Enlightenment / Awake / Sombre Thoughts / Personal Freedom / Ode To The Golden Fruit / Until My Blood... / Your Perpetual Bliss / The Cries That Swore The Moon
HELIOPOLIS, Morbid (1999)
The Serpent God / Choirs Of Bitterness / Reincarnation Of The Serpent God / Tear Down Your Walls / Resurrection / Ein Meer Aus Tränen / Dominion / Behold His Arrival / Nobody Will Miss You

APOTHEOSIS (GERMANY)
Line-Up: Bernd Golderer (vocals), Marcus Rembold (guitar), Udo Plieninger (guitar), Alexander Woydich (bass), Alexander Dallinger (drums / keyboards)

Formed in 1993 and issuing the 'Beyond The Grave - No Breeding Ground' demo the following year, after several live shows M.D.D. Records signed APOTHEOSIS.
Playing Death Metal with a Gothic touch, the band sing in both English and German and have, since the release of the first album, added keyboard player Marco to the ranks.

Albums:
A SHROUD OF BELIEF, M.D.D. 06 CD (1996)
Apotheosis / As Serenity Fades / A Shroud Of Belief / White Angel - Dusty God / A Landslide Called Eternity / Beyond The Grave / Stars Beyond Their Skies / No Breeding Ground / Total Silence
BLACK AND BLUE REALITY, M.D.D. 11CD (1997)
Black & Blue Reality / Exfarevanity / Pleasurefall / Horizon / Splendid / Release / Excuses / Vergangen / Innocence For Free / A Start Inside / Rain

A PUNTO (ARGENTINA)

Albums:
POPULAR PODER, November (1996)

ARCANE (USA)
Line-Up: Oscar Barbour (vocals), Doug Judah (guitar), Byron Hawk (guitar), Kurt Joye (bass), Kelly Sanford (drums)

Progressive Thrash Metal band ARCANE, founded in 1987, debuted with the 1989 'Mirror Deception' demo.

Albums:
DESTINATION UNKNOWN, Wild Rags (1991)
Recurrent Inception / Enshrouded Crypt / Infernal Domicile / Ancient Internecine / Life's Illusion / Impasse Of Humanity / Mirror Of Deception / Agaememnon

ARCHAIC TORSE (GERMANY)
Line-Up: Claus (vocals), Stefan (guitar), Jörg (guitar), Victor (bass), John (drums)

A Death Metal quartet.

Albums:
SNEAK ATTACK, IMF 377 0027 2 41 (1994)
Beyond The Great Divide / The Value Of Your Soul / Message To No One / Snuff / Sneak Attack / A Valediction / Forbidden Mourning / Compulsion To Kill / Fraud

ARCH ENEMY (SWEDEN)

Line-Up: Johan Liiva (vocals), Mike Amott (guitar), Christopher Amott (bass), Daniel Elandsson (drums)

Old style Death Metallers ARCH ENEMY feature ex-members of CARNAGE, CARCASS and EUCHARIST.

Frontman Johan Liiva previously played with CARNAGE and FURBOWL whilst guitarist Mike Amott, best known for his role in CARCASS, was also once a CARNAGE member early on and, in addition to ARCH ENEMY, currently also plays in SPIRITUAL BEGGARS.

Christopher Amott, Mike's younger brother, would appear to be following in his brother's footsteps by not laying all his eggs in one basket by also contributing to his side band ARMAGEDDON, whilst drummer Daniel Erlandsson occasionally with IN FLAMES and was previously with EUCHARIST.

The band contributed a cover of 'Aces High' to the Toys Factory Records tribute to IRON MAIDEN, namely the cheesily titled compilation album 'Made In Tribute'. Christopher Amott shifted to bass as the six string position was filled by WITCHERY / MERCYFUL FATE man Sharee D'Angelo.

ARCH ENEMY built up quite a global reputation with tours of Japan and Europe. The band also opened for CRADLE OF FILTH in 1999. A support slot gained by admitted nepotism as Erlandsson's elder brother had gained the CRADLE OF FILTH drummer's job.

Albums:

BLACK EARTH, Wrong Again WAR011CD (1996)
Bury Me An Angel / Dark Insanity / Eureka / Idolatress / Cosmic Retribution / Demoniality / Transmigration Macabre / Time Capsule / Fields Of Desolation
STIGMATA, Century Media (1998)
Beast Of Man / Stigmata / Sinister Mephisto / Dark Of The Sun / Let The Killing Begin / Black Earth / Tears Of The Dead / Vox Stellarum / Bridge Of Destiny
BURNING BRIDGES, Century Media 77276-2(1999)
The Immortal / Dead Inside / Pilgrim / Silverwing / Demonic Science / Seed Of Hate / Angelclaw / Burning Bridges
BURNING JAPAN LIVE 1999, Toys Factory (2000)
The Immortal / Dark Insanity / Dead Inside / Diva Satanica / Pilgrim / Silverwing / Beast Of Man / Bass Intro /

Tears Of The Dead / Bridge Of Destiny / Transmigration Macabre / Angelclaw

ARCHGOAT (FINLAND)

Extreme Death Black Metal outfit ARCHGOAT issued the 'Jesus Spawn' and 'Penis Perversor' demos prior to the controversially titled 1994 12" single.

Singles/EPs:
Angelcunt: Tales Of Desecration, Necropolis (1994)
(12" split single with BEHERIT)

ARIUS (Fremont, OH, USA)

Line-Up: Lukas Kummer (vocals / bass), Matt Moyer (guitar), Matt Davis (guitar), Shane McConnell (drums)

Ohio act ARIUS were originally assembled as EVISCERATE during 1992 with a line up of vocalist / bassist Lukas Kummer, guitarists Damon Conn and Matt Moyer and drummer Shane McConnell. Conn would decamp leaving the newly named ARIUS as a trio until the enlistment of former AHRIMAN guitarist Bryan Autullo.

ARIUS released the 1995 demo session 'The Last Suffer' after which Autullo made way for Matt Davis.

ARMAGEDDON (SWEDEN)

Line-Up: Jonas Nyrën (vocals), Christopher Amott (guitar), Martin Bengtsson (bass), Peter Wildoer (drums)

An uncompromising, brutal Metal band, ARMAGEDDON, created by members of ARCH ENEMY and IN THY DREAMS, spread the word initially with their inclusion on a Japanese released IRON MAIDEN tribute album with their version of 'Die With Your Boots On'.

Founder member and drummer Daniel Erlandsson left to form EUCHARIST prior to recording of the 1997 'Crossing The Rubicon' album.

Albums:
CROSSING THE RUBICON, War Music 970304-1 (1997)
2022 (Intro) / Godforsaken / The Juggernaut Divine / Astral Adventure / Funeral In Space / Asteroid Dominion / Galaxies Away / Faithless / Children Of The New Sun / Into The Sun

ARMOURED ANGEL (AUSTRALIA)

Singles/EPs:
Hymn Of Hate / Beyond The Sacrament / Stigmartyr / Ordained In Darkness, (199-) ('Stigmartyr' EP)

ARSEDESTROYER (SWEDEN)

Line-Up: Terje Andersson (vocals / guitar), Thorbjörn Gräslund (guitar), Peter Hirseland (bass), Kenneth Andersson (drums)

A subtly named Swedish Grindcore act. The 1998 shared album with Americans ABSTAIN is culled from live shows recorded during 1997.
ARSEDESTOYER toured Japan in 2000 sharing billing with Japan's premier scatalogically obsessed Grindsters GORE BEYOND NECROPSY.

Singles/EPs:
Arse Destroyer, Distortion (1993) (Split EP with CONFUSION)
Split, Devour (2000) (7" split single with GORE BEYOND NECROPSY)

Albums:
ARSE DESTROYER, Psychomania PMR012 (1994) (Split LP with NOISE SLAUGHTER)
MOTHER OF ALL CHAOTIC NOISECORE, Distortion DISTCD 11 (1995)
LIVE ABOARD THE M.S. STUBNITZ, In League Wit' Satan (1998) (Split album with ABSTAIN)
F.O.A.D. / Kenneth (R.I.P.) / Tg's Lilla Kuk / I Got Kas / Strategies Of Complete Assholes / This Record Is Not Compatible With The German 33/45 System / Domar's Girlfriend Likes To Flash Beaver From Stage / Ackliga Javla Syrsa / Knut's Girlfriend Likes To Flash Beaver From The Stage / Boycott Mol / Domar's Liver / Tg Is Crying (But Not For Kenneth) / Sodomizer (Featuring MC Swinger) / Matte (R.I.P.) / Partypatte 31 Ar 16 / We Actually Played 19 Songs But Nevermind / These Aren't Really Songtitles Anyway

ASHEN MORTALITY (UK)

Line-Up: Ian Arkley (vocals / guitar), Melanie Bolton (vocals / keyboards), Tim Cooper (bass), George Aytoun (drums)

West Midlands Christian Doomladen Death Metal band. ASHEN MORTALITY were created in 1993 by former SEVENTH ANGEL frontman Ian Arkley. The original line up comprised Arkley, vocalist and keyboard player Melanie Bolton, bassist Tim Cooper and drummer Ben Jones. ASHEN MORTALITY's debut eponymous demo was actually produced by Andy Wicket, the original singer of DURAN DURAN!
Following second demo 'Separation' Jones decamped to be replaced by Neal Harris for an appearance at the Greenbelt festival and tours of Holland and Germany. To promote the debut album 'Sleepless Remorse' ASHEN MORTALITY undertook support gigs to AT THE GATES, ACRIMONY and HECATE ENTHRONED with another new face on the drum stool Neil Shivlock.
George Aytoun is the latest sticksman appearing on second album 'Your Caress'.
Arkley would guest on Australian Christian Death Metal act PARAMAECIUM's third album 'A Time To Mourn'.

Albums:
SLEEPLESS REMORSE, Forsaken (1996)
Yesterday's Gone / Faded Tapestry / Separation / Sleepless Remorse / Cast The First Stone / The Darkest Of Nights / Imprisoned
YOUR CARESS, (1999)
Broken Bonds / Your Caress / In Empty Eyes / My Reflection / From This Cage / Our Eden / Through The Vale

ASHES (SWEDEN)

Swedish outfit ASHES attempted to recreate old school Death Metal on their 1997 debut album, entitled 'Death Has Made It's Call'.
The band came together the previous year, pulling in ex-PANTHYMONIUM guitarist Mourning in time for recording.

Albums:
DEATH HAS MADE IT'S CALL, Necropolis NR015 (1997)
Darker Age / Path To Eternity / The Battle / Crucified Mirror Of Me / Ashes / Like Fire / Heretic / No More Pain / Temple Of Truth / Storm / Rock n' Roll Witch

ASIATIC SPIKE

Albums:
BEASTIAL WARFARE, Don't Kill Yourself (1999)

Job Of The Year / Everyone's Nightmare / Poop Chute Riot / Eaten Alive / Between Rape and Necrophilia / Dance Of The Demons / Twilight In The Midst Of Chaos / Mexican Asylum / That Doesn't Look N.O.R. / Santa or Satan / Nordic Bloodshed / Curbstomp / Asshole Police II

AS I LAY DYING

Previously titled VISCERAL EVISCERATION.

ASPHYX (HOLLAND)
Line-Up: Martin Van Drunen (vocals / bass), Eric Daniels (guitar), Bob Bagchus (drums)

ASPHYX date back to 1989 when the band was formed by drummer Bob Bagchus with former member Tony Brookhuis and swiftly issued the first demo entitled 'Enter The Domain'.

Frontman Martin Van Drunen split from Dutch techno-thrashers PESTILENCE in late 1990 due to personality clashes within the band and, shortly after his departure, he hooked up with ASPHYX replacing former bassist / vocalist Theo Loomans.

ASPHYX went into the studio to record a projected debut album to be entitled 'Embrace The Death'. However, due to record company financial problems these tapes never saw a commercial release.

The band's second attempt, and what was to be their debut album, 'The Rack' was recorded on a minimalist budget in a deliberate attempt to achieve a deliberately primitive sound. Worldwide sales approaching 30,000 copies were boosted by a European tour alongside ENTOMBED, proving ASPHYX had chosen the right path.

'Crush The Cenotaph', issued in 1992, was a mini-album produced by Waldemar Sorychta and containing reworks of pre-Van Drunen era material and live tracks. Livework to promote the mini-album comprised an extensive European tour with BENEDICTION and BOLT-THROWER.

Clearly the tour was more enjoyable for Van Drunen than most. Clearly impressed by each other, the bassist / vocalist joined BOLT-THROWER in 1994!

The revised line-up of ASPHYX thus emerged, comprised of new vocalist / bassist Ron Van Pol, guitarist Eric Daniels and drummer Sander Van Hoof.

Further ructions hit the ASPHYX line up in 1995 as Daniels joined ETERNAL SOLSTICE and original vocalist Theo Loomanns returned. Loomanns contributed bass and guitar to the 'God Cries' album.

The 'Embrace The Death' sessions finally found a release in 1996 through Century Media with extra tracks from 'Mutilating Process'.

Despite the constant line-up changes ASPHYX continued to build on their popularity in the Death Metal market with consistent album sales. However, the band changed title to SOULBURN for 1998's 'Feeding On Angels' album. Tragically Loomans was killed the same year in a road accident.

The 2000 album found ASPHYX, back to their former title as a mark of respect to Loomans, as a duo of Wannes Gubbles, Eric Daniel and Bog Bagchus. However, after its release ASPHYX announced their retirement.

Singles/EPs:
Mutilating Process / Streams Of Ancient Wisdom, Nuclear Blast (1990)
Crush The Cenotaph / Rite Of Shades / The Krusher / Evocation (Live) / Wasteland Of Terror (Live), Century Media 799723-2 (1992) ('Crush The Cenotaph' EP)

Albums:
THE RACK, Century Media 84 9716 (1991)
The Quest Of Absurdity / Vermin / Diabolical Existence / Evocation / Wasteland Of Terror / The Sickening Dwell / Ode To A Nameless Grave / Pages In Blood / The Rack
LAST ONE ON EARTH, Century Media (1993)
M.S. Bismarck / The Krusher / Serenade In Lead / Last One On Earth / The Incarnation Of Lust / Streams Of Ancient Wisdom / Food For The Ignorant / Asphyx (Forgotten War)
ASPHYX, Century Media CD 77063 (1994)
Prelude Of The Unhonoured Funeral / Depths Of Eternity / Emperors Of Salvation / 'Til Death Do Us Part / Initiation Into The Ossuary / Incarcerated Chimaeras / Abomination Echoes / Back Into Eternity / Valleys In Oblivion / Thoughts Of An Atheist
GOD CRIES, Century Media 77117-2 (1996)
God Cries / It Awaits / My Beloved

Enemy / Died Yesterday / Cut-Throat Urges / Slaughtered In Sodom / Frozen Soul / Fear My Greed / The Blood I Spilled.
EMBRACE THE DEATH, Century Media CD 77141-2 (1996)
Intro / Embrace The Death / The Sickened Dwell / Streams Of Ancient Wisdom / Thoughts Of An Atheist / Crush The Cenotaph / Denying The Goat / Vault Of The Wailing Souls / Circle Of The Secluded / To Succubus A Whore / Eternity's Depths / Outro / Mutilating Process / Streams Of An Ancient Wisdom
ON THE RISING WINGS OF INFERNO, Century Media 77263-2 (2000)
Summoning The Storm / The Scent Of Obscurity / For They Ascend… / On The Wings Of Inferno / 06-06-2006 / Waves Of Fire / Indulge In Frenzy / Chaos In The Flesh / Marching Towards The Styx

AS SERENITY FADES (FINLAND)
Line-Up: Sami Kotiranta (vocals), Sami Vainikka (guitar), Peter Viherkanto (guitar), Henri Fagerholm (bass), Tom Henriksson (drums)

Billed as Melodic Death Metal AS SERENITY FADES first made their presence known with their 1992 demo tape 'Lowering Sunset'.

Singles/EPs:
Tear Seas / Yearning / Oriental / Earthborn, Adipocere CDAR 018 (1994) ('Earthborn' EP)

ASSISTING SORROW (KY, USA)
Line-Up: Chris Leffler (vocals / guitar), Jerry Barksdale (bass / keyboards), Mike Barnes (keyboards), Jim Higgins (drums)

ASSISTING SORROW issued a self financed album 'Under The Lies' and contributed to tribute albums for such diverse artists as KING DIAMOND, AC/DC and LED ZEPPELIN. The band folded in early 1999 with bassist Jerry Barksdale and drummer Jim Higgins joining CORONACH. Barksdale also operates as bass player with Gothic Industrial project ABSENCE OF FAITH.
Albums:
UNDER THE LIES, Assisting Sorrow (1999)

ASSORTED HEAP (GERMANY)
Line-Up: Dirk (vocals), Klaus (guitar), Gunter (guitar), Lord Meyer (bass), Marter (drums)

Death Metallers ASSORTED HEAP recorded their inaugural demo tape, 'Killing Peace', in 1988. During 1991 they wound up supporting PARADISE LOST in Germany.

Albums:
THE EXPERIENCE OF HORROR, 1 MF 377 0012 1 27 (1991)
Unexpiated Bloodshed / Experience Of Horror / Remembrance Of Tomorrow / In Vain / Sold Out Souls / Trick To Your Mind
MIND WAVES, 1 MF 337 0028 2 41 (1992)
Coloured Eyes / Holy Ground / What I Confess / Nice To Beat You / Mind Waves / Dealing With Dilemma / Cardinal Sin / Hardcore Incorrigible / Artificial Intelligence

ASSUCK (FL, USA)
Line-Up: Paul Pavlovich (vocals), Steve Heritage (guitar), Pete Jay (bass), Rob Proctor (drums)

Singles/EPs:
Necrosalvation, Rigid (1989) (7" single)
Suffering Quota, No System (1990)
Blindspot, Open (1992) (7" single)
Split, (199-) (Split 7" single with OLD)
State To State / The Thousand Mile Stare / Procession / Epilogue / A Nation's Tear, SOA (1993) ('State To State' EP)

Albums:
ANTI CAPITAL, Sound Pollution (1991)
Socialized Crucifixion / The Thousand Mile Stare / Population Index / Dogmatic / Spiritual Manipulation / Feasts Of War / October Revolution / Procession / State To State / The Perpetual Cycle / World Of Confusion / Civilization Comes, Civilization Goes / Page By Page / Sterility / Body Politic Equation / Anticapitol / Epilogue / Wall Of Shame / Suffering Quota / Parade Of The Lifeless / Blood And Cloth / Automate / Within Without / Blindspot / By Design / Spine / Infanticide
MISERY INDEX, Sound Pollution (1997)
QED / Salt Mine / Corners / Dataclast / Blight Of Element / Talon Of Dominion / Unrequited Blood / Wartorn / Sum And Substance / Riven / Reversing Denial / Lithographs / Intravenous / A Monument

To Failure / In Absence

ASTRAL RISING (FRANCE)
Line-Up: Frank Tomse (vocals / guitar), Essem (guitar), Phillipe Guiziou (bass), Jerome Lachaud (drums)

A French Death flavoured Doom act. Drummer Jerome Lauchaud split after the debut and for 1995's 'In Quest' ASTRAL RISING drafted Eric Lauuad. The band folded in 1996.

Singles/EPs:
Alpha State, Arckham (1992)

Albums:
ABEON AADEONA, Chaos 001 (1993)
Nocturnal Thoughts / ...In Awe / Odd Memories / Dawn In Cries / Skadia / Tactire Tink
IN QUEST, Active AC.95-001 (1995)
In Quest / Beggar Of The New Hopes / Wasteland / Gowns Black Viles / Anguish Feelings / Choral Fantasy / Pray In A Garden / The Realm To Come / Callioppe

ATHEIST (FL, USA)
Line-Up: Kelly Shaefer (vocals / guitar), Randy Burkey (guitar), Roger Patterson (bass),

Florida's ATHEIST started out life originally titled RAVAGE under which title the band contributed tracks 'Brain Damage' and 'On They Slay' to the 1987 'Raging Death' compilation album.
Issued a 1988 demo featuring the tracks 'No Truth', 'Choose Your Death', 'Beyond', 'On They Slay' and 'Brain Damage'.
Supported the likes of TESTAMENT, SNFU, DEATH ANGEL and OBITUARY prior to signing to European label Active Records. Scott Burns produced debut album 'Piece Of Time'.
In February 1991 ATHEIST suffered a huge blow when bassist Roger Patterson was killed. Added ex-CYNIC bassist Tony Choy to record 'Unquestionable Presence'. Choy opted to accompany PESTILENCE for their 1991 world tour.

Albums:
PIECE OF TIME, Active ATV8
Piece Of Time / Unholy War / Room With A View / On They Slay / Beyond / I Deny / Why Bother? / Life / No Truth
UNQUESTIONABLE PRESENCE,
Active ATV20 (1991)

Mother Man / Unquestionable Presence / Your Life's Retribution / Enthralled In Essence / An Incarnation's Dream / The Formative Years / Brains / And The Psychic Saw
ELEMENTS, Music For Nations MFN 150 (1993)
Green/ Water / Samba Briza / Air / Displacement / Animal / Mineral / Fire / Fractal Point / Earth / See You Again / Elements

ATOMVINTER (SWEDEN)

A Swedish Death Metal group.

Albums:
ATOMVINTER, Black Sun DISTCD 12 (1995)
Sinnes / Kurd / Hej Säpol / Nyliberal / Danska Poliser Är Harda / Sexualakt / Djävla / Tvättsvamp / Sla Tillbaka / Du / 790 Dagar / Kärra / Västra Frölunda, / Angered / Nazifasoner / Videodrome

ATRAX MORGUE (JAPAN)

Albums:
SICKNESS REPORT, (199-)
Evisceration / Massive Vulval Warts / Deformed / Brain Penetration / Sphrenix Nor / Ipoleptic / Arphenia / Chronic Disease / Slow Agony Of A Dying Organism

ATROCITY (GERMANY)
Line-Up: Alex Krull (vocals), Matthias Röderer (guitar), Richard Scharf (guitar), Oliver Klasen (bass), Michael Schwarz (drums)

Founded in Ludwigsburg during 1985, ATROCITY signed to Nuclear Blast Records and released the 'Blue Blood' EP in 1989, followed by the Scott Burns produced 'Hallucinations' album the following year.
One of ATROCITY's early incarnations included bassist Rene Tometschek who later formed MIGHTY DECIBEL releasing an EP 'Relieve The Distress'.
ATROCITY toured Europe as support to CARCASS in 1990, SODOM in 1991 and DEICIDE in 1992. In 1994 ATROCITY supported OBITUARY on their British tour following cancellation by EYEHATEGOD. In early 1995 the band underwent a line-up change, substituting Scharf and Markus Knapp for guitarist Torsten Bauer and bassist Chris Lukhamp respectively. Not content to rest on their laurels,

ATROCITY undertook some brave experimentation of sounds for their two 1995 releases. 'Die Liebe' was a joint project with electronic band DAS ICH, whilst 'Calling The Rain' was graced with an ethnic lead vocal from Yasmin Krull.

To promote the 'Willenskraft' album ATROCITY toured Germany on a package tour with strong support from IN FLAMES, HEAVENWOOD and TOTENMOND.

Experimenting further still, the 1997 single 'Shout' is ATROCITY's interpretation of TEARS FOR FEARS' hit song and also includes a version of D.A.F.'s 'Verschwende Deine Jugend'. Following the tradition of diversity set previously, the 'Shout' single proved to be a taster for the 'Werk 80' album, a collection of cover versions by pop artists such as O.M.D., DAVID BOWIE, DURAN DURAN, FRANKIE GOES TO HOLLYWOOD, HUMAN LEAGUE and even SOFT CELL.

ATROCITY's prolonged tenacity finally paid rewards when they achieved their first chart album, 'Werk 80' entering the German placings at number 33, the sales figures for which must in some respect be married to a tasteful advertising campaign featuring the two models chosen for the single and album artwork.

Singles/EPs:
Blue Blood / When The Fire Burns Over The Sea / Humans Lost Humanity, Nuclear Blast NB 23 (1989)
Deliverance (Come To My World-Mix) / Willenskraft (Remix) / Scorching Breath (Remix) / Gottes Tod, Massacre MAS CD 114 (1996) ('The Definition Of Kraft & Wille' EP)
Shout (edit) / Shout / Verschwende Deine Jugen, Massacre MAS CD141 (1997)
Tainted Love / Tainted Love (Albrin mix) / Die Deutschmaschine / Deliverance (Wow! Mix), Massacre MASCD143 (1997)
Taste Of Sin / Pictures Of Matchstick Men, Massacre (2000)

Albums:
HALLUCINATIONS, Nuclear Blast NB 038 (1990)
Deep In Your Subconsciousness / Life Is A Long And Silent River / Fatal Step / Hallucinations / Defeated Intellect / Abyss Of Addiction / Hold Out (To The End) / Last Temptation / Blue Blood / When The Fire Burns Over The Sea /

Humans Lost Humanity
TODESSEHNSUCHT, Roadrunner RR 9128 2 (1992)
Todessehnsucht / Godless Years / Unspoken Names / Defiance / Triumph At Dawn / Introduction / Sky Turned Red / Necropolis / A Prison Called Earth / Todessehnsucht Reprise / Arcangel
BLUT, Massacre CD033 (1994)
Trial / Miss Directed / In My Veins / Blood Lust Undead Trance / I'm In Darkness / Calling The Rain / Moon-Struck / Ever And Anon / Begotten Son (Of Wrath) / Into The Maze / Leicenfeier / Goddess In Black / Threnody (The Spirit Never Dies) / Soul Embrace / Land Beyond The Forest
DIE LIEBE, Swan Lake MASS CD 069 (1995)
Die Liebe / Moonstrucker / Bloodlust (Undead Trance) / Misdirected / Parentalia / Trial By Ordeal / Unschuld / Von Leid Und Elend Und Seelenqualen / Die Todgeweihten
CALLING THE RAIN, Swan Lake MASS CD071 (1995)
Calling The Rain (video edit) / Back From Eternity / Departure / Land Beyond The Forest / Migrant's Shade / Dir Geburt Eines Baumes / Calling The Rain (remix) / Ancient Sadness
WILLENSKRAFT, Massacre CD099 (1996)
Scorching Breath / Deliverence / Blood Stained Prophecy / Love Is Dead / We Are Degeneration / Willenskraft / For Ever And A Day / Seal Of Secrecy / Down Below / The Hunt
WERK 80, Massacre MAS PC0138 (1997) **33 GERMANY**
Shout / Rage Hard / Wild Boys / The Great Commandment / Send Me An Angel / Tainted Love / Der Mussolini / Being Boiled / Don't Go/ Let's Dance / Maid Of Orleans
NON PLUS ULTRA 1989-1999, Massacre (2000)
Shake Your Heads / Tainted Love / Rage Hard / Shout / Die Deutschmaschine / Siehst Du Mich Im Licht / Blue Moon / Deliverance / Gottes Tod / Land Beyond The Forest / Calling The Rain / Die Liebe / Die Todgeweihten / Willenskraft / Love Is Dead / We Are Degeneration / Trial / B.L.U.T. / Leichenfeier / Neropolis / Todessehnsucht / Godless Years / Fatal Step / Hallucinations / Blue Blood (1996 version) / Procreation (Of The Wicked)
GEMINI, Massacre (2000) **95 GERMANY**
Taste Of Sin / Zauberstab / Tanz Der Teufel / Lieberspiel / Wilder Schmetterling / Sound Of Silence / Das

11 Gebot / Sometimes… A Nightsong / Seasons In Black / Gemini / Lili Marleen

ATROX (NORWAY)
Line-Up: Monika (vocals / keyboards), Eivind (guitar), Rune (guitar), Tom (bass), Tor Arne (drums)

Atmospheric self-styled 'Schizo' Metallers ATROX, although not strictly within genre confines, possess many links to Black Metal acts. The act was founded in 1988 as SUFFOCATION, comprising guitarists Skei and Gundar Dragsten (later of GODSEND), bassist Sven, drummer Knarr and vocalist Gersa. The group evolved into ATROX during 1990 issuing the demos 'Mind Shadows' and 1993's 'Dead Leaves'. The same year found ENTROPY NOVA guitarist Tomas taking over the drum stool from Knarr - later of BLOODTHORN, a position taken the following year by Larry. Both Skei and Sven would also decamp, the former making his name with MANES. Drafted in were I FEAR guitarists Rune and Dagga, vocalist Monika (sister of 3RD AND THE MORTAL's Ann-Marie) and GODSEND bassist Tommy.
1997 also found ATROX contributing a version of HAWKWIND's 'Golden Void Part II' to a local compilation album. After the release of the debut album Gersa departed leaving Monika as sole vocalist. ATROX underwent a traumatic line up change in October of 1999 when a disagreement over musical direction forced the exit of Larry, Dagga and Tommy. MIST ENTICER members drummer Tor Arne and bassist Tom filled the role of rhythm section.
Monika, her sister Ann-Marie and Rune also operate the side project TACTILE. Eivind divides his time with MANES.
Not to be confused with either the American ATROX or the Swedish Thrash Metal ATROX that issued the 1992 single 'Land Of Silence'.

Singles/EPs:
Silence The Echoes, Danza Ipnotica (1997)

Albums:
MESMERISED, Head Not Found (1997)
Intro / Steeped In Misery As I Am / Wave / The Ocean / A Minds Escape / Flower Meadow / The Air Shed Tears / Hinc Illac La Crimac
CONTENTUM, Seasons Of Mist (2000)
Sultry Air / Unsummoned / Lizard Dance

/ Parta Rei / Gather In Me No More / Ignoramus / Letters To Earth / Serenity / Homage / What Crawls Underneath / Torture / Outro

ATROX (SWEDEN)
Line-Up: Tobbe Johansson (vocals / guitar), Johan Larsson (guitar), Pelle Nilsson (guitar), Stephan Hermansson (bass), Isti (drums)

Black Speed Metallers ATROX added three new members following the 'Land Of Silence' single release. New recruits were vocalist Nicke Erikson and guitarists Johan Gardesedt and Johan Dahlström.

Singles/EPs:
Land Of Silence / The Oldest Wisdom, PLC PLC 9201-02 (1992)

Albums:
MESMERISED, Head Not Found (1997)

AT THE GATES (SWEDEN)
Line-Up: Tomas Lindberg (vocals), Anders Bjorler (guitar), Martin Larsson (guitar), Jonas Bjorler (bass), Adrian Elandsson (drums)

A very aggressive technical Thrash act in the vein of America's ATHEIST, but with added twists and a touch of the avant garde, this Swedish quintet, was initially known as GROTESQUE, under which name they released the 'Incantation'

AT THE GATES
Photo : Martin Wickler

34

AT THE GATES
Photo: Lisa K.

album in 1991, the Gothenburg based band having formed in August 1990.

As AT THE GATES, the first product to emerge was the mini-album 'Gardens Of Grief' on Dolores Records. The outfit's line-up at this time consisted of vocalist Tomas Lindberg, guitarists Alf Svensson and Anders Bjorler, bassist Jonas Bjorler and drummer Adrian Erlandsson.

Svensson's involvement with AT THE GATES would be beaten by his colleagues as the man soon departed later, going on to form OXIPLEGATZ and releasing the 'Worlds And Worlds' album in 1996.

'The Red In The Sky Is Ours' features guest violinist Jesper Jarold. AT THE GATES toured Europe in 1992 opening for MY DYING BRIDE. Their third album 'With Fear I Kiss The Burning Darkness' was produced by noted Death Metal producer Tomas Skogsberg and again received solid reviews. AT THE GATES appeared at the MTV/Peaceville show at Nottingham's Rock City alongside ANATHEMA and MY DYING BRIDE before once more touring Europe with ANATHEMA and CRADLE OF FILTH.

'Terminal Spirit Disease' was produced by Fredrik Nordstrom and includes a selection of live tracks culled from the previous three releases alongside new studio material. To back up its release the band once more hit the road with ANATHEMA and MY DYING BRIDE. Toured Europe in early 1995 with SEANCE.

AT THE GATES switched labels moving to Earache Records. First product of this liaison was the 'Slaughter Of The Soul' album, which featured a version of Australian act SLAUGHTERLORD's track 'Legion'. KING DIAMOND guitarist Andy La Rocque guests on the track 'Cold'.

AT THE GATES also contributed their rendition of 'Captor Of Sin' to the SLAYER tribute album 'Slatanic Slaughter'.

Despite 'Slaughter Of The Soul' proving to be their highest selling effort, AT THE GATES split in late 1996. Various ex-members of AT THE GATES created THE HAUNTED fronted by former FACEDOWN singer Marco Aro.

Erlandsson founded H.E.A.L. and later joined premier British Black Metal act CRADLE OF FILTH in 1999.

Lindberg became vocalist for GREAT DECEIVER releasing the 2000 album 'Jet Black Art'. Lindberg joined DISINCARNATE in 1999, the band assembled by former DEATH / TESTAMENT / CANCER guitarist JAMES MURPHY.

By mid 2000 Lindberg was fronting LOCK UP, the side project of NAPALM DEATH men Shane Embury and Jesse Pintado with DIMMU BORGIR drummer Nick Barker.

Singles/EPs:
Souls Of The Evil Departed / At The Gates / All Life Ends / City Of The Screaming Statues, Dolores DOL 005 (1991)
Souls Of The Evil Departed / All Life Ends, Peaceville Collectors CC7 (1994)

35

(7" yellow vinyl single)

Albums:
THE RED IN THE SKY IS OURS,
Peaceville DEAF 10 (1992)
The Red In The Sky Is Ours / The
Season To Come / Kingdom Gone /
Through Gardens Of Grief / Within /
Windows / Claws Of Laughter Dead /
Neverwhere / The Scar / Night Comes,
Blood Black / City Of Screaming Statues
**WITH FEAR I KISS THE BURNING
DARKNESS**, Peaceville DEAF14 (1993)
Beyond Good And Evil / Raped By The
Light Of Christ / The Break Of Autumn /
Non-Divine / Primal Breath / The
Architects / Stardrowned / Blood Of The
Sunsets / The Burning Darkness / Ever-
Opening Flower / Through The Red
TERMINAL SPIRIT DISEASE,
Peaceville VILE 47 (1994)
The Swarm / Terminal Spirit Disease /
And The World Returned / Forever Blind
/ The Fevered Circle / The Beautiful
Wound / All Life Ends (Live) / The
Burning Darkness (Live) / Kingdom
Gone (Live)
SLAUGHTER OF THE SOUL, Earache
MOSH 143 (1995)
Blinded By Fear / Slaughter Of The Soul
/ Cold / Under A Serpent Sun / Into The
Dead Sky / Suicide Nation / World Of
Lies / Unto Others / Nausea / Need /
The Flames Of The End / Legion

AURORA BOREALIS

(Atlanta, GA, USA)
Line-Up: Ron Vento (vocals / guitar),
Jason Ian-Vaughn Eckart (bass), Derek
Roddy (drums)

Essentially a one man project of former
LESTREGUS NOSFERATUS man Ron
Vento. AURORA BOREALIS first
employed ACHERON and ANGEL
CORPSE drummer Tony Laureano for the
'Mansions Of Eternity' album. By the time
of 'Praise The Archaic - Lights Embrace'
bassist Jason Ian-Vaughn Eckart and
MALEVOLENT CREATION drummer
Derek Roddy were employed.
The band is prolific on the tribute scene
having cut 'After Forever' for the BLACK
SABBATH tribute 'Hell Rules', 'Altar Of
Sacrifice' for the SLAYER homage
'Gateway To Hell', JUDAS PRIEST's
'Metal Meltdown' for the 'Hell Bent For
Metal' opus and 'We Rock' for the DIO
collection 'Awaken The Demon'.

Albums:
MANSIONS OF ETERNITY, (199-)
Crowned With Embalment / Weighing Of
The Heart / Valley Of The Kings / Slave
To The Grave / Sixteenth Charm
**PRAISE THE ARCHAIC - LIGHTS
EMBRACE**, (199-)
Offerings Of Jade And Blood / A Gaze
Into Everdark / In The Depths Of A
Labyrinth / Aggressive Dynasty / War Of
The Rings / For Your Comprehension /
Constellation Embellished With Chaos /
Calm Before The Storm
NORTHERN LIGHTS, (199-)
Thrice Told / Enter The Halls / Images In
The Nightsky / Draco / Sky Dweller /
Hydrah / Dream God / Distant

AUTHORIZE (SWEDEN)

Line-Up: Tomas Ek (vocals), Larsa
Johansson (guitar), Jörgen Paulsson
(guitar), Putte Leander (bass),
Micke Swed (drums)

Initially known as MORBID FEAR upon
their foundation in 1988, the group
contributed the track 'Darkest Age' to the
1990 split EP 'Opinionate'.
Drummer Micke Swed left to team up with
UNDER THE SUN.

Albums:
THE SOURCE OF DOMINION,
Putrefaction PUT 007 (1991)

AUTOPSY (USA)

Line-Up: Eric Cutler (vocals / guitar),
Chris Reifert (drums / vocals), Danny
Corrales (guitar), Ken Sovari (bass)

AUTOPSY was formed in 1987 when
drummer Chris Reifert left DEATH
following their 'Scream Bloody Gore'
album. Debuted the following year with a
four-track demo comprising 'Human
Genocide', 'Embalmed', 'Stillborn' and
'Mauled To Death'.
The debut album utilizes SADUS bassist
Steve DiGeorgio for the recording
sessions but the band soon found a
temporary substitute Ken Sovari in time
for European live work with BOLT-
THROWER and PESTILENCE.
In 1990 prior to a European tour bassist
Ken Sovari left to be replaced by Eric's
bother Steve Cutler. SUFFOCATION
bassist Josh Barohn also featured as a
member the same year. Barohn was later
to found WELT and IRON LUNG.
AUTOPSY played a 1992 festival in
Detroit on a bill with MORTICIAN, VITAL

REMAINS and REPULSION in which the band played as a trio due to Eric Butler breaking his hand.

Steve Cutler departed following the 'Mental Funeral' album. AUTOPSY re-enlisted the services of DiGiorgio for the 1992 'Fiend For Blood' EP before adding ex-SUFFOCATION bassist Josh Barohn on a permanent basis.

The 'Acts Of The Unspeakable' was hyped as AUTOPSY's most 'sickest fuckin' album ever' - until 'Shitfun'.

Chris Reifert created ABCESS and by 2000 THE RAVENOUS with STORMTROOPERS OF DEATH bassist Dan Lilker and NECROPHAGIA's Killjoy.

Singles/EPs:
Retribution For The Dead / Destined To Fester / In The Grip Of Winter, Peaceville VILE 24T (1991)
Fiend For Blood / Keeper Of Decay / Squeal Like A Pig / Ravenous Freaks / A Different Kind Of Mindfuck / Dead Hole, Peaceville VILE 29T (1992)

Albums:
SEVERED SURVIVAL, Peaceville VILE (1989)
Charred Remains / Service For A Vacant Coffin / Disembowel / Gasping For Air / Ridden With Disease / Pagan Saviour / Impending Dread / Severed Survival / Critical Madness / Embalmed / Stillborn
MENTAL FUNERAL, Peaceville VILE 25 (1991)
Twisted Mass Of Burnt Decay / In The Grip Of Winter / Fleshcrawl / Torn From The Womb / Slaughterday / Dead / Robbing The Grave / Hole In The Head / Destined To Fester / Bonesaw / Dark Crusade / Mental Funeral
ACTS OF THE UNSPEAKABLE, Peaceville VILE33 (1994)
Meat / Necrocannibalistic Vomitorium / Your Rotting Face / Blackness Within / An Act Of The Unspeakable / Frozen With Fear / Spinal Extractions / Death Twitch / Skullptures / Pus-Rot / Battery Acid Enema / Lobotomized / Funerality / Tortured Moans Of Agony / Ugliness And Secretions / Orgy In Excrements / Voices / Walls Of The Coffin
SHITFUN, Peaceville VILE49 (1995)
Deathmask / Humiliate Your Corpse / Fuckdog / Praise The Children / The Birthing / Shit Eater / Formaldehigh / I Sodomise Your Corpse / Geek / Brain Damage / Blood Orgy / No More Hate / Grave Violators / Maim Rape, Kill Rape / I Shit On Your Grave / An End To The

Misery / The 24 Public Mutilations / Bathe In Fire / Bowel Ripper / Burnt To A Fuck / Excremental Ecstasy

AUTOPSY TORMENT (SWEDEN)
Line-Up: David Lee Rot (vocals), Harri (guitar), Daniel Scyphe (bass), Sexual Goatlicker (drums)

A notorious name among Death Metal circles. AUTOPSY TORMENT would spawn the equally renowned PAGAN RITES.

The band first emerged with the Grindcore 1989 demo session 'Splattered' but had adopted a more Death Metal style for the 1991 effort 'Darkest Rituals'. The band folded in 1994 as vocalist David Lee Rot and drummer Sexual Goatlicker (Karl Vincent) forged PAGAN RITES. Rot also became the singer for TRISTITIA.

However, by the following year original bass player Daniel Scyphe recreated the band with Rot, Goatlicker and Jimi on bass. A reunion show in Gothenburg witnessed a non-appearance from Rot necessitating Ustumallagen from DENIAL OF GOD deputizing.

AUTOPSY TORMENT laid down recordings for a proposed 2001 release.

AVULSED (SPAIN)
Line-Up: Dave Rotten (vocals), José 'Cabra' (guitar), Juancar (guitar), Lucky (bass), Furni (drums)

AVULSED were created in 1992 by vocalist Dave Rotten, bassist Lucky, drummer Toni and HAEMORRAGE man Luisma. With this line-up a demo tape, 'Embalmed In Blood', emerged and by November of that year guitarist Jose Cabra was enrolled.

Five months later a second effort, 'Deformed Beyond Belief' was issued as AVULSED began playing live scoring gigs with CANCER, CEREBRAL FIX, GOMORRHA and INTOXICATION pushing sales of the demo beyond the 1,200 mark.

The hard work paid off in September 1993 when Greek label Molon Lave Records offered a contract. AVULSED's 'Deformed Beyond Belief' sessions becoming one half of a split CD shared with Greek act ACID DEATH.

During December of that year Toni quit and AVULSED made up the ranks with former INTOXUCATION man Furni.

1994 found AVULSED gigging alongside

Lusimas's extreme Goregrind side project HAEMMORAGE but discontent within the AVULSED ranks as to their guitarists commitment to their act forced Lusimas dismissal as AVULSED drafted erstwhile SACROPHOBIA guitarist Juancar for gigs with HELLBOUND and VADER followed by German dates in January 1996 together with SINISTER.

Lucky departed just prior to the release of 'Eminence In Putrescence' in November 1996. The 'Carnivoracity' EP found a re-release with additional live cuts.

Upfront of American tour dates in 2000 long standing drummer Furni made his exit. AVULSED completed the schedule of gigs by utilizing the temporary services of WORMED man Andy C.

Vocalist Dave Rotten also operates Death Metal act CHRIST DENIED.

Singles/EPs:
Carnivoricity EP, (1994)

Albums:
CARNIVORISITY, Repulse RPS 007 (1995)
Carnivorisity / Cradle Of Bones / Demoniac Possession / Morgue Defilement / Bodily Ransack / As I Behold I Despise / Gangrended Divine Stigma / Cradle Of Bones / Deformed Beyond Belief / Matando Gueros
EMINENCE IN PUTRESCENCE, Repulse RPS 017 CD (1996)
Hidden Perversion / Sweet Lobotomy / Powdered Flesh / Goreality / Gangrened Divine Stigma / Frozen Meat / Ecstasy For Decayed Chunks / Killin Astral Projections / Bodily Ransack / Resistiré
CYBERGORE, Repulse RPS029CD (1998)
Frozen Beat / Addicted To The Red Bull / Sweet Bakalaotomy / Hash-Perversions / Powered Fish / Petisuis Lobotomy / Gorroneality / Pasti Vor City (Frozen Speed) / Beyond Monotony / Eminence In Popurrence
STABWOUND ORGASM, Repulse (2000)
Amidst The Macabre / Stabwound Orgasm / Blessed By Gore / Compulsive Hater / Eminence In Putrescence / Exorcismo Vaginal / Anthro-Pet-Phagus / Homeless Necrophile / Nice Rotting Eyes / Skinless / Coprotherapy / Virtual Massacre

AWAKENING (HOLLAND)

Singles/EPs:
Swimming Through The Past, Adi (1992) (7" single)

AXEGRINDER (UK)
Line-Up: Trev (vocals), Matt (bass), Steve (guitar), Daryn (drums)

An underground British Metal band that was created in 1986 from various Punk bands, including STONE THE CROWS, the band were originally titled TYRANTS OF HATE with drummer Jel at the drumstool.

As the band began to lean towards more slower, Metal material, a change of name to AXEGRINDER came about. In 1987 they recorded their 'Grind The Enemy' demo which led to interest from Peaceville Records guru Hammy. AXEGRINDER subsequently appeared on the 'A Vile Peace' compilation album which, in turn, led to an offer of a full album. AXEGRINDER later recruited guitarist Cliff Evans who, after the band's demise, formed Death Metal band FLESH.

Trev, Steve and Daryn created WARTECH enlisting bassist Chris.

Albums:
RISE OF THE SERPENT MEN, Peaceville VILE7 (1989)
Never Ending Winter / Hellstorm / Life Chain / War Machine / Evilution / Rise Of The Serpent Men / The Final War

AYDRA (ITALY)

Albums:
PSYCHO PAIN CONTROL, Dawn Of Sadness (1996)

AZRAEL (SWITZERLAND)
Line-Up: T. Hades (vocals / guitar), Boom (guitar), Hermann (bass), R.T. (drums)

A Swiss Death Metal band dating to 1991. A promotion single was recorded for Darken Art Productions during 1992 prior to their album debut in 1995.

Singles/EPs:
Infernal Decision / Ignorance, Darken Act (199-) (Split single with TARAMANZIA)

Albums:

THERE SHALL BE NO ANSWER,
Nuclear Blast NB AZ001 (1995)
Streckbank (Intro) / Inauguration Of The
Common Death / Reduced To Ashes /
Reveal Adventisies / From Chet Osiris -
Apis / Terra Incognita / Ignorant /
Gruesome Odd / Crucify The Raven /
There Schall Be No Answer / Euthanasia
/ Behind The Walls / Overlord

BABYLON SAD
(SWITZERLAND)
Line-Up: Micha Dietschy (vocals), Daniel M. Raess (guitar), Dennis Dopheide (bass), Marco Wolf (keyboards), Curtis Moffa (drums)

Switzerland's BABYLON SAD were formed by two ex-MESSIAH members, namely vocalist / bassist Reto Kühne and guitarist Daniel Raess. However, Kühne left to concentrate on side projects such as FEAR OF GOD.
BABYLON SAD's 1992 line-up comprised of Raess, ex-REACTOR vocalist Nenad Dukic, bassist Ret Kühne and ex-CALHOUN CONQUER guitarists Bruce and Christian Muzik, keyboard player Marco Wolf and ex-CALHOUN CONQUER / MEKONG DELTA / KROKUS drummer Peter Haas.
By 1993 the band had undergone a radical change, with Dukic joining SICKENING GORE. So, along with Raess and Wolf, BABYLON SAD comprised of vocalist Michael Dietschy, bassist Dennis Dopheide and drummer Curtis Moffa.
The album saw a re-release with a different cover and two extra tracks.

Albums:
KYRIE, Massacre CD026 (1993)
Alma - Tedam Redemptions / Pictures Of Paradise / Unknown Tribe / Manifest 05 / Seance / Gothic Spring / End Title / The Awakening / Wandering Spirit

BABYLON WHORES (FINLAND)
Line-Up: Ike Vil (vocals / keyboards), Antti Litmanen (guitar), Ewo Meichem (guitar), Jake Babylon (bass), Kouta (drums)

Noted exponents of "Death Rock" BABYLON WHORES mix a heady brew of Gothic Rock, 80's Thrash and Black Metal in a unique combination that has set the band apart from the pack.
The band's debut single 'Devil's Meat' released on their own Sugar Cult label saw the group comprising vocalist Ike Vil, guitarists Jussi Konittinen and Ewo Meichem, bassist M. Ways and drummer Pete Liha. Follow up 'Sloane 313' saw the bass player's job going to the suitably titled Jake Babylon. Further changes were afoot for BABYLON WHORES third release 'Trismegistos' with guitarist Antti Litmanen taking Konittinen's position and

Kouta coming in on drums.
In late 1999 Babylon Jake bailed out to found a new act DEATH FIX and was replaced by Taneli Nyholm of ABSURDUS, CRYHAVOC and PANDEMONIUM OUTCASTS. Nyholm also goes under the pseudonyms of 'Serpent', 'Daniel Rock' and 'Daniel Stuka'.
BABYLON WHORES toured America in 2000 as guests to KING DIAMOND.

Singles/EPs:
Cool / Third Eye / East Of Earth, Sugar Cult SUGAR 666 (1994) ('Devil's Meat' 7" single)
Of Blowjobs And Cocktails / Cold Hummingbird / Babylon Astronaut / Silver Apples, Sugar Cult SUGAR 667 (1995) ('Sloane 313' EP)
Love Under Will / Hellboy / Speed Doll / Beyond The Sun / Trismegistos, Sugar Cult SUGAR 668 (1996) ('Trismegistos' EP)
Errata Stigmata / Errata Stigmata (Version) / Fey (Version) Sol Niger (Video), Necropolis NR067 CD (2000)

Albums:
COLD HEAVEN, Heroine - Music For Nations MFN 226 (1997)
Deviltry / Omega Therion / Beyond The Sun / Metatron / Enchirdion For A Common Man / In Arcadia Ego / Babylon Astronaut / Flesh Of A Swine / Cold Heaven
DEGGAEL, Spinefarm SPI62CD (1998)
Dog Star A / Sol Niger / Somniferum / Omega Therion (V2) / Emerald Green / Deggael: A Rat's God
KING FEAR, Necropolis (2000)
Errata Stigmata / Radio Werewolf / Hand Of Glory / Veritas / Skeleton Farm / To Behold The Suns / Exit Eden / Sol Niger / Fey / King Fear - Song Of The Damned

BANE (Los Angeles, CA, USA)
Line-Up: Rocky Ruiz (vocals), David Renteria (guitar), Reggie Galang (guitar), Sal Fernandez (bass), Art Cotero (drums)

One of a plethora of BANEs. This Death Metal combo was founded in 1994 with bass player Sal Fernandez also handling lead vocals. The recruitment of vocalist Rocky Ruiz boosted BANE to a quintet but the band lost guitarist Roberto Lepe following a 1997 demo. His replacement was Reggie Galang.

BANISHED (Buffalo, NY, USA)
Line-Up: Tom Frost (vocals), Dave Craiglow (guitar), Gary Schipani (bass), Rick Breier (drums)

BANISHED were previously known as BAPHOMET for their 1992 album 'The Dead Shall Inherit'.
BAPHOMET's 1990 demo secured the band a deal with English label Peaceville Records. The band evolved quickly into BANISHED when threatened by legal action from the German BAPHOMET.

Singles/EPs:
Altered Minds / Cast Out The Flesh, Peaceville Collectors CC 3 (1993)

Albums:
DELIVER ME UNTO PAIN, Deaf DEAF 013 (1993)
Diseased Chaos / Deliver Me Unto Pain / Cast Out The Flesh / Skinned / Inherit His Soul / Valley Of The Dead / Succumb To The Fear / Altered Minds / Scars / Anointing The Sick / Enter The Confines / Through Deviant Eyes

BAPHOMET (GERMANY)
Line-Up: Thomas Hertler (vocals), Gernot Kerrer (guitar), Hansi Bieber (bass), Manuel Reichart (drums)

Founded during 1986 in Bietgheim, BAPHOMET released a brace of demos prior to signing with Massacre Records in 1990, releasing the debut album 'No Answers' the following year. Bass on the debut was contributed by POLTERGEIST's Marek Felis.
BAPHOMET went on the road in Europe to promote the album's release, opening for the likes of BATTLEFIELD, ATROCITY and MYSTIK. They toured again throughout Germany in October 1992 as support to CANNIBAL CORPSE. For the second album, 'Latest Jesus', which included a cover version of HALLOWS EVE's 'Lethal Tendencies', BAPHOMET supported GRAVEDIGGER in Germany.
Thomas Hertler was to quit the group after touring in support of the 'Trust' album thanks to the age old 'musical differences' excuse.

Albums:
NO ANSWERS, Massacre MASS CD001 (1991)
Median / No Answers / Past And Present / The Fence / Act Of Jealousy / Elm

Street / Time Has Come / Identified / Rise Of Baphomet / Terror Of Thoughts
LATEST JESUS, Massacre MASS CD007 (1992)
A Second To None / Lethal Tendencies / State Of Censorship / Latest Jesus / Coalition Of The Lost / Born Of No Name / Near Dawn / Full Moon Eyes
TRUST, Massacre CD027 (1993)
Betrayed / Mind The Doubt / What Went Wrong / Everlast / Intense / Low Life / Attitude / Prove / Trust

BAPHOMET (Buffalo, NY, USA)
Line-Up: Tom Frost (vocals), Dave Craiglow (guitar), Gary Schipani (bass), Rick Breier (drums)

BAPHOMET's 1990 demo secured the band a deal with English label Peaceville Records. The band evolved quickly into BANISHED when threatened by legal action from the German BAPHOMET.

Albums:
THE DEAD SHALL INHERIT, Peaceville VILE 31 (1992)
The Suffering / Through Deviant Eyes / Leave The Flesh / Valley Of The Dead / Torn Soul / We Have Eternity To Know Your Flesh / Vile Reminiscence / Boiled In Blood / The Age Of Plague / Infection Of Death / Streaks Of Blood

BATHORY (SWEDEN)
Line-Up: Quorthon (vocals / guitar), Kothaar (bass), Vvornth (drums)

A one man Extreme Metal project based around the enigmatic Quorthon (previously known as 'Ace Shot'), who was at one time rumoured to be the son of Black Mark label boss Borje Forsberg. With BATHORY Quorthon prides himself on overblown epic chunks of Metal that has attracted a loyal fan base.
BATHORY came to attention of the masses via the tracks 'The Return Of Darkness And Evil' and 'Sacrafice' that were both featured on the 'Scandinavian Metal Attack' compilation album of 1984. BATHORY was actually created a year before by Black Spade on vocals and guitar, bassist Hanoi and drummer Vans (real name Jonas Akerlund). The band toyed with various band names including NOSFERATU, MEPHISTO, ELIZABETH BATHORY and COUNTESS BATHORY before settling on BATHORY. For the 'Scandinavian Metal Attack' album Black Spade retitled himself Ace Shot and later

Quorthon.
BATHORY performed only a handful of gigs before resolving never to perform again in a deliberate intention to compound the mystique surrounding the act. An early bass player was DRILLER KILLER's Cliff. Carsten Nielsen, drummer for Danes ARTILLERY, was offered a position in BATHORY during 1985 but declined. The band nearly relented in 1986 when a European tour with CELTIC FROST and DESTRUCTION was planned. Despite Witchhunter of SODOM rehearsing with the band the touring plans were scrapped.

The rhythm section of Kothaar and Vvornth appeared on 1988's 'Blood Fire Death'.

Quorthon issued a solo album, simply titled 'Album' (Black Mark 666-9), during 1993. For reasons best known to himself Quorthon consistently refuses to take the BATHORY experience out on tour.

1995's 'Octagon' suffered a setback at the last minute before release. It was deemed that lyrics to two tracks 'Resolution Greed' and 'Genocide' were too extreme hence a cover version of the KISS classic 'Deuce' was included instead. The missing two tracks were later issued on the 'Jubileum Volume III' compilation.

A BATHORY record entitled 'Raise The Dead' was planned for release through Music For Nations, but this proposed record never appeared.

BATHORY are without doubt highly influential in the Scandinavian Black Metal scene with many later artists offering cover versions in homage.

In 1997 various Greek Black Metal acts including KAWIR, EXHUMATION and DEVISER contributed to the 'Hellas Salutes The Vikings' tribute effort. A more substantial album came the following year featuring heavyweight names such as MARDUK, GEHENNAH, DARK FUNERAL, EMPEROR, NECROPHOBIC and SATYRICON titled 'In Conspiracy With Satan'.

Singles/EPs:
The Sword / The Lake, The Woodman, Black Mark (1988) (Promotion)
Twilight Of The Gods / Under The Runes / Hammerheart, Black Mark BM CD666P (1991) (Promotion release)

Albums:
BATHORY, Tyfon / Black Mark BMCD 666-1(1984)
Hades / Reaper / Necromancy / Sacrifice / In Conspiracy With Satan / Armageddon / Raise The Dead / War
THE RETURN, Tyfon / Black Mark BMCD 666-2 (1985)
Possessed / The Rite Of Darkness / Reap Of Evil / Son Of The Damned / Sadist / The Return... / Revelation Of Doom / Total Destruction / Born For Burning / The Wind Of Mayhem / Bestial Lust (Bitch)
UNDER THE SIGN OF THE BLACK MARK, Black Mark BMCD 666-3 (1986)
Nocturnal Obedience / Massacre / Woman Of Dark Desires / Call From The Grave / Equimothorn / Enter The Eternal Fire / Chariots Of Fire / 13 Candles / Of Doom..
BLOOD FIRE DEATH, Black Mark 666-4 (1988)
Oden's Ride Over Nordland / A Fine Day To Die / The Golden Walls Of Heaven / Pace 'Till Death / Holocaust / For All Those Who Died / Dies Irae / Blood Fire Death
HAMMERHEART, Black Mark BMCD 666-5 (1990)
Shores In Flames / Valhalla / Baptized In Fire And Blood / Father To Son / Song To Hall Up High / Home Of Once Brave / One Rode To Asa Bay
TWILIGHT OF THE GODS, Black Mark BMLP666-6 (1991)
Prologue - Twilight Of The Gods - Epilogue / Through Blood By Thunder / Blood And Iron / Under The Runes / To Enter Your Mountain / Bond Of Blood / Hammerheart
JUBILEUM VOLUME 1, Black Mark BMCD 666-7 (1992)
Rider At The Gate Of Dawn / Crawl To Your Cross / Sacrifice / Dies Irae / Through Blood By Thunder / You Don't Move Me (I Don't Give A Fuck) / Odens Ride Over Nordland / A Fine Day To Die / War / Enter The Eternal Fire / Song To Hall Up High / Sadist / Under The Runes / Equimanthorn / Blood Fire Death
JUBILEUM VOLUME II, Black Mark 666-8 (1993)
The Return Of The Darkness And Evil / Burnin' Leather / One Rode To Asa Bay / The Golden Walls Of Heaven / Call From The Grave / Die In Fire / Shores In Flames / Possessed / Raise The Dead / Total Destruction / Bond Of Blood / Twilight Of The Gods
REQUIEM, Black Mark 666-10 (1994)
Requiem / Crosstitution / Necroticus / War Machine / Blood And Soul / Pax Vobiscum / Suffocate / Distinguish To Kill / Apocalypse

OCTAGON, Black Mark 666-11 (1995)
Immaculate Pinetreeroad / Born To Die /
Psychpath / Sociopath / Grey / Century /
33 Something / War Supply / Schizianity
/ A Judgement Of Posterity / Deuce
BLOOD ON ICE, Black Mark BMCD666-
12 (1996)
Intro / Blood On Ice / Man Of Iron / One
Eyed Old Man / The Sword / The Stallion
/ The Wodwoman / The Lake / Gods Of
Thunder Of Wind And Of Rain / The
Ravens / The Revenge Of Blood On Ice

BATTLELUST (SWEDEN)
Line-Up: Micke Grankvist (vocals),
Markus Terramäki (guitar), Baron De
Samedi (guitar / bass / drums)

BATTLELUST was created by
NECROMICON member Baron De
Samedi originally titled ONDSKA ('Evil').
By 1996 Samedi had left NECROMICON
and, after a brief spell as a member of
GATES OF ISHTAR, together with
Lucichrist (Patrick Tonkvist) of
EVERDAWN and resumed activities with
ONDSKA. Before long a name change to
BATTLESTORM was adopted for a demo
'The Eclipse Of The Dying Sun'.
A track 'The Acheron' was submitted to
the Fullmoon compilation album 'A
Tribute To Hell'. However, Lucichrist
would leave to be replaced by Haris Agic.
Agic was out of the picture by the time of
recording of the debut album 'Of Battle
And Ancient Warcraft'. Samedi had now
been joined by SATARIEL singer Micke
Grankvist and DARKEST SEASON
guitarist Markus Terramäki.

Albums:
**OF BATTLE AND ANCIENT
WARCRAFT**, Hammerheart (1998)
Armageddon Arrives / Retrobution /
Angel Fire / Forever Laid In Chains / The
Sword Of Death / Darkened
Descendants / Of Battle And Ancient
Warcraft / The Dawn Of The Black
Hearts / With The Blackstorms I Came /
Snow And Ice Demonmight

BATTLE OF DISARM (JAPAN)

Singles/EPs:
Split, (199-) (7" split single with HYLKIO)
Split, (199-) (7" split single with
MASSKONTROL)
In The War, Tribal War (1993)

BEHEADED (MALTA)
Line-Up: Lawrence Joyce (vocals), David
Bugeja (guitar), David Cachia (bass),
Chris Brincat (drums)

A rare Maltese Death Metal formation.
BEHEADED was founded in 1991 by the
trio of vocalist Marcel Scalpello, guitarist
David Bugeja and drummer Chris Brincat.
Later additions were guitarist Tyson
Fenech and bassist David Cachia. Under
this incarnation BEHEADED released a
1995 promotional cassette 'Souldead'.
Fenech would depart in favour of Omar
Grech for recording of the debut album
'Perpetual Mockery' issued by the
Swedish X-Treme label. Scalpelle would
then leave as BEHEADED pulled in
Lawrence Joyce for a second outing
'Resurgence Of Oblivion'.

Albums:
PERPETUAL MOCKERY, X-Treme
(1998)
RESURGENCE OF OBLIVION, Mighty
Music (2001)
Transmutation Of Veracity / Exhortation
Of Benevolence / Resurgence Of
Oblivion / Paramnesis Dream / Suffer
Some More

BELCHING BEET (GERMANY)

Singles/EPs:
**You Know That Holes Are Empty 'Cos
There's Nothing Inside**, Masters Of
Mayhem (1991) (7" EP)

Albums:
BELCHING BEET, Ecocentric (1991)
(Split album with RUPTURE)

BELIEVER (Colebrook, PA, USA)
Line-Up: Kurt Bachman (vocals / guitar),
Dave Baddorf (guitar), Howe Kraft (bass),
Joey Daub (drums)

Pennsylvanian Christian Death
Thrashers formed in 1985 by drummer
Joey Daub and vocalist Kurt Bachman
together with guitarist Dave Baddorf and
bassist Howe Kraft. Added new bassist
Wyatt Robertson in mid 1990.
The 1994 album 'Dimensions' found
BELIEVER with Jim Winter on bass and
William Keller on lead vocals. Daub
would forge a union with SACRAMENT
members guitarist Mike DiDonato and
bassist Erik Ney to create FOUNTAIN OF
TEARS for a 1999 album.
Ex-BELIEVER members later founded

SERAPH.

Albums:
EXTRACTION FROM MORTALITY, REX
Music 000-137-8902D (1989)
Unite / Vile Hypocrisy / D.O.S.
(Desolation Of Sodom) / Tormented /
Shadow Of Death / Blemished Sacrifices
/ Not Even One / Extraction From
Mortality / Stress
SANITY OBSCURE, RC Records RC
9312 (1991)
Sanity Obscure / Wisdom's Call / Non-
Point / Idols Of Ignorance / Stop The
Madness / Dies Irae (Day Of Wrath)/
Dust To Dust/ Like A Song
DIMENSIONS, Roadrunner RR 9101-1
(1994)
Gone / Future Mind / Dementia / What Is
But Cannot Be / Singularity / No Apology
/ Trilogy Of Knowledge: Intro - The Birth,
Movement I: The Lie, Movement II: The
Truth, Movement III: The Key

BELPHEGOR (AUSTRIA)
Line-Up: Märr (vocals / bass), Chris
(drums), Helmuth (chainsaw), Sigurd
(distortion)

Austria's BELPHEGOR have visions of
being the world's most brutal band.
Musically the group plays ridiculously
fast, melodies and riffs being thin on the
ground.
The band's second album was released
with two different covers, one featuring an
injured baby in the booklet. Very tasteless
and reckoned to be worse than better
known Grindcore acts have concocted.

Singles/EPs:
Obscure And Deep / Blood Stained
Ritual / Sabbath Bloody Sabbath,
Perverted Taste MOMO 003 (1995)
('Obscure And Deep' EP)

Albums:
BLOOD BATH IN PARADISE, Belphegor
BELPHEGOR 1 (1993)
Requiem In C (Intro) / Bloodbath In
Paradise / Graves Of Sorrow / Schizoid
Nightmare / Mutilated Corpses
THE LAST SUPPER, Lethal LRC 18
(1995) (1996)
The Last Supper / A Funeral Without A
Cry / Impalement Without Mercy / March
Of The Dead / The Rapture Of
Cremation / Engulfed in Eternal Frost /
D.I.E. / In Remembrance Of Hate And
Sorrow / Blood Bath In Paradise - Part 2
/ Krunifixion

IL SYMPHONY, (1996)
BLUTSABBAT, Last Episode LEP 010
(1997)
Abschwörung / Blackest Ecstasy / Purity
Through Fire / Behind The Black Moon /
Blutsabbath / No Resurrection / The
Requiem Of Hell / Untergang Der
Gekreuzigten / Path Of Sin
NECRODAEMON TERRORSATHAN,
Last Episode (2000)
Necrodaemon Terrorsathan / Vomit Upon
The Cross / Diabolical Possession / Lust
Perishes In A Thirst For Blood / S.B.S,R,
/ Sadism Unbound / Tanzwut
Totengesänge / Cremation Of Holiness /
Necrodaemon Terror Sathan Part II /
Outro Analjesus

BELSEBUB (SWEDEN)
Line-Up: Mika Savimäki (vocals / bass),
Peter Blomman (guitar),
Johnny Fagerström (drums)

Swedish Death Metal band with one EP
to their credit.

Singles/EPs:
Chemical Warfare / Infected Organs /
Masters To Reveal, Drowned M11620
(1992)

BENEATH THE REMAINS
(New York, NY, USA)

Albums:
QUEST OF THE LOST SOULS,
Released Power (1998)

BENEDICTION (UK)
Line-Up: David Ingram (vocals), Darren
Brookes (guitar), Peter Rew (guitar),
Frank Healy (bass), Ian Treacy (drums)

A Birmingham act formed in early 1989,
BENEDICTION are sadly more noted in
their home country for having supplied
vocalist Barney Greenaway to NAPALM
DEATH than their musical achievements.
However, outside of Britain,
BENEDICTION have garnered a sizeable
following through ever improving albums
and constant touring.
The group debuted with the 'Dreams You
Dread' demo in June 1989 which secured
the band a deal with German label
Nuclear Blast. Following the release of
the first album, entitled 'Subconscious
Terror', Dave Ingram stepped in for
Greenaway on vocals and contributed to
promotion activity during the year which
included British supports to PARADISE

LOST and AUTOPSY.

The band undertook a further British tour opening for BOLT-THROWER prior to recording their follow up effort 'The Grand Leveller'. Before the record came out the band undertook further headlining dates throughout 12 countries, capitalized on by selected British and German dates upon its release. 1991 shows included gigs with label mates DISMEMBER and MASSACARA.

The group endured another line-up change when bassist Paul Adams departed in late 1991, BENEDICTION favouring ex-CEREBRAL FIX man Frank Healy to take his place.

Toward the end of 1991 BENEDICTION released the 'Dark Is The Season' EP which featured a reworking of the old ANVIL chestnut 'Forged In Fire'. At the dawn of 1992 BENEDICTION hit the road once more with BOLT-THROWER on a bill including ASPHYX that enabled the band to play its first dates in Israel.

The 1993 album 'Transcend The Rubicon'opened up more new ground as BENEDICTION topped the bill of a European tour with ATHEIST and CEMETERY as support. Dates included visits to Ireland, Portugal and Mexico. The travelling cost the group the services of drummer Ian Treacy though, the skinsman quitting and being superseded by the 18 year old Neil Hutton.

In 1994 BENEDICTION supported BOLT-THROWER on their American club tour, but found themselves as headliners on latter dates as problems hit BOLT-THROWER forcing their withdrawal. BENEDICTION, with future MARSHALL LAW drummer Paul Brookes in tow, also appeared at the legendary Milwaukee Metalfest during the same year, on a bill alongside fellow heavyweights BIOHAZARD and SLAYER.

During 1995 Neil Hutton and David Ingram formed the side project WARLORD UK, releasing the 'Maximum Carnage' album on Nuclear Blast in 1996. The album included covers of AMEBIX and SLAYER songs.

More recently frontman Ingram (now named Dave Bjerregaard Ingram after his marriage) lent a helping hand to BOLT-THROWER for a batch of live dates during 1997, when their vocalist Martin Van Drunen bailed out without warning. However, the 'helping hand' turned out to be more permanent. Ingram stayed the course for a series of festival appearances but by November of 1998 had bailed out. BENEDICTION promptly

pulled in former DETHRONED frontman Dave Hunt to fill the vacated vocal position.

BENEDICTION's 1998 album 'Grind Bastard' included a cover of JUDAS PRIEST's 'Electric Eye'.

BENEDICTION
Photo : Martin Wickler

Singles/EPs:
Experimental Stage, Nuclear Blast NB057 (1992)
Foetus Noose / Forged In Fire / Dark Is The Shadow / Jumping At Shadows / Experimental Stage, Nuclear Blast NB059 (1992)
Return To The Eve, Nuclear Blast NB 058PDS (1992)
The Grotesque / Ashen Epitaph / Violation Domain (Live) / Subconscious Terror (Live) / Visions In The Shroud (Live), Nuclear Blast NB 088-2 (1994) ('The Grotesque - Ashen Epitaph' EP)

Albums:
SUBCONSCIOUS TERROR, Nuclear Blast NB033 (1990)
Intro - Portal To Your Phobias / Subconscious Terror / Artefacted Irreligion / Grizzled Finale / Eternal Eclipse / Experimental Stage / Suspended Animation / Divine Ultimatum / Spit Forth The Dead / Confess All Goodness
THE GRAND LEVELLER, Nuclear Blast 048 (1991)
Vision In The Shroud / Graveworm /

45

Jumping At Shadows / Opulence Of The Absolute / Child Of Sin / Undirected Aggression / Born In A Fever / The Grand Leveller / Senile Dementia / Return To Eve
TRANSCEND THE RUBICON, Nuclear Blast NB073 (1993)
Unfound Mortality / Nightfear / Paradox Alley / Bow To None / Painted Skulls / Violation Domain / Face Without Soul / Bleakhouse / Blood From Stone / Wrong Side Of The Grave / Artefacted - Spit Forth
THE DREAMS YOU DREAD, Nuclear Blast NB120 (1995)
Down on Whores (Leave Them All For Dead) / Certified...? / Soulstream / Where Flies Are Born / Answer To Me / Griefgiver / Denial / Negative Growth / Path Of The Serpent / Saneless Theory / The Dreams You Dread
GRIND BASTARD, Nuclear Blast (1998)
Deadfall / Agonized / West Of Hell / Magnificat (Irenicon) / Nervebomb / Electric Eye / Grind Bastard / Shadow World / Bodiless / Carcinova Angel / We The Freed / Destroyer / I

BENUMB (CA, USA)

Line-Up: Paul Pontikoff (vocals), Dave Hogarth (guitar), Rob Koperski (guitar), Tim Regan (bass), John Goteli (drums)

Californians BENUMB, led by the Russian émigré Paul Pontikoff, trod a fine line between Hardcore and Death Metal. BENUMB issued a string of shared 7" singles with the likes of SHORT HATE TEMPER, THE DUKES OF HAZZARD, SUPPRESSION and APARTMENT 213 oddly all featuring untitled tracks.
Kopeski would later be credited as penning lyrics for Nu-Metal platinum act KORN on the track 'Helmet In The Bush'. Both Pontikoff and Gotelli would found VULGAR PIGEON issuing the 'Genetic Predisposition' single and 'Summary Execution' album.

Singles/EPs:
Split, Same Day (1995) (7" split single with SHORT HATE TEMPER)
Split, Rape An Ape (1997) (7" split with THE DUKES OF HAZZARD)
Split, Stenchasaurus (1997) (7" split with APARTMENT 213)
Consumed / No Hope / A.A.D. / Deprivation / Beyond Fucked, Relapse (1997) ('Gear In The Machine' EP)
Split, Monkeybite (199-) (Split flexi single with SUPPRESSION)

Albums:
SOUL OF THE MARTYR, Relapse (1998)
Driven Out / No Regret / L.N.F. / Nothing Personal / Sick / Monetary Gain / Oblivious / Stood Up And Sold Out / C.T.O.A. / I.H.M.U.S.T. / Blind / Struggle On / Purpose / Crawl, Stagger, Fall / Self Righteous / Stuck Pig / Self Inflicted / T.P.U. / T.Y.G. / Agony I / Agony II / Consumed / No Hope / A.A.D. / Of MY Own / Deprivation / Beyond Fucked / Reoccurrence / Lost Perception / Perseverance / Overwhelmed, Overcome / Nothing For Nothing / A.D.S. / Choke
WITHERING STRANDS OF HOPE, Relapse (2000)
Synopsis Of Ignorance Within The Society At Large / Once And Never Against / Underbelly / Minimum Wage Intellectual / Pass The Buck / Suffer / Epileptic / Integration / Realization Of Fact / Oxygen Thief / Just Short Of The Line / Serenity Within Chaos / WTO: Disintegration Of The Working Class / Three Down, One To Go / Laceration Of Belief / Survival Between Maggots / Amongst The Fallen / Articulation Of Hypocrisy / Abundant Knowledge, Infinite Stupidity / Father To The Fatherless / Imminent Departure / Flesh For Flesh / Dissection Of Grace / Embodiment Of Despair / Ascend From Persecution / Years Of Unjust / Cause And Reject / Genocide / Statistics / Division Within Division / Successful Failure / Closing Arguement

BESTIALIT (SLOVAKIA)

BESTIALIT would evolve into LUNATIC GODS issuing the 'Litany By The Fire' album.

Albums:
FUCKLAND, Metal Age MAP002 (1994) (Split album with DEHYDRATED)

BETRAYER (POLAND)

Line-Up: Berial (vocals / bass), Ripper (guitar), Riju (guitar), Molly (drums)

BETRAYER is a Polish Death Metal outfit.

Albums:
CALAMITY, Morbid Noizz MN 002 (1995)
After Death / Down With The Gods / In Sacrifice / From Beyond The Graves / Maze Of Suffering / Before Long You Will Die / Wrathday / Sickness Of The

Human Race

BEWITCHED (SWEDEN)
Line-Up: Vargher (vocals / guitar), Blackheim (guitar), Wrathyr (bass), Reaper (drums)

One of a myriad of Satanic Death Metal studio project acts put together by members of other bands on the side, BEWITCHED vocalist Vargher (real name Marcus Norman) is also a member of ANCIENT WISDOM, while guitarist Blackheim (real name Anders Nyström) is in both DIABOLICAL MASQUERADE and KATATONIA.
BEWITCHED debuted with the 1995 'Hellspell' demo. Their 1996 EP 'Encyclopedia Of Evil' is made up of covers of bands such as BLACK WIDOW's 'Sacrifice', MERCYFUL FATE's 'Come To The Sabbath', VENOM's 'Warhead', CELTIC FROST's 'Circle Of The Tyrants' and BATHORY's 'Hellcult'.

Singles/EPs:
Intro / Warhead / Sacrifice / Evil / Circle Of The Tyrants / Come To The Sabbath / Hellcult, Osmose OPCD 041/SPV 076-20642 (1996) ('Encyclopedia Of Evil' EP)

Albums:
DIABOLICAL DESECRATION, Osmose OPCD034 (1996)
Hard As Steel (Hot As Hell) / Hellcult / Born Of Flames / Deathspell / Bloodthirst / Burnin' Paradise / Holy Whore / Triumph Of Evil / Firehymn / Dressed In Blood / Blade Of The Ripper / The Witches Plague / Diabolical Desecration
PENTAGRAM PRAYER, Osmose Productions OPCD 057 (1997)
Blood On The Altar / Hallways To Hell / Demondawn / Night Of The Sinner / Satan's Claw / Hellblood / Beastchild / Cremation Of The Cross / The Night Stalker / Sacrifice To Satan / Hellcult Attack / Pentagram Prayer
AT THE GATES OF HELL, Osmose Productions (1999)
Sabbath Of Sin / Heave Is Falling / Black Mass / The Devils Daughters / At The Gates Of Hell / Let The Blood Run Red / Lucifer's Legacy / The Sinner And The Saint / Enemy Of God / Infernal Necromancy

BEYOND BELIEF (HOLLAND)
Line-Up: A.J. Van Drenth (vocals / guitar), Robbie Woning (guitar), Ronnie Van Der Way (bass), Jacko Westendorp (drums)

BEWITCHED
Photo : Martin Wickler

Formed in 1986, BEYOND BELIEF feature two ex DEADHEAD members guitarist Robbie Woning and bassist Ronnie Van Der Way. Having released the 'Remind The Skull' demo in 1990, a further demo, 'Stranded', followed in 1992.

BEYOND BELIEF toured their native Holland with CREEPMINE, ANCIENT RITES and DEADHEAD.

Albums:
TOWARDS THE DIABOLICAL EXPERIMENT, Shark 029 RTD (1993)
Intro: Ave / Shapes Of Sorrow / Stranded / The Experiment / The Nameless / Silent Are The Holy / Fade Away / Untouched / Prophetic Countdown / Kissing In XTC / The Finishing Touch / Outro: Never
RAVE THE ABYSS, Shark 102 (1995)
Rave The Abyss / Cursed / Blood Beach / High On The Moon / The Burning Of Redlands / Crushed Divine / The Grand Enigma / Tyrants Of The Sun / Lost

BEYOND DAWN (NORWAY)
Line-Up: Tore Gjedrm (vocals / bass), Espen Ingierd (guitar), Petter Haavik (guitar), Einar Sjurso (drums), Dag Midbrod (Trombone)

After one demo tape BEYOND DAWN were able to release a four track record on Adipocere Records before later changing labels to Candlelight Records with whom they released 'Pity Love' in 1996.

Both albums display a very original, depressive and bizarre mixture between Death style Doom, Psychedelic and Avant Garde Rock.

Drummer Einar Sjurso guests on FLEURETY's 2000 album 'Department Of Apocalyptic Affairs'.

Albums:
LONGING FOR SCARLET DAYS,
Adipocere CD AR019 (1994)
Cold / Moonwomb / Chaosphere / Clouds Swept Away The Colours
PITY LOVE, Candlelight CANDLE 012 (1996)
When Beauty Dies / The Penance / (Never A) Bygone Tendance / As The Evening Falters, The Dogs Howl / Embers Storm / Ripe As The Night / Daughter Sunday
REVELRY, Misanthropy AMAZON14CD (1998)
Love's (Only) True Defender / Tender / Resemblance / Stuck / Three Steps For

The Chameleon (How To Seduce Modestly) / I Am A Drug / Breathe The Jackal / Life's Sweetest Reward / Chains / Phase To Phase
IN REVERIE, Eibon (1999)
Need / Rendezvous / Prey / Atmosphere / Confident As Hell / Naked / Phrase Juxtaposition / Chameleon

BEYOND SERENITY (DENMARK)
Line-Up: Carsten Holm (vocals), Morten R. Jorgensen (guitar), Johnny Larsen (guitar), Anders Duus (bass), Thomas Maaetoft (drums)

Singles/EPs:
Cold / Childhood's Important / Time Turns The Key / Angel Of Revenge, Rox BSCD 9601 (1996) ('Bursting Into Leaf' EP)

BIRDFLESH (SWEDEN)
Line-Up: Alex (vocals / guitar), Magnus (vocals / bass), Andreas (vocals / drums)

One of Scandinavia's leading Grind Metal acts. BIRDFLESH, founded in October of 1992, issued the promotional tapes 'The Butcherbitchtape' in 1994, and 'Demo Of Hell' in 1995. Two songs from this session were also issued on the 'Sometimes Death is Better 2, 3 & 4' Compilation CD Box set released by the Belgian Shiver label.

Further demos 'Fishfucked' arrived in 1997. However, in August of 1997 Alex went on an eight month sabbatical throughout South East Asia during which period BIRDFLESH was put on ice. Meantime both Andreas and Magnus worked with their other acts as well as forging a fresh Japanese inspired Grindcore band together NAPALM GORE.

With Alex back from his travels the newly reconvened BIRDFLESH released their fourth demo, 'We Were 7 Who 8 Our Neighbours On A Plate' in August 1998. The band would tour Japan in 1999 as running mates with D-RIVER.

Singles/EPs:
Split, (199-) (7" split single with CARCASS GRINDER)
Split, (199-) (7" split single with SQUASH BOWELS)
The Hungry Vagina / Trip to the Grave / Burgers of the Fucking Dead / Land of the Sick / Walk of Insanity / Mutilation Boogie & Masturbation Blues / Sweat of the Old Man / Teenage Mutilator / The Brutal Corpse / More Garlic / Bodily

Dismemberment, Burning Death BDR001 (1998) ('Trip To The Grave' 7" single)

BLACKEND (GERMANY)
Line-Up: Michael Goldschmidt (vocals / guitar), Manuel Unterhuber (guitar), Mario Unterhuber (bass), Alex Mayer (drums)

Albums:
SLOTH, MDD 12CD (1997)
Harmonies In Black / No More Confidence / Regression / Not To Deny / Separate / Retaliation Breed / Parts Of Peril / Virtual / Streams Of Perfection
MENTAL GAME MESSIAH, Massacre MAS CD0218 (1999)
DEMO '95, Gutter (1999) (Split CD with LOONATIKK)

THE BLACK LEAGUE (FINLAND)

Act founded by ex-SENTENCED and IMPALED NAZARENE bassist / singer Taneli Jarva and drummer Sir Luttinen of IMPALED NAZARENE, LEGENDA and BEHERIT.
THE BLACK LEAGUE was completed by MYTHOS, IMPALED NAZARENE and LEGENDA bassist Florida and guitarists Alexi Ranta and Maike. The latter has credits with infamous Finnish Punk bands TERVEET KADET and FAFF BEY.
Ranta also busies himself with IGNIS FATUUS whilst Florida is a members of SHADOWS OVER SHADOWLAND.

Albums:
ICHOR, Spinefarm (2000)
Doomwatcher / One Colour: Black / Deep Waters / Goin' To Hell / Avalon / We Die Alone / The Everlasting Part II / Ozymandias / Blood Of The Gods / Bunker King / Winter Winds Sing / Ecce Homo! / Night On Earth

BLACKRISE (DENMARK)

Albums:
MOONCULT, A Koffin Not Found (1997)

BLACK SHEPERD (BELGIUM)
Line-Up: Yvon Verhaegen (vocals), Igor Plint (guitar), Michel Oluf (guitar), Patrick Minnebier (bass), Alain Verhaegen (drums)

A Belgian Thrash act with Black Metal influences. Ex-BLACK SHEPERD guitarist Luc Vervelot created CONSPIRACY OF SILENCE.

Albums:
IMMORTAL AGGRESSION, Punk Etc (1988)
Immortal Aggression / State Of Decay / Make Love War / Corpses / Preacher Of Death / Trash / Another Day To Die / Kill The Priest / Animal / Lord Of The Darkness / I Am God / Evil Revenge

BLACKSTAR (UK)
Line-Up: Jeff Walker (vocals / guitar), Carlo Regadas (guitar), Mark Griffiths (guitar), Ken Owen (drums)

As CARCASS, the originators of Gore Metal, gradually evolved into a more traditional Hard Rock outfit the band's later works, such as 'Heartworks' and 'Swansong', found the band so distanced from the original concept that a split was inevitable.
Founder member and vocalist Jeff Walker resurfaced with BLACKSTAR, an act very much musically akin to latter day CARCASS. BLACKSTAR also featured two fellow erstwhile CARCASS members, guitarist Carlo Regadas and drummer Ken Owen, together with former CATHEDRAL guitarist Mark Griffiths.
BLACKSTAR cut cover versions of HÜSKER DÜ's 'The Girl Who Lives On Heaven Hill' and THIN LIZZY's 'Running Back' for the 1998 Peaceville compilation 'X'.

Albums:
BARBED WIRE SOUL, Peaceville CDVILE69 (1997)
Game Over / Smile / Sound Of Silence / Rock n' Roll Circus / New Song / Give Up The Ghost / Revolution Of The Heart / Waste Of Space / Deep Wound / Better The Devil / Instrumental

BLACK WITCHERY (FL, USA)
Line-Up: Impurath (vocals / bass), Tregenda (guitar), Vaz (drums)

BLACK WITCHERY evolved from the early 90's act IRREVERENT. By 1996 the band had retitled itself WITCHERY. A further title change occurred in 1999 as BLACK WITCHERY was adopted.
The 2000 album 'Hellstorm Of Evil Vengeance' was a shared affair with Canadian act CONQUEROR. As part of their contribution BLACK WITCHERY cut a cover of BLASPHEMY's 'Demoniac'.
BLACK WITCHERY have also contributed versions of SLAYER's 'Fight Till Death' to a Dwell Records tribute

album and KREATOR's 'Tormentor' for a Fullmoon tribute affair.

Guitarist Tregenda (Steve Childers) participated in the BURNING INSIDE project in collusion with renowned ICED EARTH, DEMONS & WIZARDS, DEATH, CONTROL DENIED and INCANTATION drummer Richard Christy and fellow axeman Michael Estes from famed Black Metal merchants ACHERON.

Singles/EPs:
Summoning Of Infernal Legions, Dark Horizon DHR002 (1999) (7" single)

Albums:
HELLSTORM OF EVIL VENGEANCE, Dark Horizon DHR004 (2000) (Split album with CONQUEROR)

BLASPHEMY (CANADA)

Line-Up: Nocturnal Grave Desecrator And Black Winds (vocals), Caller Of The Storms (guitar), Ace Gustapo Necrosleezer And Vaginal Commands (bass), 3 Black Hearts Of Damnation And Impurity (drums)

Canadian Grindcore Black Metal crew BLASPHEMY preceded their debut album with a 1989 demo 'Blood Upon The Altar'. One of the very few Black Metal acts to include a black member.

Albums:
FALLEN ANGEL OF DOOM, Wild Rags (1990)
Winds Of The Black Gods / Fallen Angel Of Doom / Hording Of Evil Vengeance / Darkness Prevails / Desecration / Ritual / Weltering In Blood / Demoniac / Goddess Of Perversity / The Desolate One
GODS OF WAR, Osmose Productions (1993)
Elders Of The Apocalypse / Blood Upon The Altar / Blasphemous Attack / Gods Of War / Intro / Atomic Nuclear Desolation / Nocturnal Slayer / Emperor Of The Black Abyss / Intro / Blasphemy / Necrosadist / War Command / Empty Chalice

BLAZING ETERNITY (DENMARK)

Line-Up: Nattevogter P.T.M. (vocals), Morten Souren Lybecker (guitar), Hunger Darkenfeld (bass), Lars Korsholm (drums)

Copenhagen's BLAZING ETERNITY would bow in with the 1996 demo 'Soer Sorte Leder' and capitalized on this with the 1998 session 'Der Hviler En Nat Under Sorte Virten Borge'. Previously the act had operated under the handle of ANCIENT SADNESS having issued a 1993 demo 'Tragedies'.

BLAZING ETERNITY's debut album of 2000 included guest sessions from SATURNUS members guitarist Kim Larsen and keyboard player Anders Nielsen.

Bass player Hunger Darkenfeld is an erstwhile VINTERMISKE member.

Albums:
TIMES AND UNKNOWN WATERS, Prophecy Productions (2000)
Concluding The Die Of Centuries / Fortable Horisorter / Of Times And Unknown Waters / Still Lost In The Autumn Of Eternity / (Sagnet Om) Manden Med Dew Sorte Hat / Dead Inside / Dark Summernights Of Eternal Twilight / End - Midnight

BLOCKHEADS (FRANCE)

Albums:
LAST TRIBES, (199-)
WATCH OUT, (199-)
FROM WOMB TO GENOCIDE, Bones Brigade (2000)
First Genocide / Generally Accepted Ideas / Polymorphic Perdition / Horned Totem / Artificial Day / Mc Dollars / Avagdu / G.O.D.S. / Opportunist / Circle Of Consumption / Dog Bomb / Between Human And Animal / Crom Cruach / Ekum / Will Nature Soon Forget / Seismosore / Moloch / Masked Masses / Unwillingly And Slow / D.Y.B.M. / Womb / Flies Reward / Paroxysm Of Speeches / Butterfly / Millennium Utopia / Regression / Haashaastaak

BLOOD (GERMANY)

Line-Up: Alex (vocals), Elsen (guitar), Ruben (guitar), Taki (bass), Ventilator (drums)

Founded in 1986 BLOOD emerged with a stream of brutally stark demo tapes 'Infernal Horror', 'Destroy Command', 'Deathcore', 'Heinous Noise', and 'Spasmo Paralytic Dreams'.

For a time they held the distinction of being the only German Grind / Death act to gain a deal in America, releasing a debut album and a series of split EPs on the Wild Rags label. BLOOD also released a split EP in 1995 with Poland's DEAD INFECTION.

For the 1993 album 'O Agios Pethane'

vocalist Alex was ousted in favour of new face Martin. Guitarist Ruben also departed making BLOOD a quartet. Martin would later resurface fronting DAWN for the 1998 'Entrance To Malevolence' album.

Singles/EPs:
Recognize Yourself, Wild Rags (1990)
Traditional Rites, (1991) (Split EP with AGATHOCLES)
Salvation To The Dead, (1991) (Split EP with IMPETIGIO)
Spittle Red Of Blood, Iron (1994)
Revelation / Morpheus / Blood For Blood, Morbid MSR 015 (1995) (7" split single with DEAD INFECTION)
Split, Iron (1998) (7" split single with INHUMANE)

Albums:
IMPULSE TO DESTROY, Wild Rags (1989)
CHRIST BAIT, 1MF (1992)
Lost Lords / And No One Cries / The Last Words / Scares Of Soul / Damnation / Harass / Join Stock Company / Final Chasm / Dogmatize / Self Immolation / Widow Path / Be Doomed / Bought Beauty / Past Belief Cessions / Mass Distortion / The Greed / Down To The Swamp / Technical Abortion / The Head Of A Dead Cat / Terrorise
O AGIOS PETHANE, 1MF 377.0034-2 (1993)
Intro (Dracula) / Kadath / Cannibal Ritual / Profanity / Submission / Sodomize The Weak / Punishment / Christbait / Dread / Wings Of Declaration / By The Way Of Grace / God Left The World / Aesta Ta Malakja Sou / Revelation / Divine Seed / Spasmoparalytic Dreams / Lamentation / Stream Of Anguish / Blood For Blood / Outro
MENTAL CONFLICTS, Morbid 550526 (1995)
Intro (Tentacles) / Insomnia / Toothache / Master's Clemency / Secrets Of Blood / Mental Conflict / Bleed For Me / Spreading The Thoughts / Blood / Stretched / Away Is Away / For Auld Lang Syne / Crown Court / Inflame / Texas Chainsaw Massacre / Naked Frozen / Blood Price / The Favour Of Ecstasy / Morpheus / I Dream Dead
DEPRAVED GODDESS, Blood (1996)

BLOODBATH (SWEDEN)
Line-Up: Dan Swanö (vocals), Mikael Akerfeldt (vocals), Blackheim (guitar), Jonas Renske (bass)

A genuine Black Metal supergroup project. The unholy union includes EDGE OF SANITY's Dan Swanö, OPETH's Mikael Akerfeldt, KATATONIA and DIABOLICAL MASQUERADE's guitarist Blackheim and KATATONIA / OCTOBER TIDE bassist Jonas Renske.

Singles/EPs:
Breeding Death / Ominous Bloodvomit / Furnace Funeral, Century Media (2000) ('Breeding Death' EP)

BLOOD COVEN (Kent, OH, USA)
Line-Up: Dann Saladin (vocals / guitar), Dave Ingram (guitar), Jason Woolard (bass), Brian Kerr (drums)

Ohio's BLOOD COVEN began life with ex SIN EATER frontman Dann Saladin. By 1993 Saladin had split away from his former act and the title BLOOD COVEN was adopted for a new venture. The band contributed a track 'Statuary' to the 'Midnight Offerings II' compilation album. Guitarist Dave Ingram was drafted and a 1995 demo 'Dark Harmonies' followed. BLOOD COVEN at this juncture also comprised of bassist Chuck Smith and drummer Andy Wiper. A further tape emerged in 1997 'Serenades For The Bleeding'.
Both Smith and Wiper bailed out of the project. Undaunted BLOOD COVEN enlisted former AD NAUSEUM drummer Brian Kerr and set about gigging minus a bassist. However, by 1996 ex-HATE THEORY four stringer Jason Woolard had been enrolled.
In their time BLOOD COVEN have guested for MERCYFUL FATE, OVERKILL and MORBID ANGEL amongst others.

Singles/EPs:
A Tribute To Warriors Lost, Blood Coven (1997) (7" single)

Albums:
ASHES OF AN AUTUMN BURNING, Bloodfiend (1998)
Ashes Of An Autumn Burning / The medium / The Burning Season / Firm Grip Of Darkness / To Reach Serenity / Kiss Of Akhkharu / The True Name Of God

BLOODCUM (USA)
Line-Up: Joey Hannemann (vocals) Bobby Tovar (guitar), George Hierro

(guitar), John Araya (bass), Jimmy Sotelo (drums)

BLOODCUM came to attention featuring SLAYER siblings. Vocalist Joey Hannemann being brother of SLAYER guitarist Jeff Hannemann and bassist John Araya playing the same instrument as his more famous brother and SLAYER frontman Tom Araya.

Albums:
BLOODCUM, Wild Rags (1987)
Son Of Sam / Harassment By Farm Animals / Belligerent Youth / Live To Kill / First To Die / Happily Married / Son Of Sam / Harassment By Farm Animals / Belligerent Youth / Live To Kill / First To Die / Happily Married
DEATH BY A CLOTHES HANGER, Wild Rags (1988)
Happily Married / Son Of Sam / Live To Kill / Good Hearted Man / Treatment Of Death / Death By A Clothes Hanger / Belligerent Youth / Harassment By Farm Animals / First To Die / Sike-O-Path

THE BLOOD DIVINE (UK)
Line-Up: Darren White (vocals), Paul Ryan (guitar), Paul Allander (guitar), Benjamin Ryan (keyboards), Was Sarginson (drums)

Colchester's THE BLOOD DIVINE came together in late 1995 as a vehicle for ex-ANATHEMA vocalist Darren White and features ex-CRADLE OF FILTH guitarists Paul Allander and Paul Ryan along with keyboard player Benjamin Ryan. Drummer Was Sarginson also plies his trade with DECEMBER MOON. Musically the band have opted for a Doomladen Death Metal stance.
In support of the 'Awaken' album dates opening for labelmates MY DYING BRIDE were undertaken in Europe prior to a batch of British headliners. Further forays into Europe saw BLOOD DIVINE appearing at many festivals, including the 'Rock In Madrid' show alongside BRUCE DICKINSON and NAPALM DEATH.
THE BLOOD DIVINE gave two cover tracks to Peaceville Records 1998 tenth anniversary compilation 'X' in JOY DIVISION's 'Love Will Tear Us Apart' and THE OSMONDS 'Crazy Horses'.
Sarginson enjoyed a brief spell as drummer for CRADLE OF FILTH. Allander quit to create a new act LILLITH with former ENTWINED keyboard player Mark Royce and ex-CENOBITE vocalist /

guitarist Mark Giltrow. The band adopted a new name of PRIMARY SLAVE but Allander was re-enlisted into the ranks of CRADLE OF FILTH in late 1999.
Benjamin Ryan founded CROWFOOT with form WITCHFINDER GENERAL, BAJJON and LIONSHEART bassist Zakk Bajjon. This band, with the addition of ex-CRADLE OF FILTH guitarist Rishi Mehta and former INCARCERATED drummer Mark Cooper became RAINMAKER 888.

Singles/EPs:
And With The Day's Dying Light, Peaceville (1996)

Albums:
AWAKEN, Peaceville CDVILE 62 (1996)
So Serene / Moonlight Adorns / Visions (Of A Post Apocalyptic World) Part One / Wilderness / These Deepest Feelings / Aureole / Oceans Rise / Artemis / In Crimson Dreams / Heart Of Ebony / Warm Summer Rain
MYSTICA, Peaceville (1997)
Mystica / As Rapture Fades / Visions In Blue / The Passion Reigns / Leaving Me Helpless / Visions Part II: Event Horizon / I Believe / Enhanced By Your Touch / Sensual Ecstasy / Fear Of A Lonely World / Prayer

BLOOD DUSTER (AUSTRALIA)
Line-Up: Tony Forde (vocals), Matt Collins (guitar), J.J. La Whore (guitar), Jason P.C. (bass), Matt Rizzo (drums)

Quite uniquely Melbourne's BLOOD DUSTER have somehow managed to mould lethal Grindcore with traditional 70's style Southern Rock and Rockabilly rhythms spiced up with a large dose of grossed out humour. The band, with an inaugural 1990 line up of bassist Jason 'P.C.' Fuller, drummer Brick and a guitarist (possibly) called Fred, opened up proceedings with the 1992 demo 'Menstrul Soup'. Brick would be forced into retiring from music suffering with a badly injured knee whilst Fred (?) reportedly also retired but in his case to a mental home!
BLOOD DUSTER signed to Wild Rags Records in America for a proposed first album. However, the record 'Fisting The Dead', would eventually emerge on the domestic Dr. Jim label. Line-up at this stage comprised of Jason P.C., drummer Shane Rout, vocalist Tony Forde and guitarist Brad. However, Rout would break ranks to join Black Metal band

LORD LUCIFER at the same time as Brad made his exit.

Second outing 'Yeest', replete with a deliberately shocking medical photograph for a cover and apparently so named as to copy exactly another local act's album title, would be re-issued by Relapse in America combined with the previous mini-album. Fin Allman was now on guitar with ORDER OF CHAOS man Matt Rizzo on drums.

For 1998's 'Str8 Outta Northcote' Rout made a return on drums as Allman departed. Latterly BLOOD DUSTER have drafted NO GRACE six stringer Matt 'Lowpartz' Collins, second guitarist Josh ('J.J. La Whore') of POD PEOPLE and reinstated Rizzo.

The quaintly titled 'Cunt' album sees a cover of IMPETIGO's 'Dis-Organ-Ized'.

Both Fuller and La Whore are members of MEGAWATT WINGED AVENGER whilst Fuller also operates Stoner band DERN RUTLIDGE.

Albums:
FISTING THE DEAD, Dr. Jim (1993)
Albert / Northcote / Motherfuckin' / Chuck / Showered With Affection Part II / Strop / Nasty Chicks
YEEST, Dr. Jim (1995)
Vulgar Taste / Kill, Kill, Kill / Bitch / Mortician / Sadomasifuck / Rectal Spawn / Grossman The Meatman / Bloodfart / Knee Deep In Menstrual Blood Part II / Chunky Bit / Simultaneous Pleasure Pinch / Theatre Of The Macabre / Gimme Some Lovin' / Raping The Elderly / Anal Feast / Fisting The Dead / Derek
YEEST, Relapse (1995)
Albert / Northcote / Motherfuckin' / Chuck / Showered With Affection Part II / Strop / Nasty Chicks / Vulgar Taste / Kill, Kill, Kill / Bitch / Mortician / Sadomasifuck / Rectal Spawn / Grossman The Meatman / Bloodfart / Knee Deep In Menstrual Blood Part II / Chunky Bit / Simultaneous Pleasure Pinch / Theatre Of The Macabre / Gimme Some Lovin' / Raping The Elderly / Anal Feast / Fisting The Dead / Derek
STR8 OUTTA NORTHCOTE, Relapse (1998)
Givin' Stiff To The Stiff / Hippie Kill Team / Metal As Fuck / I Hate Girls And Crusty Punx / Chop Chop / Tittie / Motherload / The Meat Song (Stiffy In McDonalds) / Death Squad / Instrumental I / The Simple Life / Where Does All The Money Go When Releasing A Full Length Album

/ It's Just Not Metal / Celebrating 35% Pig Fat / F.S.S. / Ooh Aah / Derek II / Roll Call / Shoved Up Your Pisshole / Ballad Of Hoyt / Pure Digital Silence
CUNT, Relapse (2000)
We Are The Word Police / Big Fat Arse / Another Slack Arsed Aussie Band / Pronstoresiffi / Pissing Contest / I Just Finished Sucking Off Metalheads In The Mens Urinals / Hoochie Mumma / I Love It When Joe Pesci Swears / Stock Takin' / Lets All Fuck / A Track Suit Is Not Appropriate Metal Apparel / The Corpse Song / Fuck You Scene Boy / Is Killing Clones Illegal / Don't Call Me Home Boy Ya Cunt / Spefeven / The Object Is To Shift Some Units / Sweet Meat / Dis-Organ-Ized

BLOODFEAST (USA)
Line-Up: Gary Markovitch (vocals), Adam Tranquilli (guitar), Lou Starita (bass), Kevin Kuzma (drums)

Initially known as BLOODLUST in 1985. Released a 4 track demo 'Suicidal Mission' in February 1986 shortly after adding second guitarist Mike Basden. Changed names to BLOODFEAST before signing to New Renaissance Records. BLOODFEAST toured America in 1988 supporting DEATH ANGEL. Parted company with guitarist Adam Tranquilli following the release of 'The Last Remains'.

Tranquili re-emerged in 1991 with his new outfit LAST REMAINS featuring Rich Caputo on vocals, Kurt Becker on second guitar, Ron McLynn on bass and drummer Adam Kieffer.

Singles/EPs:
Face Fate / R.I.P. / Bloodlust / Vampire, New Renaissance NRR 35 (1988)

Albums:
KILL FOR PLEASURE, New Renaissance NRR 16 (1987)
Menacing Thunder / Kill For Pleasure / Cannibal / Vampire / Suicidal Mission / Venomous Death / The Evil / Darkside / R.I.P.
THE LAST REMAINS, New Renaissance (1988)
CHOPPING BLOCK BLUES, Flametrader FLAME 1016CD (1990)
The Last Remains / Hunted, Stalked And Slain / Chopping Block Blues / Hitler Painted Roses / Dropping Like Flies / Born Innocent / Turn To Dust / The Chemically Imbalanced / Spasmodic /

BLOOD FROM THE SOUL (UK)
Line-Up: Lou Koller (vocals), Shane Embury (guitar / bass / drum programming)

A project involving NAPALM DEATH's Shane Embury and SICK OF IT ALL vocalist Lou Koller. BLOOD FROM THE SOUL is, more or less, an Embury solo adventure, the man recording songs that he wouldn't have been able to perform with NAPALM DEATH.

Albums:
TO SPITE THE GLAND THAT BREEDS, Earache MOSH 89 CD (1996)
Painted Life, The Image And The Helpless / On Fear And Prayer / Guinea Pig / Natures Hole / Vascular / To Spite / Suspension Of My Disbelief / Yet To Be Savoured / Blood From The Soul

BLOODLUST (USA)
Line-Up: Guy Lord (vocals), Anthony Romero (guitar), Earl Mendenhall (guitar), Sandy K. (bass), M.E. Cuestas (drums)

Following the release of their debut album, BLOODLUST split with vocalist Guy Lord and added ex-ABBATOIR man Steve Gaines, brother of STRYPER bassist Tim Gaines. Further line up shuffles witnessed the departure of guitarist Anthony Romero and drummer M.E. Cuestas.
The 'Terminal Velocity' EP of 1988 sees BLOODLUST with a line up of Gaines, guitarists Earl Mendenhall and John Lisi, together with bassist Sandy K. and drummer Graig Kasin.
BLOODLUST were later to recruit bassist Eric Meyer. In 1990 Sandy K. and John Lisi created LAST RITES.

Singles/EPs:
Terminal Velocity / City Of The Forgotten / C.T.R (Sunday's Liar) / Semper Fi / Guilty As Sin, Wild Rags WRR005 (1988)

Albums:
GUILTY AS SIN, Roadrunner RR 9744 (1985)
Soldier Of Fortune / Ride To Death / Chainsaw / Tear It Up / Bleeding For You / Too Scared To Run / Rising Power

BLOOD OF CHRIST (CANADA)
Albums:
A DREAM TO REMEMBER, Pulverizer (1997)
Moonlight Eclipse / Lonely Winter Morning / The Lost Shrine / Dreams Of Winter Landscapes / As The Roses Wither / Nocturnal Desire / Act IX - The Ancient Battles / Winter Tree... A Forest Of Tragedy / Whispers From The Past

BLO-TORCH (HOLLAND)
Line-Up: Michel (vocals), Hassan (guitar), Marvin Vriesde (guitar), Sander (bass), Pascal (drums)

Albums:
BLO-TORCH, Wicked World (1999)
Spanish Sun / Mount Ygman / King Of Karnage / In Black Sky / Panzerstorm / Quatrain / Seen To Be The Enemy / March Of The Worm / Bloodstains

BODYBAG ROMANCE (USA)
Line-Up: Zach (vocals), Chaz (guitar), Adam Wright (guitar), Aaron (bass), Adam (drums)

Death Metal band previously known for their 1997 demo 'Deeper Than What You Can See' as CALIPH.
Guitarist Adam Wright also shares duties with his other act STRONG INTENTIONS.
As CALIPH the act was fronted by singer Cody and included guitarist Jeremy who quit in June of 1999. His place was taken by Chaz, previously with Christian Death Metal act EUCHARIST.
As BODYBAG ROMANCE the band issued a further demo session 'What To Do If You Are Left Behind' and a 7" single on Fistfight Records.
BODYBAG ROMANCE's 'Gincrusher' album included a version of MOUNTAIN's 'Mississippi Queen'.

Singles/EPs:
Bodybag Romance, Fistfight (1999)

Albums:
GINCRUSHER: HYMNS OF SHIT AND GLORY, Bodybag Romance (1999)
Baptized In Shit / Bow To Q / The One I Waisted / The One That Waisted Me / The Miracle Of Grief / Mississippi Queen

BOLT-THROWER (UK)
Line-Up: Karl Willetts (vocals), Barry Thomson (guitar), Gavin Ward (guitars),

Jo-Anne Bench (bass),
Andy Whale (drums)

Founded in Birmingham during 1986 BOLT-THROWER gaining notoriety on the local Metal scene with a unique, war obsessed heaviness. At this time the band featured vocalist Alan West, guitarist Barry Thomson, bassist Gavin Ward and drummer Andy Whale. The name BOLT-THROWER is taken from a siege device in a fantasy role playing game.

Following a 1987 demo 'Concessions In Pain' the fledgling band added bassist Jo-Anne Bench, shifting Gavin Ward to second guitar. A further demo ensued, which resulted in a Radio One session on the John Peel show. This airing led to an album deal with Vinyl Solution Records, but not before West's departure.

The band added vocalist Karl Willetts to record the debut album 'In Battle There Is No Law'. Having performed well on the Earache organized 'Grindcrusher' tour of 1989 after contributing a track to the compilation album of the same name, the band then executed dates in Holland with AUTOPSY and PESTILENCE on the 'Bloodbrothers' tour.

The group's first album for Earache, 'Realm Of Chaos', was to sell in excess of 50,000 copies worldwide and utilized artwork from Games Workshop that carried on the theme of fantasy wargaming.

With the release of the 'Cenotaph' EP BOLT-THROWER once more toured Europe, this time with support from NOCTURNUS. The release of the next studio affair, 'Warmaster', saw the band's first American dates before engaging in further European shows, where they were supported by BENEDICTION and ASPHYX. However, BOLT-THROWER's first Australian tour in 1993 ended in debacle when the band were stuck without a flight home!

Eventually managing to make it back to Britain the Birmingham bunch undertook another American club tour in July 1994 with fellow brummies BENEDICTION as support, but failed to complete the schedule.

Ex-PESTILENCE, ASPHYX and SUBMISSION vocalist Martin Van Drunen joined the band in 1994 replacing the departed Willets and drummer Martin Kearn was added in the line-up shuffle.

Severing connections with Earache Records in early 1997 and signing to American label Metal Blade, before recording on a brand new album could commence, Van Drunen, suffering from a disease which made his hair fall out, quit unexpectedly on the eve of some European festivals. BOLT-THROWER killed time by throwing in a few live gigs with BENEDICTION's Dave Ingram guesting.

As BOLT-THROWER went into the studio in late 1997 it was announced that 19 year old Alex Thomas had succeeded skinsman Kearn and that Willets had rejoined.

BOLT-THROWER toured Europe in January 2001 supported by FLESHCRAWL.

Singles/EPs:
Cenotaph / Destructive Infinity / Prophet Of Hatred / Realm Of Chaos, Earache MOSH CD 33 (1991)
Spearhead / Crown Of Life / Dying Creed / Lament, Earache MOSH 73 (1993) ('Spearhead' EP)
Forgotten Existence / Attack In The Aftermath / Psychological Warfare / In Battle There Is No Law, Strange Fruit (1988) ('The Peel Sessions' EP)

Albums:
IN BATTLE THERE IS NO LAW, Vinyl Solution SOL 11 (1988)
In Battle There Is No Law / Challenge For Power / Forgotten Existence / Denial Of Destiny / Concession Of Pain / Attack In The Aftermath / Psychological Warfare / Nuclear Annihilation / Blind To Defeat
REALM OF CHAOS, Earache MOSH 13 (1989)
Eternal War / Through The Eye Of Terror / Dark Millennium / All That Remains / Lost Souls Domain / Plague Bearer / World Eater / Drowned In Torment / Realm Of Chaos / Outro
WARMASTER, Earache MOSH 35 (1991)
Unleashed (Upon Mankind) / What Dwells Within / The Shreds Of Sanity / Profane Creation / Final Revelation, Cenotaph, War Master / Rebirth Of Humanity / Afterlife
THE FOURTH CRUSADE, Earache MOSH 70 (1993)
The Fourth Crusade / Icon / Embers / Where Next To Conquer / As The World Burns / This Time It's War / Ritual / Spearhead / Celestial Sanctuary / Dying Creed / Through The Ages (Outro)
FOR VICTORY, Earache MOSH 120 (1994)
War / Remembrance / When Glory

Beckons / For Victory / Graven Image / Lest We Forget / Silent Demise / Forever Fallen / Tank (MK 1) / Armageddon Bound
MERCENARY, Metal Blade (1998)
Zeroed / Laid To waste / Return From Chaos / Mercenary / To The Last... / Powder Burns / Behind Enemy Lines / No Guts, No Glory / Sixth Chapter

BONEWIRE (UK)

Initially known as INCARCERATED, BONEWIRE's debut album was produced by LIONSHEART bassist Zakk Bajjon.

Albums:
THROWN INTO MOTION, Cacophonous NIHIL 3CD(1995)
Drowning Stain / Opium / Hollow / Beneath The Sun / Shed This Skin / As Far As The Eye / Forgive Me / Tides / Awake

BRAIN DAMAGE (SWEDEN)

Noisecore act BRAIN DAMAGE would share a split 7" single with GUT. Early nineties demo tapes included 'Reject The Rockstar Nation', 'Death To Rock Stars' and 'Boycott The Commercial Music Business'.

Singles/EPs:
Split, (199-) (7" split single with GUT)

BRIGHTER DEATH NOW

BRIGHTER DEATH NOW is the longstanding quest for the extreme Electronic Death persuasions of Roger Karmanik, founder of Cold Meat Industries. Karmanik has also recorded previously under the title of LILLE ROGER issuing 'A Celebration' in 1985 and the 1987 'Undead' single.
Adjectives simply fail in an attempt to describe BRIGHTER DEATH NOW's music. Suffice to say it is extremely uncomfortable listening.

Singles/EPs:
Nordanvinterdöd, (1996)

Albums:
GREAT DEATH I, Cold Meat Industry (1990)
Great Death I / Evisceration / Certified Dead / Gore / Death Appeal / Moribund / Laudate Dominum I
PAIN IN PROGRESS, Unclean

Productions (199-)
Shatterer Of Death / Pain In Progress / Certified Dead / Dachau-Anthem / Still Murder / Meat Processing / Heart Of Stone / Bloodshower / Bloodsex And Murders / Serapeum / Maruta Kornand / Blood On The Sheets / Death Komh / Meat Improvement
SLAUGHTERHOUSE, Functional (1993)
Dead Bones / Cadaver / Death Party / The Last Call / Grave / Death / Consumers / Grave Cracker
GREAT DEATH II, Cold Meat Industry (1996)
Great Death II / Adipocere / Anus Praeparati / Mortarium / Deathcraft / Exsurge Morto / Laudate Dominum II
NECROSE EVANGELICUM, Cold Meat Industry (1995)
Willful / Soul In Flames / Impasse / Rain, Red Rain / Deathgrant / Necrose Evangelicum
GREAT DEATH III, (1996)
Great Death III / Urinated / Female Blood / Funeral Day / Open The Gates / Angel Of Death - Laudate Dominum III
INNERWAR, Cold Meat Industry (1996)
Innerwar / American Tale / No Pain / Happy Nation / Little Baby / Sex Or Violence / No Tomorrow / War
NO SALVATION - NO TOMORROW, Cold Meat Industry (199-)
GREATEST DEATH, Cold Meat Industry (1998)
Adipocere / Anus Praeparati / Female Blood / Laudate Dominum I / Evisceration / Gore / Moratorium / Moribund / Urinated
MAY ALL BE DEAD, (1999)
I Hate You / I Wish I Was A Little Girl / Behind Curtains / Payday / Oh What A Night / Fourteen
OBSESSIS, Cold Meat Industry (2000)

BRODEQUIN (Knoxville, TN, USA)
Line-Up: Jamie Bailey (vocals / bass), Mike Bailey (guitar), Chad Wallis (drums)

Death Metal band BRODEQUIN, named after a French medieval leg crushing torture device, include former BESIEGED and ENTER SELF drummer Chad Wallis in the ranks. The debut album 'Instruments Of Torture' was self-financed but later re-issued by Extremis Records.

Albums:
INSTRUMENTS OF TORTURE, Extremis (1999)
Spinning In Agony / Soothsayer / Ambrosia / The Virgin Of Nuremburg /

Duke Of Exeter / Infested With Worms / Burnt In Effigy / Strappado / Hollow / Feast Of Flesh

BROKEN (UK)

A Yorkshire Death Metal quintet, previously known as EPITAPH, issued a purely self financed album during 1997.

Albums:
SKYTORN, Sterilized Decay (1997)

BROKEN HOPE (Chicago, IL, USA)
Line-Up: Jeremy Wagner (vocals), Brian Griffin (guitar), Shaun Glass (bass), Ryan Stanek (drums)

Very much in the Gore-Metal mould. Chicago's BROKEN HOPE have nevertheless put a healthy work ethic to their advantage touring America constantly to back up a string of blood-curdling releases.
The band formulated in 1989 when vocalist Jeremy Wagner and bassist Joe Ptacek joined CRYPT, an act featuring drummer Ryan Stanek. CRYPT folded and the trio duly founded BROKEN HOPE. The band's first demo secured a deal with Grindcore Records for their debut 'Swamped In Gore'.
BROKEN HOPE stepped up a gear by signing to Metal Blade Records for their sophomore effort 'Bowels Of Repugnance', this album seeing erstwhile SINDROME bassist Shaun Glass joining the fold. The band toured persistently and hard alongside acts such as UNLEASHED, DEICIDE and SIX FEET UNDER. A further album 'Loathing' cemented BROKEN HOPE's grip on the scene.
1995's 'Repulsive Conception' featured BROKEN HOPE's version of the TWISTED SISTER track 'Captain Howdy'. The album also saw AGENT STEEL / CANCER / DEATH guitarist JAMES MURPHY as guest on the track 'Engorged With Impiety'.
The band parted ways with Metal Blade masking any doubts over their career by touring America with support from Poland's VADER and MONSTROSITY before dates in Chile with Germany's SODOM.
Stanek, De Mumbrum and Griffin forged the side act EM SINFONIA in the ensuing downtime during which Glass departed.
The 1999 BROKEN HOPE album sees Ryan Schimmenti of New York's

DISFIGURED, Brian Hobbie of INTERNAL BLEEDING and also Mike Zwicke on session bass guitar. Griffin would act as producer for DISFIGURED's debut album 'Prelude To Dementia' as well as on INTERNAL BLEEDING's 'Driven To Conquer'.

Albums:
SWAMPED IN GORE, Grind Core International (1991)
Borivoj's Demise / Incinerated / Swamped In Gore / Bag Of Parts / Dismembered Carcass / Devourer Of Souls / Awakened By Stench / Gorehog / Gobblin' The Guts / Cannibal Crave / Claustrophobic Agnostic Dead
BOWELS OF REPUGNANCE, Metal Blade CDZORRO 64
Repugnance / The Dead Half / Coprophagia / She Came Out In Chunks / Peeled / Hobo Stew / Decimated Genitalia / Preacher Of Sodomy / Remember My Members / Waterlogged / Embryonic Tri-Clops / Drinking The Ichor / Felching Vampires
REPULSIVE CONCEPTION, Metal Blade (1995)
Dilation And Extraction / Grind Box / Chewed To Stubs / Engorged With Impiety / Swallowed Whole / Erotic Zoophilism / Pitbull Grin / Into The Necrosphere / Essence Of Human Pain / The Internal Twin / Penis Envy / For Only The Sick / Freezer Burnt / Imprim's Obscurity / Captain Howdy
LOATHING, Metal Blade (1997)
Siamese Screams / Translucence / The Cloning / Reunited / High On Formaldehyde / A Window To Hell / Skin Is In / Auction Of The Dead / He Was Raped / I Am God / Deadly Embrace
GROTESQUE BLESSINGS, Martyr Music (1999)
Wolf Among Sheep / Chemically Castrated / Necro-Fellatio / Christ Consumed / War Maggot / Earth Burner / Internal Inferno / Razor Cunt / Hate Machine

BRUJERIA (USA)

Although a supposedly anonymous Mexican Death Metal band BRUJERIA are in fact led by FEAR FACTORY guitarist Dino Cazares and drummer Raymond Herrara in collusion with FAITH NO MORE's Jim Gould.

Ex-CRADLE OF FILTH and present day DIMMU BORGIR / LOCK UP drummer Nick Barker contributed to the 2000 album 'Brujerizmo'.

Singles/EPs:
Demoniaco!, Nemesis (1990) (7" single)
Machetazos!, Alternative Tentacles (199-)
(7" single)
Tribute To Pablo Escobar, Alternative
Tentacles (1994) (7" single)
Marajuana / Matando Gueros '97 / Pito
Wilson (Live) / Henchando Chingazos
(Live) / Matando Gueros (Live), Tralla
TRCD071 (1998) (CD single)

Albums:
MATANDO GUEROS, Roadrunner RR
9061-2 (1993)
Para De Venta / Leyes Narcos /
Sacrificio / Santa Lucia / Matando
Gueros / Seis Seis Seis / Cruza La
Frontera / Grenudos Locos / Chingo De
Mecos / Narcos Satanicos / Desperado /
Culeros / Misas Negras (Sacrificio III) /
Chinga Tu Madre / Verga Del Brujo /
Estan Chingados / Molestando Ninos
Muertos / Machetazos (Sacrificio II) /
Castigo Del Brujo / Christa De La Roca
RAZA ODIADA, (199-)
Raza Odiada / Colas De Rata /
Hechando Chingazos / La Migra /
Revolucion / Consejos Narcos / Almas
De Venta / La Ley De Plomo / Los Tengo
Colgando / Sesos Humanos / Primer
Meco / El Patron / Hermanus Menendez
/ Padre Nuestro / Vitmos Satanicos
BRUJERIZMO, Roadrunner (2000)
Brujerizmo / Vayan Sin Miedo / La
Tracion / Pititis, Te Invoco / Laboratorio
Cristalitos / Division Del Norte / Marcha
De Odio / Anti-Castro / Cuiden A Los
Ninos / El Bajon / Mecosario / El
Desmadre / Sida De La Merte

BRUTAL INSANITY (USA)

Albums:
SPLIT, (2000) (Split album with
DROGHEDA)
Front Right Fatal / Hate Race / Blame
Yourself / Illvolutions / Reflections From
A Real World (Live) / Dragged Down
(Live) / Blame Yourself (Live) / Butcher
Within (Live) / Going Out Clubbing (Live)
/ Illvolution (Live) / Front Right Fatal
(Live) / Hate Race (Live)

BRUTALITY (FL, USA)

Line-Up: Scott Reigal (vocals), Don
Gates (guitar), Jay Fernandez (guitar),
Jeff Acres (bass), Jim Coker (drums)

BRUTALITY's debut album, recorded
naturally at Morrisound studios, featured
a line up of vocalist Scott Reigal,
guitarists Don Gates and Jay Fernandez,
bassist Jeff Acres and drummer Jim
Coker. Fernandez would make his exit to
be replaced by Brian Hipp for 1995's
'When The Sky Turns Black'.
By the time of BRUTALITY's last outing
'In Mourning' Both Hipp and Gates had
been superseded by former NASTY
SAVAGE man Danny Gray and erstwhile
DEGRADATION member Dana Walsh.
However, pre-recording Gray made way
for ex-EXECRATION guitarist Pete
Sykes.
Ex-member Brian Hipp would enjoy a
fleeting appearance with premier British
Black Metal band CRADLE OF FILTH
during 1995 and later resurfaced as a
member of DIABOLIC.

Singles/EPs:
Hell On Earth, Gore GORE 007 (1991)
Sadistic, (1992)

Albums:
SCREAMS OF ANGUISH, Nuclear Blast
NB 075 (1993)
These Walls Will Be Your Grave /
Ceremonial Unearthing / Sympathy /
Septicemic Plague / Crushed / Spirit
World / Exposed To The Elements /
Cries Of The Forsaken / Cryptorium /
Spawned Illusion
WHEN THE SKY TURNS BLACK,
Nuclear Blast NB115-2 (1995)
When The Sky Turns Black / Race
Defects / Awakening / Electric Funeral ?
Foul Lair / Screams Of Anguish /
Esoteric / Artistic Butchery / Violent
Generation / Shrine Of The Master
IN MOURNING, Nuclear Blast (1996)
Obsessed / The Past / Destroyed By
Society / Waiting To Be Devoured / Died
With Open Eyes / In Mourning /
Subjected To Torture / Calculated
Bloodshed / Extinction

BRUTAL NOISE (ARGENTINA)

Line-Up: Juan Paulo Barrera (vocals),
Alex Diaz (guitar), Claudio Sattler
(guitar), Facundo Ramirez (bass), Panda
Figueroa (drums)

BRUTAL NOISE was formed in 1995 under
the original title of ANO NEGRO. Switching
names to BRUTAL NOISE the 1998 demo
tape 'Mundo Septico' followed.

Albums:
IMPENDING ROT, (2000)
Impaling Cops / Butchers Song /
Apartheid '99 / Dismemborado / I'm
Waiting '99 / Without Control '99 /
Sawing The Legs / Death Spit My Face /
Chullets Suffocating Rage

BRUTAL TRUTH (USA)
Line-Up: Kevin Sharp (vocals),
Brent McCarty (guitar), Dan Lilker
(bass), Rich Hoak (drums)

BRUTAL TRUTH, Grindcore exponents
with a definite thirst for speed, were
created during a lull in NUCLEAR
ASSAULT activities when bassist Dan
Lilker (Previously with ANTHRAX /
STORMTROOPERS OF DEATH)
assembled a band to indulge his love of
hardcore. Recruiting guitarist Brent
McCarty and drummer Scott Lewis the
line up was finalized with the addition of
vocalist Kevin Sharp.
However, recordings made by the band
whilst still a trio were issued on the
bootleg EP 'The birth of ignorance' on
Liberated Records.
In time Lilker split NUCLEAR ASSAULT
to concentrate fully on BRUTAL TRUTH.
With Lilker's pedigree a deal was quickly
on the table and the band signed to
grindcore exponents Earache Records
for their debut effort 'Extreme Conditions
Demand Extreme Responses'. A 7" single
'Ill Neglect' also saw the light of day
featuring a raucous cover of THE
BUTTHOLE SURFERS 'The Shah
Sleeps In Lee Harvey's Grave'.
BRUTAL TRUTH paid their live dues in
America opening for CATHEDRAL,
CARCASS and NAPALM DEATH prior to
guesting for FEAR FACTORY in Europe.
During the tour Lewis departed and was
supplanted by former NINEFINGER man
Rich Hoak.
Pushing the boundaries of extremity even
further BRUTAL TRUTH forged a liaison
with Coventry techno act LARCENY to
record the 'Perpetual Conversion' 7", the
B side of which featured a version of
BLACK SABBATH's 'Lord Of This World'.
The 1994 album 'Need To Control' was
formatted uniquely enough to make an
impact with it being a boxed set of 5, 6, 7,
8 and 9 inch vinyl. Bonus cuts included
CELTIC FROST's 'Dethroned Emperor'
and PINK FLOYD's seminal 'Wish You
Were Here'.
Even as this album was being released
Lilker was dabbling in another project

titled EXIT 13, together with Lewis, and
guesting on the 'No Matter What The
Cause' album by Germans HOLY
MOSES up front of a BRUTAL TRUTH
tour encompassing Australia, Japan and
America.
The band, feeling that Earache Records
did not have the necessary commitment,
broke away from the label in search of
another deal. It was to be a full two years
before BRUTAL TRUTH signed up with
American label Relapse Records. During
this interim the quartet were far from
inactive. A 1995 vinyl album 'Machine
Parts' emerged which included no less
than five different live versions of
'Collateral Damage' including takes with
EXIT 13's Bill Yurkiewicz and NAPALM
DEATH's Barney Greenaway on vocals.
The band also contributed tracks to the
'Nothings Quiet On The Western Front'
compilation and issuing a split EP with
SPAZZ which included a version of DIE
KREUZEN's 'Rumburs'.
In 1997 Hoak teamed up with
CORROSION OF CONFORMITY's Mike
Dean to record a project album under the
band name of NINE FINGER.
BRUTAL TRUTH made an appearance in
a porn movie 'Studio X' in 1997. The band
played two songs live and even took a
part in acting although not in some of the
more 'animated' scenes. Lilker took time
out to resurrect STORMTROOPERS OF
DEATH as the original line up toured
America one last time.
The '97 album 'Sounds Of The Animal
Kingdom' broke BRUTAL TRUTH into
fresh audiences and includes a
somewhat unlikely cover of jazz maestro
SUN RA's 'It's After The End Of The
World'. The Japanese release added
bonus cover versions in AGATHOCLES's
'Hippie Cult', NAUSEA's 'Cybergod' and
BLACK SABBATH's 'Cornucopia'. The
latter also appeared on a split EP on
Hydrahead Records, a label that
specializes in BLACK SABBATH covers!
The band at this point were credited as
being Sharp (grunts and groans), Gurn
(fingers), Lilker (opposable thumbs) and
Hoak (sticks and stones).
BRUTAL TRUTH undertook a demanding
90 date tour of America to wind up 1997
on a touring package combining
CANNIBAL CORPSE, IMMOLATION and
OPRESSOR.
Despite steady progress and increased
sales BRUTAL TRUTH split following
completion of an Australian tour in
September 1998. Lilker resumed activity

with STORMTROOPERS OF DEATH for their 'Bigger Than The Devil' album. The bassist also operates in Black Metal band HEMLOCK.

Hoak re-emerged in 2000 with his subtly titled new band TOTAL FUCKING DESTRUCTION.

BRUTAL TRUTH's epic swansong 'Goodbye Cruel World' was made up of a twin CD set. The first CD featured a live show from Sydney, Australia which included covers of tracks by BLACK SABBATH, S.O.B., THE GERMS, THE MELVINS and AGATHOCLES whilst the second CD had bonus track rarities and the 'Machine Parts' recordings along with more live material from Japanese and New Zealand shows.

Singles/EPs:
Ill Neglect / The Shah Sleeps In Lee Harvey's Grave, Earache 7 MOSH 080 (1992)
Perpetual Conversion / Perpetual Larceny / Walking Corpse / Lord Of This World / Bedsheet, Earache MOSH 084CD (1993) (Split CD with LARCENY)
Godplayer, Earache (1994) (7" single)
B.I.T.B. / Dethroned Emperor / Painted Clowns / Wish You Were Here, Earache MOSH 110B (1994) (Free EP with 'No Need To Control' album)
Porkfarm / Rumburs / Foolish Bastard, Bovine (1996) (7" split single with SPAZZ)
Split, Deaf American (1997) (7" split single with RUPTURE)
Cornucopia, Hydrahead (1997) (Split EP with CONVERGE)

Albums:
EXTREME CONDITIONS DEMAND EXTREME RESPONSES, Earache MOSH 069 (1992)
P.S.P.I. / Birth Of Ignorance / Stench Of Prophet / Ill Neglect / Denial Of Existence / Regression-Progression / Collateral Damage / Time / Walking Corpse / Monetary Gain / Wilt / H.O.P.E. / Blockhead / Anti-Homophobe / Unjust Compromise
NEED TO CONTROL, Earache MOSH 110 (1994)
Collapse / Black Door Mine / Turn Face / Godplayer / I See Red / Iron Lung / Bite The Hand / Ordinary Madness / Media Blitz / Judgement / Brain Trust / Choice Of A New Generation / Mainliner / Displacement / Crawlspace
MACHINE PARTS, Deaf American (1995)
Spare Change / Machine Parts /

Collateral Damage (Live) / Collateral Damage (Live) / Collateral Damage (Live) / Collateral Damage (Live) / Collateral Damage (Live) / Fucktoy / Kill Trend Suicide
KILL TREND SUICIDE, Relapse RR 6498 (1997)
Blind Leading The Blind / Pass Some Down / Lets Got To War / Hypocrite Invasion / Everflow / Zombie / Homesick / Humanity's Folly / I Killed My Family / Kill Trend Suicide
SOUNDS OF THE ANIMAL KINGDOM, Relapse RR 6968 (1997)
Dementia / K.A.P. / Vision / Fuck Toy / Jiminez Cricket / Soft Mind / Average People / Blue World / Callous / Fisting / Die Laughing / Dead Smart / Sympathy Kiss / Pork Farm / Promise / Foolish Bastard / Postulate Then Liberate / Machine Parts / In The Words Of Sun Ra / Unbaptise / Cybergod
GOODBYE CRUEL WORLD! LIVE FROM PLANET EARTH+13, Relapse (1999)
Intro / Dementia / K.A.P. / Choice Of A New Generation / Birth Of Ignorance / Stench Of Profit / Walking Corpse / Sympathy Kiss / Pork Farm / Jiminez Cricket / Respect At Length / Media Blitz / Fucktoy / Ill-Neglect / Kill Trend Suicide / Cornucopia / Godplayer / I Killed My Family / Time / Denial Of Existence / Hippie Cult / Callous / Zodiac / No Sleep / Hippie Cult / Cybergod / Cornucopia / Born To Die / Spare Change / Machine Parts / Collateral Damage (Live) / Collateral Damage (Live) / Collateral Damage (Live) / Collateral Damage (Live) / Fucktoy / Kill Trend Suicide / Bubblbop Shop / Boredom's Cover No. 2 / Telly (With Bucky) / Blind Leading The Blind / Pass Some Down / Vision / Die Laughing / Let's Go To War / Zombie / Homesick / Everflow / Dead Smart / Dethroned Emperor / It's After The End Of The World / Callous / Average People / Black Door Mine / Promise / Foolish Bastard / Bite The Hand / Collateral Damage
FOR DRUG CRAZED GRINDFREAKS ONLY!, Solardisk (2000)
K.A.P. / Dead Smart / Blind Leading The Blind / Lets Go To War / Choice Of A New Generation / Walking Corpse / Fisting / Homesick / Stench Of Profit / Jiminez Cricket / Untitled

BURIAL (Westfield, MA, USA)
Line-Up: Devin Doherty (vocals), Matt Rogalski (guitar), Nick Lecrenski (guitar),

Ian Plakias (bass), Jamie Sullivan
(drums)

Death Metallers BURIAL were created in
Massachusetts during 1995. However,
the group would switch titles to LEGION
for a 1996 demo cassette before losing
their original bass player and vocalist.
New blood was added with singer Don
Marhefka and bassist Ian Plakias and by
late 1998 the band re-adopted their
former name of BURIAL. A self financed
album 'Mourning The Millennium' was
issued prior to Marhefka bowed out.
BURIAL drafted Devin Doherty as their
new frontman for appearances at the
New Jersey March Metal Meltdown
festival.

Albums:
MOURNING THE MILLENNIUM, (1998)
ENLIGHTENED WITH PAIN, Lost
Disciple (2000)

BURIED DREAMS (MEXICO)
Line-Up: Erich Olguín (vocals), Antonio
De Yta (guitar), Ndua Valdespino
(guitar), Ezequiel Mendoza (bass),
Ivan Sartos (keyboards),
Oscar Doniz (drums)

Albums:
BEYOND YOUR MIND, Oz Productions
(1997)
The Sword And The Cross / Black
Dragon / Reflexions Of The Light / The
Battle / Beyond Your Mind / Limits Of
Fantasy / Looking Through The Fire /
Irony / Moxtla / Her Beauty
PERCEPTIONS, Oz Productions (2000)
Illhamiqui / The Riddle / The Mind's
Subconscious / At The End / Cosmic
Prophecies / 360 / Perceptions / God's
Of Fire / Buried Dreams

BURNING INSIDE (USA)
Line-Up: Jamie Prim (vocals / bass),
Steve Childers (guitar), Michael Estes
(guitar), Richard Christy (drums)

Studio Metal project centred on renowned
ICED EARTH, DEMONS & WIZARDS,
DEATH, CONTROL DENIED and
INCANTATION drummer Richard Christy.
Guitarist Steve Childers is a member of
BLACK WITCHERY whilst his fellow
axeman Michael Estes is from Black
Metal merchants ACHERON.
The 2000 debut album 'The Eve Of The
Entities' was released on the Polish label
Still Dead Productions.

Albums:
THE EVE OF THE ENTITIES, Still Dead
Productions (2000)
Words Of Wyndhym / The Eve Of The
Entities / My Own / The Unknown /
Masque / Engulfed In Flames / The
Valley Of Unrest / Blood To All That Exist
/ Chapels Of Youth / Drained Of
Essence / Everlasting Sleep

BURNT BY THE SUN (USA)

Singles/EPs:
Buffy / You Will Move / Lizard Skin
Barbie / The Fish Under The Sea Dance,
Relapse (2001) ('Burnt By The Sun' EP)

BUTCHERED (BELGIUM)

Grindcore band initially created as
DISTRAUGHT during 1997 under which
title they released the 'Spheres Of
Insanity' demo.

Albums:
**NEW METHODS FOR THE ADVANCED
SADIST**, Lowlife (1999)
I Am Pain / God Of The World /
Shattered Corpse / Fed By Menstrual
Defecation / My Private Golgotha /
Another Gruesome Dream Fulfilled /
Butchery Eternally / Stiff Of Christ (Born
Too Late) / Life Of Addiction / Evolution
Into Sickness

BUZZOV.EN (Richmond, VA, USA)
Line-Up: Kirk Fisher (vocals / guitar),
Buddy Apostolis (guitar), Brian Hill
(bass), Ashley Williamson (drums)

BUZZOV.EN made a brief if lasting
impression internationally in the mid 90's
with vocalist Kirk Fisher's onstage antics
which usually ended up with the frontman
suffering self inflicted injuries.
The band was previously known as
SEWAR PUPPET.
An erstwhile BUZZOV.EN member Dixie
Collins created WEEDEATER for the
2000 album 'And Justice For Y'All'.

Singles/EPs:
Wound EP, Allied ALLIEDNO11 (1991)
Useless / Never Again, Reptilian REP 013
(1997)
Vagabond / Mainline / Red Green /
Crawl Away / Chokehold, Allied (1997)
('Chokehold' EP)

Albums:

TO A FROWN, Allied ALLIED 21CD
(1992)

SORE, Roadrunner RR 8998-2 (1994)
Sore / Hawking To Explain / Hollow /
Dome / I Don't Like You / Broken /
Pathetic / Should I / Behaved / Blinded /
Grit / This Is Not…

AT A LOSS, Off The Record (1998)
At A Loss / Lack Of / Kakkila / Loracei /
Flow / Crawl Away / Whiskey Fit / Don't
Bring Me Down / Dirtkickers / Red Green
/ Useless / Heal / Left Behind

CABAL (FRANCE)

Singles/EPs:
Severing Teeth, Nails And Scrotum / Haemogenic Bronchial Furonculosis / Worm Infestation Of Deliquescent Human Offal / Unaesthetic Genital Stump / The Scalpel / The Gift, Panx (1998) (7" single)
Necrosymphonic Orchestration Of A Staphylococcic Uragenic Affection / Lymphogramulomatosis / Nasocomial Nephritic Colitis / Worm Infestation Of Deliquescent Human Offal, Bizarre Leprous (1998) (7" split single with MUCUPURULENT)

CADAVER (NORWAY)
Line-Up: Ole Bjerkebakke (vocals / drums), Anders Odden (guitar), Espen Sollum (guitar), Rene Jansen (bass)

CADAVER's 'Hallucinating Anxiety' album was also later re-released as a split CD with CARNAGE. For the second release 'In Pains' bassist Rene Jansen made way for Eilert Solstad.
CADAVER's debut plied pure Death Metal whilst the sophomore attempt saw more technical Thrash elements creeping in. Rumours abounded that CADAVER were to return to the scene in 2000. Demos were recorded with Anders Oden plus DØDHEIMSGARD men Apollyon and Czral.

Albums:
HALLUCINATING ANXIETY, Necro (1990)
Tuba / Ignominious Eczema / Corrosive Delirium / Hallucinating Anxiety / Cannibalistic Dissection / Hypertrophyan / Petrified Eyes / Inanimate / Twisted Collapse / Abnormal Deformity / Maelstrom / Mental Abhorrence / Bodily Trauma
IN PAINS, Relativity / Earache 88561-1144-2 (1992)
Bypassed / Mr. Tumour's Misery / Into The Outside / Blurred Visions / Runaway Brain / Inner Persecution / In Distortion / Thy Misanthrope / Ins-Through-Mental / During The End

CADAVEROUS CONDITION (AUSTRIA)
Line-Up: Wolfgang Weiss (vocals), Rene Kramer (guitar), Peter Droneberger (bass), Paul Droneberger (drums)

Death Metal act CADAVEROUS CONDITION revamped the Deutsche Welle hit 'Eisbär' in true Death Metal style for their 1993 debut.
The second album 'For Love...' features a guest appearance by WEREWOLF vocalist Hagen on the track 'In June, As I Killed Time'.

Albums:
IN MELANCHOLY, Lethal LRC 008 (1993)
Katzentanz / To Be / Beautiful / Marian / The Flower / Shine / The Sadness Out Of Me / You Remain / Depart (With Me) And I Wait / May Fragments Not Dissolve / Eisbär
"FOR LOVE" I SAID, Lethal LRC 23 (1995)
M / Tayst / A Song For / All The Vastness / What The Moon Brings / In June, As I Killed Time / Your And My Dead Stars / I Love You / The Ever Bleating Fools / Cold /... And The Forgotten / Teenage Kicks
TRYST, Starry SQD 02 (1996)
Motherdust / Shine / Lakeside Down / Wings But No Body / Nostalgia / Undertaker / Up The Ass Off A Swan / Who Will Buy My Records When I'm Dead / It Really Matters / I'll Protect Myself / Meg The Gypsy / Luminous Glow / Never Want To See You (Again) / I'll Be There / Nice Device / Never Want To Sleep With You Again / Wings

CADUCITY (BELGIUM)

Albums:
THE WEILIAON WIELDER QUEST, Shiver SHRO12 (1995)
Entry: Thus Begins Our Fair Journey / Vision For The Morrigon / Praseodymium / The Whimsical Crafts Of Enchantment / Strength Of Cruid Fire / Gymbrea's Enriching Wisdom Part One, Two And Three
WHIRLER OF FATE, Shiver (1997)

CALLENISH CIRCLE (HOLLAND)
Line-Up: Patrick Savelkoul (vocals), Jos Evers (guitar)

CALLENISH CIRCLE were, in their original incarnation as GENOCIDE in 1992 by vocalist Patrick Savelkoul and guitarist Jos Evers, a straight Death Metal act. Numerous line up changes afflicted the ranks until 1994 when, opting to switch titles to CALLENISH CIRCLE, the band issued the 'Lovelorn' demo tape. The tape made an enormous impression gaining the band the honour of "Demo of the month" in the well respected Dutch Rock magazine Aardschock and eventually winding up voted third best demo of the year.

A string of contributions to various compilation releases ensued before CALLENISH CIRCLE landed a deal with Hammerheart Records. The debut album is produced by Hans Swagerman.

Singles/EPs:
Silent Tears / Escape / Broken / Mirror Of Serenity, (2000) ('Escape' EP)

Albums:
DRIFT OF EMPATHY, Hammerheart (1996)
Inner Sense / Mental Affection / Slough Of Despond / Solitude / Last Words / The Dreamers Path / Disguised Ignorance / Where The Moon Meets The Sea / Scars
GRACEFUL ... YET FORBIDDING, DSFA (2000)
No Reason / Forgotten / Inner Battle / Beyond… / Broken / Oppressed Natives / Silent Tears / Passionate Dance / Caught By Deceit / Shadows Of The Past / Alone

CANCER (UK)
Line-Up: John Walker (vocals / guitar), James Murphy (guitar), Ian Buchanan (bass), Carl Stokes (drums),

Telford based extreme Speed Metal band, CANCER's first gig was in Birmingham opening for BOMB DISNEYLAND and the initial demos were recorded at the legendary Pits studio, owned by STARFIGHTERS vocalist Steve Burton. Having been granted a deal by Vinyl Solution CANCER's debut album, 'To The Gory End', took a mere four days to record!

Erstwhile AGENT STEEL and OBITUARY guitarist JAMES MURPHY was enlisted to record the sophomore 'Death Shall Rise' and the platter was produced by noted Death Metal producer Scott Burns into the bargain. Amusingly, the album caused a great deal of controversy upon release in Europe when it was banned in Germany by the State body for censorship of works dangerous to the youth, on grounds that the album cover would incite youngsters to inflict violence upon each other!

CANCER had recorded 'Death Shall Rise' in Scott Burns' Florida home state and chose to spend further working time in America by playing the 1991 Milwaukee Metalfest and also supporting DEICIDE and OBITUARY. However, by December 1991 James Murphy had quit the band to form DISINCARNATE, later joining TESTAMENT and Danes KONKHRA.

1993 was another particularly busy year for the band, releasing third album 'The Sins Of Mankind' and performing a European tour with openers CEREBRAL

CANCER
Photo : W. Nicholas

FIX. The group also was to tour Britain and America with DEICIDE.

In 1994 the band enrolled new guitarist Barry Savage and CANCER stepped up a level upon signing to major label East West Records. Following the release of the new album, 'Black Faith', which featured a caustic take on DEEP PURPLE's 'Space Truckin', the quartet toured Britain with support act MESHUGGAH.

Stokes filled in for Telford Hardcore mongers ASSERT in 2000. The drummer also busied himself with a new Metal project titled REMISSION with Walker.

Albums:
TO THE GORY END, Vinyl Solution SOL 22 (1990)
Blood Bath / C.F.C. / Witch Hunt / Into The Acid / Imminent Catastrophe / To The Gory End / Body Count / Sentenced To The Gallows / Die Die
DEATH SHALL RISE, Vinyl Solution SOL28 (1991)
Hung, Drawn And Quartered / Tasteless Incest / Burning Casket / Death Shall Rise / Back From The Dead / Gruesome Tasks / Corpse Fire / Internal Decay
THE SINS OF MANKIND, Vinyl Solution SOL35 (1993)
The Sins Of Mankind / Cloak Of Darkness / Electro-Convulsive Therapy / Patchwork Destiny / Meat Train / Suffer For Our Sins / Pasture Of Delights At The End / Tribal Bloodshed Part I - The Conquest / Tribal Bloodshed Part II - Under The Flag
BLACK FAITH, East West 0630 10752-2 (1995)
Ants (Nemesis Ride) / Who Do You Think You Are / Face To Face / Without Cause / White Desire / Kill Date / Temple Song / Black Faith / Highest Orders / Space Truckin' / Sunburnt / Save Me From Myself

CANCEROUS GROWTH (USA)

Albums:
LATE FOR THE GRAVE, Nuclear Blast (198-)
HMMMNLMNLMM, Nuclear Blast (198-)

CANNIBAL CORPSE (FL, USA)

Line-Up: Chris Barnes (vocals), Rob Barrett (guitar), Jack Owen (guitar), Alex Webster (bass), Paul Mazurkiewicz (drums)

Undoubtedly ranking among the higher echelons of the Death Metal elite. Florida gore merchants CANNIBAL CORPSE, since their debut 1990 album 'Eaten Back To Life', which featured bassist Bob Rusay, have stayed the course over an impressive stream of uncompromising albums. The band's album artwork has remained deliberately provocative with many releases being issued in tamer variants of the original shockers. By 2000 the band had shifted half a million records.

The CANNIBAL CORPSE line up that debuted on the hard hitting 'Eaten Back To Life' comprised vocalist Chris Barnes, dual guitarists Bob Rusay and Jack Owen, bassist Alex Webster and drummer Paul Mazurkiewicz.

The stopgap mini-album 'Hammer Smashed Face' included the band's first forays into cover version territory featuring as it did renditions of POSSESSED's 'The Exorcist' and BLACK SABBATH's 'Zero The Hero'. 1994's 'The Bleeding' was the last CANNIBAL CORPSE album to feature Chris Barnes, the vocalist opting out to concentrate on his side project act SIX FEET UNDER.

CANNIBAL CORPSE's 1996 line up comprised mainstay guitarists Jack Owen and Rob Barrett, bassist Alex Webster, drummer Paul Mazurkiewicz and ex-MONSTROSITY vocalist George 'Corpsegrinder' Fisher.

Added former NEVERMORE guitarist Pat O'Brien for 1997's 'Gallery Of Suicide' album.

Ex-member Barrett founded HATEPLOW with a moonlighting Phil Fasciana of MALEVOLENT CREATION to issue the 2000 album 'The Only Law Is Survival'.

Albums:
EATEN BACK TO LIFE, Metal Blade ZORRO12 (1990)
Shredder Humans / Edible Autopsy / Put Them To Death / Mangled / Scattered Remains, Splattered Brains / Born In A Casket / Rotting Head / The Undead Will Feast / Bloody Chunks / A Skull Full Of Maggots / Buried In The Backyard
BUTCHERED AT BIRTH, Metal Blade ZORRO26 (1991)
Meat Hook Sodomy / Gutted / Living Dissection / Under This Rotted Flesh / Covered With Sores / Vomit The Soul / Butchered At Birth / Rancid Amputation / Innards Decay
TOMB OF THE MUTILATED, Metal Blade ZORRO49 (1992)
Hammer Smashed Face / I Cum Blood / Addicted To Vaginal Skin / Split Wide

Open / Necropedophile / The Cryptic Stench / Entrails Ripped From A Virgin's Cunt / Post Mortal Ejaculation / Beyond The Cemetery
HAMMER SMASHED FACE, Metal Blade ZORRO 57 (1993)
Hammer Smashed Face / The Exorcist / Zero The Hero / Meat Hook Sodomy / Shredded Humans
THE BLEEDING, Metal Blade ZORRO67 (1994)
Staring Through The Eyes Of The Dead / Fucked With A Knife / Stripped, Raped And Strangled / Pulverized / Return To The Flesh / The Pick Axe Murders / She Was Asking For It / The Bleeding / Force Fed Broken Glass / An Experiment In Homicide
VILE, Metal Blade 3984-14104-2 (1996)
Devoured By Vermin / Mummified In Barbed Wire / Perverse Suffering / Disfigured / Bloodlands / Puncture Wound Massacre / Relentless Beating / Absolute Hatred / Eaten From Inside / Orgasm Through Torture / Monolith
GALLERY OF SUICIDE, Metal Blade (1998)
I Will Kill You / Disposal Of The Body / Sentenced To Burn / Blood Drenched Execution / Gallery Of Suicide / Dismembered And Molested / From Skin To Liquid / Unite The Dead / Stabbed In The Throat / Chambers Of Blood / Headless / Every Bone Broken / Centuries Of Torment / Crushing The Despised
BLOODTHIRST, Metal Blade (1999)
Pounded Into Dust / Dead Human Collection / Unleashing The Bloodthirsty / The Spine Splitter / Ecstasy In Decay / Raped By Beast / Coffinfeeder / Hacksaw Decapitation / Blowtorch Slaughter / Sickening Metamorphosis / Condemned To Agony
LIVE CANNIBALISM, Metal Blade (2000)
Starring Through The Eyes Of The Dead / Blowtorch Slaughter / Stripped, Raped And Strangled / Fucked With A Knife / Unleashing The Bloodthirsty / Dead Human Collection / Gallery Of Suicide / Perverse Suffering / The Spine Splitter / I Will Kill You / Devoured By Vermin / Disposal Of The Body / Sacrifice / Confessions

CANT (GERMANY)
Line-Up: Alex Kirkov (vocals / guitar), Hilmar Guisk (guitar), Dimi Kirkov (bass), Christian 'Luke' Haupt (keyboards), Hansi Leinen (drums)

Germanic Death Metal.

Albums:
TIDES, CSD 100005 (1996)
Love In Your Heart / Edge Of Madness / Dreams Of Tomorrow / Take Control / Forever / Evening Sky

CANTARA (HOLLAND)
Line-Up: Dick Barelds (vocals / bass), Jens Van Der Valk (guitar), Pascal Grevings (guitar), Freddy Leenders (drums)

CANTARA's debut album is a straight down the line Death Metal offering. During 1996 the band were in the studio recording a follow up.

Albums:
DARK, Smalltime SPCD001 (1993)
Dark / The Shades Of Love / Shredding Memories (A Trilogy Part III) / Exposure Of Involuntary Frustrations (Of Misery) / Odi Et Amo (Outro)

CAPTAIN 3 LEG (USA)

Singles/EPs:
Split, Headfucker (1998) (7" split single with UNHOLY GRAVE)

CAPTOR (SWEDEN)
Line-Up: Magnus Fasth (vocals), Niklas Kullström (guitar), Fredrik Olofsson (guitar), Jacob Nordangård (bass), Angelo Mikaj (drums)

CAPTOR can trace the band history back through many line-up changes as far back as 1986. The first demo recorded in 1991 was titled 'Memento Mori'. A further tape, 'Domination', followed in 1992 which led to CAPTOR's inclusion on a compilation CD assembled by Swedish Rock magazine 'Close Up'.
Bassist / vocalist Jacob Nordangård was to lose his place following the debut album 'Lay It To Rest', CAPTOR opting to recruit two new members in his place, the jobs going to bassist Christoffer Andersson and vocalist Magnus Fasth.

Singles/EPs:
Refuse To Die / My Head / Insane / More Life / Circle Of Hate, Dolphin Productions DMPCDS 07 (1995)

Albums:
LAY IT TO REST, Euro EURO 933-CD (1995)

Intro / Traumatic Depressive Lunacy / Utilized / Aspects Of Positive Thinking / Jaws Of Lust / Domination / Let Revolution Speak / Possessed / Depression / Trail Of Death / Lay It To Rest / Fundamental Influence
DROWNED, Progress PCD 34 (1996)
So Bold As Cold / Disbelieve / Mother / Zombiehead / Hostile Reality / Refuse To Die / Insane / Lost / Confession / More Life / Pray / Sick
DOGFACE, Diehard PCD-42 (1998)
Disconnect / Bleed With Me / All My Pain / Filthy / Lofi / I Told You / Hate Is Hate / Lakafak / So / Unfair / L.F.S.

CARBIDE (Detroit, MI, USA)

Albums:
SPIRAL TERMINATION, Independency (1997)

CARBONISED (SWEDEN)
Line-Up: Jonas Derouche (vocals / guitar), Lars Rosenberg (bass), Piotr Wawrzeniuk (drums)

Formed by Lars Rosenberg as a studio quintet in 1988 CARBONISED released the 'Auto-Da-Fe' demo the following year. The band's first line-up comprised of vocalist Matti Karki, guitarists Jonas Derouche and Stefan Ekström, bassist Lars Rosenberg and drummer Markus Rüden. However, Ekström and Röden left to join MORPHEUS.
Following the release of the 'No Canonisation' 7" single during 1990 vocalist Matti Karki opted to join DISMEMBER, although the group did add ex ROBOTS drummer Piotr Wawrzeniuk. The new line-up recorded the demo 'Recarbonised' in 1990, but soon after Rosenberg left to join ENTOMBED, effectively putting CARBONISED on ice for live work. Nevertheless, CARBONISED added ex THERION member guitarist Christofer Johnsson in favour of Jonas Derouche to record the 'For The Security' debut album.
CARBONIZED were to suffer further membership problems in April 1992 when Wawrzeniuk joined THERION.

Singles/EPs:
No Canonisation / Statues / Auto Da Fe, Thrash THR 003 (1990)

Albums:
FOR THE SECURITY, Thrash THR 011 (1991)

Recarbonized / Hypnotic Aim / Euthanasia / Blinded Of The Veil / Syndrome / Reflections Of The Dark / Third Eye / Purified (From The Sulfer) / For The Security / Monument
DISHARMONISATION, Foundations 2000 FDN 2006-2 (1993)
Frozen Landscapes / Vladtepes / Lord Of Damnation / Silent Journey / Spanish Fly / Succubus / Night Shadows / The Voice Of Slained Pig / Confessions / Spacecraft / Whip Me Darling
SCREAMING MACHINES, Foundation 2000 FDN 2013-2 (1996)
My Hate / Circles / For Those Who Play / High Octane / Psychodelica / Golden Rain / Fever / I Wanna Die / Fist / Common Enemy / Screaming Machines

CARCARIASS (FRANCE)
Line-Up: Raphael Couturier (vocals / bass), Pascal Lanquetin (guitar), Bertrand Simonin (drums)

The rather obviously named CARCARIASS garnered useful exposure by having their track 'To Be With You...In Your Grave' included on a free CD included with 'Metallion' magazine. The band opened for CRADLE OF FILTH and had the song 'Brain Dead' featured on a 'Hard Rock' magazine free CD prior to signing to the Swiss Impact label for the second album 'Sidereal Torment'.

Albums:
HELL ON EARTH, Carcariass (1997)
Hell On Earth / To Be With You... In Your Grave / Dream Of Space / Carcariass / Children Slave / Brain Dead / Post Combustion / Extreme Flatulence / Hopeless
SIDEREAL TORMENT, Impact (1999)
Distributed Thinking / Indian Eviction / Die Anal / Void Attraction / Roman Hegemony / Led By Ignorance / Insect Killers / Sidereal Torments

CARCASS (UK)
Line-Up: Jeff Walker (vocals / bass), Bill Steer (guitar), Ken Owen (drums)

A Liverpool based extreme Metal band formed in 1985 and masterminded by ex NAPALM DEATH man Bill Steer and ex ELECTRO HIPPIES Jeff Walker, CARCASS' 1988 debut album, 'Reek Of Putrefaction', sparked immediate controversy with it's cover depicting a collage of human flesh.
Although CARCASS played intense

Death Metal more than extreme enough to match the visuals, the group has since claimed that the whole point of 'Reek Of Putrefaction's sleeve art was in order to get it banned. Instead, it just sold more copies. Steer departed from NAPALM DEATH to concentrate fully on CARCASS just before recording of 1989's the 'Symphonies Of Sickness'. CARCASS added Swedish guitarist Mike Amott (ex-CARNAGE) in May 1990 to thicken their live sound. Road work to promote the ensuing 'Necrotism' and the 'Tools Of The Trade' EP included last minute support dates alongside French Thrashers LOUDBLAST on DEATH's British tour when PESTILENCE pulled out. This was followed up by the epic Earache records 'Gods Of Grind' tour, featuring CARCASS, CATHEDRAL, ENTOMBED and CONFESSOR.

Unsurprisingly, record sales started to slow down when the gore factor finally wore off, with 'Necrotism' selling around 100,000 copies. Amott departed after 1994 album's 'Heartwork's completion in order to return to Sweden to form SPIRITUAL BEGGERS and ARCH ENEMY. CARCASS, meantime, endeavoured to mature in order to rid themselves of the Death Metal tag and progress musically.

The aforementioned 'Heartwork' displayed a far greater degree of musicianship than its predecessors with classic Heavy Metal influences very much on display, especially on the guitar solos. The album also benefited from an HR Giger photographed sculpture as it's cover, as opposed to the expected dead meat!

In order to replace Amott CARCASS recruited ex-VENOM guitarist, American born Mike Hickey for live work. The band toured Britain as guests to Rap Metallers BODY COUNT before a mammoth European and American tour. Sales of 'Heartwork' were strong, over 50,000 in America alone, and towards the end of the American dates the band were signed to Columbia Records. In June Hickey was replaced (later turning up in CATHEDRAL and CRONOS), by ex-DEVOID guitarist Carlo Regadas.

In late 1995 Walker opted to tour with YEAR ZERO on a temporary basis whilst CARCASS waited for Columbia Records to release the new album. However, Columbia in America dropped the band during November resulting in the departure of Steer.

Although CARCASS regrouped and resigned the already recorded album to previous label Earache, Steer's departure left his former colleagues to carry on under the new banner of BLACKSTAR adding ex-CATHEDRAL / YEAR ZERO guitarist Griff to the cause.

Steer re-emerged in 1999 fronting BLACKSMITH. By the following year he had created FIREBIRD with CATHEDRAL's Leo Smee and SPIRITUAL BEGGERS Ludwig Witt.

Singles/EPs:
Pathological / Genital Grinder II / Hepatic Tissue Fermentation, Strange Fruit SFPS 073 (1989) ('The Peel sessions' EP)
Tools Of The Trade / Incarnated Solvent Abuse / Pysofied (Still Rotten To The Gore) / Hepatic Tissue Fermentation II, Earache MOSH 49 (1992)
Heartwork / This Is Your Life / Rot n' Roll, Earache MOSH 108 (1994)

CARCASS
Photo : Martin Wickler

Albums:
REEK OF PUTREFACTION, Earache MOSH 6 (1988)
Genital Grinder / Regurgitation Of Giblets / Maggot Colony / Pyosisified (Rotten To The Gore) / Vomited Anal Tract / Fermenting Innards / Excreted Alive / Suppuration / Foeticide / Feast On Dismembered Carnage / Splattered

68

Cavities / Psychopathologist / Burnt To A Crisp / Pungent Excruciation / Oxidisede Razor Masticator / Malignant Defecation
SYMPHONIES OF SICKNESS, Earache MOSH 18 (1989)
Reek Of Putrefaction / Exhume To Consume / Excoriating Abdominal Emanation / Ruptured In Purulence / Empathalogical Necroticism / Embryonic Necropsy And Devourment / Swarming Vulgar Mass Of Infected Virulency / Cadaveric Incubator Of Endoparasites / Slash Dementia / Crepitating Bowel Erosion
NECROTISM - DESCANTING THE INSALUBRIOUS, Earache MOSH 42 (1991)
Inpropogation / Corporeal Jigsaw Quandary / Symposium Of Sickness / Pedigree Butchery / Incarnated Solvent Abuse / Carneous Cacophony / Lavaging Expectorate Of Lysergide Composition / Forensic Clinicism / The Sanguine Article
HEARTWORK, Earache MOSH 97 (1994) 54 UK
Buried Dreams / Carnal Forge / No Love Lost / Heartwork / Embodiment / This Mortal Coil / Arbeit Macht Fleish / Blind Bleeding The Blind / Doctrinal Expletives / Death Certificate
SWANSONG, Earache MOSH160 (1996) 58 UK
Keep On Rotting In The Free World / Tomorrow Belongs To Nobody / Black Star / Cross My Heart / Child's Play / Room 101 / Polarized / Generation Hexed / Firmhand / R**k The Vote / Don't Believe A Word / Go To Hell
WAKE UP AND SMELL THE...CARCASS, Earache MOSH 161 (1996)
Edge Of Darkness / Emotional Flatline / Ever Increasing Circles / Blood Splattered Banner / I Told You So / Buried Dreams / No Love Lost / Rot n' Roll / Edge Of Darkness / This Is Your Life / Rot n' Roll / Tools Of The Trade / Pyosified (Still Rotten To The Core) / Hepatic Tissue Fermentation / Genital Grinder 2 / Hepatic Tissue Fermentation / Exhume To Consume

CARCASS GRINDER (JAPAN)

Oriental Grindcore mongers CARCASS GRINDER would feature on the shared cassette 'Grind The Faces Of Rockstars' alongside UNHOLY GRAVE, SAPROGENIC ENTRAILS and IMPREGNATE TRICHOMA. Split singles would include the expected alliance with

Belgian kings of the genre AGATHOCLES as well as Sweden's BIRDFLESH.

Singles/EPs:
C.G.archy, Regurgitated Semen (1994) (7" split single with AGATHOCLES)
Split, Nat (1997) (7" split single with VIOLENT HEADACHE)
Split, (199-) (7" split single with BIRDFLESH)
Split, (199-) (CD split single with HASHDRUM)

CARDINAL SIN (SWEDEN)
Line-Up: Dan Ola Persson (vocals), Magnus Andersson (guitar), John Zweetslot (guitar), Alex Losbäck (bass), Jocke Göthberg (drums)

CARDINAL SIN, whose musicians openly state to be rooted in 80's Metal, boast ex-MARDUK members guitarist Magnus 'Devo' Andersson and drummer Jocke 'Grave' Göthberg. Guitarist John Zweetslot was previously with DISSECTION.
Following this line-up's recording of the 'Spiteful Intent' EP the rhythm section was completed with the addition of bassist Alex Losbäck and a new vocalist was added in the form of Dan Ola Persson.
Göthberg created DARKIFIED. Zweetslot is now in DECAMERON while Andersson now fronts OVERFLASH.

Singles/EPs:
Spiteful Intent / Probe With A Quest / The Cardinal Sin / Language Of Sorrow, Wrong Again WAR 010 CD (1996) ('Spiteful Intents' EP)

CARNAGE (SWEDEN)
Line-Up: Matti Karki (vocals), David Blomkvist (guitar), Mike Amott (guitar), Johnny Dordevic (bass), Fred Estby (drums)

Despite only having performed three gigs CARNAGE, who featured ex-DISMEMBER drummer Fred Estby and former CARBONISED / DISMEMBER singer Matti Karki in their line-up, play a pivotal part in the historical lineage of Swedish Death Metal.
The band debuted with a live single in 1989, which was recorded by Estby, guitarist Mike Amott, bassist Johnny Dordevic and vocalist / guitarist Johan Axelsson. Although recorded in

Stockholm it only saw a release in Mexico!

Axelsson soon left to join JESUS EXERCIZE then FURBOWL and was replaced by another ex-DISMEMBER man, namely David Blomqvist.

In the wake of the band's split Mike Amott later joined CARCASS before forming SPIRITUAL BEGGARS. Dordevic joined ENTOMBED as lead vocalist. Estby, Blomqvist and Karki reformed DISMEMBER.

Singles/EPs:
Torn Apart (Live) / Crime Against Humanity (Live) / The Day Man Lost (Live) / Infestation Of Evil (Live), Distorted Harmony DH003 (1989) (Mexican release)

Albums:
DARK RECOLLECTIONS, Necrosis NECRO34 (1990) (Split LP with CADAVER)
Dark Recollections / Torn Apart / Blasphemies Of The Flesh / Infestation Of Evil / Gentle Exhuming / Deranged From Blood / Malignant Epitaph / Self Dissection / Death Evocation / Outro

CARNAL FORGE (SWEDEN)
Line-Up: Jonas Kjellgren (vocals), Johan Magnusson (guitar), Jari Kuusisto (guitar), Petri Kuusisto (bass), Stefan Westerberg (drums)

The founding line up of CARNAL FORGE comprised DELLAMORTE man Jonas Kjellgren, drummer Stefan Westerberg of IN THY DREAMS and STEEL ATTACK personnel guitarist Jari Kuusisto and bassist Dennis Vestman. Following the debut album 'Who's Gonna Burn' Vestman departed to be replaced by another IN THY DREAMS man Petri Kuusisto.

Vocalist Jonas Kjellgren was guitarist with CENTINEX between 1999 and September 2000.

Albums:
WHO'S GONNA BURN, Wrong Again (1998)
Who's Gonna Burn / Sweet Bride / Twisted / Godzilla Is Coming Thru' / The Other Side / Part Animal - Part Machine / Born Too Late / Evilizer / Moggotman / Confuzzed
FIREDEMON, Century Media (2000)
Too Much Hell Ain't Enough For Me / Covered With Fire (I'm Hell) / I Smell

Like Death (Son Of A Bastard) / Chained / Defacer / Pull The Trigger / Uncontrollable / Firedemon / Cure Of Blasphemy / Headfucker / The Torture Will Never Stop / A Revel In Violence

CARPHARNAUM

Albums:
REALITY ONLY FANTASIZED, Carphanaum (1997)
Eternal Descent / Night Terror / Sinister Perceptions / Sightless / Drawn In Misery / Journey Beyond / Delusional Imprisonment / Soul Dissolved

CASKET (GERMANY)
Line-up: Jörg Weber (vocals / guitar), Karin Trapp (vocals), Jürgen Bischoff (guitar), Marc Fischer (bass), Tobias Demel (keyboards), Steffan Klein (drums)

CASKET were created in 1992 issuing their first demo recordings 'Voices From Beyond', the following year. A further cassette, '...But Death Comes Soon', followed in 1994 as CASKET added secondary female vocals from Karin Trapp and performed shows opening for PYOGENESIS and PANDEMONIUM.

Albums:
EMOTIONS... DREAMS OR REALITY, Serenades (1997)
Way To Happiness / Emotions... / Black Mountain / Confessions / ... Dream Or Reality / Life-Elixir / Near Heaven
TOMORROW, Serenades SR013 (1997)
A Piece Of Love / Suicide / Questions Of Life / Secrets / Last Days / No More / Feel The Fire / Tomorrow/ Tears Of Sorrow
FAITHLESS, (199-)
Not Like You / A Lover In Disguise / Let Your Hair Hang Down / Dirty Thoughts / What For / The Other Way Round / An Illusion / Not Too Far / Maybe / Way To Happiness - The Continuation

CASTLE (HOLLAND)
Line-Up: Eric (vocals), Ilja (guitar), Richard (guitar / keyboards), Lucien (bass), Jean-Marie (drums)

Tillburg based CASTLE offered Doom Death Metal on their one and only release.

Albums:
CASTLE, MMI Records 009CD (1994)
The 7th Empire / The Emperor's

Children / Alter Reality / Exposed / Travelling / Castle / Bridge Of Snow

CASTRUM (UKRAINE)
Line-Up: Georgius (vocals), Cornelius (guitar / bass / keyboards), Werkoff (drums)

CASTRUM, based in Uzhgorod in the Ukraine, are fronted by Hungarian vocalist Georgius (real name George Kudla). The band was founded in 1994 by guitarist / bassist Cornelius (real name Kornel Kontros), Georgius and drummer Lancelot. CASTRUM issued no less than three demo tapes in 1996 namely 'Burial Of Affection', 'Flames By Impiety' and 'Pleasure In The Deeds Of Horror'. After these recordings Lancelot was superseded by Werkoff.
All three members also operate in CHAMOS.

CATAMENIA (FINLAND)
Line-Up: Mika Tönning (vocals), Riku Hopeakoski (guitar), Sampo Ukkola (guitar), Heidi Riihinen (keyboards), Timo Lehtinen (bass), Toni Tervo (drums)

A Finnish Black/Death Metal sextet from Oulu, CATAMENIA opened their account in early 1998 with the release of the debut album, 'Halls Of Frozen North', through Massacre.
Produced by Gerhard Magin, the band had been signed on the strength of their 'Winds' demo of 1995. Vocalist Mike Tönning guested as lead vocalist for fellow Finns DAWN OF RELIC on their debut 'One Night In Carcosa' album.

Albums:
HALLS OF FROZEN NORTH, Massacre MAS CD0153 (1998)
Dreams Of Winterland / Into Infernal / Freezing Winds Of North / Enchanting Woods / Halls Of Frozen North / Forest Enthroned / Awake In Dark / Song Of The Nightbird / Icy Tears Of Eternity / Burning Aura / Child Of Sunset / Land Of The Autumn Winds / Pimea Yo / Outro
MORNING CRIMSON, Massacre (1999)
Aurora Borealis / Talvijön Verjot / … And Winter Descends / In Blood They Lay / Beauty Embraced By Night / Passing Moments Of Twilight Time / Cast The Stars Beyond / Morning Crimson / The Forests Of Tomorrow
CATAMENIA, Massacre (2000)
Winternacht / Talvijön Verjot / Dreams Of Winterland / Aurora Borealis / Into

Infernal / Freezing Winds Of North
ETERNAL WINTER'S PROPHECY, Massacre MAS CD0258 (2000)
Gates Of Anubis / Soror Mystica / Blackmansions / Kingdom Of Legions / Half Moons, Half Centuries / Forever Night / Dawn Of The Chosen World / Eternal Winter's Prophecy / In The Void / The Darkening Sun / In The Capricorns Cradle

CATASEXUAL URGE MOTIVATION (JAPAN)

Extreme grinding act with an obvious murder fixation. CATASEXUAL URGE MOTIVATION emerged with the 1994 'Catharsis' demo tape following this effort with further cassettes 'Rape Trauma Syndrome' in 1995 and 'Bizarre Abnormality'.
The group would be included on a 4 way split single 'Hungry Urinary Urn' alongside C.S.S.O., MALIGNANT TUMOUR and N.C.C. A shared tape 'What Do You Kill For' in 1996 witnessed an alliance with NEGLIGENT COLLATERAL COLLAPSE. The same year the band shared another tape with GOROPSY and issued a live session entitled 'Satsujin'.
The 1997 album included a cover version of IMPETIGO's 'Defiling The Grave'. CATASEXUAL URGE MOTIVATION would change their name to VAMPYRIC MOTIVES shortly after the release of the 2000 re-release of the 'Encyclopedia Of Serial Murders' album.

Singles/EPs:
Split, (199-) (7" split single with SQUASH BOWELS)
Split, (199-) (7" split single with SLOUGH)

Albums:
FANTASY WANTS VICTIM, (1996)
ENCYCLOPEDIA OF SERIAL MURDERS, Deliria (1997)
Mutilation, Rape And Serial Murder As A Modern Metaphor / Supraliminal Psychosadistic Motivation / Bleeding For Spermqueen / Hate From The Womb / I Have A Good Knife For Penetration /Philosophical Diary Of A Habitual Murderer / Joy To The Kill… Be My Victim / King Of The Degenerates In The End Of The Century / Multiple Parasexuality Disorder / Mass Murder, The Only Way To Become God / Homicidal Patterns: Disorganized-

Organized / Murder Is Art Accepted By Many Artists / The Man Who Aimed At Maximum Murder To The Greatest Pleasure / Murder Is Better Than Birth / He Shot Her Down And Ate Her Flesh, And Then Said "Excuse Me For Living But I Preferred To Be Eaten Rather Than To Eat" / What Was The Spark That Touched Off A Murder / I Am As Beautiful As I Have Killed / I'll Confess Everything That I Ever Killed 5 People And The One Was A Little Girl / Defiling The Grave / Declaration Of A Serial Killer... Mental Terrorism / Campaign For Legalized Murder / Vivid Stains In Hematomania's Delirium

CATASTROPHIC (USA)

Albums:
THE CLEANSING, Metal Blade (2001) Hate Trade / Balancing The Furies / Enemy / Lab Rats / Messiah Pacified / The Cleansing / Pain Factor / Jesters Of The Millennium / The Veil / Blood Maidens / You Must Bleed / Terraform

CAULDRON (USA)
Line-Up: Kam Lee, Pete Slate, Mark Lavenia

Kam Lee is ex-MASSACRE. Pete Slate is from EQUINOX whilst Mark Lavenia is a member of INCUBUS.

Albums:
CAULDRON, (2000)
Overblown Success Story / Automated Larceny / Carnival Of Death / Internal Reactor / Decomposition Of Humanity / What, When, Why, How, Where

CAUSTIC (DENMARK)
Line-Up: Soren Jansen (vocals), Gert Lund (guitar), Rolf Hansen (guitar), Rune H. Andersen (bass), Carsten Gierlevsen (drums)

Death Metal band with Thrash influences CAUSTIC, founded in 1991, hail from Esbjerg, releasing demo sessions 'An Integral Sense' and 'Timid Reality' the same year.

Singles/EPs:
Victim Of Ignorance / Moments In The Infinite / Lacrymose Progeny, Shiver Records SHR009 (1994) ('Moments In The Infinite' EP)

CELTIC FROST (SWITZERLAND)
Line-Up: Tom G. Warrior (vocals / guitar), Martin Eric Ain (bass), Reed St. Mark (drums)

A highly influential Zurich Thrash Metal act who pushed the musical boundaries of the genre to the limit, CELTIC FROST blended a fusion of extreme aggression with Classical and Jazz leanings to create a unique 'avant garde' eclectic style. The band rapidly built a strong fan base and, at their peak, looked set to rival the big name American Speed Metal outfits for world domination.

CELTIC FROST had a strange genesis as mentor and renowned 'death grunter' Warrior and bassist Martin Eric Ain were members of what was generally acknowledged to have been one of the worst bands ever - HELLHAMMER. Tom himself started out musically in GRAVE HILL who were heavily influenced by the NWoBHM bands such as DIAMOND HEAD and VENOM.

The original CELTIC FROST, so named after a combination of song titles on a CIRITH UNGOL album sleeve, line-up in May 1984 comprised Warrior, Ain and drummer Isaac Darso. The latter lasted precisely one rehearsal before being usurped by SCHIZO's Stephen Priestly on a temporary basis as a session drummer for recording. At this stage CELTIC FROST were still working on NWoBHM favourites such as songs by ANGELWITCH and ARAGORN.

With HELLHAMMER's reputation preceding them (magazines reviews polarized at either the genius or dreadful end of the spectrum) CELTIC FROST retained their previous deal with Noise Records by submitting a master plan detailing the names of all future releases. The strategy called for an initial demo to be entitled 'A Thousand Deaths' but the label soon persuaded the band that this should form the basis of an opening commercially available product.

CELTIC FROST's first product, the mini-album, 'Morbid Tales' was recorded with Martin Eric Ain's former colleague in SCHIZO drummer Stephen Priestly. As soon as the sessions were completed though Priestly decamped. CELTIC FROST set about negotiations with American drummer Jeff Cardelli of Seattle act LIPSTICK. However, the band hired another American, ex-CROWN drummer Reed St. Mark (real name Reid Cruickshank).

As with HELLHAMMER media views on 'Morbid Tales' ranged in their extremity from excellent to dire. The controversy stoked up by these opposing views would serve the band well. CELTIC FROST were still at this juncture wearing the stage make up later to be given the name 'corpse paint' by later generations of Black Metal bands. A further EP 'The Emperors Return' followed to equally polarized reviews and even condemnation from the band themselves. By now CELTIC FROST were being acknowledged as leaders in their field.

CELTIC FROST's inaugural live performances came with a run of shows opening for German bands BEAST and MASS in Germany and Austria. Planned shows in Italy with ASTAROTH were shelved.

Ain had been asked to leave during recording of the next album 'Into Megatherion' and CELTIC FROST pulled in Dominic Steiner of the Glam Rock act JUNK FOOD. The album, which saw the band utilizing timpanis, French horns and operatic vocals courtesy of Claudia-Maria Mokri, would be the first to be graced with lavish album sleeve artwork from the renowned artist H.R. Giger.

Friction between the band members resulted in Steiner's dismissal as soon as 'Into Megatherion' had been completed. For CELTIC FROST's debut show outside of Europe at the November 1985 'World War Three' festival in Montreal alongside VOIVOD, POSSESSED, DESTRUCTION and NASTY SAVAGE with Martin Eric Ain back in the bass position.

Warrior also worked as producer for fellow Swiss Metal band CORONOR, a gesture they repaid by becoming CELTIC FROST's roadcrew!

1986 saw CELTIC FROST back on the live circuit touring Europe sharing billing with HELLOWEEN and GRAVE DIGGER. Later shows saw a headline at a Belgian festival, the band's debut in England in London with GRAVE DIGGER and HELLOWEEN supporting and also touring in America alongside RUNNING WILD and VOIVOD.

With CELTIC FROST's status rising sharply the 'Tragic Serenades' EP was issued to keep fans happy between albums. The EP consisted of remixed tracks from 'To Megatherion' and new numbers.

'Into The Pandemonium' provided fans with another bizarre offering comprising tracks such as a cover of WALL OF VOODOO's 'Mexican Radio' and the Rap cut 'One In Their Pride'. Before the album had been recorded New York based guitarist Ritchi Desmond was briefly linked with a position in the band, but, having travelled to Switzerland to work with the group Desmond returned home citing "too many conflicting attitudes" as the reason why he failed to join CELTIC FROST. Warrior countered that Desmond brought uninvited family members along to the audition and looked nothing like his submitted photograph! Desmond was to front SABBAT for their 'Mourning Has Broken' album and subsequent disastrous tour.

During a break in recording the band played a series of European gigs with ANTHRAX, CRIMSON GLORY and even METALLICA.

For live work to promote 'Into The Pandemonium' CELTIC FROST added second guitarist Ron Marks and toured Britain in winter of 1987 with support from KREATOR then America on a bill with EXODUS and ANTHRAX. The tour succeeded in dumbfounding many of the band's established fans with such radical tracks as the aforementioned 'Mexican Radio' cover and the band was dogged throughout it's duration by legal wrangles with Noise Records. Disillusioned, Marks quit to be replaced by former JUNK FOOD guitarist Oliver Amberg.

Upon their return to Europe CELTIC FROST hit further problems when Martin Ain decided to abandon the music business entirely in favour of wedded bliss (!), so Warrior quickly drafted in Curt Victor Bryant.

CELTIC FROST was in a state of flux besieged by business and financial problems. Even an offer from director Ken Russell to lay down the soundtrack to the movie 'The Lair Of The White Worm' had to be declined because the group was in such disarray. However, the final blow to the classic line-up came when Reed St. Mark upped and left to join MINDFUNK and his position was filled by a returning Stephen Priestly. This was the line-up that was to record the disastrous 'Cold Lake' album produced by Tony Platt; a record that effectively killed the band's career in Europe.

With this effort CELTIC FROST appeared to ditch all of their former pretensions artistically and even adopted a new 'Glam' image, much to the horror of their most hardcore following. Tom dropped the 'Warrior' from his stagename and became plain old Thomas Gabriel

Fischer, sporting an L.A. GUNS T-shirt on official press photos.

It was heavily rumoured that the band had, in a SPINAL TAP style move, adopted Tom's girlfriend as manager and that the new look was her masterplan for CELTIC FROST's step into the big league. CELTIC FROST themselves maintained that tracks like 'Teaze Me' were a parody of Glam Rock, but fans were outraged and the media universally attacked the album. The European tour fared badly with audiences deserting in droves. However, in America 'Cold Lake' was in actual fact making serious sales headway and a U.S. tour beginning in March 1989 was judged a success..

In late '89 the badly bruised CELTIC FROST announced a return to their former style and regrouped with Ron Marks. Martin Eric Ain was also persuaded to put down some guest bass tracks and contribute lyrics. The 'Vanity / Nemesis' Roli Mossiman produced album was cited by many as the band's best record to date, but the legacy of 'Cold Lake' still haunted the quartet to such a degree that sales suffered.

CELTIC FROST only managed minimal touring to back up the release of 'Vanity / Nemesis' including a British tour. By now Warrior was to be seen spotted playing a guitar emblazoned with his wife's name 'Michelle', the lady in question also having become a backing singer for the band.

New management hooked up a deal with major label BMG in America. However, the deal was shelved at the last minute leaving CELTIC FROST high and dry.

A further CELTIC FROST album did emerge titled 'Parched With Thirst Am I And Dying'. The record comprised of rare material and completely reworked older tracks. Promoted as a new album it sold extremely well.

Warrior took the band into an even more radical direction when he mooted the idea of working with ex-THE TIME guitarist Jesse Johnson on a projected Funk-Metal project. Stephen Priestly meantime would perform drums for French act TREPONEM PAL's 1991 'Aggravation' album.

Following a 1992 four track demo, featuring the tracks 'Honour Thy Father', 'Seeds Of Rapture', 'Icons Alive' and 'Oh Father', the band searched in vain for a new deal. Initial tapes were laid down with Priestly on drums but sessions in Texas saw Reed St. Mark back behind the kit and Renée Hernz on bass. Nothing came of this latest venture and CELTIC FROST effectively split; Marks relocating to America to form STEPCHILD then SUBSONIC.

In 1992 Noise released a CELTIC FROST epitaph in the form of 'Parched With Thirst Am I And Dying'; a collection of rare and unreleased studio out-takes as the band bowed out.

In more recent years Martin Ain has produced the debut album from doom band SADNESS in 1995, whilst Tom Warrior was found fronting APOLLYON'S SON in 1996.

Singles/EPs:

The Usurper / Jewel Throne / Return To Eve, Noise N0041 (1986) ('Tragic Serenades' EP)

Dethroned Emperor / Circle Of The Tyrants / Morbid Tales / Suicidal Winds / Visual Aggression, Noise N0042 (1986) ('Emperor's Return' EP)

I Won't Dance / One In Their Pride / Tristesses De La Lune, Noise N094 (1986)

Wine In My Hand (Third From The Sun) / Heroes / Descent From Babylon, Noise NO (1990)

Albums:

MORBID TALES, Noise N 0017 60-1673 (1984)
Into The Crypt Of Rays / Visions Of Mortality / Procreation (Of The Wicked) / Return To Eve / Danse Macabre / Nocturnal Fear

TO MEGATHERION, Noise N0031 (1985)
Innocence And Wrath / The Usurper / Jewel Throne / Dawn Of Megiddo / Eternal Summer / Circle Of Tyrants / (Beyond The) North Winds / Fainted Eyes / Tears In A Prophet's Dream / Necromantical Screams

INTO THE PANDEMONIUM, Noise N0065 (1987)
Mexican Radio / Mesmerised / Inner Sanctum / Sorrows Of The Moon / Babylon Fell / Caress Into Oblivion / One In Their Pride / I Won't Dance / Rex Irae (Requiem-Opening) / Oriental Masquerade

COLD LAKE, Noise NUK 125 (1989)
Intro - Human / Seduce Me Tonight / Petty Obsession / (Once) They Were Eagles / Cherry Orchards / Juices Like Wine / Little Velvet / Blood On Kisses / Downtown Hanoi / Dance Sleazy / Roses Without Thorns / Tease Me / Mexican Radio (New Version)

VANITY/NEMESIS, Noise-EMI EMC 3576 (1990)
The Heart Beneath / Wine In My Hand (Third From The Sun) / Wings Of Solitude / The Name Of My Bride / This Island Earth / The Restless Seas / Phallic Tantrum / A Kiss Or A Whisper / Vanity / Nemesis / Heroes
PARCHED WITH THIRST AM I AND DYING, Noise N 191-2 (1992)
Idols Of Chagrin / A Descent To Babylon / Return To The Eve / Juices Like Wine / The Inevitable Factor / The Heart Beneath / Cherry Orchards / Tristesses De La Lune / Wings Of Solitude / The Usurper / Journey Into Fear / Downtown Hanoi / Circle Of The Tyrants / In The Chapel In The Moonlight / I Won't Dance / The Name Of My Bride / Mexican Radio / Under Apollyon's Sun

CEMETARY (SWEDEN)
Line-up: Matthias Lodmalm (vocals / guitar), Christian Saarinen (guitar), Zrinko Culjk (bass), Juhs Sievers (drums)

Swedish outfit CEMETARY'S original 1989 line-up comprised of vocalist/guitarist Matthias Lodmalm, drummer Juha Sievers and bassist Zrinko Culjak. The group's first demo, issued in 1991, was titled 'Incarnation Of Morbidity' followed by 'Articulus Mortis' setting up sufficient interest at label level to prompt Black Mark to sign the group to an album deal, with debut product arriving in 1992 in the shape of 'An Evil Shade Of Grey'.
Having issued the second album, 'Godless Beauty' in 1992, the third album, 'Black Vanity', saw the arrival of Markus Nordberg on drums, CEREMONIAL OATH's Anders Iwers on guitar and Thomas Jofesson on bass in a major re-shuffle. The group would promptly tour Europe in early 1995, supporting BOLT-THROWER.
By 1997's highly gothic influenced 'Last Confession' CEMETARY had, in effect, become a solo vehicle for Lodmalm although he was also diverting his efforts to new act SUNDOWN.
With SUNDOWN's demise in 2000 Lodmalm resurrected the band under the new title of CEMETARY 1213.

Albums:
AN EVIL SHADE OF GREY, Black Mark BMCD20 (1992)
Dead Red / Where The Rivers Of Madness Stream / Dark Illusions / Evil Shade Of Grey / Sidereal Passing / Scars / Nightmare Lake / Souldrain
GODLESS BEAUTY, Black Mark BMCD 33 (1993)
Now She Walks The Shadows / The Serpent's Kiss / And Julie Is No More / By My Own Hand / Chain / Adrift In Scarlet Twilight / In Black / Sunrise (Never Again) / Where The Fire Forever Burns
BLACK VANITY, Black Mark BMCD 59 (1994)
Bitter Seed / Ebony Rain / The Hunger Of Innocent / Scarecrow / Black Flowers Of Passion / Last departure- Serpentine Parade / Sweet Tragedy / Pale Autumn Fire / Out In Sand / Rosemary Taste The Sky
SUNDOWN, Black Mark BMCD 70 (1996)
Elysia / Closer To The Pain / Last Transmission / Sundown / Ophidian / Primal / New Dawn Coming / The Embrace / Morning Star / The Wake
LAST CONFESSIONS, Black Mark BMCD 111 (1997)
Forever / Caress The Damned / So Sad Your Sorrow / 1213 - Trancegalactica / Twin Reactor / Fields Of Fire / One Burning Night / Carbon Heart

CEMETARY 1213 (SWEDEN)
Line-Up: Matthias Lodmalm (vocals / guitar)

CEMETARY 1213 is in reality the resurrection of CEMETARY following frontman Matthias Lodmalm's decision to close down his post CEMETARY act SUNDOWN.

Albums:
THE BEAST DIVINE, Century Media (2000)
The Lightning- Firewire / Union Of The Rats / Silicon Karma (It Just Can't Be The Same) / Antichrist 3000 / The Carrier / Linking Shadows / Sunset Grace (Let Me Die Alone) / Dead Boy Wonder / Empire Of The Divine / Anthem Apocalypse

CENOTAPH (ITALY)

Trieste based Black group with Death Metal tendencies. CENOTAPH bowed in with a 1991 demo 'The Lurking Fear On Consecrated Ground' in 1991 followed up by the 'Demonolatreia Larve In Corpre Christi' tape.
Not to be confused with the plethora of other CENOTAPH's hailing from Mexico,

America, Spain and Turkey.

Albums:
THIRTEEN THRENODIES, Planet K (1994)

CENOTAPH (MEXICO)
Line-Up: Edgardo (vocals), Pala (guitar), Julio Viterbo (guitar), Curro (bass), Oscar (drums)

An illustrious Mexican Death Metal act founded in 1989. Although traditionally Death Metal musically CENOTAPH employ strong Satanic themes. Ex-member Daniel Corchado would go on to forge the highly rated and industrious act THE CHASM. He would be later joined by Julio Viterbo for THE CHASM 2000 album 'Procession To The Infraworld'.
Following a Milwaukee Metalfest performance CENOTAPH folded but recently have regrouped.

Singles/EPs:
Tenebrous Apparitions, Distorted Harmony (1990) (7" single)
The Eternal Disgrace, (1991) (7" single)

Albums:
THE GLOOMY REFLECTION OF OUR HIDDEN SORROWS, Horus Corporation (1992)
The Gloomy Reflection Of Our Hidden Sorrows: i) requiem For A Soul Required, ii) Ashes In The Rain, iii)… A Red Sky, iv) Evoked Doom, v) Tenebras Apparitions, vi) The Spiritless One, vii) Infinite Meditation Of An Uncertain Existence In The Cosmic Solitude, viii) Repulsive Odor Of Decomposition
EPIC RITES (9 EPIC TALES OF DEATH RITES), Oz Productions CDOZ001 (1996)
Intro / Crying Frost / Lorn Ends / Navegate / Towards The Umbra / As The Darkness Borns / Angered Tongues / Epic Rites / Dethroned Empire / Thornes Of Fog
RIDING ON BLACK OCEANS, (1998)
The Solitudes / Severance / Grief To Obscuro / Macabre Locus Celesta / Among The Abrupt / Infinitum Valet / The Silence Of Our Black Oceans / Soul Profundis / Ectasia Tenebrae
VALUPTUOUSLY MINCED, (199-)
Less Than Human Urinal / Life Immortal / Different Dimensional Pervation / Revenge / Valuptuously Minced / Source Of Suspicions / Chorus Throttled / Middle Ages

CENOTAPH (TURKEY)

Albums:
VOLUPTOUSLY MINCED, Hammer Muzik (1997)
PUKED GENITAL PURULENCY, Hammer Muzik (1999)
Mutilated Genitalia In Lack Of Resurrection Under Effective Punch / Superimposed Guttural Vociferations Of Ulceric Anal Turgor / Paralised, Clitoridectamized, Spreadagled, Molested Cadaver / Multipurpose Utilization From Lustly Shreddeds Scummy Vaginal Discharge / Verbalized Opinions About Intravaginal Umbilical Corded Fetus In Uterus / Sickened By His Own Pathologic Fancy Of Collecting Ingots Of Humanial Meat / Ex-Femine Promiscuous Masculine's Solified Klitoris Swallowed By Vermins In Coffins

CENOTAPH (USA)
Line-Up: Roger Scott (vocals / guitar), David Allen (bass), Darrell (drums)

Satanic Death Metal band CENOTAPH previously included ex-DEUTSCH THREAT drummer Karl 'Killer' Schmitt. He would be replaced by Darrell of LOS REACTORS.

Albums:
BLOOD RITUAL, (1989)
APOSTASY, (1993)

CENTINEX (SWEDEN)
Line-Up: Mattias Lamppu (vocals), Kenneth Wiklund (guitar), Andreas Evaldsson (guitar), Martin Schulman (bass), Joakim Gustafsson (drums)

Renowned Death Metal act that have increasingly bolstered their sound and imagery with Satanic lyrical references. CENTINEX opened their career in September 1990 issuing the debut demo cassette 'End Of Life' the following year. The band signed to Swedish label Underground for release of the album 'Subconscious Lobotomy' which saw a limited release of 1,000 copies. The CENTINEX line-up at this juncture comprised twin vocalists Erik and Mattias Lamppu, guitarist Andreas Evaldsson, bass player Martin Schulman and drummer Joakim Gustafsson.
A further three track demo session 'Under The Blackened Sky' followed. CENTINEX's next cassette release 'Transcend The Dark Chaos', released on

the band's own novelly titled Evil Shit Productions, was repressed by Sphinx Records.

The second CENTINEX full length album 'Malleus Malefaction' was recorded for the German Wild Rags label and produced by Peter Tägtgren of HYPOCRISY.

1996 saw the release of a shared 7" single in collusion with INVERTED and a fresh band line up retaining Lamppu, Schulman and Evaldsson but with new faces in UNCURBED guitarist Kenneth Wiklund and drummer Kalimaa. The band also featured on a split EP with Sweden's VOICES OF DEATH and German act BAPHOMET.

Early 1997 found CENTINEX on tour in Scandinavia as guests to CRADLE OF FILTH. However, a split in the ranks came the following year when both Lamppu and Evaldsson made their exit. It was to be July 1999 before CENTINEX enrolled UNCANNY and DELLAMORTE drummer Kennet Englund. For touring later in the year CENTINEX pulled in DELLAMORTE and CARNAL FORGE man Jonas Kjellgren on guitar and UNCURBED and DELLAMORTE vocalist Johan Jansson.

The same year had CENTINEX contributing their version of 'Ripping Corpse' to a Full Moon Productions KREATOR tribute album.

2000 witnessed yet more ructions when Kjellgren and Englund decamped. Replacements were AZURE vocalist Robban Kanto and drummer Johan.

2001 had CENTINEX sharing vinyl with the infamous American act NUNSLAUGHTER with their take on SODOM's 'Enchanted Land' for the 'Hail Germania' EP on the Belgian Painkiller label.

Singles/EPs:
Sorrow Of Burning Wasteland, (1996) (Split 7" single with INVERTED)
Shadowland / Eternal Lies, Oskorei Productions 004 (1998)
Apocalyptic Armageddon / Seeds Of Evil / Everlasting Bloodshed, Deadly Art DAP 095 (2000)
Enchanted Land, Painkiller (2001) ('Hail Germania' Split 7" with NUNSLAUGHTER)

Albums:
SUBCONSCIOUS LOBOTOMY, Underground UGR05 (1992)
Blood On My Skin / Shadows Are Astray / Dreams Of Death / Orgy In Flesh / End

Of Life / Bells Of Misery / Inhuman Dissections Of Souls / The Aspiration / Until Death Tear Us Apart
TRANSCEND THE DARK CHAOS, Sphinx SIXR 003 (1994)
MALLEUS MALEFACTION, Wild Rags WRR 043 (1995)
Upon The Ancient Ground / Dark Visions / Sorrow Of The Burning Wasteland / Transcend The Dark Chaos / Thorns Of Desolation / Eternal Lies / At The Everlasting Evil
REFLECTIONS, Diehard RRS 954 (1997)
Carnal Lust / Seven Prophecies / Before The Dawn / The Dimension Beyond / My Demon Within / In Pain / Undivined / Darkside / Into The Funeral Domain
REBORN THROUGH FLAMES, Repulse RPS 032CD (1998)
Embraced By Moonlight / Resurrected / Summon The Golden Twilight / The Beauty Of Malice / Under The Guillotine / Through Celestial Gates Molested / In The Arch Of Serenity
BLOODHUNT, Repulse RPS 042CD (1999)
Under The Pagan Glory / For Centuries Untold / Luciferian Moon / Bloodhunt / The Conquest Infernal / Like Darkened Storms / Mutilation
HELLBRIGADE, Repulse RPS 046CD (2001)
Towards Devastation / On With Eternity / The Eyes Of The Dead / Emperor Of Death / Last Redemption / Blood Conqueror / Neverending Hell / Nightbreeder / Hellbrigade

CENTURIAN (HOLLAND)
Line-Up: Seth Van Der Loo (vocals), Robert Oorthuis (guitar), Patrick Boley (bass), Wim Van Der Valk (drums)

CENTURIAN was borne out of the disintegration of INQUISITOR. The band employed the SEVERE TORTURE rhythm section of bassist Patrick Boley and drummer Seth Van Der Loo. Van Der Loo though would fulfill the vocalist's role in CENTURIAN.

However, by late 2000 both Boley and Van Der Loo had quit CENTURIAN.

Singles/EPs:
Of Purest Fire EP, (199-)

Albums:
CHOROZONIC CHAOS GODS, Full Moon Productions (1999)
Damned And Dead / The Law Of

Burning / Hail Caligula!!! / Misanthropic Luciferian Onslaught / Let Jesus Bleed / Blood For Satan / Soul Theft / Cross Of Fury / In The Name Of Chaos
FOURTEEN WORDS, (199-)
The Planet Is Ours / Count The Dead / One Day / Fourteen Words / White Is My Heart / Centurion / Retribution / The Parting (Sweet Sorrow) / Hear My Cry / Grandfather's Tale / Heed The Call
RIDES AGAIN!, (2000)
Legions Of Hate / Prelude To Valhalla / Remembrance / Thor (The Powerhead) / Rise Of The Numenor / The Fields Of Atheny / Victory Against Genocide / Only Our Rivers Run Free

CEPHALIC CARNAGE
(Denver, CO, USA)
Line-Up: Lenzig (vocals), Zac (guitar), Steve (guitar), Jawsh (bass), John (drums)

CEPHALIC CARNAGE covered a version of SLAYER's 'Jesus Saves' for the tribute album 'Gateway To Hell II' on Dwell Records. The band have also recorded a split CD with ANAL BLAST on Nightfall Records.
CEPHALIC CARNAGE toured America in 2000 on a package bill with INTERNAL BLEEDING and DEEDS OF FLESH.
Ex-bassist Doug Williams would join ORIGIN during 1999.

Albums:
CONFORMING TO ABNORMALITY, Headfucker (1998)
Anechoic Chamber / Jihad / Analytical / Wither / Regalos De Mora / Extreme Of Paranoia / AZT / Waiting For The Millenium
EXPLOITING DYSFUNCTION, Relapse (2000)
Hybrid / Driven To Insanity / Rehab / Observer To The Obliteration Of Planet Earth / On Six / Gracias / Crypto Sporidium / The Ballad Of Moon / Of Smoke / Warm Hand On A Cold Night (A Tale Of Onesomes) / Invertus Induca (The Marijuana Convictions) / Molestandos Plantas Muertos! / Eradicate Authority / Paralyzed By Fear / Exploiting Dysfunction

CEREBRAL FIX (UK)
Line-Up: Simon Forrest (vocals), Tony Warburton (guitar), Greg Fellows (guitar), Frank Healy (bass), Andy Baker (drums)

Birmingham's CEREBRAL FIX trod a fine line between Crossover Punk and Death style Thrash Metal. The band were founded at the height of the Thrash explosion in 1988 with a line up of vocalist Simon Forrest, guitarist Gregg Fellows, bassist Steve and drummer Ade none of whom had previous band experience.
CEREBRAL FIX's first demo landed them a deal with Vinyl Solution Records for 1988's 'Life Sucks And Then You Die'. However, the band had appeared on a Sounds magazine flexi-sampler just before this with the track 'Maimed To Beg'. The same year the band got some serious touring under their belts sharing a bill in Britain with BOLT-THROWER, both acts promoting debut albums on the same label.
CEREBRAL FIX lost their rhythm section in 1990 as both Steve and Ade departed, ostensibly to form another act but this never materialized. Replacements were ex-NAPALM DEATH and SACRILEGE bassist Frank Healy and former VARUKERS and SACRILEGE drummer Andy Baker. This line up turned in another demo to secure a fresh deal with Roadrunner Records.
CEREBRAL FIX set about touring once more guesting for NAPALM DEATH on their 'Harmony Corruption' dates up front of a second album 'Tower Of Spite'. Harking back to Healy and Baker's roots the bonus track on the CD was a cover of SACRILEGE's 'The Closing Irony'.
In May of 1990 the band gained the honours of supporting SEPULTURA at London's Marquee club.
1991 saw Baker leaving and in his place coming former VARUKERS and METAL MESSIAH man Kevin Frost for the 'Bastards' album. CD bonus tracks comprised of 'Maimed To Beg', the GBH cover 'No Survivors' and the DAMNED's 'Smash It Up', the latter featuring WOLFSBANE's Blaze Bayley on vocals. Promoting the album found the band guesting in Britain to OBITUARY.
1992's 'Death Erotica' had a version of DISCHARGE's 'Never Again' with NAPALM DEATH's Barney Greenaway and POP WILL EAT ITSELF's Clint on guest vocals. NAPALM DEATH's bassist Shane Embury also added vocals to the track 'Too Drunk To Funk' whilst MARSHALL LAW's Andy Pyke and SHY and SIAM vocalist Tony Mills contributed to a version of the JUDAS PRIEST hit 'Living After Midnight'.
A 1992 tour with PARADISE LOST was followed up by a European tour in 1993

alongside CANCER and GOMORRAH. Healy by this time had departed and the band pulled in the bassist from DISCHARGE to fulfil the dates.
The band folded shortly after. Healy later teamed up with BENEDICTION. Frost is back with THE VARUKERS.

Albums:
LIFE SUCKS AND THEN YOU DIE, Vinyl Solution SOL 15 (1988)
Warstorm / Cerebral Fix / Looniverse / Give Me Life / Soap Opera / Behind The Web / Product Of Disgust / Life Sucks / Power Struggle / Go / Fear Of Death / Acid Sick / Skatedrunk / Zombie / Existing Not Living
TOWER OF SPITE, Roadrunner RO 9356 1 (1990)
Unite For Who? / Enter The Turmoil / Feast Of The Fools / Chasten Of Fear / Circle Of The Earth / Tower Of Spite / Injecting Out / Quest For Midian / Forgotten Genocide / Culte Des Mortes (I)
BASTARDS, Roadracer RO 92861 (1991)
Descent Into Unconsciousness / Veil Of Tears / Beyond Jerusalem / Return To Infinity / Sphere Born / I Lost A Friend / Ritual Abuse / Mammonite / Middle Third (Mono Culture) / Maimed To Beg / No Survivors / Smash It Up
DEATHEROTICA, Under One Flag FLAG 75 (1992)
Death Erotica / World Machine / Clarissa / Haunted Eyes / Mind Within Mine / Splintered Wings / Creator Of Outcasts / Angel's Kiss / Still In Mind / Ratt Of Medusa / Never Again / Too Drunk Too Funk / Burning/ Living After Midnight

CEREBRAL TURBULENCY
(CZECH REPUBLIC)

Czech Grindsters CEREBRAL TURBULANCY issued the demo tape 'Right To Choose'. They would also share the tactfully deprecatingly titled tape 'Are Shit!' with GRIDE and MALIGNANT TUMOUR.

Albums:
AS GRAVY, Leviathan (1997)
…To The Agony / A Hunter Of The Children / Grind Hockey / Inborn Blindness / Dying Fetus / Worse Than With Wire To The Eye / Born With The Crap / The World Of Joys And Dreams / Choice Aims To The Responsibility For Own Decision / Fever 39-7 / Outro / Chemical And Bacterial Analysis Of

Cadaver / Painful Memories

CEREBROCIDE (GERMANY)
Line-Up: Thorsten Kohl (vocals), Frank Rostock (guitar), Thomas Schmidt (guitar), Mike Friedrich (bass), Jens Majer (drums)

CEREBROCIDE debuted their familiar brand of Death Metal with the 1994 demo 'Total Insane'. Following these recordings the band was wrought by a major line up change but would return in a renewed guise with the 1995 effort 'Souls'.

Albums:
SEEMING PARADISE, Cerebrocide (1997)
Intro / The Legend Of The Cross / Corruption / The Dread / City Of Fear / Life Of People / Unholy War / Servent Of Devil / Desire / Born Blind
DELUSION, Cudgel Agency CUD CD002 (1999)
Under Pressure / Teufelskreis / 8 (Captured) / Right To Die / The Other World / Braincell / Peace Of Mind / Illusion / Pedophile Man

CEREMONIAL OATH (SWEDEN)
Line-Up: Anders Friden (vocals), Anders Iwers (guitar), Mikael Andersson (guitar), Thomas Johansson (bass), Markus Nordberg (drums)

Founded in 1989 by ex-TIAMAT guitarist Anders Iwers, ex-FORSAKEN guitarist Mikael Andersson, bassist Jesper Strömblad and former CRYSTAL AGE vocalist Oscar Dronjak, CEREMONIAL OATH debuted in 1992 with a single, 'The Lost Name Of God', on Corpsegrinder Records.
Unfortunately, the band was hit by the departure of Strombold (who left to join IN FLAMES) and Dronjac (having decided to reunite with CRYSTAL AGE) following the release of the debut album 'The Book Of Truth'.
Interestingly, both Strömbold and Dronjac were to come to the fore in 1997 with their Trad Metal side project band HAMMERFALL which, with their debut album 'Glory To The Brave', quite unexpectedly broke the national German charts wide open.
CEREMONIAL OATHS's eventual second album, 'Carpet', included a guest performance by AT THE GATES vocalist Tomas Lindberg. It also featured a version of IRON MAIDEN's 'Hallowed Be

Thy Name'.
The group has also submitted a version of 'Disposable Heroes' for the METALLICA tribute album 'Metal Militia'.

Singles/EPs:
Lost Name Of God / For I Have Sinned / The Praise, Corpse Grinder CGR 005 (1992)

Albums:
THE BOOK OF TRUTH, Modern Primitive 38102242 (1993)
Prologue (Sworn To Avenge) / The Invocation / For I Have Sinned (The Praise) / Enthroned / Only Evil Prevails / Thunderworld (Welcome To Forever) / Lords Of Twilight / Ceremonial Oath / The Lost Name Of God / Book Of Truth B/ Hellbound
CARPET, Black Sun BS02 (1995)
The Day I Buried / Dreamsong / Carpet / The Shadowed End / One Of Us / Nightshade / Immortalized / Hallowed Be Thy Name

CEREMONY (HOLLAND)
Line-Up: Micha Verboom (vocals), Peter Verhoef (guitar), Johan Vd Sluijs (guitar), Ron Vd Polder (bass), Patrick Van Gelder (drums)

Singles/EPs:
Indemnicy, (1995)

Albums:
TYRANNY FROM ABOVE, Cyber Music CYBER CD6 (1993)
Inner Demon / Drowned In Terror / Solitary World / Ceremonial Resurrection / When Tears Are Falling / Humanity / Beyond The Boundaries / Of This World / Tribulation Foreseen

CHAKAL (BRAZIL)

Vocalist Korg is credited with penning the lyrics for SEPULTURA's 'To The Wall'. Vocalist Korg also sang with THE MIST, a band including ex-SEPULTURA guitarist Jairo T. in it's ranks.

Albums:
THE MAN IS HIS OWN JACKAL, Coguemelo COG036-A (1991)

CHANNEL ZERO (BELGIUM)
Line-up: Franky De Smet Van Damme (vocals), Xavier Carion (guitar), Tino Olivier De Martino (bass),

Phil Baheux (drums)

Brussels Metal act CHANNEL ZERO were created in 1990 by ex-CYCLONE members.
Having debuted in 1992 with an eponymously titled debut for Shark Records, the quartet stepped up a level with the follow-up 'Stigmatized For Life' album, which was produced by PANTERA drummer Vinnie Paul. Following its release the band toured Europe supporting BIOHAZARD, OBITUARY, PRO-PAIN, EXHORDER and NAPALM DEATH.
The band's third album, The 'Unsafe', (the second on Play It Again Sam) is notable for a guest vocal performance on one track by METHOD OF DESTRUCTION's Billy Milano.
For recording of the ensuing 'Black Fuel' CHANNEL ZERO flew to Connecticut in America in order to record, but became disillusioned with the results. Deciding upon scrapping these recordings, CHANNEL ZERO returned to Europe to complete the album with producer Attie Bauw.

Singles/EPs:
Suck My Energy (Edit) / Suck My Energy / Repetition, Play It Again Sam 977. 847 (1995)
Help / Last Gasp / All For One / Man On The Edge, Play It Again Sam (1995)
Fool's Parade (Single edit) / Multi Flower Nursery / Fool's Parade, Play It Again Sam (1996)

Albums:
CHANNEL ZERO, Shark 032 (1992)
No Light (At The End Of The Tunnel) / Tales Of Worship / The Pioneer / Succeed Or Bleed / Never Alone / Inspiration To Violence / Painful Jokes / Save Me / Animation / Run With The Torch
STIGMATISED FOR LIFE, Play It Again Sam BIAS 259CD (1994)
Gold / Testimony / Unleash The Dog / Chrome Dome / Repetition / America / Stigmatized For Life / Play A Little / Big Now / Last Gap
UNSAFE, Play It Again Sam BIAS 290CD (1995)
Suck My Energy / Heroin / Bad To The Bone / Help / Lonely / Run W.T.T. / Why / No More / Unsafe / Dashboard Devils / As A Boy / Man On The Edge
BLACK FUEL, Play It Again Sam BIAS 350 CD (1996)
Black Fuel / Mastermind / Call On Me /

Fool's Parade / Self Control / Misery / The Hill / Love-Hate Satellite / Caveman / Put It In / Wasted / Outro
LIVE, Play It Again Sam (1998)

CHAOS AND TECHNOCRACY
(ITALY)

An Italian Death Metal band with Thrash Punk leanings.

Singles/EPs:
Abstract Reflections / Programmed By Society / Path Of Life / Thinking / Abstract Reflections (Live), Whiplash WHI 001 (1995) ('Abstract… And More' EP)

THE CHASM (OH, USA)
Line-Up: Daniel Corchada (vocals / guitar), Julio Viterbo (guitar), Alfonso Polo (bass), Antonio Leon (drums)

Mexican Death Black band THE CHASM, who opened their career with the demo 'Awaiting The Day Of Liberation', relocated to Ohio. The band's mentor and founder is former CENOTAPH man guitarist Daniel Corchada.
Corchada would loan himself out to the infamous INCANTATION in mid 1997. The group has undergone many changes in line up and by 1999 was down to a duo of Corchado and drummer Antonio Leon. Numbers were boosted with the recruitment of another erstwhile CENOTAPH member Julio Viterbo.
The 2000 album 'Processions To The Infraworld' saw the enlistment of bassist Roberto V. but he would soon bail out in favour of former ALLUSION four stringer Alfonso Polo.
THE CHASM has cut versions of KREATOR and DESTRUCTION songs for tribute albums.

Albums:
PROCREATION OF THE INNER TEMPLE, Bellphegot BELLCD 95011-2 (1994)
Conqueror Of The Mourningstar / A Dream Of An Astral Spectrum (To An Eternal Hate) / Confessions Of Strange Anxiety / Honoris Lux Infinitus (A Whipper To The Moon) / The Day Of Liberation / The Lonely Walker (My Pride And My Wrath) / The Cosmos Within / Stair To Aspirations
FOR THE LOST YEARS, Reborn CD001 (1995)
The Gravefields / Secret Winds Of Temptation / The Pastfinder / Deathcult

For Eternity / Ascention Of Majestic Ruins / Our Time will Come… / Procreation Of The Inner Temple / An Arcanum Faded / Torn (By The Sunrise) / My Tideless Seas / Lost Yesterdays Impossible Tomorrows
DEATHCULT FOR ETERNITY: THE TRIUMPH, Oz Productions (1998)
Revenge Rises-Drowned In Mournful Blood / No Mercy (Our Time Is Near) / I'm The Hateful Raven / A Portal To Nowhere / Channeling The Bleeding Over The Dream's Remains / Possessed By Past Tragedies (Tragic Shadows) / Apocalypse / In Superior Torment… / The Triumph (Of My Loss)
PROCESSIONS TO THE INFRAWORLD, Dwell (2000)
Spectral Sons Of Mictlan / The Scars Of My Journey / At The Edge Of Nebulah Mortis / Fading… / Return Of The Banished / Cosmic Landscapes Of Sorrow / Architects Of Melancholic Apocalypses / Storm Of Revelations

CHEMICAL BREATH (BELGIUM)
Line-Up: Alain Chernouh (vocals / guitar), Rene Rockx (guitar), Surgen Maes (bass), Andy Missotten (drums)

Death Metal act from Maasmechelen that included former VIRULENT AGGRESSION guitarist Rene Rockx. CHEMICAL BREATH folded in 1996 but would reunite with a line up of Rockx, former GARBAGE personnel Bob Schillemans and Chris Sibbald along with Gerrie Verstrehen and Menno Corbeek. The band would dissolve for the final time in 1998 with Rockx becoming bass player for EXCAVATION.
EXCAVATION, along with Corbeek, would become BEYOND. Rockx would reunite with former CHEMICAL BREATH vocalist Alain Chernouh in FORM.

Albums:
FATAL EXPOSURE, Crypta DA 8210-2 (1992)
The Advantage Of Disbelief / Arachnid / Erased From Existence / Chamber Of Lost / Deny Fear / Hideous Perspectives / Several Hours To Judgement / Lost Tribes / Mutilation
VALUES, Crypta 8206-2 (1994)
I Persist My Opinion / Awaiting The Miracles / A Core Undesired / Inexpectibal Being / Message To The Mystic / Reduce Your Value / The Open Field / Admiring The Open End

CHILDREN OF BODOM (FINLAND)

Line-Up: Alex Laiho (vocals / guitar), Ale Kuoppala (guitar), Henkka 'Blacksmith' Seppäiä (bass), Janne Viljami Wirman (keyboards), Jaska Raatikainen (drums)

Espoo based Black Death metal act named after Finland's infamous Lake Bodom, the scene of a horrific series of murders. The band was previously titled INHEARTED. Founder member and vocalist Alex Laiho made his name as part of THY SERPENT maintaining CHILDREN OF BODOM, created in 1993 with drummer Jaska Raatikainen, as a going concern.

The band supported DIMMU BORGIR on their 1997 Finnish dates and would also feature on the high profile compilation album 'Metallilitto'. The praise received for this release scored the band a deal with Spinefarm Records. CHILDREN OF BODOM's debut album 'Something Wild' was an instant best seller and sales were strengthened when the band also scored a priority licensing deal with Germany's Nuclear Blast Records.

Later the same year the industrious Laiho would team up with IMPALED NAZARENE and would also form part of Kimberley Goss' SINERGY line ups.

CHILDREN OF BODOM would quite spectacularly land a national number 1 single with 'Downfall' in early 1999.

Wirman, under the title of WARMAN, cut a solo album in 2000 titled 'Unknown Soldier'.

The B side to CHILDREN OF BODOM's 2000 single 'Hate Me' features a cover version of W.A.S.P.'s 'Hellion'. The ensuing album 'Follow The Reaper' found the Japanese version with an extra bonus track, a version of OZZY OSBOURNE's 'Shot In The Dark'.

CHILDREN OF BODOM supported PRIMAL FEAR for a German tour in February 2001.

Singles/EPs:
Downfall / No Command, Spinefarm (1999) **1 FINLAND**
Hate Me / Hellion, Spinefarm (2000)

Albums:
SOMETHING WILD, Nuclear Blast NB 308-2 (1998)
Deadnight Warrior / In The Shadows / Red Light In My Eyes (Part I) / Red Light In My Eyes (Part II) / Lake Bodom / The Nail / Touch Like Angel Of Death
HATEBREEDER, Nuclear Blast (1999)
Warheart / Silent Night, Bodom Night / Hatebreeder / Bed Of Razors / Towards Dead End / Black Widow / Wrath Within / Children Of Bodom / Down Fall
TOKYO WARHEARTS-LIVE, Nuclear Blast (1999)
Intro / Silent Night, Bodom Night / Lake Bodom / Bed Of Razors / War Of Razors / Deadnight Warrior / Hatebreeder / Touch The Angel Of Death / Downfall / Towards Dead End
FOLLOW THE REAPER, Nuclear Blast (2000)
Follow The Reaper / Bodom After Midnight / Children Of Decadence / Every Time I Die / Mask Of Sanity / Taste Of My Scythe / Hate Me / Northern Comfort / Kissing The Shadows / Hellion

CHILDREN OF BODOM
Photo : Martin Wickler

CHOR CHOREA (GERMANY)

Line-Up: Veit Ulmann (vocals / guitar), Jens Busch (guitar), Andy Bahr (bass), Mario Hesse (drums)

Previously known as DEFCON, issuing the 1990 album 'Suicide' under that moniker, the group changed its title to CHOR CHOREA in 1991; releasing the demo tape, 'Triumph', the following year. More demos followed. 'Mental Maze' appeared in 1993 and 'Inner Stage' a year later and, having toured with KREATOR, POLTERGEIST, RAGE and MESSIAH bassist Andy Bahr was replaced with Jens Semrau.

Albums:
EXPERIENCE, Crosswire CROSS 002 (1995)
People / Because / Why / We Try / '67 / Dreams / November / The Meat Inspector / Crossroads / Repetitions / Breit / Cyberlife

CHRIST DENIED (SPAIN)
Line-Up: Dave Rotten (vocals), David Nigger (guitar / bass / programming)

Studio duo of former INTOXICATION man David Nigger and AVULSED's Dave Rotten. The latter also operates in Grindcore band ANEAMIA. The 'Got What He Deserved' album includes a cover of ONSLAUGHT's 'Angel Of Death'.
CHRIST DENIED have also cut a version of PYREXIA's 'The Uncertain' for a split EP shared with ABORTED in 2000.

Singles/EPs:
Daethronation / Hierarchy Of Hypocrisy / Christophobia / No Salvation / Overlord, Morbid (1995) ('The Horned God' double split 7" single with HAEMORRAGE)
The Uncertain, Soulreaper (2000) (Split single with ABORTED)

Albums:
... GOT WHAT HE DESERVED, Gulli GR005 (1996)
Banish The Vanished / A Monk's Wet Dream / Pay To Pray / Deserved No Less / Useless Sinless Life / No Salvation / Misery / Angels Of Death / Body Of Christ / Hierarchy Of Hypocrisy
CHRIST DENIED, Soulreaper (2000) (Split CD with ABORTED)

CHRONICAL DIARRHOEA (USA)

Speedcore. The 'Abstract Says' 7" single included cover versions of NEGATIVE APPROACH and S.S.D. songs.

Singles/EPs:
Abstract Carnage, Off The Disk OTD 06 (1989)

Albums:
ROYAL DIARRHOEA, (198-)
SALOMO SAYS, Nuclear Blast (1988)
Shit World / The Influence / J.R.'s / B.S.I. / Profile Less Nation / Trademark Abortion / A Contradiction / 007 / Hate You / Indescribable / Other Attitudes /

Doomshock / The Never Ending, Indescribable. Incredible, Irregular Hardcore Mosh / Flower Power / Attack Of The Blurr Demons / Senseless Lyrics / Ommes Kills / Joe's Choice / Uncle Ben's Favourite Blues / Chemical Terrorism / Sick Of You / Ha?
ABSTRACT CARNAGE, Nuclear Blast (1990)
Go Slow / The Expert / Hell Commander / Pressure / Supervising Neighbours / Fast Food / Problems / Glue / Passion / Sad Is True / Acid Freak / Flower Power

CHRONICICAL DISTURBANCE (CANADA)
Line-Up: Alain Lefedvre (vocals / guitar), Alain Deslauries (guitar), Pierre Delorre (bass), Francois Richard (drums)

Albums:
FOGGY CREEK, S.A. Butcher (1990)
Foggy Creek / Crust And Crumbs / Chronic Confusion / Sordid End / Starless / Another Day In The Ratrace / Open Season / No Tomorrow / Doctor Death / Prejudice

CHRONIC DECAY (SWEDEN)
Line-Up: Jocke Hammar (vocals / guitar), Roger (guitar), Gunnar Norgren (bass), Micke Karlsson (drums)

Singles/EPs:
Ecstasy In Pain / 1st Of September / Dark Before Dawn, Studiefrämjandet SFRS 613 (1990)
Silent Prayer / Vision Of A Madman, Studiefrämjandet SFRCS 9305 (1993) (Split EP with EXANTHEMA & RETURN TO HEAVEN)

CIANIDE (Chicago, IL, USA)
Line-Up: Mike Perun (vocals / bass), Steve Coroll (guitar), Jim Bresnahen (guitar), Andy Kuizin (drums)

Chicago Death Metal act created as a trio of singer / bassist Mike Perun, guitarist Steve Caroll and drummer Jeff Kabella during 1989. After a 1990 demo entitled 'Funeral' CIANIDE struck a deal with the Grindcore International label for their 1992 debut 'The Dying Truth'. Second effort 'A Descent Into Hell' during 1994 included a version of SLAUGHTER's 'Death Dealer'.
Kabella left in 1995 and was replaced by Andy Kuizin for 1996's limited edition release 'Rage War'. Second guitarist Jim Bresnahen was drafted for 1998's 'Death, Doom And Destruction'.

Caroll also operates as the lead vocalist for Black Death Thrashers LORDES WERRE appearing on their 1999 'Demon Crusades' album.

Albums:
THE DYING TRUTH, Grindcore International (1992)
Mindscrape / Human Cesspool / The Suffering / Scourges At The Pillar / Crawling Chaos / The Dying Truth / Funeral / Second Life
A DESCENT INTO HELL, (1994)
Gates Of Slumber / Eulogy / The Undead March / The Luciferian Twilight / Beyond The Fallen Horizon / Darkness / Death Dealer / Mountains In Thunder
RAGE WAR, (1996)
DEATH, DOOM AND DESTRUCTION, (1998)
Rage War / This World Will Burn / Metal Never Bends / Envy And Hatred / Salvation / The Power To Destroy / Deadly Spawn / (We Are All) Doomed
DIVIDE AND CONQUER, Merciless MRCD0013 (2000)

CIBORIUM (PORTUGAL)
Line-Up: José Carlos Marques (vocals / guitar), João Lopes (guitar), João Pereira (bass), Antónia Beirade (keyboards), Nuno Marecos (drums)

Portuguese Gothic flavoured Death Metal. Debuted with a 1996 demo 'On The Strayed Pyx'.

Albums:
COLOSSAL CRAGS, Grade (1999)
The Wraith / Thy Soot / Catalepsy / Scion / Avigarzitor / Lugubrious Voyager

CIBORIUM (Baltimore, MD, USA)
Line-Up: Ian Davis (vocals), Justin Ethem (guitar), Ryan Taylor), Tony Montalvo (drums)

"Hyperspeed" Death Metal band CIBORIUM began life as a school act in 1994 and have endured many line up fluctuations over the years. The band issued two demos, 'Envision Of Death' and 'Abomination' prior to recording the debut album 'Make Them Die Slowly'.

Albums:
MAKE THEM DIE SLOWLY, (2000)

CINERARY (CA, USA)
Line-Up: Matti Way (vocals), Danny Louise (guitar), Mike Dooley (bass), Rick Myers (drums)

CINERARY evolved from INCESTUOUS, an act founded in 1999 by ex-GORGASM drummer Derek Hoffman. A series of line up changes led to the solo INCESTUOUS release 'Brass Knuckle Abortion' after which the band opted for a name change to CINERARY.
Personnel at this point were ex-DISGORGE vocalist Matti Way, former SMEGMA / CUMCHRIST guitarist Danny Louise ('Wrench'), Mike Dooley from CORPSE VOMIT on bass and DISGORGE drummer Ricky Myers. Founder member Hoffman had rejoined GORGASM in January 2001 and would also be found deputizing for LIVIDITY.
Wrench also operates BRETHREN with ex-INCESTUOUS and DYSPHORIA vocalist 'Sick' Nick Hernandez, Jeff and Jim from CIANIDE and Nefarious of MACABRE.

COALESCE (Kansas City, USA)
Line-Up: Sean Ingram (vocals), Jes Steineger (guitar), Nathan Ellis (bass), James Dewees (drums)

News emerged in the spring of 2001 that Ingram and Dewees were involved in a twin drummer collaboration billed as AMERICAN SPECTATOR in union with ZAO drummer Jesse Smith together with TFU personnel bassist Don Clark and guitarist Ryan Clark.

Albums:
FUNCTIONING ON IMPATIENCE, (1998)
012: REVOLUTION IN JUST LISTENING, Relapse (1999)
What Happens On The Road Always Comes Home / Cowards.Com / Burn Everything That Bears Our Name / White The Jackass Operation Spins Its Wheels / Sometimes Selling Out Is Waking Up / Where The Hell Is Ricky Thorne These Days? / Jesus In The Year 2000 / Next On The Shit List / Counting Murders And Drinking Beer (The $46,000 Escape) / They Always Come In Fall

COCK AND BALL TORTURE
(GERMANY)
Line-Up: Sascha (vocals / drums)

The delightfully named Grindcore act COCK AND BALL TORTURE was created in 1997 by erstwhile CARNAL

TOMB members. Their first product, the demo tape 'Cocktales', would be later re-issued on CD in 1998 in a limited run of 550 copies but would run foul of the censors due to its pornographic cover art. Shredded Records would give the EP a further re-release of 1000 copies with different artwork.

COCK AND BALL TORTURE have shared a string of split singles and EPs with the likes of LIBIDO AIRBAG, Poland's SQUASH BOWELS, GROSSMEMBER and Mexico's DISGORGE.

Singles/EPs:
Cocktales, Cock And Ball Torture (1998)
The Taste Of Animal Sperm (The Orgasm Of A Hyena) / After Master / Fresh Ejaculata / Scrotum Blast / Horney Hosier / The Cock And Ball Torture / Cuntkiller / Sperm-Orgy / She Sucks As Hard As She Can / Hymen / Phrenetic Pussy Slasher / Frenzy Lesbians / Pussy Commando / Drowned In Sperm / Randy Rectum Fistfuck / Colonel Cunt, Shredded (1998) ('Cocktales' EP)
Veni, Vidi, Spunky, Bizarre Leprous (1999) (7" split single with SQUASH BOWELS)
Tapir Tits / Scato Scampi / Pinguine / Dingo Dong, Stuhlgang (2000) ('Zoophilia' split CD single with LIBIDO AIRBAG)
Anal Cadaver, Noweakshit (2000) (7" split single with GROSSMEMBER)
Big Tits, Big Dicks, Flesh Feast (2001) (7" split single with LAST DAYS OF HUMANITY)
Split, Lofty Storm LSR011 (2001) (7" split single with DISGORGE)

Albums:
OPUS (SY) VI, Shredded (2000)
Anal Sex Terror / Candy Teen Pussy Pleasers / Feakal Fatal / Anna'n'ass / Fat Sex Mama / Spunky Monkey / King Anus III / Big Tit Slappers / Lesbian Duo Dildo Fuck / Spank Me / Fuck Me / Fill Me / Rosetta Twist / Panda Penis / Koala Cunt / Bi-Bee / Anal Lilly Pissing Chick / Fist Fuck Family / Torture'lini Ball'o'nese / Important Impotence / Juicy Lucy / Vulvurine Cooze Blues / Whorrorbitch

COERCION (SWEDEN)
Line-Up: Keneth Nyman (vocals / bass), Rickard Thulin (guitar), Pelle Ekegren (drums)

Swedish Death Metal act COERCION came together in 1992 as a quintet of frontman Kenneth Nyman, guitarists Rickard Thulin and L. Ortega, bassist Pelle Liljenberg and drummer G. Johnston.

By the following year the first demo 'Headway' had emerged and COERCION would follow this with a further tape 'Human Failure'. COERCION's line-up had evolved by this point as S. Persson had taken Ortega's position. The band scored a deal with domestic label Chaos Records but much to their frustration no product was instigated. However, German label Perverted Taste would pick up the band for the debut album 'Forever Dead'. New members at this juncture, with the departure of Persson, were guitarist Steffe Söderberg and drummer Tor Frykholm.

Shortly after these sessions Frykholm broke ranks and Pelle Ekegren took over drum duties. COERCION's turmoil did not end there though as Liljenberg would make his exit immediately prior to gigs in Germany and Poland on a package bill with IMPENDING DOOM, CRYPTIC TALES and PURGATORY.

With Söderberg also leaving COERCION trimmed down to a trio to record the sophomore album 'Delete'.

Albums:
FOREVER DEAD, Perverted Taste PT021 (1997)
Coughing Blood / Blind Witness / Cursed With Existence / Dead Meat / Crawling In Filth / Breeding The Enemy / Down We Go / Human Failure / March / Forever Dead / Scattered / Grief (Beyond Relief)
DELETE, Perverted Taste PT025 (1999)
Come The Storm / Once I Cared / Eclipsed / Mental Turmoil / The Pointless Routine / Delete / Burst / Anticlimax / Without Aim / Discontinued / Life Denied / Evolution Reversal

COMECON (SWEDEN)
Line-Up: Martin Van Drunen (vocals), Pelle Strom (guitar), Rasmus Ekman (guitar), Anders Green (drums)

Previously known in a more Hardcore vein as KRIXJHÄLTERS under which title they released three records, an eponymous debut EP, the 1987 mini album 'Hjälter Skelter' and 1989's full blown album 'Evilution'. A musical shift was adopted and a name change to

OMNITRON ensured in an effort for more global recognition.

Going back to their Hardcore Metal roots the band renamed themselves again, this time to COMECON, and engaged ENTOMBED vocalist L.G. Petrov as a guest on the debut 'Megatrends In Brutality' album. Whilst Martin Van Drunen, (formerly with ASPHYX) contributed vocals to 'Converging conspiracies', drums being handled by Fredrik Palsson.

Obviously intent on sticking to tradition, the band's third album, 'Fable Frolic', found MORGOTH frontman Marc Grewe singing lead!

Singles/EPs:
Branded By Sunlight, CBR CBR S 134 (1991) (Split 7" promotion with MERCILESS)

Albums:
MEGATRENDS IN BRUTALITY, Century Media 9735 (1991)
Dog Days / Slope / Ulcer / The Mule / Conductor Of Ashes / Teton Tantrums / Omnivorous Excess / Good Boy Benito / Armed Solution / The Future Belongs To Us / Wash Away The Filth
CONVERGING CONSPIRACIES, Century Media CD 77057 (1993)
Democrator / The Ethno-Surge / Community / Aerie / Bled-Burn / Morticide / Worms / Pinhole View / The Whole World / God Told Me To / Dipstick / The House That Man Built
FABLE FROLIC, Century Media CD 77094-2 (1995)
Soft, Creamy Lather / How I Won The War / Bovine Inspiration / Frogs / Ways Of Wisdom (Serves Two) / Propelling Scythes / The Family Album / Imploder / It Wears Me Down / Anaconda Charms Grass Snake / Icons Of Urine / Sunday Stroll / Canvas Of History

COMPOS MENTIS (SWEDEN)

Albums:
QUADROLOGY OF SORROW, (2000)

CONCEPTION (NORWAY)
Line-Up: Roy S. Kahn (vocals), Tøre Ostby (guitar), Hans C. Gjestvang (keyboards), Ingar Amlien (bass), Arve Heimdal (drums)

Massively talented act centred upon the virtuoso guitar talents of Tøre Ostby. CONCEPTION bass player Ingar Amlien was previously in late 70's act ROCQUEFIRE alongside future TNT guitarist Ronnie Le Tekrö.

CONCEPTION's debut self-financed album, produced by VICTORY guitarist Tommy Newton, was re-released in 1993 by Noise Records.

CONCEPTION also featured on the Noise live video of 1993, 'The Power Of Metal', alongside RAGE and GAMMA RAY. CONCEPTION utilized the services of keyboard player Hans C. Gjestvang for a brief period.

Supported SKYCLAD on their '94 British club tour and also put in some dates with TROUBLE and THRESHOLD.

The group's majestic fourth album 'Flow' found CONCEPTION evolving from Death Metal into a monstrous Hard Rock act. The album found the band in receipt of rave reviews throughout Europe, although the critical acclaim, unsurprisingly, stopped at the front door of the major British Rock press.

CONCEPTION duly folded with vocalist Roy Kahn joining American Metal band KAMELOT. Guitarist Tøre Ostby and bassist Ingar Amlien founded A.R.K. with VAGABOND / THE SNAKES / MUNDUS IMPERIUM singer Jorn Lande and TNT / YNGWIE MALMSTEEN drummer John Macaluso.

Amlien forged a Black Metal project CREST OF DARKNESS, releasing three albums to date. The 1999 CREST OF DARKNESS release 'The Ogress' sees both Kahn and Heimdal contributing.

Singles/EPs:
Roll The Fire / Silent Crying, Noise N0218-3 (1994)

Albums:
THE LAST SUNSET, Conception CSFCD 9101 (1991)
Prevision / Building A Force / War Of Hate / Bowed Down With Sorrow / Fairy's Dance / Another World / Elegy / The Last Sunset / Live To Survive / Among The Gods
PARALLEL MINDS, Noise N0218 (1994)
Water Confines / Roll The Fire / And I Close My Eyes / Silent Crying / Parallel Minds / Silver Shine / My Decision / The Promiser / Wolf's Lair / Soliloquy
IN YOUR MULTITUDE, Noise N0229-2 (1995)
Under A Mourning Star / Missionary Man / Retrospect / Guilt / Sanctuary / A Million Gods / Some Wounds / Carnal Compression / Solar Serpent / In Your

Multitude
FLOW, Noise N 0274-2 (1997)
Gethsemane / Angel (Come Walk With
Me) / A Virtual Lovestory / Flow / Cry /
Reach Out / Tell Me When I'm Gone /
Hold On / Cardinal Sin / Would It Be The
Same

CONSOLATION (HOLLAND)
Line-Up: Manoloxx (vocals), Yehudi
(guitar), Dennis (guitar), Rein (bass),
Toep (drums)

Originally known as GORE-FLIX and
formed in 1989, the Dutch quintet
changed titles to CONSOLATION due to
increasing line-up changes.
Under the new handle the group
submitted the track 'Eye Of The Storm' to
the 1992 compilation album 'And Justice
For None' before new vocalist Manoloxx
was added later in the year.
Having signed to Displeased Records,
CONSOLATION released their debut CD,
a split effort with NEMBRONIC
HAMMERDEATH, in 1993, following it up
in 1996 with the 'Brave Melvin From The
Southern Point' record.

Singles/EPs:
The Truth, (1995)

Albums:
BEAUTY FILTH, Displeased (1993)
(Split album with NEMBRONIC
HAMMERDEATH)
We Mourn / Christianity Exposed /
Crusaders / Beautyfilth / No Hope, No
Fear / Locked / Part-Time God / Snowfall
**BRAVE MELVIN FROM THE
SOUTHERN POINT**, Displeased D-
00031 (1996)
Murder / Ephemera / Godmode / A
Clean Whistle And American Meat /
Moribund / Truckload Of Hatred / Red
Rum / Stahlhelm / The Truth / Dominion
Fails / Brave Melvin From The Southern
Point / Sin / The Darkest Black
STAHLPLAAT, Displeased (1998)
Fireblade / Motocation / Cold Blooded
Cold / Camel Song / Dead Thrill /
Holocauster / Route 666 / Killjoy /
Funeral Pyre / Murder Death Kill /
Hellwalker I: Beyond The Darkest Black /
Hellwalker II: Wheels Of Steel /
Hellwalker III: Black Tar / Speedstar

CONSPIRACY OF SILENCE
(BELGIUM)
Line-Up: Danny Goris (vocals), Geert
Van De Meutter (guitar), Luc Vervloet
(guitar), Richard Lepelaar (bass), Kurt
Bertels (drums)

CONSPIRACY OF SILENCE, featuring
former BLACK SHEPARD guitarist Luc
Vervloet, were founded in 1992. A 1993
demo preceded their mini-CD.

Singles/EPs:
The Freak Parade / We Who Are
Faceless / Flesh Burned Black /
Cathedral Of Rain, Shiver SHR013
(1994) ('Conspiracy Of Silence' EP)

CONSPIRATOR (GERMANY)
Line-Up: Lars Schutze (vocals), Sven
Gerstner (guitar), Jan Körle (guitar),
Matthias Busse (bass), Hinnerk Gerds
(drums)

In 1993 CONSPIRATOR released the
demo 'A Deadly State Of Mind' and added
ex-JET BLACK drummer Hinnerk Gerds
shortly afterwards.

Albums:
SEPTIC SOULS, Crossroads CR 01 002
94 (1994)
Intro / My Pain Is Your Pleasure / Saint
Or Sinner / Nothing To Feel For / Too
Angry To Live / Slaves Of Pain / Killing
To Survive / Save Me From Tomorrow /
Flesh And Blood / Revenge
(Conspirators Are Back) / Insecticide

CONTRADICTION (GERMANY)
Line-Up: Oliver Lux (vocals / guitar),
Oliver Kämper (guitar), Lars Fischbach
(bass), Kay Fischer (drums)

CONTRADICTION were formed in 1989
and the group's first demo, 'Deadly
Games', was recorded the following year
followed by a second tape entitled 'Old
Demon'.

Albums:
RULES OF PEACE, Contradiction 4242
190571 (1993)
Lie / Chains Of Misery / Change Your
Mind / Kingdom Of The Damned /
Submissive Servant / So What? / Trilogy
Of Darkness / Despising The Rules Of
Peace / Nuclear Disaster / Pray To Me /
The Hunter
ALL WE HATE!, Strictly Stone 95001
(1995)
All We Hate / Red Line / Dic(K)tator /
Disorder Unleashed / Pretender /
Lifetime / Do You Wanna Die? / Land Of
Insanity / Scars On My Soul / 50% Off /

Voices / Wake Up

CONTROL DENIED (USA)
Line-Up: Chuck Schuldiner (vocals / guitar), Shannon Hamm, Brian Benson (bass), Tim Aymer, Richard Christy (drums)

DEATH protagonist Chuck Schuldiner put his main act on ice generating a new project CONTROL DENIED very much in the Power Metal mould. Originally Schuldiner was to work with the original WINTER'S BANE vocalist but he was to be lured away for a more permanent liaison with WICKED WAYS.
CONTROL DENIED was now down to Schuldiner, bassist Brian Benson and drummer Chris Williams.
Although CONTROL DENIED recorded an album's worth of material and received offers from various labels Williams upped and left forcing Schuldiner into a rethink. The outcome was somewhat inevitable and DEATH announced their reformation in October with a line up of Schuldiner, Hamm, drummer Richard Christy and a returning Steve DiGeorgio on bass, the latter still retaining his fulltime participation in SADUS.
DEATH duly returned to the scene by signing to the aggressive Nuclear Blast label for 1998's 'Sound Of Perseverance', an album which saw a further progression towards straight heavy metal. Schuldiner was aided in this effort by Hamm, Christy and bassist Scott Clendenin. The album included a stab at JUDAS PRIEST's 'Painkiller'.
The CONTROL DENIED album finally found a release in 1999.
2000 found Christy back on the drumstool aiding fellow Deathsters INCANTATION for their live commitments following this with a stint with ICED EARTH. Christy also runs a side project band BURNING INSIDE with BLACK WITCHERY guitarist Steve Childers and ACHERON's Michael Estes.

Albums:
THE FRAGILE ART OF EXISTENCE, Nuclear Blast (1999)
Consumed / Breaking The Broken / Expect The Unexpected / What If? / When The Link Becomes Missing / Believe / Cut Down / The Fragile Art Of Existence

CONVERGE (Boston, MA, USA)

CONVERGE's 1999 release 'The Poachers Diaries' is a split CD with Virginia's AGORAPHOBIC NOSEBLEED.

Albums:
PETITIONING THE EMPTY SKY, (199-)
The Saddest Day / Forsaken / Albatross / Dread / Shingles / Buried But Breathing / Farewell Note To This City / Color The Blood Red / For Your Antithesis / Homesong
CARING AND KILLING, (199-)
Shallow Breathing / I Abstain / Two Day Romance / Fact Leaves Its Ghost / Becoming A Stranger / Antithesis / Dead / Tied To My Neck / Divinity / Blind / Shy / Down / Zodiac / Yesterday / Savoir Salvation / But Life Goes On
WHEN FOREVER COMES CRASHING, (199-)
My Usual Everything / The High Cost Of Playing God / In Harms Way / Conduit / The Lowest Common Denominator / Towing Jehovah / When Forever Comes Crashing / Ten Cents / Year Of The Swine / Letterbomb / Love As Arson
THE POACHER DIARIES, Relapse RR 6409 (199-) (Split CD with AGORAPHOBIC NOSEBLEED)

CONVULSE (FINLAND)
Line-Up: Rami Jamsa (vocals / guitar), Toni Hankala (guitar), Juha Telenius (bass), Janne Mikulanan (drums)

CONVULSE deal in Death Metal with Rock n' Roll elements. Added vocalist Kimmo Hakkila and drummer Perr Lind in 1995.

Singles/EPs:
Lost Equilibrium / Memories, Relapse (1993)

Albums:
WORLD WITHOUT GOD, Thrash THR013 (1992)
REFLECTIONS, Nuclear Blast NB 114-2 (1994)
Intro / The Rite Of Sunshine / The Green Is Grey / Years Of Decay / Memories / The Nation Cries / Crying Back Yesterday / Lost Equilibrium / The New Arrival

CORONACH (KY, USA)
Line-Up: Eric Best (vocals / guitar), Michael Meyer (guitar), Adam Howell (bass), Jerry Barksdale (keyboards), Jim

Higgins (drums)

Kentucky Black-tinged Death Metal. Both drummer Jim Higgins and keyboard player Jerry Barksdale are erstwhile members of ASSISTING SORROW. Barksdale also operates as a member of the Gothic Industrial project of former OMINOUS EROTICA man William J. Butler entitled ABSENCE OF FAITH.

Singles/EPs:
The Gift Of Foresight, Splatter Tribe (2000)

CORONER (SWITZERLAND)
Line-Up: Ron Royce (vocals / bass), Tommy T. Baron (guitar), Marquis Marky (drums)

Zurich Metal band CORONER achieved European success with a distinct brand of experimental avant garde Metal in the tradition of CELTIC FROST and, in the early part of their career, the band hardly toured - which added to the mystique.
Originally formed in 1984 with guitarist Oliver Amberg (later to join CELTIC FROST), Tom Warrior, mainstay of CELTIC FROST, contributed vocals to CORONER's first demo, 'Death Cult', before new guitarist Tommy T. Baron and drummer Marquis Marky joined CELTIC FROST's American 'Tragic Serenades' tour as road crew. From then on CORONER were continually blighted by comparisons to CELTIC FROST, not helped by Noise Records (CELTIC FROST's label) signing the Swiss trio for good measure!
CORONER's first album, 'R.I.P.', received good reviews and went on to sell over 50,000 units in Europe, and the distinct lack of gigs was more by circumstance than planning. A proposed European tour supporting METHOD OF DESTRUCTION was cancelled by the headliners when protesters threatened to sabotage the tour.
The second album, 'Punishment For Decadence', was produced by Guy Bidmead and emerged a year after CORONER's 1987 debut, featuring a cover of the JIMI HENDRIX classic 'Purple Haze'. Once more the band were unable to tour properly to promote the album, with a planned American jaunt with SABBAT and RAGE being cancelled at the last minute and British dates postponed when the band were incarcerated by British customs for lack of

work permits! CORONER did, however, manage to snatch a few support shows to SACRED REICH later in the year.
1989 brought CORONER's third album, 'No More Colour', produced by Pete Hinton and it would be in support of this release that the band finally CORONER toured Europe in 1990 with strong support from cult Texans WATCHTOWER.
In 1993 CORONER supported Canadians ANNIHILATOR on a British tour and, although still utilizing the services of Mark and Royce, CORONER had by 1995, to all intents and purposes, become a solo vehicle for Baron.
Marquis Marky turned up again in 1999 as part of Thomas Fischer's APOLLYON SON. Fortunately he had reverted to his real name of Mark Edelmann.

Singles/EPs:
Die By My Hand / Tunnel Of Pain, Noise NO136-6 (1989)
Purple Haze / Masked Jackal, Noise 7HAZE3 (1989)
I Want You (She's So Heavy) / Divine Step, Noise NO0177-7 (Limited Edition Promotion)

Albums:
R.I.P., Noise N0075 (1987)
Intro / Reborn Through Hate / When Angels Die / Intro (Nosferatu) / Nosferatu / Suicide Command / Spiral Dream / R.I.P. / Coma / Fried Alive / Intro (Totentanz) / Totentanz / Outro
PUNISHMENT FOR DECADENCE, Noise NUK 119 (1988)
Intro - Absorbed / Masked Jackal / Arc-Lite / Skeleton On Your Shoulders / Sudden Fall / Shadow Of A Lost Dream / Newbreed / Voyage To Eternity
NO MORE COLOR, Noise NUK 138 (1989)
Die By My Hand / No Need To Be Human / Read My Scars / D.O.A. / Mistress Of Deception / Tunnel Of Pain / Why It Hurts / Last Entertainment
MENTAL VORTEX, Noise N0177-1 (1991)
Divine Step (Conspectu Mortis) / Son Of Lilith / Semtex Revolution / Sirens / Metamorphosius / Pale Sister / About Life / I Want You (She's So Heavy)
GRIN, Noise NO2010-2 (1993)
Dream Path / The Lethargic Age / Internal Conflicts / Caveat (To The Coming) / Serpent Moves / Still Thinking / Theme For Silence / Paralized, Mesmerised / Grin (Nails Hurt) / Host

CORONER, Noise N0212-2 (1995)
Between Worlds / The Favorite Game / Shifter / Serpent Moves / Snow Crystal / Divine Step (Conspectu Mortis) / Gliding Above While Being Below / Der Mussolini / Last Entertainment (TV Bizarre) / Reborn Through Hate / Golden Cashmere Sleeper (Part 1) / Golden Cashmere Sleeper (Part 2) / Masked Jackal / I Want You (She's So Heavy) / Grin (No Religion Remix) / Purple Haze (Radio Live Cut)

CORPSE (RUSSIA)

Eastern European Death Metal.

Singles/EPs:
Remembrance Of Cold Embodiments, Final Holocaust (199-) (Split single with NECRO K.I.L.L. DOZER)

CORPSE (USA)

Albums:
FROM THE GRAVE, (1997)

CORPSE VOMIT (DENMARK)

Not to be confused with the American CORPSE VOMIT. Confusingly both acts claim true rights to the name. CORPSE VOMIT's album release was delayed by many years due to the controversial nature of the sleeve artwork.
There are rumours that CORPSE VOMIT frontman 'Molesting Mike' is in reality the vocalist with WITHERING SURFACE.

Albums:
DROWNING IN PUKE, Mighty Music PMZ007 (2000)

CORPSE VOMIT (USA)
Line-Up: Matt McClelland, Pat Clancy (guitar), Mike Dooley (bass), Garrett Scanlon

Founded in 1993 by Matt McClelland, Pat Clancy and Garrett Scanlon. Two years later CORPSE VOMIT added bass player Brice Dalzell as the act issued the demos 'Gathering Chemical Children' and 'Bastards Of Forever Filth'.
Dalzell left in 1998 as CORPSE VOMIT enlisted Mike Dooling of CINERARY.
McClelland, Scanlan and Clancy also operate CUMCHRIST. Scanlan and Clancy also have another side project entitled L.S.B.

Albums:
RAPING THE EARS OF THOSE ABOVE, (1999)
Sons Of Famine / Maggot Lamb / Waste / Seas Of Excrement / Mind Scabs / Gathering Chemical Children / Sleeping Dismay / Death Meddle / Crawling Visions / Nothing

COUNTERBLAST (SWEDEN)
Line-Up: Martin Letell (vocals), Stefan Hakeskog (guitar), Andreas Ågren (bass), Håkan Paulsson (keyboards), Håkan Andersson (drums)

Apocalyptic blend of Thrash, Hardcore and Crustcore.

Singles/EPs:
Prospect / Remain, Skuld SKULD023 (1995)

Albums:
BALANCE OF PAIN, Skuld E.B. 010 (1996)
Prelude Pain / Independence / Disembodiment / Balance Of Pain / Depression / In League With Baldrick / The European Empire Of Capitalism / Beneath The Surface

CRACK UP (GERMANY)
Line-Up: Tim Schnetgöke (vocals / bass), Dirk Oschaltz (guitar), Helvin Pour (guitar), Frank Schlinkert (drums)

CRACK UP are a Death Metal act produced by former HOLY MOSES man Andy Classen.

Albums:
BLOOD IS GOOD, Corrosion CR 6-501-2 (1996)
Blood Is Life / Unburden / Wounded / Voices / Failing / Forever In Me? / Hatred Unfolds / Cycle Of Need / Painted Black / Fading Away
FROM THE GROUND, Nuclear Blast NB CD 257-2 (1997)
From The Ground / Razzberry / Cracked Pack / Money Will Roll Right In / Broomer / Rats / Swab / Glorius / Blood On The Floor / For Fake / Sappy Restrain / Dysorientated / Burrrn! / Worthless / To The Sky
HEADS WILL ROLL, (199-)
Well Come / So Far No Good / Only With The Devil / The Assassin / Harder They Fall / Off Kilter / Next Big Thing / Hell's Day / For 2nds I Thought I'd Rather Be Dead / In A Hole / Modern Art

/ Into The Dirt / Demon / Bad Mongo
DEAD END RUN, (199-)
It's Shit / Dead End Run / Maximum
Speed / Stallknecht / Dead Good
Motherfucker / Higher / Whores Suck It /
Well In The Night / I'm The Only Way /
Cut / Microcosm / Heavy Hearted King /
Better Dance / Everflow / Rock The Coffin

CRANIUM (SWEDEN)
Line-Up: Chainsaw Demon (vocals),
Fredrik Söderberg (guitar), Grave Raper
(guitar), Necro Nudist (drums)

CRANIUM's history dates back to 1985
founded by brothers bassist Phillip Von
Segebaden and guitarist Gustaf. The act
was rounded off with guitarist Fredrik
Söderberg and drummer Fredrik
Engqvist. The band changed titles to
LEGION for the 1986 demo 'The Dawn'
but soon folded.
Söderburg would found OBDURACY
then the highly rated DAWN.
By 1996 the band reformed as CRANIUM
once more to release the 'Speed Metal
Satan' mini-album comprising early 80's
tracks re-recorded. The band, now with
Phillip Von Segebaden retitled 'Chainsaw
Demon', employed the services of DAWN
drummer Jocke Petterson before he
decamped to THY PRIMORDIAL rebilling
himself as Morth.
For the 'Speed Metal Slaughter' album
UTUMNO man Johan Hallberg was
recruited although under the pseudonym
of Necro Nudist.
Phillip Von Segebaden also has a side
project band DEFENDER.

Albums:
SPEED METAL SATAN, Necropolis
(1997)
Lucifer's Breath (The Storm To Come) /
Storm Of Steel And Hate / Riders Of
Damnation / Bestial Butcher / Raped By
Demons
SPEED METAL SLAUGHTER,
Necropolis (1998)
Slaughter On The Dance Floor /
Lawnmower Lover / Dentist Of Death /
S.R.T. (Satanic Rescue Team) / A Devil
On The Drums - Sluts Of Satan /
Graveyard Romance / Satanic Holiday
SPEED METAL SENTENCE, (1999)
Speed Metal Sentence / Nymphomaniac
Nuns / Full Moon Fistbanger / Satanic
Sect / Pestilential Penis / Samurai Satan
/ Taxi Terror / Cranium-Crushers Of
Christ

CREEPMIME (UK / HOLLAND)
Line-Up: Rogier Hakkaart (vocals /
guitar), Andy Judd (guitar), Mark Hope
(bass), Frank Brama (drums)

CREEPMIME debuted with the 1992
demo 'Anthems For A Doomed Youth'
and, having gained a deal with Mascot
Records appeared with the 'Shadows'
album (produced by Patrick Mameli of
PESTILENCE) the following year.

Albums:
SHADOWS, Mascot M7006 2 (1993)
The Fruit Of III Virtue / A Serenade For
The Tragic / Suffer The Shadows / The
Way Of All Flesh / Chinese Whispers /
Soon Ripe, Soon Rotten / Gather The
Shattered / My Soul Flayed / Bare
CHIAROSCURO, Mascot M7015-2
(1996)
The Colours Still Unwinds / Scarlet Man
/ In The Flesh / Clarity / Diced /
Chiaroscuro / Black Widower / Fools
Paradise / King Of Misrule / Gods
Thoughts

CREMATION (HOLLAND)

CREMATION issued the demos 'Waiting
For The Sun' in 1995, 'Rapture' in 1998
and 'Sempiternal Hatred' in 1999 before
sharing space with PULVERIZER for the
split EP 'Futile Felicity'.
CREMATION men Michiel and Benito
founded NAIL OF CHRIST with vocalist
Henri in 2001 releasing the demo 'To
Challenge The Source Of Chaos'.
In April 2000 guitarist Paul Baayens
teamed up with the reformed
THANATOS.

Singles/EPs:
Futile Existence / Deceptive Felicity,
(2000) (Split EP with PULVERIZER)

CREMATORIUM (Whittier, CA, USA)
Line-Up: Dan Tracy (vocals), Mark
Uehlein (guitar), Alex Villalobos (bass),
Frank Escalon (drums)

Californian Deathsters, founded by the
Escalon brothers Frank and Marvin in
1990, debuted with the 1993 demo 'Dark
Manifestation'. The follow up cassette
'Unholy Massacre' led to the 'Epicidiums
Of The Damned' album.
CREMATORIUM offered their homage to
JUDAS PRIEST by including their version
of 'Breaking The Law' to the 'Hell Bent
For Metal' tribute album.

Albums:
EPICEDIUMS OF THE DAMNED,
Crematorium (1997)
Lands Plagued / Disbelief / Coma Of
The Soul / Unholy Massacre / Corporate
Malignance / Painless, Lifeless /
Sufferance Of Life / Unfound Face /
Dismal

CREMATORY (SWEDEN)
Line-Up: Stefan Harvik (vocals), Urban
Skytt (guitar), Johan Hansson (bass),
Mats Nordrup (drums)

CREMATORY drummer Mats Nordrup
was formerly with GENERAL SURGERY
and was a founder member of Goregrind
act REGURGITATE. Guitarist Urban Skytt
and bassist Johan Hansson have now
formed a new version of
REGURGITATED.
Former URA KAIPA man Mikael Lindevall
was also in the ranks of CREMATORY
before he joined PROBOSCIS.

Singles/EPs:
Into Celephaes / Chunks Of Flesh /
Denial / On Consecrated Ground, MBR
MANGLED 4 (1992)

CREMATORY
Photo : Darius Ramzani

CRIMSON THORN
(Minneapolis, MN, USA)
Line-Up: Luke Renno (vocals / bass),
Miles Sunde (guitar), Andy Kopesky
(guitar), Kevin Sundberg (drums)

Christian Death Metal act CRIMSON
THORN heralded their coming with the
demo session 'The Plagued'. At this
stage the band comprised vocalist /
bassist Luke Renno, guitarists Miles
Sunde and Paul Jongeward and drummer
Dave Quast. By the time of recording the
debut album 'Unearthed' Quast had
made way for Kevin Sundberg. This
album, originally released on the Atomic
label would be re-released by the R.E.X.
concern with different artwork and once
more by Morphine Records coupled with
tracks from 'The Plagued' demo.
The 'Dissection' album, originally issued
on Morphine but later remarketed by Little
Rose Productions, includes a cover
version of STRYPER's 'Loud n' Clear'.
CRIMSON THORN would contribute a
track to the 2001 LIVING SACRIFICE
tribute album.

Albums:
UNEARTHED, Atomic (1995)
Unearthed / Decrepit / Cultivate Decay /
Ignorant Self / Your Carcass /
Asphyxiated / Malignant Masters /
Defaced / Comatose / Imminent Wrath /
No Exceptions
DISSECTION, Morphine (1999)
Beaten Beyond / Eternal Life / Deepest
Affliction / Dissection / Putrid
Condemnation / All Authority / Blood
Letting / My Salvation / I Ask / 2nd
Timothy / Grave Of Rebirth / Psallo /
Loud n' Clear

CRIPPLE BASTARDS (ITALY)
Line-Up: Giulio The Bastard (vocals),
Alberto The Crippler (guitar),
Fulvio Hatebox (guitar), Andrea (bass),
Al Mazzotti (drums)

Asti based Grindcore act CRIPPLE
BASTARDS have over the years forged
alliances with many of their international
colleagues on a series of split singles.
The group came into being when
teenagers vocalist / guitarist Alberto (16)
and drummer Giulio (13) teamed up with
the Punk-Metal band GRIMCORPSES.
By 1988 an extreme Metal direction had
been decided upon and a name switch to
CRIPPLE BASTARDS highlighted this
shift. The group also put in their debut
'gig' at a friends birthday party.
The band did get to record a demo in
1989 (a blistering 25 songs in six
minutes!) but somehow neglected to
distribute it. The two protagonists started
a side Hardcore band DISSONANCE in

1990 together with friend Luigi on drums. This unit would see the first occasion Giulio took up lead vocals. Both DISSONANCE and CRIPPLE BASTARDS would share cassette space with K.S.G. (yet another extra-curricular project of Giulio and Alberto - this time a sombre ambient affair) for a three-way demo tape with CRIPPLE BASTARD laying down no less than 64 tracks. This tape would be given away free by the group members at other bands gigs.

In 1991 DISSONANCE folded but K.S.G. scored five tracks included on the 'Killed By The Machinery Of Sorrow' compilation. CRIPPLE BASTARDS meantime cut their second demo. The band put in their first proper gig proudly announcing that, bar a handful of determined fans, they cleared the venue! 1992 saw CRIPPLE BASTARDS inaugural vinyl appearance with the band donating two tracks from their 1991 demo to the 'Son Of Bblleeauurrggh!' compilation on Slap A Ham Records. In August the band, still a duo of Giulio on vocals along with drums and Alberto on guitar, put in their first foreign show at the Croatian 'Melody' festival. Shortly after the act drafted drummer Michele Delemont but would remain without a bass player for some time to come. Not content with resting on their laurels Giulio and Alberto struck up another side outing HARSH FEELINGS.

Two shared tape releases emerged on the bands own E.U. label in 1993. Live recordings from their Croatian festival performance were allied with tracks from Belgians AGATHOCLES and another 40 demo tracks featured alongside DARK SEASON songs. The band somehow managed to squeeze no less than 44 tracks onto their shared 1993 7" single with Spain's VIOLENT HEADACHE. These tracks were recorded in 1991 as a duo of Giulio and Alberto on a small cassette recorder in the band's rehearsal room. Although he appears on the sleeve artwork drummer Michele did not perform although he did feature on the rare 1993 split single with W.B.I. Early material from the bands GRIMCORPSES era was released on a cassette with more recent CRIPPLE BASTARDS, HARSH FEELINGS and FILTHY CHARITY material.

The band, back to a deadly duo minus Michele, would also manage to put in live dates in Germany. Other recordings that year included 6 new originals for a split single with SOCIAL GENOCIDE, 5

PATARENI cover versions for a tribute album 'Obrade', an AGATHOCLES cover for the 'Kill Your Idols' compilation and even a BEATLES cover.

1994 would prove a taxing year for the band as Alberto struggled with a drug problem. Nevertheless split releases with PSYCHOTIC NOISE and SENSELESS APOCALYPSE. The EP 'Frammenti Di Vita' comprised solely of cover versions with CRIPPLE BASTARDS paying homage to extreme Italian acts such as INDEGESTI, WRETCHED, NEGAZIONE, NABAT, UNDERAGE, IMPACT and BLUE VOMIT. A further split 7" on the German Regurgitated Semen label, in collaboration with PATARENI, included a cover of the KING CRIMSON classic '21st Century Schizoid Man'. However, after these songs were laid to rest Michele quit the band but was persuaded to stay on in order to conclude recording commitments. CRIPPLE BASTARDS did put in a batch of Italian and German gigs with a stand in drummer. Before the end of the year CRIPPLE BASTARD's tenure without a bassist was ended when Brazilian Eduardo joined the band.

In 1995 a whole slew of split singles arrived with PSYCHOTIC NOISE on the Belgian Grinding Madness label, with CAPITALIST CASUALTIES on the American Wiggy Bits double 10" release and PREPARATION H for another American label Vicious Interference. With Michele still hanging on the band recorded a mass of material throughout the year that would see the light of day on the full length 'Your Lies In Check' album, a split album with SUPPRESSION and yet more split singles. Some material was also bootlegged in South America on a single split with WRETCHED.

CRIPPLE BASTARDS finally replaced Michele with ex-ARTURO man Paulo. An impromptu live jam with Giulio gusting for IMPACT would surface on a split 10" single with PATARENI.

Eduardo returned to Brazil in May of 1996 and a temporary replacement was found in the form of ARTURO's Stefano. This liaison soon broke down as both ARTURO men departed. CRIPPLE BASTARDS remained as a duo until STUNTPLASTICPARK man Gaba made an entrance. The state would intervene though and after just two shows Gaba was forced out in order to fulfil his military service duties. Paulo would deputize in the studio to cut some tracks for a HUSKER DU tribute album on Beserk

Records before quitting again. The group laid down some more material with Giulio on drums once more until former WELCH and ACREDINE man Walter Dr. Tomas took the post. A new bassist was found in Gigi Pacino.

The new look quartet would perform at some chaotic Italian Hardcore festivals before a date in Slovenia before recording tracks for a split single with I.R.F. Further gigs at Italian Punk festivals followed before Pacino broke ranks. More live shows, this time in Austria, were completed without a bassist but upon their return Panz took the four string position.

As 1997 turned into 1998 there were rumblings of disquiet from founder member Alberto. Although persuaded to stay the course for the next round of recordings by the time of CRIPPLE BASTARDS support tour of Italy to Brazilians RATOS DE PORAO it was with ex-HATEBOX man Fulvio on guitar alongside Alberto. Yet again line up problems would blight the band with Panz being fired and Alberto finally packing his bags. ENTROPIA drummer Andrea duly filled the bass slot for a tour of Slovenia, Croatia, Czech Republic and Germany. A series of Belgian shows would see Alberto returning for these and the next round of studio recordings.

1999 predictably saw CRIPPLE BASTARDS in turmoil once again as Dr. Tomas made his exit. Al Mazzotti of Punk band STINKING POLECATS was pulled in for live work although Dr. Tomas remained in place for recordings. Tragedy would strike in the midst of European dates though as the band was involved in a serious crash which injured Mazzotti's hand.

Singles/EPs:
Useful- Useless / Conceptual Indistinction / Zakljucenje / Look In Your Dish / Toxic Sex / Without A Shadow Of Justice / Shame Of You / Ecologicial Carnage / Flagged Pain / Fucked…Original Expressions / Standing Violent / Civilized Torment / Resumption! / Thick Glasses Division / HC Funeral / Incurableness Of A Stigmatization / Sick Of Pleasure / I.H.P. / Far Away From My Best Friends / Self Instruction / Against The Stream / Stealthy Loneliness / Rending Aphthous Fevers / What Can Be… / Animal-Respect / Outside World / Stylized Fear / A Sort Of Repulsion Called 'Intelligence' / My Last Hours / Windows / Mortuary

Slab / Irenic / Rigid Freedom / Sincere Smiles / Act Like A Rose / Psychosexuality / Breathing For Fun / Something Wrong / Equality / Alternative- Dressed Puppets / Turn The Corner / Sarcastic Gloom / Allegorical Masturbations / I Dare You, Psychomania (1991) (7" split single with VIOLENT HEADACHE)
Paranoic / Without A Shadow Of Justice / Round Table / T.L.O.H. / War Spoils / Bane / Frightened-Neglected / What I Thought, Useless USE 001 (1993) ('War Spoils' 7" split single with W.B.I. 500 copies)
S.L.U.T.S. / Living Monuments / Radije Volim… / Offensive Death / 0:01 / Bonds Of Enmity / Miniaturized Eden / Prisons / The Opinion Of The Poor / Stimmung / Imposed Mortification / Vital Dreams / More Frustrations / Falling Wish / My Serenity - Dealing With A Pressing Problem, A-Wat (1993) ('Life's Built On Thoughts' EP)
Life In General / Disagreeable Selections / 21st Century Schizoid Man / Hydrophobic Web / Mass Media / Grimcorpses, Regurgitated Semen (1993) ('21st Century Schizoid Man'. 7" split single with PATERNI)
Spero Venga La Guerra / Incubo Di Morte / Troia / Sporca Naia / Mass Media / Vaffanculo / La Nostra Violenza, Ecocentric (1993) ('Frammenti Di Vita' EP)
Split, A.D.P. (199-) (7" split single with $OCIAL GENOCIDE)
Images Of War - Images Of Pain / My Mind Invades / Blue Penguins / Italia Di Merda / Peasants / Self Justice Punks / 1974 / Something Wrong / Walk Away / Ragman, View Beyond (199-) (7" split single with SENSELESS APOCALYPSE)
Split, Grinding Madness (199-) (7" split single with PSYCHOTIC NOISE)
Split, Vicious Interference (199-) (7" split single with PREPARATION H)
Split, Upground (199-) (7" split single with CARCASS GRINDER)
Split, Bovine (199-) (7" split single with SUPPRESSION)
Split, Bootleg (199-) (7" split single with WRETCHED)
Split, (199-) (10" split single with PATERNI)
Massacrecore, Denied A Custom (1997)
Good Taste In Assholism, MCR Company (1998) (7" split single with I.R.F.)
Dawn Of Ecology, Havin' A Spazz (1999) (7" split single with POPULAR EASY LISTENING MUSIC ENSEMBLE)

Extreme Glorification Of Violence, Nat (1999)
Live To Hate People, Applequince (199-) (3" CD single)
Split, S.O.A. (199-) (7" split single with COMRADES)
Il Grande Silenzio, Rhetoric (199-)

Albums:
BEST CRIMES, (199-)
YOUR LIES IN CHECK, Ecocentric (1997)
Being Ripped Off / Without A Shadow Of Justice / Prejudices And Walls / Images Of War - Images Of Pain / Imposed Mortification / Prospettive Limitate / Intelligence Means... / Disagreeable Selections / Caught In Your Silence / Prisons / Irenic / September 18th 1993 / A Dispetto Della Discrezione / Watching Through My Chaos / Newscast Slave / Round Table / Italia Di Merda / The Outside World / My Mind Invades / Danas Je Dan Za Lijencine / More Frustrations / Stimmung / Ghiacciaio / What I Thought / Negative Fractures / Ratings / Paranoic / Frightened-Neglected / 1974 / Milicija Die! / Walk Away / Nichilismo Ampliato / Vital Dreams / Blue Penguins / Bonds Of Enmity / Ragman / Windows / Rending Aphthous Fevers / Bane / Living Monuments / War Spoils / We Can Work It Out / Self Justice Punks / Incorporated Grave / D.S.S. (Double Scented Shit) / Sexist Society... Must Destroy It! / The Last Shipwrecked / Intransigent Simpathy / Polizia, Una Razza De Estinguere / Cormorant / Life In General / Hydrophobic Web / Padroni / Useful-Useless / More Restrictions. Why? / Miniaturized Eden / Something Wrong / 21st Century Schizoid Man / Devozioni? / Nothing On Earth / Invito Alla Riservatezza / Come E Falso Dio / Radije Volim... / S.L.U.T.S. / Grimcorpses / Offensive Death / My Serenity / Dealing With A Pressing Problem / Necrospore

CRONIC DISORDER

(Cherryville, NC, USA)
Line-Up: Doug Canipe (vocals / bass), Chip Whitesides (guitar), Brad Sellars (drums)

Retro Death Thrash act dubbed by themselves as "The drunkest band in the world". Self released the debut album 'Dead To The World' which unusually featured a Death Metal workout of a JOHNNY CASH song. Danish label Mighty Music would re-release the album under a new title of 'Torture Test' with all new artwork. The original intention was for the band to record new material as additional tracks for the re-release, but guitarist Chip Whiteside broke his hand, scuppering these plans.
CRONIC DISORDER have also cut a version of the KISS track 'All American Man' for a tribute album.

Albums:
DEAD TO THE WORLD, (2000)
TORTURE TEST, Mighty Music (2001)

THE CROWN (SWEDEN)

Line-Up: Johan Lindstrandt (vocals), Marcus Sunesson (guitar), Marko Trevonen (guitar), Magnus Osfelt (bass), Janne Saarenpaa (drums)

Death Metal act previously titled CROWN OF THORNS under which title they released the albums 'The Burning' and 'Eternal Death'. Persistent legal pressure from the American AOR act of the same name forced a name change. With their new simplified title the band toured Europe in early 1998 on a billing with SACRILEGE resulting directly in a deal with American label Metal Blade for third album 'Hell Is Here'.
To promote the record THE CROWN embarked on further European dates on a Black Metal festival package bill of IMPALED NAZARENE, EMPEROR, MORBID ANGEL and PECCATUM. A further cover version ensued, this time a crack at BATHORY's 'Burnin' Leather' for the 'Power From The North' compilation.
THE CROWN toured Europe in December 2000 as part of an almighty Death Metal package that included ENSLAVED, MORBID ANGEL, BEHEMOTH, HYPNOS and DYING FETUS.

Albums:
HELL IS HERE, Metal Blade (1998)
The Poison / At The End / 1999 - Revolution 666 / Dying Of The Heart / Electric Night / Black Lightning / The Devil And The Darkness / Give You Hell / Body And Soul / Mysterion / Death By My Side
DEATHRACE KING, Metal Blade (2000)
Deathexplosion / Executioner (Slayer Of The Light) / Back From The Grave / Devil Gate Ride / Vengeance / Angel Rebel / I Won't Follow / Blitzkrieg

Witchcraft / Dead Man's Song / Total Satan / Killing Star (Superbia Luxuria XXX)

CROWN OF THORNS (SWEDEN)
Line-Up: Johan Lindstrandt (vocals), Marcus Sunesson (guitar), Marko Trevonen (guitar), Magnus Osfelt (bass), Janne Saarenpaa (drums)

Not to be confused with Jean Beouvoir's American Melodic Rock act, Sweden's CROWN OF THORNS, founded in 1990 by ex-IMPIOUS vocalist Johan Lindstrandt and very much in the Grindcore mould, are a much heavier proposition altogether. CROWN OF THORNS first hit the tape trading scene with an impressive demo, 1993's 'Forever Heaven Gone'. Shortly after it's release the band got to play the Swedish Hultsfred festival alongside ENTOMBED and IGGY POP but lost guitarist Robert Österberg to Punk act ÖLHÄVERS. His replacement was Marcus Sunesson who cut his teeth with the 1994 demo 'Forget The Light'. This tape scored them a deal with Black Sun Records for the debut album 'The Burning'. CROWN OF THORNS also made their mark on the SLAYER tribute album 'Slaytanic Slaughter' contributing their take on 'Mandatory Suicide'.
The band's sophomore outing 'Eternal Death' continued the trend and yet again the Swedes were adding to another tribute album, this time nailing a cover of 'Arise' for the SEPULTURA homage 'Sepultural Feast'.
Continued threat of litigation from the American CROWN OF THORNS resulted in the band adopting the title THE CROWN in 1997. Undaunted the band toured Europe in early 1998 on a billing with SACRILEGE resulting directly in a deal with American label Metal Blade for third album 'Hell Is Here'.

Albums:
THE BURNING, Black Sun (1995)
Of Good And Evil / Soulicide Demon-Might / Godless / The Lord Of The Rings / I Crawl / Forever Heaven Gone / Earthborn / Neverending Dreams / Night Of The Swords / Candles / Forget The Light
ETERNAL DEATH, Black Sun (1997)
Angels Die / Beautiful Evil Soul / In Bitterness And Sorrow / The Black Heart / World Within / The Serpent Garden / Kill (The Priest) / Misery Speaks /

Hunger / Death Of God

CRUSHER (FRANCE)
Line-Up: Crass (vocals), Pascal Thomas (guitar), Raph Jouguet (bass), Charly Meniz (drums)

Previously known as FRAYEURS, under this title the band who would be CRUSHER formed in 1987, releasing two demos 'Frayeur Or Die' and 'A Step Forward' before changing the band name in 1992.
A new demo, 'Collective Hypnosis', secured a support slot to PROTECTOR on their German tour and a deal from Noise Records; debut album 'Corporal Punishment' arriving in the stores during 1993.

Albums:
CORPORAL PUNISHMENT, Noise N0205-2 (1993)
Collective Hypnosis / Corporal Punishment / Fury Settles / Sense Of Powerlessness / All For A Holy Cause / Adventure For Sale / Actions Speak Louder Than Words / Infanticide / Immigrant Exploitation / Profit Of a Billion Deaths / Modernism Keeps Killing
UNDERMINE, Noise N0231-3 (1993)
Storm Brewing / Undermine / Sell The Vaticans Wealth / The Right To Be Different / In Your Face / Hell On Earth / Man Submits
UNDERDRIVE, Semetary (1994)

CRUST (GERMANY)
Line-Up: Marco (vocals), Matthias (guitar), Sven (guitar), Gunnar (bass), Sebastian (drums)

CRUST are a traditional Death Metal from the north of Germany.

Albums:
SHAPES OF INNER URGE, Invasion (1996)
Intro / The River Will Flow / Decomposition / Grass / Menace My Logical Mind / Land Of Behind / Color Code: Red / Drop Dead / First Breath / Darkside

CRY HAVOC (FINLAND)
Line-Up: Kaapro Ikonen (vocals), Jouni Lilja (guitar), Risto Lipponen (guitar), Kari Myöhänan (bass), Pauli Tolvahen (drums)

CRY HAVOC began their musical journey entitled PREPROPHECY issuing the Death Metal demos 'A Tomb Of Sanity' in 1993 and it's follow up 'Season Of Sorrows'. A name switch to RAVENSFALL saw the addition of ABSURDUS rhythm section bassist Taneli Nyholm and drummer Matti Roiha in 1996. However, when ABSURDUS were signed by the British Candlelight label Nyholm and Roiha disembarked back to their priority act. (Nyholm, billed as 'Daniel Stuka', would later join BABYLON WHORES).

A deal was struck with a Singapore based label and RAVENSFALL began preparation for recording of a debut album. Fate intervened when the label in question folded leaving the band high and dry. Noted label Spinefarm came to their rescue and the band, now billed as CRYHAVOC, cut their debut entitled 'Sweet Briars'.

Sales of the album were high (no doubt aided by the artistic sleeve photo cover imagery) and 'Pitch Black Blues' emerged in 1999.

Albums:
SWEET BRIARS, Nuclear Blast NB 326-2 (1998)
Bloodtie / Repent (Whore) / Come With Me / Wolfdance / Pagan Uprise / I Fade Away / Armageddon Y'Know / Misanthropy
PITCH BLACK BLUES, Spinefarm (1999)
Cryscythe / Metamorphosis / The Wind / Snowsong / Spree / The Serpent And Eve / Wild At Heart / Pitch Black Ink

CRYOGENIC (GERMANY)
Line-Up: Sven (vocals), Johanna (vocals), Harpokrates (guitar), Imperus (guitar), Jormundgander (bass), Theehomok (keyboards), Trismegistos (drums)

Berlin's CRYOGENIC had their debut album 'Celephais' produced by the noted figure of Harris Johns. The band, then in 1993 with early members singer Ruben and guitarist Niddhoggar, heralded their arrival with the demo 'Ignis Occultus In'.

Albums:
CELEPHAIS, Solistitium SOL034 (1999)
Celephais - Overture / Wanderer / Die Rueckkehr / Fimbulwinter / Nactwache / Ignis Occultus In... / Processia Nocturna - Teil I / Processia Nocturna - Teil I /

Celephais / Celephais - Finale
EGO NORIA, (199-)
Analysis / Directionally One / Death By Misadventure / Conspiracy Theory / Have My Head / Fall On / T.Y.T.D. (Too Young To Die) / Full Grown State / Stalemate / Redneck / Shock Value
SUSPENDED ANIMATION, (199-)
One Minute Hit / Mind Over Soul / Severed / Junc / Death Becomes You / Mary Belle / Destructive Minds / Numerical Superiority / Bring It On

CRYPTIC (GERMANY)

Albums:
CRYPTIC, Noise Variations (1998) (Split album with FESTERING SALIVA and VIVESECTION)
Shrinkhead Butt Plug / A Gulp Of Putrid Body Liquids / Matul Isle / Bodyshaper / Steel Erection
CIRCULAR SAW FETISH, Noise Variations (1998)

CRYPTICAL REALM (BELGIUM)

CRYPTICAL REALM opened proceedings with the 1996 demo 'Jus Caedis' followed up by a live cassette 'Celtic Rage'.

The 'La Tené' EP was limited to a mere 100 copies.

Although CRYPTICAL REALM is firmly centred upon multi instrumentalist Bart Uytterhaegen, other contributing musicians included the soprano vocals of Wendy Supere, guest vocals from Sven of ANESTHESY and Hugo Tack on bass and keyboards.

Singles/EPs:
Death Wish / Fall Into Your Darkest Dream / Golgota (Live) / The Celtic Rage (Live), (1998) ('La Tené' EP)

Albums:
OPUS INFINITY, (1999)
Intro / Imman Curaig Maldruin Inso / The Excalibur Sonate: The Lady In The Lake / The Three Nights Of Samhain / Opus Infinity / The Excalibur Sonate II: The Uther Pendragon Pact

CRYPTIC REVELATION (JAPAN)

Albums:
THE TRUTH IS OUT THERE, (1999)

CRYPT OF KERBEROS (SWEDEN)
Line-Up: Christian Eriksson (vocals),
Johan Löhnroth (guitar), Peter Petersson
(guitar), Stefan Karlsson (bass), Jessica
Stranbdell (keyboards), Mikael Sjöberg
(drums)

Founded in 1990 under the original
moniker of MACRODEX, releasing a
demo cassette under that title, the group
transformed itself into CRYPT OF
KERBEROS. After the release of the
'Visions Beyond Darkness' single guitarist
Johan Löhnroth and drummer Mikael
Sjöberg split and Jonas Strandell and
Mattias Bough were drafted in to fill the
respective vacancies.
Although CRYPT OF KERBEROS issued
a follow up single in 1992 and the 'World
Of Myths' album in 1995, the group has
now folded, guitarist Peter Petersson
becoming a member of ARCANA.

Singles/EPs:
Visions Beyond Darkness / Darkest
Rites, Sunabel SUNABEL 001 (1991)
Cyclone Of Insanity / The Ancient War,
Adipocere AR004 (1992)

Albums:
WORLD OF MYTHS, Adipocere CDAR
913 (1995)
The Canticle / Cyclone Of Insanity /
Dream... / Stormbringer / The Ancient
War / Nocturnal Grasp / The Sleeping
God / World Of Myths

CRYPTOPSY (CANADA)
Line-Up: Mike DiSavo (vocals),
Jon Levasseur (guitar), Alex Auburn
(guitar), Eric Langlois (bass),
Flo Mounier (drums)

Montreal's CRYPTOPSY was created by
erstwhile NECROSIS personnel vocalist
Lord Worm, guitarist Steve Thibault and
renowned speed drummer Flo Mounier
together with former REACTOR guitarist
Dave Galea. The band was rounded off
by bassist Kevin Weagle for the opening
four song demo session 'Ungentle
Exhumation'.
CRYPTOPSY's debut album, 'Blasphemy
Made Flesh produced by Rod Shearer,
was issued in 1994 after which Galea
broke ranks to be superseded by Jon
Levasseur. Weagle also left the fold as
CRYPTOPSY pulled in replacement
Martin Fergusson.
The band signed to the Swedish Wrong
Again concern for the follow up 'Non So

Vile', produced by OBLIVEON guitarist
Pierre Rémillard. Further line up
tribulations saw the exit of both
Fergusson and Thibault. Eric Langlois
was enrolled as bassist as CRYPTOPSY
cut their third album, this time for
Germany's Century Media label, as a
quartet. Guitarist Miguel Roy was added
after recording.
CRYPTOPSY suffered another major
blow when Lord Worm decided to retire
from the band. However, this move was
on good terms as the previous incumbent
introduced the band to his replacement,
ex-INFESTATION vocalist Mike DiSavo.
Promoting 'Whisper Supremacy', which
featured Lord Worm on backing vocals,
CRYPTOPSY undertook their inaugural
American tour sharing billing with NILE,
OPPRESSOR and GORGUTS. Further
shows in 1999 saw Roy out of the picture
replaced by former SEISME six stringer
Alex Auburn as the band hit the road in
the States for another round, this time
with Poles VADER. The group would also
put in a European showing at the
prestigious Dutch Dynamo festival as well
as dates in Japan.
Promoting fourth album 'And Then You'll
Beg' witnessed the 'Pain Cometh' tour
with support from CANDIRA.

Albums:
BLASPHEMY MADE FLESH, Invasion
(1994)
Defenstration / Abigor / Open Face
Surgery / Serial Messiah / Born Headless
/ Swine Of The Cross / Gravaged (A
Cryptopsy) / Memories Of Blood / Mutant
Christ / Pathological Frolic
NONE SO VILE, Wrong Again (1996)
Crown Of Horns / Slit Your Guts /
Graves Of Your Fathers / Dead And
Dripping / Benedictive Convulsions /
Phobophile / Lichmistress / Orgiastic
Disembowelment
WHISPER SUPREMACY, Century Media
(1998)
Emaciate / Cold Hate, Warm Blood /
Loathe / White Worms / Flame To The
Surface / Depths You've Fallen /
Faceless Unknown / Serpent's Coil
AND THEN YOU'LL BEG, Century
Media (2000)
...And Then It Passes / We Bleed /
Voice Of Unreason / My Prodigal Sun /
Shroud / Soar And Envision Sore Vision
/ Equivalent Equilibrium / Back To The
Worms / Screams Go Unheard

CRYSTAL AGE (SWEDEN)
Line-Up: Oscar Dronjac (vocals / guitar),
Moses Jonathon Elfström (guitar),
Fredrick Larsson (bass), Hans Nilsson
(drums)

CRYSTAL AGE, a Death Metal band
forged by ex-CEREMONIAL OATH
vocalist / guitarist Oscar Dronjac, covered
METALLICA's 'Damage Inc.' for the 1994
Black Sun Records tribute album 'Metal
Militia', before unleashing their debut
album the following year.
Interestingly, a band created by Dronjac
and bassist Frederick Larsson purely for
fun in 1993 was later to overtake
CRYSTAL AGE. The trad-Metal
renaissance band HAMMERFALL, which
included Dronjac's erstwhile
CEREMONIAL OATH colleague drummer
Jesper Strömbold (Also of IN FLAMES)
as well as members of DARK
TRANQUILITY, exploded into the national
German charts during 1997 with their
debut album 'Glory To The Brave'.

Albums:
FAR BEYOND DIVINE, Vic VIC2 (1995)
Far Beyond Divine Horizons / Fortune
And Glory / The Beauty Of Evil / Son Of
Time / Wind Walker / Crystals Of The
Wise / On Blooded Wings / Tempt Not
Thy Maker / Star Destroyer / Retaliation

C.S.S.O. (JAPAN)
Line-Up: Narutoshi (vocals), Sumito
(guitar), Takeshi (drums)

Notorious Grindcore act C.S.S.O.
(CLOTTED SYMMETRIC SEXUAL
ORGAN) began life entitled GUSTRIC
JUICE with a line up of vocalist Narutoshi,
guitarist Sumito, drummer Takashi and
Gan-Tyan. The band's singer would
depart for MAGGOTY CORPSE whilst
Sumito teamed up with GRUDGE.
However, the pair would return to action
with GUSTRIC JUICE soon evolving the
band into ALTERNATIVE DEADBODY.
Under this new guise the band cut a
demo with MAGGOTY CORPSE
drummer Junji sessioning. Shortly after
recording the band morphed again into
C.S.S.O. pulling in EUTHANASIA
drummer Makato then Susumu.
During 1996 C.S.S.O. toured Europe
sharing billing with Poland's DEAD
INFECTION and Spain's
HAEMORRHAGE. This union resulted in
the release of a split EP in collusion with
DEAD INFECTION.

The band's shared EP in alliance with
Austria's MASTIC SCUM: RAPE included
versions of NAPALM DEATH's 'Control'
and CARCASS' 'Genital Grinder'. In 1998
Susumu made way for Takeshi.
2000 found the group appearing on the
'Transoriental X-Press' shared album
combined with French artists
DESECRATION and INFECTED PUSSY.
The year would also see the group's
debut European album release 'Nagrö
Läuxes VIII' on Germany's Morbid
Records.
C.S.S.O. would also contribute their
version of 'Cannibal Ballet' to the
IMPETIGO tribute album 'Wizards Of
Gore'. Further split EP's ensued with
Australians THE BLOODY VICE and
Sweden's BIRDFLESH.

Singles/EPs:
Tijikuwa Hejimagari / Bra Bara Man /
I'm Sorry I Was Born / Boric Acid
Dumpling, Morbid (1993) (7" split EP
with THE MEATSHITS)
Putrid Cadaver Part II / Zombie Fuck /
Nuclear Karate Man, M.M.I. (1994)
(7" split EP with VIVISECTION)
Alkanoid / Itch / Putrid Cadaver Part II /
Zombie Fuck, Gulli (1994) (7" split EP
with BLAST OF SILENCE)
Split, Underground Warder (1997)
(7" split EP with DEMISOR)
Genital Grinder / Slithering Maceration
Of Ulcerous Facial Tissue (Sampling
version) / General Surgery / Fear?! (70's
mix) / Regurgitate / Control, Ohne
Maulkorb Productions (1997) (7" split EP
with MASTIC SCUM and RAPE)
Baka Sen / Worst, Morbid (1998)
('Worst' 7" split single with DEAD
INFECTION)
Hungry Urinary Urn, Bizarre Leprous
Productions (1999) (7" split EP with
MALIGNANT TUMOUR, NEGLIGENT
URGE COLLAPSE and CATASEXUAL
URGE MOTIVATION)
Living Dead A Go Go, The Spew
Records (2001)
(7" split EP with THE BLOODY VICE)
Split, Ubble Gubble (2001)
(7" split with BIRDFLESH)

Albums:
C.S.S.O., Relapse (1997)
Shake It Up Bokan / Diversion Of
Former Customary Trite Composition /
Don't Play Guitar Sitting On Chair / Long
Hair Mathematics Teacher / Hey Tonny!
(a.k.a. Anal Bloody Anal) / Eclectic Birth
GRINDWORK, Grindwork (1999) (Split

album with NASUM, VIVESECTION and RETALIATION)
NAGRÖ LÄUXES VIII, Morbid (2000)
Daddy's Home / Explanatory Notes Of Pilferige / 256 / Very, Very Blue Belly / Perversion / Kyushikanga / Spartan / Intro / Bara Bara Man / Richly Coloured Moist Elegy / I'd Chokyo / Alkanoid / Rolling The Zen / Psycho 65 / Boric Acid Dumpling / Penisnatcher / The Song Without Rice / A Trigonometrical Of Mokuba / Intro / Zombie Fuck
TRANSORIENTAL X-PRESS, Necrophile Productions (2000) (Split album with DESECRATION and INFECTED PUSSY)
LIVE, Riot City Japan (2000)
Into The Dogma / Into The Dead / (Japanese title) / (Japanese title) / Terrorize / 305 / Hail Impetigo / The Kill / I Hope You Die In A Hotel Fire / Impro Session / 893 K / Alkanoid
ARE YOU EXCREMENTS, Morbid (2001)

CUCUMIS SATIVUS (GERMANY)
Line-Up: Markus Söllner (vocals), Volker Meissner (guitar), Boris Kluge (keyboards), Jürgen Kämmler (drums)

Punk Death Metal band. Released two demos under the name of GORGON GLASS before a name switch in 1994 to CUCUMIS SATIVUS as more NWoBHM and Psychedelic influences crept in.

Albums:
AN EROTIC FUNERAL, Cucumis Sativus CS010194 (1994)
Flowers In The Sea / River Of No Return / Return Of God / Twilight Symphony / Wrong / Slow Psychic Terror/ Poem / Mental Suffering / Lovesickness / Slow Psychic Terror ('91 version)

CUTTHROAT (JAPAN)
Line-Up: Mirai (vocals), Shinichi (guitar), Yasuyuki (bass), Youhei (drums)

CUTTHROAT was a 1999 project forged by the alliance of two of Japan's most esteemed extreme acts SIGH and ABIGAIL. CUTTHROAT signed to Greek label Iso666 for the subtly titled 'Rape, Rape, Rape' album.

Albums:
RAPE, RAPE, RAPE, Iso666 (2000)
HATE BREEDS RAGE, (2001)
Nothing To Give / What A Mess / Power Place / Our Father / Keeplock / Hate Breeds Rage / Hard Way / Want No Longer / This Would / I Never Wanted / 'How Much For That Weed, Fool'

CYANOTIC (DENMARK)
Line-Up: Jan Rasmussen (vocals), Jacob Krogholt (guitar), Martin Olsen (guitar), Claus Larsen (bass), Niels Jørgenson (drums)

Metal act CYANOTIC issued a brace of demos prior to self financing their 'Sapphire Season' album produced by ex INVOCATOR man Jacob Hansen. The album saw a later release licensed through Nordic Metal Records.

Albums:
SAPPHIRE SEASON, Nordic Metal NMCD1096 (1996)
A Mirage To Cherish / Solitary King / Inside The Avalanche Maze / Dethroned / Embryonic Wonder / Echoes In The Wasteland / Forest Of Oblivion / Sapphire Sea / Salvation Accomplished

CYBERGRIND

Side project of MORTIFICATION guitarist Michael Carlisle.

Albums:
TRANSCEND, (2000)

CYBORG (DENMARK)
Line-Up: J. Mann (vocals), B. Lund (guitar), J. Petersen (guitar), K. Johansen (bass), J. Bonnesen (drums)

CYBORG were created in 1993 with an unlikely line-up of the bizarrely titled Crusher Of Non-Intelligent Livechips on vocals, guitarists Mad Dog Process Exterminator and Infernalizer Of Undeveloped Human Brains and drummer Infector of the New World. This group released the 1993 demo 'Cybernetic Orgasm'.
By 1996 only Crusher Of Non-Intelligent Livechips, more commonly known as J. Mann, was left, adding KONKHRA guitarist B. Lund and members of DETEST to regenerate CYBORG.

Albums:
CHRONICLES, Die Hard RRS951 (1996)
Cyberchrist / Falling / Chronicles / Father Of Lies / Sow The Child / Day Of The Dog / Powermind / Wrapped In Human Tissue

CYNIC (FL, USA)
Line-Up: Paul Masvidal (vocals / guitar),
Jason Gobel (guitar), Tony Choy (bass),
Sean Reinert (drums)

CYNIC were more noted for their
individual members contributions to other
acts.
Bassist Tony Choy contributed bass parts
to the ATHEIST album 'Unquestionable
Presence' before joining Dutch thrashers
PESTILENCE for their 'Testimony Of The
Ancients' album and following world tour.
Guitarist Paul Masvidal and drummer
Sean Reinert played on DEATH's 1992
album 'Human' then opted to join
DEATH's 1992 American and European
tour on a temporary basis.
Masvidal also contributed heavily to
MASTER's 'And On The Seventh Day
God Created Master' album. Guitarist
Jason   Gobel   guests   on
MONSTROSITY's 'Imperial Doom' album
and also filled in for live shows.
CYNIC recorded a 1992 three track demo
for Roadrunner Records. Following the
album release Masvidal reunited with
DEATH on a permanent basis.
Reinert joined GORDION KNOT but by
2000 was involved with AGHORA.
Malone also contributes to the debut
AGHORA album.

Albums:
FOCUS, Roadrunner RR 91692 (1993)
Veil Of Maya / Celestial Voyage / The
Eagle Nature / Sentiment / I'm But A
Wave To… / Uroboric Forms / Textures /
How Could I

DAARGESIN
(GERMANY)
Line-Up: Ingo (vocals / guitar / pan pipes), Jürgen (guitar), Thomas (bass), Festus (drums)

Death Metal act from Erlangen

Albums:
DAARGESIN, D&S DSR CD022 (1995)
Stonehenge / Daargesin / Powersound Tractor / Mendacity / Chaos / Blasphemy / Paranoya / Misanthropic Attitude / Maggots / The Death

DAEMON (SWEDEN)
Line-Up: Anders Lundemark (vocals / guitar), Morgan Pitt (bass), Nicke Andersson (drums)

Death Metal project convened by KONKHRA members together with ENTOMBED's Nicke Andersson. The album is produced by DISMEMBER's Fred Estby.

Albums:
SEVEN DEADLY SINS, Die Hard RRS947 (1996)
Sloth / Wrath / Greed / Lust / Gluttony / Pride / Envy / The Eight Sin

DAHMER (CANADA)
Line-Up: Sebastian Dionne (vocals / bass), Ti-Fred (guitar), Yvan (drums)

Canadian Death-Grindcore act with an uncompromising intent to shock. Named after one of the twentieth century's most infamous mass murderers DAHMER use the serial killer theme throughout all of their controversial releases. DAHMER began with a union in 1995 of guitarists Sebastian Dionne and John with drummer Yvan. Seb would switch instruments to bass. However, due to the guitarist's work commitments the band's debut split single was recorded minus John and indeed without any bass guitar. He would return after recording as DAHMER added second guitarist Ti-Fred. DAHMER issued a self titled demo and a three way split cassette shared with CARCASS GRINDER and DIARRHÉE MENTALE, the latter being Dionne's side project band.
DAHMER's line-up, minus John once more, settled down to the trio of Seb, Fred and Yvan with Seb handling bass and vocals.

A stream of split 7" singles would follow including alliances with SATURATION, I.R.F., APARTMENT 213, Spain's DENAK and fellow Canucks WADGE. The band's shared single with SUPPRESSION 'Let's Dance' on Germany's Yellow Dog label displayed DAHMER's wry sense of sick humour as the sleeve depicted a pair of severed feet. The '9 Trak' single, issued on the Canadian Spineless label, would be released with no less than three different covers.
The cover artwork to the 'Dahmerized' album was particularly horrific featuring a photograph of severed head, hands and genitalia. The album itself is made up of songs many of which are titled after notorious murderers.
Latterly DAHMER have mixed in political and social commentry in their lyrics alongside the tried and tested murder fixation.

Singles/EPs:
Dean Corll / Dahmer The Milwaukiller / Herman Webster Mudgett / Jonestown / V-Gang / Strong Or Weak Person?, Yellow Dog, (199-) ('Let's Dance' 7" split single with SUPPRESSION)
Bastards / T'as Raison / Heritage Front / David Berkowitz / Indiens / Tueurs En Série / Homophobes / Harvey Murray Glatman, Obnoxious Cadaver (1995) ('Bastards' 7" split single with UNDINISM)
Premières Nations / Serbert Mullin / William George Bonin / Randy Stephen Kraft / Thomas Hamilton / Harvey Murray Glatman / Friedrich Haarmann / Henry Lee Lucas / Edmund Emil Kemper III, Spineless (199-) ('9 Trak' 7" single)
Société Industrielle / Ta Religion... Tes Problèmes / Foncez, Slightly Fast (199-) ('Great Samu Is Back!!!' 7" split single with I.R.F.)
Pseudo Underground / Emportez Notre Race, Spineless (1998) (7" split single with SATURATION)
Marcel Petiot / Tact De Bonnes Raisons, Doomsday Machine (199-)
Consummateurs Leaders / Unabomber / James Oliver Huberty, (199-) (7" split single with JEAN X SEBERG)
Mes Ancêtres, Je M'En Sacre / Crock-O (Une Preséntation De Provigo), Trashart (199-) (7" split single with APARTMENT 213)
Donald Harvey / Peter Kurten / Carl Panzram, Spineless (199-) (7" split single with DENAK)
Split, Clean Plate (2000) (7" split single with WADGE)

Albums:
DAHMERIZED, Clean Plate P.O.B. 709 (199-)
The Hillside Stranglers/ Douglas Daniel Clark / Adolfo De Jesus De Constanzo / Mark Essex / John George Haigh / Albert Hamilton Fish / Jeanne Moulinet Weber / Simoneau / In, Cool, Branché, Sensass & Flyé / David Berkowitz / Bastards / Les Dieux De l'Underground / Gary Michael Heidnick / Just Another Dis-Clone Song / Tueurs En Série / Dennis Andrews Nilsen / Pedro Alfonso Lopez / Edward Gein / John Wayne Gacy / Positif
DAHMER, (199-) (Split album with FRANK AND THE BITCHES)

DAMNABLE (POLAND)

Singles/EPs:
Split, (1997) (7" split single with HAEMORRHAGE)

Albums:
INPERDITION, (199-)

DAMNATION (POLAND)
Line-Up: Les (vocals / guitar), Bart (guitar), Nergal (bass), Inferno (drums)

Black Death Metal act DAMNATION feature two members of BEHEMOTH: vocalist / guitarist Les and bassist Nergal. The band formed in 1991 releasing their first demo 'Everlasting Sickness' in 1993. A further tape, 'Forbidden Spaces', followed the next year which led to a deal with Polish label Pagan Records.
Following the debut album's release bassist Dagon was replaced by Nergal. 1997 saw DAMNATION cutting the track 'Porwany Obledem' in homage to Polish extreme Metal pioneers KAT. With DAMNATION's profile rising sharply Pagan Records would issue the band's 'Forbidden Spaces' demo as part of a split album shared with BEHEMOTH. An EP, 'Coronation', followed comprising three new tracks and a re-recording of 'Land Of Degradation'. The same year also saw the induction of former CONDEMNATION bass player Arthur. Touring Poland in April of 1998 DAMNATION formed part of a package bill with LUX OCCULTA and SACRIVERSUM. Further afield the band played at the German 'Fuck The Commerce II' festival and the Belgian 'With A Dragons Blaze' event.
Vocalist Les was to create a side project

titled HELL-BORN together with BEHEMOTH's Lord Ravenlock releasing an eponymous album.
In 2000 DAMNATION's latest release 'Resist' scored international distribution being released by Metal Mind in Poland, Cudgel Agency in Germany and Dark Realm in America. DAMNATION had now shaped up as a quartet of vocalist Raven, guitarists Les and Bart, bassist Holoc and drummer Varien.
More recently DAMNATION have spread their talents across the burgeoning tribute market, featuring on no less than two MORBID ANGEL tributes, donating 'Bleed For The Devil' to a Dwell Records album and 'Blasphemy Of The Holy Ghost' to a Hellfire effort. The band also appears on the Necropolis Records KING DIAMOND tribute with their take on 'A Mansion In Darkness' and offer 'Tribulation' to a No Mercy Records POSSESSED tribute compilation.

Singles/EPs:
Coronation / Spell Master / Sworn To The Darkside / The Land Of Degradation, Last Episode 007300-2 LEP (1997) ('Coronation' EP)

Albums:
REBORN, Pagan Moon CD 002 (1995)
Pagan Prayer - The Antichrist / The Land Of Degradation / Leaving Into New Reality / From Broken Cross (Bleeding Jesus) / Time Of Prophets / Infestation - Maldoror Is Dead / Forbidden Spaces / The Ruling Truth / Behind The Walls Of Tears / Reborn (Outro)
REBEL SOULS, Last Epitaph Productions LEP010 (1996)
Prelude To Rebellion / Who Your God Is / Son Of Fire / Rebel Souls / Azarath - Watching In Darkness / From The Abyssland / Deliverance / Might Returns
FORBIDDEN SPACES, Last Epitaph (1997) (Split album with BEHEMOTH)
RESIST, Cudgel Agency CUD007 (2000)
Your Pain Is Not For Me / In Resistance / Confession / Voices Of An Unknown Dimension / Absence In Humanity / Forsaken By Destiny / Against My Enemies / Invisible Force / Down Of My Feet

DARK (GERMANY)
Line-Up: Michael Löchter (vocals), Thorsten Schmitt (guitar). Mathias Fickert (guitar), Christian Betz (bass), Jochen Donauer (drums)

DARK were created in 1991 as a covers act playing the Death Metal favourites by such artists as SEPULTURA, DEATH and MORBID ANGEL.

DARK's first compositions of their own surfaced on the 1994 demo 'Visions', a cassette which was limited to 300 soon-sold-out copies.

Vocalist Michael Lochter would lose his place for the third album 'Revolution'. Guitarist Mathias Fickert took the lead vocal role on the record which included an ambitious stab at U2's Pride (In The Name Of Love).

DARK drummer Jochen Donauer would session on the debut album from Progressive Metal band SUNBLAZE.

Albums:
ENDLESS DREAMS OF SADNESS, G.U.N. GUN 117 BMG 74321 44768-2 (1997)
Endless Dreams... / Nemesis Of Neglect / Dawn Of The Gods / When Love Is Gone / Gaias Masterpiece / Fool / A Taste Of Fear / In Darkness / Brainsickness / Dagobar / Embedded In Illusions / Visions / ... Of Sadness
SEDUCTION, G.U.N. GUN 74321 50237-2 (1997)
Another Journey / Dark Clouds Rising / Bloodred Sunrise / Broken Down / My Desire / Love And Seduction / Sands Of Time / This Falling Veil / Shadowdancer / Angeltear / The Flood
REVOLUTION, G.U.N. (1999)
Deadzone / Eyes Wide Open / Pride (In The Name Of Love) / Cradle Of Darkness / Unreal / Marble Halls / Edge Of Infinity / Spacedrift / May B!

DARK MILLENNIUM (GERMANY)
Line-Up: Christian Mertens (vocals), Hilton Thiessen (guitar), Michael Burmann (guitar), Klaus Pachura (bass), Christoph Hesse (drums)

DARK MILLENNIUM were created in 1989 when ex-DESPAIR bassist Klaus Pachura teamed up with guitarist Hilton Thiessen and drummer Christoph Hesse. The band debuted with an out and out Thrash demo entitled 'The Apocryphal Wisdom'. Various members came and went as DARK MILLENNIUM evolved into a more Death Metal vein. A second demo 'Of Sceptre Their Ashes May Be' was enough to secure a deal with Massacre Records.

Thiesson later formed CHERUB.

Albums:
ASHORE THE CELESTIAL BURDEN, Massacre MASSCD010 (1992)
Mission / Dead In Love / Of Sceptre Their Ashes May Be / Mechanismeffects / Fatehistory / Peace In My Hands / My Repertory Of Grey / The Mindartist / In And For Nothing / Myth
DIANA READ PEACE, Massacre MASS CD022 (1993)
Mission / Dead In Love / Of Sceptre Their Ashes May Be / Brotherhood Sleep / Back To Treasureland / Mechanismeffects / Fatehistory / Peace In My Hands / My Repertory Of Grey / The Mindartist / In And For Nothing / Pandemonium / Myth

DARKSEED (GERMANY)
Line-Up: Stefan Hertrich (vocals / guitar), Andi Wecker (guitar), Thomas Herrmann (guitar), Rico Galvagno (bass), Harald Winkler (drums)

Melodic Death Metal with a strong Gothic flavouring dating back to 1992. The band, named after the 'Darkseed' computer game and initially founded by vocalist / guitarist Stefan Hertrich and drummer Harald Winkler as a covers band came to prominence with their 'Sharing The Grave' and 'Darksome Thoughts' demos. At this stage DARKSEED included Turkish guitarist Tarkan Duval. He in turn was superseded by Andy Wecker as the band supported ANATHEMA in their home town of Munich.

Prior to the 'Romantic Tales' EP for Invasion Records guitarist Thomas Herrmann was ousted in favour of Jacek Dworok in August of 1992. Although DARKSEED now had their commercial debut released the band would fold with Wecker and Winkler creating a more grunge influenced outfit. Hertlich resolved himself to resurrect DARKSEED and cut a private six song demo which soon enticed Winkler back into the fold. By November of 1995 Wecker was also reinducted as was guitarist Thomas Hermann and bassist Rico Galvagno. This unit set about a sequel to the 'Romantic Tales' release. Although artwork was made up for what was to be 'Romantic Tales II' the project was shelved and the group signed to the Serenades label for 1996's 'Midnight Solemny Dance' album.

DARKSEED's next step was to ink a deal with the burgeoning Nuclear Blast label. This new dawn did not exactly get off to a good start when after an industry gig at the Cologne Popkomm festival alongside MOONSPELL, CREMATORY and PYOGENESIS, Wecker was unceremoniously fired.

The band drafted guitarist Daniel Kirsten and drummer Willy Wurm for recording of their Nuclear Blast debut 'Spellcraft'. Between the studio sessions and the album's release DARKSEED put in shows supporting AMORPHIS, later captured on a live compilation video. 'Spellcraft' was issued in March of 1997 and DARKSEED set about promotion by hooking up with LACRIMOSA, SECRET DISCOVERY and THE GALLERY for a month long bout of touring. Further shows saw the act included among the ranks for the 10th anniversary Nuclear Blast festivals in Germany sharing the stage with THERION, DIMMU BORGIR, IN FLAMES and CREMATORY.

In December of 1997 Kirsten broke ranks necessitating DARKSEED employing a session guitarist for an appearance at the Austrian 'Mind Over Matter' festival. The gap was finally plugged in July of the following year when Tom Gilcher was enlisted. Unfortunately though the band was struck a severe blow when they learned of the death of ex-member Andy Wecker. The young guitarist had succumbed to cancer.

A further Nuclear Blast album 'Give Me Light' ensued in March of 1999 but strangely its release was a low key affair and a subdued DARKSEED managed a mere handful of gigs that year. Before the year was out both Galvagno and Wurm were out of the picture.

DARKSEED signed to major label Sony for a projected 2001 album provisionally titled 'Astral Adventure'.

Vocalist Stefan Hertrichj also operates in SCULPTURE.

Singles/EPs:
Dream Recalled On Waking / In Broken Images / Above The Edge Of Doom / A Charm For Sound Sleeping, Invasion IR 010 (1994) ('Romantic Tales' EP)

Albums:
MIDNIGHT SOLEMNLY DANCE, Serenades SR 008 (1996)
Watchful Spirit's Care / Lysander / Love's Heavy Burden / The Sealing Day / Forgetfulness / Like To A Silver Bow / Chariot Wheels / The Bolt Of Cupid Fell / Night Mislead / My Worldly Task Is Done / Winter Noon
SPELLCRAFT, Nuclear Blast NB 221-2

(1997)
Craft Her Spell / Pall Whatever Falls / Self Pity Sick / You Will Come / That Kills My Heard / Walk In Me/ Spirits / Nevermight / Senca
ROMANTIC TALES, Serenades (1998)
Dream Recalled On Waking / In Broken Images / Above The Edge Of Doom / A Charm For Soul Sleeping / Last Dream / Frozen Tears / Atoned To Cries / Luctu Perditus / Atoned To Cries (Rough mix)
GIVE ME LIGHT, Nuclear Blast (1999)
Dancing With The Lion / Cold / Echoes Of Tomorrow / Cosmic Shining / Journey To The Spirit World / Give Me Light / Flying Together / Echoes Of Tomorrow (Acoustic version) / Spiral Of Mystery / Desire
DIVING INTO DARKNESS, Nuclear Blast (2000)
Forever Darkness / I Deny You / Counting Moments / Can't Find You / Autumn / Rain / Hopelessness / Left Alone / Downwards / Cold Under Water / Many Wills

DARK TRANQUILLITY (SWEDEN)
Line-Up: Anders Friden (vocals), Fredrik Johansson (guitar), Niklas Sundin (guitar), Martin Henriksson (bass), Anders Jivarp (drums)

DARK TRANQUILITY date back to 1989, but started life under the rather bizarre moniker of SCEPTIC BOILER!

Changing names to DARK TRANQUILITY, the band issued two rare 7" singles. The first of these 1992 efforts, the 'Trial Of Life Decayed' EP, was limited to a thousand copies while only a mere five hundred pressings were made of the 'A Moonclad Reflection' EP. Both these recordings were re-released in Poland the following year on Carnage Records.

In the wake of the release of the 'Skydancer' debut album vocalist Anders Friden left for IN FLAMES and was replaced by Mikael Stanne for the second album 'The Gallery'. In between these albums DARK TRANQUILITY contributed a version of 'My Friend Misery' to the METALLICA tribute album 'Metal Militia' which was released on Black Sun Records in 1994

Stanne contributed guest vocal on DENIAL's debut EP 'Rape Of The Century'. Perhaps a more significant moment in the band's history was the decision taken by Stanne and Sundin to create a trad-Metal side project with former CEREMONIAL OATH drummer Jesper Strömbold and CRYSTAL AGE guitarist Oscar Dronjac titled HAMMERFALL.

With the original intention of creating a non-serious, kickabout band, HAMMERFALL signed to Nuclear Blast and quite amazingly shifted over 50,000 copies of their debut album 'Glory To The Brave' in Germany alone. Unfortunately for Stanne this was after he had dropped out of the band to concentrate on DARK TRANQUILITY.

In November 1997 DARK TRANQUILITY headlined the Osmose touring extravaganza known as the 'World Domination' tour in headlining over ENSLAVED, BEWITCHED, SWORDMASTER, DEMONIAC and DELLAMORTE.

The band toured Japan in 1999 with Finnish act CHILDREN OF BODOM. The band also performed to their biggest audience the same year as part of the Italian 'Gods Of Metal' festival headlined by IRON MAIDEN.

DARK TRANQUILITY added bassist Michael Nicklasson and keyboard player Martin Brändström for 2000's 'The Haven'.

Singles/EPs:
Mid Vinter / Beyond Enlightenment / Void Of Tranquility, Guttaral (1992) ('Trial Of Life Decayed' EP. Limited edition of 1000)
Unfurled By Dawn / Yesterworld, Exhumed Productions CORPSE001 (1992) ('A Moonclad Reflection' EP. Limited edition of 500)
Of Chaos And Eternal Night / With The Flaming Shades Of Fall / Away, Delight, Away / Alone, Spinefarm SPI23CD (1995) ('Of Chaos And Eternal Night' EP)
Zodijackyl Light / Razorfever / Shadowlit Facade / Archetype, Osmose OPMCD 049 (1995) ('Enter Suicidal Angels' EP)

Albums:
SKYDANCER, Spinefarm SPI 16CD (1993)
Nightfall By The Shore Of Time / Crimson Winds / A Bolt Of Blazing Gold / In Tears Bereaved / Skywards / Through Ebony Archways / Shadow Duet / My Faeryland Forgotten / Alone
THE GALLERY, Osmose Productions OPCD 033 (1995)
Punish My Heaven / Silence, And The Firmament Withdrew / Edenspring / The Dying Line / The Gallery / The One Brooding Warning / Midway Through Infinity / Lethe / The Emptiness From Which I Fed / Mine Is The Grandeur...

And... / Of Melancholy Burning
SKYDANCER + CHAOS AND ETERNAL LIGHT, Spinefarm SP143CD (1996)
Nightfall By The Shore Of Time / Crimson Winds / A Bolt Of Blazing Gold / In Tears Bereaved / Skywards / Through Ebony Archways / Shadow Duet / My Faeryland Forgotten / Alone / Of Chaos And Eternal Night / With The Flaming Shades Of Fall / Away, Delight, Away / Alone '94
THE MIND'S I, Osmose Productions (1997)
Dreamlore Degenerate / Zodijackyl Light / Hedon / Scythe, Rage And Roses / Constant / Dissolution Factor Red / Insanity's Crescendo / Still Moving Sinews / Atom Heart 243.5 / Tidal Tantrum / Tongues / The Mind's Eye
PROJECTOR, Century Media (1999)
Freewill / Therin / Undo Control / Auctioned / To A Bitter Halt / The Sun Fired Blanks / Nether Noras / Day To End / Dobermann / On Your Time
HAVEN, Century Media 215668 (2000)
The Wonders At Your Feet / Not Built To Last / Indifferent Suns / Feasts Of Burden / Haven / The Same / Fabric / Ego Drama / Rundown / Emptier Still / At Loss For Words

DAWN (GERMANY)

Albums:
ENTRANCE TO MALEVOLENCE, Revenge Productions (1998)
Intro / Surrender To The Apocalypse / Entrance To Malevolence / Blackened Tomorrow / Relentless Havoc

DAWN (SWEDEN)
Line-Up: Henke Fors (vocals), Andreas Fullmestad (guitar), Fredrik Söderberg (guitar), Lars Tängmark (bass), Karsten Larsson (drums)

OBDURACY guitarist Andreas Fullmested and MORGUE guitarist Fredrik Söderberg formed DAWN in late 1991 after they left their respective acts. Previous to OBDURACY Söderberg had been a member of the mid 80's acts CRANIUM and LEGION.

Membership was completed with additions from FUNERAL FEAST and MESENTARY. Two demo cassettes followed in 1992's 'Demo 1' and 'Apparition' in 1993, with the latter being eventually released as a 7" EP the same year on a shared EP with

PYPHOMGERTUM.
The DAWN debut album arrived in 1995 and it's title is translated as 'When The Sun Sets Forever' and boasts lyrics in medieval Swedish.
Outside the confines of DAWN vocalist Henke Fors has found the time to perform temporary vocal duties for fellow Swedes IN FLAMES appearing on their debut mini-album. The singer also found time to create an extreme Black Metal band called NIDEN DIV. 187 with A CANOUROUS QUINTET guitarist Leo Pignon and members of THY PRIMORDIAL, releasing two albums for Necropolis Records: 'Towards Judgement' and 'Impergium'.
Extra-curricular activity clearly being contagious in Swedish Death Metal circles, DAWN bassist Lars Tängmark also has a side project with the Gothic act THE WOUNDED MEADOW.
DAWN reappeared in 1996 with the mini-album 'Sorgh Pa Sverte Vingar Flogh' (or, translated. 'Sorrow Flew On Black Wings') and featured a cover version of INFERNAL MAJESTY's 'Night Of The Living Dead'.
Söderberg would resurrect his old group CRANIUM as a side project during 1998 issuing three albums.
DAWN's drummer Jocke Petterson is also known as Morth in THY PRIMORDIAL and has sessioned with both UNMOORED and CRANIUM.

Singles/EPs:
The Eternal Forest EP, Bellphegot (1993) (Split EP with PYPHOMGERTUM)
Vya Kal / Sorrow Flew On Black Wings / Soil Of Dead Earth / Night Of The Living Dead, Necropolis NR 6664 (1996) ('Sorgh Pa Svarte Vingar Flogh' EP)

Albums:
NAER SOLEN GAR NIBER EVOGHER, Necropolis NR006 (1995)
Eyesland / The Ethereal Forest / Diabolical Beauty / In The Depths Of My Soul / Ginom Renande Lughier / As The Tears Fall / Svarter Skiner Solen / Everflaming
SLAUGHTERSUN (CROWN OF THE TRIARCHY), Necropolis NR021 (1998)
The Knell And The World / Falcula / To Achieve The Ancestral Powers / Ride The Wings Of Pestilence / The Aphelion Deserts / Stalkers Blessing / Malediction Murder

DAWN OF RELIC (FINLAND)
Line-Up: Rauli Roininen (guitar), Teemu Luukinen (guitar), Pekka Mustonen (bass), Pekka Malo (keyboards), Jukka Zaan Juntunen (drums)

DAWN OF RELIC's 1994 demo 'Of The Ambience', which featured vocalist Jarmo Juntunen, resulted in their signing to Earache Records subsidiary Wicked World. The band's unique brand of Black Metal is heavily infused with H.P. Lovecraft references.
Session vocalists for the 'One Night In Carcosa' album were CATAMENIA's Mika Tönning and HORNA's Nazgul Von Armageddon.

Albums:
ONE NIGHT IN CARCOSA, Wicked World (1999)
Fimbulveir / When Aldebaran Is Visible / The Last Dance Of Sarnath / Kadath Opened: Part I: To Dream, Part II: Through The Cavern Of Flame, Part III: Nether Seas Boiling / Welkins Gar / Just A River / Oceans
WRATHCAST, (2000)
Wrathcast / N.W.S. / Scions Of The Blackened Soil / Awakenings / The Wall Of Tartarean Well's / Dawn Of Relic / No Sign Of The Dawn / Harvest Moon / Instru-Mentally-III

DBX (USA)
Line-Up: Dave Brockie (vocals / guitar), Mike Derks (guitar), Dave Roberts (drums)

A side outlet for GWAR man Dave Brockie. DBX (THE DAVE BROCKIE EXPERIENCE) also includes GWAR members guitarist Mike Derks and drummer Dave Roberts.

Albums:
DIARRHEA OF A MADMAN, (2001)
40,000 Times / Too Much Stuff / You Want to Suck My Dick / Pants / Faggot on Fire / Helium Creed Beat Stall / The Dance of Europe / Iranian Masturbator Washing Yourself / Servant of Death's Head / Two Smart Guys Fight (About Michaelangelo) / The Pennington Lark / I Clean Up Real Good / Great News! / Masturbate / I Saw Three Forms / Calling Dr. Fong

DEAD (GERMANY)
Line-Up: Dany (vocals / guitar), Uwe (bass / guitar), Peter (drums)

DEAD issued the demo tapes 'Far Beyond Driven' and 'Slaves To Abysmal Perversity'. DEAD also released a split effort with THE MEATSHITS (which included a G.G. ALLIN cover 'Highest Power'), GUT and Swedes REGURGITATE.

Singles/EPs:
Slaves To Abysmal Perversity, (199-)
Wanted For Kinky Sessions, (1995)
Recognize: Spread Your Legs... / Rectal Punishment / Receive My Golden Shower / Highest Power, Gulli GR007 (1995) ('Dead' 7" split single with THE MEATSHITS)
Split, (199-) (7" split single with GUT)

Albums:
DEAD, Poserslaughter SPV 084-57712 (1994) (Split album with REGURGITATE)
Intro - Bound To Please / For Lovers Of The New Bizarre / Far Beyond Your Imagination / Mental Erection / Sodomy My Carnal Abuse / Come & Obey! / Indomitable Lasciviousness / Woman From Sodom
YOU'LL NEVER KNOW PLEASURE UNTIL YOU'RE DEAD, Poserslaughter SPV 084-57742 (1995)
Rectal Punishment / Receive My Golden Shower / Penicide / You'll Never Know Pleasure... / Slaves To Abysmal Perversity / XXL Cunt / Body Fluids Are My Favourite Fetish / Delicious Taste Of Vaginal Excrements / Highest Power / Thrusted To The Limits Of All Delights / Journey To Extacy / Die When You Die / Hey Baby Why Don't You Love Me? / Skin Deep Between Her Thighs / Recognize: Spread Your Legs Whore (Part I)
V.I.P., (199-)

DEAD BEGINNERS (FINLAND)
Line-Up: T. Sitomaniemi, E. Lahdenperä

DEAD BEGINNERS were previously titled AUTUMN VERSES. The band in their previous guise would record a further two projected albums for release post the 'Tunes Of Disconsolation' debut. However, the recordings were shelved only to be combined for issue as the 'Sinners Rebellion' under the act's new name of DEAD BEGINNERS.

Albums:
SINNER'S REBELLION, Spikefarm (2000)
Calling Ruby / Treason Via Magdalene / The Wounderable One / The Paragon And The Beast Of Burden / Arradeus 2000 / Ex Cathedra / The Illfated / Sinner's Rebellion / Dead Beginners

DEADEN (USA)

Albums:
HYMNS OF THE SICK, (199-)

DEADHORSE (TX, USA)
Line-Up: Michael Haaga (vocals / guitar), Greg Martin (guitar), Allen Price (bass), Ronny Guyote (drums)

Relapse Records reissued both DEADHORSE albums in 1999 with bonus tracks from the band's 1988 demo 'Death Rides A Dead Horse' and 1994's 'Feed Me' tape.

Albums:
HORSECORE: AN UNRELATED STORY THAT'S TIME CONSUMING, Deadhorse (1989)
Murder Song / Born Believing / Crushing Of The Irate / Hank / Bewah / World War Whatever / Forgive / Army Surplus / Piece Of Veal / Mindless Zombies / Adult Book Store / Flowers For The Dead / Too Close To Home / Scottish Hell / Subhumanity
PEACEFUL DEATH AND PRETTY FLOWERS, Big Chief 9 26716-21 (1992)
Cod Piece Face / Turn / La La Song / Like Asrielle / The Latent Stage / Peaceful Death / Eulogy / Snowdogs / The Lark Nest / Medulla Oblongata / Aplo / Rock Lobster / Sawbone / Every God For Himself / Turn / Medulla Oblongata / Waiting For The Sun

DEAD INFECTION (POLAND)
Line-Up: Jaro (vocals), Cyjan (drums)

Goregrinders DEAD INFECTION would issue the demo tapes 'World Full Of Remains' and 'Start Human Slaughter' prior to a split live cassette shared with INFECTED PUSSY.
DEAD INFECTION released a split EP with Germany's BLOOD in 1995 and further split efforts with C.S.S.O. and MALIGNANT TUMOUR..

Singles/EPs:
From The Anatomical Deeps / Life Of A Surgeon / Her Heart In Your Hands /

The Firing Ground, Morbid MSR 015 (1995) ('Party's Over' 7" split single with BLOOD)
Mrs. Irena / Poppy Seed Cake / Mysterious Wine / Flying Shit In The Outer Space / Gas From Ass / After Accident (Part II), Morbid (1997) (7" split single with C.S.S.O.)
You Can't Help Falling In Love / No Pate, No Mind / He Makes Shit Who Makes Shit Last / Death By The Master Key / We Are Polish / Where Is The General? / Uncontrollable Flatulence, Morbid (1998) ('No Pate - No Mind' 7" split single with MALIGNANT TUMOUR)

Albums:
SURGICAL DISEMBOWELMENT, Morbid MR 010 CD (1994)
Maggots In Your Flesh / Pathological View On The Alimentary Canal / Torsions / Undergo An Operation / After Accident / Xenomorph / Let Me Vomit / Spattered Birth / Start Human Slaughter / Deformed Creature
A CHAPTER OF ACCIDENTS, Morbid MR020 (1995)
From The Anatomical Deeps / Autophagia / The End Of Love / Hospital / Incident Of Corsica / Airplane's Catastrophe / Little John's Story / Her Heart In Your Hand / Ambulance / Colitis Ulcerosa / Life Of A Surgeon / Fire In The Forest / Damaged Elevator / The Firing Ground / Tragedy At The Railway Station / Don't Turn His Crushed Face On Me / Torn By The Lion Apart / The Merry-Go-Round
HUMAN SLAUGHTER... TIL REMAINS, Morbid (1997)
THE GREATEST SHITS, Obscene Productions (1998)

DEATH (Tampa, FL, USA)

Originally formed in 1984, the band's early demos were recorded with the founding trio of vocalist / guitarist Chuck Schuldiner, guitarist Rick Rozz and drummer Kam Lee under the name of MANTAS. Further tapes as DEATH were recorded but Schuldiner was to put the band on ice joining San Francisco's SLAUGHTER for a brief tenure. After resurrecting DEATH with drummer Chris Reifert, more recording ensued landing the band a deal.
DEATH's first album 'Scream Bloody Gore', a somewhat pedestrian and all too predictable Death Metal outing, was to be an unreliable marker for what was to come. DEATH, centred on the erratic

talent of Schuldiner, were to develop into a finely honed and technically proficient leader of the genre over successive releases.
The band's line-up for 'Scream Bloody Gore' was Schuldiner handling vocals, guitar and bass, guitarist John Hand and drummer Reifert.
Reifert departed in 1987 to form AUTOPSY, releasing a four track demo in 1988 and a string of notoriously sickening albums thereafter.
DEATH toured Europe in 1989 with support act DESPAIR prior to American dates with DARK ANGEL. However, before recording the third album Rozz returned to his act MASSACRE.
For the 'Spiritual Healing' album in 1990 DEATH comprised Schuldiner, bassist Terry Butler and drummer Bill Andrews. Rehearsals were held with guitarist Mark Carter before erstwhile AGENT STEEL / HALLOWS EVE man JAMES MURPHY was drafted in.
Following the album's release Murphy was unceremoniously fired, later joining OBITUARY, British thrash act CANCER, TESTAMENT and Danes KONKHRA as well as issuing solo albums. DEATH set about touring initially as a trio before adding CYNIC's Paul Masvidal on a temporary basis.
1990 American dates with CARCASS and PESTILENCE were completed using the services of ex-EVIL DEAD guitarist Albert Gonzales. DEATH then enlisted ex-ROTTING CORPSE guitarist Walter Thrashler for the remaining dates of their American tour with KREATOR.
Somewhat bizarrely DEATH toured Britain with KREATOR minus Schuldiner who reportedly was advised to stay in America for health reasons. Ex-DEVASTATION drummer Louis Carrisalez filled in on vocals whilst Thrashler substituted on guitar. The fans refused to accept a touring line up minus Schuldiner and the dates were far from a success. Upon their return to America both Butler and Andrews joined MASSACRE.
Schuldiner was quick to resurrect the band finally managing to attain the services of CYNIC's Paul Masvidal full time. Masvidal had in between stints with DEATH guested on the MASTER album of 1991 'On The Seventh Day God Created Master'. Alongside them were former SADUS bassist Steve DiGeorgio and CYNIC drummer Sean Reinert.
For DEATH's 1992 touring line-Schuldiner was joined by Masvidal,

Reinert and bassist Scott Carino. Toured Britain in February with support from PESTILENCE and VIOGRESSION.

Added ex-DARK ANGEL drummer Gene Hoglan in 1994. DEATH's line up now comprising Schuldiner, Hoglan, ex-KING DIAMOND guitarist Andy LaRocque and the reinstated bassist Steve DiGeorgio. Carino went to FESTER and in 2000 was a member of LOWBROW.

Toured America in 1994 with support from Dutch act GOREFEST. The 'Symbolic' album was to have been recorded with LaRocque and former WATCHTOWER and RETARDED ELF bassist Doug Keyser but the guitarist was committed to recording of the KING DIAMOND album 'The Spider's Lullaby' and no fee could be agreed for the bassist.

DiGeorgio and LaRocque departed in early 1995 to be replaced by ex-PAIN PRINCIPLE bassist Kelly Conlan and guitarist Bobby Koeble. DEATH toured America with NEVERMORE the same year.

Schuldiner changed tack completely later the same year putting DEATH on ice and generating a new project CONTROL DENIED very much in the power metal mould. Originally Schuldiner was to work with the original WINTER'S BANE vocalist but he was to be lured away for a more permanent liaison with WICKED WAYS.

CONTROL DENIED was now down to Schuldiner, bassist Brian Benson and drummer Chris Williams.

Although CONTROL DENIED recorded an album's worth of material and received offers from various labels Williams upped and left forcing Schuldiner into a rethink.

The outcome was somewhat inevitable and DEATH announced their reformation in October with a line up of Schuldiner, guitarist Shannon Hamm, ex-BURNING INSIDE and ACHERON drummer Richard Christy and a returning Steve DiGeorgio on bass, the latter still retaining his fulltime participation in SADUS.

DiGeorgio reunited with another ex-DEATH man guitarist JAMES MURPHY for one of his side projects DISINCARNATE.

DEATH duly returned to the scene by signing to the aggressive Nuclear Blast label for 1998's 'Sound Of Perseverance', an album which saw a further progression towards straight heavy metal. Schuldiner was aided in this effort by Hamm, Christy and bassist Scott Clendenin. The album included a stab at JUDAS PRIEST's 'Painkiller'.

Ex-DEATH drummer Gene Hoglan would turn up on the drums for cult Norwegian outfit OLD MAN'S CHILD's 1998 album 'Ill Natured Spiritual Invasion'. He would later work with Canadian talent DEVIN TOWNSEND with a new project JUST CAUSE.

Meantime touring found DEATH on the road in America sharing the bill with high profile Swedes HAMMERFALL.

Although 1999 heralded the welcome release of Schuldiner's CONTROL DENIED album fate dealt a cruel blow when it was announced that the frontman was diagnosed with a brain tumour. The frontman had an operation in January and spent the bulk of the year in recuperation.

2000 found Christy back on the drum

stool aiding fellow Deathsters INCANTATION for their live commitments before touring with ICED EARTH. Veteran British Hardcore merchants NAPALM DEATH paid homage in their own oblique way by including a DEATH cover on their 'Leaders Not Followers' album, although the song in question was from an early demo and does not appear on any official DEATH release.

Albums:
SCREAM BLOODY GORE, Under One Flag FLAG 12 (1987)
Infernal Death / Zombie Ritual / Denial Of Life / Sacrificial / Mutilation / Regurgitated Guts / Baptized In Blood / Torn To Pieces / Evil Dead / Scream Bloody Gore / Beyond The Unholy Grave / Land Of No Return
LEPROSY, Under One Flag FLAG 24 (1988)
Leprosy / Born Dead / Forgotten Past / Left To Die / Pull The Plug / Open Casket / Primitive Ways / Choke On It
SPIRITUAL HEALING, Under One Flag FLAG 38 (1990)
Living Monstrosity / Altering The Future / Defensive Personalities / Within The Mind / Spiritual Healing / Low Life / Genetic Reconstruction / Killing Spree
HUMAN, Roadrunner RC 9238 (1991)
Flattening Of Emotions / Suicide Machine / Together As One / Secret Face / Lack Of Comprehension / See Through Dreams / Cosmic Sea / Vacant Planets
FATE (BEST OF) Under One Flag FLAG 71 (1992)
Zombie Ritual / Together As One / Open Casket / Spiritual Healing / Mutilation / Suicide Machine / Altering The Future / Baptized In Blood / Left To Die / Pull The Plug
INDIVIDUAL THOUGHT PATTERNS, Roadrunner RR 9079CD (1993)
Overactive Imagination / Jealousy / Trapped In A Corner / Nothing Is Everything / Mentally Blind / Individual Thought Patterns / Destiny / Out Of Touch / Philosopher / In Human Form
SYMBOLIC, Roadrunner RR 8957-2 (1995)
Symbolic / Zero Tolerance / Empty Words / Sacred Serenity / 1,000 Eyes / Without Judgement / Crystal Mountain / Misanthrope / Perennial Quest
SOUND OF PERSEVERANCE, Nuclear Blast 27361 63372 (1998)
Scavenger Of Human Sorrow / Bite The Pain / Spirit Crusher / Story To Tell / Flesh And The Power It Holds / Voice Of

The Soul / To Forgive Is To Suffer / A Moment Of Clarity / Painkiller

DEATH RAGE (ITALY)

Albums:
SELF CONDITIONED, SELF LIMITED, Shark 011 (1989)
DOWN IN THE DEPTH OF SICKNESS, Metal Master (1990)

DEATH SENTENCE
(CZECH REPUBLIC)

Albums:
THE WORLD DESPAIRES..., (1997)
Screams Of The Shadows / The Last / Faces From My Dreams / The Flames Of Hope In My Head / The World Despaires... / Death Is Only Life / Walpurgis Night / Dead World / Obituary Memories / Decameron

DEATHSTRIKE (Chicago, IL, USA)

Another project from Paul Speckmann of ABOMINATION and MASTER. The 1991 Nuclear Blast release was a pressing of an earlier 1995 demo.

Albums:
FUCKING DEATH, Nuclear Blast (1991)
The Truth / Mangled Dehumanization / Pay To Die / Re-Entry And Destruction / The Final Countdown / Man Killed America - Embryonic Misc. / Pervert / Remorseless Poison

DEATH THREAT (USA)

Albums:
PEACE AND SECURITY, Triple Crown (2000)

DEATH VOMIT (RUSSIA)

DEATH VOMIT not surprisingly deal in Death Metal. Vocals are sure to be inspiring if a little messy!

Albums:
DEATH VOMIT, Metalagen (199-)

DEATHWITCH (SWEDEN)
Line-Up: Af Necrohell (guitar), Lady Death (bass), Terror (drums)

DEATHWITCH is a side project act of SACRAMENTUM drummer Niklas 'Terror' Rudolfsson. The mysterious

Reaper adds vocals to the debut album. 1998's 'The Ultimate Death' was produced by former KING DIAMOND guitarist Andy LaRocque. DEATHWITCH's line up for this opus being Terror switching from drums to vocals, Doomentor on guitar, DISSECTION bassist Peter Palmdahl and new drummer Horror.

Rudolfsson issued a side project album 'Enter The Realm Of Death' under the band name RUNEMAGICK in 1999.

Albums:
TRIUMPHANT DEVASTATION, Desecration DR001 (1996)
Intro - Black Dawn / Triumphant Devastation / Flag Of Black Death / Unholy Destruction / Soul Crusher / Bestial Mutilation / Storm Of Damnation / Infernal Gates Of Hell / Under The Black Wings / Deathwitch / Nocturnal Sacrifice / Sadistic Sodomizer
DAWN OF ARMAGGEDON, Necropolis DR02 (1997)
Intro - Dawn Of War / Ichora Shall Bleed / Angel Execution / Wrath Of Sathanas / Hellfuck Sodomy / Dawn Of Armageddon / Eternal Fornication / Blasphemous Desecration / Beast Of Holocaust / Diabolical Tormentor / Desecration Of The White Christ / Outro (Armageddon) / Infernal Gate (demo) / Triumphant Devastation (demo) / Beast Of Holocaust (demo) / Evil Blood (demo) / Wrath Of Sathanas (demo) / Nocturnal Sacrifice (demo)
THE ULTIMATE DEATH, Necropolis (1998)
Prelude To Grand Darkness / The Ultimate Death / Necromancers Rites / Violent Carnage / Dark Gift / Grave Symphony / Condemned To The Grave / Witches Morbid Lust / Prelude To Grand Conquest / Monumental Massacre / Revel In Sin / Monster Perversion / Death Machine / Pestilent Pandemonium / Demon Sabbath / Dawn Of Ymodus Millenium
MONUMENTAL MUTILATIONS, Necropolis NR035 (1999)
The Return Of Evil / Demonic Witch / Possessed Sadist / Fire Fuck / Jehova Shall Bleed / Total Cremation / Black Beast / Sacrifice In Fire / The Rite Of Darkness / Terror Doom / Flag Of Black Death / Executioner 1999 / Necromancer

DECAMERON (SWEDEN)

Line-Up: Alex Losbäck (vocals / bass) / Johannes Losbäck (guitar), Johan Norrman (guitar), Tobias Kjellgren (drums)

Previously known as NECROFOBIC, the Swedes changed titles to DECAMERON in 1991 and released their first demo in 1992 titled 'My Grave Is Calling'. Frontman Alex Losbäck also moonlighted with RUNEMAGICK in the early 90's.

Drummer Tobias Kjellgren is ex-SWORDMASTER. One of the band's original guitarists Johan Norrman quit to join DISSECTION in mid 1994 and also joined SACRAMENTUM.

DECAMERON soldiered on utilizing the temporary services of LORD BELIAL guitarist Dark. A permanent member was later found in Johnny Lehto. Drummer Tobias Kellgren departed following completion of the debut album, which was issued in 1996.

Kjellgren would later joined DISSECTION in December 1995.

Albums:
MY SHADOW..., No Fashion NFR013CD (1996)
Mörker / Carpe Nocem / Our Time Has Come / Satanised / Le Roi Triste / The Scar Of Damnation / Sexual Immortality / Skabma / My Shadow... / Prophecy Of Life To Come / Mistress Of Sacrifice

DECAPITATED (POLAND)

Line-Up: Sauron (vocals), Vogg (guitar), Martin (bass), Vitek (drums)

Teenage Death Metal act DECAPITATED averaged an age of just 17 by the time of their debut album but incredibly drummer Vitek was a mere twelve years old upon their formation in 1996. In 1997 the trio of vocalist Sauron, guitarist Vogg and Vitek added the 13 year old bassist Martin.

DECAPITATED debuted with the demos 'Crematorial Gates' in 1997 and 1998's 'The Eye Of Horus'.

The first album, recorded for Earache subsidiary Wicked World, was produced by VADER's Peter Wiwczarek and sees a cover of SLAYER's 'Mandatory Suicide'. DECAPITATED's early demos were pressed up onto CD by Poland's Metal Mind Productions entitled 'The First Damned'.

Toured as support to VADER in early 2001.

Albums:
WINDS OF CREATION, Wicked World
(2000)
Winds Of Creation / Blessed / The First
Damned / Way To Salvation / The Eye
Of Horus / Human's Dust Nine Steps /
Dance Macabre / Mandatory Suicide
THE FIRST DAMNED, Metal Mind
Productions (2001)
Winds Of Creation / Blessed / The First
Damned / Way To Salvation / The Eye
Of Horus / Human's Dust Nine Steps /
Dance Macabre / Mandatory Suicide

DECAY OF SALVATION (CA, USA)
Line-Up: Jaime (vocals), Bryant (guitar),
John Cardenas (guitar), Robert (bass),
Bill Makela (drums)

Albums:
SUFFER, (1999)

DECEASED (VA, USA)
Line-Up: King Fowley (vocals / drums),
Mike Smith (guitar), Mark Adams
(guitar), Lez Snyder (bass)

Band leader King Fowley also owns Old
Metal Records, a label specializing in re-
releasing 80's Metal underground
classics. DECEASED were founded in
the mid 80's and opened up proceedings
with the inaugural 1987 demo session
'Evil Side Of Religion'. Pre-DECEASED
vocalist and drummer Kingsly 'King'
Fowley had paid his dues with school
band SLACK TYDE and the 1982 unit
MESSENGER.
As DECEASED, Fowley, with guitarists
Doug Souther and Mark Adams played
their debut gig in April 1986 performing a
set of covers such as SODOM,
BATHORY, SLAYER and MOTÖRHEAD
at a friends house. Progress was swift
and soon DECEASED were becoming a
draw on the local club circuit.
However, tragedy would strike the band
in March of 1988 when bass player Rob
Sterzel, along with two friends of the
band, was killed in a hit and run incident.
Stopping his car to change a flat tyre the
three friends were mown down by a van
driver. Needless to say the media had a
field day when it was revealed Rob's
band was titled DECEASED.
Following this huge setback the 1989 set
'One Night In The Cemetery' ensued. Two
further cassettes ensued with 'Birth By
Radiation' and 1990's 'Nuclear Exorcist'
before DECEASED hooked up with
Death Metal specialists Relapse Records

for the debut album 'Luck Of The Corpse'.
Frictions within the band though led to
DECEASED performing to record the live
'Gutwrench' single minus Souther. Shortly
after recording Souther quit with Mike
Smith taking his place.
The 1995 release 'Death Metal From The
Grave' comprises early demo material
with live cuts and a cover version of
VENOM's 'Die Hard'.
DECEASED's 2000 album 'Supernatural
Addiction' was produced by Simon
Effemey. The band's live album includes
a cover version of KROKUS's
'Headhunter'.
DECEASED also cut various other covers
for tribute albums and laid down in quick
succession their takes on SODOM's
'Witching Hour', AUTOPSY's 'Charred
Remains' and KREATOR's 'Tormentor'.
Fowley also operates the Trad Metal act
OCTOBER 31 as well as DOOMSTONE.

Singles/EPs:
Gutwrench, Relapse (199-) (7" single)

Albums:
LUCK OF THE CORPSE, Relapse
(1991)
Fading Survival / The Cemetery's Full /
Experimenting With Failure / Futuristic
Doom / Haunted Cerebellum / Decrepit
Coma / Shrieks From The Hearse /
Psychedelic Warriors / Feasting On
Skulls / Birth By Radiation / Gutwrench
**THE THIRTEEEN FRIGHTENED
SOULS**, Relapse (1992)
The 13 Frightened Souls / Robotic
Village / Voivod / Planet Graveyard /
Nuclear Exorcist
THE BLUEPRINTS FOR MADNESS,
Relapse (1995)
Morbid Shape In Black / The Triangle /
Island Of The Unknown / The Blueprints
For Madness / The Creek Of The Dead /
Mind Vampires / Into The Bizarre /
Alternative Dimensions / Midnight /
Negative Darkness / A Reproduction Of
Tragedy
DEATH METAL FROM THE GRAVE,
Relapse (1995)
Immune To Burial / Worship The Coffin /
Birth By Radiation / Vomiting Blood /
Virus / Deformed Tomorrows / Nuclear
Exorcist / Shrieks From The Hearse / A
Trip To The Morgue / After The
Bloodshed / Sick Thrash / Futuristic
Doom (Live) / Fading Survival (Live) /
Haunted Cerebellum (Live) / Robotic
Village (Live) / Die Hard
FEARLESS UNDEAD MACHINES,

Relapse RR 6957 (1997)
The Silent Creature / Contamination / Fearless Undead Machines / From The Ground They Came / Night Of The Deceased / Graphic Repulsion / Mysterious Research / Beyond Science / Unhuman Drama / The Psychic / Destiny
SUPERNATURAL ADDICTION, Relapse (2000)
The Premonition / Dark Chilling Heartbeat / A Very Familiar Stranger / Frozen Screams / The Doll With The Hideous Spirit / The Hanging Soldier / Chambers Of The Wailing Blind / Ely's Dementia
UP THE TOMBSTONES - LIVE 2000, Thrash Corner (2000)
The Silent Creature / The Premonition / The 13 Frightened Souls / Robotic Village / The Triangle / Dark Chilling Heartbeat / Fearless Undead Machines / The Psychic / Headhunter / Sick Thrash

DECOLLATION (SWEDEN)
Line-Up: John Lesley (vocals / guitar), John Jeremiah (guitar), Charles Von Weissenberg (bass), Nick Sheilds (keyboards), Chris Steele (drums)

Despite their anglicised pseudonyms DECOLLATION are all Swedish natives. Bassist Charles Von Weissenberg (real name Tomas Johansson) is ex CEREMONIAL OATH whilst drummer Chris Steele (real name Kristian Wåhlin) is ex GROTESQUE and LIERS IN WAIT. Both Wåhlin and vocalist John Lesley (real name Johan Österberg) are now in DIABOLIQUE.

Singles/EPs:
Dawn Of Resurrection / Point Of No Return / The Godborn / Cursed Lands, Listenable POSH0004 (1992) ('Cursed Lands' EP)

DECOMPOSING SERENITY
(AUSTRALIA)

Grinding Noisecore Aussies DECOMPOSING SERENITY debuted with the oddly titled 'Rectify The Anal Bombshell' demo in 1996. A brace of shared 7" singles followed. An album emerged in 2000 in alliance with Brazilians VOMITO.

Singles/EPs:
Split, (199-) (7" split single with SADISTIC LINGHAM CULT)
Blood Was Drawn / Enthral The Internal Fungus / Women's Severed Feet / Facial

Distortion / Bestial Consumption Of Faeces, Prolapse 02 (1998) (7" split single with VISCERA)

Albums:
DECOMPOSING SERENITY, Lofty Storm Productions (2000) (Split album with VOMITO)
Six Nails & A Foot / Body Parts Are For Me / By The Time You Read This, I Will Be Cut In Half / Aftertaste Of Human Flesh / His Contorted Corpse With Holes In His Throat / Give The Children Her Severed Head / Childproof Anus Modification / Blood-Soaked Dragonflies & Fairy Dust / Women's Severed Feet / Blood Was Drawn / Enthral The Internal Fungus / Crunchy Serene Dragonfly / Crunchy Serene Dragonfly / Childproof Anus Modification / Nocturnal Symphonies Of Blood

DECORYAH (FINLAND)
Line-Up: Jukka Vuorinen (vocals / guitar), Jani Kakko (guitar / bass), Jonne Valtonen (keyboards), Mikko Laine (drums)

DECORYAH, although dating back to 1989, only released their debut demo 'Whispers From The Depth' in 1992. A second demo, entitled 'Cosmos Silence', was released at the close of the year. This tape provoked attention from Switzerland's Witchhunt Records prompting a 7" single release.

Singles/EPs:
Ebonies, Witchhunt (1993)

Albums:
WISDOM FLOATS, Witchhunt WIHU 9416 (1995)
Astral Mirage Of Paradise / Wisdom Floats / Monoliths / Beryllos / Reaching Melancholia / Circle Immortality / When The Echoes Start To Fade / Cosmos Silence / Intra-Mental Ecstasy / Ebonies / Infinity Awaits
FALL - DARK WATERS, Metal Blade 3984-14111-2 (1996)
Fall - Dark Waters / Submerged Seconds / Envisioned (Waters?) / Some Drops Behind The Essence / Endless Is The Stream / Gloria Absurdiah / Wintry Fluids (Portal) / She Came To Me In The Form Of Water / She Wept In The Woods

DEEDS OF FLESH (USA)

Line-Up: Jacoby Kingston (vocals / bass), Erik Lindmark (guitar), Jared Deaver (guitar), Mike Hamilton (drums)

DEEDS OF FLESH was forged by ex T.H.C. and CHARLIE CHRIST members Jacoby Kingston, Eric Lindmark and drummer Joey Heaslet in 1993.
Following the self financed 'Gradually Melting' EP DEEDS OF FLESH signed to Relapse Records for their sophomore effort 'Trading Pieces'.
With the issuing of third album 'Inbreeding The Anthropophagi' Heaslet made his exit and was supplanted by Brad Palmer. The band also pulled in erstwhile VILE guitarist Jim Tkacz.
Heaslet made his return for the 'Path Of The Weakening' album after which Tkacz decamped. His position was filled by former PSYPHERIA and IMPALED guitarist Jared Deaver. Later in the year the drum stool was taken over by Mike Hamilton of VILE.
Kingston was unable to fulfill a November 1998 tour of Brazil necessitating the recruitment of DEPRECATED man Derek Boyer to fill in.

Singles/EPs:
Three Minute Crawlspace / Gradually Melted / Human Sandbags / Feelings Of Metal Through Flesh, (199-) ('Gradually Melted' EP)

Albums:
TRADING PIECES, Repulse (1996)
Carnivorous Ways / Born Then Torn Apart / Trading Pieces / Hunting Humans / Impious Offerings / Acid Troops / Deeds Of Flesh / Erected On Stakes / Chunks In The Shower / Blasted / Outro
INBREEDING THE ANTHROPOPHAGI, Repulse (1998)
End Of All / Deeding Time / Breeding The Anthropophagi / Infecting them With Falsehood / Canvas Of Flesh / Ritual Of Battle / Fly Shrine / Gradually Melted
PATH OF THE WEAKENING, Erebos ERE 017 (1999)
Indigenous To The Appalling (Mutinous Humans) / Lustmord / Path Of The Weakening / Summarily Killed / Sounds Of Loud Reigns / Execute The Anthropophagi / I Die On My Own Terms / Sense Of The Diabolic / A Violent God
MARK OF THE LEGION, Unique Leaders Entertainment (2001)

DEEP RED (FINLAND)

Line-Up: Dani Andersson (vocals), Ile Paasonen (guitar), Antti Oinonen (guitar), Henkka Laine (bass), Teemu Mutka (drums)

Brutal Death Metal act DEEP RED came into being during 1999 issuing the three track opening demo 'Yours In Murder'. A further effort 'All Will See Rebirth' saw the inclusion of new members vocalist Dani Andersson and bassist Henrik Laine. The band would sign to the American Blunt Force label, owned by Death Metal veterans DYING FETUS, for their debut 'Prophetic Luster' opus.
DEEP RED contributed their version of 'Trap Them And Kill Them' to a 2001 IMPETIGO tribute album.

Albums:
PROPHETIC LUSTER, Blunt Force (2001)

DEFACED CREATION (SWEDEN)

Line-Up: Thomas Dahlström (vocals), Jörgen Bylander (guitar), Zeb Nilsson (bass), Arrtu Malkku (drums)

Anti-Christian tinged Death Metal act DEFACED CREATION bowed in with the 1994 demo 'Santeria'. The band had been forged by guitarist Jörgen Bylander, vocalist Thomas Dahlström and bassist Zeb Nilsson. A second guitarist Stefan Dahlberg broke ranks after the demo recording.
A further eponymous demo session arrived in 1995 followed by the EP 'Resurrection'. DEFACED CREATION teamed up with ACTERNUM for the split 'Fall' EP of 1997 which featured a new rhythm section of bass player Jock Wassberg and drummer Arrtu Malkku. The band, with Johan Hjelm now on bass, also shared space in 1998 on the 'Infernal' EP with STANDING OUT.
DEFACED CREATION toured Europe as part of the 'Brutal Summer' package including DYING FETUS and DERANGED.
Bylander is also a member of Death Metal band CONDAMNED.

Singles/EPs:
Resurrection, Paranoya Syndrome (1996)
Fall, Paranoya Syndrome (1997) (Split EP with ACTERNUM)
Infernal, Rockaway (1998) (Split EP with STANDING OUT)

Albums:
SERENITY IN CHAOS, Vod VODCD005
(2000)
Baptized In Fire / Macabre Exposure Of
Fleshly Devotion / Fire Temple / Kill The
Light / Devastation / Return In Black /
Cannibalistic Feast / Stillborn / The
Victorious Underworld / Infernal /
Enslave The Christians / Fall

DEFECATION (UK / USA)
Line-Up: Mick Harris (vocals / drums),
Mitch Harris (guitar)

Recorded in 1989 by ex-NAPALM
DEATH / present day SCORN drummer
Mick Harris and American RIGHTEOUS
PIGS / NAPALM DEATH guitarist Mitch
Harris, DEFECATION's album was
produced by Dan Lilker of NUCLEAR
ASSAULT.

Albums:
PURITY DILUTION, Nuclear Blast (1992)
Intro - Megaton / Vestige Of Earthly
Remains / Life On Earth Is Fucking
Cancerous / Contagion / Predominance /
Recovery / Side Effects / Mutual Trust /
Popular Belief / Scrutiny / Under
Estimation / Granted Wish

DEFENDER (SWEDEN)

DEFENDER is the side project act of
AFFLICTED bassist Philip Von
Segebaden. The man is also a member
of the notorious CRANIUM where he
goes under the title Chainsaw Demon.

Albums:
THEY CAME OVER THE HIGH PASS,
Necropolis NR043 (1999)
They Came Over The High Pass / The
Siege Of Armengar / High Himalayan
Valley / Summit Day / Dragon / City In
The Clouds / Maze Of The Minotaur /
Nomads Of The Stars

DEFILED (JAPAN)

Albums:
ERUPTED WRATH, Nightfall (1999)
Fall Into Dilemma / Nihilism / Rush Of
Hostility / Erupted Wrath / Defiled /
Boiled In Limbo / Addicted To Occult
Oath / Crush The Enemy Rising / Depths
Of Psycho / Defeat Of Sanity

DEFLESHED (SWEDEN)
Line-Up: Lars Löfven (vocals / guitar),
Gustaf Jorde (bass), Matte Modin
(drums)

DEFLESHED are purveyors of
predictable Death Metal, heavy on gross
lyrics and impenetrable vocals.
DEFLESHED was forged during 1991
with an inaugural line up of guitarist Lars
Löfven, Kristoffer Griedl and drummer
Oskar Karlsson. This line up managed an
eponymous demo before fracturing.
Second session 'Abrah Kadavrah' saw
the inclusion of erstwhile
CREMATORIUM bassist Gustaf Jorde
and lead vocals from Johan Hedman.
Progress was such that DEFLESHED
were included on the Nuclear Blast
'Grindcore' compilation and had three
tracks from the demo issued as a 7"
courtesy of the Italian Miscarriage label.
Bassist Gustaf Jorde was added prior to
recording of debut album 'Ma Belle
Scalpelle' for the German Invasion
Records concern.
Karlsson left for GATES OF ISHTAR (also
SCHEITAN and RAISED FIST) and in his
stead came Matte Modin in time for the
'Abrah Kadavhrah' album.
In 1998 DEFLESHED contributed their
version of SEPULTURA's 'Beneath The
Remains' for a tribute album.
DEFLESHED toured Europe as support
to CANNIBAL CORPSE in 1999. By 2000
Modin had bailed out to join DARK
FUNERAL.
The band toured Japan during March of
2001.

Singles/EPs:
Obsculum Obscenum / Satanic Source
/ Phlegm, Miscarriage MS002 (1993)

Albums:
MA BELLE SCALPELLE, Invasion
IR009 (1994)
Gathering Flies / Moribiance Blue Cafe /
Simply Fall Towards / Many Mangled
Maggots / Ma Belle Scalpelle
ABRAH KADAVRAH, Invasion IR019
(1995)
Beaten, Loved And Eaten / Mary Bloody
Mary / With A Gambrel / In Chains And
Leather / Abrah Kadavrah / Gone With
The Feaces / Anatomically Incorrect / On
Gorgeous Grounds / Body Art... /
...Pierced Through The Heart
UNDER THE BLADE, Invasion IR 032
(1997)
Farewell To The Flesh / Entering My

Yesterdays / Eat The Meat Raw / Sons Of Spellcraft And Starfalls / Metalbounded / Under The Blade / Thorns Of A Black Rose / Cinderella's Return And Departure / Walking The Moons Of Mars / Metallic Warlust / Curse The Gods
DEATH... THE HIGH COST OF LIVING, War Music (1999)
FAST FORWARD, War Music (1999)
The Return Of The Flesh / The Heat From Another Sun / Fast Forward / The Iron And The Maiden / Proud To Be Dead / Snowballing Blood / Wilder Than Fire / Feeding Fatal Fairies / Lightning Strikes Twice / Domination Of The Sub Queen / Speeding The Ways

DEHUMANISED (New York, NY, USA)

Albums:
PROPHECIES FORETOLD, Pathos (1988)
Kingdom Of Cruelty / Fade Into Obscurity / Solitary Demise / Infinite Despair / Doomed To Die / Terminal Punishment / Condemned / Drawn By Blood

DEICIDE (FL, USA)
Line-Up: Glenn Benton (vocals / bass), Eric Hoffman (guitar), Brian Hoffman (guitar), Steve Asheim (drums)

DEICIDE, emerging from the cult troupe AMON in 1987, were the first American Black Metal band to push the novelty factor into the realms of the dangerous. Early shows had arch-protagonist vocalist / bassist Glen Benton drenched in the blood of a pig bedecked in studded body armour sporting an upside down cross the frontman had burned into his own forehead.
Further controversy was whipped up after the second album 'Legion' when two New Jersey teenagers tortured and killed a dog leaving it's carcass hanging in a tree. When questioned by authorities the youngsters claimed inspiration from DEICIDE.
The band built up a loyal fanbase with surprising speed and Roadrunner Records were quick off the mark in re-issuing the AMON demos re-credited to DEICIDE and marketed as 'Amon: Feasting The Beast'.
The singer's more than vocal appreciation of a Satanic belief system, his willingness to engage in media sponsored set discussions on good and evil with church members (including the late former TWELFTH NIGHT vocalist and vicar GEOFF MANN) and his apparent witnessed shooting of squirrels in his house (!) put DEICIDE firmly in the Black Metal camp.
So vociferous was the media against DEICIDE that their notoriety spread into areas not normally troubled by Black Metal. Benton's comments regarding his supposed treatment of animals led to bomb threats which blighted a European tour. A more pointed message left with the media from the Animal Militia organization informed Benton he would be killed if he stepped on English soil. DEICIDE's British and European shows went according to plan until the Scandinavian leg when a bomb planted at the Fryshuset club in Stockholm, Sweden exploded. However, it was unclear as to the object of the assault as support band GOREFEST had also received death threats from another source.
Benton, whose first son he tactfully named Daemon, rather intriguingly voiced premonitions that he will die aged 33. Needless to say his 33rd Birthday passed without event.
Quite remarkably for a Black Metal band DEICIDE has maintained a rock solid line up since it's inception and continues to maintain a strong unyielding fan base. Latest release 'Insinerate Hymn' is as uncompromising as ever.

Albums:
DEICIDE, Roadrunner RO 9381 (1990)
Lunatic Of God's Creation / Sacrificial Suicide / Oblivious To Evil / Dead By Dawn / Blasphericion / Deicide / Carnage In The Temple Of The Damned / Mephistopheles / Day Of Darkness / Crucifixion
LEGION, Roadrunner RC 91922 (1992)
Satan Spawns The Caco-Daemon / Dead But Dreaming / Repent To Die / Trifixion / Behead The Prophet (No Lord Shall Live) / Holy Deception / In Hell I Burn / Revocate The Agitator
AMON: FEASTING THE BEAST, Roadrunner RR 91112 (1993)
Lunatic Of God's Creation / Sacrificial Suicide / Crucifixation / Carnage In The Temple Of The Damned / Dead By Dawn / Blasphereion / Feasting The Beast / Day Of Darkness / Oblivious To Nothing
ONCE UPON THE CROSS, Roadrunner RR 8949-2 (1995)
Once Upon The Cross / Christ Denied / When Satan Rules His World / Kill The Christian / Trick Or Betrayed / They Are

All Children Of The Underworld / Behind The Light They Shall Rise / To Be Dead / Confessional Rape
SERPENTS OF THE LIGHT, Roadrunner RR 8811-2 (1997)
Serpents Of The Light / Bastard Of Christ / Blame It On God / This Hell We're In / I Am No One / Slaves To The Cross / Creatures Of Habit / Believe The Lie / The Truth Above
WHEN SATAN LIVES, Roadrunner (1998)
When Satan Rules His World / Blame It On God / Bastard Of Christ / They Are The Children Of The Underworld / Serpents Of The Light / Dead But Dreaming / Slave To The Cross / Believe The Lie / Trick Or Betrayed / Behind The Light Thou Shall Rise / Deicide / Father Baker's Dead By Dawn / Sacrificial Suicide
INSINERATE HYMN, Roadrunner RR 8570-2 (2000)
Bible Basher / Forever Hate You / Standing In The Flames / Remnant Of A Hopeless Path / The Gift That Keeps On Giving / Halls Of Warship / Suffer Again / Worst Enemy / Apocalyptic Fear / Refusal Of Penance

DE INFERNALI (SWEDEN)

Actually the solo project of DISSECTION's Jon Nodveidt, DE INFERNALI's album features EDGE OF SANITY's Dan Swäno singing lead vocal on the track 'Sign Of The Dark'.

Albums:
SYMPHONIA DE INFERNALI, Nuclear Blast (1997)
Into The Labyrinths Of Desolation / Ave Satan / Orcus Cursus / Sign Of The Dark / Revival / Paroxysmal Winds / Forever Gone / Atomic Age / Liberation / X

DELIVERANCE (UK)
Line-Up: Kris Krowe (bass / vocals), Sin (guitar), Master Daniels (drums)

Albums:
DEVIL'S MEAT, Metalworks VOV666 (1987)
Desire / Your Death / Rotten To The Core / Devil's Meat / R.I.P. / Killing For Jesus / Deliverance / Twenty One Steps To Hell
EVIL FRIENDSHIP, AVM (1989)
Dies Irae / Tongues Of Lies / Lord Of Vice / Bell, Book And Scandal / No Way Out / Alive Forever / The Drowning / Turn Me To Stone / Evil Friendship /

Rabid / Trooper Of Death / Requiem
BOOK OF LIES, Metalworks (199-)
The Devil's Instrument Parts I-III / Nightmare / Sympathy / Book Of Lies / Runaway / The Evil / Tear Down The Walls / R.I.P.
THE ULTIMATE REVENGE, Griffin GN 5931-2 (1993)
The Devil's Instrument Parts I-III / Turn Me To Stone / Devil Friendship / Deliverance / Bell, Book And Scandal / Runaway / Troopers Of Death / Alive Forever / R.I.P. / 21 Steps To Hell / The Evil / Vision / Stealer Of Dreams / The Church Of Deliverance

DEMANTOR (GERMANY)

Albums:
YOUR ONLY SATISFACTION, Galdre (1997)
White Chappel / The Church / Death's Door / Your Only Satisfaction / Shadows / Behind His Face / Buried Alive / Moments In The Laboratories / Dangerous Worship / Isolate / Army Of Corpses / Publish Lies / Scientology / Destroy (The Picture Of Jesus)

DEMENTIA (HOLLAND)
Line-Up: Arno Burtner (vocals / guitar), Marc Faber (guitar), Ron Van Dijk (bass), Spike Baker (drums)

Den Haag Death Thrash metal men DEMENTIA came together at the tail end of the 80's. By the 'Watching At Dawn' album DEMENTIA had developed a pure Thrash style.

Albums:
WATCHING THE DAWN, Dementia (1995)
Ignorance Is Bullshit / Destiny / Inside Your World / Contradictory Emotions / C.T.P.K. / Thorn In Our Side / Regression

DEMENTOR (CZECH REPUBLIC)
Line-Up: Rene Blahusiah (vocals / guitar), Roman Calpas (guitar), Miro Kucej (bass), Milos Hornak (drums)

Founded as far back as 1988 the present day line-up of Black Death Metal band DEMENTOR features none of the original line up. DEMENTOR bowed in as a trio of guitarist Roman Lukac and siblings Lubos Gazdfik on bass and brother Roman on drums. Some time later vocalist Rene Blahusiah was added to the ranks and it was to be this personality that would prove to be the staying power of the band.

DEMENTOR opened proceedings with the 1992 demo 'The Extinction Of Christianity' before striking a deal with Czech label Immortal Souls Productions for the cassette album 'The Church Dies'. Signing to Spanish label Qabalah Productions. At this stage Blahusiah had been joined by guitarist Roman Calpos, bassist Miro Kucej and drummer Milos Hornak.

DEMENTOR signed to the infamous French concern Osmose Productions for a 2001 album.

Albums:
THE CHURCH DIES, Immortal Souls Productions (1994) (Cassette album)
KILL THE THOUGHT OF CHRIST, Immortal Souls Productions (1997)
Devils Rebirth / The False Faith / Time For Death / Waiting For Death / Love / Requiem To The Cursed Lust / The Art Of Blasphemy / Taste Of Dead Meat / Gates Of Eternity / The Eyes Of The Beast
THE ART OF BLASPHEMY, Qabalah Productions (1999)
In The Name Of God / Kill The Thought Of Christ / The Law Of Karma / The Lost Humanity / Fate Of Emptiness / Rotting God / Suppuration Of My Soul / Mortal Melody / Prometheans
ENSLAVE THE WEAK, Osmose Productions (2001)

DEMIGOD (FINLAND)
Line-Up: Esa Linden (vocals), Mika Naapasalo (guitar), Jussi Kiiski (guitar), Tero Laitinen (bass), Seppo Taatila (drums)

Cult Death Metal act split after only one album. In 1993 Seppo Taatila joined ADRAMELCH. Esa Linden would also join ADRAMELCH in 1996.

Albums:
SLUMBER OF SULLEN EYES, Drowned DC008 (1992)
Intro / As I Behold I Despise / Dead Soul / The Forlorn / Tears Of God / Slumber Of Sullen Eyes / Embrace The Darkness - Blood Of The Perished / Fear Obscures From Within / Transmigration Beyond Eternities / Towards The Shrouded Infinity / Perpetual Ascent / Darkened

DEMILICH (FINLAND)
Line-Up: Antti Boman (vocals / guitar), Aki Hytonen (guitar), Ville Koistinen (bass), Mikko Virnes (drums)

Without a doubt DEMILICH offer up a unique sick brand of Sludge Death Metal overladen with extreme guttural vocals. Antti Boman's singing style is so outrageous that the band felt the need in the CD booklet to explain that no effects were used during recording.

DEMILICH's debut was released by American label Necropolis and licensed by Repulse.

The European version adds four songs from the demo 'The Four Instructive Tales Of... Decomposition'.

Albums:
NESPITHE, Repulse RPS 014 (1995)
When The Sun Drank The Weight Of Water / The Sixteenth Six Tooth Son Of Fourteen Four Regional Dimensions (Still Unlamed) / Inherited Rowel Levitation - Reduced With Any Effort / The Echo (Replacement) / The Putrefying Road In The Nineteenth Extremity (...Somewhere Inside The Bowels Of Endlessness) / (Within) The Chamber Of Whispering Eyes / And You'll Remain... (In Pieces Of Nothingness) / Erecshyrinol / The Planet That Once Used To Absorb Flesh In Order To Achieve Divinity And Immortality (Suffocated To The Flesh That It Desired) / The Cry / Raped Embalment Beauty Sleep / Introduction - Embalmed Beauty Sleep / Two Independent Organisms - One Suppurating Deformity / And The Slimy Flying Creatures Reproduce In Your Brains / The Uncontrollable Regret Of The Rotting Flesh

DEMOLITION HAMMER
(New York, NY, USA)
Line-Up: Steve Reynolds (vocals / bass), James Reilly (guitar), Derek Sykes (guitar), Vinny Daze (drums)

Deathsters DEMOLITION HAMMER hail from New York. Debuted with the 1987 demo tape 'Skull Fracturing Nightmare' followed by a further session in 1989 'Necrology'. The band had their 1990 debut 'Tortured Existence' recorded at Morris Sound Studios in Tampa and produced by Scott Burns.

DEMOLITION HAMMER were down to a trio by 1994 of Reynolds, Sykes and drummer Alex Marquez.

Albums:
TORTURED EXISTENCE, Century
Media 0897132 (1990)
.44 Calibre Brain Surgery / Neanderthal /
Gelid Remains / Crippling Velocity /
Infectious Hospital Waste / Hydrophobia
/ Parricidal Epitaph / Mercenary
Aggression / Cataclysm
EPIDEMIC OF VIOLENCE, Century
Media CM 7728-2 (1992)
Skull Fracturing Nightmare / Human
Dissection / Pyroclastic Annihilation /
Envenomed / Carnivorous Obsession /
Orgy Of Destruction / Epidemic Of
Violence / Omnivore / Aborticide
TIMEBOMB, Century Media CM 77071-2
(1994)
Under The Table / Power Struggle /
Mindrot / Bread And Water / Missing:
5.7.'89 / Waste / Unidentified / Blowtorch
/ Mongoloid / Time Bomb

DEMON DAGGER (PORTUGAL)
Line-Up: Pedro Mendes (vocals), Vitor
Carvalho (guitar), José Figueiredo
(bass), Miguel Carvalho (drums)

DEMON DAGGER date back to 1995.
The band was founded as a quartet of
vocalist Pedro Mendes, guitarist Vitor
Carvalho, bassist José Silva and
drummer Miguel Carvalho.
Silva departed in 1997. A 1997 demo
featured W.C. NOISE guitarist Rodolfo
Carduso as guest.

Singles/EPs:
Soul Of Steel / A Stand Below, Recital
(1999)

Albums:
AFTERSHOCK, Recital BOX002 (2000)
Etched Face / Sinking / Wrecking
Wrench / A Stand Below / Broadmoor /
Corundura Pursuit / Don't Look Back /
Sinful Bles-sin / Sweet Turning Sour /
Frenzy Wraith / Soul Of Steel

DEMONIAC (NEW ZEALAND)
Line-Up: Behemoth (vocals), Heimdall
(guitar), Shred (guitar), Diccon (bass),
Matej (drums)

New Zealand Black Metal band
DEMONIAC issued the 1994 demo 'The
Birth Of Diabolical Blood'. DEMONIAC
relocated to England during 1997 to take
part in the 'World Domination' tour of
Europe headlined by DARK

TRANQUILITY and ENSLAVED.
Frontman Behemoth (real name Lindsey
Duncan) would relinquish the bass role in
1998 to former ADORIOR man Chris
Hastings as singer Adromelech exited. By
2000 the position was in the hands of
erstwhile VOICE OF DESTRUCTION
bassist Diccon. Drums were handed over
to new Slovenian recruit Matej.
DEMONIAC landed themselves in hot
water when it was learned the track
'Myths Of Metal' included the lyric "Hitler
metal, Sieg Heil". Facing a ban on the
album from the German authorities the
band issued a swift apology. Denying any
racist slur the group pointed out that the
band's guitarists Heimdall (real name
Sam Totman) was of Maori descent whilst
the band's other six stringer Shred (real
name Herman Li) was from Hong Kong.

Singles/EPs:
Moonblood, United Blasphemy (199-)

Albums:
PREPARE FOR WAR, Evil Omen EOR
003 CD (1995)
Intro (Prologue Of War) / Prepare For
War / The Birth Of Diabolic Blood / The
Earth Calls Me / Missein Anthropos /
Hammer Of Damnation / The Return Of
The Darkness And Evil / Celtic Sword Of
Iron / A Narain / Evocation / Chaoist /
So Bar Gar / Dormant Entity / Final
(Epilogue Of War)
STORMBLADE, Evil Omen EOR 005 CD
(1997)
Burn The Witch / Domination / Red Light
/ Into The Cavern Light / Hatred Is Purity
/ Fight The War / Red Headed Maniac /
Nigger Slut / Stormblade
THE FIRE AND THE WIND, Osmose
Productions OPCD082 (1999)
The Eagle Spreads Its Wings / Daggers
And Ice / Demonic Spell / Night Demons
/ Myths Of Metal / Sons Of The Master /
The Fire And The Wind

DENAK (SPAIN)

The 1998 split single shared with fellow
Spaniards HAEMORRHAGE includes a
version of IMPETIGO's 'Boneyard'.

Singles/EPs:
Siempre Yo / Generacion? Que? / Sin
Argumentos / Siempre Agobiado /
Boneyard, Upground (1998) (7" split
single with HAEMORRHAGE)
Untitled / Grita / Nunca Cesan De Dar
Vueltas, Dwie Strony Medalu (1999) (7"

split single with ABSTAIN)
Split, (199-) (7" split single with
DAHMER)

DENETHOR (HOLLAND)
Line-Up: Dracul (vocals), Schmerzen
(guitar), Profane (bass), Nocturnasz
(drums)

Corpsepainted DENETHOR was the
creation of former OBSCURITY members
Schmerzen and vocalist Myst. 1995 saw
the addition of female vocalist Gineke but
her tenure was brief. Myst departed in
September 1997 in favour of the fire
breathing Dracul.
Although DENETHOR released a 1997
demo session the band had folded by
1998.

DEPRAVITY (FINLAND)
Line-Up: Martti (vocals), Olli (guitar),
Enska (guitar), Pete (bass), Matti
(drums)

Albums:
SILENCE OF THE CENTURIES,
Adipocere CD AR017 (1993)
Silence Of The Centuries / Sleepy
Ocean / Remasquerade /
Phantasmagoria / Vacuum Of Thoughts

DEPRECATED (USA)
Line-Up: A.J. Magana (vocals), John
Remmen (guitar), Matt Sotelo (guitar),
Derek Boyer (bass), Torrey Moores
(drums)

Founded in 1996 by former DISGORGE
members vocalist A.J. Magana, bassist
Derek Boyer and drummer Torrey
Moores. DEPRECATED's first guitarist
was Adam Heast.
During November of 1998 Boyer filled in
for DEEDS OF FLESH vocalist Jacony
Kingston for a series of shows in Brazil.
DEPRECATED pulled in VEHEMENCE /
BRIDES OF CHRIST guitarist John
Chavez for recording of 'Engulfing
Visions'. Meantime DEPRECATED
members turned up deputizing for other
acts with A.J. Magana fronting
DISGORGE as temporary replacement
for Matti Way and bass player Derek
Bowyer teaming up with DYING FETUS
in 2001.
The band added former DECREPIT
BIRTH guitarist Matt Sotelo but found that
Magana had joined DISGORGE on a full
time basis appearing on their 'Dissecting
The Apostles' opus.

Singles/EPs:
Deriding His Creation / Mentally
Deprived / Realization Of Betrayal /
Induced Deception, (199-) ('Deriding his
Creation' EP)

DEPRESION (AUSTRIA)
Line-Up: Daniel, Milan, Radim, Alex

Albums:
DEPRESION, Depresion (1997)
Intro / Time To Die / Life Of My Soul /
Mendacious Faith / Bitches Of Your Mind
/ Depressions / Face Of Religion /
Torture Of Defenceless / Yearning /
Kladivo Na Carodejnice

DERANGED (SWEDEN)
Line-Up: Per Gyllenbäck (vocals), Johan
Axelsson (guitar), Jean-Paul Asenov
(bass), Rikard Werman (drums)

Yet another Scandinavian act attempting
to out-gross the originators of the genre.
DERANGED actually engaged guitarist
Mike Amott, later of CARCASS and
SPIRITUAL BEGGARS, to play on the
'Architects Of Perversion' mini-album and
in spite of initial scepticism on the
international scene, DERANGED soon
forged their own distinct path, becoming
renowned as one of the very heaviest of
Swedish acts.
In 1995, after the release of the 7" single
'On The Medical Slab', bassist Jean-Paul
Asenov was sacked and superseded by
Mikael Bergman. The latter's stay with
the band was fairly shortlived and he was
fired shortly after his appointment, which
led to guitarist Johan Axelsson
performing bass duties on the 'Rated X'
sessions prior to the band recruiting
former INVERTED bassist Dan
Bengtsson.
DERANGED have a cover of the VENOM
track 'In League With Satan' on the 1992
Primitive Art Records tribute album
'Promoters Of The Third World War'.
The band also contribute the original cut
'Hammer Cottered Rectum' to the 1993
Repluse Records compilation
'Sometimes Dead Is Better'.
For the 1997 'High On Blood' album
DERANGED replaced Gyllenback with
MOONSTRUCK man Fredrik Sandberg.
DERANGED set about touring Europe
alongside DYING FETUS and DEFACED
CREATION with another bout of dates
with VOMITORY. However, Sandberg
was replaced almost immediately after.
The new man behind the microphone for

the 1999 effort 'Ill' was Johan Anderberg of MURDER CORPORATION. DERANGED would then trim down to a trio with the departure of Bengtsson.

Singles/EPs:
Orgy Of Infanticide Exposed Corpses (Part II) / The Confessions Of A Necrophile / Nervus Thoralicius L: Ongus (Part II), Obliteration OR001 (1993)
Upon The Medical Slab / Red Disorder, MMI MMI 015 (1995)
Internal Vaginal Bleeding / The Bowels Of My Dismay / Majestic Hole / Sculptures Of The Dead, Repulse RPS 010B (1995)

Albums:
ARCHITECTS OF PERVERSION, Repulse RPS002 (1994)
RATED X, Repulse RPS 010 (1995)
Black Semen Vengeance / Killing Spree / (Clim) Axe / Narcissistic Sleighride / Unleash My Hunger... / Razor Tongue / I'm The Love Undertaker / ...As A Wolf / Sixteen And Dead / Paint It Black
HIGH ON BLOOD, Regain (1997)
Razor Divine / Humanity Feeds On Filth / (Eroti)kill / Raised On Human Sin / High On Blood / Robber Of Life / Nailed Ejaculation / By Knife… / Haunted By Natural Danger / With The Silence Came Horror / Experience The Flesh
III, Listenable (1999)
Ripped, Raped, Randomized / Compulsive Urge To Kill / Consume Excrete / Laugh At Human Tragedies / Through The Realm Of Torture / Festering / Ill / Thrill Kill / I Thrive On Suffering / Death Tripping / Razor (rection)

DESCEND (Cleveland, OH, USA)

Albums:
DESCEND, Cutting Edge (2000) (Split album with ALL THAT IS EVIL)
Unseen / Visions To Come / Toutasis Strikes / To Infinity We Shall Fall

DESCENDENT (Toledo, OH, USA)
Line-Up: Brian Norwalk (vocals), Tom Martin (guitar), Scott Brauer (bass), Scott MacEachern (drums)

Albums:
DEGENERATION, (1995)
Self Submissive / The Heir Apparent / Godseed / Dereal - In Isolation / My Own, My Enemy / Release

DESECRATION (ITALY)
Line-Up: Steve Macpherson (vocals / keyboards), Francesco Conte (guitar), Jurij G. Ricotti (guitar), Fabio Fraschini (bass), Gaetano Verderame (drums)

Technical Death Metal with keyboards.

Albums:
THE VALLEY OF ETERNAL, Zasko Lab Z16 Dsml 93 (1993)
Experiment 49 / Reincarnation Of Soul / Corpse Embodiment / The Valley Of Eternal Suffering / Premature Explant / Corrosive Infection

DESECRATION (UK)

Opened proceedings with the gory 'Mangled Remains' demo of 1992. DESECRATION's debut album 'Gore And Perversion's cover artwork was so extreme the record remained without a label for a lengthy period. Eventually Arctic Serenades felt brave enough to sign the act only to have the first pressing seized by the police under the obscene publications act.
Without a drummer vocalist Ollie took up the role for second album 'Murder In Mind'. DESECRATION toured the UK supporting CANNIBAL CORPSE, IMMORTAL and THUS DEFILED prior to European dates with VADER and MORTICIAN.
The third album 'Inhuman' was produced by Dave Chang.

Albums:
GORE AND PERVERSION, Arctic Serenades (199-)
MURDER IN MIND, Copro (2000)
INHUMAN, Copro CD-COPO13 (2001)
Insane Savagery / Turning Black / Dig Up, Dig In / Asphyxiate On Blood / Life Of Gore / Inhuman / Another Obscene Publication / Death You'll Face / Killer Row / A Message For The Censor

DESIRE (PORTUGAL)
Line-Up: Tear (vocals), Mist (guitar), Eclipse (guitar), Dawn (keyboards), Flame (drums)

DESIRE was originally titled INCARNATED upon their foundation in 1992 by vocalist Tear and drummer Flame. Although a promo single 'Death Blessed By A God', was issued by September 1994 the band decided upon a name change to DESIRE.

The 'Infinity...' album included contributions from female vocalist Joana Pereira, bassist Jaime Souza and ex-guitarist Luis Lamelas.

Second guitarist Eclipse was added following the debut album release. Although having been a going concern for some years DESIRE have played live on only a handful of occasions.

Albums:
INFINITY... A TIMELESS JOURNEY THROUGH AN EMOTIONAL DREAM, Skyfall SKY 85.003 (1996)
Chapter I: (Prologue) / Chapter II: (Leaving) This Land Of The Eternal Desires / Chapter III: A Ride In The Dream Crow / Chapter IV: The Purest Dreamer / Chapter V: In Delight With The Mermaid / Chapter VI: Forever Dreaming... (Shadow Dance) / Chapter VII: Epilogue

DESPAIR (GERMANY)
Line-Up: Robert Kampf (vocals), Marek Grzeszek (guitar), Waldemar Sorychta (guitar), Klaus Pachura (bass), Markus Freiwald (drums)

DESPAIR formed in 1986 with vocalist Robert Kampf, although the group swapped Kampf shortly after the release of the Harris John's produced 'History Of Hate' for new vocalist Andreas Henschel in 1988 as the former became head of record label Century Media.

DESPAIR were perennials on the German Metal scene having opened for the likes of DEATH and DEATH ANGEL even before landing a deal. With a record under their belts further touring in Europe ensued as guests to acts such as ANNIHILATOR and OVERKILL.

Drummer Markus Freiwald joined FLAMING ANGER then VOODOO CULT. Guitarist Waldemar Sorychta founded GRIP INC. with ex-SLAYER drummer DAVE LOMBARDO and is also now an accomplished producer in his own right.

Singles/EPs:
Slow Death (Live) / History Of Hate (Live) / Young And Uncertain (Live), Century Media (1991)

Albums:
HISTORY OF HATE, Century Media 08 9702-1 (1988)
The Enigma / Freedom Now / History Of Hate / Constructing The Apocalypse / Slow Death / Outconditioned / Slaves Of

Power / Joy Division / Never Trust
DECAY OF HUMANITY, Century Media 08 9712 (1990)
Decay Of Humanity / Cry For Liberty / Delusion / Victims Of Vanity / A Distant Territory / Silent Screaming / Radiated / Satanic Verses
BEYOND ALL REASON, Century Media 08 9726 1 (1992)
Beyond Comprehension / Deaf And Blind / Imported Love / The Day Of Desperation / In The Deep / Rage In The Eyes / Burnt Out Souls / Son Of The Wild / Crossed In Sorrow

DESULTORY (SWEDEN)
Line-Up: Klas Morberg (guitar / vocals), Stefan Poge (guitars), Jens Almgren (bass), Thomas Johnson (drums)

Ronninge based Death Metal band formed in 1989, DESULTORY recorded a 1991 demo at the renowned Sunlight Studios with producer Tomas Skogsberg titled 'Death Unfolds'. This demo, together with a later effort 'Visions', were released together as the 'Forever Gone' limited edition mini-album in 1992.

The band toured Britain with CANNIBAL CORPSE in 1994 and by the third album DESULTORY had trimmed down to a trio of Johnson, Morberg and his brother Häkan Morberg on guitar.

Albums:
FOREVER GONE, HOK HOK LP002 (1992)
INTO ETERNITY, Metal Blade ZORRO 52 (1993)
Into Eternity / Depression / Tears / The Chill Within / Visions / Twisted Emotions / Forever Gone / Passed Away / Asleep
BITTERNESS, Metal Blade ZORRO 77(1994)
Life Shatters / Left Behind / A Closing Eye / Taste Of Tragedy / Bleeding / Among Mortals / Enslaved / Winter / Cold Bitterness
SWALLOW THE SNAKE, Metal Blade 3984-14109-2 (1996)
Mushroom Smile / The Bitter Man / Before Today, Beyond Tomorrow / Swallow The Snake / In My Veins / Blizzard In My Blood / Zone Traveller / Beneath / King Of The Valley And The Western Sky / Nothing Dies / Silent Suffering

DETERIORATE (USA)

Previously a straight forward Death Metal band DETERIORATE would evolve into a more Black incarnation with later releases. The band folded in 1997. Erstwhile members of DETERIORATE would form ZAHGURIM.

Albums:
ROTTING IN HELL, JL America (1993)
Agonized Display / A Thousand Years Of Anguish / Cannibal Autopsy / Devoured / The Sufferance / Rotting In Hell / Asphyxiation Cremation / Shadows Of Death / Beyond The Grave / Decomposed Anatomy
THE SENECTUOUS ENTRANCE, Pulverizer (1996)
The Senectous Entrance / In The Presence Of Eurus / Xipe Totec / Stealing Strength For The Ivory Bear / Kiev 1237 / Religious Fatum / Ode To A Mortal / Darea Come… / Gather The Nebbish… / Evaporated Battle Ground

DETEST (DENMARK)
Line-Up: Peter Jørgensen (vocals), Ole Christiansen (guitar), Hardy Akira Madsen (guitar), Peter Frandsen (bass), Brian Andersen (drums)

Brøndby based DETEST supported DEATH and CARCASS in Denmark and appeared at the Roskilde Festival.

Albums:
DORVAL, Progress Red Labels PRL010 (1995)
The Assault On Dorval / The Process Of Doom (Preface Of Invasion) / A Black Sea Rose / Inhaled Through The Body / Unavoidable Encounter / Defiled / Dorval (Revenging Hour) / Bound / (Chapter VI) Legio / Deathbreed (The Description Of Legio) / Gathering Of Darkness (The Conclusion) / Shadows Of Dissolution / Obscurity Devised

DEUTERONOMIUM (FINLAND)
Line-Up: Kalle Paju (guitar), Manu Lehtinen (bass)

A Christian Death Metal act whose second album 'Here To Stay' is highly revered among certain circles. The band began life with a line up of Jarno Lehtinen, Miika Partala, Manu Lehtinen and Tapio Laakjo debuting with a 1993 demo 'Paths Of Righteousness'. A second session 'Crosshope' in 1996 led to the first album 'Street Corner Queen' which brewed a heady mixture of sounds as diverse as Black Metal and Reggae! Following the 'Here To Stay' album DEUTERONOMIUM were down to a duo of guitarist Kalle Paju and bassist Manu Lehtinen.

Singles/EPs:
Crosshope / Thinking / Tribal Eagle / Blue Moment, (1997) ('Tribal Eagle' EP)
To Die And Gain / Misleader / To Die And Gain (Demo version), Little Rose Productions (1999)

Albums:
STREET CORNER QUEEN, Little Rose Productions (1998)
Street Corner Queen / Druglord / Spell Of Hell / The Fall / Empty Shell / Human Nature / Bonsai People / Black Raven / C.C.R. / III / Northern Prairie
HERE TO STAY, Little Rose Productions (1999)
Whirlwind / To Die And Gain / S.S. / My God / terminator / Statue Of Liberty / Comeback / Fool / Here To Stay / Christ Addict / D.D.D. / Millstone / Dead End

DEVOID (UK)
Line-Up: Loui Fellows (vocals), Carlo Regadas (guitars), Jim Dawson (guitars), Paul Craig (bass), Stuy (drums)

A Liverpool based Death Metal band. Fellows quit in 1992. Regadas later went on to join CARCASS in 1994.

Albums:
BLACKENED EMPIRE, Skysaw SAW 7 (1992)
Entangled / Banished From Humanity / Relentless Anguish / Obsession Syndrome / Live Through My Pain / Burning Rage / Defiance

DEVOURMENT (USA)
Line-Up: Wayne Knupp (vocals), Brian (guitar / bass), Brad Fincher (drums)

Ultra-brutal Death Metal band DEVOURMENT is led by erstwhile MEATUS vocalist Wayne Knupp.

Albums:
MOLESTING THE DECAPITATED, United Guttural (1999)
Festering Vomitous Mass / Postmortal Coprohagia / Choking On Bile / Molesting The Decapitated / Self Disembowelment / Fucked To Death / Devour The Damned /

Shroud Of Encryption
1.3.8., Corpse Gristle (2000)
Babykiller / Shroud Of Encryption ('97) / Festering Vomitous Mass ('97) / Choking On Bile ('97) / Festering Vomitous Mass ('99) / Postmortal Coprophagia / Choking On Bile ('99) / Molesting The Decapitated / Self Disembowelment / Fucked To Death / Devour The Damned / Shroud Of Encryption ('99)

DEW OF NOTHING (MEXICO)

Albums:
DOUBLEWEIRD, Sempiternal Productions SP007 (2000)
Dew Of Nothing (Intro) / Seven Caves / Woman Kind / Wings Eye / Art Upon Perception Of Time / Proud Of Damned / Nightmare's Lake / Levels Of Sycho Path / Intruder And Holy Hate / Doubleweird (Outro)

DIABLERIE (FINLAND)
Line-Up: Henri Villberg (vocals), Kimmo Tukainen (guitar), Eric Lundén (guitar), Alessi Ahokas (bass), Juha Suorsa (keyboards), Antti Ruokola (drums)

Created in late 1997 by former CEREMONY OF ECLIPSE members vocalist Henri Villberg and guitarist Kimmo Tukainen. Original second guitarist Jukka Gråstén would decamp after recording of the 'Astro' demo necessitating bassist Erik Lundén covering the guitar role and the enrollment of Alessi Ahokas on bass.
Ahokas has credits with RAPTURE, EXCELSIOR, PROPHET and SNOWGARDEN. Lundén has a side band entitled STILL LIFE. Villberg has sessioned as guest 'growling' vocalist for PROPHET.

Albums:
SERAPHYDE, Avantgarde (2001)
Dystphia Show / Nervine / Float / Astronomicon / Weltschmerzen / Until Death Do Us Apart / Nations Collide / Bitter Utopia / Death Wired To The Bleak / Seraphyde / Oppressions

DIABLOS RISING
(FINLAND / GREECE)
Line-Up: Mikka Luttinen, Magus Vampyr Daoloth

Industrial Black Death Metal project by Mikka Luttinen of IMPALED NAZARENE and Magus Vampyr Daoloth of NECROMANTIA, DIABLOS RISING's debut album features one Phillip Glass inspired track that is three minutes of complete silence!
Daoloth formed a further side project RAISM in 1996, issuing an album 'The Very Best Of Pain'.

Singles/EPs:
S.N.T.F., Kron-H (1995) (7" single)

Albums:
666, Osmose Productions OPCD023 (1995)
Genocide - I Am God / Vinnum Sabbati / Give Me Blood Or Give Me Death / Satanas Lead Us Through / Sorcery - Scientia Maxima / 666 / X-X-ST
BLOOD, VAMPIRISM AND SADISM, Kron-H 001 (1995)
Satanic Propaganda / Blood Lunar Cult / Blood Communion / Ilsa / Sadism Unbound / Mantle Of Suffering / Necrommanteion / Ashes To Ashes, Flesh To Dust

DIABOLIC (Tampa, FL, USA)
Line-Up: Paul Ouellette (vocals), Briam Malone (guitar), Brian Hipp (guitar), Ed Webb (bass), Aantor Coates (drums)

Tampa blasphemous Black Death Metal band DIABOLIC feature former HORROR OF HORRORS, EULOGY and EXMORTIS drummer Aantor Coates. Bassist Ed Webb is also a former EULOGY member.
DIABOLIC's June 1997 demo 'City Of The Dead' would be reissued as a mini-album by Fadeless Records. The act's debut gig came with a high-profile appearance sharing the stage with heavyweights VADER, MONSTROSITY and BROKEN HOPE. The band took to the road with gusto appearing in 1998 at the Milwaukee Metalfest and New York Demonfest, the New England Death And Hardcore festival and the Texan November To Dismember gig in 1999.
Touring in America saw DIABOLIC as part of the 'Death Metal Massacre' package alongside CANNIBAL CORPSE, GOD DETHRONED and HATE ETERNAL. The tour, although a great success, was marred by the band having all their equipment stolen after the first gig. Undaunted, DIABOLIC put in further touring supporting MORBID ANGEL the same year.
Ouellette would later be sacked for alleged "weakness" as bass player Ed

126

Webb took over lead vocal duties. The band would also draft former BRUTALITY and CRADLE OF FILTH guitarist Brian Hipp. With this line up DIABOLIC cut a version of SLAYER's 'Killing Fields' for a tribute album.

Later shows would see erstwhile ANGEL CORPSE guitarist Gene Palubicki filling in.

Albums:
CITY OF THE DEAD, Fadeless (1999)
Denounce God / City Of The Dead / Vortex / Encarta / Inborn
SUPREME EVIL, The Plague (2000)
Insacred / Sacrament Of Fiends / Ancient Hatred / Treacherous Scriptures / Grave Warnings / Rack Of Torment / View With Abhorrence / Dwelling Spirits / Wicked Inclination / Supreme Evil
SUBTERRANIAL MAGNETUDE, (2000)

DIABOLICAL (PARAGUAY)

Albums:
SACRED REMAINS, (199-)
Monstrous Birth / (Nothing) Sacred Remains / Enslaved By Darkness / The Morning Madness / Innocencia Mortis / Never Again / Final Retribution / I Hate… / Black Sepulcher / Totally Insane / Abandoned
DOMINUS INFERNAL, Icarus (2000)
Revelation Of The Infernal Power / The Laws Of Hell / Ready For The Ceremony / The Ancient God Serpent / Unholy Darkness For The Occult Abyss / Almighty Force Of Truth / Three Lords From Hell / The Warriors / Recibe El Nuebo Fuego

DIABOLIQUE (SWEDEN)
Line-Up: Kristian Wählin (vocals / guitar), Johan Österberg (guitar), Bino Carlsson (bass), Hans Nilsson (drums)

DIABOLIQUE is the brainchild of GROTESQUE and LIERS IN WAIT founder Kristian Wahlin. Guitarist Johan Österberg is ex-DECOLLATION. Drummer Hans Nilsson is another LIERS IN WAIT member and also has credits with LUCIFERION and DIMENSION ZERO.
The debut album was produced by KING DIAMOND's Andy La Rocque.
Wählin also goes under the pseudonym of Necrolord as cover artist for many Black Metal bands.

Albums:
WEDDING THE GROTESQUE, Black Sun (1997)
Dark Man / Shaven Angel Forms / Blood Of Summer / Sacrificial Highway / The Unchaste Bittersweet / Sorrow Piercing Art / The Smiling Black / Beggar Whipped In Wine / The Diabolique
THE DIABOLIQUE, Listenable POSH 011 (1998)
Stealing The Fire From Heaven / Blood Of Summer / Beggar Whipped In Wine / Sorrows Piercing Art / Deep Shame Of God
THE BLACK FLOWER, Black Sun (1999)
Catholic / Dark Rivers Of The Heart / Absinthe / And Deepest Sadness / Yesmine / Eternal Summer / Cannula / Morphine / A Golden Girl From Somewhere / Silver / Play In The Dark
BUTTERFLIES, Necropolis NR044CD (2000)
Rain / Losing You / Butterflies / Summer Of Her Heart / Stolen Moments / Beneath The Shade

DICHOTIC (CANADA)
Line-Up: Roland Kinley (vocals), Richard Guy (guitar), Jeff Galder (guitar), Scott Armstrong (bass), Neil Grandy (drums)

Halifax, Nova Scotia Death Metal act DICHOTIC have self-financed two albums to date.

Albums:
COLLAPSE INTO DESPAIR, Discorporate Music (1998)
Solely In Opposites / God Complex / Touching The Timeless / Heed To Instincts / Out Of Spite / Love Stained Splatter / Unholy Exhumation
LOWEST COMMON DENOMINATOR, Discorporate Music (1999)
Spilling / Exhumation / Fisting / Precise / Failed Expectations / Smothered / Cyclical Retardation / (Sic.) / Dead Simple

DIES IRAE (POLAND)

Offshoot act from VADER men Mauser and Docent.

Albums:
IMMOLATED, Metal Blade 3984143562 (2000)
Zonak / Message Of Aiwas / Sirius / Immolated / The Nameless City / Bestride Shatak / Turning Point / Hidden

Love / Lion Of Knowledge / Unheavenly Salvation / Fear Of God / Blasphemous Words

DIM MAK (USA)

Line-Up: Scott Ruth (vocals), Shaune Kelley (guitar), Dennis Carroll (bass), Branson Thomas (drums)

DIM MAK consist of former RIPPING CORPSE members guitarist Shaune Kelley, vocalist Scott Ruth and drummer Brandon Thomas together with ex-TORTURE KRYPT bassist Dennis Carroll. Eschewing the gore and occult leanings of their former acts DIM MAK, named after an ancient Chinese martial art technique the 'death touch', made their presence felt with numerous compilation appearances prior to signing to the Singapore based Dies Irae label for their 'Enter The Dragon' album.

Albums:
ENTER THE DRAGON, Dies Irae (1999)
Spirit Of The Dragon / Defy The Clouds / Feel The Pain / Cobra's Eyes / Between Two Fires / Royal Ass Whipping / Insect To Insect / No Rope A Dope / Warchild / Sorry / Tribulations / Gas Poured On Flame / Dark With Demons

DISAFFECTED (PORTUGAL)

DISAFFECTED was created in January 1991 issuing two demos prior to gigging. A tape of a rehearsal landed the band a deal with Skyfall Records in 1995 although shortly after the release of 'Vast' DISAFFECTED lost both their vocalist and drummer Quim Aries, the latter going on to join SACRED SIN.
The debut album, which includes a cover of ACHERON's 'Thou Art Lord', was produced by Marsten Bailey, the Englishman responsible for the HEAVENWOOD album 'Diva'.

Albums:
VAST, Skyfall (1995)
Cold Tranquility / No Feelings Left / Unlimited Vision / The Praxis Of The Non Being / Dreaming I / Dream II (Another Form) / Allusion / Dead Like My Dreams / Vast - The Long Tomorrow / … And Flesh Will Be My Bride / Thou Art Lord

DISASSOCIATE (Brooklyn, NY, USA)
Line-Up: Ralphy Boy (vocals), Ricardo Sheets (guitar), Cn (samples), Xb (bass), Xd (drums)

An illustrious name on the underground circuit DISASSOCIATE blend an abrasive mix of sonically charged Metal, Punk and Hardcore. DISASSOCIATE were created in mid 1992 with an inaugural line up of ex-JESUS CHRUST man Ralphy Boy on vocals, former CHOKING VICTIM drummer Squirt, Nick on bass, JESUS CHRUST guitarist M.M. Fury with NAUSEA and THORNS drummer Roy Mayorga on second guitar. The latter would journey on to CRISIS, PALE DEMONS and by 2000 OZZY OSBOURNE.
By August the band had trimmed down to Ralphy Boy, M.M. Fury, Squirt and second guitarist Smegs. Shortly after erstwhile SEIZURE bassist John Munera made the line up complete. The band soon fractured though with both Smegs and squirt bailing out.
Ralphy Boy, M.M. Fury and Munera persevered drafting Lawrence Sux from Jazz Grindcore act DANK SINATRA. This version of DISASSOCIATE cut the debut demo tape 'Partytime'.
Live work was to be undertaken with SOCIAL OUTCAST and MISERY but Sux was arrested on the eve of the show. Disillusioned, Munera quit, leaving DISASSOCIATE as a duo.
During this period of flux Fury temped with DENIED before DISASSOCIATE was reactivated with the addition of BLACK RAIN members Bones 23 on bass and drummer Thom Furtado. This version of the band cut the notorious 'Murder The Mind' 7" single'. Initially issued in a black and white sleeve adorned with graphic medical photographs of malformed babies the EP was released as 800 black vinyl, 100 green and a further 100 transparent discs. An even more limited run of just 20 copies came with a full colour sleeve. The same year found DISASSOCIATE contributing the track 'Institutional Hate' to a four way shared EP with RECTIFY, BATTLE OF DISARM and VOMITOSE 'Fukt Az Punx' issued on Squat Or Rot Records. More exposure came with their inclusion on the Sound Pollution 'Fuckin' Noise Terror' compilation. The band would then issue a cassette release 'Live In Singapore'.
With the completion of an East Coast tour to promote the single Furtado departed and DISASSOCIATE plugged the gap with MALIGNANCY's John Bedpan. The band actually moved into a full-on Black Metal incarnation during this period complete with corpse paint. Line-up

ructions soon put an end to this as Bedpan drifted off to enter the world of catering!

The drum stool was quickly occupied by Alex Hernandez of FALLEN CHRIST. Fury had previously been jamming in a side project with Hernandez dubbed DOWN LAW.

With Hernandez on board the band recorded the first CD 'Controlled Power'. Issued in 1996 the Japanese version of the album came complete with tracks from the previous 'Live In Singapore' outing. The same year saw a video release 'Years In Question' and another compilation appearance, this time on the Resevoir 'Nothing's Quiet On The Western Front' collection. However, DISASSOCIATE's fluidity on the drummer front reared its head again when Hernandez jumped ship to IMMOLATION. Joe Darkside of DARKSIDE NYC and ALL OUT WAR stepped in for gigs with CATHEDRAL in America and the act's first Japanese shows.

Predictably the group hit drummer problems again although did perform at least one show with both Darkside and Furtado on two kits. For American dates with CORRUPTED and HELLCHILD the act enrolled Haroldo Mardones. It came as no surprise that a new face was soon behind the kit, namely Scott Bates.

1997 witnessed the inclusion of live tracks from DISASSOCIATE as part of the Angst Records compilation 'Where's My Shoe?'. Another fleeting showing came with the use of the 10 second track 'Phatboy' on the ambitious 73 band 7" EP 'Blleeeeaaauuurrrgghhh!!' compilation on Slap A Ham.

DISASSOCIATE's 1998 album 'Symbols, Signals & Noise' was produced by Steve Austin of TODAY IS THE DAY and would prompt a further tour of Japan. Austin would also handle the reins for 2000's 'Imperfect World'.

Singles/EPs:
Army Of Losers / Born Against / Fight / Pigsday / I Eat Your Skin / 3 A.M. Brawl / Murder The Mind, Splifford Productions SP001 (1993) ('Murder The Mind' 7" EP)

Albums:
CONTROLLED POWER, Devastating Soundworks DS003 (1996)
Anti Justice / People / Zombie Dance / Envy The Dead / In Heat / Black Triangle / Life In A Bottle / Controlled Power / A

Long Hard Battle / Bedpan's FPD / Crustier Than You / Brainwashed / Their Freedom / Ice Bong / Warning
SYMBOLS, SIGNALS & NOISE, Devastating Soundworks DS004 (1998)
IMPERFECT WORLD, Thick (2000)
Intro / The Reign Of The Superpowers / The Price Of Freedom / Bad Fish / Bill Clinton Is A Nymphomaniac / Family Life / Fractal Basin Boundaries - A Strange Attractor / Los Cabrones / Untitled / The Whistle Song / Fallout / From Yesterday 'Til Today / Operation Hemp / Imperfect World / Information Warfare / Hear Them Cry / Flight 800 / Sit And Rot / Bad Science

DISASTROUS MURMUR (AUSTRIA)
Line-Up: Harald Bezdek (vocals / guitar), Walter Schweiger (bass), Manfred Perack (drums)

DISASTROUS MURMUR managed to compose an entire album based on various means of horrific torture. Which was nice... Premier American Death Metal act MORTICIAN would cover 'Extra Uterine Pregnancy' on their 2001 album 'Domain Of Death'.

Singles/EPs:
Black n' Bad / Stick Around, Murena MR 11/86 (1986)

Albums:
RHAPSODIES IN RED, Osmose Productions OPLP 004 (1992)
Disgorged Bowel Movement / Extra Uterine Pregnancy Part 2 / Dinner Is Served / Trash, Chunk And Garbage / Masked Killer / Flesh... Is What I Need / Satisfaction In The morgue / Into The Dungeon / Desecrating The Grave / Drowned In Blood
FOLTER, Lethal LRC 848 (1994)
The Oral Rectal And Vaginal Pear / Breaking By Means Of The Wheel (Germany 1550-1750) / The Punishment Collar / The Judas Cradle / The Headcrusher / Unfleshed To The Bone / The Saw (Spain 18th Century) / Heretic's Pincers / The Grate
...AND HUNGRY ARE THE LOST, Perverted Taste (2001)

DISBELIEF (GERMANY)
Line-Up: Karsten Jäger (vocals), Tommy Fritsch (guitar), Olly Lenz (guitar), Joe Trunk (bass), Kai Bergerin (drums)

DISBELIEF, Nuclear Blast (1997)
Follow / Away / My Life / Scattered
Product / God? Master! / In A Cage /
Soul Massacre / Why Emotional? /
Against The Shadow / The Harmony
Within / Behind Those Eyes
INFECTED, Grind Syndicate SYN003
(1998)
Infected / Mindstrip / First / Fetish 97 /
Again / Down / Pounding / Without A
Kiss / Now
WORST ENEMY, Massacre MAS
CD0278 (2001)

DISCIPLES OF MOCKERY (USA)

Line-Up: Craig Pillard (vocals / guitar),
Mike Boyce (guitar), Ronnie Deo (bass),
Jim Roe (drums)

DISCIPLES OF MOCKERY was founded
by the exodus of INCANTATION
members guitarist Craig Pillard, bassist
Ronnie Deo and drummer Jim Roe in
alliance with former ROTTING CORPSE
man Mike Boyce on second guitar.

The band cut a notorious 3 track live in
the studio promotional CD soon dubbed
the 'Red' single before cutting the debut
album 'Prelude To Apocalypse'.
Manufactured in a limited run of a mere
1,000 copies, the album was produced by
Paul Crook of ANTHRAX.

Pillard departed in 1994 relocating to
New York. In the midst of a well
documented heroin addiction Pillard
teamed up with both CATTLE PRESS
and Doom act CEREMONIUM. Freeing
himself from his drug habit the man
journeyed back home where he reunited
with Deo and Roe in WOMB.

The 'Red' single was combined with
WOMB tracks for a split CD release by
Necroharmonic Productions. The same
label would also reissue the one and only
album.

Albums:
PRELUDE TO APOCALYPSE, (1998)

DISCORDANCE AXIS

(New York, NY, USA)
Line-Up: Eva 05 (vocals), Qon (guitar),
Dave Witte (drums)

Grindcore unit founded by former
HUMAN REMAINS / EXIT 13 drummer
Dave Witte. Other members go under
pseudonyms although Eva 05 is in
actuality Jon Chang and Qon is guitarist
Rob Marton.

DISCORDANCE AXIS were founded in
1992 emanating from the dissolving of
SEDITION. The band bowed in with a
split 7" single in alliance with COSMIC
HURSE. At this stage the band was
actually intended to be a purely one off
recording project. Nevertheless
DISCORDANCE AXIS returned shortly
after to cut tracks for another split affair,
this time shared with HELLCHILD. The
recordings came dangerously close to
being consigned to the vaults as the
studio time was originally slated for the
recording of a debut album. Apparently
the band members got into an argument
and disbanded. Three months later the
differences were resolved and the tracks
that had been cut were issued on the
single.

Yet again DISCORDANCE AXIS pursued
the split 7" idea in collusion with
CAPITALIST CASUALTIES. The band
contributed live tracks to a single
intended for a miserly production run of
just 200 copies. A mistake in the pressing
plant left 25 over-runs though and these
were released with different cover artwork
to the main issue.

DISCORDANCE AXIS had their fourth
split 7" in 1994 with DEF MASTER.
These songs are notable for having no
bass guitar at all. Released on the
Japanese HG Fact label the single saw a
run of 2000 copies. Finally the band got
around to their debut album 'Ulterior'
released in 1995 by Devour Records.
When work in the studio was completed
Witte broke ranks to concentrate on
HUMAN REMAINS full time. Undaunted
the band drafted Rob Proctor of ASSUCK
for a tour of Japan the same year. After
these dates Witte returned.

Yet another split 7" ensued, this time with
PLUTOCRACY on the Slap A Ham label.
The record came about by accident
though as Plutocracy's tracks were
supposed to be back to back with songs
donated by ASSUCK. When Assuck's
tapes failed to arrive DISCORDANCE
AXIS plugged the gap.

In 1998 the band put together another
split effort, this time with Japanese band
MELT BANANA. A cover version of MELT
BANANA's 'So Unfilial Rule' was
countered by their Japanese colleagues
responding in kind by covering 'One
Dimensional'.

After DISCORDANCE AXIS had released
their second full length album 'Jouhou'
Marten, suffering from tendonitis, quit.
Steve Procopio of HUMAN REMAINS

soon made up the numbers as the band delved into electro sounds for the 1997 single 'Necropolitan'.

1998 saw 'Jouhou' reissued with a compliment of bonus tracks and a brace of live tracks appearing on the 'Snarl Out' compilation album on Slightly Fast Records. Devour Records also collated early, live and rare tracks for the 'Original Sound Version' album.

The 2000 album 'The Inalienable Dreamless' benefited from an international release in both vinyl and CD formats. There was even an ultra limited edition boxed version restricted to just six copies.

Witte created side project ATOMSMASHER in 2000 in union with OLD guitarist James Plotkin and JANSKY NOISE's Speedranch.

Witte is also a member of BURNT BY THE SUN with his former HUMAN REMAINS colleague Teddy Patterson.

In March of 2001 DISCORDANCE AXIS was reportedly laid to rest. Marten had been forced out again due to an illness which provoked pain when subjected to loud noises. Not the best complaint to have when a member of a Grindcore band! Former member Procopio was pulled in to fulfill Japanese tour commitments.

Witte forged an alliance with SPAZZ mainman Chris Dodge to issue the joint venture album 'East West Blast Fest'.

Singles/EPs:
Split, Pulp (1992) (Split 7" single with COSMIC HURSE. 500 copies)
Split, HG Fact (1993) (Split 7" with HELLCHILD)
Split, Pulp (1993) (Split 7" with CAPITALIST CASUALTIES. 225 copies)
Split, HG Fact (1994) (Split 7" single with DEF MASTER. 2000 copies)
Split, Slap A Ham (1995) (Split 7" single with PLUTOCRACY)
Information Sniper / Amphetamine Hollow Tip / Tokyo / So Unfilial Rule / Junk Utopia / Continuity, HG Fact (1995) (Split 7" with MELT BANANA)
Necropilitan, HG Fact (1997)
Split, (2001) (Split 7" single with CORRUPTED)

Albums:
ULTERIOR, Devour (1995)
JOUHOU, Devour (1997)
Vertigo Index / Panoptic / Aperture Of Pinholes / Information Sniper / Carcass Lottery / Come Apart Together, Come

Together Alone / Rain Perimeter / A Broken Tomorrow / Attrition / Nikola Tesla / Flow My Tears The Policeman Said / Jouhou / Damage Style / Arther Scalpul / A Crack In The Cataracts / Numb(ers) / Ashtray Ballpoint / Typeface / Reciprocity / Reincarnation /Alzheimer
ORIGINAL SOUND VERSION, Devour (1998)
THE INALIENABLE DREAMLESS, Hydrahead (2000)
Castration Rite / The Inalienable Dreamless / Sound Out The Braille / Oratorio In Grey Vacuum Sleeve / Angel Present / The Necropolitan / Pattern Blue / The End Of Rebirth / Loveless / Radiant Arkham / Use Of Weapons / Compiling Autumn / Jigsaw / The Third Children / A Leaden Stride To Nowhere / Drowned

DISFEAR (SWEDEN)
Line-Up: Jeppe Lerjerud (vocals), Björn Pettersson (guitar), Henke Frykaman (bass), Robin Wiberg (drums)

Nykoping Crustcore unit DISFEAR released a split EP with UNCURBED in 1995. Original drummer Jallo Lehto would be superseded by Robin Wiberg.

Albums:
A BRUTAL SIGHT OF FEAR, Lost And Found LF060CD (1993)
A Brutal Side Of War / Judgement Day / Forced To Conform / No Hope Of Survival / Religion / Min Elegi / Undergang / Vietnam Idaq / Det Sista Kriget
SOUL SCARS, Distortion DISTCD 13 (1995)
Soul Scars / Left To Die / The Ultimate Disaster / To Hell And Back / Weak / Sobriety / The Price Of Ignorance / All This Fear / Do As You're Told / The True Face Of War / Grim Reality / After The Revival / Anxious / Disavowed
EVERYDAY SLAUGHTER, Osmose Productions (1997)
With Each Dawn I Die / Anthem Of Agony / Crimescene: Worldwide / A Race For Power / Spectre Of Genocide / Everyday Slaughter / Subsistence / Totalitarian Control / Frustration / Aftermath / Overkill / Captured By Life / … In Fear

DISFIGURED (Hicksville, NY, USA)
Line-Up: Joe Reilly (vocals), John Luyster (guitar), Ryan Schimmenti (bass), Jean Paul Matiuk (drums)

New York's DISFIGURED, renowned for bassist Ryan Schimmenti's predilection for wearing Graham Bonnet style Hawaiian shirts, was created in 1996 as a trio of former CREHATE members guitarist John Luyster and drummer Jean Paul Matiuk along with SCHIMMENTI. Later former REPUDIATION man Joe Reilly took over lead vocals.

DISFIGURED's debut album 'Prelude To Dementia', recorded in Illinois and produced by BROKEN HOPE's Brian Griffin, includes an unaccredited take on AC/DC's 'Dirty Deeds Done Dirt Cheap' with guest vocals from Frank Rini of INTERNAL BLEEDING and a guitar solo from Chris Matiuk. FLESHGRIND's Rick Lipscomb also adds guest vocals to 'Ridden With Disgust' and 'Witness Your Creation'.

Schimmenti would perform session bass duties on BROKEN HOPE's 'Grotesque Bleedings' album and would later join INTERNAL BLEEDING as temporary frontman supplanting Frank Rini.

Singles/EPs:
Split, (1997) (Split 7" single with REPUDIATION)

Albums:
PRELUDE TO DEMENTIA, Severed (1999)

DISGORGE (MEXICO)

Grinding Deathsters DISGORGE arrived with the 1995 demo cassette 'Through The Innards'. Previously the band had made their reputation on the live circuit in Mexico and an appearance on the live compilation video 'Audio Visual Aberration II' issued by Bellphegot Records. A second three track cassette emerged in 1996 prompting tour dates which spread into such far flung places as El Salvador and Guatemala. In Mexico itself DISGORGE supported visiting artists such as CANNIBAL CORPSE, MACABRE, INCANTATION and KATAKLYSM.

A further tape entitled 'Chronic Corpora Infest' arrived in 1997 and was later re-issued in CD format by American Line Productions. The following year a split 7" single in alliance with Polish Grind merchants SQUASH BOWELS was issued in the Czech Republic. DISGORGE's 1999 'Infestour' took them outside of Mexico into Nicaragua, Costa Rica and back to Guatemala and El Salvador. Domestic dates billed the 'Tormentour' included gigs with

SHAMASH and BURIED DREAMS. DISGORGE's second album 'Forensick' was released by the Spanish Death Metal specialists Repulse Records.

Singles/EPs:
Split, (1998) (7" split single with SQUASH BOWELS)
Split, Lofty Storm LSR011 (2001) (7" split single with COCK AND BALL TORTURE)

Albums:
CHRONIC CORPORA INFEST, Perpetual (1997)
FORENSICK, Repulse (1999)

DISGORGE (USA)

Line-Up: Matti Way (vocals), Tony Freithoffer (guitar), Eric Flesy (bass), Rick Myers (drums)

DISGORGE was created during 1992 by frontman Bryan Ugartechea, guitarist Tony Freithoffer and drummer Ricky Myers. This line up cut the opening demo 'Cognitive Lust Of Mutilation' the same year but a relocation to San Diego saw the departure of Ugartechea. By the time of DISGORGE's second demo session in 1995 Matti Way had taken over on lead vocals and Eric Flesy had took the bass position.

Further ructions occurred after the debut 1998 album 'Cranial Impalement' with both Freithoffer and Flesy decamping. New faces were guitarist Diego Sanchez and former STRANGULATION bassist Ben Marlin. The line up predictably would not last.

DISGORGE members vocalist A.J. Magana, bassist Derek Boyer and drummer Torrey Moores all founded DEPRECATED during 1996.

Following the departure of Matti Way to former GORGASM drummer Derek Hoffman's act INCESTUOUS (later CINERARY) the band utilized the temporary services of DEPRECATED's A.J. Magana. This position became a permanent fixture as Magana rejoined the act full time for recording of the 'Dissecting The Apostles' album.

Ricky Myers also joined CINERARY in early 2001.

DISGORGE toured Europe in March of 2001 headlining over GOREOPSY and SANATORIUM.

Albums:
CRANIAL IMPALEMENT, Extremities Productions (1998)

Deranged Epidemic / Atonement / Cognitive Lust Of Mutilation / Period Of Agony / Cranial Impalment / Penetrate The Unfledged / Malodorous Oblation / Carnally Decimated
SHE LAY GUTTED, Erebos ERE 018 (2000)
Revelations XVIII / She Lay Gutted / Exhuming The Disemboweled / Compost Devourment / Sodomise The Bleeding / False Conception / Womb Full Of Scabs / Disfigured Catacombs / Purifying The Cavity

DISGRACE (FINLAND)
Line-Up: Jukka Taskinen (vocals / guitar), Riku Sanaksenaho (guitar), Jussi Selonen (bass), Miska Koski (drums)

Although starting life as a straightforward extreme Metal outfit DISGRACE would evolve into a groovy mixture of Death Metal and 50's Rock n' Roll. DISGRACE's debut album 'Grey Misery' on the Modern Primitive label featured guitarist Toni Stranius. The band cut another album for Modern Primitive but the label collapsed before it could be released. Stranius was replaced by Anton Kupias for the 1995 effort 'Superhumandome'.
By 2000 the band were billing themselves as vocalist Oral Chimpanzee, guitarists Anal Chimpanzee and Jimbo Mini Golf, bass player C.C. Less and drummer King Nobody.

Singles/EPs:
Depths Of Gods / Deprive My Innermost Soul / Incinerate / Offering, Seraphic Decay SCAM 007 (1990) ('Depths Of Gods' EP)
Sunwheel / Malachia's Grin / Fields / Love Mountain / Icon / Radioblast, Crawfish Recordings FISH001 (1994) ('Vacuum Horror, Horror Vacuums' EP)
Gula / Cut It Off / Down On Elvis / She Loves, Greatest Vinyl Collections GVC 101 (1998)
Furvival EP, Scapegoat (2000)

Albums:
GREY MISERY, Modern Primitive (1992)
My Dark Paradise / Unity's Interlude Dyes Blind Tomorrow / Abtruse Myth / Obscurity In The Azure / The Chasm / And Below Lies Infinity / Waves Of Hypocrisy Seas / Debris / Immortality's Open Lake / Transcendental Dimension
SUPERHUMANDOME, Morbid SPV 084-12652 CD (1995)
Boneplay / Mean Relief / Distress /

Dome / One Spiral / Bait / Forever / Ride / The Earth Silence / Christaddictsense / Spleen
IF YOU'RE LOOKING FOR TROUBLE, Metamorphos (1998)
Psyche Rodeo / The Supremes / Cut It Off / Deadbeat / Tequila Desert / Speed Up / Greyhound / She Loves / Rock n' Roll / Explode - Explode / Roadkill Theme

DISGUST (UK)
Line-Up: Dean Jones (vocals), Dave Ellesmere (guitar), Gary Sumner (guitar), Lee Barrett (bass), Steve Beatty (drums)

On the brutal borderline between Punk and Death Metal DISGUST were assembled by the head of the Plastic Head distribution network drummer Steve Beatty, an ex-member of MASS. Joining him were EXTREME NOISE TERROR bassist Lee Barrett, guitarist Dave Ellesmere of DISCHARGE and THE INSANE, fellow guitarist Gary Sumner of THE INSANE and BLITZKRIEG and another EXTREME NOISE TERROR member vocalist Dean Jones.
The second album, produced by ex-SABBAT guitarist Andy Sneap, had ex-CRACK / BLANK GENERATION guitarist Kneil Brown joining in as well as a surprise inclusion of erstwhile MOTÖRHEAD guitarist WURZEL.
DISGUST's album covers depicting victims of war are not noted for their subtlety.

Albums:
BRUTALITY OF WAR, Earache (1994)
Intro / Mother Earth / As Millions Suffer / An Horrific End / Thrown Into Oblivion / Civilization Decays / Relentless Slaughter / And Still… / The Light Of Death / What Kind Of Mind / You Have No Right / Sea Of Tears / The Anguished Cry / Life Erased / Outro
A WORLD OF NO BEAUTY, Nuclear Blast 27361 62322 (1996)
Intro / The Result Of War / Remember / Eden / The Last Embrace / A Mothers Bleeding Heart / Can Your Eyes See / Just Another War Crime / Evil Trade / Blood Soaked Soil / The Wounds Are Never Healed / Hymn For A Dying Planet

DISGUSTING (NORWAY)
Line-Up: Ken (vocals / guitar), Lasse (vocals / guitar), Erik (vocals / bass), Lars (vocals / drums)

Albums:
SHAPESHIFTER BIRTH BLUES, Head Not Found HNF007 (199-)
Fuch-Sia / Me And My Mind / Chronological Perversity / We're Always Here (The Talamasca) / Slimy / Voluspa / My Shade / Calamity / Shapeshifterbirthblues / Gasp At Your Final Breath

DISHARMONIC ORCHESTRA
(AUSTRIA)
Line-Up: Patrick Klopf (vocals / guitar), Harald Bezdek (bass), Martin Messner (drums)

DISHARMONIC ORCHESTRA, as their name implies, are an experimental trio unafraid to mix Metal with Rap and Grindcore. The band was founded in 1987 by vocalist / guitarist Patrick Klopf and drummer Martin Messner. Two demos resulted in 1987 'The Unequalled Visual Response Mechanism' and 'Requiem For The Forrest' before bassist Harald Bezek departed.
The band drafted Herwig Zamernik in for live dates and soon scored a deal with German extreme label Nuclear Blast. The firsts fruits of this union was a split album with fellow Austrians PUNGENT STENCH and an EP 'Successive Substitution'.
In order to promote their first full length album 'Expositions Prophylaxe' the trio set out on a series of German festival dates with ATROCITY, CARCASS, ENTOMBED and PUNGENT STENCH. A club tour of America ensued on a billing including AUTOPSY, CANNIBAL CORPSE, IMMOLATION and REPULSION. 1992 was sealed with European dates with ENTOMBED and SINISTER.
Signing to the SPV Steamhammer label DISHARMONIC ORCHESTRA issued the 'Pleasuredome' album before calling it a day.
DISHARMONIC ORCHESTRA were among the first European bands to tour Israel.

Singles/EPs:
Successive Substitution, Nuclear Blast NB (1990)

Albums:
SPLIT LP, Nuclear Blast NB019 (1989)
(Split LP with PUNGENT STENCH)
Dehumanoid / Distorted Mind / Putrid Stench / Shredded Illusion /

Compulsorily Screaming / Interposition / Animal Suffocation
EXPOSITIONS PROPHYLAXE, Nuclear Blast NB 037 (1990)
Introphlaxe / Inexorable Logic / Life Disintegrating / Sick Dishonourableness / Successive Substitution / Accelerated Evolution / Psycoanalysis / Quintessentially / Unnecessary Institution / Hypophysis / Disappeared With Hermaphrodite Choids / Disharmonisation / The Unequalled Visual Response Mechanism
NOT TO BE UNIDIMENSIONAL CONSCIOUS, Nuclear Blast NB062 (1992)
Perishing Passion / A Mental Sequence / Addicted / Seas With Missing Pleasure / The Return Of The Living Beat / Idiosyncrasy / Like Madness From Above / Time Frame / Mind Seduction
PLEASURE DOME, Steamhammer SPV 084-76772 (1994)
Hyperact / Recommended Suicide / The Silence I Observe / Feel Like Fever Now / The Sick Deep Under / Getting Me Nowhere / Pleasuredome / Stuck In Something / Fall Colours Fall / Overwhelming Tranquility / Where Can I Park My Horse / Off The Road / Sunday Mood

DISINCARNATE (USA)
Line-Up: Tomas Lindberg (vocals), James Murphy (guitar), Steve DiGeorgio (bass), Nick Barker (drums)

Although a veteran journeyman guitarist for hire on the Death scene guitarist JAMES MURPHY (whose credits include AGENT STEEL, DEATH, TESTAMENT, CANCER, OBITUARY and KONKHRA) also made time for his own act DISINCARNATE.
The 1993 Colin Richardson produced album 'Dreams Of The Carrion Kind' had Murphy working with fellow guitarist Jason Carman, vocalist Bryan Cegon and drummer Tommy Viator. Guesting vocalists were CANCER's John Walker and MY DYING BRIDE man Aaron Stainthorpe.
The band was reassembled in 1999 with a line up of Murphy, ex AT THE GATES singer Tomas Lindberg, SADUS / DEATH bassist Steve DiGeorgio and CRADLE OF FILTH drummer Nick Barker. Before any product could be issued Barker joined DIMMU BORGIR.
Murphy has issued two solo albums to date 'Convergence' in 1996 and 1999's 'Feeding The Machine'. DiGeorgio joined

ICED EARTH.

Albums:
DREAMS OF THE CARRION KIND, Roadrunner (1993)
De Profundis / Stench Of Paradise Burning / Beyond The Flesh / In Sufferance / Monarch Of The Sleeping Marches / Soul Erosion / Entranced / Confine Of Shadows / Deadspawn / Sea Of Tears / Immemorial Dream

DISINTER (Chicago, IL, USA)
Line-Up: Zion (vocals), Preston (guitar), Mike (guitar), Bats (bass), Tom (drums)

Old school Death Metal band founded in 1990 as a side project from EYEGOUGER and PAIN guitarist Preston with GORGASM's Tom Tangalos for a 1991 demo tape 'Disinterra Et Corpus'. DISINTER was put on one side whilst Preston concentrated on EYEGOUGER. The band was resurrected in 1996 for a demo 'Storm Of The Witch' with Evil Ed on vocals. The 'Desecrated' album followed for Pulverizer Records. Zion took over from Evil Ed as frontman.
After the 1997 'With The Blood' demo drummer Dave Chiarella (also a member of FUNERAL NATION) left to join USURPER, retitling himself Dave Hellstorm. DISINTER pulled in drummer Tom to plug the gap.

Singles/EPs:
The Beauty Of Suffering EP, Disinter (1997)

Albums:
DESECRATED, Pulverizer (1997)
WELCOME TO OBLIVION, Morbid MR 079 (2000)
The Sleeper Awakens / Welcome To Oblivion / Followed From Death / That Which Is Owned / Descendants Of Darkness / Holy Parasites / The Battle Rages On / Twisted Soul / Field Of Screams / Earthen Interment: Torn From The Grave

DISMAL EUPHONY (NORWAY)
Line-Up: Keltziva (vocals), Kristoffer Austrheim (guitar / bass / drums), Elin (keyboards)

Hafrsfjord's DISMAL EUPHONY released the demo 'Spellbound' on CD prior to a name change to SORIA MORIA SLOTT. However, upon signing to Napalm Records the band reverted back to their previous title.
During early 1997 the band lost both their bass player and second guitarist. New recruits to DISMAL EUPHONY in 2000 were bassist Etland Casperson (reputedly of MR. CUCUMBER!) and APOSTACY keyboard player Axel Henriksen.

Singles/EPs:
Dismal Euphony / A Winter's Tale / Spellbound / The Mournful Silence, Napalm NPR 018 (1996) ('Dismal Euphony' EP)
Lady Ablaze / Abandon / Cabinet Bizarre / 150 MPH / Bortgag, Napalm NPR 072 (2000) ('Lady Ablaze' EP)

Albums:
SORIA MORIA SLOTT, Napalm NPR 021 (1997)
Prolog / Et Vintereventyr / Nattan Loftet Sitt Tunge Ansikt / Alvedans / Trolloundet / Ekko / Isgrav, Det Siste Hvilested / Epilog
AUTUMN LEAVES (THE REBEL LION OF TIDES), Napalm NPR 033 (1997)
An Autumn Leaf In The Circles Of Time / Simply Dead / A Thousand Rivers / Mistress Tears / Carven / Spire / In Remembrance Of A Shroud / Splendid Horror
ALL LITTLE DEVILS, Napalm (1999)
Days Of Sodom / Rage Of Fire / Victory / All Little Devils / Lunatic / Psycho Path / Shine For Me Misery / Scenario / Dead Words
PYTHON ZERO, Nuclear Blast (2001)
Critical Mass / Python Zero / Zentinel / Needle / Magma / Birth Reverse / Plasma Pool / Flyineye

DISMEMBER (SWEDEN)
Line-Up: Matti Karki (vocals), David Blomqvist (guitar, Robert Senneback (guitars), Richard Cabeza (bass), Fred Estby (drums)

Swedish extreme Death Metallers DISMEMBER were formed in 1988 as a trio of vocalist/bassist Robert Senneback, guitarist David Blomqvist and drummer Fred Estby. This initial line-up only maintained itself for just over a year but did release two demos in the shape of 'Dismembered' and 'Last Blasphemies'.
The original DISMEMBER folded in late 1989 with Estby joining forces with CARNAGE and Blomqvist opting for ENTOMBED. However, shortly before recording of the debut CARNAGE album

Blomqvist jumped ship from his new act to join the band.

CARNAGE dissolved when guitarist Mike Amott quit to CARCASS leaving Estby, Blomqvist and vocalist Matti Karki to resurrect DISMEMBER. Still a trio, this new line-up released the Tomas Skogsberg produced 'Reborn In Blasphemy' demo before inviting Senneback, then a member of UNLEASHED, to resume his position in the band. DISMEMBER also augmented their sound with the addition of ex-CARBONISED bassist Richard Cabeza.

Having signed to Germany's Nuclear Blast label, the first hard product to arrive was the inclusion of two of the latest demo tracks on the 'Death Is Just The Beginning' compilation album.

DISMEMBER garnered huge media attention in 1991 when their 'Like An Ever Flowing Stream' debut album was confiscated by British and Australian customs for being 'indecent and obscene' (hence the title of their 1993 album). Her Majesty's customs had objected to song titles and lyrics such as 'Skin Her Alive' and 'Brutal Orgy Of Flesh'. The subsequent court case shot DISMEMBER's name to the forefront of the current wave of Death metal acts.

The band toured Europe opening for MORBID ANGEL in June 1991 but these dates were curtailed due to disagreements between the two acts. Further live shows included DISMEMBER's appearance at the Rock Hard festivals alongside DEATH, PESTILENCE and NAPALM DEATH.

The band's notoriety was capitalized on by the 1992 mini-album 'Pieces' which saw more live shows in Europe, touring in conjunction with OBITUARY and NAPALM DEATH. A second full album, 'Indecent And Obscene', gave their fans more of the same formula which had so outraged H.M. customs. DISMEMBER followed the record's release with a bout of touring in America in 1993 with SUFFOCATION and DEICIDE before hooking up with MORBID ANGEL once more for a European tour.

Following a lay off period DISMEMBER returned to the fray in early 1995 as part of the Nuclear Blast organized festivals alongside labelmates MESHUGGAH, HYPOCRISY and BENEDICTION. A single, 'Casket Garden', was released as a taster for the new album.

'Massive Killing Capacity' gave DISMEMBER their first German chart album.

Whilst gaining notoriety within the DISMEMBER ranks bassist Richard Cabeza also moonlights for UNANIMATED and DAMNATION.

2000 also saw Karkki and Cabeza in collusion with ENTOMBED's Uffe Cederlund and Peter Stjärnvind for their MURDER SQUAD project.

Singles/EPs:

Skin Her Alive / Defective Decay, Nuclear Blast NB047 PDS (1991)
Pieces / I Wish You Hell / Carnal Tomb / Soon To Be Dead, Nuclear Blast NB060 (1992)
Pieces / I Wish You Hell / Carnal Tomb / Soon To Be Dead / Deathvocation, Nuclear Blast NB 060 MS 55-29575 (1992) ('Pieces' 12" EP)
Casket Garden / Wardead / Justifiable Homicide, Nuclear Blast NB130-2 (1995)
Misanthropic / Pagan Saviour / Shadowlands / Afterimage / Shapeshifter, Nuclear Blast NB LC 7027 (1997)

Albums:

LIKE AN EVER FLOWING STREAM, Nuclear Blast NB047 (1991)
Override Of The Overture / Soon To Be Dead / Bleed For Me / And So Is Life / Dismembered / Skin Her Alive / Sickening Art / In Death's Sleep / Deathevocation / Defective Decay
INDECENT AND OBSCENE, Nuclear Blast NB077 (1993)
Fleshless / Skinfather / Sorrowfilled / Case Obscene / Souldevourer / Reborn In Blasphemy / Eviscerated (Bitch) / 9th Circle / Dreaming In Red
MASSIVE KILLING CAPACITY, Nuclear Blast NB (1995)
I Saw Them Die / Massive Killing Capacity / On Frozen Fields / Crime Divine / To The Bone / Wardead / Hallucigenia / Collection By Blood / Casket Garden / Nenia / Life - Another Shape Of Sorrow
DEATH METAL, Nuclear Blast NB 27361 62502 (1997)
Of Fire / Trendkiller / Misanthopic / Let The Napalm Rain / Live For The Fear Of Pain / Stillborn Ways / Killing Compassion / Bred For War / When Hatred Killed The Light / Ceremonial Comedy / Silent Are The Watchers / Mistweaver

DISMEMBERED FETUS
(Denver, CO, USA)
Line-Up: Creep (vocals), Mike (guitar), Ace (bass), Jeremy (drums)

Denver's uncompromising DISMEM-BERED FETUS, whose logo includes the disturbing inclusion of a hanging baby, were created in 1991 and originally fronted by the ubiquitous figure of Mephistopheles Fetusgrubber. He would depart in 1994.
Leading up to the 1996 'Generation Of Hate' album DISMEMBERED FETUS issued two demos in 1994, 'Hate' and 'Broken Neck' as well as a 1995 session 'I Don't Feel So Fuckin' Good'. Ex-members would create EAR BLEEDING DISORDER.

Singles/EPs:
Split, (199-) (7" split single with VOMIT SPAWN)

Albums:
GENERATION OF HATE, Dismembered Fetus (1996)
Intro / Maggots / Noise 1 / Colfax / Noise 2 / Ebola / Noise 3 / Bloody Vomit / Noise 4 / Ode To Nathan / Noise 5 / Beaten To Death / Noise 6 / Whores / Noise 7 / Shot On Everyone / Noise 8 / Panic Attack / Noise 9 / Dogrape / Lesbian Grandma / Oooka Mooka / Bloody Vaginal Discharge / Noise 10 / Gutted / Noise 11 / Godfuck / Noise 12 / Violent Planet / Noise 13 / Generation Of Hate

DISORDERED (USA)

Albums:
DOCUMENTARY OF DISGUST, (199-)

DISPATCHED (SWEDEN)
Line-Up: Krister Andersson (vocals), Daniel Lundberg (guitar), Jonas Kimberg (bass), Emanuel Åström (drums)

Gnesta based Death Metallers DISPATCHED were created in 1991. Adopted a fresh rhythm section following the 'Blue Fire' single release in 1995 New members were ex-MARBLE ICON bassist Fredrik Larsson and drummer Emanuel Lundberg.
DISPATCHED folded but mentor guitarist Daniel Lundberg reformed the act in 1996. The 2000 album sees a raunchy cover version of EUROPE's 'The Final Countdown'.

Singles/EPs:
Blue Fire / Is Born / Awaiting The End / Red Zone, Exhumed CORPSE 06 (1995)

Albums:
MOTHERWAR, MFN (2000)
Intro / Motherwar / To Sleep You Go / She's Lost / Down / Templar / The Final Countdown / Silver Waves / Dispatched

DISRUPT (MA, USA)
Line-Up: Jay Stiles (vocals), Jeff Hayward (guitar), Terry Savanstano (guitar), Bob Palombo (bass), Randy Odierno (drums)

The core of DISRUPT would later found the ultra Sludge Doom band GRIEF. Drummer Randy Odierno would at first switch to bass, then back to drums before finally leaving GRIEF.
Singer Jay Stiles would also make his presence felt with STATE OF FEAR. In alliance with DISRUPT guitarist Jeff Hayward he also features in CHICKEN CHEST AND THE BIRD BOYS.

Singles/EPs:
Deprived, (199-)
Doomed To Extinction, (199-)
Rid The Cancer, (1989)
Split, (199-) (7" split single with TUOMIOPAIVAN LAPSET)
Split, Crust (199-) (7" split single with WARCOLLAPSE)
Split, Dam (1991) (7" split single with RESIST)
Split, Adversity (1991) (7" split single with DESTROY)
Split, Desperate Attempt (199-) (7" split single with DISDAIN)
Smash Divisions, S.O.A. (1991)
Refuse Planet, Relapse (1991)
Deprived, Relapse (1991)
Split, Sludge (1993) (7" split single with SAUNA)

Albums:
UNREST, Relapse (1994)
Domestic Prison / Mass Graves / Complaint / A Life's A Life / Pay For… / Unrest / Reality Distortion / Down My Throat / Tortured In Entirety / Religion Is A Fraud / We Stand Corrected / Faction Disaster / Human Garbage / Without Sincerity / Neglected / Same Old Shit / For What? / Squandered / Mindlock / Green To Grey / Critics / Dog Eat Dog / Deprived / Give It Back / Victims Of Tradition / Exorbitant Prices Must Diminish / Smash Divisions / Lack Of

Intelligence / No Values / Solidarity
REFUSE PLANET, (199-) (Split album with DESTROY)
Dog Eat Dog / Suffocation / Subject To Suffering / No Values / Inebriated / Refuse Planet / G.A.M.E. / Consumed By The System

DISSECT (HOLLAND)
Line-Up: Vincent Scheerman (vocals / guitar), Philip Nugteren (guitar), Ricardo Etman (bass), Edwin De Waard (drums)

Albums:
SWALLOW SWOUMING MASS, Cyber Music CYBER CD5 (1992)
Vanished Into The Void / Exterion Tumours / Gals Of The Eternal Solstice / Z. Day / Presage To The Eternity / Swallow Swouming Mass / Pulsating Blood / Growls Of Death / Spontaneous Diarhoea

DISSECTION (SWEDEN)
Line-Up: Jon Nodtveidt (vocals / guitar), John Zwetsloot (guitar), Peter Palmdahl (bass), Ole Öhman (drums)

Gothenburg Death Metallers DISSECTION date back to their formation in 1989 by ex-OPTHALAMIA and THE BLACK vocalist / guitarist Jon Nodveidt's and bassist Peter Palmdahl.
The band's first offering was the demo 'The Grief Prophecy' in 1990 followed by a limited edition single on the French label Corpsegrinder Records. A further demo in 1992 led to an album deal with another French label, namely No Fashion.
Nodtveidt was already operating his side project THE BLACK at this stage going under the pseudonym of Rietas.
Following the release of 'The Somberlain' album in late 1993 guitarist John Zwetsloot was to leave and in came replacement Johan Norman, previously with DECAMERON and SACRAMENTUM. Meantime Nodtveidt extra curricular act THE BLACK released their debut record 'The Priest Of Satan'.
DISSECTION signed to Germany's Nuclear Blast label in early 1995 but not before releasing two tracks on a compilation album for Wrong Again Records namely a cover of TORMENTOR's 'Elizabeth Bathory' and an original 'Where Dead Angels Lie'. The Swedes have also contributed SLAYER's 'Anti-Christ' to the Black Sun Records compilation 'Slatanic Slaughter'.

The band toured Europe with label mates DISMEMBER in December 1995. For these shows DISSECTION debuted a new drummer, Tobias Kjellgren, ex-of SWORDMASTER and DECAMERON. The departing Öhlman temporarily teamed up with SWORDMASTER then joined OPHTHALAMIA.
Having started 1996 touring America on a bill alongside AT THE GATES and MORBID ANGEL DISSECTION's return shows in Europe were on a bill with SATYRICON and GORGOROTH.
During a down period in the band's activity frontman Jon Nodvelt created a dark ambient side project titled DE INFERNALI during 1997. Fans were kept interested with the Necropolis Records release 'The Past Is Alive' which collected together the early demos and singles as well as two tracks from SATANIZED, yet another side project outfit that included Nodtveidt, guitarist Johan Norman and drummer Kjellgren.
As 1998 dawned DISSECTION's future was thrown into doubt when Nodtveidt, in keeping with recent Black Metal musicians behaviour patterns, was arrested on suspicion of the murder of an Algerian homosexual. Nodtveidt would ultimately be imprisoned for the crime.
Palmdahl joined RUNEMAGICK for 'The Supreme Force Of Eternity' album. The bassist also appeared on the 1998 album from DEATHWITCH 'Ultimate Death'.

Singles/EPs:
Into Infinite Obscurity / Shadows Over A Lost Kingdom / Son Of The Mourning, Corpsegrinder CGR 003 (1990)
Where Dead Angels Lie (Demo Version) / Elisabeth Bathory / The Anti-Christ / Feathers Fell / Son Of the Mourning / Where Dead Angels Lie (Album Version), Nuclear Blast NB 1672 (1996) ('Where Dead Angels Lie' EP)

Albums:
THE SOMBERLAIN, No Fashion NFR 006 (1993)
Black Horizons / The Somberlaine / Crimson Towers / A Land Forlorn / Heaven's Damnation / Frozen / Into Infinite Obscurity / In The Cold Winds Of Nowhere / The Grief Prophecy / Shadows Over A Lost Kingdom / Mistress Of The Bleeding Sorrow / Feathers Fell
STORM OF THE LIGHT'S BANE, Nuclear Blast NB129 (1995)
At The Fathomless Depths / Soulreaper / Night's Blood / Where Dead Angels Lie /

Feather's Fell / Unhallowed / Thorns Of Crimson Death / Retribution: Storm Of The Light's Bane / No Dreams Breed In Breathless Sleep
THE PAST IS A LIVE (THE EARLY MISCHIEF), Necropolis NR017 (1996)
Shadows Over A Lost Kingdom / Frozen / Feathers Fell / Son Of The Mourning / Mistress Of The Bleeding Sorrow / In The Cold Winds Of Nowhere / Into Infinite Obscurity / The Call Of The Mist / Severed Into Shreds / Satanized / Born In Fire

DIVINE EMBRACE (GERMANY)
Line-Up: Stefan Hebes (vocals), Thomas Naumann (guitar), Rolf Prakett (guitar), Ingo Rieger (bass), Frank Hoffmeister (drums)

A Progressive Death Metal combo. DIVINE EMBRACE drummer Jorg Burkhardt took his leave in January 2000 being replaced by Frank Hoffmeister.

Albums:
TALES OF AVALON, (2000)
The Tale Of The Betrayers Inevitable Death / Recurring Ceremony / Mystique Island / Another Sanctuary / Regions Of The Grail / Lament / From Father To Son / The Guest / Traveller In Time

DIVINE SIN (SWEDEN)
Line-Up: Fredde Lundberg (vocals), Micke Andersson (guitar), Peter Halvarsson (guitar), Buddy Goude (bass), Martin Knutar (drums)

Albums:
WINTERLAND, Black Mark BMCD 83 (1995)
Gates Of Everbe / Children Of Conformity / Dead Again / Memories / All Alone / A Twilight Dream / Winterland / Years Of Sorrow / Endless Sleep / My Best Nightmare / In The Wake Of Perfection

DOG FACED GODS (SWEDEN)
Line-Up: Johnny Wranning (vocals), Conny Jonsson (guitar), Peter Tuthill (bass), Richard Evensand (drums)

DOG FACED GODS were named after the TESTAMENT song. Vocalist Johnny Wranning and guitarist Conny Jonsson also have credits with EBONY TEARS. Wranning is also an ex-MISCREANT member. Before too long all the membership of EBONY TEARS were involved with DOG FACED GODS

operating both bands in tandem.
Pelle Saether of ZELLO produced and added guest vocals to the 1998 album. Keyboards came courtesy of ZELLO's Mats Olsson.

Albums:
RANDOM CHAOS THEORY IN ACTION, GNW GNW04 (1998)
Blindfolded / The Man Inside / God All Over / Face My Rage / Fractured Image / Dirge / Prozac 3105 / Purge / All Worlds Collide / Swallowtail / The Chaos

DOLORIAN (FINLAND)
Line-Up: Antti Haapapuro (vocals / guitar), A. Kukkohori (bass / drums), J. Ontero (keyboards)

A multi-faceted act DOLORIAN, based in Oulu and previously entitled TEMPLES BEYOND, employ elements of Black and Death Metal slowed down to a labouring Doom crawl. The band themselves describe their music as leaving the listener "spiritually cramped".

Albums:
WHEN ALL LAUGHTER HAS GONE, Avantgarde (1999)
Desolated Colours / My Weary Eyes / A Part Of Darkness / When All Laughter Has Gone / Collapsed / Fields / With Scorn I Perish

DOMINION (UK)
Line-Up: Michelle Richfield (vocals), Mass Firth (vocals / guitar), Arno Cagna (vocals / guitar), Danny North (bass), Bill Law (drums)

Starting life as Thrash influenced outfit BLASPHEMER in 1995 over numerous demo recordings BLASPHEMER evolved into DOMINION promoting session singer and erstwhile ballet student Michelle Richfield to the lead vocalist role. However, her angelic strains still compete in the mix with the Death growls of guitarists Mass Firth and Arno Cagna.
The track 'Alive?' on the debut features MY DYING BRIDE's Ade on vocals.
DOMINION offered two bizarre cover versions to the 1998 Peaceville Records compilation album 'X' in TEARS FOR FEARS 'Shout' and the ROLLING STONES 'Paint It Black'.
Drummer Bill Law joined MY DYING BRIDE for their '34.788%... Complete' album in 1998.

Albums:
INTERFACE, Peaceville CDVILE63
(1996)
Tears From The Star / Milennium /
Silhouettes / Alive? / Weaving Fear / The
Voyage / Deep Into Me / Impulse /
Conspire To Me / Hollowvision
BLACKOUT, Peaceville (1997)
Blackout / Release / Covet / Distortion / Ill
Effect / Today's Tomorrow / Down / Prism
/ Threshold / Unseen / Fuelling Nothing

DOMINUS (DENMARK)
Line-Up: Michael Poulsen (vocals /
guitar), Mads Hansen (guitar), Jesper
Olsen (bass), Jess Larsen (drums)

Ringsted Death Metal act founded by
Poulsen in 1991, DOMINUS released a
self titled demo followed up by a further
tape 'Astaroth' in early 1993. The band's
first commercially available product came
in the form of a track donated to the
second in the series of 'Fuck You, We're
From Denmark' compilation albums on
Progress Records.
Poulsen, a lecturer in Positive Nordic
Satanism (!), engaged himself in TV
discussions concerning his Black Metal
stance with a priest on Scandinavian TV.
DOMINUS signed to Greek label Molon
Lave releasing a 7" single. The band's
first album, 'View To A Dim', saw the band
returning to Progress Records. At live
shows Poulsen addresses his audience
in native Norwegian tongue.
Following the debut album DOMINUS
had a line-up shift, adding ex-
ILLDISPOSED drummer Lars Hald and
bassist Anders Nielsen.
1997's 'Vol. Beat' found DOMINUS
adopting a radical musical shift towards
50's Rock n' Roll inspired beat Metal!
Quite aptly, the album was recorded at
Jailhouse studios by Tommy Hansen.

Singles/EPs:
Sidereal Path Of Colours / De-Ice
Dreams, Molon Lave MLR SP 031
(1994)

Albums:
A VIEW TO A DIM, Progress RRS 942
(1995)
Symphony Of The Goddess / Tears In
Black / Bring Down The Roars / Spiritual
Mountain / Awakening Of The
Overthrown / View To The Dim / Lost
Behind Scars / A Sign From The Cryptic
Winter / The Blaze Of Valhalla / Sidereal
Path Of Colours / The Raven's Eye /

Weiv Ot Eht Mid
THE FIRST NINE, Progress PCD30
(1996)
Dancing With Magic / Soul Damnation /
Final Journey / The Burning Maid /
Ancient Emperor / Next Living Obliging /
Confront The 9 / Second Palace / The
Crystal Demon / Final Journey (Part II)
VOL. BEAT, Progress PCD-40 (1997)
No Matter What... / Swine For A While,
Pigs For A Week / The Path / Give Me
The Reason / Beat, Booze, The Hooker's
Lose / Billy Gun/ Me And I / Action
Please / How Sweet They Kill / From The
Cradle Goes The Bell / The Call
GODFALLOS, Diehard PCD-57 (2000)
Thine / The Act Of Organic Plastic / Seed
From The Beast / Manipulated Destiny /
Call No. 3 / Hypercane / The Face That
Wouldn't Show / Antichrist / Cabbage / To
Seek Her Scent / Angelsitter

DOOM (UK)
Line-Up: Jon Pickering (vocals / bass),
Brian Talbot (guitar), Stick (drums)

DOOM started life as THE
SUBVERTERS, an outfit that comprised
of vocalist / bassist Jon Pickering,
guitarist Brian Talbot and drummer Jason
Hodges. Following a change of drummer
to Mick Harris, the band rallied around the
new title of DOOM.
However, Harris would depart for
NAPALM DEATH and so new drummer
Stick was added as DOOM's line-up
evolved during 1987 This period of
transition saw Pickering handing over
bass duties to Pete Nash so as to be able
to concentrate on lead vocals.
DOOM recorded a demo in August 1987
for Peaceville Records; two tracks of
which found their way onto the 'A Vile
Peace' compilation album. Nash had
broken his wrist prior to these sessions so
NAPALM DEATH bassist Jim Whitley
filled in.
A further demo cassette, 'War Is Big
Business', was made available for sale at
gigs before DOOM recorded their debut
album 'War Crimes-Inhuman Beings' for
Peaceville Records. A further demo,
'Domesday', bridged the gap upfront of
the 1988 album 'Bury The Debt - Not The
Dead' (a split album with Sweden's NO
SECURITY). DOOM were also invited to
record two sessions for Radio One's John
Peel show around this point.
At the close of a lengthy European tour
Talbot announced he was leaving,
necessitating Pickering switching to
guitar and DOOM soldiered on into 1990

before splitting.

Following the group's demise Pickering formed POLICE BASTARD, whilst drummer Stick joined EXTREME NOIZE TERROR then DIRT.

But DOOM was by no means dead and buried. The band reformed two years after they first split in order to tour Japan, but shortly after broke up once more. Talbot and Stick brought in ex-GENITAL DEFORMITIES vocalist Tom Croft and bassist Paul Mallen to quickly resurrect the name. This line-up recorded a split album with Finland's SELFISH and a split 7" single with HIATUS, although Mallen was to leave and in his stead came ex-LARGACTYL bassist Scoot.

A further split 7" was released with EXTINCTION OF MANKIND followed by the tactfully titled 'Fuck Peaceville' album and 'Hail To Sweden' single.

DOOM's 1996 tour of Sweden saw both Scoot and Croft opting to jump ship so BLOOD SUCKING FREAKS bassist Denis Boardman and vocalist Wayne Southworth were drafted in for the live dates. A permanent bassist was eventually found in ex-SUFFER man Chris Gasgoyne.

Singles/EPs:

Doomed, Peaceville (1993)

Police Bastard / Relief Part Two / Diseased / Circles / A Means To An End, Discarded (1989)

Lost The Fight, Flat Earth (1994)

Doomed To Extinction, Ecocentric (1994) (split EP with EXTINCTION OF MANKIND)

Hail To Sweden, Pandora's Box (1995)

Monarchy Zoo / Raining Napalm/ Want Not Need / Dig Your Grave / Doomed, Discipline FIST 2 (1996)

Albums:

WAR CRIMES – INHUMAN BEINGS, Peaceville VILE 4 (1988)
Confusion / Life Lock / Slave To Convention / A Dream To Come True / Drowning In The Mainstream / Same Mind / Relief / After The Bomb / Stop-Gap / Scared / Sick Joke / Natural Abuse / Exploitation / Beat The Boss / Money Drug / Fear Of The Future / No Religion / Phobia For Change / Multinationals / Obscenity / War Crimes

BURY THE DEBT - NOT THE DEAD, Peaceville VILE 11 (1989)
No Thought / Black Monday / Nazi Die / Agree To Differ / War On Our Doorstep / Bury The Debt (Not The Dead) / Life In Freedom, Governed By Equality / Days Go By / Sold Out Scene / Free Yourself

TOTAL DOOM, Peaceville VILE 11CD (1989)
Confusion / Life Lock / Slave To Convention / A Dream To Come True / Drowning In The Mainstream / Same Mind / Relief / After The Bomb / Stop-Gap / Scared / Sick Joke / Natural Abuse / Exploitation / Beat The Boss / Money Drug / Fear Of The Future / No Religion / Phobia For Change / Multinationals / Obscenity / War Crimes / No Thought / Black Monday / Nazi Die / Agree To Differ / War On Our Doorstep / Bury The Debt (Not The Dead) / Life In Freedom, Governed By Equality / Days Go By / Sold Out Scene / Free Yourself / Relief Part II / Police Bastard / Diseased / Circles / A Means To An End / Sick Joke ('89)

PEEL SESSIONS, Strange Fruit SFPMCD 203 (1989)
Symptom Of The Universe / Multinationals / Exploitation / Circles / No Religion / Relief / Sold Out / War Crimes / Means To An End / Dream To Come True / Natural Abuse / Days Go By / Life Lock / Bury The Debt / Life In Freedom / Money Drug / Fear Of The Future

DOOMED FROM THE START, Discipline DISCLP5 (1993)
Relief / Slave To Convention / Fear Of The Future / A Dream To Come True / Exploitation / Beat The Boss / Obscenity / After The Bomb / Terminal Filth Wimpcore Killer / Life Lock / A Dream To Come True / Circles / Black Monday / Sold Out Scene / Bury The Debt (Not The Dead) / Agree To Differ / Diseased / Nazi Die / Police Bastard / Reality / Worthless Nothing / Happy Pill / Trash Breeds Trash / Dropout / Dig Your Grave / No Justice / Canvas Of Lies / No Thought / Life In Freedom / Means To An End

THE GREATEST INVENTION, Discipline DISCLP10 (1993)
Happy Pill / Dig Your Grave / Trash Breeds Trash / Dropout / Worthless Nothing / No Justice / Silent Scream / My Pornography / Same Mind

DOOM / SELFISH, (1995)

FUCK PEACEVILLE, Profane Existence (1996)
Confusion / Lifelock / Slave To Convention / After The Bomb / Multinationals / Circles / War Crimes / Relief / Sold Out / No Thought / Free Yourself / Police Bastard / War On Your Doorstep / Obscenity / Sick Joke / Exploitation / Phobia For Change / A Dream To Come True / Relief (Part II) /

141

Beat The Boss / Agree To Differ / Life Is Freedom, Governed By Love / No Religion / Same Mind / Drowning In The Mainstream / Natural Abuse / Scared / Bury The Debt (Not The Dead) / Money Drug / Fear Of The Future / Nazi Die / Diseased / Days Go By / Stop Gap System / Black Monday / Means To An End / Bastard File In The Urethra Of Paul Halmshaw
RUSH HOUR OF THE GODS, Flat Earth (1996)

DOXODEMON (SINGAPORE)
Line-Up: Paat (vocals), Pearce Arai (guitar), Sham (guitar), Joehanis (bass), Azli (drums)

Black Grindcore act founded as LIBATION during 1992 by NECRONANISM vocalist / bassist Paat, guitarist Ash and drummer Zul. This group would switch names to ITNOS for the less than tactfully titled EP 'Christ Mary Bitch' released on the Dutch Superior Creation label in 1994.
ITNOS folded with Zul (as Dajjal) joined ABBATOIR and IMPIETY.
Paat reassembled a new band with erstwhile MIXES guitarist Jumaat and former MARTYRDOM drummer Azli for the promotional cassette 'Hymnenic Promonancy'. By 1997 the band had filled out with second guitarist Sham, previously an OSSUARY member.
December 1998 witnessed further changes with the enlistment of ex-HARVESTER guitarist Pearce Arai and former OSSUARY and MARTYRDOM bassist Joehanis. With this line-up the group adopted the new title of DOXODEMON.

Albums:
EVANESCE, Darkartz (1999)

DRACONIS (Los Angeles, CA, USA)

Albums:
OVERLORDS OF THE GREYING DAWN, Dark Realm (1999)
Overlords Of The Greying Dawn / Black Horde Of Blasphemy / When Darkness Lasts Forever / Descending The Shadowed Passage To Nocturnal Realms / Medieval Spirits From The Seven Gates / The Oracle Of Eternal Doom / Alongside Subconscious Souls Of eternity / Unseen Reflections Of Interdimensional Transfixions / Beneath The Dismal Aura Of Stormfog / Cryptic

Chasms Shroud The Everdark
THE HIGHEST OF ALL DARK POWERS, Greying Dawn (1999)

DRAINED (MA, USA)
Line-Up: Bob Mendell (vocals), Neal Delongchamp (guitar), Mike Cardoso (bass), Roger Chouinard (drums)

Albums:
SUSPENSION OF DISBELIEF, Martyr Music Group (1999)

DRAWN AND QUARTERED
(Seattle, WA, USA)
Line-Up: Herb Burke (vocals), Kelly Kuciemba (guitar), Greg Reeves (bass), Matt Cason (drums)

Uncompromising Death Metal band initially founded as PLAGUE BEARER. Evolved into DRAWN AND QUARTERED in 1996 drafting bassist Greg Reeves the following year. DRAWN AND QUARTERED issued demos and had their track 'Open Mind' included on the compilation album 'Eat The Evidence' issued on Morta Coil Records. Drummer Mtt Cason also operates in side act SERPENT'S AEON. Other band members have also resurrected PLAGUE BEARER.

Albums:
TO KILL IS HUMAN, Moribund (1999)
Ministry Of Torture / Machete Bloodbath / The Hills Run Red / Open Mind / Carnal Copulation / To Kill Is Human / Implements Of Hell / Christian Extinction / Broken On The Wheel / Punishment By Burning Torment / Mangled Beyond Recognition

DR. DEATH (GERMANY)
Line-Up: M.K. (vocals / keyboards), M.P. (guitar), T.H. (guitar), S.Q. (bass), C.P. (keyboards), V.S. (drums)

Progressive Death Metal act.

Albums:
CRASH COURSE IN THE GARDEN OF CHRIST, Dr. Death DMP 012 (1994)
The Room Of Souls / Crash Course In The Garden Of Christ / I Summon You / On The Way / To Utopia / Ocean Of Tears / Epoh Dnoyeb
PREAPOCALYPTIC VISIONS, A.M. Music Disaster 10011 (1996)
Forever Falling / In The Name Of God / Dark Side / Dying Hour / After Life / Marked By Life / Perfect World / Real

Face / The Search For The Lost Dreams / Blind / Time Of The Awakening / When Emotion Dies

DREAMS OF DAMNATION (USA)
Line-Up: Charlie Silva (vocals / bass), Jimmy Durkin (guitar), Al Mendez (drums)

DREAMS OF DAMNATION are led by former DARK ANGEL guitarist Jimmy Durkin and the gargantuan figure of Brazilian Charlie Silva.

Albums:
LET THE VIOLENCE BEGIN, Necropolis NR064 CD (2000)
Blood To Free A Soul / Unholy Invocation / Cremation Day / Demonic Celebration / Hammer Of Sickness / Release Me

DRILLER KILLER (SWEDEN)
Line-Up: Cliff (vocals / guitars), Manuel (bass), Chris (drums)

Death Punk band DRILLER KILLER include MACHINE GUN KELLY members Cliff (Clifford Lundberg) on guitar and bassist Robert Jörgensson on bass.
DRILLER KILLER's debut album 'Totalfuckinghate' came packaged with almost obligatory tasteless, offensive, snuff movie style cover artwork.
DRILLER KILLER offered a split CD with the notorious IMPALED NAZARENE in 2000.

Albums:
TOTALFUCKINGHATE, Distortion DISTCD 15 (1995)
Fucked For Life / This Means War / From Out Of Nowhere / Wrong Again / Food For Worms / Skaneland / Speed D'Mon / Re-Arranged Face / Ruled By None / Wanna Be's / Power Hour / From Out Of Nowhere (Chip n' Dale Dope Remix)
FUCK THE WORLD, Osmose Productions (1997)
Tomorrow / HS 69 / Sick Shit / Fuck The World / Weekend Warrior / Freeman / Beaten Down / Hellcome / Thrill Of The Pill / Blind Naked n' Covered With Shit / Still Alive / Times Up / Suffering Is Human / I Couldn't Care Less / Down The Drain / Lies
IMPALED NAZARENE VS DRILLER KILLER, Solardisk (2000)
AND THE WINNER IS..., Osmose Productions OPCD 105 (2000)
Man Overbored / No Rules / Fire In The Hole / Legalize Murder Now / Obsessed

By Speed / Sliced / B.O.F.G. / Cyanide Kick / Last Man Standing / Skin n' Bones / Gated Communities / Loose Screws / The No Good People

DRIPPING (NJ, USA)
Line-Up: Frank Bleakley (vocals), Sebastian Russo (guitar), Tom Keiffer (bass), Bruce Moallem (drums)

New Jersey Death Metal convened in late 2000 by former CADAVERMENT personnel guitarist Sebastian Russo and drummer Bruce Moallem. Initial line up included DECEMBER vocalist / guitarist Jerry Sammarco and bassist Tom Keiffer. Sammarco would quit before the end of the year. The band would soon be boosted back to quartet status with the inclusion of erstwhile UNHALLOWED, CARRION and COMATOSE RUST man Frank Bleakley.

D-RIVER (JAPAN)

D-RIVER's second album 'Utagoroshi Minaemon' was recorded at Morrisound Studios in Tampa, Florida and produced by former BRUTAL TRUTH man Rich Hoak and ex-ICED EARTH drummer Mark Prator.

Albums:
UTAGOROSHI MINAEMON, Bellwood (2000)

DROGHEDA (Akron, OH, USA)
Line-Up: Buddy Mitchell (vocals / guitar), Dan Haynes (bass), John Roddy (drums)

Ultra Speed Grindcore. The band was named DROGHEDA by an early member and it was only later it was discovered there was an Irish brass band of the same title! An eponymous demo arrived in 1993 followed by the 'Unearthly' cassette in 1994. A third demo, 'Kill Extremist', led to a deal with the Wild Rags label for the debut album 'Pogramist' in 1996. The same year also saw a split 7" single with fellow Grindsters MORTICITE.
1997 brought forth a split tape shared with DISMEMBERED FETUS. Further split efforts found the band in alliance with FATE OF ICARUS, BRUTAL INSANITY and DYSMORFIC.

Singles/EPs:
Pipe Bomb Bombardment / Rapid Fire Sniper / Sledge Of Oppression / Terrorist Grind Regime / Mustard Gas Asphyxia / Murderholes / Chaos Kill / Siege - Destroy / Kill, Maim And Leisure,

Extremist (1996) (7" split single with MORTICITE)
Split, (1998) (7" split single with FALL OF ICARUS)

Albums:
POGROMIST, Wild Rags (1996)
CELEBRATING 5 YEARS OF VIOLENCE, Wild Rags (1997)
Horrorist / Celebration Of Violence / Revenge Overkill / Maggot Spawn / Abandoned The Flesh / Spiralling Alcoholic Demise / Introgression / Blood In The Face / Mindbleed / Death By Doses / Terror, Fucking Terror / Godgrinder / Clean Up The Chunks / Hate Is My Only Reason To Live / Karnivorkian / Desperation Madness / Drogheda / Rejoice / Stygian Nightmare / Obscure Magical Rhetoric / Lords Of Chaos / Carcass Dweller / Of Pain / Darkening Amoral Morality / Caries / Break My Body / Cunthunter / Set Your Own Pace / Lettered Pigs / Untitled
AGENTS OF PRIMORDIAL CREATURES AND ULTIMATE CREATION, Extremist (1999) (Split album with DYSMORFIC)
Enemy Of God / Maximum Carnage Potential / Dead To Rights / Ruptured / Homicided / Rally Around The Mask / Impending Theocracy / Agents Of Primordial Creation And Ultimate Destruction / Techno-Terrorism / A Handful Of Us - Destroy A Nation Of You / Concertina Headwrap / Thorough Domestic Beating / Frenzied Stand-Off / Kill Zone Delirium / Master Disease / 100 Megaton Kill / Black Gods' Shadow / Destination: Extreme / Devastating Hate Bomb / Manifesto / Terminal Depopulation Experiment / Raging Class Riot / Gouging My Way To Experiment / Gunpoint Confession / Blacklisted / Crackhead Going Fast
SPLIT, (2000) (Split album with BRUTAL INSANITY)
Of Pain / Drogheda / Spiralling Alcoholic Demise / Carcass Dweller / Karnivorkian / Terror, Fucking Terror / Lords Of Chaos / Maggot Spawn / Death By Doses

DYING FETUS (Baltimore, MD, USA)
Line-Up: John Gallagher (vocals / guitar), Sparky Voyles (guitar), Jason Netherton (bass), Kevin Talley (drums)

DYING FETUS, originally titled for maximum shock value DEAD FETUS, was forged in 1991. Drafted guitarist Brian Latta in 1994 and issued a compilation of their demos commercially as the 'Infatuation With Malevolence' CD in 1995. This self-financed release led in turn to a deal with Pulverizer

Records for the 1996 follow up 'Purification Through Violence'. Promoting this outing DYING FETUS toured America on a package bill with MONSTROSITY and Canadians KATAKLYSM.
Dying Fetus signed to German label Morbid Records for 1998's 'Killing On Adrenaline'. The record betrayed some of DYING FETUS's Hardcore leanings as the band included an INTEGRITY cover song. A subsequent nine week touring spree included a headline performance at the Morbid Metalfest in Germany. However, Latta would leave in December of 1998 as DYING FETUS promoted one of their road crew Sparky Voyles to plug the gap. The band would also enlist former DEITY drummer Kevin Talley.
Setting up their own custom label Blunt Force the group re-issued the 'Infatuation With Malevolence' debut complete with extra live tracks recorded in Germany. 2000 bowed in with the six track mini-album 'Grotesque Impalement' and a showing at another German festival, this time headlining the 'Fuck The Commerce III' festival. Before the year was out DYING FETUS had released the full length 'Destroy The Opposition' album through Death Metal specialists Relapse.
Netherton departed in January 2001 to found MISERY INDEX. His initial replacement being Sean from GARDEN OF SHADOWS. DYING FETUS toured America as part of the 'Death Across America' tour billed alongside Poland's VADER CEPHALIC CARNAGE and DEEDS OF FLESH. The band drafted DEPRECATED bass player Derek Bowyer during 2001 and vocalist Vince Matthews, a veteran of SADISTIC TORMENT, MUCOUS MEMBRANE and AUTUMN DAWN.
Gallagher, Voyles and Talley also operate a Hardcore side outfit named KNUCKLE DEEP.

Albums:
INFATUATION WITH MALEVOLENCE, Wild Rags (1995)
PURIFICATION THROUGH VIOLENCE, Pulverizer (1996)
Blunt Force Trauma / Beaten Into Submission / Skull Fucked / Permanently Disfigured / Raped On The Altar / Nothing Left To Pray For / Nocturnal Crucifixion / Skum (Fuck The Weak)
KILLING ON ADRENALINE, Morbid MR042 (1998)
Killing On Adrenaline / Procreate The Malformed / Fornication Terrorists / We Are The Enemy / Kill Your Mother, Rape Your Dog / Absolute Defiance / Judgement Day / Intentional Manslaughter
INFATUATION WITH MALEVOLENCE, Blunt Force BFR003 (1999)
Eviscerated Offspring / Your Blood Is My

144

Wine / … And The Weak Shall Be
Crushed / Visualize Permanent
Damnation / Purged Of My Worldly Being
/ Bathe In Entrails / Nocturnal Crucifixion
/ Grotesque Impalement / Vomiting The
Fetal Embryo / Tearing Inside The Womb
/ Intentional Manslaughter (Live) / Kill
Your Mother, Rape Your Dog (Live) /
Skull Fucked (Live)
GROTESQUE IMPALEMENT, Blunt
Force BFR004 (2000)
Grotesque Impalement / Streaks Of
Blood / Bringing Back The Glory /
Tearing Inside The Womb / Final Scream
(Prelude To Evil: Davey's Nightmare) /
Hail Mighty North - Forest Trolls Of
Satan
DESTROY THE OPPOSITION, Relapse
(2000)
Praise The Lord (Opium Of The Masses)
/ Destroy The Opposition / Born In
Sodom /Epidemic Of Hate / Pissing In
The Mainstream / In Times Of War / For
Us Or Against Us / Justifiable Homicide

DYSMORFIC

Albums:
HUMAN DISCOUNT, Extremist (1999)
(Split album with DROGHEDA)
Human Waste / Psychopathia Sexualis /
Life / When You Die / Abomination /
Nothing / Beating The Dead

EAR BLEEDING DISORDER
(Denver, CO, USA)

Grindcore merchants EAR BLEEDING DISORDER include former members of DISMEMBERED FETUS. The band uniquely shared a 4-way split album with fellow Grindsters EXHUMED, NECROSE and Spaniards EXCRETED ALIVE on the Brazilian Lofty Storm Productions label.
A split 7" single was issued in collaboration with Mexican Grind band LAUGHING DAY.

Singles/EPs:
Split, Riotous Assembly RIOT003 (199-) (7" split single with LAUGHING DAY)

Albums:
CHORDS OF CHAOS, Lofty Storm Productions (1996) (4-way split album with EXHUMED, EXCRETED ALIVE and NECROSE)
Token Of Disgust / Hungry System / Star Wars / Morbid / $300 And A Hand Job / Autodidactic Murder / Pigsblood / Nubie Blast / Reasons / K Song / Story Of A Terrorist / Kill The DJ / Terror Style / Higher Source / MN 21 / Cryptic Slaughter / Why Try?

EBONY TEARS (SWEDEN)
Line-Up: Johnny Wranning (vocals), Conny Jonson (guitar), Thomas Thun (bass), Iman Zolgharnian (drums)

EBONY TEARS vocalist Johnny Wranning also operates with MISCREANT and DOG FACED GODS. Guitarist Conny Jonson is also a DOG FACED GODS man. Eventually the membership of DOG FACED GODS mirrored EBONY TEARS with the recruitment of ex-BULLDOZER bassist Peter Tuthill and drummer Richard Evensand with the two bands functioning in tandem.

Albums:
TORTURA INSOMNIA, Black Sun (1998)
Moonlight / Freak Jesus / Nectars Of Eden / With Tears In My Eyes / Involuntary Existence / Opacity / Spoonbender / Evergrey / Skunk Hour
A HANDFUL OF NOTHING, Black Sun (1999)
Inferno / Harvester Of Pain / A Handful Of Nothing / Scenario / When Depression Speaks / Erised / Cosmical

Transformation / The End

EDGE OF SANITY (SWEDEN)
Line-Up: Dan Swanö (vocals), Dread (guitar), Sami Nerberg (guitar), Anders Lundberg (bass), Benny Larsson (drums)

Influential Metallers noted the involvement of mentor Dan Swano (a big name on the Swedish music scene renowned for his production and involvement in other acts as diverse as UNICORN, PAN-THY-MONIUM, GODSEND, WOUNDED KNEE and NIGHTINGALE among others). EDGE OF SANITY came together in 1989. Guitarist Sami Nerberg was previously with Punk act F.Z.Ö. while Swano and bassist Anders Lundberg had been in another Punk band by the name of ULANBATOR.
EDGE OF SANITY debuted with the demo tape 'Kur-Nu-Gi-A' and the band has managed to sustain a stable line-up. The act signed to the Black Mark label in 1990 recording their debut 'Nothing But Death Remains' at the legendary Montezuma Studios, home previously to THERION, HEXENHAUS, BATHORY, CANDLEMASS and CREMATORY among others.
Their 1995 EP 'Until Eternity Ends' contains a version of THE POLICE's hit 'Invisible Sun'. Don't be fooled by the one credited track on 1996's 'Crimson' album- the song is over 40 minutes in duration.
Despite a prolific recording schedule various members of EDGE OF INSANITY have found the time to work on other projects. Guitarist Dread (real name Andreas Axelsson) contributes to LUCKY SEVEN and sang lead vocal on Deathsters MARDUK's first album. Drummer Benny Larsson also records with OPHTHALMIA under the pseudonym 'Winter', whilst Swano sang lead vocals for Danish Metallers MACERATION on their 'A Serenade Of Agony' album using the nom de plume of Day Disyraah.
In 1996 Swano united with OPETH's Mikael Akerfelt to create an impromptu retro Metal project entitled STEEL. Never intended as a serious venture STEEL nevertheless came to the attention of Near Dark Productions who would issue two tracks on a picture disc single in 1998.
Somewhat surprisingly the 1997 album 'Cryptic' found Swanö no longer involved and his position was taken by PAN-THY-MONIUM / DARKIFIED vocalist Robban

Karlsson.
Swanö created the project band BLOODBATH with OPETH's Mikael Akerfeldt and KATATONIA men Blackheim and Jonas Renske in 2000. As 2001 came around it emerged that the boundless Swanö had instigated yet another new band project entitled KARABOUDJAN.

Singles/EPs:
Until Eternity Ends / Eternal Eclipse / Bleed / Invisible Sun, Black Mark BMCD 58 (1994)
Sacrificed, Black Mark BMCD 37-P (1994) (Radio Promotion release)

Albums:
NOTHING BUT DEATH REMAINS, Black Mark BMCD 10 (1991)
Tales... / Human Aberration / Maze Of Existence / The Dead / Decepted By The Cross / Angel Of Distress / Impulsive Necroplasma / Immortal Souls
UNORTHODOX, Black Mark BMCD 18 (1992)
Unorthodox / Enigma / Incipience To The Butchery / In The Veins / Darker Than Black / Human Aberration / Everlasting / After Afterlife / Beyond The Unknown / Nocturnal / Curfew For The Damned / Cold Sun / Day Of Maturity / Requiscon By Page / Dead But Dreaming / When All Is Said
THE SPECTRAL SORROWS, Black Mark BMCD37 (1994)
The Spectral Sorrows / Darkday / Livin' Hell / Lost / The Masque / Blood Of My Enemies / Jesus Cries / Across The Fields Of Forever / On The Other Side / Sacrificed / Waiting To Die / Feedin' The Charlatan / A Serenade For The Dead
PURGATORY AFTERGLOW, Black Mark BMCD 61(1994)
Twilight / Of Farksome Origin / Blood Colored / Silent / Black Tears / Elegy / Velvet Dreams / Enter Chaos / The Sinner And The Sadness / Song Of Sirens
CRIMSON, Black Mark BMCD 68 (1996)
Crimson
INFERNAL, Black Mark BMCD 108 (1996)
Hell Is Where The Heart Is / Helter Skelter / 15:36 / The Bleakness Of It All / Damned (By The Damned) / Forever Together Forever / Losing Myself / Hollow / Inferno / Burn The Sun / The Last Song
CRYPTIC, Black Mark BMCD 125 (1997)
Hell Written / Uncontrol Me / No Destiny / Demon I / Not Of This World / Dead I Walk / Born, Breed, Bleeding / Bleed You Dry
EVOLUTION, Black Mark (2000)
Pernicious Anguish / Immortal Souls / Maze Of Existence / The Dead / Angel Of Distress / Everlasting / After Afterlife / Human Aberration / Kill The Police / When All Is Said / Blood Of My Enemies / Elegy

EISENVATER (GERMANY)
Line-Up: Markus Lipka (vocals / guitar), Jim Sudmann (vocals / guitar), Marek Gibney (bass), Jörg Grzedzicki (drums)

Extreme act somewhere between Grindcore and Death Metal. Following the debut drummer Grzedzicki departed to make way for Peter Belendier.

Albums:
EISENVATER, We Bite WB 1-089-2 (1992)
Dre Säuger / Fleisch / Der Greuel / Mutter / Blind / Die Lüge / Hund / Gudrun / Aggressos Apathis / Ayay!
EISENVATER II, We Bite WB 1-101-2 (1994)
Salut / Kaiserschnitt / Heimat / Ich Spreche Von Dir / Zahn / Schwartzkopf / Pakka / Schwächling / Erektion
EISENVATER III, We Bite WB 1-131-2 (1995)
Arbeit / Krampf / Unsere Liebe / Fleischgeld / Idiot / Krätzmilbe / Motorprügel / Predictum / Hawaii

ELECTROCUTION (ITALY)
Line-Up: Alex Guadagnoli (vocals), Mick Montaguti (guitar), Max Canali (bass), Luca Canali (drums)

Death Metallers founded by the rhythm section of the Canali brothers.

Albums:
INSIDE THE UNREAL, Rosemary's Baby Discs 800171920065 (1994)
Premature Burial / Rising Of Infection / They Died Without Crosses / Growing Into The Flesh (Bleed To Death) / Body's Decay / Ghost Of The Past / Under The Wings Only Remains / Back To The Leprosy Death / Behind The Truth / Bells Of The End.

ELECTRO HIPPIES (UK)
Line-Up: Andy (vocals / guitar), Doom (bass), Simon (drums)

Liverpool Grindcore act ELECTRO

147

HIPPIES forte was primitive bass heavy and gruelling non-formula Rock. Former ELECTRO HIPPIES man Jeff Walker created Gore-mongers CARCASS.

Albums:
PLAY LOUD OR DIE, Necrosis NECRO1 (1986)
Acid Rain / Wings Of Death / Theme Toon / The Reaper / Profit From Death / Run Ronald / Terror Eyes / Am I Punk Yet? / Vivisection / The Horns Of Hades
PEEL SESSIONS, Strange Fruit SFSP042 (1987)
Sheep / Starve The City (To Feed The Poor) / Meltdown / Escape / Dead End / Thought / Chickens / Mother / Mega-Armageddon Death
THE ONLY GOOD PUNK IS A DEAD ONE, Peaceville VILE002 (1988)
Faith / Acid Rain / Run Ronald / Scum / BP / Unity / Terror Eyes / So Wicked / Profit / Freddy's Revenge / Mistake / Things Of Beauty / Protest / Gas Joe Pearce / Lies / Tortured Tears / D.I.Y. (Not D.R.I.) / Suck / Deception
ELECTRO HIPPIES LIVE, Peaceville VILE013 (1989)
THE PEACEVILLE RECORDINGS, Peaceville (199-)
Faith / Acid Rain / Run Ronald / Scum / B.P. / Terror Eyes / So Wicked / Profit / Freddy's Revenge / Mistake / Things Of Beauty / Protest / Gas Joe Pearce Lies / Tortured Tears / Turkey / D.I.Y. (Not D.R.I.) / Suck / Deception / Could You Look Me In The Eyes / Sometimes I'm So Glad / Reject / Escape / Mega-Armageddon Death Part 3 / Mother / Faith / Unity / Sleep / City / Acid Rain / Run Ronald / Chickens / So Wicked / Profit / Meltdown / Mega-Armageddon Death / Mega-Armageddon Death (Extended version) / Silver Machine

ELYSIAN FIELDS (GREECE)
Line-Up: Bill (vocals / guitar), Michalis Katsikas (guitar / bass)

Death Metal band previously known as DESULPHARIZE for their inaugural demo 'Nihilistic Era'. The title ELYSIAN FIELDS was adopted in 1994.
Guitarist Michalis Katsikas also operates HAVORUM.

Albums:
ADELAIN, Unisound (1995)
I Of Forever / As One / Unsentiment - I Was Dying Once Again / Of Purity And Black / Foredoomed Elegy / Father

Forgive Them (For They Don't Know) / Elysian Fields / Deicide - The Auspice
WE... THE ENLIGHTENED, Wicked World WICK02CD (1998)
Their Blood Be On Us / I Am The Unknown Sky / Until The Night Cries Rise In Your Heart / … And The Everdawn Faded Away / Shall They Come Forth Unto Us / Arcana Caelestia / The End Shall Be Tragically Fulfilled / The Last Star Of Heaven Falls / Wither, Oh Divine, Wither

EMBALMER (OH, USA)

Albums:
THERE WAS BLOOD EVERYWHERE, Relapse (1997)
There Was Blood Everywhere / The NecroFiling Cabinet / Blood Sucking Freaks / May The Wounds Bleed Forever / Rotten Body Fluids / Morbid Confessions / Bonebox / The Cellar

EMBODYMENT (Dallas, TX, USA)
Line-Up: Sean Corbray (vocals), Andrew Godwin (guitar), Derrick (guitar), Jason (bass), Mark Garza (drums)

A highly regarded Christian Death Metal unit initially led by highly rated vocalist Kris McCaddon. EMBODYMENT's inaugural 1993 line up comprised of McCaddon, guitarists Andrew Godwin and James Lanigan, bass player Kevin Donnini and drummer Mark Garza. LIVING SACRIFICE frontman Bruce Fitzhugh would guest on the 1998 Barry Poynter produced debut 'Embrace The Eternal'.
Although EMBODYMENT garnered praise for their first album they horrified many fans by adopting a radical Nu-Metal direction for 2000's 'The Narrow Scope Of Things'. EMBODYMENT were fronted by Sean Corbray for this release.

Albums:
EMBRACE THE ETERNAL, Solid State (1998)
20 Tongues / Breed / Swine / Blinded / Religious Infamy / Strength / Golgotha / Carnival Chair / Embrace / Outro
1993-1999 DEMOS, Embodyment (1999)
Cryptic Descension / Dismembering Death / Stillborn Natality / Entropy / Shroud Of Darkness / Legion Of Damnation / Apocalypse Of The Suffering / Persecute Me / Golgotha / Religious Infamy
THE NARROW SCOPE OF THINGS,

(2000)
Winter Kiss / Pendulum / One Less
Addiction / Greedy Hands / Confessions
/ Assembly Line Humans / Prelude /
Killing The Me In Me / Critical Error /
Ballad / One Less Addiction (Acoustic) /
The Aftermath Of A Closure
HOLD YOUR BREATH, (2001)

EMBRACED (SWEDEN)
Line-Up: Kalle Johansen (vocals),
Michael Hakansson (vocals / bass),
Davor Jepic (guitar), Peter Mardklint
(guitar), Julius Chmielewski (keyboards),
Daniel Lindberg (drums)

The 'Amorous Anathema' release is in
fact EMBRACED's demo re-released on
CD format. EMBRACED members
bassist Michael Hakansson and keyboard
player Sven Karlsson joined EVERGREY
in late 2000.
Hakansson also has credits with
MORTUM.

Albums:
WITHIN, Regain RR0008 (2000)
Solitude Of My Own / Within Me / The
Fallen / Putrefaction / Era Of Changes /
Nightmare Drama / Sacred Tears /
Blessed Are Those / Outro
AMOROUS ANATHEMA, Regain (2000)
A Dying Flame / The End... And Here
We All Die / Nightfall / Princess Of
Twilight / Into The Unknown / Memento
Of Emotions / The Beautiful Flow Of An
Autumn Passion / Dirge Of The
Masquerade

THE EMBRACED (NORWAY)
Line-Up: Mads Eriksen (vocals), Geir
Frode Stavsoien (guitar), Rune Holm
(guitar), Daniel Seth (bass), Jorgen
Bjornstrom (drums)

Albums:
**IN MY DREAMS... I AM
ARMAGEDDON**, Aftermath Music
(1998)
In My Dreams... I Am Armageddon /
Dreamspawn / Remnants Of A Scorched
World / Remains Of Life / Split / The
Last Embrace / The Demon Storm / As
Darkness Falls / Autumn Leaves
THE BIRTH, Invasion (1999)
The Birth / A Path That Never Ends /
The Beautiful Angels / The Plague
Divine / Apart / Daughter Of The Lupus
Moon / Thymus / Last Departure / The
Song Of Death

EMBRACING (SWEDEN)
Line-Up: Henrik Nygren (vocals), André
Nylund (guitar), Richard Magnusson
(guitar), Ola Andersson (bass), Matthias
Holmgren (drums/ keyboards)

High standard Death Metal.

Albums:
I BEAR THE BURDEN OF TIME,
Invasion IR 022 (1996)
Winterburn / Shades Embrace / On
Wings Of Sadness / My Dragon Banner /
I Bear The Burden Of Time / They
Seldom Return / Thirst For Blood /
Eternal Sear / Shapeless / A Last Breath
Of Night
DREAMS LEFT BEHIND, Invasion IR
031 (1998)
Drown Inside The Illusion / Morningdew /
Stolen Memories / Only Greedy Gods /
Killers Nature / Long Time No seen / For
The Angels For Me / The Good Old
Days / Name It Tomorrow / Dreams Left
Behind / Lay The Rose Upon Her Grave

EMINENZ (GERMANY)
Line-Up: Leviathan (vocals), Darkman
(guitar), Karsten Breitung (guitar),
Butcher (bass), Henry Kuhnert (drums)

EMINENZ were a union of ex-Death
Metal musicians, the previous influences
plainly audible on the two albums.
Guitarist Karsten Breitung also operates
BELMEZ.

Albums:
EXORIAL, Lethal LRC9666 (1994)
Introduction Black Thoughts / Jesus Wept
Nevermore / Demons From The Black
Abyss / Angel Rip Angel / The Unholy
(Preachers Of Darkness) / Blasphemy /
Ghost / Demons Awake / Only Flesh /
Dark Millennium / Exorial / Outro
THE HERETIC, Lethal LRC24 (1996)
Demons Cross The Fiery Path /
Bloodred Nights / Day Of Battle, Night
Of Thunder / Lucifers Return / Thousand
Blasphemies / The Gate / Necronomicon
Exmortis / The Heretic / Lucifers Return
ANTI GENESIS, (199-)
Nocturnal Horizon / God's Downfall /
Praise The Death / Army Of Immortals /
Apocalypse / Triumph Of The
Nightforces / Grey Souls / Conspiracy Of
The Witches / Anti Genesis
THE BLACKEST DIMENSION, Last
Episode LEP 045 (2000)
Exorials Return / Voices / Diabolical
Majesty / Darkness Come Over Us /

Seraph's Flight / Sink In Oblivion / Warriors / Demons Warpath / Sentenced To Victory

ENCHANTMENT (UK)
Line-Up: Paul Jones (vocals), Marc (guitar), Steve (guitar), Mark (bass), Chris (drums)

A mixture of Gothic, Thrash and Death Metal ENCHANTMENT's debut recording, the demo tape 'A Tear For The Young Eloquence', was produced by Peaceville Records boss Hammy.
The group was later snapped up by the German label Century Media.

Albums:
DANCE THE MARBLE NAKED, Century Media (1994)
Kneading With Honey / My Oceans Vast / The Touch Of A Crown / Carve Me In Sand / Summer For The Dames / God Send / Of Acorns That Gather / Meadows

ENDLESS (GERMANY)
Line-Up: Tom Küchler (vocals), Eric Hofmann (guitar / keyboards), André Hager (bass), Jan Erdtel (keyboards), Sven Drechsler (drums)

Albums:
BEYOND THE ABYSS, Spirit (199-)
Calamity / Church In Chaos / Plastic Flowers / Brocken Der Zerfalls / Wake Again In Heaven (Sometimes) / Death Kiss / Walking Flame / Elaine / Love Is The Real Drug
FIRE, Spirit 27361 61932 (1996)
Beyond The Abyss / Expiratory Death / Twilight Of Delusion / Cascade / Between The Devil And The Deep Sea / Angel Shield / Desire To Rule / Victim Of Fire / Son Of Time / Confidential Eyes / Endzeitgedanken / No Reason (Destroy Mix) / Virgin Eyes

ENDLESS TEARS (FRANCE)
Line-Up: Vince (vocals / guitar), Philippe (guitar), Francois (bass), Roulo (drums)

After the release of two demos this four-piece band from Talant recorded their first, self-financed CD.
'Emotion' finds this bi-lingual outfit (lyrics are in French and English) offering technical, melancholic Thrash Metal.

Albums:
EMOTION, ENT001 (1994)
Emotion / Sacrifice-Le Poete / Lies / Retour / Sister Love / L'Acte / Wait / Le Dernier Survivant

END ZONE (RUSSIA)
Line-Up: Igor Lobanov (vocals / guitar), Oleg Mishin (guitar / keyboards), Roman Senkin (bass), Valeri Dedov (drums)

Death Metal band END ZONE include a cover of SODOM's 'Remember The Fallen' on their 1995 'First Bequest' album.

Albums:
FIRST BEQUEST, (1995)
From The Distance / Conqueror Night / Dangerous Gift / Ulterior Solitude / Oblivion Flow / S.O.D. / The Edge Of String / Questions With No Answer / Remember The Fallen / Candlestick To Parcass / Last Hope Of Suffered Soul / The Castle Of Woman Of Mine / Rock n' Roll
ECLECTICA, (199-)
Alpha / The Vortex Of Reality / Khovanschina (Final) / Dual Infinity / The Remedy / Refuse-Resist / Afterwards

ENEMY SOIL (Sterling, VA, USA)
Line-Up: J.R. (vocals), Richard Johnson (guitar), Brian (bass), Omid (drums)

North Virginia Ultra-Speed Grindcore act ENEMY SOIL, led by guitarist Richard Johnson, endured many line-up changes over the years. For many of the bands early works a drum machine was proudly in evidence. Founder member Mason would later turn up in INITIAL STATE and FRODUS.
The band's first appearance came with a 1993 shared cassette in alliance with PARASITIC UNFESTATION. The following years saw a split 7" in union with Canadians WADGE. A string of split releases followed with Japanese band DESPERATE CORRUPTION in 1996, with ABSTAIN, AGORAPHOBIC NOSEBLEED, CORRUPTED and REVERSAL OF MAN in 1997. The 1998 album 'Fractured Theology' was only issued on 3" CD format.
The 2001 career retrospective album 'Smashes To The State' include numerous unreleased versions of songs plus covers of EXTREME NOISE TERROR's 'Murder', WADGE's 'Pass The Blame', TERRORIZER's 'Corporation Pull In' and the CRO-MAGS 'Don't Tread On Me'.
ENEMY SOIL finally folded in early 1999

with the bulk of the band membership founding INDEX.

Singles/EPs:
Split, Break It Out (1994) (7" split single with WADGE)
Group Think / Sentencing / Common Ground / Fall Of Empire / Trapped In A Routine, Relapse (1995) ('Casualties Of Progress' 7" single)
Split, Bovine (1996) (7" split single with DESPERATE CORRUPTION)
War Parade, Slap A Ham (1996) (7" single)
Split, Fistheldhigh (1997) (7" split single with REVERSAL OF MAN)
Split, Bovine (1997) (7" split single with AGORAPHOBIC NOSEBLEED)
The Weathermen / Group Think / Small Man, Big Mouth / Soln Witness / Sentencing, Clean Plate CP13 (1997) ('Live At Fiesta Grande' 7" flexi single)
Hypocrisy / Partisan Loyalty / Drugged Conscience / Direct Action / Corporation Pull-In, Dwie Story Medalu (1998) ('Live In Virginia' 7" single)
Split, Sacapuntas (1999) (7" split single with PG.99)

Albums:
RUINS OF EDEN, Clean Plate (1997)
FRACTURED THEOLOGY, Profane Existence (1998)
Ministry Of Deception / The Crusade / Charade / A Moment Of Clarity / Incapacitated / My Religion / Nothing Answer Part III / Scapegoat / On Display / Machinery / Self Gratification / Ageism / Sanctified Homicide / Fall Of Empire / Partisan Loyalty (Live)
SMASHES TO THE STATE, Bones Brigade (2001)
Sanctioned Homicide / The Weathermen - Enemy Soil / Content In Slavery / Solemn Witness / Resistance / Hypocrisy / The Weathermen / Expendable / Ignorance Manifest / Solemn Witness / Conditioned / Obey / Group Think / Sentencing / Common Ground / Expendable / Abort The Soul / P.I.B. / Sickness Part I / Sickness Part II / Ageism / Partisan Loyalty / Nothing Answers / Pass The Blame / Burden Of A Vacant Cross / Conditioned / Murder / Introduction / Lost / Hypocrisy / Façade / Enough / Evolution / Sentencing / Clone / Combustion / Obey / Common Ground / Direct Action? / Drugged Conscience / Group Think / After The Fact / Waiting List / The Body Politic / The Weathermen / Introduction - Hypocrisy / Partisan Loyalty / Drugged Conscience / Direct Action? / Corporation Pull In / Recombustion / The Body Politic / Death Sentence / Elitist Disciples / Ministry Of Deception / The Crusade / Charade / A Moment Of Clarity / Incapacitated / My Religion / Nothing Answers Part II / Scapegoat / On Display / Machinery / Self Gratification / Ageism / Sanctioned Homicide / Fall Of Empire / Partisan Loyalty / Don't Tread On Me / Obsequious / Fashionable Activism

ENGORGE (HOLLAND)

Albums:
AWAITING TO SUBSIDE, (199-)
Disapproval Existence / The Solitude Within The End / Shattered Mind / Seducting The Odd / The One Thing Standing / Awaiting To Subside / Graceful Century / Indignation / Hate Of The Disordered

ENGORGE (NJ, USA)

New Jersey's ENGORGE comprise erstwhile DISCIPLES OF MOCKERY and NEBULA 666 members, After an initial demo 'Enchanted By The Battles Of Azazel' ENGORGE issued an extremely rare album. The 'Within The Realms Of Blasphemous Fornication' CD was pressed in only 100 copies.
A further demo 'Grave Desecration' was issued in 2000. Kyle of ENGORGE was previously a stand in drummer for Death Metal act MORTICIAN.
Not to be confused with the Dutch Death Metal act of the same name that released the 'Awaiting To Subside' album.

Albums:
WITHIN THE REALMS OF BLASPHEMOUS FORNICATION, Engorge (1999)

ENGORGED (NY, USA)

Albums:
DEATH METAL ATTACK 2, Razorback (1999)
Engorged / House Of The Dead / In Support Of Multi National Corp. / F.A.N.G.S. / Cobra H.I.S.S. / XVY Triad / Genital Finder / Chemically Castrated / Carpet Sharkin' / Sealed With A Klip (Kipland P. Kinkle) / Death Metal Attack II / Engorged / Huge Gaping Hole / XVY Triad / Death Metal Attack / Kings Of Beer / Legalize Child Porn / Raping The Full House Twins / Vomiting Butchers /

Fangs / Encore

ENSHROUD (MALTA)
Line-Up: Conrad Borg (vocals), Josef Bajada (guitar), Carlo Aquilina (guitar), Sean Pollacco (bass), Gordan Zammit (keyboards), Kenneth Pace (drums)

Black Death Metallers ENSHROUD came onto the scene in 1997. With keyboard player Charlotte Schembri the band submitted the track 'Miseries' to the 'Tomorrows Millionaires' compilation album on Toppling Colossus Records. ENSHROUD lost the services of Schembri but added vocalist Conrad Borg and keyboard player Gordan Zammit during 1999.

ENSLAVEMENT OF BEAUTY (NORWAY)
Line-Up: Ole Alexander Myrholt (vocals), Tony Eugene Tunheim (guitar), Hans Age Holmen (bass), Asgeir Mickelson (drums)

ENSLAVEMENT OF BEAUTY started out in 1995 as a duo of vocalist Ole Alexander Myrholt and guitarist Tony Eugene Tunheim. Following the debut 'Traces O' Red' album the group added bassist Hans Age Holmen and SPIRAL ARCHITECT and BORKNAGER drummer Asgeir Mickelson.

Albums:
TRACES O' RED, Head Not Found HNF061CD (1999)
In Thro' The Cave Of Impressions / Traces O' Red - The Fall And Rise Of Vitality / Be Thou My Lethe And Bleeding Quietus / Dreams / Something Unique / The Poem Of Dark Subconscious Desire / Eerily Seductive / My Irreverent Pilgrimage / And I Still I Wither / I Dedicate My Beauty To The Stars

ENTER MY SILENCE (FINLAND)
Line-Up: Mikko Kotomaki (vocals), Arto Huttunen (guitar), Tuomas Jappinen (guitar), Ville Lapio (bass), Teemu Hokkanen (drums)

A melodic Death Metal crew previously operating as CAPTIVITY. Created in 1995 a series of demos were issued before bassist Ville Lapio made his exit in 1998 necessitating guitarist Arto Huttunen switching instruments to plug the gap. As 1998 drew to a close the band adopted a new title of ENTER MY SILENCE issuing the four track EP 'Sophia's Eye'.

Lapio made his return as ENTER MY SILENCE signed up to the Danish Mighty Music concern for debut album 'Remote Controlled Scythe'. Lead vocals were laid down by a guesting Mikko Kotomaki of FUNERIS NOCTURNUM.

Singles/EPs:
Neverdawn / Sophia / The Tide Will Turn / Plastic Night, (1998) ('Sophia's Eye' EP)

Albums:
REMOTE CONTROLLED SCYTHE, Mighty Music PMZ014-2 (2000)
Six. Nothing / Irrelevant / Inhale-Exhale / Articulate / Split / Nevernity / Filter X / The Loss Of The Leading One / Mindfall Effect

ENTITY (SWEDEN)
Line-Up: Danne Persson (vocals), Jimmy Svensson (guitar), Tompa Gustafsson (bass / keyboards), Tomas Hedlund (drums)

Singles/EPs:
The Lasting Scar / My Inner War / Leave The Kiss To Die, Megagrind (1995)
The Payment, Megagrind MGREP004 (1995)

ENTOMBED (SWEDEN)
Line-Up: Lars Göran Petrov (vocals), Uffe Cedarland (guitar), Alex Hellid (guitar), Jorgen Sandström (bass), Nicke Andersson (drums)

In the plethora of Death Metal bands to have emerged ENTOMBED have proven themselves as ranking among the elite. Never less than skull crushingly heavy, the band have carved their own niche in the market with deft musicianship and a unique perspective and the band's 1993 album 'Wolverine Blues' is generally acknow-ledged to be a masterpiece of the genre. Originally known as NIHLIST, under which name they recorded the 'Drowned', 'But Life Goes On' and 'Premature Autopsy' demos, bassist Johnny Hedlund formed UNLEASHED and NIHILIST folded to reunite a matter of days later retitled ENTOMBED.
The first demo the band recorded as ENTOMBED was titled 'Only Shreds Remain' and following the release of the 'Left Hand Path' debut album in 1990 (with both guitarists handling bass duties in the studio) ENTOMBED recruited a permanent bass player in CARBONISED / MONASTARY man Lars Rosenberg.

1991 was quite an eventful year for the Swedish outfit. Vocalist Göran Petrov was fired in July after personal clashes within the band and was replaced by ex-CARNAGE vocalist Johnny Dordevic. However, the 'Crawl' single was recorded with vocalist Orvar Safstrom of NIRVANA 2002 stepping in on a temporary basis following the split with Petrov.

In the Autumn the band toured America alongside fellow Swedes UNLEASHED and headliners MORBID ANGEL, although by the middle of the following year Johnny Dordevic had left to have his position filled by the reinstated Goran Petrov. In his sabbatical from ENTOMBED the vocalist had recorded with both COMECON and MORBID.

In 1994 ENTOMBED, promoting the landmark 'Wolverine Blues' album released in 1993, toured Europe heavily as guests to NAPALM DEATH. General opinion was that ENTOMBED consistently stole the show from a flagging headliner. Subsequent American dates were only marred by the band having to play as a trio in Canada minus Goran Petrov and Sandström losing their passports when ENTOMBED's tour van was stolen in Cleveland. ENTOMBED persevered with a show in Toronto utilizing guitarist Uffe Cederland as lead vocalist. Further chaos was to impinge itself though when, for the second show in Montreal, Cederland lost his voice completely, prompting the band to invite audience members to participate to plug the gap!

Aside from 'The Singles Compilation' album released by Earache the only other ENTOMBED product to see release during 1994 was the 'Out Of Hand' 7" single, which saw the band covering tracks by such diverse influences as KISS and REPULSION.

Mid-way through 1995 bassist Rosenberg opted to join THERION, having filled in on a temporary basis for live work. ENTOMBED would add ex-GRAVE bassist Jörgen Sandström in his place and would part company with Earache Records in 1996 to sign with major label East West. However, despite finalizing recording of a projected album the band found themselves embroiled in record company politics and the album was shelved. Luckily, a deal was hastily negotiated between East West and leading independent Music For Nations in order for 'To Ride, Shoot Straight And Speak The Truth' to be released in 1997. Digipack versions of the album came with

a free 'Family Favourites' EP which saw ENTOMBED ripping through BLACK SABBATH's 'Under The Sun', VENOM's 'Bursting Out', KING CRIMSON's '21st Century Schizoid Man' and MC5's 'Kick Out The Jams'.

Aside from ENTOMBED, drummer Nicke Andersson also began to dabble with a side Punk project known as THE HELLACOPTERS with Dick Hakansson (a.k.a. Dregan) from BACKYARD BABIES. Andersson issued his first full length album for THE HELLACOPTERS in late 1996 to laudatory reviews. The band received such acclaim, even being requested to support KISS on their Scandinavian dates, that Andersson felt obliged to quit his parent act to concentrate fully on THE HELLACOPTERS.

In 1996 Cederland and Andersson released the 'Seven Deadly Sins' album together with KONKHRA's vocalist Anders Lundemark under the band name DAEMON. Incidentally, Uffe Cederland also dabbled with a Punk crew titled HAYSTACK together with BACKYARD BABIES bassist Johan Blomqvist, the band releasing a 1998 album 'Slave Me'. ENTOMBED, now with MERCILESS, FACE DOWN, REGURGITATE and LOUD PIPES drummer Peter 'Flinta' Stjarnwind, put in an American tour to kick off 1998.

Opting for a complete rethink after the artistic failure of 'Same Difference' ENTOMBED went back to the very basics. The 2000 album 'Uprising', costing a miserly £4,000, being deliberately under produced and harking back to past glories. Not only was the old logo revived but the album cover was in fact the artwork from their original 'But Life Goes On' demo tape. If that was not enough ENTOMBED reworked the title track from 'Left Hand Path' retitling it 'Say It In Slugs'. With ENTOMBED's star in the ascension once again former label Earache issued a set of live tapes culled from a 1992 London Astoria show for the 'Monkey Puss - Live In London' album.

2000 also saw Cederlund and Stjärnvind in collusion with DISMEMBER's Matti Karki and Richard Cabeza for their MURDER SQUAD project album 'Unsane, Insane And Mentally Damaged'. Another ENTOMBED offshoot, the Thrash band BORN OF FIRE, would see Stjarnvind and Cabeza in alliance with Dimman and ex-UNLEASHED and present day LOUD PIPES and TERRA FIRMA bassist Fredda Lindgren.

ENTOMBED
Photo : Martin Wickler

Crawl / Forsaken, Earache MOSH 38 (1991) (12" single)
Crawl / Forsaken / Bitter Loss, Earache MOSH 38T (1991) (12" single)
Stranger Aeons/ Dusk/ Shreds Of Flesh, Earache MOSH52 (1992)
Hollowman / Serpent Speech / Wolverine Blues / Bonehouse / Put Off The Scent / Hellraiser, Earache MOSH 94 (1993) ('Hollowman' EP) 26 SWEDEN
State Of Emergency, King Kong KK004 (1993) (Split EP with TEDDY BEAR & DOLL SQUAD)
Out Of Hand / God Of Thunder / Blackbreath, Earache MOSH 114 (1994)
Night Of The Vampire, Earache MOSH132 (1995) (with NEW BOMB TURKS)
Kick Out The Jams / 21st Century Schizoid Man / Bursting Out / Under The Sun, Music For Nations DISC 2 (1997) ('Family Favourites' free EP with album)
Wreckage / Tear It Loose / Satan / Lost / Ballad Of Hollis Brown, Music For Nations CDMGNM233 (1997)
A Mesmirization Eclipse / Vice By Proxy / Black Juju / Sentimental Funeral, Man's Ruin MR099 (1999) ('Black Juju' EP)

Albums:
LEFT HAND PATH, Earache MOSH 21 (1990)
Left Hand Path / Drowned / Revel In Flesh / When Life Has Ceased / Supposed To Rot / But Life Goes On / Bitter Loss / Morbid Devourment / Deceased / Truth Beyond / Carnal Leftovers
CLANDESTINE, Earache MOSH 37 (1991) 44 SWEDEN
Crawl / Severe Burns / Living Dead / Through The Colonnades / Stranger Aeons / Blessed Be / Sinners Bleed / Chaos Breed / Evilyn
WOLVERINE BLUES, Earache MOSH82 (1993)
Eyemaster / Rotten Soil / Wolverine Blues / Demon / Contempt / Full Of Hell / Blood Song / Hollowman / Heavens Die / Out Of Hand
TO RIDE, SHOOT STRAIGHT AND SPEAK THE TRUTH, Music For Nations MFN 216 (1997) 7 SWEDEN, 75 UK
To Ride, Shoot Straight And Speak The Truth / Like This With The Devil / Lights Out / Wound /L They / Somewhat Peculiar / DCLXVI / Parasight / Damn Deal Done / Put Me Out / Just As Sad /

Boats / Mr Uffe's Horrorshow / Wreckage
WRECKAGE, Pony Canyon PCCY 01207 (1997) (Japanese release)
Wreckage / Lights Out (Live) / Just As Sad (Live) / L They (Live) / Wreckage (Indie Cart) / Kick Out The Jams / Tear It Loose / 21st Century Schizoid Man / Bursting Out / Under The Sun
SAME DIFFERENCE, (1998)
Addiction King / The Supreme Good / Clauses / Kick In The Head / Same Difference / Close But Nowhere Near / What You Need / High Waters / 20-20 Vision / The Day, The Earth / Smart Aleck / Jack Worm / Wolf Tickets
MONKEY PUSS - LIVE IN LONDON, Earache (1999)
Living Dead / Revel In Flesh / Stranger Aeons / Crawl / But Life Goes On / Sinners Bleed / Evilyn / The Truth Beyond / Drowned / Left Hand Path
UPRISING, Metal Is (2000)
Seeing Red / Say It In Slugs / Won't Back Down / Insanity's Contagious / Something Out Of Nothing / Scottish Hell / Time Out / The Itch / Returning To Madness / Come Clean / In The Flesh

ENTRAILS MASSACRE
(GERMANY)
Line-Up: Danilo Posselt (vocals), Stephen Hasse (guitar), Robert Gross (bass), Daniel Brosch (drums)

Rostock based Grind Crustcore act ENTRAILS MASSACRE have been ardent in their philosophy of spreading the cause worldwide forging alliances with numerous international acts for co-operations for both touring and single releases.
The band was first assembled in 1991 with former SUDDEN DEATH vocalist Janek and ex-LILITH members guitarists Christoph and Matze and drummer Daniel Brosch. The latter having credits with HEKATOMBE, ANAL TRACT and SUDDEN DEATH.
During 1992, the year in which their debut single emerged - a split affair with ACOUSTIC GRINDER, a radical overhaul of the band membership saw the inclusion of bassist Enrico and guitarist Ricardo. Danilo Posselt of WOJCCZESH and NEGATIVE APPROACH would become the bands new singer and erstwhile WOJCZECH man Stephan Kurth would take over four string duties in 1993 after deputizing on bass for the earlier 'Deepest Wish' demo. This tape included one side of live

material recorded in Romnitz, original studio tracks and a cover of ACOUSTIC GRINDER's 'Can't Ignore This Fucking War'.

The band's first overseas expedition came with a 1994 tour of Peru, the band utilizing the temporary services of WOJCZECH drummer Heinz for these dates. The bass position also saw a switch with ex AWAKE MORTEM man Mischa Buhrmeister being enlisted.

Further releases saw split single collaborations with ROT from Brazil (limited to 800 copies), ANUS PRAETOR (limited to 500 copies) and a shared live cassette with NYCTOPHOBIC. Another split tape 'Smash The Ignorance!' had the band rubbing shoulders with AGATHOCLES, INCISIVE and WOJCZECH.

1996 witnessed the departure of Kurth and the recruitment of former WOJCZECH and AUTHORS OF DOOM guitarist Stefan Strech. Releases included a split single 'Escaltriante', graced in cover artwork depicting a photograph of a mutilated baby and including a cover version of AGATHOCLES 'Consuming Endoderme Pus', with NYCTOPHOBIC.

In 1997 ENTRAILS MASSACRE toured Brazil with session bass handled by Raik of PERSOPHONE replacing Buhrmeister. Returning home ENTRAILS MASSACRE took part in the 'Bastards Have Landed' European tour sharing billing with WOJCZECH and Belgians CORNUCOPIA. Records issued that year comprised a split single with Japan's premier Grindsters UNHOLY GRAVE.

In 1998 the band arranged for their Brazilian touring colleagues ROT and ABUSO SONORO to tour Germany as a package billing. Shared cassette releases saw unions with Sweden's ARSEDESTROYER and Peruvians T.S.M. and CADAVER INCUBADOU. Live tapes were also issued in collusion with ULTRAPASSIV and a three-way split shared with ACROHOLIA and YACOPSAE.

The following year an experiment at female lead vocals was tried with SCUMFUCK's Loretta handling the mike but this idea was soon abandoned. Guitarist Stephan Haase, previously with HEKATOME and PAINFUL DEATH, was also enrolled. Further touring in Brazil found ENTRAILS MASSACRE as a trio.

Latterly ENTRAILS MASSACRE have continued their tradition of split releases with South Africa's GROINCHURN, KONSTRUKT, SUB-CUT, Americans GODSTOMPER and Brazilian acts CRUEL FACE and MANIFEST.

Robert Gross of WORSHIP took the bass role in 2000.

Singles/EPs:
Isis & Osiris / Visceral Combustion / Entrails Massacre, Regurgitated Semen RSR001 (1992) (7" split single with ACOUSTIC GRINDER)
Older Age / Mistake / Die Nacht / Reams Turn Into Chaos / In Memory Of, Regurgitated Semen RSR012 (1995) ('Die Nacht' 7" split single with ROT)
Harbour Of Identity / Far Away So Close / Entrails Massacre, Gulli GR003 (1995) ('Harbour Of Identity' 7" split single with ANUS PRAETOR)
Trouble / Saw Her Face / Just Friends / I Am Innocent / Another Spirit / Consuming Endoderme Pus, T&M T&M001 (1996) ('Escaltriante' 7" split single with NYCTOPHOBIC)
Misstegoitisch / Should Happen In The Future / Panic Oppressions / Misery In A Long Time / It's My View / Past / ...Use Your Favour Hour, Nat NAT008 (1997) (7" split single with UNHOLY GRAVE)
Split, Absurd (1999) (12" split single with SUB-CUT)
Split, Towerviolence Headfukka (2000) (7" split single with CRUEL FACE)
Split, Towerviolence Headfukka (2000) (7" split single with MANIFEST)
Split, Rescued For Life (2001) (7" split single with GODSTOMPER)

ENTWINED (UK)

Line-Up: Stephen John Tovey (vocals), Lee James (guitar), Simon (bass), James Southgate (drums)

ENTWINED feature erstwhile ESTRANGED members vocalist Stephen John Tovey, bassist Simon and drummer James Southgate. Guitarist Lee James has credits with MORTAL TIDE and METAL STORM. As ENTWINED the band bowed in with the demos 'XIII' and 'Hot Cherished Mask'.

ENTWINED supported MORBID ANGEL on their 1998 European tour but would fold shortly after.

Albums:
DANCING UNDER GLASS, Earache (1998)
The Sound Of Her Wings / Shed Nightward Beauty / Under A Killing Moon / The Forgotten / A Moments Sadness /

The Sacrifice Of Spring / Red Winter / Heaven Rise / XIII

EPIDEMIC (GREECE)
Line-Up: Jimmy Murphy (vocals / bass), Olly (guitar), Alex De Paduani (guitar), Slaughter (drums)

Singles/EPs:
Intro - Addiction / Waiting The Execution / Artificial Peace / Religious Greed, Epidemic EPI 1 (1991) ('Artificial Peace' EP)

Albums:
INDUSTRIAL, Soundphaze SIR CD 9402 (1994)
Hatred's Impression / Suffer Alone / Suicide Material / Suppressive Carmine / What Is Free / Anger / Industrial Solidarity / Fragments To The Greed / Absolution

EPIDEMIC (San Francisco, CA, USA)
Line-Up: Carl Fulli (vocals), Erik Moggridge (guitar), Guy Higbey (guitar), Mark Bodine (bass), Bob Cochran (drums)

EPIDEMIC debuted with the 'Immortal Minority' demo. A further demo tape in 1989 secured an album deal with Metalcore Records. Following EPIDEMIC's break-up, guitarist Erik Moggridge would unite with former MACHINE HEAD drummer Will Carroll and bassist Max Barnett to create the Stoner Death Metal band OLD GRANDAD.

Albums:
THE TRUTH OF WHAT WILL BE, Metalcore CRE4CD (1990)
DECAMERON, Metal Blade CDZORRO 50 (1992)
Circle Of Fools / Insanity Plea / Vision Divine / Hate / Unknown / Live Your Death / Factor Red / Blown Doors / Territories / Tornado / Three Witches / Lord War
EXIT PARADISE, Metal Blade CDZORRO 79 (1994)
Void / Vulture / Deaden / Lament / Exit Paradise / Institution Of Ignorance / Section 13 / Everlasting Lie / Written In Blood / To Escape The Void
EPIDEMIC, Rage (1994)

EPITAPH (SWEDEN)
Line-Up: Johan Enocksson (vocals / drums), Manne Svensson (guitar), Nicke Hagen (bass)

Swedish Metal band EPITAPH were previously known as DARK ABBEY and the first album, a split effort with fellow Swedes EXCRUCIATE, was recorded with ex-HYPOCRISY members Jonas Österberg (guitar) and Lars Sköke (drums)

Albums:
EPITAPH, Infest INF002 (1991) (Split LP with EXCRUCIATE)
TRANQUILITY, World Fluid WRFD502 (1992)

EQUINOX (FL, USA)
Line-Up: Darkness (vocals / bass), Pete Slate (guitar), Tony Blakk (guitar), Stephen Spillers (drums)

A retro-Black defiled Death Metal band from central Florida created during the winter of 1992 by erstwhile ACHERON guitarist Pete Slate, former INCUBUS bassist Mark Lavenia, vocalist Darkness and drummer Stephen Spillers.
EQUINOX debuted with the demo cassette 'Anthem To The Moon' following which Lavenia decamped. Darkness took over the bass role as the band also inducted another ACHERON veteran guitarist Tony Blakk. With this line up the band cut 'Upon The Throne Of Eternity' single.
During the autumn 1995 the group secured a deal with the Greek Unisound concern for the debut full length album 'Return To Mystery'.
By 2000 Lavernia had reunited with Slate in an alliance with ex-MASSACRE drummer Kam Lee founding CAULDRON.

Singles/EPs:
Upon The Throne Of Eternity, Deathlike Silence (1995) (7" single)

Albums:
RETURN TO MYSTERY, Unisound (1996)
Rites Of Red Giving / Return To Mystery / Until The Dawn's Mist / The Mourning River / Valley Of The Kings / Dreams Of The Winter Solstice / Winds Of Autumn / Infernal Atavism (Descend To Tetragrammaton) / Path To Eternal Ruin
JOURNEY INTO OBLIVION, Still Dead (1999)

ESTATIC FEAR (AUSTRIA)
Line-Up: Beowulf (vocals / bass), Stauff (guitar), Calix Miseriae (guitar /

keyboards), Astaroth Magus (drums)

This Doom / Death / Black / Gothic Metal band, featuring guitarist Calix Miseriae (real name Matthias Kogler), was formed in 1993 and has featured a stable line-up since 1994.
On the debut album, which features strong medieval themes, the band was assisted by female vocalist Marion and the flute playing of Petra Hölzl.
Drummer Astaroth Magus ('Milan Dejak') also operates in ASTAROTH, THIRD MOON and SEPTIC CEMETARY.

Albums:
SOMNIUM OBMUTUM, CCP 100151-2 (1996)
Des Nachtens Suss' Gedone / Somnium Obmutum / As Autumn Calls / Ode To Solitude
A SOMBRE DANCE, CCP 100197-2 (199-)
Intro (Unisomo Lute Instrumental) / Chapter I / Chapter II / Chapter III / Chapter IV / Chapter V / Chapter VI / Chapter VII / Chapter VIII / Chapter IX

ETERNAL DIRGE (GERMANY)
Line-Up: Timo (vocals / guitar), Pethe (guitar), Boelmi (bass), Ralf (drums)

This self styled "Neo pagan psycho metal" band, from Marl, Westfalia, was formed in the mid 80s and released several demos before 'We Are The Dead' led to a record deal.
Both of ETERNAL DIRGE's albums highlight the group's brand of Death / Thrash Metal with keyboard leanings on a grand scale. Indeed, during the recording of the 'Khaos Magick' album permanent keyboardist Sascha R. joined the group.

Albums:
MORBUS ASCENDIT, HASS Production (1994)
Out The Eons / The Crawling Chaos / Exploring The Depths / Blind Idiot God / The Decadence Within / We Are The Dead / Sinustis Maxillaris / Evolved Mutations
KHAOS MAGICK, Moribund MR024 (1996)
I, Unameable / The Threshold Of Sensation / Anthem To The Seeds (Of Pure Demise) / Feaster From The Stars / Rending The Veils / Kallisti / Like Roses In A Garden Of Weed / In Praise Of Biocide / Hymn To Pan / My Sweet Satan

ETERNAL OATH (SWEDEN)
Line-Up: Joni Maensivu (vocals), Peter Nagy (guitar / drums), Petri Tarvainen (guitar), Peter Wendin (bass), Par Almquist (keyboards), Tad Jonsson (drums)

Peter Nagy has credits with HYPOCRITE. Martin Viklander also has credits on bass guitar for the 1996 debut 'So Silent' outing.

Albums:
SO SILENT, N Wrapped Media NWM01 (1996)
The Dawn / Harmonic Souls Departed / So Silent / Insanity / Eternal Rest / Dream Of Rising
THROUGH THE EYES OF HATRED, Pulverized (2000)

ETERNAL PASSION (GERMANY)
Line-Up: Jürgen Hofmann (vocals), Armin Binder (guitar), Günther Rascher (guitar), Bernhard Atzesberger (bass), Dieter Kasberger (keyboards), Freddy Pongratz (drums)

A Doom / Death Metal act.

Albums:
THE SLEEPING RIVER, Gin Phonic GIN001 (1995)
The Past Is Like The Future / Yearning / Land Of Melancholy / Awake / Darkside / Waiting For Death (Live Studio Track)

ETERNAL PEACE (GERMANY)
Line-Up: D. Kaczmaerk (vocals), O. Martin (guitar), J. Dietrich (guitar), B. Kern (keyboards), J. Irmscher (drums)

This five-piece band plays diverse Death Metal with atmosphere. A few of the songs on the 'Schinderaas' album are delivered in the band's native tongue.

Albums:
SCHINDERAAS, Noiselab SJR 112 (1995)
Sacrifice / Schinderaas / Anfissa / Sölnergrab / LDarkness / Autumns Day / Requiem / Outro

ETERNAL REST (GERMANY)
Line-Up: Skip Danko (vocals), Klaus (guitar), Akki (guitar), Gregor (bass), Friedel (drums)

Singles/EPs:
Flamingo Road / Nic's Way / My

Pizzaman Is A Terrorist / The Wave / Crying, Strange Ways (1995)

Albums:
HAGEN - THEESFELD, Strange Ways WAY 121 (1995)
Jazz / Nic's Way / Unborn / I Come There / Take Me To Hospital / The Wave / Patriot Disease / Session / My Pizzaman Is A Terrorist / Harry Fisch Jr. / Bigger / Dirty Old Song / I Go There - Dub

ETERNAL SADNESS (GERMANY)
Line-Up: Wolfgang Lutsch (vocals / guitar), Alex Hagenauer (vocals / guitar), Jörg Mensche (bass), Timo Lechner (keyboards), Tom Hemmerlein (drums)

This five-piece band mixes Death Metal with Gothic Metal and Techno Thrash. ETERNAL SADNESS have played with BOLT-THROWER in their time and received some glowing press coverage.

Albums:
ELATION, Eternal Sadness (1996)
Elation / Shadows From The Past / Autumn / Descending Glances / Drowned Fate / Like A Mourner / Your Beauty / Dance Of The Dawn

ETERNAL SOLSTICE (HOLLAND)
Line-Up: Kees Van Schouten (vocals), Philip Nutgren (guitar), Victor Van Drie (guitar), Ramon Soeterbroek (bass), Mischa Kak (drums)

Founded in 1989 by vocalist Kees Van Scouten, guitarist Philip Nutgren, bassist Ramon Soeterbroek and original drummer Edwin Roor, when the latter departed two ex-SEMPITERNAL DETHREIGN musicians were added in drummer Mischa Hak and guitarist Victor Van Drie. Hak was also playing drums with MOURNING.
ETERNAL SOLSTICE began recording a proposed split album with MOURNING in 1990 but Van Schouten departed leaving Souterbroek to handle lead vocal duties. It took a further two years for this split album to see a release on Midian Creations Records, during which time ETERNAL SOLSTICE split.
The band were reformed the following year by Nutgren and Soeterbroek together with drummer Eric Boekoe. A demo followed, but the band splintered once more leaving Soeterbroek handling lead vocals. Although drummer Mische Hak performed on the debut full length

album 'The Wish Is Father To The Thought', which included a cover of SODOM's 'Outbreak Of Evil', ETERNAL SOLSTICE found a permanent drummer in ex-MOURNING man Andre Van Der Ree.
The band augmented their sound in early 1996 by welcoming ex-ASPHYX guitarist Eric Daniels into the ranks.

Albums:
ETERNAL SOLSTICE, Midian Creations (1992) (Split LP with MOURNING)
THE WISH IS FATHER TO THE THOUGHT, Displeased (1994)
God In The Flesh / Torn Apart / Chamber Of Morpheus / Act Of Settlement / Blasphemous Sermons / Dragged Down To Rot / Sleep Of Death / Demonic Fertilizer / Wrapped In Darkness / Outbreak Of Evil
HORRIBLE WITHIN, Poseidon PP-35020 (1995)
Unholy Trinity DV / Culpable Homicide / The Ceremony Has Begun / Mask The Face Of Death / One Last Vision (Prepare) / By Your Command / T.W.I.F.T.T.T. / Eager For Death / A Wish Beyond / Worn With Age
DEMONIC FERTILIZER, Poseidon (1997)
Insects / Deep Sleep / Melancholic '97 / Rebirth In Ice / Obscuration / In The Year 2525 / Demonic Fertilizer II / Thrall To The Gallows / Turn Of The Century

ETERNAL SUFFERING (USA)
Line-Up: Wayne Sarantopoulos (vocals), Brian Evans (guitar), Chris Glover (guitar), Jon Landolfi (bass), Chad Connell (drums)

Death Metal incarnation put together in early 1994 initially as PUTRID by guitarist Brian Evans and drummer Chad Connell. Later recruits were former ESTRANGLEMENT singer Wayne Sarantopoulos and bass player Chris Glover. With this new membership a new title of DISGORGE was chosen, later adopting the revised herald of ETERNAL SUFFERING upon discovering the existence of their Mexican and Californian namesakes.
ETERNAL SUFFERING's debut demo arrived in 1996 titled 'Remain Forever In Misery' and the full length 'Drowning In Tragedy' capitalized on interest. Following recording the band inducted bass player Jon Landolfi.

Albums:
DROWNING IN TRAGEDY, Extremities Productions (1998)
Midnight's Embrace / My Once Shadowed Desire / Drown In The Candles Flame / Let The Dark Water Flow / The Warmth In Her Torment / Trail Of Blood To The Altar / Love Can Never Conquer Hate / Buried Under Blackened Tears / Rise / To Sadness, Betrothed

ETERNAL TEARS OF SORROW
(FINLAND)
Line-Up: Altti Veteläinen (vocals), Antti Talala (guitar), Jarmo Puolakanaho (guitar), Olli Pekka-Torro (guitar / keyboards), Pasi Hiltula (keyboards), Petri Sankala (drums)

Death Metal act with Black overtones although the band themselves are reluctant to label their brand of music 'black'. The group rose from the ashes of an early 90's act ANDROMEDA which comprised of Altti Verläinen on bass, Jarmo Puolakanaho on guitar, vocalist Mikko Komulainen, guitarist Olli Pekka Törrö and drummer Petri Sankala. ANDROMEDA folded after their rehearsal rooms burnt down but did manage a 1993 demo 'Beyond The Fantasy'.
By the following year Verläinen, Törrö and Puolakanaho founded ETERNAL TEARS OF SORROW bowing in with the tape 'The Seven Goddesses Of Frost'. The group was far from happy with the end result citing the facts that it had been recorded at school on a four track! Fortunately a follow up session 'Bard's Burial' secured a deal with the Swedish X-treme Records label. However, although the 'Sinner's Serenade' opus was laid down in 1996 it was to be September 1997 before its release.
The band switched to the Finnish Spinefarm concern for sophomore outing 'Vild Mánnu'. In 1999 Törrö decamped and new members Antti Talala on guitar, bassist / keyboard player Pasi Hiltula and erstwhile ANDROMEDA colleague drummer Petri Sankula were welcomed into the fold.
The 'Chaotic Beauty' album, which includes a cover of EDGE OF SANITY's 'Black Tears', was produced by Mikko Karmila featured backing vocals from SINERGY's Kimberley Goss.
Touring to promote the album resulted in the exit of Talala with Antti Kokko taking his position.

Albums:
SINNERS SERENADE, X-Treme XTR003 (1997)
Another One Falls Asleep / The Law Of The Flames / Dirge / Into The Deepest Waters / Sinners Serenade / My God, The Evil wind / March / Bard's Burial / The Son Of The Forest / Empty Eyes
VILD MÁNNU, Spinefarm SPI68CD (1999)
Northern Doom / Burning Flames Embrace / Goashem / Scars Of Wisdom / Nightwinds Lullaby / Raven (In Your Eyes) / Vild Mánnu / Coronach / Nodde Rahgan / Seita
CHAOTIC BEAUTY, Spinefarm (2000)
Shattered Soul / Blood Of Faith Stains My Hands / Autumn's Grief / The Seventh Eclipse / Bride Of The Crimson Sea / Black Tears / Tar Of Chaos / Bhéan Sidhe / Nocturnal Strains / Flight Of Icarus / Coronach / Nightwinds Lullaby / Burning Flames Embrace

ETHERIAL WINDS (HOLLAND)
Line-Up: Henri (vocals / keyboards), Bert (guitar), Freddy (bass), Micha (drums)

Previously known as EMBITTER, this Dutch band became ETHERIAL WINDS in 1992. They supply a mixture of Doom and Death Metal.

Albums:
SAVED, MMI 008 (1995)
Calmed (Intro) / Into The Serene / Winter / Benevolence Of The Opaque / In Depression / Endless (Outro)
FIND THE WAY... TOGETHER, Massacre MASS CD059 (1995)
Together / Entrance / Hymne Of Gladness / Elements Of Sorrow / Wish / Hunger / Can't You Sleep / Tragedy

EUCHARIST (SWEDEN)
Line-Up: Markus Johnsson (vocals / guitar), Thomas Einarsson (guitar), Tobias Gustafsson (bass), Daniel Erlandsson (drums)

One of the first bands to combine Death Metal with strong melodies, these so called pioneers of the 'Göthenburg style' released their debut 'A Velvet Creation' in 1993 although a 1992 demo (recorded whilst most of the band were still only sixteen!) and an EP 'Greeting Immortality' had preceded it. The debut album was actually recorded under strenuous conditions, the band disliking each other so much they had actually officially split up before commencement of recording. Vocalist / guitarist Markus Johnsson was in particular so disgusted he refused to record any guitars for the album.

Drummer Daniel Erlandsson later joined IN FLAMES, LIERS IN WAIT and DIABOLIQUE.

EUCHARIST reconvened once more in the late 90's cutting two tracks 'The Predictable End' and 'Wounded And Alone' for 1995's Wrong Again Records compilation 'War'.

Singles/EPs:
Greeting Immortality, Obscure Plasma (1993)

Albums:
A VELVET CREATION, Wrong Again WAR001 (1993)
Greeting Immortality / The Religion Of The Blood-Red Velvet / March Of The Insurrection / My Bleeding Tears / Floating / A Velvet Creation / Into The Cosmic Sphere / Once My Eye Moved Mountains
MIRROR WORLDS, War Music (1998)
Mirror Worlds / Dissolving / With The Sun / The Eucharist / Demons / Fallen… / In Nakedness / Bloodred Stars

EUCHARIST (USA)
Line-Up: Stacey (vocals), Chaz (guitar), Derek (guitar), Matt (bass), Jeremy (drums)

A Christian Death Metal act that made quite an impression upon the scene but would ultimately fold. Guitarist Chaz joined the secular act CALIPH which morphed into BODYBAG ROMANCE.
Fellow guitarist Derek founded THISFIREWITHIN along with drummer Jeremy. Bassist Matt joined SARAH'S CHILD and Ska act 13TH TRIBE.

EVENVAST (ITALY)
Line-Up: Antonietta Scilipoti (vocals), Luca Martello (guitar), Diego Maniscalco (bass), Roberto Risso (drums)

EVENVAST include the former CHAOS AND TECHNOCRACY duo of vocalist Antonietta Scilipoti and guitarist Luca Martello.

Singles/EPs:
Over / The Valley Surrounding Me (Part I) / Petit Monde / Slippin' The Stealth, ARS Metalli (2000) ('Where The Trees Still Speak' EP)

Albums:
HEAR ME OUT, Black Lotus BLRCD 009 (1999)
Never Know Me / Once Again / The One You Wish / Foolish Game / Memory / Energy / Believe Me / Ru
DAWNING GLOOM, ARS Metalli (2001)

THE EVERDAWN (SWEDEN)
Line-Up: Pierre Törnkvist (vocals / guitar / bass), Patrick Törnkvist (guitar), Niklas Svensson (bass), Oskar Karlsson (drums)

THE EVERDAWN were created by erstwhile GATES OF ISHTAR members drummer Oskar Karlsson and bassist Niclas Svensson together with former SCHEITAN guitarist Pierre Törnkvist. In fact, all three - previous to the formation of GATES OF ISHTAR in 1994 - had been members of DECORTITION.
Svensson and Törnkvist also have credits in THE MOANING.

Singles/EPs:
The Everdawn / Nightborn / The Silent Winter Sky / Opera Of The Damned, Black Diamond IRS (1996) ('Opera Of The Damned' EP)

Albums:
POEMS – BURN THE PAST, Invasion (1997)
Territory Loss / When The Sunset Forever Fades / Needlework / Where Pain Never Dies / Autumn, Sombre Autumn / Burn / Poems / Opera Of The Damned

EVEREVE (GERMANY)
Line-Up: Tom Sedotschenko (vocals), Thorsten Weißenberger (guitar), Stephan Kiefer (guitar), Stefan Müller (bass), MZ Eve 51 (keyboards), Marc Werner (drums)

EVEREVE made quite an impact with their Nuclear Blast debut album 'Seasons'. However, a second effort 'Stormbirds' saw progress stalling despite roadwork in Europe with CREMATORY.
1999 would see former VERMILION FIELDS singer Benjamin Richter take Tom Sedotschenko's position. Tragically the troubled Sedotschenko would commit suicide on May 1st.
Although not charting in Europe the 'Regrets' album would achieve the dubious distinction of being number one on the Lebanese independent radio charts for a three week run! In September

of 1999 EVEREVE put in European dates on a package billing with HYPOCRISY and COVENANT.

In January of 2000 drummer Marc Werner departed making way for the mysterious MC Wifebeater, actually Martin Claas. Signing to Massacre Records for the 2001 album 'E-Mania' EVEREVE would dispense with Richter's services as keyboard player MZ Eve 51 (real name Michael Zeissl) took over the role.

Singles/EPs:
Intro / Darkmere / Salvation / Stormbirds / Autumn Child, Promo-Split-CD (1995) (Promotion Split CD with PARRACIDE)

Albums:
SEASONS, Nuclear Blast NB222-2 (1996)
Prologue: The Bride Wears Black / A New Winter / The Phoenix, Spring / The Dancer, Under A Summer Sky / Twilight / Autumn Leaves / Untergehen Und Auferstehen / To Learn Silent Oblivion / A Winternight Depression / Epilogue
STORMBIRDS, Nuclear Blast (1998)
Embittered / Fields Of Ashes / Escape / On Lucid Wings / Martyrium / The Failure / The Downfall / Dedications / Stormbirds / As I Breathe The Dawn / Spleen / Universe / A Past For You / Valse Bizarre
REGRETS, Nuclear Blast (1999)
Misery's Dawn / Fall Into Oblivion / Holyman / Redemption / House Of The Rising Sun / The Eclipse Of The Seventh Sun / Passion And Demise / Dies Irae (Grave New World) / Where No Shadows Fall / House Of The Rising Sun (Club edition)
E-MANIA, Massacre (2001)

EVIL DEAD (USA)
Line-Up: Phil Flores (vocals), Juan Garcia (guitar), Albert Gonzales (guitar), Mel Sanchez (bass), Rob Alaniz (drums)

EVIL DEAD, a band who were unafraid to take Death Metal to new levels of extremity, were created by guitarist Juan Garcia after he abandoned AGENT STEEL in 1988. Garcia's previous credits also included ABATTOIR.

Indeed, the original version of EVIL DEAD included ex-ABATTOIR bassist Mel Sanchez and ex-NECROPHILIA drummer Rob Alaniz. ABATTOIR guitarist Mark Caro was invited to join early on but the liaison didn't pan out and he quickly left the scene after recording a three track demo tape.

Guitarist Albert Gonzalez and vocalist Phil Flores were added a year later and EVIL DEAD would go on to score a deal with the German label Steamhammer Records.

The group debuted with the 'Rise Above' EP in 1989 and followed it up with the full blown album 'Annihilation Of Civilization' the same year.

The Japanese version of 'Annihilation Of Civilization' included bonus tracks from the European only released EP.

EVIL DEAD fragmented before their second album, Albert Gonzales was fired and would join DEATH for touring duties. Rob Alaniz walked out (forming RISE in the process) but Flores and Garcia regrouped by adding guitarist Dan Flores and bassist Karlos Medina (after Sanchez split) for 1991's 'The Underworld'. Drums on the album, which included a version of the SCORPIONS 'He's A Woman, She's A Man', were supplied by Doug Clawson and backing vocals by METAL CHURCH man David Wayne. DEATH drummer Gene Hoglan also guested.

Singles/EPs:
Rise Above / Run Again / Sloe Death / S.T. Riff, Steamhammer 557590 (1989)

Albums:
ANNIHILATION OF CIVILIZATION, Steamhammer 847603 (1989)
F.C.I.: The Awakening / Annihilation Of Civilization / Living God / Future Shock / Holy Trials / Gone Shooting / Parricide / Unauthorised Exploitation / B.O.H.I.C.A.
THE UNDERWORLD, Steamhammer 084 76362 (1991)
Intro (Comshell 5) / Global Warming / Branded / Welcome To Kuwait / Critic-Cynic / The 'Hood / The Underworld / He's A Woman, She's A Man / Process Elimination / Labyrinth Of The Mind / Reap What You Sow
LIVE... FROM THE DEPTHS OF THE UNDERWORLD, Steamhammer (1992)

EVIL INCARNATE (USA)
Line-Up: Mike Eisenhauer (vocals / bass), Rob Rigney (guitar), Dave Gally (guitar), Andy Vehnekamp (drums)

Previously known as APOLLYON and forged by erstwhile NUM SKULL members frontman Mike Eisenhauer and guitarist Tom Brandauer in 1994. A series of demos started with 'Beyond Blasphemy' and 'Deliverance From

Salvation'. Brandauer departed and was replaced by former MORBID CORPSES and FEAR SPAWNED RELIGION man Dave Gally. The third effort 'Christ Destroyed' was issued before Deathgasm Records compiled these early recordings for the 'Blood Of The Saints' album. These recording were also issued on cassette by the Czech label Ramu Records.

EVIL INCARNATE have also offered tribute to VENOM, SLAYER and BLACK SABBATH by appearing on various tribute albums.

EVIL INCARNATE drummer Andy Vehnekamp is better known as a member of JUNGLE ROT.

Brandauer returned following the exit of Gally.

A second album entitled 'Blackest Hymns Of God's Disgrace' was recorded in 2000.

Albums:
BLOOD OF THE SAINTS, Deathgasm (2000)
First Born Of The Wicked / Last Suffer Of Nazarene / Blood Of The Saints / Heaven Lay Burned / His Only Bastard Son / Twist Of The Serpents Head / Raised From The Deep / The Sacrificial Lamb / Dead Corpse Of Jesus Christ / Sculpture Of Impurity

EVILUTION (New Haven, CT, USA)

Albums:
SHRINE OF DESECRATION, Pure Death (1998)
Act Of Attrition / The Rebirth Of Azazel / Cowering Messiah / Nailed To The Cross / Baptimisal Rite To Deity / Shrine Of Desecration / In Constant Obscure / Extracted From The Womb

EVILWAR (BRAZIL)
Line-Up: Sabatan (vocals), Azarack (guitar), Typhon Seth (bass), Ichthys Niger (drums)

EVILWAR, founded in mid 1999, include former MURDER RAPE personnel vocalist Sabatan, guitarist Azarack and drummer Ichthys Niger. Both Azarack and Niger also have credits with INSANE DEVOTION.

Albums:
UNHOLY MARCH, (2000)

EVISCERATION (PORTUGAL)

Albums:
HYMN TO THE MONSTROUS, (1995)
Farewell To Earth, Heaven And Sun / Torments Of A Dying Victim - Hymns To The Monstrous / Consumed Act / Fever Hallucinations / A Morbid Sensation Of Cold / (The Art Of) Empalement / Profound Wounds / A Strong Temptation To Kill / In The Flesh / Dead Foetus / Dismembering Process Of A Four Month Child / Extremities Brutalized / Outro

EVOKE (UK)

EVOKE, a Mansfield based Black Metal band, debuted with a 1994 demo tape before eventually issuing two singles during 1997, the second of which is a split 7" green vinyl affair shared with Germany's KADATH.

Singles/EPs:
Behold The Twilight / Await The Inevitable, Megagrind (1997)
As I Bleed / Among Mere Mortals, Paranoia Syndrome (1997) (Split 7" with KADATH)

Albums:
DREAMING INTO REALITY, (1997)
Intro / The Sign Of Solitude / Through Blood Stared Eyes / Body Rites / Among Mere Mortals / No Repeat / Rouge / Die Before My Eyes / When Beauty Dies / Equanimity Lost / Manipulate The Ridicule / As I Bleed / While You Decay I Live
THE FURY WRITTEN, System Shock (2000)

EXCESS OF CRUELTY (BELGIUM)
Line-Up: Johan (vocals), Joris (guitar), Jan (guitar), Gerry (bass), Joeri (drums)

Created by a union of former KOROS DAGANAT and NEX personnel during 1991 EXCESS OF CRUELTY began life as a Grindcore unit but would soon start to tread down the path of Black inspired Death Metal.

The band first gelled when the Metal band NEX's rhythm section of drummer Joeri and bassist Raf teamed up with vocalist Johan and guitarist Joris from Hardcore group KOROS DAGANAT. This initial incarnation of EXCESS OF CRUELTY issued a Grind influenced demo but by their second effort 'Infinite Solitariness' the band had become a fully

fledged Death Metal operation.
A 7" single 'Thoughts Of A Forlorn Existence' ensued prior to a further demo 'Stream To Aljira' in 1992. Two years later a further cassette 'Catharsis Tranquillitatis' emerged before the enrollment of second guitarist Jan. The 1996 tape 'Fionnuala' precipitated the departure of Raf and the recruitment of CHEMICAL BREATH four stringer Gerry.

Singles/EPs:
Thoughts Of A Forlorn Existence, Lowland (1992)

Albums:
UNDER THE IVY OF ITHAMOR, Wood Nymph (1997)
The Dreamweavers Illusion / Wafts From Birch And Briar Breath / The Reaper Of The Harvest / Fionuala / Nangara / Beholding The Crimson Tide / When At Eventide / Under The Ivy Of Ithamor / Solemn Sounds Of The Soul / Northern Shekinah Light / The Trooper

EXCISION (INDONESIA)

A solo project of former INNER WARFARE and present day KEKAL guitarist Jefray. EXCISION first broke cover with the demo 'Manipulation Of Response' then had a track 'Purpose' included on the American compilation album 'Last Minutes Of Suffering' issued on Loud Cat Productions. EXCISION followed this with a cassette release in 1998 'The Quality Of Mankind'.
The debut album 'Visi' includes assistance from the enigmatically titled vocalist sf/y. EXCISION have also shared a 2000 cassette release with WORLDHATE.

Albums:
VISI, (2000)
Broken / To Change Horizons / I See / The Killing Fields / View From The Balcony / Visi / My Time Is Eternity / Changing Horizons / If I Have To Die / I See (Reprise)

EXCREMENT (FINLAND)
Line-Up: Antti Oinonen (vocals / guitar), Sami Keltikangas (guitar), Jusi Hokkala (bass), Seppo Santala (drums)

Albums:
SCORCHED, Invasion (1995)
Intro / Corpse Fucking Art / Scorched / Sleep / Distortion / Covered With Feces

EXCRETED ALIVE (SPAIN)

Albums:
CHORDS OF CHAOS, Lofty Storm Productions (1996) (4-way split album with EXHUMED, EAR BLEEDING DISORDER and NECROSE)
Your Useless Majesty / Crude Reality / Your Music Business / Slave Of A Vice / Are Squeezing The Neck / Metaphor

EXCRETION (SWEDEN)
Line-Up: Thomas Wahlström (vocals / bass), Christoffer Holm (guitar), Anders Hanser (guitar), Tommy Otemark (drums)

Swedish Death Metal quartet. Stolle Holm is also credited with guitar.

Albums:
VOICE OF HARMONY, Wrong Again WAR007 (1995)
Forever Closed Eyes / I Am / Darkness Falls / That Once Been Given / Life Passion Ends / Those Silent Days / Suicide Silence / The Final Part Of Sleep / Voice Of Harmony

EXCRUCIATE (SWEDEN)
Line-Up: Lars Levin (vocals), Johan Rudberg (guitar), Hempa Brynolfsson (guitar), Fredrik Isaksson (bass), Per Ax (drums)

EXCRUCIATE started life as a trio in 1989 with guitarists Hempa Brynolfsson and Johan Melander together with drummer Per Ax. This line-up recorded the 'Mutilation Of The Past' demo the following year before adding bassist Fredrik Isaksson and vocalist Christian Carlsson.
Following the band's commercial debut, a split album with EPITAPH, Carlsson made way for ex-MASTICATION singer Lars Levin. In 1992 Melander opted to leave and in his stead came another erstwhile MASTICATION member Johan Rudberg.
Strangely EXCRUCIATE folded soon after the 1993 album 'Passages Of Life'.

Albums:
EXCRUCIATE, Infest INF002 (1991) (Split LP with EPITAPH)
PASSAGE O FLIFE, Thrash 852 314 (1993)

EXHUMATION (GREECE)
Line-Up: John Nokteridis (vocals), Marios Iliopoulos (guitar), Panagiotis

Giatzoglu (guitar), Thomas Bairachtaris (keyboards), Pantelis Athanasiadis (drums)

The 1998 album 'Dance Across The Past' has guest appearances from Kimberley Goss of DIMMU BORGIR and SINERGY and Jesper Strombald of IN FLAMES. EXHUMATION folded in 2000 with guitarist Mario creating NIGHTRAGE.

Albums:
SEAS OF ETERNAL SILENCE, Diehard RRS956 (1997)
Seas Of Eternal Silence / Dreamy Recollectzion / Beyond The Eyes Of The Universe / Forgotten Days / Passing Suns / Ceaseless Sorrow / Guilts Of Innocence / Monuments
DANCE ACROSS THE PAST, Holy (1998)

EXHUMATOR (BELARUS)
Line-Up: Alexander Bourei (vocals / guitar), Pavel Bolokhov (bass), Jouri Golovach (drums)

Extreme Metal act EXHUMATOR was forged in Minsk, capitol of Belarus, in 1989. The band started out as a quartet of vocalist Slava Korsakov, guitarist Vova Lisishin, bassist Igor Silnichenko and drummer Anton Arkhipov. This line-up cut the debut album 'Welcome And Die' and the follow up EP 'Arising Of Suspicions'.
Vadim Akimov was added on lead vocals in 1992 to appear on the sophomore album 'Resurrected'. The bass position then switched to accommodate Pavel Bolokhov.
The 1994 demo 'Sacrificial Bleeding' would be the last recording made by Akimov who died the following year. Undaunted EXHUMATOR relocated to Western Europe in order to further their career. Settling in Brussels EXHUMATOR were by now a trio of Bourei, Bolokhov and drummer Jouri Golovach.

Singles/EPs:
Arising Of Suspicions EP, (1993)

Albums:
WELCOME AND DIE, (1990)
RESURRECTED, (1993)

EXHUMATOR (GERMANY)

Albums:
DIE FOR WHATEVER BUT, Exhumator (1995)

IN YOUR FACE, (1996)

EXHUMED (CA, USA)
Line-Up: Matt Harvey (vocals / guitar), Mike Bearns (guitar), Bud Burke (bass), Col Jones (drums)

Brutal Death Metal in its most undiluted state. California's EXHUMED have made unrelenting progress despite being wrought into ever new incarnations by constant line-up changes over the years. The band first made their mark in 1991 with an inaugural roster of frontman Jake Giardina, guitarist Derrel Houdashelt and Matt Harvey, bassist Ben Marrs and drummer Col Jones.
EXHUMED debuted with a stark statement of intent with the demo 'Dissecting The Caseated Omentum'. A 7" single 'Excreting Innards' proved there was to be no concessions to compromise. Ramming the point home EXHUMED would garner valuable exposure for their sick artform guesting for visiting dignitaries such as AUTOPSY, ENTOMBED, CANNIBAL CORPSE and MORBID ANGEL. A whole slew of uncompromising demo cassettes would ensue beginning with 'Gorgasm'.
With the dismissal of Marrs in November of 1993 Ross Sewage would front the band as Giardina deputized on bass for 1993's 'Grotesque Putrefied Brains'. Further touring had the band out with heavyweights DISMEMBER, SUFFOCATION and VADER.
Another promotional tape was offered titled 'Cadaveric Splatter Platter'. These sessions had Harvey responsible for both guitar and bass as Giardina bade his farewell. Mark Smith would come in on bass but would soon decamp. Matt Widener was later inducted as permanent bassist. The revised band cut a further demo session 'Horrific Expulsion Of Gore' in late 1994. The following year witnessed an exclusive new track 'Necro-Fornicator' being contributed the Morbid Metal compilation album 'Deterioration Of The Senses' and a shared live cassette in alliance with notorious Spanish Death Metal brethren HAEMMORHAGE. However, Widener would vacate his position and Sewage wound up adding bass guitar to his duties. Having his own graphics company Sewage would be responsible for much of EXHUMED's horrifically graphic artwork.
Another rare track 'Intercourse With A Limbless Cadaver' was included on the 'Orchestrated Chaos' compilation put out

by Soulside Records in March of 1996. EXHUMED would share space with the equally twisted Ohian act HEMDALE on a split album 'In The Name Of Gore' the same year. Further ructions saw the release of Houdashelt and the swift substitution with INFANTICIDE man Leon Del Muerte.

Del Muerte would figure on recordings made for a four-way split EP 'Chords Of Chaos' for Lofty Storm Productions which paired EXHUMED off with NECROSE, BLEEDING DISORDER and EXCRETED ALIVE. The new guitarist would also feature on the compilation track 'Bleeding Heap Of Menstrual Carnage' donated to the 'Accidental Double Homicide' collection on Satan's Pimp Records before leaving the ranks to join IMPALED. For a time Ross Sewage would also deputize as bassist for IMPALED sharing his duties with EXHUMED.

Down to a trio EXHUMED set out on a support tour of America guesting for MORTIIS before hooking up with the European extravaganza 'Grind Over Europe II'. This gargantuan Death package nestled EXHUMED in amongst the likes of VOMITORY, AGATHOCLES, DERANGED, KADATH, HEMDALE and NYCTOPHOBIC. With the fulfillment of these dates EXHUMED, limbering up for dates in Mexico, was back up to strength as a quartet with the induction of ex-BURIAL guitarist Mike Bearns.

The band signed to Death Metal aficionados Relapse Records for the 1998 'Gore Metal' full length debut. The album saw production courtesy of former TESTAMENT, DEATH and CANCER guitarist JAMES MURPHY. Not neglecting the singles market 1998 proved fruitful for EXHUMED collectors as the band graced no less than three split affairs in cahoots with RETALIATION on the 'Tales Of The Exhumed' release for the Italian Headfucker concern, NYCTOPHOBIC as part of the 'Totally Fucking Dead' issue on Germany's Revenge Production label. A further single with PANTALONES ABAJO MARINERO for 'Indignities To The Dead' also made it out that year.

Sewage would bow out from EXHUMED in 1999 shortly after showings at the Massachusetts Metal & Hardcore Festival and the March Metal Meltdown event. Erstwhile PALE EXISTENCE bassist Bud Burke would fill the gap as EXHUMED undertook the Relapse 'Contamination' American tour alongside labelmates TODAY IS THE DAY, BENUMB, NASUM, CEPHALIC CARNAGE, SOILENT GREEN and MORGION.

The 2000 album 'Slaughtercult' would see a later re-issue as a saw shaped CD picture disc. Japanese versions came with an extra four bonus tracks. Touring to promote the album had EXHUMED on the road with VULGAR PIGEON, ABCESS and IMPALED. As 2001 broke EXHUMED kept up the tradition of the split 7" releases cutting a further effort with SANITY'S DAWN entitled 'Emeticide'.

Singles/EPs:
Excreting Innards, After World (1992)
Split, 625 Productions (1996) (Split 7" single with PALE EXISTENCE)
Instruments Of Hell, Open Wound (1997) (Split 7" single with NO COMPLY)
Indignities To The Dead, Discos Al Pacino (1998) (Split 7" single with PANTALONES ABAJO MARINERO)
Totally Fucking Dead, Revenge Productions (1998) (Split 7" single with NYCTOPHOBIC)
Tales Of The Exhumed, Headfucker (1998) (Split 7" single with RETALIATION)
Emeticide, Deadly Art Productions (2001) (Split 7" with SANITY'S DAWN)

Albums:
CHORDS OF CHAOS, Lofty Storm Productions (1996)
Excreting Innards / Vagiterian / Grotesque Putrefied Brains / The Exquisite Flavour Of Gastro-Anal Tripe (Cadaveric Splatter Platter Part II) / Sex, Drinks And Metal
IN THE NAME OF GORE, Visceral Productions VP004 (1996) (Split album with HEMDALE)
Horrendous Member Dismemberment / Septicemia (Festering Sphinctral Malignancy Part II) / Masochistic Copramania / Necrovores: Decomposing The Inanimate / Disinterred, Digested And Debauched / Bone Fucker / The Naked And The Dead / Necro Transvestite / Torso / Dissecting The Caseated Omentum / Death Metal
GORE METAL, Relapse (1998)
Necromaniac / Open The Abscess / Postmortem Procedures / Limb From Limb / Emulceation / Casket Krusher / Death Mask / In My Inhuman Slaughterhouse / Sepulcharal Slaughter / Vagiterian II / Blazing Corpse / Deadest Of The Dead / Sodomy And Lust
SLAUGHTERCULT, Relapse (2000)

Decrepit Crescendo / Forged In Fire (Formed In Flame) / A Lesson In Pathology / This Axe Was Made To Grind / Carnal Epitaph / Dinnertime In The Morgue / Fester Forever / Deep Red / Infester / Slave To The Casket / Slaughtercult / Funeral Fuck / Vacant Grave

EXIT 13 (USA)
Line-Up: Bill Yurkiewicz (vocals), Steve O'Donnel (guitar), Dan Lilker (bass), Scott Lewis (drums)

Grind merchants EXIT 13 are the result of an extra-curricular project assembled by Relapse Records boss Bill Yurkiewicz on vocals, guitarist Steve O'Donnel, and BRUTAL TRUTH's Dan Lilker on bass together with his former band mate drummer Scott Lewis.
A former EXIT 13 drummer Dave Witte was to create DISCORDANCE AXIS and ATOMSMASHER.
A further release in 1995 'Just A Few More' was issued under the revised band tag of EXIT 23.

Albums:
ETHOS MUSICK, Roadrunner RR 6913-2 (1994)

EXIT 23 (USA)
Line-Up: Bill Yurkiewicz (vocals), Steve O'Donnel (guitar), Dan Lilker (bass), Scott Lewis (drums)

Grind merchants EXIT 23 was an extension of an extra-curricular project assembled by Relapse Records boss Bill Yurkiewicz on vocals, guitarist Steve O'Donnel, and BRUTAL TRUTH's Dan Lilker on bass together with his former band mate drummer Scott Lewis originally billed EXIT 13.
EXIT 13 first issued the 1994 album 'Ethos Musick'.

Albums:
JUST A FEW MORE, Roadrunner RR 6966CD (1995)

EXMORTEM (DENMARK)
Line-Up: Søren Lønne (vocals / bass), Henrik Kolle (guitar), Mike Neilsen (drums)

Originally known as MORDOR this Danish Death Metal band date back to 1992 with a line-up of guitarist Henrik Kolle, drummer Mike Neilsen and bassist

Mads Weng. It wasn't to be until 1993 when the band added a vocalist in Søren Lønne, recording the 'Souls Of Purity' demo.
Still, as MORDOR the band contributed the track 'In Command' to the Progress Records compilation 'Fuck You We're From Denmark. Volume II' in 1994. Weng left soon after it's release and Lønne took over bass duties.
Signing to new label Euphonious the band, aware of at least three other Metal acts titled MORDOR, adopted the new title of EXMORTEM.
Following the album's release the band augmented it's sound with the addition of second guitarist Martin Thim.

Albums:
LABYRINTHS OF HORROR,
Euphonious PHONI001CD (1995)
Intoxicated By Death / In The Dark Of The Moon / Bloodshed Of The Holy / In Command / Creation Of Evil / Dark Thy Kingdom / Punishment For The Weak / Labyrinths Of Horror / Necromonicon The Gateway To The Seven Mighty Gates Of Reincarnation
DEJECTED IN OBSCURITY,
Euphonious PHONI 008 (1998)
Creatures Of The Night / Born Into The World Of Darkness / Deathcult / Land Of No Return / No Redemption / Materialization / Behold The Mighty Ravenholt / Obsessed / Dwell In Darkness / Dawn Of Reincarnation

EXOCET (GERMANY)
Line-Up: Dirk Mylius (vocals), Stephan Hämmerling (guitar), Patrick Stein (guitar), Tom Merker (bass), Steffan Kolditz (drums)

EXOCET, formed in 1989, first demoed in late 1992 with their 'Apocalyptic Visions' tape. The group subsequently played various support dates to the likes of CREMATORY, ATROCITY and POST MORTEM and also appeared at the 1994 'Thrash Against Trash' festival headlined by KREATOR. The 'Confusion' album was produced by former ANGEL DUST / SCANNER singer S.L. Coe.
Supported CREMATORY on their 1995 European tour.

Albums:
CONFUSION, Massacre MASSCD068 (1995)
Hypocrite / I Kill Now / Commercial Overkill / The Martyr / Abyss Of

Sexuality / Chemical Profit War / In Hate / Apocalyptic Visions / Retaliation / My Nuclear Safety / Unborn / More Bass

EXORCISM (PA, USA)

EXORCISM, a one man venture, trade in Black Death Metal. A demo 'Suspended Above The Flesh' was issued in 1997 preceding a string of self-financed releases.

Albums:
AFTERLIFE, (1998)
VANISH INTO THE DEPTHS, (1999)
A JOURNEY INTO THE NIGHT CHASM, Nascent Frost Productions (2000)

EXOTO (BELGIUM)
Line-Up: Chris (vocals), Wilek (guitar), Flip (guitar), Vic (bass), Molly (drums)

The leading Death Metal act in Belgium and the Netherlands, EXOTO formed in 1989 and released a live cassette entitled 'Waiting For The Maggots' in 1990. A studio recorded tape, 'And Then You Die', followed in 1991 and gained the honour of being voted 'Demo Of The Month' in the influential Dutch Rock mag 'Aardschock', going on to sell 1,600 copies.
A third demo, 'The Fifth Season', spawned two tracks that would appear on the 'Ashes' EP released by the Midian Creations label in 1992 before the group's first album, 'Carnival Of Souls', arrived in 1994.
Sadly, original drummer Didier was killed in a traffic accident later the same year. This traumatic event would lead to the band recording the 'A Tribute To Didier' tape in 1995. Still, having been signed by Black Mark Productions after the response by fans to 'Carnival Of Souls' EXOTO were to release the 'A Thousand Dreams Ago' album the same year.

Singles/EPs:
Ashes EP, Midian Creation (1992)

Albums:
CARNIVAL OF SOULS, Tessa (1994)
A THOUSAND DREAMS AGO, Black Mark BMCD 81 (1995)
The World Before You / Behind Your Mind / Scream Inside / Waveyard / She / Spirit Within Me / Anxious For The Light / Deny The Pain / Thoughts / The Fifth Season / Second Murder / No Regret

EXPIRATION (SPAIN)
Line-Up: Carlos (vocals), Felix 'Lombriz' (guitar), Ed Brain (guitar), Angel (bass), Sergio 'Larva' (drums)

After the band's 'Deviated' EP EXPIRATION vocalist Carlos left and was replaced by Guanche 'Artemi'.
In their time EXPIRATION have played with the likes of AVULSED, DERANGED and GOLGOTHA.

Singles/EPs:
Deviated / Don't Bury Me / The Hidden Voices / Maze Of Sadness / Number Four, Expiration EXP-001 (1996)

EXPULSION (SWEDEN)
Line-Up: Anders Holmberg (vocals / bass), Stefan Lagergren (guitar), Calle Fransson (drums)

EXPULSION date back to a 1988 band titled RIVER'S EDGE. The initial line-up for EXPULSION featured former TIAMAT members guitarist Stefan Lagergren (guitar), Anders Holmberg (bass) and Calle Fransson (drums).
The band released its first demo tape, 'Cerebral Cessation', in 1989 and also contributed the track 'Certain Corpses Never Decay' to the compilation cassette 'Hymns Of The Dead Volume Two'. Later the same year EXPULSION recorded a second demo entitled 'Veiled In The Mist Of Mystery'. This tape landed the band a deal with Putrefaction Records for whom they were to record the single 'Soul Upheaval' / 'Lain Hidden'. However, this remains unreleased.
Another blow was struck when various members found themselves with impending terms of compulsory national military service. Holmberg thus decided to put the band on ice and joined TRANQUILLITY.
Lagergren and Fransson reformed EXPULSION in 1991 adding vocalist Fredrik Thornqvist and female bassist Chelsea Krook. The following year EXPULSION augmented their sound with the enlistment of second guitarist Chris Vowden. The band's first gig, supporting GRAVE, soon followed.
Chelsea Krook departed and the returning Anders Holmberg signed up once more in time to record the debut single, a self-financed effort.
EXPULSION promptly featured three tracks - 'The Other Side', 'Soul Upheaval' and 'As The Last One Leaves' - to the Evil

Omen Records compilation album 'Vociferous and Machiavellian Hate'. Coincidentally a further EXPULSION track, 'Let The Raven's Fly', was featured on the Growing Deaf label's compilation 'History Of Things To Come'.

EXPULSION's long awaited debut album, 'Overflow', appeared in 1994 and offered a guest appearance from TIAMAT vocalist Johan Edlund on the track 'At The Madness End'.

Singles/EPs:
Bitter Twist Of Fate / With Aged Hands / Lain Hidden / In A Whirling Dust, Dodsmetallfirma Expulsion (1993) (Limited edition of 600 copies)

Albums:
OVERFLOW, Godhead GOD011 (1994)
Don't Leave Me To Bleed / Let The Raven's Fly / Fallen / With Aged Hands / Dreamvoyage / The Other Side / The Anatomical Range / As The Last One Leaves / At The Madness End / Overflow

EXTERMINATOR (BELGIUM)

Albums:
MIRROR IMAGES, Exterminator (2000)

EXTOL (NORWAY)
Line-Up: Christer Espevoll (guitar), Emil Nicolaisen (guitar), Eystein Holm (bass), David Husvik (drums)

EXTRA HOT SAUCE (USA)

Side project act of NUCLEAR ASSAULT and BRUTAL TRUTH bassist Dan Lilker. EXTRA HOT SAUCE's 1988 album 'Taco Of Death' included a version of BLACK SABBATH's 'Paranoid' compacted down to a mere 90 seconds.

Albums:
TACO OF DEATH, Peaceville VILE 8 (1988)
Intro: AIDS / Passive Terrorism / Tony's Dilemma / Cluless Fucks / I Need A Job / Communication Breakdown / The Cheeba Man / Free Bird?

EXTREMA (ITALY)
Line-Up: Gianluca Perotti (vocals), Andrea Boria (guitar), Tommy Massara (guitar), Alex Ghilardotti (bass), Christiano Dalla Pellegrina (drums)

The above EXTREMA line-up recorded the 'We Fuckin' Care' single and the group would tour in Italy as support to SLAYER on the American group's 'Reign In Blood' tour. Although a highly popular live act in their native country it took ten years for EXTREMA to issue their debut album in 1992, by which point the group comprised vocalist Tommy Massara, guitarist Gianluca Perotti and Giolio Loglio, bassist Mattioa Bigi and drummer Chris Dalla Pellegrina.

The live EP of 1993 vintage was only ever released in Italy and featured a cover of the DEAD KENNEDYS 'Too Drunk To Fuck'.

Guitarist Giolio Loglio quit the group before they recorded 1995's 'The Positive Pressure (Of Injustice)' album.

Singles/EPs:
We Fuckin' Care, Extrema (1988)
Lawyer's Incx. / Child O' Boogaow / Modern Times / Displaced / Join Hands / Too Drunk To Fuck, Rosemary's Baby Discs BABE 13 CD (1993) ('Proud, Powerful n' Alive' EP)

Albums:
TENSION AT THE SEAMS, Rosemary's Baby Discs 08-110052 (1992)
Join Hands / Child O' Boogaow / Displaced / Truth This Everybody / Modern Times / Double Face / Road Pirats / Lawyers Incx. / And The Rage Awaits / For Good The Die / Life
THE POSITIVE PRESSURE (OF INJUSTICE), Flying FLY 190 CD (1995)
This Toy / The Positive Pressure (Of Injustice) / Fear / Money Talks / Confusion / Grey / Like Brothers / To Hell / On Your Feet, On Your Knees / Tell Me

EXTREME NOIZE TERROR (UK)
Line-Up: Dean Jones (vocals), Phil Vane (vocals), Pete Hurley (guitar), Ali Firouzbakht (guitar), Lee Barrett (bass), Pig Killer (drums)

Formed in 1985 and signed to Manic Ears Records after just one gig (the first product being a split LP with Punk outfit CHAOS UK titled 'Radioactive'), Ipswich Punk Metal merchants EXTREME NOIZE TERROR achieved a great deal of Pop notoriety by performing on KLF's hit single '3AM Eternal'

In the group's formative period NAPALM DEATH drummer Micky Harris could be found on vocals, but would leave during 1987 to form SCORN. The same year the band recorded numerous sessions for Radio One DJ John Peel but suffered other changes in personnel with bassist Jerry Clay leaving to make way for Mark Gardiner. Harris was superseded by ex-DOOM drummer Stig (Tony Dickens) and the band recorded their first full length album 'A Holocaust In Your Head', although Gardiner also departed in favour of Mark Bailey.

1990 found Jones and Firouzbakht guesting on RAW NOISE's 'Sound Of Destruction' single.

Following a tour of Japan ENT recorded their third John Peel session and it was this recording that brought the band's unique sound to the attention of KLF mainman Bill Drummond and the two united to record the hit single '3 AM Eternal'. An album, entitled 'The Black Room', was also recorded but never released. Nevertheless, EXTREME NOISE TERROR had their moment of glory at the 1992 Brit Awards when band members fired blanks from machine guns at the audience.

During 1994 the band lost drummer Stig (who quit to join D.I.R.T.) although his position was filled by original skinbasher Pig Killer. Mark Bailey was also replaced during this period by Lee Barrett, who was also a member of DISGUST.

In early 1997 Vane, who also plied his trade with OPTIMUM WOUND PROFILE, was announced as the new vocalist for NAPALM DEATH supplanting the departed Barney Greenaway. Vane had previously been asked by NAPALM DEATH to fill in for Greenaway on an American tour during 1996 due to Barney's fear of flying! Amazingly, Greenaway was, within days, fronting EXTREME NOISE TERROR! And whilst Vane recorded a split EP with NAPALM DEATH he was soon to return to the TERROR, with Greenaway rejoining NAPALM DEATH, but not before he had laid down vocals for the 'Damage 381' album.

For their Earache tenure the band employed former DECEMBER MOON / CRADLE OF FILTH drummer Was Sarginson, although by 2000 he had been supplanted by the 19 year old Zac. Band members put in an appearance on the 2000 RAW NOISE album 'The Terror Continues'. By 2001 EXTREME NOISE TERROR were being fronted by FAILED HUMANITY vocalist Adam Catchpole for the 'Being And Nothing' album.

Singles/EPs:
Are You That Desperate, Crust (199-)

Albums:
RADIOACTIVE, Manic Ears ACHE 1 (1986) (Split LP with CHAOS UK)
System Shit / No Threat / Human Error / Murder / False Profit / Show Us You Care / You Really Make Me Sick / Fucked Up System / Real Life / Only In It For The Music
PEEL SESSION, Strange Fruit SFPS048 (1987)
False Profit / Another Nail In The Coffin / Use Your Mind / Carry On Screaming / Human Error / Conned Through Life / Only In It For The Music Part Two
A HOLOCAUST IN YOUR HEAD, Hurt HURT 1 (1987)
Statement / Take The Strain / Show Us You Care / Use Your Mind / Only In It For The Music / Deceived / Conned Thru Life / Innocence To Ignorance / Another Nail In The Coffin
PEEL SESSIONS, Strange Fruit SFPMA208 (1987)
False Profit / Use Your Mind / Human Error / Only In It For The Music / Subliminal Music / Punk - Fact And Fiction / Deceived / Another Nail In The Coffin / Carry On Screaming / Conned Thru Life / Work For Never / Third World Genocide / I Am A Bloody Fool / In It For Life / Shock Treatment
SPLIT, Sink Below SINK1 (1989) (Split album with FILTHKICK)
Intro / In It For Life / Subliminal Music Mind Control / Work For Bever / Punk: Fact Or Faction / Cruelty To Carnivores / Damaging
PHONOPHOBIA, Vinyl Japan DISC 1 X (1992)
Pray To Be Moved / Knee Deep In Shit / Self Decay / Moral Bondage / Just Think About It / Lame Brain / What Do
RETRO-BUTION (TEN YEARS OF TERROR), Earache MOSH 83 (1995)
Raping The Earth / Bullshit Propaganda / Lame Brain / Work For Never / We The Helpless / Invisible War / Subliminal / Human Error / Murder / Think About It / Pray To Be Saved / Conned Through Life / Deceived / Third World Genocide
DAMAGE 381, Earache MOSH 173 (1997)
BEING AND NOTHING, Candlelight CANDLE075CD (2001)

170

FACE DOWN (SWEDEN)
Line-Up: Marco Aro (vocals), Joacim Karlsson (guitar), Jaokim Harju (bass), Henrik Blomqvist (keyboards), Richard Bång (drums)

Originally titled MACHINE GOD upon their formation in 1993 by ex-AFFLICTED / PROBOCSIS bassist Joakim Harju, the quite brutal FACE DOWN found themselves snapped up by Roadrunner and this resulted in the release of the critically acclaimed 'Mindfield' debut album.
However, drummer Richard Bång left after the album was completed and had his vacant space occupied by ex-UNANIMATED / MERCILESS man Peter Sjärnvind.
A second album, 'The Twisted Rule The Wicked', emerged through new label Nuclear Blast in 1997.
Aro joined THE HAUNTED with ex members of AT THE GATES.

Albums:
MINDFIELD, Roadrunner RR 8902 (1995)
Wear / Kill The Pain / Human / Holy Race / Demon Seed / Save Me, Kill Me / Colors / Twelve Rounds / Hatred / One Eyed Man
THE TWISTED RULE THE WICKED, Nuclear Blast NB 194-2 (1997)
Dead Breed / Self Appointed God / Waste / Life Relentless / Autumn Scars / Bed Of Roaches / Top Of The World / Slender Messiah / For Your Misery / Embrace The Moment / Cleansweep / With Unseeing Eyes

FAILED HUMANITY (UK)

Vocalist Adam Catchpole would also divide his duties with EXTREME NOISE TERROR.

Albums:
THE SOUND OF RAZORS THROUGH FLESH, Candlelight CANDLE058CD (2001)
The Sound Of Razors Through Flesh / Your Blood My Blood / Unleashed Defiance / Trust No One / To Die A Thousand Times / Full Of Hate / Darkness Descends / Kicked To Death / The Rise They Fall

FEAST ETERNAL
(Traverse, MI, USA)

Line-Up: T.J. Humlinski (vocals / bass), John Greenman (guitar), Matt Skrzypczak (drums)

Albums:
PRISONS OF FLESH, (1999)
Immersion / Forgetting God / Dead Eyes / Flight Of The Fallen / Of Service And Suffering / Ashes To Dust / Prisons Of Flesh / Into Eternity

FERMENTING INNARDS
(GERMANY)
Line-Up: Mario Weinhold (vocals), Rico Spiller (guitar / bass), Andreas Hilbert (guitar / bass / keyboards), Marek Kassubeck (drums)

Originally a Death Metal outfit, this East German group rapidly turned into more of a Black Metal touting outfit.

Singles/EPs:
In Hate / Innocent Or Incident / Drowned / Eternal Sadness, Invasion IR 006 (199-) ('Drowned' EP)

Albums:
MYST, Invasion IR 016 (1995)
Blood And Thunder / Myst / Those Burning Thorns / Hatefid / Transfiguration Of The Withered Beauty / Eternal Sadness / Mourning / The Rising In Northern Storm / Svantfeldet Hat / Battles On Ice

FERTILIZER (GERMANY)
Line-Up: Daniel Wagner (vocals), Markus Münch (guitar), Marcus Beck (bass), Dennis Emmel (drums)

A Death / Thrash Metal quartet formed in 1990, FERTILIZER released the 'Environmental Glutton' demo a year later.
In 1993 guitarist Frank Lemmart joined the group and, in 1994, FERTILIZER issued their debut album.
The four piece have toured with PYOGENESIS, DISASTROUS MURMER and RU DEAD? throughout Germany.

Albums:
A PAINTING OF ANNOYANCE, Invasion / SPV 0077.141532 (1994)
Solar Vertigo / Traumstunde / T.U.S.C. / Feelharmony Melodream Overdose / Under The Oath Of... / 2nd Service / Time Dune

FESTER (NORWAY)

Line-Up: Rolf Tommy Simonsen (vocals / guitar), Tiger Mathisen (vocals / guitar), Jörgen Skjolden (bass), Jan Skjolden (drums)

This Norwegian outfit combine Doom / Death Metal with a brand of Black Metal that, on the 'Silence' album, incorporates mainly whispered vocals!

Albums:
WINTER OF SIN, No Fashion NFR 002 (1994)
Winter Of Sin / Senses Are The True You / The Ancient Gods Wore Black / Entering... / Victory!!! / Liberation / As The Swords Clinch The Air / A Dogfight Leaves A Trace / The Commitments That Shattered
SILENCE, Lethal LRC 756 (1995)
Dream / Silent Is The Raven / Frustrations / The Maze / The Conformists / Voices From The Woods / Elisabeta In My World Of Thoughts / Growing Thirst / Nar Noen Dor

FETISH 69 (AUSTRIA)

Line-Up: Christian Fetish (vocals), Robert Lepenik (guitar), Wolfgang Messner (guitar), Astrid Kleber (bass), Stephan Stasny (drums), Martin Koch (visuals/video), Kim Pil Jung (samples)

FETISH 69 first came to prominence with their 'Sexual Warfare' demo of 1988 which soon sold out. This was followed by the flexi-single 'Pigblood'.
In 1990 the band included the track 'Headhunter' on an Austrian 7" compilation EP published by a Rock magazine. This was capitalized on by the 12" 'Pumpgun Erotic' single and shows with HENRY ROLLINS. American interest saw two songs culled from the 'Pumpgun Erotic' single released in the States as a limited edition 7". Further American exposure came from the inclusion of the track 'Deep Scar Man' on the 'Dope, Guns And Fucking In The Streets' compilation album. Rounded off 1991 with dates alongside TREPONEM PAL and BOSSHOG.
1992 provided yet more valuable promotion by inclusions on no less than three compilation albums; 'Soul Rape', 'Boiler Live Pool' and Nuclear Blast's 'Death Is Just The Beginning'. FETISH 69 also released a split EP with LOS TRES HOMBRES (a pseudonym for PUNGENT STENCH).

The band toured Europe as support to SKREW in 1993 in which year they released 'Brute Force', which was recorded with PUNGENT STENCH guitarist Martin Shirenc.
In 1995 vocalist Christian Fetish released the book 'Kinokiller', a tome documenting mass murderers in movies. A year later FETISH 69 returned to the scene with the 'Purge' album and a brand new line-up consisting of Fetish, guitarist Robert Lepenik, bassist Christoph Baumgartner, drummer Rainer Binder and sampling expert Kim Pil Jung.

Singles/EPs:
Pigblood, (1988) (Flexi)
Pumpgun Erotic, Play With Fire (1990) Why Not / Jack & Bianca (Fireworks) / Daddy Cool, Why Not WNR CD 1 (1992) (Split EP with LOS TRES HOMBRES)

Albums:
BRUTE FORCE, Intellectual Convulsions SPASM051 (1993)
Void / Marooned / Stares To Nowhere / Stomachturner / Tough Center - Harter Kern / Hellville (Pop. 7000)
ANTIBODY, Nuclear Blast NB087-2 (1995)
Hyperventilator / Wrecked Joe / Versus Nature / Fireworks / Pigsblood / No Nothing / Stomachturner / Antibody / Being Boiled / Hogditch (Pigblood reprise)
PURGE, Community COM 1005-222-2 (1996)
Kickback / Born Invisible / Hatefriends / Head Gun-Mindrill / Adrenalizer / Release / Tools / Pushing The Cranium / Purifier / Targets / Waiting Room / Skinhole / Purge
GEEK, Doxa (1999)

FINALLY DECEASED (GERMANY)

Line-Up: Lars Reichmann (vocals / guitar), Martin Staszak (bass), Martin Mengels (drums)

An old school Death Metal band, after the release of the 'Blessed By Demons' EP FINALLY DECEASED released a demo produced by Andy Classen and played the Wacken Open Air Festival in 1994. Oddly, the group were promptly barred from ever playing the event again due to claims that they were 'too evil'!!

Singles/EPs:
Blessed By Demons / Darkened Soul / As I Die / The One Who Cares, WWR 94

004 07 (1994) ('Blessed By Demons' EP) (1994)

FINAL SACRIFICE (GERMANY)
Line-Up: Michael Jopp (vocals), Thomas Klemm (guitar), Axel Keiser (guitar), Uwe Schmitz (bass), Markus Euler (drums)

Singles/EPs:
Manifestation / The End Is Near / Shut Your Mouth / Hate Is In Your Mind / At Death's Door / Psychical Waste, Final Sacrifice (1996) ('Manifestation' EP)

FLAMES (GREECE)
Line-Up: Nigel Foxxe (vocals), Chris Lee (guitar), Andy Kirk (bass), Gus Collin (drums)

FLAMES significantly changed line-up for the 'Summon The Dead' album bringing in vocalist Alex Oznek, guitarist Athan Schitsos and drummer George Adrian. Mainman Nigel Foxxe later formed THANATOS and NIGEL FOXXE'S INC releasing an album.
Foxxe would later figure in FORTRESS UNDER SIEGE.

Albums:
MADE IN HELL, (1985)
MERCILESS SLAUGHTER, Famous Music (1986)
Murder / Legend / Beloved Dead / Moorgile / Werewolf On The Hunt / Cocksuckin' Slave / Evil / Infidel
LIVE IN THE SLAUGHTERHOUSE, Famous Music (1987)
SUMMON THE DEAD, Famous Music FM0053 (1988)
Eastern Front / Summon The Dead / Kill For Mummy / Alcohol And Beer / Legend II (The Demon's Mind) / Legions Of Death / Avenger / Slaughterhouse / Ballad Of A Skinbeating Maniac
LAST PROPHECY, Famous Music (1989)
Revenge / Deathra / Agnostic Front / Destiny Of Hate / Red Terror / Silo / Acid Rain / Drinking All Night
NOMEN ILLI MORS, Molon Lave (1991)
IN AGONY WE RISE, (1992)

FLEGMA (SWEDEN)
Line-Up: Kalle Metz (vocals), Martin Olsson (guitar), Jörgen Lindhe (guitar), Richard Lion (bass), Martin Brorsson (drums)

Having released their full blown debut album, 'Blind Acceptance' in 1992,

FLEGMA added ex OBSCURITY guitarist Jörgen Lindhe to the line-up following 1994's 'Flesh To Dust' album. This also found them offering a cover of the KISS track 'I Stole Your Love'. In addition the band have contributed tracks to both VENOM and METALLICA tribute albums with 'Leave Me In Hell' on the VENOM tribute 'Promoters Of The Third World War' on Primitive Art Records and 'The Thing That Should Not Be' on Black Sun Records 'Metal Militia' METALLICA tribute album.

Singles/EPs:
Eine Kleine Schlachtmusik, Insane INSANE 001 (1990)

Albums:
BLIND ACCEPTANCE, Black Rose BRR001 (1992)
FLESH TO DUST, Black Rose BRR002 (1994)
Rotting Away / Crown Of Thorns / Drowning / Walk In Confusion / Shadow Of A Silhouette / Father / Enticed / As The World Watches / I Stole Your Love / Flesh To Dust

THE FLESH (NORWAY)
Line-Up: Einar Fredriksen (vocals / bass), Espen Simonsen (guitar), Morten Vaeng (guitar), Anders Eek (drums)

THE FLESH are a very brutal Death Metal band formed in 1993 in Drammen, near Oslo. The quartet features two ex-members of FUNERAL (bassist Einar Fredriksen and drummer Anders Eek) and was originally conceived as a side project from the duo's mothership.
Prior to debuting with the 'Storming The Heaven's Gate' EP THE FLESH had received some rave reviews for their 'Icecold Macabre Lust' demo.

Singles/EPs:
The Weeping Of Wrists / Inadvertent Battery / Last Day Of Your Life / Inhuman Misbehaviour, Arctic Serenades SERE 004 (1995) ('Storming The Heaven's Gate' EP)

FLESHCRAVE (CANADA)
Line-Up: Gianmarco (vocals / guitar), Claudio (guitar), Jay (bass), Tom Drums)

Toronto's FLESHCRAVE began life as a Thrash Metal outfit entitled BLACK WIDOW. In this incarnation the band, comprising vocalist / guitarist Gianmarco, guitarist Mike, bass player Mark and drummer Tom, played mainly METALLICA and SEPULTURA covers.

By 1997 the band had adopted a Death Metal stance and retitled themselves INHUMATION adding new guitarist Claudio as Mike shifted duties to bass. A further name change to FLESHCRAVE saw the exit of Claudio and the recruitment of Joe on bass.

Latterly Jay has taken the four string position and Claudio has made his return.

FLESHCRAWL (GERMANY)

Line-Up: Alex Pretzer (vocals), Stefan Hanus (guitar), Mike Hanus (guitar), Markus Amann (bass), Bastian Herzog (drums)

FLESHCRAWL's first demo tape in 1991 was titled 'Festering Flesh'. This was quickly followed by the self financed mini-album 'Lost In A Grave".

1993's 'Impurity' release was produced by EDGE OF SANITY's Dan Swano.

Prior to recording the third album, 'Bloodsoul', bassist Amann quit, leaving Mike Hanus to take up four string duty.

Although the group pursued a Doomier direction in the early part of their career they have since progressed into a pure Death Metal outfit with increasingly Satanic lyrical tendencies. The 'Bloodred Massacre' album includes a version of SLAYER's 'Necrophiliac'.

2000 found FLESHCRAWL on tour in Europe as part of the 'No Mercy' festival package alongside Poland's VADER, America's VITAL REMAINS and Brazilians REBAELLIUN.

FLESHCRAWL's 'As Blood Rains From The Sky...' album sees covers of EXCITER's 'Swords Of Darkness' and CARNAGE's 'The Day Man Lost'.

Singles/EPs:
Lost In A Grave EP, Morbid (1991)

Albums:
DESCEND INTO THE ABSURD, Black Mark BMCD 27 (1992)
Between Shadows They Crawl / Phrenetic Tendencies / Perpetual Dawn / Purulent Bowel Erosion / Lost In A Grave / Never To Die Again / Festering Flesh / Infected Subconscious / Evoke The Excess
IMPURITY, Black Mark BMCD 48 (1993)
From The Dead To The Living / Withering Life / Reincarnation / Subordinated / Disfigured / After

Obliteration / Stiffen Souls / Center Of Hate / Inevitable End / Incineration
BLOODSOUL, Black Mark BMCD 88 (1996)
Bloodsoul / In The Dead Of Night / Embalmed Beauty Sleep / Contribution Suicide / The Age Of Chaos / Recycling The Corpses / Nocturnal Funeral / Tomb Of Memories
BLOODRED MASSACRE, (199-)
Hellspawn / Dark Dimension / Bloodred Massacre / Awaiting The End / The Messenger / Through The Veil Of Dawn / Necrophiliac / Beyond Belief / Slaughter At Dawn
AS BLOOD RAINS FROM THE SKY ... WE WALK THE PATH OF ENDLESS FIRE, Metal Blade (2000)
March Of The Dead / Path Of The Endless Fire / Under The Banner Of Death / As Blood Rain From The Sky / Embraced By Evil / The Dark Side Of My Soul / Swords Of Darkness / Impure Massacre Of Bloody Souls / Creation Of Wrath / Graves Of The Tortures / Feed The Demon's Heart / The Day Man Lost

FLESHGRIND (IL, USA)

Line-Up: Rich Lipscomb (vocals / guitar), Steve Murray (guitar), James Genenz (bass), Alan Collado (drums)

Incarnated during 1993, FLESHGRIND's initial line-up roster included vocalist / guitarist Rich Lipscomb, Steve Murray on guitar, bassist Casey Ryba and drummer Dave Barbolla. This unit recorded the 'Holy Pedophile' demo produced by BROKEN HOPE's Brian Griffin. The bands next effort, 1995's 'Sorrow Breeds Hatred (Bleed On Me)' again produced by Griffin, led to a deal with the Pulveriser label for the 'Destined For Defilement' album.

The album saw the exit of Ryba in favour of Ray Vasquez. However, it transpired that Pulverizer were unable to manufacture the CD and so FLESHGRIND issued the album on their own imprint.

Both Vasquez and Barbolla broke away from the band as FLESHGRIND inducted drummer Alan Collado of EUPHORIC EVISCERATION and James Genenz of Doom band AVERNUS. Touring ensued with Canadian dates in union with SUFFOCATION and an American nationwide tour with MORTICIAN.

Lipscomb would add guest session vocals to DISFIGURED's debut album 'Prelude To Dementia' appearing on the tracks 'Witness Your Creation' and

'Ridden With Disgust'.

Albums:
DESTINED FOR DEFILEMENT,
Fleshgrind (1998)
Whacked / Burning Your World /
Chamber Of Obscurity / Sordid
Degradation / Rape Culture / Lurid
Impurity / Organ Harvest / Frozen In A
Voiceless Scream / Litany Of Murder
THE SEEDS OF ABYSMAL TORMENT,
Season Of Mist (2001)
Destroying Your Will / Desire For Control
/ Monarch Of Misery / Disdain The
Mournful / The Deviating Ceremonies /
Hatred Embodied / Seas Of Harrow / A
Legion Of Illusions / The Supreme Art Of
Derangement / Hogtied And Hatefucked

FLESH GRINDER (BRAZIL)
Line-Up: Chacal (vocals / guitar), Fabio
(vocals / guitar), Rogerio (bass), Johnny
(drums)

FLESH GRINDER employ some truly
horrific photographic artwork on their
albums. The artwork for the 2001 album
'Libido Corporis' was so extreme release
was delayed until the band could find a
printer willing to handle the product. Not
for the faint-hearted.

Albums:
ANATOMY AND SURGERY, Lofty Storm
LSR003 (1997)
Intro: Cerebral Draw / Opthamologic
Laceration In An Insane Moribund /
Tissue Injury Caused By An Apparent
Immunologic Reaction Of Host / Embolia
/ Surgical Considerations About
Embryologic Malformations / Anatomy In
Surgery / Congenital Abnormalities Of
Basic Mechanics Of Excretory Tubules /
Boneyard / Hemorrhagical Convultions
Of The Gastric Ligaments / Abberations
Of The Immune Response Seen In Viral
Immunity
S.P.L.A.T.T.E.R., Lofty Storm LSR005
(1999)
Intro (Stomachal Emanation) / Chronic
Mucocutaneous Candiasis /
S.P.L.A.T.T.E.R. / Technics To Extract
The Female Reproductive System Thru
Anal Canal / Cutaneous Anaphilaxis /
Cavernous Sinus Thrombosis /
Granulomatous Inflammation With
Elliptical Macrophages / Acute Syndrome
Resembling Infectious Monucleosis /
The Amorphous (Nongibrous) / Chronic
And Recurrent Regurgitant Lung
Disease / Adverse Effects Seen In
Immunologically Compromised Hosts /
The Adagio Of Pathologist / Developing
Malignant Cancerous Tissue In The 8th
Inch Of The Large Intestine
**FROM ROTTEN PROCESS... TO
SPLATTER**, Millennium (2000) (Split
album with LYMPATHIC PHLEGM)
LIBIDO CORPORIS, Demise (2001)

THE FORSAKEN (SWEDEN)
Line-Up: Anders Sjöholm (vocals),
Stefan Holm (guitar), Patrick Persson
(guitar), Michael Hakansson (bass),
Nicke Grabowski (drums)

THE FORSAKEN, previously titled
SEPTIC BREED, offer Death Metal with
Satanic overtones. Vocalist Anders
Sjöholm also fronts MASSGRAV and
OMINOUS whilst bass player Michael
Hakansson plays with EVERGREY and
EMBRACED.

Albums:
MANIFEST OF HATE, Century Media
(2001)
Seers Hatred / Deamon Breed / Betrayal
Within Individuals / Collection Of
Thoughts / Soulshade / Intro - Manifest
Of Hate / Dehumanised Perspective /
Truth Of God / Incinerate / Inseminated
By The Beast

FUCK ON THE BEACH (JAPAN)

A bizarre Japanese amalgam of
Grindcore, Thrash Metal and Baywatch!

Singles/EPs:
Fastcore On The Beach, Slap A Ham
SLAP042 (1998)
Split, Regurgited Semen RSR024 (1999)
(7" split single with FLÄCHENBRAND)

Albums:
POWER VIOLENCE FOREVER, Slap A
Ham SLAP051 (1998)
ENDLESS SUMMER, Slap A Ham
SLAP057 (2001)
Fuck On The Beach / Something I Don't
Want To Know / Too Sad To Be Alone /
All The World / Broken Back Hole /
Alone In Your Room / She Used To Cry
For It / Tired My Life / Betrayed Again / I
Have Never Seen Myself / Ride On
Timing / Fuck Forever

FUNERAL NATION (USA)
Line-Up: Mike Pahl (vocals / bass), Chaz
(guitar), Dave Chiarella (drums)

FUNERAL NATION drummer Dave Chiarella also shared employment with DISINTER. Chiarella joined USURPER in 1997 retitling himself Dave Hellstorm.

Albums:
REIGN OF DEATH, Turbo (1991)
Your Time Has Come / State Of Insanity / Reign Of Death / Midnight Hour / Sign Of Baphomet

FUNERAL ORATION (ITALY)
Line-Up: The Old Nick (vocals), Luca (guitar / keyboards), Fabban (bass), Rodolfo (drums)

A Death Metal band formed in 1989 not to be confused with the Dutch Hardcore band of the same name. FUNERAL ORATION has only one surviving member from the original line-up, guitarist Luca being that man.
Having released two demos 'Domine A Morte' and 'XXX A.S. 1995 E.V.' and a 7" EP. FUNERAL ORATION toured Italy extensively before line-up changes forced the group to adopt a slightly bizarre Black Metal direction in 1993.
Having issued a new, two track demo and the 'Christic Depravations' live video Avantgarde Records stepped in to offer the Italian outfit a deal, with debut album 'Sursum Luna' arriving in 1996.

Albums:
SURSUM LUNA, Avantgarde AV 017 (1996)
Beltane's Night / Pregnant Whore / Intermezzo I / Me A Morte Libera Domine / Intermezzo II / The Age Of Apotheosis / Intermezzo III / Sursum Luna (Lunesta Trilogia) / Intermezzo IV / Stigmata / Intermezzo V / Pagan Joy / Finale

FURBOWL (SWEDEN)
Line-Up: Johan Axelsson (vocals / guitar), Nicke Stenemo (guitar / keyboards), Johan Liiva (bass), Max Thornell (drums)

A Växjö based Death Goth Metal band formed in 1991 by ex-CARNAGE man Johan Axelsson and former JESUS EXERCISE drummer Max Thornell, FURBOWL's first demo, 'The Nightfall Of Your Heart' featured the ever busy ex-CARCASS guitarist Mike Amott making a guest appearance.
Bassist Johan Liiva would join Amott in his late 90's act ARCH ENEMY.
Subsequent to the release of debut album 'Those Shredded Dreams', Axelsson left to be superseded by Per Jungberger and after 'The Autumn Years' album emerged in 1994 the band have, more recently, adopted the new name WONDERFLOW.

Albums:
THOSE SHREDDED DREAMS, Step One SOROO4 (1992)
Damage Done / Nothing Forever / Razorblades / Desertion / Sharkheaven / Those Shredded Dreams
THE AUTUMN YEARS, Black Mark BMCD47 (1994)
Bury The Hatchet / Cold World / Dead And Gone / The Needle / Is This Dignity / Weakend / Baby Burn / Stabbed / Road Less Travelled / Still Breathing

GARDENIAN (SWEDEN)
Line-Up: Jim Kjell (vocals),
Niclas Engelin (guitar),
Hákan Skoger (bass), Thym
Blom (drums)

Melodic Death Metal from a
Gothenburg act founded by frontman Jim
Kjell and drummer Thym Blom. Later
recruits were former IDIOTS RULE and
SARCAZM guitarist Niclas Engelin and
bassist Hákan Skoger. GARDENIAN's
Nuclear Blast debut 'Soulburner' includes
guest lead vocals from ex-ARTCH
vocalist Erik Hawk.
The band were championed in their early
years by Jesper Strombald of IN
FLAMES who secured the deal with
Listenable records.

Albums:
TWO FEET STAND, Listenable
POSH008 (1997)
Two Feet Stand / Flipside Of Reality /
The Downfall / Awake Of Abuse /
Netherworld / Do Me Now / Murder… /
Freedom / Mindless Domination /
The Silent Fall
SOULBURNER, Nuclear Blast (1999)
As A True King / Powertool / Deserted /
Soulburner / If Tomorrow's Gone / Small
Electric Space / Chaos In Flesh /
Ecstasy Of Life / Tell The World I'm
Sorry / Loss / Black Days
SINDUSTRIES, Nuclear Blast NB 533-2
(2000)
Self Proclaimed Messiah / Doom And
Gloom / Long Snap To Zero /
Courageous / Heartless / The Suffering /
Scissor Fight / Sonic Death Monkey /
Sindustries / Funeral

GARDEN OF SHADOWS
(Gaithersburg, MD, USA)
Line-Up: Chad (vocals), Mary (guitar),
Brian (guitar / keyboards), Sean (bass),
Bret (drums)

Mystically inspired epic Death Metal from
Maryland with evident influences directly
culled from the Greek Metal scene. The
band previously operated under the guise
of FUNERAL OPERA.
GARDEN OF SHADOWS, who employ
female ex-BIOVORE guitarist Mary, came
into being during 1995 but would soon
after dispense with their rhythm section of
bass player Dave and drummer Kevin.
Former SADISTIC TORMENT man Bret
took the drumming position.
In 1997 the band cut the demo 'Heart Of

The Corona' after which new bass player
Sean was inducted. He too soon
decamped to be superseded by Owen to
record the eight and a half minute track
'Shards Of The Sphere'. This song would
be added to the original demo recordings
for a CD release on X Rated Records.
Owen would switch to guitar as keyboard
player Scott left. Further fluctuations in
the line-up witnessed the departure of
Owen and the reinlistment of Sean on
bass. Signing to the British Wicked World
label, a subsidiary of the Earache
concern, GARDEN OF SHADOWS set to
work on the 'Oracle Moon' album taking a
break to perform at the Czech 'Brutal
Assault' festival.
Sean would join DYING FETUS in
February 2001 as GARDEN OF
SHADOWS utilized the temporary
services of the bassist of FROM WITHIN
for live work.

Albums:
HEART OF THE CORONA, X Rated
(1998)
Heart Of The Corona / Lovely Cold /
Company In Solitude / Apollonian Realm
/ Shards Of The Sphere
ORACLE MOON, Wicked World (2000)
Oracle Moon / Citadel Of Dreams / Into
Infinity / Dissolution Of The Forms /
Continuum / Desert Shadows / Twilight
Odyssey

GATES OF ISHTAR (SWEDEN)
Line-Up: Mikael Sandorf (vocals), Tomas
Jutenfäldt (guitar), Andreas Johansson
(guitar), Niklas Svensson (bass), Oskar
Karlsson (drums)

Very young Lulea based GATES OF
ISHTAR were created at the end of 1994.
Drummer Oskar Karlsson and bassist
Niclas Svenssson were previously with
DECORTITION.
The band released a modestly titled
demo tape the following year modestly
titled 'Best Demo Of '95' which landed
them a deal with Finnish label Spinefarm
Records.
The debut album, although typical Death
Metal, did also include a cover version of
the W.A.S.P. hit 'I Wanna Be Somebody'
and GATES OF ISHTAR were to
subsequently tour with the likes of AT
THE GATES, DARK TRANQUILITY and
LUCIFERION.
However, both Karlsson and Svensson
departed and formed THE EVERDAWN
together with ex-DECORTITION and

SCHEITAN man Pierre Törnkvist and wound up releasing the 1997 album 'Poems- Burn The Past'.

GATES OF ISHTAR's own 1997 album, 'The Dawn Of Flames', was the last album recorded at the legendary Unisound studios.

Apparently former NECROMICON member Baron De Samedi was briefly a GATES OF ISHTAR member prior to forging BATTLELUST.

Albums:
A BLOOD RED PATH, Spinefarm SPI 31 CD (1996)
Inania / Where The Winds Of Darkness Blow / The Silence / Tears / The Dreaming Glade / When Day Light's Gone / Into Seasons Of Frost / A Bloodred Path / I Wanna Be Somebody
THE DAWN OF FLAMES, Invasion (1997)
Perpetual Dawn / Trail Of Tears / Forever Scarred / Dream Field / Dawn Of Flames / Eternal Sin / No Time / The Embrace Of Winter / Where The Winds Of Darkness Blows / A Bloodred Path / The Dreaming Glade / The Silence
AT DUSK AND FOREVER, Invasion (1998)
Wounds / The Nightfall / At Dusk And Forever / Battles To Come / The Burning Sky / Never Alone Again / Always / Red Hot / Forever Beach

GEHENNAH (SWEDEN)
Line-Up: Mr. Violence (vocals), Rob Stringburner (guitar), Ripper Olsson (bass), Hellcop (drums)

GEHENNAH made their presence known via two now infamous demos 1993's subtly titled 'Kill' and the following year's 'Brilliant Loud Overlords Of Destruction'. A deal with Primitive Art Records was struck for the 'Hardrocker' album after which GEHENNAH launched the 'No Fucking Christmas' EP, in a limited run of 500 golden vinyl copies.

GEHENNAH's next effort 'King Of The Sidewalk' saw the band signing up to French Black Metal experts Osmose Productions. Although disowned by the band as rushed and underproduced the album made sufficient impact to score a European 1996 tour billed alongside IMPALED NAZARENE and ANGELCORPSE.

With GEHENNAH gaining ground Primitive Art Records reissued both 'Hardrocker' and 'No Fucking Christmas'

in vinyl format although only 100 copies of each surfaced.

A split EP with RISE AND SHINE was also recorded.

Ronnie 'Ripper' Olson also shares his duties with VOMITORY whilst Michael 'Hellcop' Birgersson operates with DAWN OF DECAY.

Members of GEHENNAH contributed to the SATANARCHY band project of 2000 with personnel from RISE AND SHINE and FURBOWL.

Singles/EPs:
Satanclaws / Merry Shitmas, Primitive Art PAR005 (1995) ('No Fucking Christmas' EP)

Albums:
HARD ROCKER, Primitive Art PAR004 (1995)
Hardrocker / Skeletons In Leather / Say Hello To Mr. Fist / Brilliant Loud Overlords Of Destruction / Winter Of War / Beerzerk / I Am The Wolf / Blood Metal / Crucifucked / Bombraid Over Paradise / The House / Gehennah / Piss Off, I'm Drinking / Psycho Slut
KING OF THE SIDEWALK, Osmose OPCD 046 (1996)
Rock n' Roll Patrol / Hellstorm / Bitch With A Bulletbelt / King Of The Sidewalk / (You're The) Devil In Disguise / Bang Your Heads For Satan / Chickenrace / Tough Guys Don't Look Good / Saturdaynight Blasphemer / Bulldozer / Demolition Team
DECIBEL REBEL, Osmose OPCD 065 (1998)
Beat That Poser Down / Six Pack Queen / Hangover / Decibel Rebel / Hellhole Bar / Get Out Of My Way / Under The Table Again / Street Metal Gangfighters / Rocking Through The Kill / 666, Drunks And Rock n' Roll / I Fucked Your Mom / We Love Alcohol

GENERAL SURGERY (SWEDEN)
Line-Up: Richard Cabeza (vocals), Grant McWilliams (bass), Jonas De Rouche (guitar), Matti Karki (drums)

Formed in 1989 GENERAL SURGERY is the side project of various members of Swedish Death Metal acts.

The original line-up comprised then UNLEASHED guitarist Richard Cabeza on vocals, CARBONISED guitarist Jonas De Rouche, Grant McWilliams on bass and then CARBONISED vocalist Matti Karki on drums. The project's first demo was titled 'Erosive Offals'.

McWilliams departed prior to the second demo 'Pestiferous Anthropophagia'. GENERAL SURGERY's line-up then virtually disintegrated, leaving only Karkki remaining.

New recruits were AFFLICTED guitarist Joacim Carlsson and drummer Matts Nordrup. Grant McWilliams also rejoined. GENERAL SURGERY were then offered a deal by American label Grind 'Til Global Perfection. Tracks were recorded which would eventually become the 'Internecine Prurience' demo. Following recording of further songs with producer Tomas Skogsberg, Karkki quit to concentrate full time as vocalist for DISMEMBER.

The tracks recorded for the American EP were to surface as the 'Necrology' EP on Relapse Records in 1991. The initial 1000 copies came in blood red vinyl and, as the pressings soon sold out, Relapse reissued the EP on CD, with two extra tracks, in 1994.

Nordrup would surface in CREMATORY and REGURGITATE.

Albums:
NECROLOGY, Nuclear Blast NB092-2 (1994)
Ominous Lamentation / Slithering Maceration Of Ulcerous Facial Tissue / Grotesque Maceration Of Mortified Flesh / Severe Catatonia In Pathology / Crimson Concerto / The Succulent Aftermath Of A Subdoural Haemorrhage / An Orgy Of Flying Limbs And Gore

GENETIC WISDOM (HOLLAND)
Line-Up: Mike Lucarelli (vocals), Peter Slootbeck (guitar), Ralph Christian Roelvink (guitar), Ger Knol (bass), Ronny Scholten (drums)

The original 1990 line-up of GENETIC WISDOM comprised guitarists Ralph Roelvink and GJ Aaltink, vocalist Dennuz Bos and drummer Ronny Scholten.

This line-up recorded the 'Genetic Wisdom' demo prior to Aaltink being superseded by Peter Slootbeck and the band bringing in bassist Bo Brinkman. A further demo entitled 'Trivial Destiny' was released before the band landed a deal with Mascot Records.

Upon release of the debut album, 'The Fear Dimension' in 1992, Bos was asked to leave and in came ex-SACROSANCT vocalist Mike Lucarelli.

1993's 'Humanity On Parole' album featured guest sessions by GOREFEST

vocalist Jan Chris De Koeyer and CREEPMIME's Andy Judd. Brinkman was replaced by bassist Ger Knol after the album launch.

Albums:
THE FEAR DIMENSION, Mascot M7002-2 (1992)
Preservance Kills The Game / Why Don't You? / Unfortunate Childhood / Psycho Love / Afraid Of Life / Inside The Triangle (Of Death) / Visual Fastfood / Radical Hatred
HUMANITY ON PAROLE, Mascot M7008-2 (1993)
The Pain / Too Good To Be True / Forced / Get Out / Intentions Rule The World / Dedicated / Mirror Images / Don't Fight The Feeling / Used To It / Dragons To Slay / Face The Facts

GENOCIDE (PORTUGAL)

Albums:
GENOCIDE, Musica Alternativa MA041 (1995)
Obscure Brain / Black Plague / Brutal Evolution / World Lying / Die By Allergy / Human Thoughts / Silent Song / Mind Despair / Twisted Corpses

GENOCIDIO (BRAZIL)

GENECIDIO covered HELLHAMMER's 'Aggressor' as a secret uncredited track.

Albums:
ONE OF THEM, (1998)
DEPRESSION, (1999)
HOCTAE DROM, (1999)
POSTHUMOUS, (2000)
Pilgrim / Condemnation / Lilit And Nahemah / The Sphere Of Lilit / The Sphere Of Nahemah / Black Depth / Luciferic Man / Goodbye Kisses / Cloister / Ways / Black Planet / Illusions

GHOSTORM (LITHUANIA)
Line-Up: Marius (vocals), Omenas (guitar), Tarailia (guitar), Andius (bass), Smarve (drums)

GHOSTORM, a technical Death Metal band, debuted with a 1993 demo 'The End Of All Songs' and would follow it up with the Black Mark released 'Frozen In Fire' two years later.

The album was recorded at Unisound studios in Sweden and produced by EDGE OF SANITY's Dan Swano.

Albums:
FROZEN IN FIRE, Black Mark BMCD 65 (1995)
Fraud Of Dark / There / Solitude / Frost / Dreamland / Come Back / The Sea / At Boundary / Unnormal

GOATSBLOOD (CANADA)

Albums:
GOATSBLOOD, Rage Of Achilles (2001)

GOD FORBID (Brunswick, NJ, USA)
Line-Up: Bryon Davis (vocals), Doc Coyle (guitar), Dallas Coyle (guitar), John Outcalt (bass), Corey Pierce (drums)

New Jersey's GOD FORBID, founded by drummer Corey Pierce and ex FEINT 13 guitarist Dallas Coyle issued early product on the independent 9 Volt label. The band had evolved from its earlier inception as MANIFEST DESTINY through to INSALUBRIOUS before settling on GOD FORBID. During May of 1997 GOD FORBID were joined by vocalist Bryon Davis and in September of the same year by erstwhile WOMB bassist John 'Beeker' Outcalt.
Guitarist Doc Coyle would deputize on a temporary basis for AS DARKNESS FALLS in 1998.
Upon signing to German concern Century Media for the highly praised 'Determination' album GOD FORBID upped their American touring plans appearing with AMEN and SHADOW FALL for a March tour then hooking up with the NEVERMORE / OPETH / CHILDREN OF BODOM dates in April.

Singles/EPs:
Mind Eraser / Habeeber / Madman / Nosferatu / Inside, 9 Volt 9V001 (199-) ('Out Of Misery' EP)

Albums:
REJECT THE SICKNESS, 9 Volt 9V008 (1999)
Amendment / Reject The Sickness / N2 / No Sympathy / Assed Out / Ashes Of Humanity (Regret) / Dark Waters / Heartless / Weather The Storm / The Century Fades
DETERMINATION, Century Media (2001)
Dawn Of The New Millennium / Nothing / Broken Promise / Divide My Destiny / Network / Wicked / Determination Part I / Determination Part II / God's Last Gift / A

Reflection Of The Past / Dead Words on Deaf Ears

GODKILLER (MONACO)

Extreme Satanic Death Metallers GODKILLER hail, quite bizarrely from the millionaire's playground known as the principality of Monaco!
Formed in 1994 the band released their debut demo 'Ad Majorem Satanae Gloriam" the same year. It was a tape GODKILLER swiftly capitalized on in February of the following year by offering a further tape entitled 'The Warlord'. The group has since released two albums.
GODKILLER concentrate on medieval paganistic themes and are so fundamentalist in their beliefs that mainman Duke Satanael even denounces Anton La Vey's Church of Satan as being 'weak'!!
Recent GODKILLER outings have veered towards the electronic. 'Deliverance' even quotes passages from the Bible.

Albums:
THE REBIRTH OF THE MIDDLE AGES, Wounded Love (1996)
Hymn For The Black Knights / From The Castle In The Fog / Path To The Unholy Frozen Empire / Blood On My Swordblade / The Neverending Reign Of The Black Knights
IN GOD WE TRUST, Wounded Love (1997)
THE END OF THE WORLD, Wounded Love 737323 (1998)
The End Of The World / The Inner Pain / Down Under Ground / Following The Funeral Path / Day Of Suffering / Nothing Left But Silence / Still Alive / Waste Of Time / De Profundis
DELIVERANCE, Wounded Love WLR021 (2000)
Nothing Is Sacred / Wailing / At Dusk / When All Hope Is Gone / Dust To Dust / Far My Days Are Vanity / Wisdom / I Am A Stranger In The Earth / Deliverance

GODSEND (UK)
Line-Up: Bob Reid (vocals), Andy Sneap (guitar), Wayne Banks (bass), Mole (drums)

Nottingham trad Thrash Metal band, GODSEND featured ex-SABBAT men Andy Sneap and Wayne Banks and former SLEEZEPATROL drummer, Mole (real name Ian Etheridge).
Having released the 'Heavier Than A

Death In The Family' four track demo in 1993 (comprising 'Self Sacrifice', 'Dressed In Skin', 'Realms' and 'Mind Flying', the group added new bassist Jason Birnie in early 1995 and recorded a new four track demo titled 'When Man Plays God'.

GODSEND broke up in 1996 despite offers of record deals. Mole later sessioned for WRAITH. Sneap continued an engineering and production career, gaining a credit on the 1996 release from DEARLY BEHEADED and later STUCK MOJO. Sneap is now a highly rated producer much in demand.

By 1998 Mole had his own tribute act on the circuit titled MOLETALLICA.

<u>Albums:</u>
GODSEND, Stay Free STAY 006CD (1994)

GOLEM (GERMANY)

GOLEM, a Grind style Death Metal band, formed in 1990 although were hit with the death of two band members in separate car accidents during 1992 and 1993.

Having recorded a solitary demo the group was signed by Invasion Records and released the debut album, 'Eternity: The Weeping Horizons' in 1996.

<u>Albums:</u>
ETERNITY: THE WEEPING HORIZONS, Invasion IR 021 (1996)
Throne Of Confinement / Mental Force / In My Favorite Darkness / Dedication / Emotionally Astray / Incarnated Beast / Message From The Past / The Fall / Beyond The Future Skies

GOLEM (USA)

<u>Singles/EPs:</u>
Visceral Killer, Cannibalized Serial Killer KILL 002 (1993)

GOLGOTHA (SPAIN)

Line-Up: Amon Lopez (vocals), Vicente J. Paya (guitar), Ivan Ramos (guitar), Toni Soler (bass), Jose Nunez (keyboards), Ruben Alarcon (drums)

More of a project than an actual band, Spain's GOLGOTHA was the brainchild of UNBOUNDED TERROR's Vicente J. Paya, who felt he needed a vehicle for songs that he'd written that didn't fit the concept of his main outfit.

The debut GOLGOTHA release, the

'Caves Of Mind' mini-album, received glowing reviews in Europe and this gave Paya the incentive to put something a little bit more permanent together, adding DEHUMANIZED members Ivan Ramos and Ruben Alarcon amongst others.

GOLGOTHA are believed to be one of the few Spanish acts to truly have what it takes to break on an international scale.

<u>Albums:</u>
CAVES OF MIND, Repulse (1994)
MELANCHOLY, Repulse (1995)
Lonely / Lake Of Memories / Nothing / Raceflections / Lost / Immaterial Deceptions / Stillness / Virtualis Demens / Caves Of Mind

GOMORRAH (UK)

Line-Up: Sven Olafson (vocals), Mike Prior (guitar), Jose Griffin (guitar), John Clark (bass), Fran Robinson (drums)

A Death Metal act that impressed on the 'Underground Titans' club tour. The band's first album, 'Reflections Of Inanimate Matter', features a surprising guest appearance by ex-MARILLION vocalist FISH.

GOMORRAH toured Britain with WARP SPASM in 1994. Signed to Black Mark in 1995.

<u>Albums:</u>
REFLECTIONS OF INANIMATE MATTER, Megapulse MEGAP1CD (1994)
Without Trace / Defiance Sewer-Cide / Another Bleak Horizon / Rejoice In Flames / Seasons / Human Trophies
CARESS THE GROTESQUE, Black Mark BMCD 107 (1996)
Perfection Dies / Fireball / Master, Infinity & Separation / Void Existence / Feed On Me / Driven Hard / 33 Utopia / Override / Mask / Triggered

GORE (HOLLAND)

Line-Up: Marij Hell (bass / vocals), Pieter De Sury (guitar), Danny A. Lommen (drums)

GORE's original drummer Danny Lommen departed in favour of Casper Brotzmann. 'Wrede - The Cruel Peace' was co-produced by the famous Steve Albini and featured new guitarists Frankie Stroo and Joen Bentley.

Albums:
HARDGORE, Eksakt (1987)
MEANMAN'S DREAM, Red Rhino RAVE 1-A (1988)
Mean Man's Dream / Search / Love / Last Steps / Chainsaw / The Bank / Back Home / Loaded / Meat Machine / Out For Sex
WREDE - THE CRUEL PEACE, Megadisc (1988)
The Breeding (Linede) / A Cruel Peace (Wrede) / Garden Of Evil (Het Bos) / Death Has Come (De Dodd)
GORE LIFE LONG DEADLINE, SPV 084-36162 (1993)
Bad Ideas Obsession / Battle Of Stones / Treat / No Respect / Rustproof Rape / Nobody's Driven / Harder Break / The Concentration Connection / Master Of Mirrors / Kick Ass / Hanging Grounds / Waste Taste / Sleep-Well / Lifelong Deadline / Isis / The Real Mother Fucker / Cleared By Recognition / Waiting Time / Shock Exchange / Morrowland

GORE (BRAZIL)
Line-Up: Robot (vocals / bass), Lizandro (guitar), Rubem Zachis (drums)

Rio De Janeiro Grind act GORE are among the very sickest of the sick. The band think nothing of using the most depraved of photographic images for record sleeves. A burst of gut wrenching demo sessions heralded GORE's arrival opening with the 1992 tape 'Psychonecropsypatholic', 1993's 'Open Doors To The Morgue' and 1994's 'To A Life Consumed By Decay'.
The band took a mere 3 days to record their debut 1996 album 'Consumed By Slow Decay'. In 2000 GORE featured tracks on the 'Six Ways To The Holocaust' compilation album and shared a split 7" single with WTN for Mexican label American Line Productions. A split album with LAST DAYS OF HUMANITY also emerged.
2001 found the release of another shared album, this time with NEURO-VISCERAL EXHUMATION and the full length 'Ungrotesque'.

Singles/EPs:
Split, American Line Productions (2000) (7" split single with WTN)

Albums:
CONSUMED BY SLOW DECAY, Lofty Storm LSR001 (1995)
Fetus Jejuni / Incomplete Evacuation / Hysterical Extraction Of Facial Tissue / Intestinal Pestilence / Dissimulated Incabation And Maximum Infection / Phlatulent Manifestation Of Alcaligenes Feacalis / Exposed Guts / Syndrome Of Intensive Regurgitation / Attenuated Mutant Worms / Inquisitive Corporal Recremation / Unfinished Radiation / Frenetic Fetischism For Human Pieces In Decomposition / Human Limbs Mutilated / Cycle Of Suffocation / Cannibal Zoophilism With Extreme Sexual Aberration / Consummated Cancer
SPLIT, Halflife (2000) (split album with LAST DAYS OF HUMANITY)
SPLIT, Disgorgment Of Squash Bodies (2001) (Split album with NEURO-VISCERAL EXHUMATION)
UNGROTESQUE, Halflife (2001)

GORE BEYOND NECROPSY
(JAPAN)

Grind act GORE BEYOND NECROPSY set the scene with the disturbing 1992 demo 'I Recommend You Amputation'. First product was the 7" EP 'This Is An EP You Want' in 1993 followed by a 1994 live tape.
Their shared album with notorious Electro-Anarchists MERZBOW 'Rectal Anarchy' was far from subtle, the album cover graced by an enlarged anus and the song content comprising warped cover versions. In 1997 GORE BEYOND NECROPSY toured Australia with WARSORE and returned the compliment by arranging Japanese dates for WARSORE and issuing a split 7" single.
The band managed to cram over 50 tracks into just under 25 minutes on their 1999 album 'Noise A Go Go'.
A split single with Swedish Grindsters ARSEDESTROYER arrived in 2000 and the pair toured Japan the same year.

Singles/EPs:
This Is An EP You Want, M.M.I. (1993)
Split, Blurred (1995) (7" split single with SENSELESS APOCALYPSE)
Split, Mangrove (1995) (7" split single with MERZBOW)
Faecal Noise Holocaust, Cyillusions (1995)
Split, (199-) (7" split single with DISGORGE)
Split, Mink (199-) (7" split single with MINCH)
Split, Steralized Decay (1998) (7" split single with WARSORE)

Sounds Like Shit, Blurred (1998)
Split, Devour (2000) (7" split single with ARSEDESTROYER)

Albums:
RECTAL ANARCHY, Relapse (199-)
(Split album with MERZBOW)
NOISE A GO GO, Relapse (1999)
Intro / Faecal Gor Gore Attack / Chain Of Torture / Horrendous Nazi Infection / Gore Gore Warscars / Mild Shit Taste / Brainwashed Media Slave / Garbage In The Sewage / Sulfuric Acid Dream / Poultry Within / Kill The Cock Rock Greedy Hog / Intro / Dead Dog Idolization / Fartstorm / Deaf, Dumb, Blind / Filth Sounds Of Hatred / Cock Rock Asshole / Gurgling Spiral Repulsion / Global Tumor / Negative Thoughts Whirling Around / Born Deformed / Raping The Arse / Cock Rock Roach / Trash Of The Hemorrhoids / Mind Plague / Puke Yourself / The Worst Shit In The World / Boiling Detestation / Noise A Go Go! / Intro / Arsebleed / Horrendously Analdrilled / From The Cradle To The Grave / Dead Life Goes On / Subliminal State Control / Cock Rock Incineration / Pain To Be Slain / Shittier Than Shit / Instant Necropsy / Power Of Media Arrogant Mass Control / Uncleanly Devoured Visions / It's The Gore Gore Goreality / Intro / Huma BBQ Burning Hell / Stench Of Carnage... / Corporate Ghouls / Driller Killer From Outer Space / Disease Bondage / The End Of Life / Intro / Bad Taste Grotesqueen / Divine's Dead / Grudge / Harshit Shock / Chaos, Disorder & Confusion / Steaming, Bubbling Cadaverous Odor / Shitgobbling Hate Generation / Outro
GO FILTH GO, Infernal (1999)

GOREDEATH (MI, USA)
Line-Up: Corey Lasley (vocals / drums), Adam Cruz (vocals / guitar)

A Christian Death Metal duo. Both drummer Corey Lasley and guitarist Adam Cruz handle lead vocals with Lasley giving up the grunts and growls whilst Cruz wails the high pitched screams.
Lasley is also president of the extreme Christian Metal label Laceration Productions, has a side project entitled BETROTH and acts as producer for the 'Unblack' Metal band GRIM.

Albums:
CAST INTO DARKNESS, Laceration

Productions LP002 (2000)
Cast Into Darkness - The Burning / God Damned Lucifer / Souls Hacked To Shreds (Chainsawed) / Goreified / Pathetic Sins / Annihilation Of The False Realm (Where Reality Dies) / Drowned In Vomit (Vomitorium) / Deception Of The Raven / Chant The Lullaby Of Death As The Fetus Is Disposed / Cast Into Darkness - Damned To Flames

GOREFEST (HOLLAND)
Line-Up: Jan Chris De Koeyer (vocals / bass), Frank Haarthorn (guitar), Alex Van Schiak (guitar), Marc Hoogedoorn (drums)

A highly influential Death Metal act on the Dutch scene, GOREFEST emerged in late 1989 with the above listed line-up and swiftly debuted with the 'Tangled In Gore' demo recorded in December 1989, which led to a great deal of record company interest.
A further demo, titled 'Horrors In A Retarded Mind', secured a support tour in Belgium and Holland to CARCASS and a deal with Foundation 2000 Records. Live tracks from the CARCASS tour were subsequently included on the D.F.S.A. compilation 'Where Is Your God Now?'.
Although GOREFEST parted company with guitarist Alex Van Scaik in 1990 they toured Europe with REVENANT before suffering another departure, this time losing the services of drummer Mark Hoogedorn. However, following the release of the debut album, 'Mindloss', GOREFEST complemented their line-up by adding former ELEGY drummer Ed Warby and guitarist Boudewyn Bonebakker.
The group toured as support to DEICIDE in Europe in 1992 before a successful American tour opening for DEATH ensued.
After a break of nearly two years a brand new studio effort 'Soul Survivor' surfaced through Nuclear Blast in 1996. GOREFEST performed at the Dynamo festival the same year.
In early 1998 the group, promoting 'Chapter 13' for fresh label SPV, scored a major coup as the support band for JUDAS PRIEST's comeback 'Jugulator' tour that was set to open in Europe during March.

Singles/EPs:
Live Misery, Cenotaph (1991)
Fear / Raven / Horrors '94 / Fear (Live),

Nuclear Blast NB122 (1994)
Freedom (Single Edit) / Tired Moon / Goddess In Black (Orchestral Version) / Freedom (Album Version), Nuclear Blast (1996)

Albums:
MINDLOSS, Foundation 2000 (1990)
Intro / Mental Misery / Putrid Stench Of Human Remains / Foetal Carnage / Tangled In Gore / Confessions Of A Serial Killer / Horrors In A Retarded Mind / Loss Of Flesh / Decomposed / Gorefest
FALSE, Nuclear Blast NB069 (1993)
The Glorious Dead / State Of Mind / Reality- When You Die / Get A Life / False / Second Face / Infamous Existence / From Ignorance To Oblivion / The Mass Insanity
THE EINDHOVEN INSANITY - LIVE AT THE DYNAMO, Nuclear Blast NB091-2 (1993)
The Glorious Dead / State Of Mind / Get A Life / Mental Misery / From Ignorance To Oblivion / Reality - When You Die / The Mass Insanity / Confessions Of A Serial Killer / Eindhoven Roar
ERASE, Nuclear Blast NB110 (1994)
Low / Erase / I Walk My Way / Fear / Seeds Of Hate / Peace Of Paper / Goddess In Black / To Hell And Back
SOUL SURVIVOR, Nuclear Blast NB 143-2 (1996)
Freedom / Forty Shades / River / Electric Poet / Soul Survivor / Blood Is Thick / Dogday / Demon Seed / Chameleon / Dragonman
CHAPTER 13, SPV Steamhammer 085-18862 P (1998)
Chapter Thirteen / Broken Wing / Nothingness / Smile / The Idiot / Repentance / Bordello / F.S. 2000 / All Is Well / Unsung / Super Reality / Serve The Masses

GOREMENT (SWEDEN)
Line-Up: Jimmy Karlsson (vocals), Patrik Fernlund (guitar), Daniel Eriksson (guitar), Nicklas Lilja (bass), Mattias Berglund (drums)

Albums:
THE ENDING QUEST, Crypta DA 8207-2 (1994)
My Ending Quest / Vale Of Tears / Human Relic / The Memorial / The Lost Breed / Silent Hymn (For The Dead) / Sea Of Silence / Obsequies Of Mankind / Darkness Of The Dead / Into Shadows

GOREAPHOBIA (USA)

GOREAPHOBIA fell apart soon after the EP release. Vocalist / bassist Mezzadurus went on to create BLOODSTORM recording the 1997 album 'The Atlantean Wardragon' as well as putting himself out to loan to ABSU for live work.

Singles/EPs:
Omen Of Masochism, Relapse RR015 (1993)

GOREROTTED (UK)
Line-Up: Mr. Gore (vocals), Baby Slice (vocals), Dick Splash (guitar), Fluffy (guitar), Mr. Smith (bass), Rushy (drums)

London Gore Metal act. Lost vocalist Graham 'Nutty Strangeways' Hodis in late 1999. Ex-BEYOND FEAR bassist Steve, also of 7TH CHILD, also operates a side project entitled INFECTED DISARRAY.
This new unit would include GOREROTTED drummer John Insane (also of ZARATHUSTRA and BRUTAL INSANITY), guitarist Lal, second guitarist Paul of BRAINCHOKE and SUFFERING and fronted by former ZARATHUSTRA singer Eddie.

Singles/EPs:
Limb From Limb / Her Gash I Did Slash / Stab Me Til I Cum / Carrion Smelling, (1999) ('Her Gash I Did Slash' EP)

Albums:
MUTILATED IN MINUTES, Dead Again (2001)
Hack Sore / Bed 'Em, Behead 'Em / Stab Me Till I Cum / Cut, Gut, Beaten, Eaten / Corpse Fucking Art / Put Your Bits In A Concrete Mix / Mutilated In Minutes, Severed In Seconds / Gagged, Shagged, Bodybagged / Severed, Sawn And Sold As Porn

GORGASM (Chicago, IL, USA)
Line-Up: Tom Tangalos (vocals / guitar), Tom Leski (vocals / guitar), Russ Powell (vocals / bass), Derek Hoffman (drums)

A notorious name in Death Metal circles fronted by former DISINTER man Tom Tangelos. Chicago's GORGASM's repute is well justified, their particular brand of brutally harsh Metal inspiring many.
The band was created out of the disintegration of CREMATORIUM during 1994 with an inaugural demo being cut in

1996 before the arrival of powerhouse drummer Derek Hoffman.

Tangalos would take time out during 1998 to act as guest lead vocalist foe AD INFINITUM, appearing on their 'Dies Irae' demo.

Hoffman would decamp to found the equally illustrious INCESTUOUS in alliance with ex-DISGORGE vocalist Matti Way, former SMEGMA / CUMCHRIST guitarist Danny Louise ('Wrench') and Mike Dooley from CORPSE VOMIT on bass recording the 'Brass Knuckle Abortion' album. INCESTUOUS would in turn, following Hoffman's departure and his replacement by Ricky Myers of DISGORGE, became CINERARY.

In January of 2001 Hoffman regrouped with GORGASM to cut the much anticipated second album 'Bleeding Profusely'. The drummer would also be seen on the live circuit deputizing for LIVIDITY.

Albums:
STABWOUNDS INTERCOURSE, Pulverizer (1998)
Necrosodomy / Disemboweled / Stabwounds Intercourse / Coprophiliac / Horrendous Rebirth / Clitoral Circumcision
BLEEDING PROFUSELY, Gorgasm (2001)
Bleeding Profusely / Morbid Overgrowth / Stripped To Bone / Fucking The Viscera / Voracious / The Essence Of Putrefaction / Post Coital Truncation / Severed Ecstasy / Lesbian Stool Orgy / Fisticunt / Disemboweled

GORGON (FRANCE)
Line-Up: Chris (vocals / guitar / keyboards), Brice (guitar), Joel (bass), Seb (drums)

French Death Metallers GORGON were founded around the 1992 demo tape 'Call From Unknown Depths' which led directly to a deal with the Italian label Wounded Love Records for the 'Immortal Horde' EP.

In 1995 GORGON released their first, full length album with a dose of brutal Death Metal. The band also contributed songs to a number of compilation albums and played shows with SAMAEL, MERCYLESS and SADIST.

Indeed, guitarist Khaos was to join Swiss outfit SAMAEL during 1996!

Singles/EPs:
Immortal Horde - EP, Wounded Love (1993)

Albums:
THE LADY RIDES A BLACK HORSE, Dungeon 001 (1995)
Among Fogs Of Oblivion (Intro) / Tower Of Gargoyles / The Lady Rides A Black Horse / Call From Unknown Depths / As A Stone / The Union / At The Memory Of The Past / Elizabeth / Swallowed Thoughts / Immortal Horde / The Day Required
REIGN OF OBSCENITY, Gorgon (1997)

GORGUTS (CANADA)
Line-Up: Luc LeMay (vocals), Sylvian Marcoux (guitar), Eric Giguere (bass), Stephane Provender (drums)

Highly regarded and innovative Jazz flavoured Death Metal act GORGUTS was founded during 1989. By 1992 the quartet, spearheaded by the unmistakable gut wrenching growls of vocalist Luc LeMay, comprised guitarist Sylvian Marcoux, bass player Eric Giguere and drummer Stephane Provender. GORGUTS returned from a 1993 European tour promoting the second album 'Erosion Of Sanity' to discover they had been dropped by Roadrunner Records. The band also splintered at this juncture losing both their drummer and a guitarist. New faces were PURULENCE guitarist Steve Hurdle and PSYCHIC THROB bass player Steve.

Following the recording of the Pierre Remillard produced 'Obscura' opus GORGUTS drafted Steve McDonald as drummer in September 1998 to replace the recently departed Patrick Robert. With this line up GORGUTS undertook the 'Death Across America' tour alongside running mates NILE, CRYPTOPSY and OPPRESSOR.

Before the close of 1999 guitarist Daniel Mongrain, whilst retaining his ties to his own act MARTYR, would join GORGUTS replacing Hurdle and appearing on their 'From Wizdom To Hate' album.

Luc LeMay would guest on MARTYR's 2000 album 'Warp Zone'.

Albums:
CONSIDERED DEAD, Roadrunner RC 92731 (1991)
...And Then Comes Lividity / Still And Cold / Disincarnated / Considered Dead / Rottenatomy / Bodily Corrupted / Waste

Of Mortality / Drifting Remains / Hermatological Allergy / Inoculated Life
EROSION OF SANITY, Roadrunner RR91142 (1993)
With The Flesh He'll Create / Condemned To Obscurity / Erosion Of Sanity / Orphans Of Sickness / Hideous Infirmity / Path Beyond Premonition / Odours Of Existence / Dormant Misery
OBSCURA, Olympic Recordings 008 633 129-2 (1999)
Obscura / Earthly Love / The Carnal State / Nostalgia / The Art Of Sombre Ecstasy / Clouded / Subtle Body / Rapturous Grief / La Vie Est Prelude / Illuminatus / Faceless Ones / Sweet Silence
FROM WISDOM TO HATE, (2000)
Inverted / Behave Through Mythos / From Wisdom To Hate / The Quest For Equilibrium / Unearthing The Past / Elusive Treasures / Das Martyrium Des... / Testimonial Ruins

GORTICIAN (Washington, LA, USA)
Line-Up: Timothy Archer (vocals / bass), Tony Buzby (guitar), Jason Christie (drums)

Although a renowned name in underground circles GORTICIAN's historical background is shrouded in mystery due to a campaign of misinformation emanating from the band themselves. The group was convened around 1990 by frontman Junior, former GRENDEL and MAD MONK man Timothy Archer, guitarist Tony Buzby and drummer Ronnie Berthelot. This initial line-up would splinter within weeks as Matt took over the drumstool and Junior bailed out.

By 1993 GORTICIAN had settled on a power trio line up of Archer on vocals and bass, Buzby on guitar and drummer Jason Christie, the latter previously with Las Vegas act ENTITY. Reportedly the band's three track demo 'Eaten, Beaten & Crucified', with guest guitars from CHAOS HORDE guitarist Mike, was deemed so offensive the band was jailed under obscenity laws. Various stories put the group members sentences as ranging from three months in jail to a few hours incarceration with a $50 fine. There is also an urban legend that PMRC campaigner Tipper Gore incited her followers to burn the entire production run of the cassette with only one copy escaping her wrath.

GORTICIAN finally got around to a commercial release with the 2000 'Transmigration Into Hell' album released on their own Bleeding Erection label. Earlier works, including a less than reverential take on the STRAY CATS 'Stray Cat Strut' anthem, were collected on the compilation 'The Wonder Years'. Christie, under his pseudonym of High C, also operates in the Rap Metal side project THE GUYS WHO WEAR BLACK TOO MUCH led by Lord Vic Naughty of RAMPAGE.

GORTICIAN, with guest vocalist Jeremy Whitman of DESPONDENCY, would contribute their version of VENOM's '1000 Days In Sodom' to an online tribute album.

Albums:
TRANSMIGRATION INTO HELL, Bleeding Erection (2000)
The Next Religion / Alien Abduction / Avatar In The Abattoir / Labyrinths Animator / The Avengers / Olmec Assimilation / Blazing Morgue / Empire Of Perversion / Knight Of The Brazen Serpent / In The Shadow Of The Accursed Mountains / Hypocrisy And Downfall / Twilight Cycle
THE WONDER YEARS, Unsung Heroes (2000)
Kick The Chair / Orgy With The Dead / The Next Religion / Alien Abduction / Casarian Salad / Vagina Dentata / Orgy With The Dead (1993 version) / Vagina Dentata (1993 version) / Beaten, Mocked And Crucified (1993 version) / Ugly Police Incident / Death Trip / Mind Of A Lunatic / Stray Cat Strut / Alien Abduction (Special Surgery mix)

GRAVE (SWEDEN)
Line-Up: Jörgen Sandström (vocals / guitar), Ola Lindgren (guitar), Jonas Torndal (bass), Jensa Paulsson (drums)

GRAVE are one of the founders of the Swedish Death / Doom Metal scene releasing their first demo, 'Sick Disgust Eternal', in 1987 following a name change from CORPSE. Two further demos, 1988's 'Sexual Mutilation' and 1989's 'Anatomia Corporis Humanum' gained the band an enviable cult status. The latter demo was also to be issued as a four track EP.

The band toured Europe as guests to Florida thrashers MALEVOLENT CREATION in September 1991 shortly followed by dates opening for ENTOMBED.

In 1992 bassist Jonas Torndal quit and frontman Jörgen Sandström took over four string duties. Following the release of 1994's 'Soulless' GRAVE toured America in a headlining capacity prior to hooking up with the CANNIBAL CORPSE and SAMAEL tour as support. Further dates had the band putting in an appearance on the 'Full Of Hate' festivals and acting as openers for MORBID ANGEL.

Following this bout of activity Sandström wound up joining ENTOMBED in 1995. GRAVE persevered as a duo with Lindgren now responsible for vocals for the 1996 Tomas Skogsberg produced 'Hating Life' record.

GRAVE
Photo : Martin Wickler

Singles/EPs:
Extremely Rotten Flesh / Brutally Deceased / Septic Excrements / Reborned Miscarriage, M.B.R. (1989)
...And Here I Die... Satisfied / I Need You / Black Dawn / Tremendous Pain / Day Of Mourning / Inhuman, Century Media 77066-2 (1993) ('...And Here I Die...Satisfied' EP)

Albums:
GRAVE, Prophecy SRT 91L2878 (1991) (Split LP with. DEVOLUTION)
INTO THE GRAVE, Century Media 84 9721 (1992)
Deformed / In Love / For Your God / Obscure Infinity / Hating Life / Into The Grave / Extremely Rotten Flesh /

Haunted / Day Of Mourning / Inhuman / Banished To Live
SOULESS, Century Media CD 77070 (1994)
Turning Black / Soulless / I Need You / Bullets Are Mine / Bloodshed / Judas / Unknown / And Here I Die / Genocide / Rain / Scars
YOU'LL NEVER SEE, Century Media CD 9733 (1995)
You'll Never See / Now And Forever / Morbid Way To Die / Obsessed / Grief / Severing Flesh / Brutally Deceased / Christ(ns)anity
HATING LIFE, Century Media 77106-2 (1996)
Worth The Wait / Restrained / Winternight / Two Of Me / Beauty Within / Lovesong / Sorrowfilled Moon / Harvest Day / Redress / Still Hating Life
EXTREMELY ROTTEN LIVE, Century Media (1997)
Extremely Rotten Flesh / Turning Black / Restrained / Winternight / Haunted / Two Of Me / Hating Life / You'll Never See / Lovesong / Sorrowfilled Moon / Rain / Soulless / And Here I Die... / Into The Grave / Reborn Miscarriage

THE GREAT DECEIVER (SWEDEN)
Line-Up: Tomas Lindberg (vocals), Kristian Wahlin (guitar), Johan Osterberg (guitar), Matti Lundell (bass), Hans Nilsson (drums)

THE GREAT DECEIVER's 2000 mini album 'Jet Black Art' sees ex-AT THE GATES and present day THE HAUNTED frontman Tomas Lindberg on vocals. The bands pedigree also boasts guitarists Kristian Wahlin ('Necrolord') and Johan Osterberg as well as drummer Hans Nilsson all of Black Metal band DIABOLIQUE. Both Wahlin and Nilsson also lay claim to membership of LIERS IN WAIT whilst Osterberg has previous credits with DECOLLATION.

Albums:
JET BLACK ART, Trustkill TK30 (2000)
Cornered Rat / Jet Black Art / Suffering Redefined / The End Made Flesh And Blood / Desperate And Empty

THE GREAT KAT (NY, USA)

Reckoned by many to be as mad as a March hare and hailed as a genius by some, The Great Kat, real name Katherine Thomas, first reared her head in 1987 touting herself as the world's fastest guitarist and only true musician. Having attended the famed Julliard School Of Music Kat signed to Roadrunner and recorded her debut album, the unsubtle 'Worship Me Or Die' to an interesting array of opinion from the world's Metal press.

By 1989 Kat had seemingly found suitable musicians in order to tour with, the lucky duo being bassist Chip Marshall and drummer Kevin Dedario. Later releases have been short on duration if crammed to the hilt with energy. The 1998 'Bloody Vivaldi' opus features a take on Vivaldi's much loved 'Four Seasons', the 39 second hyper blast of 'Blood' and also Sarasate's 'Carmen's Fantasy'. The 2000 release 'Rossini's Rape' plumbed even deeper into the realms of the truly disturbing with workouts of Rossini's 'William Tell Overture' and Bazzini's 'The Road Of The Goblins'.

Singles/EPs:
Satan Says EP, (198-)

Albums:
WORSHIP ME OR DIE, Roadracer RO 95892 (1987)
Metal Messiah / Kat Possessed / Death To You / Satan Goes To Church / Worship Me Or Die / Demons / Speed Death / Kill The Mothers / Ashes To Dust / Satan Says / Metal Massacre
BEETHOVEN ON SPEED, Roadracer RO 93732 (1990)
Beethoven On Speed / Flight Of The Bumble-Bee / Funeral March / God / Sex And Violins / Gripping Obsession / Worshipping Bodies / Total Tyrant / Ultra-Dead / Revenge Of The Mongrel / Kat Abuse / Made In Japan / Beethoven Mosh (5th Symphony) / Paganinni's 24th Caprice / Guitar Concerto In Blood Minor / Back To The Future: For Geniuses Only
DIGITAL BEETHOVEN ON CYBERSPEED, Blood And Guts Music (1996)
Goddess / Cyerspeed / Wagner's 'Ride Of The Valkyries' / Paganini's 'Caprice #9' / Bach's 'Partita #3'
GUITAR GODDESS, Blood And Guts Music (1997)
Rossini's 'The Barber Of Seville' / Dominatrix / Feast Of The Dead / Sarasate's Gypsy Violin Waltz 'Zigerneriveisen'
BLOODY VIVALDI, Great Kat (1998)
Vivaldi's 'The Four Seasons' / Torture Chamber / Blood / Sarasate's 'Carmen's Fantasy'

ROSSINI'S RAPE, TPR (2000)
Rossini's 'William Tell Overture' / Sodomize / Castration / Bazzini's 'The Road Of The Goblins'

GRIEF (USA)
Line-Up: Jeff (vocals), Terry (guitar), Randy (bass), Rick (drums)

Albums:
COME TO GRIEF, Century Media 77087-2 (1994)
Earthworm / Hate Grows Stronger / World Of Hurt / I Hate You / Ruined / Fed Up / Stricken / Come To Grief

GRIEF OF EMERALD (SWEDEN)
Line-Up: Johnny Lehto (vocals / guitar), Anders Tång (bass), Robert Bengtsson (keyboards), Jonas Blum (drums)

GRIEF OF EMERALD was founded by former DECAMORON and ODERU man Johnny Lehto with bassist Anders Tång of NECROFEAST and MASTEMO. The band later added NIDEN DIV 187 drummer Fredrik.
An album provisionally titled 'Signs From A Stormy Past' was recorded for Scottish label Deviation but was shelved. Some tracks from these sessions were used for the 'Nightspawn' mini album.
Fredrik made an exit being replaced by Jonas Blum of RUNEMAGICK and DEATHWITCH for the 'Malformed Seed' album.

Albums:
NIGHTSPAWN, Listenable POSH013 (1998)
The Beginning / Winds Of Vengeance / Warsworn / Famine / Revival / Nightspawn / Day Of Doom / Trinitia Damnation / The Second Dynasty
MALFORMED SEED, Listenable (2000)
Like The Plague We Shall Spread / Wingless / Threshold To Fire / Nightstalker Pentagram Warrior / Holy Book - Holy Shit / Beaten Beyond Recognition / Malformed Seed / Life Has Lost

GRIFFIN (NORWAY)
Line-Up: Tommy Sebastian (vocals), Kai Nergaard (guitar), Marcus (guitar), Johnny Wangberg (bass), Marius Karlsen (drums)

Initially a project of BLOODTHORN guitarist Kai Nergaard and ATROX and BETHZAIDA man Tommy Sebastian

GRIFFIN would evolve from a kickabout rehearsal hobby to a fully fledged band. Second guitarist Marcus was added in December 2000. GRIFFIN cut tracks for a limited edition EP in early 2001 comprising of live tracks and cover renditions of TURBONEGRO's 'Bad Mongo' and IRON MAIDEN's 'Wrathchild'.

Albums:
WASTELAND SERENADES, Season Of Mist (2000)
Mechanized Reality / The Usurper / Spite Keeps Me Silent / Obsession / New Business Capitalized / Hunger Strike / Always Closing / Punishment Macabre / Exit 2000 / Wasteland Serenade / Dream Of Dreamers (Bliss 2)

GRINNING GHOUL (BELGIUM)
Line-Up: Sven Van Den Broeck (vocals), Patrick Smolderen (guitar), Mattijs Buys (guitar), Patrick Maes (bass), Leslie Andries (drums)

A Black infused Death Metal act known originally as CACODAEMON upon their formation in 1991. As CACODAEMON the band comprised of vocalist Necrodaemon (Sven Van Den Broeck), guitarist Occulta, bass player Steven Heirweg and drummer Thae Pazumon (Leslie Andries).
During 1992 Occulta left to concentrate on his other act the Black Metal band AVATAR as Heirweg was also given his marching orders. Regrouping by drafting guitarists Spawn Demon and Mattijs Buys the band evolved into GRINNING GHOUL and later brought themselves up to full strength with the addition of bassist Filip De Winter. This line up issued the 1996 demo tape 'Al Azif' and performed their inaugural gig shortly after on a billing with AVATAR and ORCHRIST.
GRINNING GHOUL was then assailed by line-up problems. Van Den Broeck quit but then made a return. Spawn Demon made his exit to be supplanted by Patrick Smolderen and in 1999 De Winter's position was taken by Patrick 'Metal Pat' Maes. In this revised formation GRINNING GHOUL laid down their debut 2000 album 'Beyond The Mirror'. However, gigs to promote the album were curtailed when Maes broke his arm.

Albums:
BEYOND THE MIRROR, (2000)
Grinning Ghoul / Grimwood Ghost /

Hellfyres & Vempyres / Anger Is A Gift / Act Of Terror / Moon Hate / Black Theatre For Tomorrow / Humanity / Spawn The Rage / Outro

GRIP INC. (USA)
Line-Up: Gus Chambers (vocals), Waldemayr Sorychta (guitars), Jason Vie Brooks (bass), Dave Lombardo (drums)

GRIP INC are most noted for their inclusion of ex-SLAYER drummer DAVE LOMBARDO, a man who whilst with his former unit often topped the 'best drummer' polls in magazines for many years. His relationship with his erstwhile band mates in SLAYER was known to be fragile and his departure was no surprise. However, it took a few years to re-emerge with GRIP INC.
The band also feature British ex-21 GUNS vocalist Gus Chambers, former HEATHEN bassist Jason Vie Brooks and ex VOODOO CULT guitarist Waldemayr Sorychta. (Lombardo had met Sorychta whilst laying down drums on a VOODOO CULT album as special guest). A fledgling version of GRIP INC. also included ex-OVERKILL guitarist Bobby Gustafson but his tenure was a brief one.
Lombardo later enjoyed a stint with TESTAMENT and issued a solo album, the pseudo classical 'Vivaldi'. The drummer would also forge FANTOMAS with ex-FAITH NO MORE singer Mike Patton.
Vie Brooks formed part of the 2000 HEATHEN reunion.

Albums:
THE POWER OF INNER STRENGTH, SPV Steamhammer 085 76922 (1995)
Uno / Savage Seas / Hostage To Heaven / Monster Among Us / Guilty Of Innocence / Innate Affliction / Colors Of Death / Ostracized / Cleanse The Seed / Heretic War Chant / Longest Hate
NEMESIS, SPV 085-18322 (1996)
Pathetic Liar / Portrait Of Henry / Empress (Of Rancor) / Descending Darkness / War Between One / Scream At The Sky / Silent Stranger / The Summoning / Rusty Nail / Myth Or Man / Code Of Silence

GROINCHURN (SOUTH AFRICA)
Line-Up: Christo Bester (vocals / bass), Mark Chapman (vocals / guitar), Sergio Christina (drums)

South Africa's premier Metal outfit. The

obviously Grind act GROINCHURN convened in 1994 as a trio of vocalist / bassist Christo Bester, vocalist / guitarist Mark Chapman and drummer Sergio Christina. This line up has remained steadfast until the present day.

GROINCHURN debuted with the demos 'Human Filth' and 'Every Dog Has Its Decay'. 1995 witnessed a glut of 7" single releases with GROINCHURN sharing split 7" singles with CAPTAIN 3 LEG for the American Fudgeworthy label and WOYCZECH on the German Painart imprint. A live 7" EP entitled 'Totally Fucking Alive' was also issued by the Czech label Icy Illusion.

Promoting the inaugural album 'Six Times Nine' GROINCHURN toured Europe with KRABATHOR and SANITY'S DAWN securing a deal with the German Morbid label along the way. Fudgeworthy would also issue the record in America on a limited edition 10" vinyl format.

Second album 'Fink' witnessed the band returning the favour to KRABATHOR as both acts put in a string of South African shows. GROINCHURN would also bring CYROGENIC over for gigs in their homeland too before renewed touring efforts in Europe.

GROINCHURN were back in action with KRABATHOR once more in Europe during 2000 promoting the 'Whoaml' release prior to American shows with TOTAL FUCKING DESTRUCTION.

Singles/EPs:
Split, Fudgeworthy (1995) (7" split single with CAPTAIN 3 LEG)
Split, Painart (1995) (7" split single with WOYCZECH)
Totally Fucking Alive EP, Icy Illusion (1995)
Bow To The Gimplord / I Don't Think So / Stayin' Alive, Morbid (1998) ('I Don't Think So' 7" split single with HAEMORRHAGE)

Albums:
SIX TIMES NINE, Morbid (1997)
FINK, Morbid (1998)
Generic / Repetition Works / Already Dead / Change Is Change / Whole / More / Ugly People / Bridges Burn / Principles Of Mass Suggestion / The Big Picture / Just Passing Through / More Different Than Different / Being Ripped Off / Open / What About Them Injuns / Sein / The Clock Is Ticking / I Want To Be White / Hollow / Ninety Nine / I Will Say It
ALREADY DEAD, Morbid (1998)

Already Dead / Let's Put The Fun Back Into Fundamentalists / Satan Spawn, The Idiots / Toad-Lee / Genocidal Tendency / Contraceive
WHOAMI, Morbid MR74 (2000)
Everything You Know's A Lie / Untitled / Fickle World / Quiet Please / Rotaludom / Blown Off Course / Da Vitameen Green / Coughin' / Eluide / Killkillkill / Re-Evolution / Puppy Love / Buy The Way

GROPE (DENMARK)
Line-Up: Per Ebdrup (vocals), Tue Madsen (guitar), Jimmy Thorsø (bass), Anders Gyldenøhr (drums)

Founded in 1994, GROPE debuted with the delightfully titled 'What Do Faggots Want?' demo. GROPE featured covers of both METALLICA and SLAYER on the 'Metal Militia' and 'Slatanic Slaughter' tribute albums.

GROPE adventurously covered BJÖRK's 'Army Of Me' for the 'Soul Pieces' EP. This would prove a portent of what was to come as GROPE's 1997 album 'Desert Storm' betrayed Grunge leanings. Sadly bassist Jimmy Thorsø would lose his battle against cancer. By the 2000 effort 'Intercooler', which saw the inclusion of new singer Alex Clausen and bassist Oberst, GROPE had evolved far away from their Death Metal roots into an American influenced Stoner band.

Singles/EPs:
Soul Pieces / Army Of Me / Interlock / Tears Correct, Progress PCD 26 (1995)

Albums:
PRIMATES, Progress RRS 941 (1995)
The Primate / Nothing Ever Ends / Under / Enemy / Fuck / Raw / Parasite / Watch Me Rule / Bleeding / Murder In A Box / 5-6-7-8 / Ignorance / Dead / Blind
THE FURY, Progress PCD 27 (1996)
Manipulated / Soul Pieces / Without Pain / The Day Will Come / Stonesun / Cold Hand / The Choice You Make / Second / Bloodred / Damned / Mørke / Killed Again / Midnight
DESERT STORM, Progress PCD 29 (1997)
Pacified / Trapped In A Bottle / While You Can / Perfect Queen / The Flower / Desert Storm / OK For Now / Dayton Thunder Kings / It's P.R.S. / Song Of Fear / Around / Murmur / Madman's Medicine / In The Name Of Hate / In The Garden Of Eden
INTERCOOLER, Die Hard (2000)

Someone Died In You / Hope For The Best / Freakshow Gallery / Six Feet Under And Far Away / Just Like The Devil / Reverend Jones / Reason To Fear / I Fell For You / Bazar / Busorama / Cupid's Shotgun / This Time Of Year

GROTESQUE (SWEDEN)
Line-Up: Tomas Lindberg (vocals), Alf Svensson (guitar), Kristian "Bullen" Wahlin (guitar), Thomas Eriksson (drums)

A Death Metal band created by ex-ORAL guitarist Alf Svensson, GROTESQUE later evolved into the highly regarded AT THE GATES.
Guitarist Kristian Wahlin joined LIERS IN WAIT. Svensson formed OXIPEGATZ. By 2000 Tomas Lindberg was fronting THE HAUNTED..

Albums:
INCANTATIONS, Dolores DOL004 (1991)
Incantations / Spawn of Azahoth / Nocturnal Blasphemies / Submit To Death / Blood Runs From The Altar
IN THE EMBRACE OF EVIL, Black Sun BS007 (1996)
Thirteen Bells Of Doom / Blood Runs From The Altar / Submit To Death / Fall Into Decay / Seven Gates / Angels Blood / Nocturnal Blasphemies / Spawn Of Azathoth / Incantation / Church Of The Pentagram / Ripped From The Cross

GUIDANCE OF SIN (SWEDEN)
Line-Up: Leini (vocals), Jeppe Lofgren (guitar), Linus Nirbrandt (guitar), L.E. Simnell (bass), Tob Sillman (drums)

Swedish "Death Rollers" founded by guitarists Jeppe Lofgren and Linus Nirbrandt, both formerly with the highly rated A CANOUROUS QUINTET. The act was originally conceived as a side project act with ex-SANGUINARY vocalist Leini and AMON AMARTH and MARDUK drummer Fredrik Andersson. Interest in the groups endeavours following a 1997 demo 'Soul Disparity' prompted a deal with the Mighty Music Label for the album 'Soul Seducer'.
Following this album GUIDANCE OF SIN pulled in erstwhile SANGUINARY bassist L.E. Limnell. Andersson would decamp to concentrate on AMON AMARTH and Tob Sillman duly filled the vacancy.
The 2000 released '6106' album sees a cover of MOTÖRHEAD's 'Killed By Death'.

Singles/EPs:
Acts, Nocturnal Music (2000)

Albums:
SOUL SEDUCER, Mighty Music (1999)
Guided By Sin / Soul Seducer / Desire-Prosecution / Dawn Of The New Religion / Fated… / Goddess Of Lies / Soul Disparity / Turning To Reality / The God Who Didn't Forgive
6106, Mighty Music (2000)
Man's Journey / Don't Let God Come Near / In the Hour of Peril / Nosferatu's Head / Breaking the Circle / Acts / Rock of the 20's / 6106 / The Primeval Myth of a Vampyre / Killed by Death

GUILLOTINE (SWEDEN)

Deliberately Germanic 80's style Death-Thrash from the Spider Erikkson led GUILLOTINE.

Albums:
UNDER THE GUILLOTINE, Necropolis NR020 (1997)
Executioner / Grave Desecrator / Leprosy / Guillotine / Death Penalty / Crucifixion / Night Stalker / Tormentor / Total Mayhem / Violence

GURD (SWITZERLAND)
Line-Up: V.O. Pulver (vocals / guitar), Tommy B. (guitar), Marek (bass), Tobias Roth (drums)

GURD were formed in January 1994 by ex-POLTERGEIST guitarist V.O. Pulver. Guitarist Tommy B. is ex-EROTIC JESUS.
GURD have toured as support to KREATOR, CORONER, SODOM, PRO-PAIN and BODY COUNT. Their work ethic paid off and by 1996 the band had signed to Century Media releasing third album 'D-Fect' and a remix offering the following year.
Further extensive touring ensued with the likes of STUCK MOJO, PRO-PAIN and LIFE OF AGONY prior to the recording of 1998's 'Down The Drain' with producer Tomas Skogsberg. Further dates followed upon its release with PRO-PAIN.
GURD underwent a drastic overhaul though with three quarters of the band decamping leaving Pulver alone to carry on the name. He duly reforged GURD pulling in former SWAMP TERRORISTS personnel guitarist Spring and bassist Andrej. New face behind the drumkit for the 2000 album 'Bedlam' was ex-JERK man Tschibu.

Albums:
GURD, C&C CC 6243 (1995)
Get Up / You Won't Make It / I.O.U.
Nothing / Enough / The Mant (Groovy) /
Scum / Cut It Out / The Way You Want /
Distinction / Gone So Far / Ceasefire /
Don't Ask Me
ADDICTED, Major CC035 (1995)
HxHxHx / Learn / Chill Out / Feel The
Silence / Ghost Dance / Face To Face /
Red House / Give In / Down And Out /
Too Vicious / Higher
D-FECT, Century Media 77150-2 (1996)
What Do You Live For / No Sleep /
We've Been Told / Fever Of Pain /
Bullshit / Human Existence / Go Go Go /
Look Away / This Place / Read My Lips /
Think / Heaven Sent / Lose Myself
D-FECT-THE REMIXES, Century Media
77176-2 (1997)
Get Up (Caveman remix) / Heaven Sent
(stop Denying edit) / Go Go Go (Vibe
Master remix) / We've Been Told (Powder
Rose remix) / Bullshit (Splatter remix) /
Heaven Sent (Sweet remix) / Insane / 102
DOWN THE DRAIN, Century Media CD
77203-2 (1998)
Down The Drain / Head Full Of Shit /
Dead Or Alive / Bow My Head / I
Remember / My Future / T.R.T.L. / Time
To Forget / Caught / Help Me / Survive /
Skin Up!!
BEDLAM, Century Media (2000)
Masterplan / Big Shot / Bedlam /
Stardust / Always / Rule The Pit /
V.U.L.T. / Take My Hand / Golden Age /
Shed No Tears / Defiance / We Will
resist / War Machine

GUT (GERMANY)
Line-Up: Oliver (vocals), Joe (guitar),
Michael (bass), Tim (drums)

GUT is the less than politically correct
side project of PYOGENESIS members
guitarist Joe and drummer Tim.

Singles/EPs:
Split, Regurgitated Semen RSR009
(1994) (7" split single with BRAIN
DAMAGE)
Split, Regurgitated Semen RSR010
(1994) (7" split single with RETALIATION)

Albums:
ODOUR OF TORTURE, Regurgitated
Semen RSR 013 (1995)
Wound Fuck / Perpetual Sperm Injection
/ Cuntshredder / The Taboo Room / Eat
My Cum (Choke On Me) / Consequence /
Dildo Delirium / Cripple Bitch / Triple

Penetration / Dissected Homo-Foreskin /
Sperm Poisoning / Grotesque
Deformities / Cunt Catheter / Twat
Amputation / Disgusting Corpse
Dissection / Bodyscraper / Vomitorium
Of Maggot Infested Cunts / Drastic
Dissection / I'll Make You Dead / Lips -
The Passage To Pleasure / She Died
With Her Legs Spread / Faggot Colony /
Revel In Cunt Slime / Hot Power Shower -
Raping Pregnant Leather Whores /
Embalmed In Pig Sperm / Cock Contest
/ Addicted To Animal Sex / Gorgamatron
/ Schwanlose Amphibie / Cavier Dinner /
Art Of Butchery / Dykeslayer / Anal
Sushi / Diarrhea Shower / Defaced Slut /
Afterburner / Knocked Out Bitch /
Confessions Of A Necrophile / Odour Of
Torture
THE SINGLES COLLECTION, Deliria
Noise Outfitters (2000)
Art Of Butchery / Mawkish: Undead &
Pulverized Vagina Putrefaction In
Dehydrawlic Sperm Soup /
Consequence (Ulcerous Phlegm) /
Wound Fuck / Corroded In Bestialized &
Gorefying Wormjizz / They Squeal Like
Pigs / Intro: Women In Decay /
Grotesque Deformities / Disgusting
Corpse Dissection / Bizarre Reality Of
Beastiality / Hyperintestinal Vulva
Desecration / I'll Make You Dead 1/
Septic Oral Sex / Drastic Mutilation /
Confessions Of A Necrophile / Spermatic
Suffocation / Sperminator / Intestinal
Cumshot / Dead Girls Don't Say No /
Vagina Berserker / Pussy Grinder / Anal
Sushi / Revel In Cunt Slime / Fistful Of
Sperm / Inverted Pussyfix / Cripple Bitch
/ Atomic Nuclear Desolation

GWAR (Richmond, VA, USA)
Line-Up: Oderus Urungus (vocals),
Slymenstra Hymen (vocals), Balsac, The
Jaws Of Death (guitar), Flattus Maximus
(guitar), Beefcake The Mighty (bass),
Nippleus Erectus (drums)

GWAR burst onto the Metal scene
flaunting some of the most outrageous
stage costumes ever graced by a Rock
band. Offering a heady brew of Sci Fi and
a fixation with porn GWAR succeeded in
shocking the establishment from the off
and the high quality theatrics soon drew
in legions of supporters.
The band claimed a lineage millions of
years in antiquity as a group of rebel
space pirates titled 'Scumdogs Of The
Universe'. Supposedly banished to planet
earth GWAR claimed responsibility for
the extinction of the dinosaurs, the

emergence of mankind and the destruction of Atlantis. For these heinous deeds they were imprisoned in Antarctica until their escape in time for debut album 'Hell-O' in 1989.

The outlandish costumes hid the alter ego personas of vocalist Dave Brockie ('Oderus Urungus'), guitarist Mike Derks ('Balsac, The Jaws Of Death'), guitarist Zack Blair ('Flattus Maximus') and bassist Casey Orr ('Beefcake The Mighty').

Needless to say their origins lay not in Antarctica but Richmond, Virginia. Pre GWAR Brockie had been a member of the Hardcore trio DEATH PIGGY which had released three single throughout the 80's 'Love War', 'Death Rules The Fairway' and 'R45'. In 1985 Brockie and DEATH PIGGY drummer Sean Sumner teamed up with director Hunter Jackson who was planning a movie entitled 'Scumdogs Of The Universe'. The costumes for this intended movie would provide the catalyst for the first GWAR incarnation. For a while both Brockie and Sumner divided their duties between DEATH PIGGY and GWAR but Sumner's lifestyle would finally catch up with him. The drummer was imprisoned for attempted murder.

In 1995 the full membership of GWAR released an album 'You Have The Right To Remain Silent' under their real names billing themselves as the X-COPS. Touring to promote the album without revealing their identities as the GWAR characters proved a struggle. Tragically the year after original GWAR drummer Sean Sumner would take his own life.

Another former GWAR drummer Jim Thompson founded BIO RITMO for a Spanish language Metal album. For their 2000 American dates GWAR redrafted 'The Sexecutioner' and 'Sleazy P. Martini'. The dates were supported by AMEN and LAMB OF GOD.

The GWAR 2000 album 'Slave Gang Singles' was only issued to the bands fan club members.

In 2001 Dave Brockie emerged with his DBX (THE DAVE BROCKIE EXPERIENCE) project album 'Diarrhea Of A Madman'. Also featured in DBX were GWAR men guitarist Mike Derks and drummer Dave Roberts ('Jizmak Da Jusha'). Having first revealed the identity of the band to the media in order to avoid the previous calamity with their X-COPS venture DBX would tour America. Also on the billing for these shows was RAWG - actually the full compliment of GWAR sans costumes.

Singles/EPs:

The Road Behind / Overture In N Minor / Krak Down / Voodoo Summoning / Captain Crunch / Have You Seen Me?, Metal Balde (1994) ('The Road Behind' EP)

Albums:

HELL-O, Shimmy Disc 010 (1989)
Time For Death / AEIOU / Americanised / I'm In Love (With A Dead Dog) / Slütman City / World O Filth/ War Toy / Captain Crünch / Püre As The Arctic Snow / Je M'Appelle J Cöusteaü / GWAR Theme / Bone Meal / Öllie North / Techno's Song / U Ain't Shit / Rock & Roll Pärty Töwn
SCUMDOGS OF THE UNIVERSE, Master MASCD 001 (1990)
The Salamaniser / Maggots / Sick Of You / Slaughterama / Kingqueen / Horror Of Yig / Vlad The Impaler / Black And Huge / Love Surgery / Sexecutioner
AMERICA MUST BE DESTROYED, Metal Blade ZORRO 037 (1991)
Ham On The Bone / Crack In The Egg / Gor-Gor / Have You Seen Me? / The Morality Squad / America Must Be Destroyed / Gilded Lily / Poor Ole Tom / Rock 'N' Roll Never Felt So Good / Blimey / The Road Behind / Pussy Planet
THE ROAD BEHIND, Metal Blade 3984-17004-2 (1992)
The Road Behind / Overture In N Minor / Krakdown / Voodoo Summoning / Captain Crunch / Have You Seen Me? / SFW
THIS TOILET EARTH, Metal Blade ZORRO 63 (1994)
Saddam A Go-Go / Penis I See / Cat Steel / Jack The World / Sonderkommando / Bad Bad Men / Pepperoni / The Insidious Soliloquy Of Skulhedface / B.D.F. / Fight / The Issue Of Tissue (Spacecake) / Pocket Pool / Slap U around / Krak Down / Filthy Flow / The Obliteration Of Flab Quarv 7
RAGNORAK, Metal Blade 3984-17001-2 (1995)
Meat Sandwich / The New Plague / Whargoul / Rag Na Rock / Dirty, Filthy / Stalin's Organs / Knife In Her Guts / Think You Outta Know This / Martyr Dumb / Nudged / Fire in The Loins / Surf Of Syn / Crush Kill Destroy / No One But The Brave
CARNIVAL OF CHAOS, Metal Blade 3984-14125-2(1997)
Penguin Attack / Let's Blame The Lightman / First Rule Is / Sammy / Endless Apocalypse / Billy Bad Ass / Hate Love Songs / Letter From The Scallop Boat / Pre-School Prostitute / If

I Could Be That / In Her Fear / Back To
Iraq / I Stuck On My Thumb / The
Private Pain Of Techno Destructo /
Gonna Kill U / Sex Cow / Antarctican
Drinking Song / Don't Need A Man
WE KILL EVERYTHING, Metal Blade
(1999)
Babyraper / Fish Fuck / The Performer /
A Short History of the End of the World
Escape from the Moose Lodge / Tune
from Da Moon / Jiggle the Handle / Nitro
Burnin' Funny Bong / Jagermonsta / My
Girlie Ways / The Master has a Butt / We
Kill Everything / Child / Penile Drip /
Mary Anne / Friend / Fuckin' an Animal
SLAVE GANG SINGLES, Slave Pit
(2000)
Drop Drawers / Don's Bong Is Gone /
The Ballad Of Vincent Bologlioni / Asian
People / Mexican Prick Fish / The
Needle / B-Day Boy / Every Little Thing
She Do / Masturbate / White Boy Can't
Dance / Stuck With Us Sucka / GWAR
Babies Cartoon Theme / Flesh Column
Battle I, II, III & IV / My Truck, My Dog
And Prison

HADEZ (PERU)
Line-Up: Ron King (vocals),
John Agressor (guitar),
Walter Crucifer (guitar),
Frank Silent (bass),
O.A.D.M. (drums)

Peruvian Black Death Metal outfit
HADEZ, founded in 1989, debuted with
the 'Extreme Badness On The World'
demo.

Albums:
AQUELAREE, Brutal (1996)
IF YOU DIE A THOUSAND TIMES,
Conquistador (199-)

HAEMORRHAGE (SPAIN)

Spain's HAEMORRHAGE are noted not
only for the ferocity of their unique brand
of Goregrind but their stomach churning
single and album covers. Indeed, the
1999 split single with Czech act
INGROWING depicts a truly horrendous
photograph of a young child mauled by a
dog. Debuted with the 'Grotesque
Embryopathology' demo and have also
issued a split promo CD on Morbid
Records with CHRIST DENIED in
addition to 1995's 'Emetic Cult' album.
The 2000 album 'Loathesongs' includes
many cover versions, not only of the
expected kind with renditions tracks by
CARCASS, DEFECATION, ENTOMBED,
REGURGITATE, IMPALED NAZARENE,
IMPETIGO and SUICIDAL TENDENCIES
of but also a take on UFO's 'Doctor
Doctor'.
HAEMORRHAGE donated a version of
'Staph Terrorist' to the Razorback
IMPETIGO tribute album 'Wizards Of
Gore'.
The 2001 album 'Scalpel, Scissors And
Other Forensic Instruments', on the
Czech Copremesis label, collated early
HAEMORRHAGE material including
cover versions of KORTATU's 'Zu
Atrapatu Artek' and GENERAL
SURGERY's 'Slithering Of The Ulcerous
Facial Tissue'.
Guitarist Lucima was previously a
member of AVULSED.

Singles/EPs:
Grotesque Embryopathology /
Fermented Post Mortem Disgorgement /
Cadaveric Metamorphose / Anatomized /
Via Anal Introspection, Morbid Single
Productions MSP 03 (1994) ('Obnoxious'
7" split single with CHRIST DENIED)

Decom-Poser / Malignant Cancroid
Formation / Excavating The Iliac Fossa,
(1997) (7" split single with DAMNABLE)
Enshrouded In Putilage / Surgery For
The Dead / Slithering Maceration Of
Ulcerous Facial Tissue, Morbid (1998)
('Surgery For The Dead' 7" split single
with GROINCHURN)
**The Sickening Aroma Of A Rectal
Carcinoma** / Cirrhoetic Liver Distillation /
Worm Infested Cavities / Zu Atrapatu
Artek, Upground (1998) (7" split single
with DENAK)
Putrefaction (I Still Remind) /
Anatomized / Rectovaginal Tissue,
Copremesis (1999) (7" split single with
INGROWING)

Albums:
EMETIC CULT, Steamhammer SPV 84-
12482 (1995)
Necromantic / Uncontrollable Proliferation
Of Neoplasm / Decrepit Dejection /
Dilacerate The Sweet Diabetic Diabolism
/ Deranged For Loathsome / Excavating
The Iliac Fossa / Grotesque
Embryopathology / Intravenous
Molestation Of Obstructionist Arteries (O-
Pus) / Via Anal Inspection / Fermented
Post Mortem Disgorgement / Cadaveric
Metamorphose / Anatomised / Pernicious
Dyseptic Inoculation / Foetal Mincer /
Expectorating Pulmonary Mucu-purulence
GRUME, Morbid (1997)
Incinerator Of Cadaveric Leftovers /
Exquisite Eschatology / Torrentlike
Eventeration / Dissect, Exhume,
Devour… / Putrescent Necromorphism /
Cartilageous Pulped Offals / Decom-
Posers / Fragments (Anatomical Blues) /
In Nephritic Blue / Ectopic Eye /
Intravenous Molestation Of
Obstructionist Arteries (O-Pus II) /
Rectovaginal Fistula / Formaldehyde /
Far Beyond The Forensic Patholgy
LOATHE SONGS, Morbid (2000)
Intro - Megaton / Vestige Of The Earthly
Remains / Pyosfied (Rotten To The
Core) / Premature Autopsy / Disgorging
Fetus / Oozing Molten Gristle / Dear
Uncle Creepy / Fascist Pig / M.A.D. /
Satanic Masowhore / Doctor Doctor
**SCALPEL, SCISSORS AND OTHER
FORENSIC INSTRUMENTS**,
Copremesis (2001)
Decom-Poser / Fragments (Anatomical
Relics) / Dissect, Exhume, Devour,… /
Torrent Like Eventeration / Malignant
Canceroid Formation / Intravenous
Molestation / Excavating The Iliac Fossa
/ Uncontrollable Proliferation Of
Neoplasm / Rectovaginal Fistula /

Enshrouded In Putrilage / Surgery For The Dead / Slithering Maceration Of Ulcerous Facial Tissue / The Sickening Aroma Of A Rectal Carcinoma / Cirrhoetic Liver Distillation / Worm Infested Cavities / Zu Atrapatu Artek / Extreme Ulceration

HAGGARD (GERMANY)
Line-Up: Asis Nasseri (vocals / guitar), Markus Reisinger (vocals / guitar), Taki Saile (vocals / piano), Andreas Nad (bass), Vera Hoffman (violin), Katherina Quast (cello), Luz Marsen (drums)

HAGGARD were founded in late 1991 and released their first demo, 'Introduction', the following year; the band touring heavily supporting the likes of DEICIDE, BIOHAZARD, AGRESSOR, ANATHEMA and PYOGENESIS.
1993 saw HAGGARD's first self financed mini album 'Progressive' and in 1994 they toured Europe as support to AMORPHIS and DESULTORY.
In 1995 the group issued the 'Once… Upon A December's Dawn' promo tape touring with Danes ILLDISPOSED. HAGGARD took a line up roster out on the road comprising of 16 people.
The follow up album 'And Thou Shalt Trust… The Seer'. An ambitious affair with German, English and Latin lyrics atop a heady mix of Metal. Classical and mediaeval music.
HAGGARD toured alongside RAGE in 1997.

Albums:
PROGRESSIVE, Progressive (1993)
Charity Absurd / Mind Mutilation / Incapsuled / Progressive / Daddy Was Her First Man
ONCE… UPON A DECEMBER'S DAWN, Progressive (1995) (Cassette release)
Perpetual Motions / The Tragedy / Afterlife / The Lost Forgiveness / Circle Of Dreams
AND THOU SHALT TRUST… THE SEER, Serenades SR011 (1997)
Chapter 1: The Day As Heaven Wept / Chapter 2: Origin Of A Crystal Soul / Chapter 3: In A Pale Moon's Shadow / Chapter 4: De La Morte Noire / Chapter 5: Lost (Robin's song) / Chapter 6: A Midnight Gathering
AWAKEN THE CENTURIES, Drakkar (2000)

HARMONY (SWEDEN)
Line-Up: Pehr (vocals / bass), Peter (guitar), Kjell (drums)

This Swedish Death Metal trio became TORMENT after releasing a split EP with SERENADE and went on to release a full length album through We Bite Records.

Singles/EPs:
Cold Atmosphere / The Radiance From A Star / The Lonely Kingdom / Conjuration / Mountains Of Frost / Mysterious, Arctic Serenades SERE 008 (1995) ('The Radiance From A Star' EP, Split CD with SERENADE)

HARMONY DIES (GERMANY)
Line-Up: Martin Pomp (vocals / bass), Mike Hoffman (guitar), Kai Mertens (guitar), Robert Kotlarski (drums)

A Death Metal act from Berlin.

Singles/EPs:
Decision For War / Slaughtered / Eternal Cycle / Like Yourself / Where The Dead Are, Harmony Dies (1996) ('Slaughtered' EP)

HATE ETERNAL (USA)
Line-Up: Erik Rutan (vocals / guitar), Alex Webster (bass), Tim Yeung (drums)

HATE ETERNAL, alongside ALAS, is one of the two bands led by MORBID ANGEL and ex-RIPPING CORPSE guitarist Erik Rutan and CANNIBAL CORPSE bassist Alex Webster
For recording of the 'Conquering The Throne' album HATE ETERNAL pulled in ex-INTERCINE bassist Jared Anderson and SUFFOCATION's guitarist Doug Cerrito.
Rutan still assists MORBID ANGEL as live guitarist and is a noted producer, having handled Brazilian act KRISIUN's 2000 album.
HATE ETERNAL toured as support to CANNIBAL CORPSE and DETHRONED. The band's latest line up including former MALEVOLENT CREATION drummer Derek Roddy.
Rutan also operates a Symphonic female-fronted Metal project titled ALAS.

Albums:
CONQUERING THE THRONE, (1999)
Praise Of The Almighty / Dogma Condemned / Catacombs / Nailed To Obscurity / By His Own Decree / The

Creed Of Chaotic Divinity / Dethroned / Sacrilege Of Hate / Spiritual Holocaust / Darkness By Oath / Saturated By Dejection

HATE OVER GROWN (PORTUGAL)
Line-Up: Tiago Contreiras (vocals), Marco Farröpo (guitar), Joäo Paulo Dias (bass), Rui Freire (drums)

A Portuguese Industrial Death Metal band.

<u>Albums:</u>
SEED, Musica Alternativa MA 061 (1995)
Crapload / Snail / Down / Lame Short-Haired Muthfu Of Lies / Nothing / Factory Tongue / Bend / Too Damn Brief / Fillin' The Blanks / This Song Hurts / Seed

HATEPLOW (USA)
Line-Up: Kyle Symon (vocals), Phil Fasciana (guitar), Rob Barrett (guitar), Julian Hollowell (bass), Dave Culross (drums)

HATEPLOW, initially convened as an amateur studio project, feature MALEVOLENT CREATION guitarists Rob Barrett and Phil Fasciana. Barrett is also an erstwhile member of CANNIBAL CORPSE.
HATEPLOW was first assembled with drummer Larry Hawke in 1994. With the project becoming a more serious venture ex SICKNESS vocalist Kyle Symon and former REVENANT bassist Tim Scott were inducted to make up the numbers as a deal was scored with Pavement Records.
However, just before recording of the debut album 'Everybody Dies' Hawke was arrested and sentenced to a lengthy jail sentence. Thankfully for the band Hawke was able to lay down his drum tracks before being incarcerated. Tragedy would strike later though as Hawke, trying to save the life of his pet dog, died in a fire at his home in May of 1997.
Former MALEVOLENT CREATION and SUFFOCATION man Dave Culross would take the drummers position for the second album 'The Only Law Is Survival'. The bass position would also undergo a change with the inclusion of Doug Humlack.
Just prior to a February 2001 European jaunt alongside IN AETURNUM and MALEVOLENT CREATION Humlack backed out. Julian Hollowell, a.k.a. Xaphan - guitarist with Black Metal

merchants KULT OV AZAZEL, would fill in on four string duties.

<u>Albums:</u>
EVERYBODY DIES, Pavement Music (1998)
Everybody Dies / Stalker / Prison Bitch / $20 Blow Job / Challenged / The Gift Giver / Crackdown / In The Ditch / Ass To Mouth Resuscitation / Compound / Ante Up / Anally Annie / Denial / Born With Both - Sunshine Of Your Love - Pepe Lopez Song
THE ONLY LAW IS SURVIVAL, Pavement Music (2000)
The Only Law Is Survival / Shattered By Disease / F.T.M. / Emotional Catastrophe / Should I Care? / Outcast / Addicted To Porn / Traitor / Without Weapons / Payback / Incarcerated (Intent To Sell) / Random Acts Of Violence / Resurgence Of Hate

HATE SQUAD (GERMANY)
Line-Up: Burkhard Schmidt (vocals), Mark Künnemann (guitar), Tim Baurmeister (bass), Helge Dolgener (drums)

Formed in 1993 HATE SQUAD, a band displaying some Hardcore and Death Metal influences to their Thrash style, attracted the attention of G.U.N. Records with their 'Theater Of Hate' demo, leading to a deal and the recording of the '94 debut album of the same title.
Ex-SARGANT FURY and ZENITH bassist Bauke De Groot joined the group after the record hit the stores in order that Tim Baurmeister could concentrate on guitar. His new axe partner Mark Künnemann would depart after second album 'I.Q. Zero' and was replaced by Markus Fenske for a tour with KREATOR. 1995's 'Sub Zero' album proved to be a collection of remixed tracks lent new life by artists such as ATARI TEENAGE RIOT, DIE KRUPPS, T.A.S.S. and GIGANTOR.
Following the release of 'Sub-Zero' both Bauermeister and De Groot quit (the former joining RYKERS); the band only replacing De Groot with former HEATHEN and GRIP INC. man Jason Vie Brooks in order to begin work on a proper third album.
Vie Brooks formed part of the 2000 HEATHEN reunion.

<u>Singles/EPs:</u>
Not My God / Terror / March Or Die

(Stormtroopers Of Death Medley): A) March Of The Stormtroopers Of Death / B) United Forces / C) Freddy Krüger / D) The Ballad Of Jimi Hendrix, G.U.N. GUN 076 BMG 74321 31787-2 (1995) (Promotion release)

Albums:
THEATER OF HATE, G.U.N. GUN 049 BMG 74321 24672-2 (1994)
Cause And Effect / Self-Defence (Is No Offense) / Love-Hate / Theater Of Hate / Perverse Insanity / Bastards / Mindloss / Condemned To Die / Hardness Of Life / Free At Last
I.Q. ZERO, G.U.N. GUN 075 BMG 74321 31447-2 (1995)
Not My God / BDD / My Truth / IQ Zero / Dishonesty / Crucified / Different From You / Terror / Respect
SUB-ZERO, G.U.N. GUN 096 BMG 74321 37580-2 (1995)
Not My God (Die Krupps Remix) / BDD (The Speed Remix) / IQ Zero (TASS Remix) / Different From You (Biochip C Remix) / Every Second Counts (Gigantor Remix) / Not My God (Alec Empire Remix) / Every Second Counts
PZYCO!, G.U.N. GUN 129 BMG 74321 43582-2 (1997)
Who Dares Wins / Freedom Speaks / Mission Done / Psyco! / Synthetic Twins / Just A Dream / Change / Get Loaded / The Senseless Fall / B.T.C. 97

THE HAUNTED (SWEDEN)
Line-Up: Marco Aro (vocals), Jensen (guitar), Anders Bjorler (guitar), Jonas Bjorler (bass), Per Moller Jensen (drums)

A Death / Thrash act with strong Black Metal links. THE HAUNTED was founded by former SÉANCE guitarist Jensen during the summer of 1996 bringing in erstwhile INFESTATION, AT THE GATES and TERROR guitarist Anders Bjorler together with drummer Adrian Erlandsson. THE HAUNTED also drafted former DISSECTION and CARDINAL SIN man John Zweetsloot on bass. Zweetsloot's tenure would be brief and another ex AT THE GATES man Jonas Bjorler would take his place.
The band attempted to lure in a lead vocalist and discussions were held with Toxine of SATANIC SLAUGHTER and WITCHERY, and Rogga of MERCILESS. Ultimately it would be Peter Dolving of MARY BEATS JANE that landed the job.
During 1997 Erlandsson created the side project HYPERHUG. Within time he would decamp from THE HAUNTED to concentrate on this act full time. THE HAUNTED attempted to fill the drum position with DISSECTION and OPTHALAMIA man Ole Öhman. Fate intervened when HYPERHUG's singer damaged his hearing curtailing the group. Erlandsson rejoined his former colleagues.
A deal was soon struck with Earache Records and THE HAUNTED undertook touring in Europe with NAPALM DEATH. Shortly after Dolving quit to found ZEN MONKEY. His replacement was FACEDOWN's Marco Aro. With this new line up the band toured the European festival circuit in 1999.
THE HAUNTED was offered the support slot to TESTAMENT's American dates the same year but in mid rehearsal for these shows Erlandsson quit to join premier British Black Metal band CRADLE OF FILTH. The tour went ahead with Per Moller Jensen of KONKHRA and INVOCATOR fame.

Albums:
THE HAUNTED, Earache (1999)
Hate Song / Chasm / In Vein / Undead / Choke Hold / Three Times / Bullet Hole / Now You Know / Shattered / Soul Fracture / Blood Rust / Forensick
THE HAUNTED MADE ME DO IT, Earache (2000)
Dark Intentions / Bury Your Dead / Trespass / Leech / Hollow Ground / Revelation / The World Burns / Human Debris / Silencer / Under The Surface / Victim Iced

HELLHAMMER (SWITZERLAND)
Line-Up: Satanic Slaughter (vocals / guitar), Savage Damage (bass), Bloodhunter (drums)

Formerly known as HAMMERHEAD, this bizarre and primitive extreme Metal outfit was founded in 1982.
Previous to HAMMERHEAD frontman Thomas Gabriel Fischer and bassist Steve had been involved with various fledgling acts emulating their NWoBHM heroes VENOM.
During the August of 1982 Fischer, transferring from bass to guitar, was now fronting a trio of Priestly and drummer Jörg Neubart. Inspired apparently by Newcastle NWoBHM band RAVEN and their Gallagher brothers team Fischer and Priestly adopted the joint stage surnames of 'Warrior'. Neubart became 'Bruce Day'.

Their debut demo, 'Triumph Of Death', was widely regarded as one of the worst examples of a Heavy Metal band ever! 'Metal Forces' magazine editor Bernard Doe in particular cited it as the most appalling thing he had ever heard. History however would dictate that HELLHAMMER would later be recognized as one of the root catalysts of the Black Metal genre.

Although in later years band members have admitted their knowledge of music was basic to say the least when the HELLHAMMER recordings were made nevertheless the band were in possession of an artistic vision which would undoubtedly shape the Metal scene over many years.

In 1983 HELLHAMMER enrolled bass player Martin Eric Ain and drummer Stephen Priestly from SCHIZO. However, invited to submit a fresh demo to Berlin's Noise Records HELLHAMMER very nearly split as Ain felt he did not have the necessary talent to go through with the session!

Still, positive or negative press encouraged Noise to sign the band and the Berlin based label released the 'Apocalyptic Raids' EP which had no details as to what RPM the record should be played at; sounding just as strange at 33RPM as it did at 45!

Metal Blade Records released the EP in America with an extra two tracks.

HELLHAMMER mainman 'Satanic Slaughter' later swopped identities to become Tom G. Warrior and started the avant garde Metal legends CELTIC FROST in May of 1984 retaining the deal with Noise. CELTIC FROST issued a stream of critically praised outings before fizzling out.

Still an influence in some circles over ten years later, Sweden's ABYSS covered the HELLHAMMER track 'Massacra' on their 1995 album 'The Other Side'.

Warrior forged a new project in the late 90's billed as APOLLYON SUN.

Singles/EPs:
The Third Of The Storms (Evoked Damnation) / Massacra / Triumph Of Death / Horus / Agressor, Noise N008 50-1668 (1984) ('Apocolyptic Raids' EP)

HEMDALE (OH, USA)

HEMDALE's 1996 split album shared with EXHUMED included a cover of 'Curse The Gods' by German Thrashers

DESTRUCTION.

Albums:
IN THE NAME OF GORE, Visceral Productions (1996) (Split album with EXHUMED)
Delicious Gory Fun / Pus Filled Carcass / Overflow / Bathing In Mucus And Bile / Tasty Hemorrhoidal Tissue / Brutally Mauled Human Remains / Succulent Torso Crescendo / It Burns… And It Just Plain Smells Bad / Are You Pornophoric / Demented Surgical Incest / Artificial Masturbation / Licking Mental Patients Cum Off The Sheets / Curse The Gods

HEMLOCK (Brooklyn, NY, USA)

Black Metal act that include former ANTHRAX, NUCLEAR ASSAULT and BRUTAL TRUTH bassist Dan Lilker. Besides HEMLOCK Lilker still operates in STORMTROOPERS OF DEATH. HEMLOCK issued a split EP in 1997 shared with BLACK ARMY JACKET.

Singles/EPs:
Split, Sound Views (1997) (Split EP with BLACK ARMY JACKET)

Albums:
CRUSH THE RACE OF GOD, Head Not Found (1997)
FUNERAL MASK, Head Not Found (1997)
Frozen Tears / Way Of The Wolf / Hemlock / Black Dawn / October Sunrise / Necrofuck / Loyal To Evil / Reign Of Death / Funeral Mask
LUST FOR FIRE, Full Moon Productions (1998)

HERESIARH (LATVIA)
Line-Up: Rasa (vocals), Morguelder Dragonseye (vocals / keyboards), Hater, Mourn Majesty, Burial Jester, Kalutun (drums)

HERESIAH is a union of noted Latvian outfits ALFHEIM and DARK REIGN. The band was forged when DARK REIGN members Burial Jester, Mourn Majesty and drummer Kaludun joined forces with ALFHEIM refugees Hater and Morguelder Dragonseye. The whole project is fronted by the female soprano vocals of Rasa of NEGLECTED FIELDS. Drummer Kalutun also performs as a member of SKYFORGER and BLIZZARD.

Albums:
MYTHICAL BEASTS AND MEDIEVAL WARFARE, Demolition DEMCD 103 (2000)
All Hail The Wyverns / Horns Of War / Dragons Domain / The Crownless King / The Cruel Bard / Saga Of The Shield Maid- Part I: The Old Forest (Of Lament), Part II: Of Her Triumph / Higher Than Hills / Trollstorm / Elfwine / Wolfghosts (In Winter)

HETSHEADS (SWEDEN)
Line-Up: Anders Strokirk (vocals / guitar), Stabel (guitar), Fredda (bass), Freimann (drums)

HETSHEADS are now known as BLACKSHINE. Vocalist Anders Strokirk also plays with NECROPHOBIC.

Albums:
WE HAIL THE POSSESSED, Repulse (1995)
Dissolution By Catatonia / Remonstrating The Preserver / Paganization / Brutal Exhordation / Cast In Silver / Phlebotomize (Fade Away In Silence) / When The Time Has Come / For His Sake

HEXECUTION (UK)

In early 1999 vocalist Skitzo gave up singing to concentrate on bass duties.

Singles/EPs:
Beyond All Evil EP, Copro (1998)

HIDEOUS MANGLEUS
(Allenport, PA, USA)
Line-Up: Sam Biles (vocals), Feev (guitar), Joel Bonde (bass), Curt Bonde (drums)

The obviously Death Metal act HIDEOUS MANGLEUS debuted with the delightfully titled 1990 demo 'All Your Friends Are Dead'. A 7" single 'We Live…You Sleep' followed on the French Thrash label before another outing for the German Ecocentric concern.
Ecocentric would also issue the debut album which once more used the title 'All Your Friends Are Dead'. However, due to distributor concern the record was retitled 'Hideous Heads' for later pressings.
HIDEOUS MANGLEUS reformed in 2000 signing to the Spanish Repulse label.

Singles/EPs:
We Live… You Sleep, Thrash (1991) (7" single)
Unearthing Grandma's Grave, Ecocentric (1992) (7" single)

Albums:
ALL YOUR FRIENDS ARE DEAD, Ecocentric (1993)
Play Dumb / Gnawing At Your Guts / Experiments (In The Morgue) / Self Devourment / Body Bag / Degeneration / Mutated / Deadtime / Burning Children / Malignant Ignorance / Allergic / Cranial Disrupture / Nutra Death / Technological Abortion / Mutiny /Sickening / Support The Core / Reforming (Cold Limbs) / Child Funeral / Eldraphobic / Retarded / Teenage Leper / Infravision / Naïve World / Question Your Motives / Divine Intervention / Skullfuck / Too Fast For Love / Season Of The Dead

HOLOCAUSTO CANIBAL
(PORTUGAL)

Albums:
GONORREIA VISCERAL, So Die Music (2000)
Vagina Convulsa / Holocausto Canibal / Empalamento / Septicemia Vaginal / Carnificina Psicopata / Gorgasmos… Orgasmicos Espasmos Gore / Faixa Oito

HOMICIDE (GERMANY)
Line-Up: Matarru (vocals), Shocker (guitar), Mentor (guitar), M. (bass), Zarathrusta (drums)

HOMICIDE include DARK BEFORE DAWN guitarist Mentor in the ranks. The band's first drummer Doomhammer was succeeded by Zarathrusta.

Albums:
SLAUGHTERS LEGACY, Undercover (2000)
Intro / Black Crusade / Slaughters Legacy / When Steel Gets Red / Raped By The Cross / Tiefen Der Ewigkiet / Triumph Of Death

HORRIFIED (GREECE)
Line-Up: Gore (vocals), Stavros (guitar), Thanos (bass), Stelios (drums)

A melodic Death Metal band, HORRIFIED's debut album was originally only released on vinyl before being re-issued on CD in 1994 with the two tracks from the single as bonus cuts.

Singles/EPs:
Seperial Dominion / Astral Submersion, (199-) ('The Ancient Whisper Of Wisdom' EP)

Albums:
IN THE GARDEN OF THE UNEARTHLY DELIGHTS, Black Power BPR008 (1991)
The Awakening / Elisaph / Early Dawn Enraged / Crawling Silence / Down At The Valley Of The Great Encounter / Dying Forest / Baptized In Venereal Blood / Poetry Of War / Unbridled God / Dancing Next To Dying Souls

HOUSE OF USHER (SWEDEN)
Line-Up: Jani Ruhala (vocals), Mattias Kenhed (guitar), Martin Larsson (guitar), Stefan Källarsson (bass), Jani Myllärinen (drums)

Singles/EPs:
Revengeance / Rather Black, Obscure Plasma 911002 (1991)

HOUWITSER (HOLLAND)
Line-Up: Arjaan Kampmann (vocals), Theo Van Eekelen (bass), Aad Kloosterwaard (drums)

HOUWITSER is a Death Grind side project from SINISTER's Mike and drummer Aad Kloosterwaard in conjunction with JUDGEMENT DAY's Theo Van Eekelen.
Both Kloosterwaard and Van Eekelen are also members of the reformed THANATOS.

Albums:
DEATH BUT NOT BURIED, Displeased (1999)
Intro / Dead's A Fact / Shredded To Pieces / Terror Legion / Sixtynineher / Monkey In Control / Ravishing Chaos / D.P.W. / Sliced And Diced / War, Blood And Honey / Fistfull Of Vixen / Worlds Parasites / Support Satan / Trip Of Fire / I Shape The Suffering
EMBRACE DAMNATION, Displeased (2000)
Onslaught Of Hate / Feeding On Fools / Embrace Domination / Catenated / Stabbing Overdose / Command Respect / Vile Amputation / Feel The Consequences / Unholy Orgasm / Leeches Come / Consuming Cadavers / Mercifully Mutilated

HYBERNOID (UK)
Line-Up: Dunk Goodenough (vocals), Dave Evans (guitar), Andy Bennett (guitar), Andy J. Bennett (bass), Paul Stansfield (drums), Paula Smith (vocals)

HYBERNOID debuted with the 'Opthaphobia' demo before signing to Displeased Records following a second demo entitled 'Well Of Grief'. This tape was backed up by an ambitious accompanying surreal video and duly landed the band a deal.
The 'Technology' single was only released in America.

Singles/EPs:
Dust In The Wind / Mind / Liberty, Displeased D-00026 (1993)
Technology / Regressions / Akeldama, Psycho Slaughter PS008 (1993)
World Of Ruin / Sear, Displeased D-00036 (1994)

Albums:
THE LAST DAY BEGINS?, Displeased D-00028 (1994)
Revery / Reality Wave / World Of Ruin / Ash In The Sky / Permafrost / Life Fade / Akeldema / Skin / Mind-Liberty
TODAY'S TOMORROW YESTERDAY, Displeased D-00042 (1996)
Dread The Time / Today's Tomorrow Yesterday / Menali / Strive To Convert / Skin III / Akelkama / Dust In The Wind / Mind-Liberty / World Of Ruin / Sear / When Two Lives

HYDRA (JAPAN)

Albums:
EXHIBITION OF MALICE, Obsidean Factory (1999)

HYPNOS (CZECH REPUBLIC)
Line-Up: Bruno (vocals / bass), R.A.D. (guitar), Skull (drums)

Trio HYPNOS are in fact KRABATHOR men vocalist Bruno and drummer Skull. The 2000 album 'In Blood We Trust' sees Mike of IMPALED NAZARENE involved. An accompanying EP saw HYPNOS covering BULLDOZER's 'The Cave'
HYPNOS toured Europe in December 2000 as part of an almighty Death Metal package that included ENSLAVED, MORBID ANGEL, BEHEMOTH, THE CROWN and DYING FETUS.

Singles/EPs:
Infernational / Breeding The Scum / The Cave / In Blood We Trust, Morbid (2000) ('Hypnos' EP)

Albums:
IN BLOOD WE TRUST, Morbid (2000)
Incantation / Burn The Angels Down / Fatal Shrine Of Sky / Infernational / Lovesong / Open The Gates Of Hell / Sacrilegious / Across The Battlefields / Breeding The Scum / In Blood We Trust / After The Carnage (Outro)
XXX, (2001)
Intro / The End Of God / X / Nath And Her Gun / XX / Phantasma Plasma / Mother / XXX / Neverland / XXXX? / Riddle / Mother (Father Edit) / The End Of God (Resurrection mix)

HYPNOSIA (SWEDEN)
Line-Up: Cab Castervall (vocals / guitar),

HYPNOSIA cover POSSESSED's 'My Belief' on their 2000 album 'Extreme Hatred'.

Albums:
EXTREME HATRED, Hammerheart (2000)
Extreme Hatred / Circle Of The Flesh / The Last Remains / Operation Clean Sweep / Comatose / Act Of Lunacy / Gates Of Cirith Ungol / My Belief / Hang 'Em High / Traumatic Suffering

HYPOCRISY (SWEDEN)
Line-up: Masse Broberg (vocals), Peter Tägtren (guitar), Jonas Österberg (guitar), Mikael Hedlund (bass), Lars Szöke (drums)

HYPOCRISY was formed by guitarist Peter Tägtren in October 1991 and were initially known as SEDITIOUS. Both Tägtren and drummer Lars Szöke had previously been members of CONQUEST, an act dating back as far as 1984. Tägtren had returned from America where he had been a member of MALEVOLENT CREATION and MELTDOWN. HYPOCRISY's line-up was augmented by ex-EPITAPH guitarist Jonas Österberg and erstwhile VOTARY vocalist Masse Broberg.
As HYPOCRISY the band soon secured a deal with Germany's Nuclear Blast Records issuing the debut 'Penetralia' album in 1992.
For the second album HYPOCRISY were down to a quartet, with Peter Tägtren

handling guitars. Tour dates included shows with DEICIDE and CANNIBAL CORPSE. However, on tour vocalist Masse Broberg suffered a breakdown, necessitating Tagtren taking over lead vocals. Following the dates HYPOCRISY decided to carry on as a trio releasing the 'Inferior Devotees' mini-album which included the SLAYER cover 'Black Magic'. This track also appeared on the SLAYER tribute compilation album 'Slatanic Slaughter Volume One'.
In 1995 HYPOCRISY toured such far flung places as Mexico and Portugal promoting their 'Fourth Dimension' album.

HYPOCRISY
Photo : Martin Wickler

During 1996, the year in which the band released the 'Maximum Abduction' mini-album (which included a cover of KISS' 'Strange Ways') Tägtren fulfilled duties as stand in guitarist for MARDUK on their European tour as well as working on a solo project PAIN.
Tägtren, Hedlund and Szöke also pursued a side project act THE ABYSS having so far released two albums; 'The Other Side' and 'Summon The Beast'.
As the seventh album, 1997's 'The Final Chapter' saw the light of day, Tägtren announced that this would signal HYPOCRISY's final fling, citing that he wished to concentrate on PAIN. However, this announcement combined with the resulting good reviews granted to 'The

Final Chapter' persuaded Tägtren to change his mind. By now HYPOCRISY had shifted its lyrical content away from the evil from below to the evil from above with increasing alien themes and album imagery.

HYPOCRISY issued their first live album 'Destroys Wacken' followed by another critically acclaimed studio album simply titled 'Hypocrisy'. The man also involved himself in the commercially successful LOCK UP project with NAPALM DEATH bassist Shane Embury and guitarist Jesse Pintado with DIMMU BORGIR drummer Nick Barker. Although the LOCK UP album sold spectacularly well in Germany Tägtgren backed out of the project before live work ensued.

2000 found Tägtren busier than ever with a further PAIN album 'Rebirth' as well as a fresh HYPOCRISY effort 'Into The Abyss'.

Singles/EPs:
Pleasure Of Molestation / Exclamation Of A Necrofag / Necromonicon / Attachment To The Ancestor, Relapse RR 6040 (1993)
Roswell 47 / Carved Up / Request Denied / Strange Ways, Nuclear Blast NB 145 (1996)
('Maximum Abduction' EP)

HYPOCRISY
Photo : Martin Wickler

Albums:
PENETRALIA, Nuclear Blast NB067-2 27361 60552 (1992)
Impotent God / Suffering Souls / Nightmare / Jesus Fall / God Is A ... / Left To Rot / Burn By The Cross / To Escape Is To Die / Take The Throne / Penetralia
OSCULUM OSCENUM, Nuclear Blast NB 080-2 (1993)
Pleasure Of Molestation / Exclamation Of A Necrofag / Osculum Obscenum / Necromonicon / Black Metal / Inferior Devotees / Infant Sacrifices / Attachment To The Ancestor / Althotas
INFERIOR DEVOTEES, Nuclear Blast NA RED6104-2 (1994)
Inferior Devotees / Symbol Of Baphomet / Mental Emotions / God Is A Lie / Black Magic
THE FOURTH DIMENSION, Nuclear Blast NB112-2 / 2736168940 (1995)
Apocalypse / Mind Corruption / Reincarnation / Reborn / Black Forest / Never To Return / Path To Babylon / Slaughtered / Orgy In Blood / The North Wind / T.E.M.P.T. / The Fourth Dimension / The Arrival Of The Demons / The Abyss
ABDUCTED, Nuclear Blast NB133-2/27361 61332 (1996)
The Gathering / Roswell / Killing Art / The Arrival Of The Demons (Part Two) / Buried / Abducted / Paradox / Point Of No Return / When The Candle Fades / Carved Up / Reflections / Slippin' Away / Drained
THE FINAL CHAPTER, Nuclear Blast NB 283-2 (1997)
Inseminated Adoption / A Coming Race / Dominion / Inquire Within / Last Vanguard / Request Denied / Through The Window Of Time / Shamateur / Adjusting The Sun / Lies / Evil Invaders / The Final Chapter
HYPOCRISY DESTROYS WACKEN, Nuclear Blast NB 110493 (1999)
Roswell / Inseminated Adoption / A Coming Race / Apocalypse / Osculum Obscenum / Buried / Let It Rot / The Fourth Dimension / Pleasure Of Molestation / Killing Art / The Final Chapter / Time Warp / Til The End / Fuck U / Beginning Of The End
HYPOCRISY, Nuclear Blast (1999)
Fractured Millenium / Apocalyptic Hybrid / Fusion Programmed Minds / Elastic Inverted Vision / Reversal Reflection / Until The End / Paranormal Mysteries / Time Warp / Disconnect Magnetic Corridors
INTO THE ABYSS, Nuclear Blast NB 529-2 (2000) **64 GERMANY**

203

Legions Descend / Blinded /
Resurrected / Unleash The Beast /
Digital Prophecy / Fire In The Sky / Total
Eclipse / Unfold The Sorrow /
Sodomized / Deathrow (No Regrets)

HYPOCRITE (SWEDEN)
Line-Up: Johan Haller (vocals / bass),
Nicke Åberg (guitar), Henrik Hedborg
(guitar), Peter Nagy (drums)

Stockholm Death Metallers HYPOCRITE
started out life in 1989 under the name of
DARK TERROR.
HYPOCRITE's single is a split effort with
ELECTROCUTION on the Italian Molten
Metal label. Drummer Peter Nagy also
plays for MÖRK GRYNING and
ETERNAL OATH.

Singles/EPs:
Heaven's Tears, Molten Metal
MOLTEN010 (1994) (Split single with
ELECTROCUTION)

Albums:
EDGE OF EXISTENCE, Offworld OW005
(1996)
Vita Dolorosa / Deep Within This Flower
Of Sin / Edge Of Existence / The
Scream... / Voices From The Dark Side /
Heaven's Tears / A Black Wound / When
I'm Gone / Sanctuary Of The Sleeping
God / Welcome To Abaddon / Forsaken
by Christ / Beyond The Edge

ILLDISPOSED (DENMARK)
Line-Up: Bo Summer (vocals), Lasse Bak (guitar), Hans Wagner (guitar), Ronnie Bak (bass), Lars Hold (drums)

Aarhus based ILLDISPOSED date from early 1991 and the group's first demo was titled 'The Winter Of Our Discontempt', which led to a deal with Nuclear Blast Records.

In late 1992 the band contributed the track 'Reversed' to the Progress Red label's 'Fuck You, We're From Denmark' compilation album and toured Europe as support to WARGASM and SINISTER in December 1993.

During 1994 Envoldsen left to join ANGEL ACCELERATOR DEATH and guitarist Martin Gilsted stepped in to replace Hans Wagner who was suffering from alcohol problems. Summer took time out to produce the 'Gummizild' demo for fellow Danes MERCENARY.

In early 1995 drummer Lars Hald took over for a few live shows. The 1995 album 'Submit' saw Rolf Rognvard Hansen taking over the drumstool as Hald teamed up with PANZERCHRIST.

Live shows in Germany to promote the album, noted for guitarist Lasse Bak performing many gigs stark naked, saw ILLDISPOSED playing alongside HAGGARD and DISGUST.

The 1998 effort 'There's Something Rotten...' found Gillsted supplanted by ex roadie Tore Mogensen.

Summer joined PANZERCHRIST for their third album 'Soul Collector'.

The 2000 album 'Retro' was entirely composed of cover versions. Bands honoured included CARCASS, AUTOPSY, DARKTHRONE, VENOM, AC/DC and MOTÖRHEAD.

Albums:
FOUR DEPRESSIVE SEASONS,
Nuclear Blast NB 103 (1994)
Forbidden Summer Poetry / Reversed / Weeping Souls Of Autumn Desires / Life Equals Zero (A Love Song) / Deathwork Orange / The Winter Of Discontempt / Wardance Of The Technocracy / Never Ceasing Melancholic Spring / Inherit The Spring / With The Lost Souls On Our Side
RETURN FROM TOMORROW - ATTITUDES AND LONG TERM ADJUSTMENT OF PATIENTS SURVIVING CARDIAC ARREST,
Nuclear Blast SPV 56- 1416732 (1994)
Depersonalisation / Return From

Tomorrow / On Death And Dying / Darkness Weaves With Many Shades / Impact / Withering Teardrops / Instrumental Outro
HELVEDE - MUSIC DEFINING HATRED 1992-1995. UNRELEASED AND MISSPELLED, Relapse RRS 945 (1995)
A Deathwork Orange (Introsection) / The Winter Of Our Discontempt / A Darkening Age / With The Lost Souls On Our Side / Inherit The Wind / Soulstorm / Teardrops / Darkness Weaves With Many Shades / To be Continued / Withering Teardrops / Instrumental / Die Kingdom
SUBMIT, Progress PCD 21 (1995)
Purity Of Sadness / A Frame Of Mind / Vesuvio / The Hidden Acne / Memories Expanded / Slow Death Factory / Submit / Flogging A Dead Horse / Die Kingdom
THERE'S SOMETHING ROTTEN IN THE STATE OF DENMARK, Serious Entertainment SE013CD (1998)
Psychic Cyclus I-III / Pimp / Near The Gates / We Lie In The Snow / Not A Vision - 1991 / Wake Up Dead / Instrumentally Illdisposed / There's Something Rotten... / Horsens Highway
RETRO, Diehard PCD 41 (2000)

IMMOLATION (New York, NY, USA)
Line-Up: Ross Dolan (vocals / bass), Thomas Wilkinson (guitar), Robert Vigna (guitar), Craig Smilowski (drums)

Anti-Christian Metal band IMMOLATION was created in February of 1988 by frontman Russ Dolan, drummer Neal and two erstwhile RIGOR MORTIS members guitarists Robert Vigna and Thomas Wilkinson. Two demos ensued prior to the 'Dawn Of Possession' album and the recruitment of drummer Craig Smilowski. IMMOLATION would later add former FALLEN CHRIST and DISASSOCIATE drummer Alex Hernandez for the 'Hereinafter' album. Touring saw shows in Europe with CANNIBAL CORPSE.

IMMOLATION toured America in 2000 sharing billing with SIX FEET UNDER. John McEntee deputized for Vigna on later tours. With Vigna returning to action former ANGEL CORPSE man Bill Taylor would take over from Wilkinson in 2001. Touring in Europe during May found IMMOLATION as headliners over DERANGED, DESTROYER 666, DECAPITATED and SOUL DEMISE.

Albums:
DAWN OF POSSESSION, Roadrunner (1991)

IMMOLATION
Photo : Martin Wickler

Intro - Everlasting Fire / Despondent Souls / Dawn Of Possession / Those Left Behind / Internal Decadence / No Forgiveness (Without Bloodshed) / Burial Ground / After My Prayers / Fall In Disease / Immolation
STEPPING ON ANGELS... BEFORE DAWN, Repulse (1995)
Relentless Torment / Holocaust / Rigor Mortis / Warriors Of Doom / Immolation / Dawn Of Possession / Internal Decadence / Burial Ground / Despondent Souls / Infectious Blood / Despondent Souls (1990) / Burial Ground (Live) / Infectious Blood (Live) / Immolation (Live) / Despondent Souls (Live) / Dawn Of Possession (Live)
HEREINAFTER, Metal Blade 3984-14102-2 (1997)
Nailed To Gold / Burn With Jesus / Here In After / I Feel Nothing / Away From God / Towards Earth / Under The Supreme / Christ's Cage
FAILURES FOR GODS, Metal Blade (1999)
Once Ordained / No Jesus, No Beast / Failures For Gods / Unsaved / God Made Filth / Stench Of High Heaven / Your Angel Died / The Devil I Know
CLOSE TO A WORLD BELOW, Metal Blade (2000)
Higher Coward / Father, You're Not A

Father / Furthest From The Truth / Fall From A High Place / Unpardonable Son / Lost Passion / Put My Hand In The Fire / Close To A World Below

IMMORTAL CRINGE
(Denver, CO, USA)
Line-Up: Phil Boller (vocals / guitar), Ken Snook (guitar), Jeff Gleason (bass), Vic Duran (drums)

Albums:
UNDYING FEAR, Demolition DEMCD 109 (2000)
Intro / Diminished / Glass Room / B.C. / Undying Few / Drunken Guy / Mend Your Trend / Aimless / Sea

IMMORTAL DOMINION
(Fort Collins, CO, USA)

Singles/EPs:
Canyon Curse / Animated Adrenaline / Brighter Days / I Won't Kill You / Demon Voices, Immortal Dominion (1996) ('Birth' EP)

Albums:
ENDURE, Immortal Dominion (1999)
Demon Voices / Time To Die / Water Of Life / Hydrotomb / Brighter Days / Metal

Licker / Endure / I Won't Kill You / Piece Of Meat / 1000 lbs Of Glory

IMMORTALIS (GERMANY)

IMMORTALIS' debut album was produced by ex-HOLY MOSES guitarist Andy Classen and featured a cover of VENOM's 'Countess Bathory'.

Albums:
INDICIUM DE MORTUIS, Morbid 08457062 (1991)
Burning Existence / Subordinate Gods / Bleeding Inheritance / Quo Vadis (Everlasting Life) / Indicium De Mortuis / My Requiem / Voices Of Forgotten Souls / Blasphemous Process / Countess Bathory

IMPALED (CA, USA)
Line-Up: Leon Del Muerte (vocals / guitar), Sean McGrath (guitar), Ross Sewage (bass), Raul Varela (drums)

IMPALED feature erstwhile members of EXHUMED. Founded in 1995 by erstwhile INFANTICIDE personnel guitarist Jared Deaver, bassist Ron Dorn and vocalist Jeremy Frye alongside INHUMATION guitarist Sean McGrath and drummer Raul Varela. Almost as soon as the band had gelled Frye decamped suddenly necessitating Deaver and McGrath to assume shared lead vocal duties.
With this line up IMPALED issued the 1997 four track demo 'Septic Vomit'. However, quite alarmingly Deaver would contract throat cancer forcing him to forsake vocal duties. Leon Del Muerte of EXHUMED and INFANTICIDE was enlisted as lead singer for support gigs to SUFFOCATION and DEICIDE.
A second demo ensued with Dorn's position on bass being taken by Tom Persons of Black Metal act ENTHRONED. Bad luck forced its hand once more though as Deaver was injured and Persons decamped back to ENTHRONED. Plugging the gap Del Muerte took over Deaver's guitar role and EXHUMED Ross Sewage was implemented on bass.
This incarnation of IMPALED cut the 'From Here To Colostomy' demo with the track 'Immaculate Defecation' being donated to the Razorback compilation 'Gore Is Your Master'. Other songs from this session would figure on a split 7" single release issued by Italian label

Headfucker Records in union with CEPHALIC CARNAGE.
IMPALED contributed their rendition of 'I Work For The Streetcleaner' to the 2001 Razorback Records IMPETIGO tribute album 'Wizards Of Gore'.

Albums:
THE DEAD SHALL DEAD REMAIN, Death Vomit (2000)
Introduction / Faeces Of Death / Flesh And Blood / Trocar / Spirits Of The Dead / Immaculate Defecation / Faecal Rites / Back To The Grave / All That Rots / Gorenography / Bloodbath / XXX
CHOICE CUTS, Death Vomit DVR010 (2001)

IMPALED NAZARENE (FINLAND)
Line-Up: Sir Mikka Luttinen (vocals / drums), Dr J-Ace (guitar), The Fuck You Man (bass), Mr. ML GD 6th (keyboards)

IMPALED NAZERENE date back to 1990 and have created a unique niche market for themselves in the Death Metal scene. The band lean more towards Punk and have landed themselves in hot water with the Finnish authorities by branding Russians as "Red scum". Bassist 'The fuck you man' is in fact SENTENCED's Taneli Jarva.
The band's inaugural line up comprised of Mika Luttinen on vocals, guitarists Ari Holappa and Mika Pääkkö, bass player Anti Pihkala and drummer Kimmo Luttinen. Both Luttinen brothers were previously members of MUTILATION.
IMPALED NAZARENE's presence was first felt in 1991 when the debut demo emerged titled 'Shemhamforash'. The tape was laid down on a primitive two track and saw the departure of Pihkala in favour of Harri Holonen. In April of 1991 IMPALED NAZARENE put in their first live gig as support to BEHERIT. Further shows ensued as openers to SENTENCED.
The second session 'Taog Eht Fo Htao Eht' quickly followed capitalized on by a festival appearance at the 'Days Of Darkness' event alongside AMORPHIS.
A 7" single 'Goat Perversion' was released by the Italian Nosferatu concern after which both Holappa and Halonen decamped. Undeterred IMPALED NAZARENE gigged for a while as a power trio. New recruit Taneli Jarva is drafted for a second single for French label Osmose Productions pairing 'Sadogoat' with a JOHNNY CASH cover

'Ghost Riders'! However, Pääkkö broke ranks and Jarno Anttila deputizes on guitar. This roll would soon turn into a full time tenure.

The debut full length album 'Tol Cormpt Norz Norz Norz' saw initial limited edition copies including an extra thirteen tracks comprising the earlier demos. IMPALED NAZARENE's third single 'Satanic Masowhore' was backed on the flip side with a cover version of EXTREME NOISE TERROR's 'Conned Thru Life'. Sales were strong enough to break the Finnish national top forty album charts.

Toured Europe with ANCIENT RITES in early 1994 up front of recording third album 'Suomi Finland Perkele'. The record's perceived right wing lyrics draw controversy and instructions were issued by French authorities to withdraw the album from the stores. Fortunately sales were not unduly harmed as misinformation led to the band's previous album being removed from racks. Embroiled in the resulting press frenzy IMPALED NAZARENE set out on tour around Europe with American's ABSU and Australia's SADISTIK EXEKUTION.

However, by the following year founder member Sir Luttinen had decamped to concentrate on his solo project LEGENDA. A planned mini-album, provisionally titled 'Hamnasnas', was shelved due to in fighting in the band. After Luttinen's departure he also operated in parallel BEHERIT and would session for CATAMENIA. Reima Kellokoski took the IMPALED NAZARENE drum stool for October tour dates in Europe with MINISTRY OF TERROR and KRABATHOR. The group also put in their first British show headlining a Halloween event at London's Astoria.

In early 1996 added ex-BELIAL bassist Lehto Saari, who replaced 'The Fuck You Man' Jarva immediately after recording of the 'Latex Cult' and 'Motorpenis' outings. Both Jarva and the wayward Luttinen would later found THE BLACK LEAGUE. The 'Motorpenis' mini-album features covers of tracks from Finnish Punk acts FAFFBEY and TERVEET KADET as well as GANG GREEN's 'Alkohol'. April of 1996 had the band out on their lengthiest trek around Europe to date as part of the 'No Mercy' touring festival. IMPALED NAZARENE sharing the stage with CANNIBAL CORPSE, IMMOLATION, ROTTING CHRIST, KRABATHOR and GRAVE.

Recovering after these dates the band laid down an exclusive track 'I Am The Killer Of Trolls' for the compilation album 'World Domination II'. 1996 was rounded off by a further bout of European touring with ANGEL CORPSE and GEHENNAH. The band found themselves back in trouble in 1997 when the Hare Krishna movement objected to the use of artwork on the 'Ugra Karma' album.

During the summer of 1998 the group put in further prominent international shows playing the Milwaukee Metalfest, gigs in Canada and a series of dates in Mexico. In September of 1998 the band drafted THY SERPENT, CHILDREN OF BODOM and SINERGY guitarist Alex Laiho. However, Laiho's commitments kept him out of the line up for another round of European shows this time with DRILLER KILLER and RITUAL CARNAGE. Laiho did perform with the band in February of 1999 on their second visit to America and Mexico but cut short his commitment returning to Finland. Nevertheless, IMPALED NAZARENE undertook their first Japanese shows as a quartet. The band would not let up the live work and by April were back in Europe as part of the 'No Mercy III' festivals in alliance with PECCATUM, LIMBONIC ART, THE CROWN, EMPEROR and MORBID ANGEL. Still as a four piece the band also put in shows in far flung Australia and New Zealand.

IMPALED NAZARENE's 2000 release saw a split effort with DRILLER KILLER. In early 2001 it was announced that both Laiho and Lehtosaari had fled the fold with new members plugging the gap being guitarist Teemu Raimovanta and bass player Mikael Arnkil.

The band's status is such that several bootleg singles and albums exist, most notably 'Live In The Name Of Satan'.

Singles/EPs:
Noisrevrep Taog / In The Name Of Satan / Noisrevrep Eht Retfa / Damnation, Nosferatu (1991) ('Goat Perversion' 7" single)
Sado Goat / Ghost Riders, Osmose Productions (1992) (7" single)
Satanic Masowhore / Conned Thru Life, Osmose Productions OPEP003 (1993) (7" single)
Motorpenis, Osmose Productions SPV 076 20622-2 CD (1996)

Albums:
TOL CORMPT NORZ NORZ NORZ,
Osmose Productions OPCD010 (1993)
Apolokia / I Al Purg Vompo / My Blessing
(The Beginning Of The End) / Apolokia
II: Aikolopa 666 / In The Name Of Satan
/ Impure Orgies / Goat Perversion / The
Forest (The Darkness) / Mortification
Blood Red Razor Blade / The God
(Symmetry Of Penis) / Condemned To
Hell / The Dog (Art Of Vagina) / The
Crucified / Apolokia III: Agony / Body-
Mind-Soul / Hoath: Darbs Lucifero /
Apolokia Finale XXVII AS / Damnation
(Raping The Angels)
UGRA KARMA, Osmose Productions
OPCD018 (1994)
Goatzied / The Horny And The Horned /
Sadhu Satana / Chaosgoat Law / Hate /
Gott Ist Tot (Antichrist War Mix) / Coraxo
/ Soul Rape / Kali-Yuga / Cyberchrist /
False Jehova / Sadistic 666 - Under A
Golden Shower
SUOMI FINLAND PERKELE, Osmose
Productions OPCD026 (1995)
Intro / Vituursen Multi Huipennus / Blood
Is Thicker Than Water / Steel Vagina /
Total War - Winter War / Quasb - The
Burning / Kuolema Kaikille (Paitsi Meille)
/ Let's Fucking Die / Genocide /
Ghettoblaster / The Oath Of The Goat
LATEX CULT, Osmose Productions
OPCD038 (1996)
66 6 S Foreplay / 1999: Karmakeddon
Warriors / Violence I Crave / Bashing In
Heads / Motorpenis / Zum Kotzen / Alien
Militant / Goat War / Punishment Is
Absolute / When All Golden Turned To
Shit / Masterbator / The Burning Of
Provinciestraat / I Eat Pussy For
Breakfast / Delirium Tremens
RAPTURE, Osmose Productions
OPCD069 (1998)
Penis Et Circes / 6th Degree Mindfuck /
Iron Fist With An Iron Will / Angels
Rectums Do Bleed / We're Satan's
Generation / Goatvomit And Gasmasks /
Fallout Theory In Practice / Burst
Command 'Til War / Healers Of The Red
Plague / The Pillory / The Return Of The
Nuclear Gods / Vitutation / J.C.S. /
Nuclear Metal Retaliation / Inbred /
Phallus Maleficarum
NIHIL, Osmose Productions (2000)
Cogito Ergo Sum / Human Proof / Wrath
Of The Goat / Angel Rectums Still Bleed -
The Sequel / Porteclipse Era / Nothing's
Sacred / Zero Tolerance / Assault The
Weak / How The Laughter Died / Nihil
**IMPALED NAZARENE VS DRILLER
KILLER**, Solardisk (2000)

DECADE OF DECADENCE, Osmose
Productions OPCD 108 (2000)
Intro / Condemned To Hell / The
Crucified / Disgust Suite Op. I / Morbid
Fate / Disgust Suite Op. II / Worms In
Rectum / Conned Thru Life /
Crucifixation / Nuctermeron Of
Necromanteion / Condemned To Hell /
Impurity Of Doom / The Crucified /
Infernus / Morbid Fate / Ave Satanas / In
The Name Of Satan / Fall To Fornication
/ Damnation (Raping The Angels) /
Noisrevrep Taag / In The Name Of Satan
/ Noisrevrep Taag / Damnation (Raping
The Angels) / The Black Vomit / Ghost
Riders / Sadogoat / I Am The Killer Of
Trolls / Kill Yourself / Burst Command Til
War / Nuclear Metal Retaliation /
Instrumental I / Instrumental II /
Instrumental III

IMPALER (UK)
Line-Up: Edd (vocals / bass), Chris Dew
(guitar), Paul Mariotti (guitar), Nick
Adams (drums)

Formed in 1988 as a Death Metal /
Hardcore unit under the original monicker
of CARNAGE, line-up changes and
several other names later the group
settled on IMPALER and forged a Death
Metal style on two demos and supported
acts like CANCER, CARCASS and
BENEDICTION.
Not to be confused with the industrious
Punk / Thrash American IMPALER.

Albums:
CHARNAL DEITY, Deaf 7 (1992)
The Dead Know Dreams - Avowal To Hell
/ Imminence Of The Final Punishment /
Malignant Dreams / Accursed Domain /
Internally Rotting / Impaler Of Souls /
Astral Corpse / Engulfed / Total Carnage
/ Repel Your Faith

IMPERATOR (POLAND)
Line-Up: Bariel (vocals / guitar), Mefisto
(bass), Carol (drums)

One of the true veterans of the Polish
extreme Metal scene. IMPERATOR was
founded in the mid 80's as a duo of
vocalist / guitarist Bariel and drummer
Adrian. Even in these formative days
IMPERATOR's raison d'être was
uncompromising Metal.
Mefisto was added on bass guitar during
September 1985 in order to fulfill the
band's debut live shows. The first demo
tape 'Endless Sacrifice' surfaced in 1986

followed by a live cassette titled 'Deathlive'. For IMPERATOR's third demo, 1987's 'Eternal Might', Moloch took over drum duties. The band's burgeoning status kindled the interest of Euronymous of Deathlike Silence Records but as negotiations between the two parties dragged on IMPERATOR opted to sign to local label Nameless Records. Unfortunately due to Nameless being a Polish company distribution worldwide was severely restricted.

Pagan Records re-issued the debut in 1997 with bonus tracks.

Albums:
THE TIME BEFORE TIME, Nameless (1991)
Eternal Might / Abhorrence / Necromonicon / Persecutor / Defunct Dimension / External Extinction / Ancient Race
THE TIME BEFORE TIME, Pagan Moon CD 007 (1997)
Eternal Might / Abhorrence / Necromonicon / Persecutor / Defunct Dimension / External Extinction / Ancient Race / Love Is The Law (Love Under Will) / The Rest Is Silence

IMPERIUM (HOLLAND)
Line-Up: André Vuurboom (vocals), Michel Cerrone (guitar), Rob Cerrone (guitar), Remco Nijkamp (bass), Patrick Gerritzen (drums)

A combination of technical Thrash Metal and Progressive Power Metal forged by ex-SACROSANCT member guitarist Michel Cerrone. Dutch outfit IMPERIUM scored a deal with Mascot Records after one demo.

Albums:
TOO SHORT A SEASON, Mascot M 7005-2 (1993)
Too Short A Season / Play Of Passion / Chemical Dreams / Silenced / Left Meaningless / ...To The Things That Were... / Messiah Mask / Slip Of The Tongue / Awakening

IMPETIGO (Bloomington, IL, USA)
Line-Up: Stevo De Caixo (vocals / bass), Mark (guitar), Scotty (guitar), Dan (drums)

Pioneering Death Metal band from Illinois created in 1987 as a trio of Stevo De Caixeo on vocals and bass, guitarist Mark and drummer Dan. Following the debut demo 'All We Need Is Cheez' second guitarist Scotty was added.

A 1989 demo 'Giallo' secured a deal with German label Wild Rags. However, their new record company's printers refuse to press up sleeves for the debut album 'Ultimo Mondo Cannibale' fearing possible legal action. The local Bloomington council also banned the artwork deeming it obscene and pornographic. The album eventually emerged with toned down artwork.

A now rare 7" single 'Biuo Omega' followed then a split EP shared with German band BLOOD and the 'Faceless' EP before a second full length outing 'Horror Of The Zombies'.

IMPETIGO only managed some 30 gigs during the band's lifetime before folding in 1993. De Caixeo later founded INSOMNIA but after recording an as yet unreleased album this act folded.

IMPETIGO's underground status was such that a 2000 tribute album 'Wizards Of Gore' emerged on Razorback Records featuring such artists as BLOOD DUSTER, MORTICIAN, IMPALED, DECEASED, EXHUMED, INGROWING, SANITY's DAWN, BLOOD, LIVIDITY and VASTION.

All of the band's demos have been re-released on CD format.

Singles/EPs:
Harbinger Of Death / Revenge Of The Scabby Man / Dear Uncle Creepy / Bitch Death Teenage Mucous Monsters From Hell, Wild Rags (1992) ('Biuo Omega' EP)
Boneyard / Cannibal Apocalypse, Iron (1991) (Split EP with BLOOD)
Sinister Urge / Faceless / Dis-Organised / Bloody Pit Of Horror, Wild Rags WRR031 (1991) ('Faceless' EP)
H.B.O. Theme - Who's Fucking Who? (Live) / My Lai / Jane Fonda Sucks, Bloodbath BIMI021 (1999) (Split EP with TRANSGRESSOR)

Albums:
ULTIMO MONDO CANNIBALE, Wild Rags WRR020 (1990)
Maggots / Dis-Organ-Ised / Intense Mortification / Revenge Of The Scabby Man / Veneral Warts / Bloody Pit Of Horror / Dear Uncle Creepy / Bitch Death Teenage Mucous Monsters From Hell / Zombie / Jane Fonda Sucks (Part 2) / Red Wigglers / Harbinger Of Death / Unadulterated Brutality / Mortado / Heart Of Illinois / My Lai
HORROR OF THE ZOMBIES, Wild Rags

WRR035 (1992)
Boneyard / Work For The Streetcleaner / Wizard Of Gore / Morturia / Cannibale Ballet / Trap Them And Kill Them / Cannibal Lust / Defiling The Grave / Staph Terrorist / Breakfast In The Manchester Morgue (Let Sleeping Corpses Lie)
BIUO OMEGA, Obscene Productions (2000)
Harbinger Of Death / Revenge Of The Scabby Man / Dear Uncle Creepy / Bitch Death Teenage Mucous Monsters From Hell / H.B.O. Theme: Who's Fucking Who? (Live) / My Lai / Jane Fonda Sucks

IMPIOUS (SWEDEN)
Line-Up: Martin Akesson (vocals / guitar), Valle Adzic (guitar), Robin Sorqvist (bass), Ulf Johansson (drums)

Trollhaten based Death Metal act. Created in the mid 90's IMPIOUS originally relied on a drum machine for initial demos but would draft Ulf Johansson in time for their inaugural gig in May 1995 supporting LORD BELIAL.
A second demo tape 'The Suffering' was produced by KING DIAMOND guitarist Any La Rocque.

Albums:
EVILIZED, Black Sun (1998)
Dying I Live / Don't Kiss My Grave / Born To Suffer / Haven (A Leap In The Dark) / Facing The Nails / Anthem For The Afflicted / The Faded Paradise / Painted Soul / Extreme Pestilence / Inside / Evilization
TERROR SUCCEEDS, Black Sun BS21 (2000)

IMPULSE MANSLAUGHTER
(Chicago, IL, USA)
Line-Up: Karl Patton (vocals), Chris Hanley (guitar), Nick Stevens (bass), Glen Herman (drums)

IMPULSE MANSLAUGHTER's 1988 album 'Logical End' included cover versions of MOTÖRHEAD's 'Stone Deaf Forever' and the ROLLING STONES 'Paint It Black'.

Albums:
BURN ONE NAKED AND NUKE IT, Impulse Manslaughter (1986)
HE WHO LAUGHS LAST..., Nuclear Blast (1987)
Batman And The Oracle Of Pevile Savage / Vomit Heads / We're All Bored

Here / Suffer In Silence / Walls / They Start The War / Premature Evacuation / Crimes / Too Late / Pills / This World / Sedation / Cheer Up You Fucker / Kein Spiel / Oatmeal II / 1987 Schitzoid Sam / Pattonstein's Disease / Piss Me Off
LOGICAL END, Walkthrufyre (1988)
Drag/ Face It / Not Quite Sure / Missing Children / Gimme Shelter / Crimson Dreams / No Deals / Let Them Die / Stone Dead Forever / Borderline Retard
SOMETIMES, Nuclear Blast (1992)

IN BATTLE (SWEDEN)
Line-Up: Wiklund (drums / vocals), Fröléti (guitar / bass)

IN BATTLE was a "War Metal" amalgamation in 1996 of ODHINN members guitarist Fröléti, Ostlund and drummer Wiklund with SETHERIAL's Lord Moloch and Lord Alastor Mysteriis. IN BATTLE's line up for the 1998 album was down to a duo of Wiklund and Fröléti.

Albums:
IN BATTLE, Napalm (1997)
Ruler Of The Northern Sphere / I Ofred Vi Drar Fram / The Nocturnal Moan / Enchant Me / År Av Köld / Doom Of The Unbeloved / Odhinn / A Sign Of Northern Triumph And Glory / De Hängdas Furste / Lokes Ätt / Helhorde / In Battle
THE RAGE OF THE NORTHMEN, Napalm (1998)
From The Flesh And Bones Of Our Enemies / The Rage Of The Northmen / The Sceptre Of Hate / The Conqueror / The Destroyer Of Souls / Muspelheim The Dominion Of The Flame / Storms Of War / Armies Of The Northern Realms / Endless War

INCANTATION (New Jersey, USA)
Line-Up: Craig Pillard (vocals / guitar), John McEntee (guitar), Ronnie Deo (bass), Jim Roe (drums)

A highly influential act that straddle the borderline between Black and Death Metal. INCANTATION are cited by many of todays acts as being a direct inspiration.
INCANTATION came together with a line-up of erstwhile BLOOD THIRTY DEATH members guitarist Brett Makowski and bassist Aragon Amori. Ex-REVENANT man John McEntree and Paul Ledney, previously with G.G. Allin's CONNECTICUT COCKSUCKERS.
A major fall out occurred with McEntree

being left alone as Makowski, Amori and Ledney decamped en masse to found the notorious Black Metal act PROFANATICA releasing a string of highly controversial EPs.

Following INCANTATION's debut album 'Onward To Golgotha' frontman Craig Pillard broke away from the group. Before long bassist Ronnie Deo and drummer Jim Roe joined him to found WOMB, an act that evolved into DISCIPLES OF MOCKERY.

Competition between DISCIPLES OF MOCKERY and INCANTATION was so fierce that at the 1994 Deathstock festival in New York Pillard's band played a full set of INCANTATION numbers just before INCANTATION themselves took the stage!

Confusion reigned in Death Metal circles when INCANTION's 1994 album 'Mortal Throne Of Nazarene' was re-released under the new title of 'Upon The Throne Of Apocalypse' with a reversed track order and a sticker proclaiming 'Pagan Disciples Of Mockery'!! (Later Pillard's mob became WOMB again but reverted to DISCIPLES OF MOCKERY for the 1999 three track promotion CD).

Amidst all this INCANTATION relocated entirely to Ohio with only founder member John McEntee creating a completely revised line up. INCANTATION performed a short tour of Mexico in 1995 sharing a bill with IMMOLATION and ACID BATH.

An American tour with Swedes GRAVE was nearly curtailed when INCANTATION's bassist decided not to go along for the ride. Stoically the band carried on without bass as a trio of McEntee, guitarist Dwayne Morris and drummer Kyle Severn. However, INCANTION finally settled on bassist Rob Yench.

The band later pulled in frontman Daniel Corchado but for shows in Argentina during 1996 DEATHRUNE's Mike Saez took the position on a temporary basis.

The 1997 album, produced by Bill Korecky, features a cover of DEATH's 'Scream Bloody Gore'.

By 2000 INCANTION's roster had shifted once more. Corchado opted out to concentrate on his other act THE CHASM and in came the aforementioned Mike Saez. The album was recorded with session drummer Dave Culross of MALEVOLENT CREATION and the band pulled in DEATH, CONTROL DENIED and ICED EARTH man Richard Christy for tour work.

Kyle Severn meantime involved himself with the high profile WOLFEN SOCIETY project featuring ACHERON's Vincent Crowley, VITAL REMAINS singer Jeff Gruslin and DARK FUNERAL guitarist Lord Ahriman.

INCANTATION geared up for a month long tour of the States in early 2001 in alliance with IMMOLATION and GOATWHORE. However, the dates would be abruptly curtailed at a gig in Queens, New York. The band's van was broken into outside the Voodoo Lounge venue before the show then various band members and friends became embroiled in a vicious fight. Saez had stepped in to prevent a fight involving his former DEATHRUNE bandmate Chris Shaw. As it turned out Shaw was stabbed in the back and face no less than seven times. The intervening Saez also received major wounds to his arm. Another friend Pete Schulz also received deep lacerations to the arm.

The attacker fled from the venue but was chased and caught by Kyle Severn who apprehended the man and held him until police caught up with him. The injuries to Saez were so severe that the tour was cancelled. Saez would later be rushed into hospital at a later date with stomach pains but would make a full recovery.

Singles/EPs:
Entrantment Of Evil, Seraphic Decay (1990)

Albums:
ONWARD TO GOLGOTHA, Relapse (1992)
Golgotha / Devoured Death / Blasphemous Creation / Rotting Spiritual Embodiment / Unholy Massacre / Entrantment Of Evil / Christening The Afterbirth / Immortal Cessation / Profanation / Deliverance Of Horrific Prophecies / Eternal Torture
MORTAL THRONE OF NAZARENE, Relapse (1994)
Demonic Incarnate / Emaciated Holy Figure / Iconclasm Of Catholicism / Essence Ablaze / Nocturnal Dominium / The Ibex Moon / Blissful Bloodshower / Abolishment Of Immaculate Serenity
THE FORESAKEN MOURNING OF ANGELIC ANGUISH, Relapse RR 6974 (1997)
Shadows From The Ancient Empire / Lusting Congregation Of Perpetual Damnation (Extreme Eden) / Triumph In Blasphemy (Interlude) / Forsaken Mourning Of Angelic Anguish / Scream

Bloody Gore / Twisted Sacrilegious Journey Into The Darkest Neurotic Delirium / Outro / The Ibex Moon / Blasphemous Cremation / Essence Ablaze / Blissful Bloodshower
DIABOLICAL CONQUEST, Relapse (1998)
Impending Diabolic Conquest / Desecration (Of The Heavenly Gracefullness) / Disciples Of Blasphemous Reprisal / Unheavenly Skies / United In Repugnance / Shadows From The Ancient Empire / Ethereal Misery / Masters Of Infernal Damnation / Horde Of Bestial Flames
THE INFERNAL STORM, Relapse (2000)
Anoint The Chosen / Extinguishing Salvation / Impetuous Rage / Sempiternal Pandemonium / Lustful Demise / Heaven Departed / Apocalyptic Destroyer Of Angels / Nocturnal Kingdom Of Demonic Enlightenment

INCESTUOUS (CA, USA)
Line-Up: Matti Way (vocals), Danny Louise (guitar), Mike Dooley (bass), Rick Myers (drums)

INCESTUOUS was an act founded in 1999 by ex-GORGASM drummer Derek Hoffman. A series of line up changes led to the solo INCESTUOUS release 'Brass Knuckle Abortion' after which the band opted for a name change to CINERARY. Personnel at this point were ex-DYSPHORIA vocalist 'Sick' Nick Hernandez, former SMEGMA / CUMCHRIST guitarist Danny Louise ('Wrench'), Mike Dooley from CORPSE VOMIT on bass. Following recording of the album former DISGORGE vocalist Matti Way took the role of frontman. Founder member Hoffman had rejoined GORGASM in January 2001 and INCESTUOUS plugged the gap with Ricky Myers of DISGORGE.
Wrench also operates BRETHREN with ex-INCESTUOUS and DYSPHORIA vocalist 'Sick' Nick Hernandez, Jeff and Jim from CIANIDE and Nefarious of MACABRE.

Albums:
BRASS KNUCKLE ABORTION, United Guttural (1999)

INCUBATOR (GERMANY)
Line-Up: Chris (vocals), Sven (guitar), Micha (guitar), Steve (bass), Dominique (drums)

A rather eccentric German Death Metal band, INCUBATOR debuted in 1991 with 'Symphonies Of Spiritual Cannibalism' and engaged ex HOLY MOSES man Andy Classen to produce 1992's 'McGillroy The Housefly'.
The third album, 'Hirnnektar', is notable for featuring a cover of PINK FLOYD's 'Set The Controls For The Heart Of The Sun'.

Albums:
SYMPHONIES OF SPIRITUAL CANNIBALISM, (1991)
McGILLROY THE HOUSEFLY, West Virginia CD 084-57242 (1992)
Thinkin' Green - Believe In Grey / Prisons Of Gore / (No Name) / Raped By A Stranger / Chaos Ego / Identität / Stories Enter Controlled Dept / Brain Eliminator / Games Of A Moon murder / Forced / Playing A Game...
HIRNNEKTAR, Steamhammer SPV 084-76732 (1993)
Taste Yourself / Leben / Spiritätze / Words Can't Hurt / And I Live In Between / S.K.S. Syndrom / So Sad (In The Mind Of Us All / Set The Controls For The Heart Of The Sun / Your Life Is Done
DIVINE COMEDY, Godz Greed (2000)
Ashes Of Tomorrow / Your Vision / Cold / Untitled / Curse / Sphere In Flames / Borderline

INCUBUS (New Orleans, LA, USA)
Line up- Francis M. Howard (guitar), Luiz Carlos (guitar), Andre Luiz Oliveira (bass), Moyses M. Howard (drums)

New Orleans Death-Thrashers centred upon the Brazilian siblings Francis M. Howard and Moyses M. Howard. INCUBUS, created in 1986, debuted with a 1987 demo 'Supernatural Death' which saw the employ of vocalist / bassist Scot W. Latour. This led in turn to a deal with Brutal Records for the first album 'Serpent Temptation'. The album gained an international release through the Metalworks concern.
INCUBUS, now with Mark Lavenia supplanting Latour and signed to German label Nuclear Blast, augmented their line-up with guitarist Luiz Carlos during the 'Beyond The Unknown' album although the sessions were cut entirely by the versitile Howard brothers. Once the album was complete Andre Luiz Olveira was added on bass. The departed Lavenia united with veteran ACHERON

guitarist Pete Slate creating EQUINOX for a brace of albums,

During 1999 after a lengthy hiatus, due to the presence of the California INCUBUS, the band underwent a change of name to OPPROBRIUM to release the 2000 album 'Discerning Forces' produced by Harris Johns.

Lavenia teamed up with ex-MASSACRE drummer Kam Lee and ACHERON and EQUINOX man Pete Slate to found project act CAULDRON in 2000.

Singles/EPs:
God Died On His Knees, Gore (1988)

Albums:
SERPENT TEMPTATION, Metalworks VOV 674 (1988)
The Battle Of Armageddon / Voices From The Grave / Sadistic Sinner / Incubus / Blaspheming Prophets / Hunger For Power / Serpent Temptation / Underground Killers
BEYOND THE UNKNOWN, Nuclear Blast (1990)
Certain Accuracy / The Deceived Ones / Curse Of The Damned Cities / Beyond The Unknown / Freezing Torment / Massacre Of The Unborn / On The Burial Ground / Mortify

INDUNGEON (SWEDEN)
Line-Up: Mournlord (vocals / drums), Asmodeus (guitar), Cethulhv (guitar), L.V. Manngarmr (bass)

INDUNGEON is a project established in 1996 by Stefan Wienerhall and Karl Beckmann of MITHOTYN and THY PRIMORDIAL vocalist Michael Andersson and bassist J. Albrektsson. The act's debut demo was impressive enough to be repressed onto CD by American label Full Moon Productions. 'Machinegunnery Of Doom' includes a cover of BATHORY's 'Fire In Fire'.

Both Beckmann and Wienerhall would later create the Power Metal band FALCONER.

Albums:
MACHINEGUNNERY OF DOOM, Full Moon Productions (1997)
THE MISANTHROPOCALYPSE, (1999)
Genocide / Powers Unbound / Misanthropocalypse / Sentenced To The Flames / Mutilated / Propaganda Of War / Final Conflict / Battletank No. II

INFAMY (Los Angeles, CA, USA)

INFAMY, who emerged with the 1995 demo cassette 'Count The Dead', include former INSIDIOUS guitarist Mark Casillas. INFAMY suffered a tragic setback shortly after recording of the debut album 'The Blood Shall Flow' when frontman Joshua 'Jagger' Heatly died suddenly in March 1998.

Albums:
THE BLOOD SHALL FLOW, Qabalah Productions QAB005 (1998)
The Maggots Are In Me / Bodily Disemboweled / Onslaught Of Carnage / Cranial Implosion / Putrid Infestation / Salem's Burning / Mass Cremation / Lacerated / The Blood Shall Flow / Cryptobiosis

INFECTED PUSSY (FRANCE)

A Grindcore act with a sense of humour. INFECTED PUSSY have shared cassette releases with SUBLIME CADAVERIC DECOMPOSITION, Poland's SQUASH BOWELS and DEAD INFECTION as well as a four way demo with ORAL CLIMAX, TERMINAL 8 and DISOBEY.

Despite being limited to a 7" vinyl single format INFECTED PUSSY managed to cram over 50 songs onto their 'Touch Me' release.

Singles/EPs:
Touch Me, (199-) (7" single)

Albums:
SPLIT, Fleshfeast (2000) (Split album with MUCUPURULENT)

INFERIA (FINLAND)
Line-Up: Reijo Kortesniemi (vocals), Jani Huttunen (guitar), Jani Nikkilä (guitar), Petri Malinen (bass), Tero Järvinen (drums)

Singles/EPs:
Under The Skin Of The Split Body / The Art Of Self Mutilation / Lunatics Anal Fanatics / Spawned At The Dawn / They Bleed And Bleed, Invasion IR007 (1995) ('Spawned At The Dawn' EP) (1995)

INFERNAL BEAUTY (BELGIUM)
Line-Up: Thomas (vocals), Kristof (guitar / keyboards), Bart (guitar), Pieter (bass), Sara (keyboards), Joachim (drums)

INFERNAL BEAUTY formed in 1994,

albeit under a different name. Originally founding members Maarten (vocals) and Kristof (guitar) pursued an avant garde direction, although once bassist Pieter and drummer Joachim joined the fold the Death Metal sound became more progressive.

After a few months rehearsing as a quartet Maarten opted to leave due, it seems, his voice not being up to the extreme style INFERNAL BEAUTY wished to offer. He was replaced by Thomas and, after completing gigs opening for SADIST, EXTERMINATOR and AVATAR in August 1995, the group completed their first demo ('Drakensquar') which was voted 'Demo Of The Month' in the Dutch Rock mag 'Aardschock'.

The success of the demo led to a deal with Hammerheart Records and the first album would contain a remixed version of the 'Drakensquar' ('Ruler Of Darkness') demo.

Novelly, the band's lyrics are in 'Drakensliny', a language peculiar to the band and invented by Joachim.

Albums:
DARKENSQUAR, Hammerheart (1997)
Revüro Eud Vis Squarderik / Alcatara (As The Forest Calls) / Io Lindipnig / Atheria / Tis Emprio / Sinitiöm Eud Sanctimo / Victro Eud Vis Squaderik

INFERNAL MAJESTY (CANADA)
Line-Up: Chris Bailey (vocals), Steve Terror (guitar), Kenny Hallman (guitar), Psychopath (bass), Rick Nemes (drums)

Following Thrash Metal band INFERNAL MAJESTY's debut 1987 album 'None Shall Defy' the band released the 'Nigresent Dissolution' and 'Creation Of Chaos' demos.

Dutch label Displeased re-issued the debut album with bonus tracks culled from the demo sessions. The 1999 'Chaos In Copenhagen' album added extra tracks of INFERNAL MAJESTY cover versions by CHRIST DENIED and DAWN.

Albums:
NONE SHALL DEFY, Roadrunner (1987)
UNHOLIER THAN THOU, Hypnotic HYP 1062 (1998)
Unholier Than Thou / The Hunted / Gone The Way Of All Flesh / Black Infernal World / Roman Song / Where Is Your God? / Death Toll / Art Of War

NONE SHALL DEFY, Displeased (1997)
Overlord / R.I.P. / Night Of The Living Dead / S.O.S. / None Shall Defy / Skeletons In The Closet / Anthology Of Death / Path Of The Psycho / Into The Unknown / Hell On Earth
CHAOS IN COPENHAGEN, Hypnotic (1999)
Birth Of Power / Unholier Than Thou / Where Is Your God? / R.I.P. / Night Of The Living Dead / S.O.S. / Night Of The Living Dead (DAWN) / Overlord (CHRIST DENIED)

INFERNAL TORMENT (DENMARK)
Line-Up: Scott Jensen (vocals), Jacob Hansen (guitar), Poul Winhyer (guitar), Steffan Larsen (bass), Martin Boris (drums)

Sick, sick, sick Death Metallers, INFERNAL TORMENT concoct some rather Extreme Metal allied to lyrics that put better known Grind acts to shame! INFERNAL TORMENT sing about bizarre sexual practices, such as eating excreta, in lurid detail. After seeking legal advice the band's record company only agreed to print the lyrics on the sleeve of the debut album if they were in reverse type and the first 3000 copies of their debut album even came complete with a free sick bag!

INFERNAL TORMENT formed in 1993 and released various demos, including the 'Instincts' tape, before contributing the track 'No Longer A Virgin' to the 'Fuck You, We're From Denmark' compilation album on Progress Records in 1994 and supported INVOCATOR on tour later the same year.

The band added ex-CONDEMNED guitarist Poul Winther prior to recording the debut album, the CD cover for which was immediately banned thus garnering INFERNAL TORMENT further promotion.

Albums:
MAN'S TRUE NATURE, Progress RRS 949 (1995)
Taking Advantage Of A Virgin / Motherfuck / Uncontrollable / Perverted / Instincts / The Undertaker / Baby Battering Bill / No Longer A Virgin / On The Hunt For Fresh Flesh / When Daddy Comes Home
BIRTH RATE ZERO, Progress PCD 45 (1997)
The Razor Twist / Product Of Society / Birthrate Zero / The End Of Civilization / 443556 / Murder The World / Race /

Eliminate / Inhaled / Fuck The Whales

INFESTATION (UK)
Line-Up: David Samuel (vocals), Giusseppe Cutispoto (guitar), Jeremy Gray (guitar), Declan Malone (drums)

Promising British Black Death Metal crew INFESTATION emerged in 1996. The band was dealt a blow in 1998 when drummer Dave Hirschmeiner joined the premier league act CRADLE OF FILTH. His replacement for the 'Mass Immolation' debut album was Declan Malone.

Singles/EPs:
Curse Of Creation EP, Infestation (1998)

Albums:
MASS IMMOLATION, Lunasound LUNA001CD (2000)
Necrospawn / Book Of Lies / Legions Of Death / Desecrate / The Hunt / Evil, Evil / Carrion / Black Pope / Butcher Knife / Curse Of Creation / Infest / Demons Of Darkness / Prophet Of Doom / Self Impaled

INFEST DEAD (SWEDEN)

A Death Metal project from EDGE OF SANITY's Dan Swanö based upon the temple of Lucifer and the burning of believers in Jesus Christ.

Singles/EPs:
The Rising / I'll Be Black / In The Spell Of Satan / Save Me From The Hands Of Christ / Fucked By Satan / Burn Me (Without The Grace Of God), Invasion IR 020 (1996) ('Killing Christ' EP)

Albums:
HELLFUCK, Invasion IR 026 (1997)
Rebirth (Intro) / The Desecration Of Christ / Infest The Dead / The New Empire / Mercenary, Merciless / Born Nailed / Susej Ilik Ot Tolp Eht / Blaspheme The Abyss / Polterchrist / Sacrifice The Saviour / Hellfuck / Darkness Complete / Haunting The Fly / Heaven Denied / Salvation Incomplete / Bewitch The Virgin / Angeldemon / World Inverted / Son Of The Darkside / Hellborn / Satanic / Amen (Outro)
JESUSATAN, (1999)
Resurrection / Christiansanity / Born To Burn / Jesusatan / Undead Screaming Sins / The Burning Of The Son / Sinister / Evil / Antichristian Song / Black Knight

INFESTER (USA)

Singles/EPs:
Darkness Unveiled, Moribund (1992) (7" single)

Albums:
TO DEPTHS, IN DEGRADATION, Moribund DEAD 06 (1995)
To Depths, In Degradation / Chamber Of Reunion / Braided Into Palsy / Epicurean Entrails / A Viscidy Slippery Secretion / A Higher Art Of Immutable Beauty / Clouds Of Consciousness / Exoriation Killz The Bliss / Meplectic Exhumation / Outro

IN FLAMES (SWEDEN)
Line-Up: Anders Friden (vocals), Jesper Strömbold (guitar), Glenn Ljungström (guitar), Johan Larsson (bass), Björn Gelotte (drums)

A Swedish Death Metal band founded in late 1990 the quintet only assumed the name IN FLAMES in 1993 after a few line up changes. The band's debut, three track demo secured a deal with Wrong Again Records.
IN FLAMES line-up for the debut album comprised of vocalist Mikael Stanne, guitarists Glenn Ljungström and Carl Näslund, bassist Johan Larsson and drummer Jesper Strömbald.
By the time of the 'Subterranean' album in 1995 IN FLAMES had added ex-EUCHARIST drummer Daniel Erlandsson. Session vocals were handled by Henke Fors.
Upon the album's release the band found a new frontman in ex-CEREMONIAL OATH and DARK TRANQUILITY singer Anders Friden as Erlandsson lost his place to Björn Gelotte.
Following two critically acclaimed albums IN FLAMES contributed a cover version of 'Eye Of the Beholder' for the METALLICA tribute album 'Metal Militia Volume 1'. Being as the band had no lead vocalist at this juncture, ANCIENT SLUMBER frontman Robert Dahne lent his lungs for this recording.
IN FLAMES eventually re-enlisted Friden in time to record 'The Jester Race', the album that was to really push the band to the forefront. Backed up by numerous laudatory press reviews IN FLAMES set out on the Spring 'Out Of The Darkness' festival package in Germany together with DIMMU BORGIR, CRADLE OF FILTH and DISSECTION.
Jesper Strömbold was to enter the

national German charts in late 1997, although not with IN FLAMES. The guitarist was the unofficial sixth member of trad-Metal outfit HAMMERFALL. The fellow Swedes debut peaked at number 34 in the charts with the 'Glory To The Brave' debut bearing many co-write credits to Strömbold.

With IN FLAMES on hold the band took the opportunity to realign their line-up, dispensing with Ljungström and Larsson. Two new players - guitarist Niklas Engelin and bassist Peter Ewars - were quickly slotted in time for recording of 1998's 'Whoracle' album.

Obviously, not wishing to enter the realms of predictability, quite surreally the album included a version of DEPECHE MODE's 'Everything Counts'.

IN FLAMES toured America in 2000 on a billing with EARTH CRISIS and SKINLAB.

Albums:
LUNAR STRAIN, Wrong Again WAR003 (1994)
Behind Space / Lunar Strain / Starforsaken / Dreamscape / Everlost (Part I) / Everlost (Part II) / Hårgalåten / In Flames / Upon An Oaken Throne / Clad In Shadows
SUBTERRANEAN, Wrong Again WAR006 (1995)
Stand Ablaze / Ever Dying / Subterranean / Timeless / Biosphere
THE JESTER RACE, Nuclear Blast NB168 (1996)
Moonsheild / The Jester's Dance / Artifacts Of The Black Rain / Graveland / Lord Hypnos / Dead Eternity / The Jester Race / December Flower / Wayfearer / Dead God In Me
WHORACLE, Nuclear Blast (1997) **78 GERMANY**
Jotun / Food For The Gods / Gyroscope / Dialogue With The Stars / The Hive / Jester Script Transfigured / Morphing Into Primal / Worlds Within The Margin / Episode 666 / Everything Counts / Whoracle
CLAYMAN, Nuclear Blast NB 499-2 (2000) **22 FINLAND, 43 GERMANY, 17 SWEDEN**
Bullet Ride / Pinball Map / Only For The Weak / … As The Future Repeats Today / Square Nothing / Clay Man / Satellites And Astronauts / Brush The Dust Away / Swim / Suburban Me / Another Day In Quicksand

INGROWING (CZECH REPUBLIC)

INGROWING included their version of 'Bitch Death Teenage Mucous Monster From Hell' to the 2001 Razorback IMPETIGO tribute album 'Wizards Of Gore'.

Singles/EPs:
Sexual Inferiority / Cyberspace Floats Through Me / Radio Hit, Copremesis (1999) ('Creation Of Another Future' 7" split single with HAEMORRHAGE)

Albums:
CYBERSPACE, Tentamen (1998)
Underture / Cyberspace Floats Through Me / Touretted / Polyanghuulaar Dereems / Sunken / Surreal Ego Ravening / We Crated Another Future / Sexual Inferiority / Mournful Inferiority / Mournful Dejection / Synergy Pertual (The Unplugged Factory… Unperpetualism) / Intro / Virus Bioforge / Just Only Weeping Decadence / Sadomasochistic Grind-Mind Fucker / Agnosis / Pithecanthrope Syndrome / Cortex Combustion

INHUMATE (FRANCE)
Line-Up: Christophe (vocals), David (guitar), Fred (bass), Yannick (drums)

Grind band created in 1990 by guitarist David, bassist Fred, vocalist Olivier and drummer Stephane. By the following year Stephane had vacated his position for APOPLEXY and Sebastien had taken over the lead vocal spot. New drummer was Valentin.

In 1993 INHUMATE cut their debut demo 'Abstract Suffering'. In late 1994 the band saw Valentin leave for LES MARAUDERS and Sebastien decamp to CEREBAL COMMOTION. New faces were singer Christophe and drummer Yannick, bother former GOD EATER personnel.

Albums:
INTERNAL LIFE, Grind Your Soul GYS001 (1996)
Alone / My Sweet Love / Putrefaction / Blood / Welcome / D.P.B. / Piece Of Meat / Screams / I Want To Kill Some... / Tatanka / The Dream / Why? / Obsession / Earth Fucking Earth / The Bullet / Incest (Just A Kiss)
EX-PULSION, Grind Your Soul GYS002 (1997)
The Key / Therapy For Dogs / Sodomy /

The Chose One / Perfection / In Quest / Blind / Efluves / Grind Inc. / Desperate / Trance / History / Mother Fuck Her Grindub
GROWTH, Grind Your Soul GYS003 (2000)
I Want To Kill Some...(Part III) / Underground / Copyright / The Fright / Clock / Grind God / Time / The Golden Cage / Vanite? / N.S.C. / Urges! / Karamazov / Grind To The Core / Satyriasis / Bread And Games / Muensterturm / D.I.Y.F.

INHUME (HOLLAND)
Line-Up: Johan (vocals), Joost (vocals), Harold (guitar), Ben (guitar), Loek Peeters (bass), Michiel (drums)

Dutch Grindcore act INHUME was convened in late 1994 issuing an inaugural demo tape at the close of 1995. Early live work found the band guesting for AGATHOCLES, DEAD INFECTION, BENEDICTION, ALTAR and NYCTOPHOBIC among others.
A live shared cassette with SUPPOSITORY was issued in 1996 followed up by a further split tape in union with Equador's MUNDO DE MIERDA. 1997 saw further studio work for a promotional demo produced by Erwin Hermsen of MANGLED. A European tour in collaboration with Swedish acts DERANGED and VOMITORY was arranged but curtailed when guitarist Richard and drummer Roel broke ranks. Replacements would be found in guitarist Harold and NEE drummer Michiel. The latter's tenure proved fleeting though as after a matter of days he would quit to concentrate on his main act. Nevertheless, a split single with BLOOD would be embarked upon.
As 1999 opened SINISTER's Erik De Windt took the drum stool but only lasted a few months after which the circle was closed as original drummer Roel was re-enlisted.
Vocalist Joost, bassist Loek and guitarist Ben are also members of DROWNING IN TEARS. Loek Peeters and Harold are also in MANGLED and the bassist also holds down duties in DISRUPT.

Singles/EPs:
Split, (199-) (7" split single with BLOOD)

Albums:
DECOMPOSING FROM INSIDE, Bones Brigade (2000)

Gargling Guts / Squirming Parasites / Human Fucking Guinea Pig / Schizophrenic Pulp / Unforeseen Annihilation / Forbidden Hunger / Airplane Crash / Splenetic Views / Blood, Sperm, Shit / Tiamat / Meatcleaver / Tumorhead / Foul Mouths Below / Inescapable Destiny / Regressive Progressive / The Missing Limb / Dead Man Walking / Destructive Impulse / Invisible Death

INIQUITY (DENMARK)
Line-Up: Brian Petrwosky (vocals / guitar), Lars Friis (guitar), Thomas Christensen (bass), Jesper Frost (drums)

Death Metal band INIQUITY date to 1989 releasing the debut demotape 'Words Of Despair' in 1991. Further demos, such as 1992's 'Entering Deception', and various appearances on compilation albums followed before their debut album.
Production for 1999's 'Five Across The Eyes' was handled by ex-INVOCATOR frontman Jacob Hanson.

Albums:
BRUTAL YOUTH '94, (1995)
SERANADIUM, Progress RRS953 (1996)
Tranquil Seizure / Prophecy Of The Dying Watcher / Serendadium / Spectral Scent / Mockery Retained To Obturate / Encysted And Dormant / Son Of Cosmos / Retorn
FIVE ACROSS THE EYES, Mighty Music (1999)
Inhale The Ghost / Surgical Orb / Sidereal Seas / Random Bludgeon Battery / From Tarnished Soil / Reminiscence / Pyres Of Atonement / The Rigormortified Grip / Forensic Alliance / Cocooned

INIURIA (SWEDEN)
Line-Up: J. Johannessen (vocals), H. Dahlberg (guitar), S. Karlsson (guitar), J. Landhäll (bass), P. Pelander (drums)

After the release of a promotion cassette, a further demo entitled 'Forgiveness' followed in 1993.
This Swedish Death Metal band finally released their debut EP in 1995.

Singles/EPs:
The Heavenly Choir / Father Of Heaven / God Of Thunder, Iniuria (1995) ('All The Leaves Has Fallen' EP)

IN-QUEST (BELGIUM)

Grind act IN-QUEST emerged with the demos 'Xylad Valox' in 1996.

Singles/EPs:
Rewarded With Ingratitude, (199-) (7" split single with SARCASTIC TERROR)

Albums:
EXTRUSION: BATTLEHYMNS, (1997)
Extrusion: Battlehymns / Matrimonium / Encrust Excrement Crevice / Anti-Disestablishmentarianism / Xylad Valox / Opus: Questor Mastodon / Inspiration Of The Madness - Goddess Of Insanity / Coroner's Inquest
OPERATION CITADEL, Shiver SHR035 (1999)

INQUISICIÓN (CHILE)

Line-Up: Pedro Galán (vocals), Manalo Schafler (guitar), Christian Maturana (bass), Carlos Hernández (drums)

Santiago's INQUISICIÓN was founded in 1993 by TORTURER guitarist Manalo Schafler together with drummer Carlos Hernández initially billed as SANTA INQUISICIÓN. The act was fronted by erstwhile PANZER vocalist Freddy Alexis. By 1995 the band title had been shortened to simply INQUISICIÓN and augmented their sound with bassist Christian Maturans, previously with PSYKIS.
The 1998 album 'In Nomine' is a collection of earlier demos released on CD format. In March 1999 Alexis made way for new singer Pedro Galán.

Albums:
STEEL VENGEANCE, Dreamland Music (1997)
Innocent Sinner / Sed Diabolus / Pagan Rites / Steel Vengeance / Fate Was Sealed / Message In Black / Torturer / The Ancient Light / Into The Labyrinth
IN NOMINI, Toxic (1998)
Innocent Sinner / Sed Diabolus / Pagan Rites / Fate Was Sealed / The Ancient Light / Torture / Into The Labyrinth / Mayday's Eve / Bats In The Bellfry / Holy Fire / The Dream Quest Of The Unknown Avalon
BLACK LEATHER FROM HELL, (1998)
Dragonslayer / Black Leather From Hell / Army Of Darkness / Midnight Avenger / The Axis Of The Mist / Witchcraft / Extermination / Devil Mistress / Mensage Oculto

INQUISITION (AUSTRIA)

Line-Up: Bernhard Wöhrer (vocals / keyboards), Stefan Kühteubl (guitar), Christian Küberl (guitar), Franz Woltr (bass / violin), Thomas Kaindl (drums)

A Death Metal act formed in 1991, after two demos (1993's 'Forgotten & Denied' and the ensuing 'Krank') the band had the number 'After The Sepulture' placed on a Nuclear Blast Records compilation album.
The band were to eventually issue product through NSM with 'Krank' in 1996.

Albums:
KRANK, NSM 12555 (1996)
Prelude For The Sick / A Tale About An Unattainable Aim: I) The Request / II) The Years Of Begging / III) The Hour Of Death / Heroes Of The Evening? / The Lighthouseman / Noch Nicht Einmal Gelebt / Braindead / Krank

INQUISITOR (HOLLAND)

Line-Up: Alex (vocals), Erik (guitar), Hans (bass), Wim (drums)

Formed in 1992 from the merging of Dutch outfits MENTICIDE and DESULTORY. INQUISITOR soon became known for a style of hectic Thrash Metal with strong Death Metal influences.
Having debuted with the 'Blasphemous Accusations' demo after several line-up changes a second demo ('Your Pain Will Be Exquisite') led to a deal with Shiver Records.
The debut album caused problems however as the cover artwork was deemed obscene and was forced to be censored.
INQUISITOR became CENTURION in the late 90's debuting with the 'Of Purest Fire' EP.

Albums:
WALPURGIS - SABBATH OF LUST, Shiver (1996)
Damnation For The Holy / Consuming Christ / Condemned Saints / Trial Of Denial / Chaos In Eden / Jehova's Downfall / Crypt Of Confession / Unholy Seeds / Cry Of The Christians / Fallen Missionary / Inquisitor

IN RUINS (USA)
Line-Up: J. Michael (vocals / guitar), Jason (bass), Sean James (drums)

Philadelphia Death Black act previously known as BLACK THORNS.

Albums:
FOUR SEASONS OF GREY, Metal Blade (1998)
The Haunted Moon / Four Seasons Of Grey / Nocturne / Vampire, Garden Of Thorns / Forest Of The Impaled / Black Thorns / Beyond The Black Lake / The Gathering Storm

INSANIA (CZECH REPUBLIC)

Albums:
CROSSFADE, (1994)

INTENSE HAMMER RAGE (AUSTRALIA)

Line-Up: Chris (vocals / bass), Ricey (vocals / guitar), A.B. (vocals / drums)

Tazmanian trio INTENSE HAMMER RAGE go all out to shock with their brand of gut churning Grindcore. The band themselves subtly describe their own particular brand of Death Metal as "Putridfoulfesteringdeathgrindcuntcore". INTENSE HAMMER RAGE announced their arrival with a 1995 tape 'The 24cm Makita Brand Circular Saw' capitalized on by the following years 'Massive Sphinkta Release'. Although a quartet at this stage the band would dispense with their vocalist, for reasons as the band put it succinctly of being "lazy, whinging, so called vocalist".
1998 witnessed INTENSE HAMMER RAGE's debut CD 'Devogrindporngorecoreaphile'. With the expected obscene cover artwork the album swiftly sold out of its first production run. American label Extremist Records would re-issue the record as half of a shared release with DROGHEDA.
Further recordings resulted in the 'Gory B' eight song session released on cassette in Japan by Obliteration Records. The band, utilizing their subtly titled own label Slut Kunting Whore Productions, would later issue it on CD. A Spanish label, Flesh Feast Productions, would also pick up 'Gory B' pairing it for CD release with the 'Massive Sphinkta Release' demo.
American label Razorback put out the

2001 album 'Avagoyamugs'. For the same label the band donated their cover version of 'Defiling The Grave' for an IMPETIGO tribute album 'Wizards Of Gore'. Split singles in collaboration with ENGORGED and N.V.E. were also planned for 2001.

Albums:
DEVOGRINDPORNGORECOREAPHILE, Intense Hammer Rage (1998)
There's A Baby On My Knob / Reclusive Existence Of A Forgotten Entity / I Blame You / The Mechanism Of Defecation / Siamese Sluts Of Fused Flesh / Fucking Dead Babies 'Couse I'm A Sick Cunt / Axx-Scenting The Gore / I Dreamt I Had A Vagina / With Her Cunt She Fucks / Pussy Lips Kissing To The Wrist / Wetbones / Look Inside Her Insides / Human Pie /Pervert The Meat / Gore, Gore And More Fucking Gore / Addicted To The Splatter / Leaking, Reeking Pregnant Cunt / Sticky Mucoid Discharge
DEVOGRINDPORNGORECOREAPHILE, Extremist (1999) (Split album with DROGHEDA)
GORY B, Obliteration (1999) (Japanese cassette release)
GORY B, Slut Kunting Whore Productions (1999)
GORY B / MASSIVE SPHINKTA RELEASE, Flesh Feast Productions (1999) (Spanish release)
AVAGOYAMUGS, Razorback (2000)

INTENSE MUTILATION (USA)
Line-Up: Pungent Vomit (vocals / guitar), Fetus Fucker (bass), Jack Shit (drums)

Singles/EPs:
Blowin' In The Wind / Stagediver, New Renaissance NRR 55 (1989)

Albums:
SAFE SEX, New Renaissance (1989)
Safe Sex / Foreplay / Raghead / Vacuam Cleaner Love (The Hoover Manoeuvre) / P.T.L. - Part Thy Legs / Shit Stains / Just Say No / The Tenths Mutilation / Cunnilingus With A Razor / Blowin' In The Wind / A Short Burst Of Noise / Addicted To Crack / Duck Fuck / Stagediver / Mr. Chamber's Testicles / Chew Me, Chew Me / Eat Shit And Prosper / Horizontal Butter Churning / The ABC Song / Rent A Placenta / You Can Fuck Your Fetus And Eat It Too / Just Say No (Reprise) / Afterbirth Casserole / Saran Rap / Fuck You

INTERNAL BLEEDING
(New York, NY, USA)
Line-Up: Ray Lebron (vocals), Chris Pervelis (guitar), Guy Marchais (guitar), Jason Carbone (bass), Brian Tolley (drums)

Billing themselves as "Total fucking slam" INTERNAL BLEEDING debuted in 1991 with a line up of singer Brian Richards, guitarists Chris Pervalis and Anthony Miola, bassist Tom Slobowski and drummer Brian Tolley. The band would endure repeated line-up changes with only Pervalis and Tolley remaining as anchors. 1991 had the band releasing the 'One Dollar' demo followed by a second effort 'Invocation Of Evil' in 1993.

Richards would be replaced by the wonderfully named Eric Wigger but by the time of the debut album 'Voracious Contempt' Frank Rini was fronting the band. Although the album was mixed by Scott Burns the band were far from happy with the end result although in Death Metal circles the album is regarded as a near classic of the genre.

Toured America during 1996 on a Death Metal package bill alongside SIX FEET UNDER and IMMOLATION. Rini, who when he wasn't growling for a Death Metal band was plugging away at his day job as a policeman, would guest on DISFIGURED's 'Prelude To Dementia' album.

Rini made way for the former DISFIGURED Hawaiian shirt obsessed man Ryan Schimmenti. This liaison proved only temporary though as INTERNAL BLEEDING drafted Ray Lebron for the 'Driven To Conquer' album. The record was produced by Brian Griffin of BROKEN HOPE.

Miola would make his exit to have his place taken by ex-PYREXIA man Guy Marchias. Jason Carbone would take Hobbie's position in 2000.

Singles/EPs:
Perpetual Degradation, (1995)

Albums:
VORACIOUS CONTEMPT, Pavement (1996)
Languish In Despair / Anointed In Servitude / Reflection Of Ignorance / Epoch Of Barbarity / Gutted Human Sacrifice / God Of Subservience / Prophet Of The Blasphemers / Humanicide / Inhuman Suffering / Despoilement Of Rotting Flesh

THE EXTINCTION OF BENEVOLENCE, Pavement (1997)
Prepare For Extinction / Ocular Introspection / Prevaricate / Ruthless Inhumanity / Plagued By Catharsis / Conformed To Obscurity / Genetic Messiah / Cycle Of Vehemence
DRIVEN TO CONQUER, (1999)
Rage / Driven To Conquer / Falling Down / Six Shots In Dallas / Conditioned / Inhuman '99 / Invisible / Slave Soul / Anthem For A Doomed Youth

INTERNAL DECAY (SWEDEN)
Line-Up: Kim Blomqvist (vocals), Micke Jacobsson (guitar), Willy Maturna (guitar), Kenny (bass), Karim Elomary (keyboards), Thomas Sjöblom (drums)

INTERNAL DECAY were formed as CRITICAL STATE in 1987. A further name change to SUBLIMINAL FEAR occurred before finalizing on INTERNAL DECAY, with a demo cassette release in 1991.

Following the debut album release guitarist Willy Maturna lost his place to ex-EXCRUCIATE man Hempa Brynolfsson.

Albums:
A FORGOTTEN DREAM, Euro Records EURO934CD (1993)

INTERNAL SUFFERING
(COLUMBIA)
Line-Up: Fabio (vocals), Leandro (guitar), Andres (bass), Edwin (drums)

INTERNAL SUFFERING, previously entitled SUFFER, feature erstwhile RITUAL guitarist Leandro. The band supported visitors to Colombia INCANTATION and SODOM during 1997. Original drummer Jorge would decamp to be replaced with Edwin as the band signed with the Spanish Repulse concern for their debut album 'Supreme Knowledge Domain'. However, after recording Edwin made his exit and Fabio took the drum stool. In a round of musical chairs this new enlistee would soon break ranks and Edwin was inducted back into the fold.

INTERNAL SUFFERING cut the 6 track mini-album 'Unmercyful Examination' for the Japanese Macabre Mementos label and followed this with a split album 'Vatican's Bombardment' shared with Americans STENCH OF DECREPITY.

Touring in 2001 found INTERNAL SUFFERING on the road in America alongside BRODEQUIN and Japan's

VOMIT REMNANTS.

Albums:
SUPREME KNOWLEDGE DOMAIN,
Supreme Music SM001 (2000)
Mighty Triumphant Return / Valley Of The
Impaled / Evil Sorcerers / Daemons
Awakening / Outside Dwellers / Threshold
Into The Unknown / Enter The Gate Of
Death / Beyond The Mystic Portal Of
Madness / Supreme Knowledge Domain /
Summoning The Ancient Ones
UNMERCYFUL EXAMINATION,
Macabre Mementos (2001)
Unmercyful Examination / Dominating
Thunderous Force / Breeders Of Chaos /
Outside Dwellers (New Hyper Brutality
Impaled Version) / Catacombs Devourer
/ Decapitation Of The Weak
VATICAN'S BOMBARDMENT,
Fleshfeast Productions (2001) (Split
album with STENCH OF DECREPITY)

INTESTINAL BLEEDING (BELGIUM)

Singles/EPs:
Split, (1997) (7" split single with
ACROHOLIA)
Split, (199-) (7" split single with
CORNUCOPIA)

Albums:
INTESTINAL BLEEDING, (199-) (Split
album with ROT)

INTESTINAL DISEASE (BELGIUM)

INTESTINAL DISEASE's shared 1996
album with Brazilians ROT 'Defying The
Wisdom Of Authority' includes a cover
version of ROT's 'Reality Based On Lies'.
By way of recompense ROT would cover
INTESTINAL DISEASE's 'World
Abruption'.

Singles/EPs:
Split, (199-) (7" split single with
CORNUCOPIA)

Albums:
**DEFYING THE WISDOM OF
AUTHORITY**, (1996) (Split album with
ROT)
Repetitive Cliché / Painted Cloud / No I'm
Not / Chaotic Dream / De Idealist / Reject
/ This Community Is Not For Me / Burning
/ People Leave / Reality Based On Lies /
Conform Or Live / Happy Depression /
Teachers In The School / Compact
Dazzle Shit / It's Time For Change

INTESTINAL DISGORGE (BRAZIL)
Line-Up: Pissy (vocals), Josh (guitar),
Nick (bass), Ryan (drums)

Grindcore merchants INTESTINAL
DISGORGE bowed in with the 1999
demo 'Festering Excrement'. A split
cassette with EJACULATED WHORE
followed prior to an appearance on a 4-
way compilation tape in collaboration with
SLOUGH, DEMONIC ORGY and
ABOSRAINE BOSOM.
The band would split up before the
release of their 2001 album 'Whore
Splattered Walls'.

Albums:
**DROWNED IN EXCREMENTAL
SLUDGE**, Lofty Storm LSR006 (2000)
Rectum Grinder / Plastered In Runny
Filth / Toilet Intercourse / Bathing In
Fecal Bathwater / Corrosion Of Green
Anal Walls / Gastrointestinal Splatter
Spray / Gorging On Fizzing Malignant
Entrails / Imbibing Rancid Micturation /
Intestinal Collapse And Melting /
Extensive Obliteration Of The Rectal
Orifice / Exploding Juicy Cancerous
Guts / Caked In Grimy Rectal Filth /
Vomiting Rancid Grime / Sleeping In
Grime Soaked Bedsheets / Swimming In
Child Innards / Torrents Of Festering
Purulency / Trembling In Torrents Of
Diarrhea / Life Story Of A Coprophagic /
Soaking Wet With Urination /
Disemboweled And Deliciously
Barbecued / Foaming Genital
Corpulence / Colonic Eruption /
Butchered Rotting Human Carcasses /
Soaked With Intestinal Chyme /
Cascade Of Gastrointestinal Crap /
Bloody Feces Syndrome / Vomiting
Fecal Paste / Face Down In A Toilet Full
Of Vomit And Feces / Pictures Of
Blistered Genitalia
WHORE SPLATTERED WALLS, Lofty
Storm (2001)

INTESTINE BAALISM (JAPAN)

Albums:
ANANATOMY OF THE BEAST, (199-)
Corporal Celebration / An Anatomy Of
The Beast / Alastor Possess /
Energumenus (The Rebirth Of The
Cursed Creation) / Blasphemy
Resurrected / A Place Their Gods Left
Behind / Burn Thou In Effigy / Tyrant

INTOXICATE (SWITZERLAND)
Line-Up: Marcel (vocals), Thomas (guitar), Ivo (guitar), Ivo C. (bass), Josh (drums)

Singles/EPs:
Sacred Inquisition / Global Disaster / Silent Killing, Intoxicate TR 94031 (1994) ('Silent Killing' EP)

INVERSION (USA)

Despite the uncompromising song titles INVERSION are in fact a well disguised Christian Death Metal act. Guest drummer on 'The Nature Of Depravity' is Dave Campbell of DEATH LIST, OBLITERATION and SICKENED.

Albums:
THE NATURE OF DEPRAVITY, (2000)

INVOCATOR (DENMARK)
Line-Up: Jacob Hansen (vocals / guitar), Jacob Schultz (guitar), Jesper M. Jensens (bass), Per M. Jensens (drums)

A pioneering Death Metal band dating back to 1986 that went under their original title of BLACK CREED, the group's first demo tape was 'Genetic Confusion' in 1988 followed by 'Alterations' the following year. After gigs with EDGE OF SANITY and ENTOMBED the band signed to Swedish label Black Mark.
The band's debut album 'Excursion Demise' sold around 10,000 copies in Europe, prompting INVOCATOR to record a further album 'Weave The Apocalypse' and they opened for PARADISE LOST in Europe during 1994.
1995's 'Early Years' album comprised the band's original demo tapes plus covers of ARTILLERY and DARK ANGEL tracks. The same year found Jacob Hansen aiding fellow Danish Death Metallers MERCENARY with production on their 'Supremacy' EP.
Jacob Schultz was replaced by guitarist Perle Hansen for the 'Dying To Live' album.

Albums:
EXCURSIONS DEMISE, Black Mark BMCD12 (1992)
Excursion Demise (...To A Twisted Recess Of Mind) / Forsaken Ones / The Persistence From Memorial Chasm / Absurd Temptation / Schismatic Injective Therapy / Occurrence Concealed /

Beyond Insufferable Dormancy / Inner Contrarieties / Alterations
WEAVE THE APOCALYPSE, Black Mark BMCD 34 (1993)
Through The Nether To The Sun / From My Skull It Rains / Desert Sands / Condition Critical / Breed Of Sin / Doomed To Be / Lost At Birth / Land Of Misery / The Afterbirth / Weave The Apocalypse
EARLY YEARS, Die Hard RRS943 (1995)
Dismal Serfage / Insurrected Despair / Restraint Life / The Scars Remain / Alterations / Occurrence Concealed / The Persistence From Memorial Chasm / Pursuit Of A Rising Necessity / The Eternal War / The Promise Of Agony
DYING TO LIVE, Progress PCD20 (1995)
Dying To Live / Kristendom / Shattered Self / King In A World Of Fools / Search / South Of No North / Living Is It / Astray / For A While / Hole

IRONIA (SPAIN)

Singles/EPs:
Split, (199-) (7" split single with FINAL EXIT)

223

JUDGEMENT DAY
(HOLLAND)
Line-Up: Jeroen Dammers
(vocals), Simone (vocals),
Wim Van Burken (guitar),
Theo Van Eekelen (guitar),
Bus Van Den Bogaard
(bass), Nolo (drums)

A Dutch Death Metal band, JUDGEMENT DAY have toured with SINISTER, PUNGENT STENCH and KRABATHOR. In addition to their debut album of 1996 vintage the group have had three songs featured on the 'Effigy Of The Possessed' compilation album.
JUDGEMENT DAY boasts the inclusion of veterans from such acts as CENTURION and PLEUROSY. Bass player Theo Van Eekelen also performs in HOUWITSER and the reformed THANATOS.
The 7" single released on Damnation Records includes a cover version of SLAUGHTER's 'F.O.D.'.

Singles/EPs:
To Conjure Conjoint Confusion, Damnation (2000) (7" single)

Albums:
CIR - CUM - CIS - ION OF THE MAR - TYR, Arctic Serenades EFFI 006 (1996)
Horror Pain / Daily Rituals / The Old Tree / Sexual Intercourse / Invisible Downfall / Clouds Of Mordor / Pathology Of Crowding

JULIE LAUGHS NO MORE
(SWEDEN)
Line-Up: Danne (vocals), Blomman (vocals / guitar), Thomas (guitar), Babbaen (bass), Ronnie B. (drums)

Albums:
WHEN ONLY DARKNESS REMAINS, Voices Of Wonder (1999)
Only Darkness Remains / Morbid Dreams / Domains Of Darkness / The Cold Awakening / The Ashes Of The Midnight Sun / Silent Waters / Everything Dies

JUNGLE ROT (Kenosha, WI, USA)
Line-Up: Dave Matrise (vocals / guitar), Kevin Forsythe (guitar), Chris Djurcic (bass), Jim Garcia (drums)

JUNGLE ROT's own particular brand 'Deathgroove', along with their themed album cover artwork's based on the ubiquitous figure of Sergeant Rot, has set them apart from the pack. The band, named after the Vietnamese war version of trenchfoot, arrived in 1994 with a line up of vocalist / guitarist Jim Bell, vocalist / guitarist Dave Matrise, bassist Chris Djurcic and ex-PRISONER drummer Jim Harte.
With this line up JUNGLE ROT cut the opening demo 'Rip Off Your Face'. A second demo, 1996's 'Skin The Living', witnessed such a volume of sales that the sessions were re-released on CD format in 1998 by Pure Death Records. A latter line up saw the percussion station taken by erstwhile EVIL INCARNATE man Andy Vehnekamp.
JUNGLE ROT's second album 'Slaughter The Weak' was originally issued by Pulverizer Records in 1998. Label problems saw a swift re-release, with different artwork, the following year by Pavement Records. Meantime a third round of artwork graced the European version licensed to Germany's Morbid Records with the original depictions of dead bodies removed.
With JUNGLE ROT on a roll a mini-album 'Darkness Foretold' was quickly released. The record included the brand new title track, live material and cover versions of CARNIVORE's 'Jesus Hitler', SLAYER's 'Fight Till Death' and SODOM's 'Agent Orange'. This record has proven to be quite a collectors item as it came with a JUNGLE ROT 'Sergeant Rot' comic the cover of which is covered in the by now expected, entrails, brains and gouged eyes.
JUNGLE ROT underwent a major line-up overhaul when founding member Jim Bell departed. Former CYANOSIS man Kevin Forsythe took the role and his CYANOSIS colleague Jim Garcia took the drum position from previous incumbent Shawn Johnson.
Keeping up with tradition JUNGLE ROT's 2001 album 'Dead And Buried', released on Olympic Records, saw a European license through Season Of Mist Records but with the artwork (you guessed it - dead bodies...) revised to accommodate the censor.

Albums:
SKIN THE LIVING, Pure Death (1998)
Demon Souls / Destruction And Misery / Eternal Agony / Killing Spree / Rotten Bodies / Black Candle Mass / Awaiting The End / Tomb Of Armenus / Decapitated / Screaming For Life
SLAUGHTER THE WEAK, Pulverizer (1998)

Left For Dead / Gore Bag / Infectious /
Demigorgon / Consumed In Darkness /
Murder One / Butchering Death / World
Of Hate / Deadly Force
DARKNESS FORETOLD, Sounds Of
Death (1998)
Agent Orange / Fight Till Death / Jesus
Hitler / Darkness Foretold / Tomb Of
Armenus (Live) / Eternal Agony (Live) /
Consumed In Darkness (Live)
DEAD AND BURIED, Olympic 216
(2001)
Intro / Immersed In Pain / Virus /
Misplaced Anger / Humans Shall Pay /
Strangulation Mutilation / Red Skies /
Killing Machine / Dead And Buried /
Psychotic Cremation / Afterlife / Circle Of
Death - Jungle Rot / Another Fix

KAT (POLAND)
Line-Up: Roman Kostrzewski (vocals), Poitr Luczyk (guitar), Wojciech Mrowiec (guitar), Tomasz Jagus (bass), Irseneusz Loth (drums)

KAT were amongst the first Polish Metal bands to make a breakthrough into Western European Rock circles in the mid 80s. KAT's debut Polish release '666' was reissued for the Western market in the toned down form of 'Metal And Hell'. Following the 1989 album 'Oddech Wymarlich Swiatów' ("The Breath Of Dead Worlds") KAT underwent line up changes. Losing guitarist Wojciech Mrowiec and bass player Tomasz Jagus the band would regroup with bassist K. Oset and guitar player J. Regulsji.
The 1992 'Bastard' album found KAT operating more furiously than ever before but the act calmed down considerably for the 1994 'Ballady' effort. Later work has seen KAT back on track.
The 1997 mini-album 'Badz Wariatem, Zagraj Z Latem' (Get Crazy, Play With Kat') the band reworked earlier material alongside new tracks and Techno remixes.
KAT vocalist Roman Kostrzewski has also issued a double album inspired by Anton La Vey's 'Satanic Bible'.

Singles/EPs:
Ostatni Tabor / Noce Szatana, MMPR (1985) (7" single)

Albums:
666, Silverton (1986)
Metal I Pieklo / Diabelsk Dom Cz. I / Morderca / Masz Mnie Wampirze / Czas Zemsty / Nole Szatana / Diabelski Dom Cz. III / Wyrocznia / 666 / Czarne Zasepy
METAL AND HELL, Ambush (1986)
Metal And Hell / Killer / Time To Revenge / Devil's House Part I / (You Got Me) Vampire / Devil's Child / Black Hosts / Oracle / Devil's House Part II / 666
38 MINUTES OF LIVE, Silverton (1988)
ODDECH WYMARLYCH SWIATÓW, Metal Mind (1994)
BASTARD, Silverton (1992)
W Bezsztalnej Bryle Uwieziony / Zawieszony Sznur / Bastard / Ojcze Samotni / N.D.C. / Piwniczne Widziadia / W Sadzie Smiertelnego Piekna / Odmiency / Lza Dla Cieriow Minionych
BALLADY, Silverton (1994)
Legenda Wyshiona / Glos Z Ciemnosci /

Talizman / Lza Dla Cienlow Minionych / Delirium Tremens / Czas Zemsty / Robak / Bez Pamieci / Niewinnosc
RÓZE MILOSCI NAJCHETNIEJ PRZYJMUJA SIE NA GROBACH, Silverton (1995)
Odi Profanum Vulgus / Purpurowe Gody / Plaszcz Skrytobojcy / Stworzylem Pieknarzecz / Slodki Krem / Wierze / Strzez Sie Plucia Pod Wiater / Szmaragd Bazyliszka
BADZ WARIATEM, ZAGRAJ Z KATEM, Silverton (1997)
SZYDERCZE ZWIERCIADO, Silverton (1997)

KATAKLYSM (CANADA)
Line-Up: Aquarius Sylvian Mars Venus (vocals), Jean Francois Dagenais (guitar), Maurizio Lacono (bass), Max Duhamal (drums)

Canadian Death Black act KATAKLYSM opened proceedings with the demo tape 'The Death Gate Cycle Of Reincarnation'. Line up initially was vocalist Aquarius Sylvian Mars Venus (Sylvian Houde), guitarist Stephan Core, bassist Maurizio Lacono and drummer Ariel Saide. The band signed to the German label Nuclear Blast for a debut 1993 album 'The Mystical Gate Of Reincarnation'.
Promoting the sophomore 'Sorcery' effort KATAKLYSM put in their inaugural European shows, including dates with DEICIDE, and became the first Canadian band to tour Mexico.
KATAKLYSM's drummer Max Duhamel was forced to leave the band in late 1995 following cartilage damage to his right knee. His replacement was American Nick Miller.
The band then switched to the Canadian Hypnotic label for the experimental 'Victim Of The Fallen World' album. However, this record saw limited distribution. By 1998 Duhamel had made his return as the band welcomed in new bassist Stephane Barbe.
Resigning with their former label Nuclear Blast KATAKLYSM cut the 2000 'The Prophecy' outing. Guests included Rob of NECROMONICON and Mike DeSaho of CRYPTOPSY.

Singles/EPs:
Vision The Chaos (Kataklysm Part I) / Shrine Of Life (Chapter III - Reborn Through Death version II), Boundless (1994) (7" single)

Albums:

THE MYSTICAL GATE OF REINCARNATION, Nuclear Blast NB093 (1993)
The Mystical Gate Of Reincarnation: Trilogy, I) Frozen In Time (Chapter One - Will Of Suicide), II) Mystical Plane Of Evil (Chapter Two - Enigma Of The Unknown), III) Shrine Of Life (Chapter Three - Reborn Through Death / The Orb Of Uncreation

SORCERY, Nuclear Blast NB108 (1995)
Sorcery / The Rebirth Of Creation: Trilogy, I) Mould In A Breed (Chapter One - Bestial Propagation), II) Whirlwind Of Withered Blossoms (Chapter Two - Forgotten Ancestors), III) Feeling The Neverworld (Chapter Three - An Infinite Transmigration) / Elder God / The Resurrected Portal Of Heaven: Trilogy, I) Garden Of Dreams (Chapter One - Supernatural Appearance), II) Once... Upon Possession (Chapter Two - Legacy Of Both Lores), III) Dead Zygote (Chapter Three - Dethroned Son) / World Of Treason

THE TEMPLE OF KNOWLEDGE, Nuclear Blast NB 157-2 (1996)
The Transflamed Memories (Trinity, I) The Unholy Signature (Segment One- Utterly Significant, II) Beckoning The Xul (Segment II - In The Midst Of The Azonei's Dominion), III) Point Of Evanescence (Segment III - Of Sheer Perseverance) / Through The Core Of

The Damned (Trinity IV) Fathers From The Suns (Act 1 - The Occurred Barrier), V) Enhanced By The Lore (Act 2 - Scholarship Ordained), VI) In Parallel Horizons (Act 3 - Spontaneous Aura Projection) / Era of Aquarius (Trinity VII) The Awakener (Epoch 1 - Summon The Legends), VIII) Maelstrom 2010 (Epoch 2 - Omens About The Great Infernos), IX) Exode Of Evils (Epoch 3 - Ladder Of Thousand Parsecs) / L'Odysee

VICTIM OF THE FALLEN WORLD, Hypnotic (1998)
As My World Burns / Imminent Downfall / Feared Resistance / Caged In / Portraits Of Anger / Extreme To The Core / Courage Through Hope / A View From Inside / (God) Head / Embracing Europa / Remember / World Of Treason II

NORTHERN HYPERBLAST LIVE, Hypnotic (1999)
Maelstrom 2010 / Exode Of Evils / Enchant By The Lore / Sorcery / Elder God / Fathers From The Sun / Point Of Evanescence / Beckoning Of The Xul / The Awakener / Once… Upon Possession / The Unholy Signature / The Orb Of Uncreation / In Parallel Horizons / Vision The Chaos / Shrine Of Life

THE PROPHECY (STIGMATA OF THE IMMACULATE), Nuclear Blast NB 470-2 (2000)
1999: 6661: 2000 / Manifestation / Stormland / Breeding The Everlasting / Laments Of Fear And Despair / Astral

Empire / Gateway To Extinction / Machiavellion / Renaissance

KATATONIA (SWEDEN)
Line-Up: Sombreius Blackheim (vocals / guitar), Israphel Wing (bass), Lord Seth (drums)

KATATONIA started life as a duo of guitar Sombreius Blackheim (real name Anders Nyström) and vocalist / drummer Lord Seth (real name Jonas Renske) in 1987. The group issued the 1992 demo 'JHVA Elohin Meth' which was later released in CD form by Dutch label Vic Records.
In late 1992 KATATONIA added bassist Israphael Wing (real name Guillaume Le Hucke) signing to No Fashion Records.
In addition to the material listed below the band have also contributed two tracks ('Black Erotica' and 'Love Of The Swan') to the Wrong Again Records compilation album 'W.A.R.' in 1995. Further recordings of interest included a split 7" EP with PRIMORDIAL the following year. Blackheim also has a side project band titled BEWITCHED releasing the 'Diabolical Desecration' album on Osmose Records in 1996. Seth is working on his OCTOBER TIDE project.
KATATONIA performed a short British tour in late 1996 with support acts IN THE WOODS and VOICE OF DESTRUCTION.
Blackheim and Seth also pursued another Death Metal project titled DIABOLICAL MASQUERADE. In 2000 the pair forged Black Metal project act BLOODBATH with EDGE OF SANITY's industrious Dan Swanö and OPETH's Mikael Akerfeldt.

Singles/EPs:
Midvinter Gates (Prologue) / Without God / Palace Of Frost / The Northern Silence / Crimson Tears (Epilogue), Vic VIC 1 (1994) ('Jhva Elohim Meth...The Revival' EP)
Funeral Wedding / Shades Of Emerald Fields / For Funerals To Come... / Epistal, Avantgarde AV 009 (1995) ('For Funerals To Come' EP)
Scarlet Heavens EP, Misanthropy (1996) (Split EP with PRIMORDIAL)
Nowhere / At Last / Inside The Fall, Avantgarde (1997) ('Sounds Of Decay' EP)
Saw You Drown / Scarlet Heavens, Avantgarde (1997)

Albums:
DANCE OF THE DECEMBER SOULS, No Fashion 005 (1995)
Seven Dreaming Souls / Gateways Of Bereavement / In Silence Enshrined / Without God / Elohim Meth / Velvet Thorns (Of Drynwhyl) / Tomb Of Insomnia / Dancing December
BRAVE MURDER DAY, Avantgarde AV022 (1996)
Brave / Murder / Day / Rainroom / 12 / Endtime
DISCOURAGE ONES, Avantgarde AV 029 (1998)
I Break / Stalemate / Deadhouse / Relention / Cold Ways / Gone / Last Resort / Nerve / Saw You Drown / Instrumental / Distrust
TONIGHT'S DECISION, (199-)
For My Demons / I Am Nothing / In Death, A Song / Had To (Leave) / This Punishment / Right Into The Bliss / No Good Can Come Of This / Strained / A Darkness Coming / Nightmares By The Sea / Black Session
SINGLES COLLECTION, (199-)
Midvinter Gates (Prologue) / Without God / Palace Of Frost / The Northern Silence / Crimson Tears (Epilogue) / Funeral Wedding / Shades Of Emerald Fields / For Funerals To Come... / Epistal / Nowhere / At Last / Inside The Fall
TEARGAS, Peaceville (2001)
LAST FAIR DEAL GONE DOWN, Peaceville (2001)
Dispossession / Chrome / We Will Bury You / Teargas / I Transpire / Tonights Music / Clean Today / The Future Of Speech / Passing Bird / Sweet Nurse / Don't Tell A Soul

KAZJUROL (SWEDEN)
Line-Up: Kjelle (vocals), Pontus (guitar), Tban (guitar), Hakan (bass), Bonden (drums)

KAZJUROL began as a purely amateur project by members of Hardcore band RESCUES IN FUTURE. The band's first commercial release came with a track on a German compilation single entitled 'Breaking The Silence' in 1986.
The interest generated by the single track prompted the recording of a demo cassette titled 'A Lesson In Love', which surfaced in 1988.
The band eventually released their debut album, 'Dance Tarantella', in 1990 which saw vocalist Kjelle replaced by Tomas Bengtsson. However, by the next release, the 'Bodyslam' EP KAZJUROL had found another frontman in Henka 'Gator'

Ahlberg. The EP featured covers of tracks by BAD BRAINS, VENOM, STORMTROOPERS OF DEATH and CRO-MAGS.

The band further displayed their Hardcore / Punk leanings with a cover of a DISCHARGE track on the Burning Heart Records 1991 compilation 'A Tribute Of Memories'.

However, KAZJUROL eventually split, with both guitarists forming Hardcore act BAD DREAMS ALWAYS.

Singles/EPs:
Messengers Of Death / Stagedive To Hell / Who Needs You?, Uproar UPROAR 004 (1987)
We Gotta Know / United Forces / Pay To Cum / Countess Bathory, Burning Heart Heartcore 001 (1991) ('Bodyslam' EP)
Hallucinations / Dance Tarentella / Blue Eyed Devils, Burning Heart Heartcore 002 (1991)

Albums:
DANCE TARANTULA, Active ATV12 (1990)
A Clockwork Out Of Order / Moment 22 / Than / Honesty, The Right Excuse / Dance Tarantella / Blind Illusions / Three Minator / Echoes From The Past / Stagedive To Hell

KEKAL (INDONESIA)
Line-Up: Jeff (vocals / guitar), Leo (guitar), Azhar (vocals / bass)

KEKAL, dating to August 1995, are an extreme Metal band moulding elements of Death, Black and Progressive styles into one unsavoury whole. Debuted with a 1996 demo entitled 'Contre Spiritualia Nequitiae'. The act originally included vocalist Harry who quit following the debut album leaving KEKAL as a trio with guitarist Jeff taking the lead vocal role. Second album 'Beyond The Dead' would see a release in America on the Fleshwalker label.
Guitarist Jeff (as 'Jefray') is an ex-INNER WARFARE member and also pursues a one man side project EXCISION releasing the 'Visi' album in 2000.

Albums:
BEYOND THE GLIMPSE OF DREAMS, Candlelight Productions (1998)
Rotting Youth / Armageddon / Spirits / Deceived Minds / The Conversion / Behind Those Images / Reality / Escaping

Eternal Suffering / A Day The Hatred Dies / My Eternal Lover
EMBRACE THE DEAD, THT Productions (1999)
Longing For Truth / Embrace The Dead / The Fearless And The Dedicated / Healing / The Final Call / From Within / Scripture Before Struggle / Millennium
THE PAINFUL EXPERIENCE, (2001)

KILLENGOD (AUSTRALIA)
Line-Up: Errol Nyp (vocals), Daniel Maynard (guitar), Corey Pagan (guitar), Daniel Maynard (bass), Jonathon Dao (drums)

Brisbane Death Metal with Black overtones. KILLENGOD was convened in 1994 as a trio of guitarist Errol Nyp, bass player Drexlar Roberts and drummer Jonathon Dao. Initially both Nyp and Dao would handle lead vocals with the guitarist handling the guttural growls whilst Dao emitted the ear piercing screams.
KILLENGOD's commercial debut came with the inclusion of their track 'Blasphemous Priest' included on a local compilation album. Following the first album 'Transcendual Consciousness' Roberts would depart as KILLENGOD pulled in bass player Daniel Maynard and second guitarist Corey Pagan.

Albums:
TRANSCENDUAL CONSCIOUSNESS, Warhead WHCD13 (199-)
Ever Death Flow / Funeral Fuck / Soul Mutilation / Believe In Divination / Experimental Evidence / Transcendual Consciousness / Luceferic Leviathan / Nordic Messiah
INTO THE ANCIENT MOON, Repulse (1998)
Ode To An Ancient Moon / Dominated Spirit / Temporary Skin / Thirteenth Universe / Masquerade Of The Masters / Lorde Of Whores / My Intention / Inhaling The Corpse / Everlasting Egypt / Black Miracle / Blasphemous Priest

KILLING ADDICTION
(Ocala, FL, USA)
Line-Up: Pat Bailey (vocals / bass), Chad Bailey (guitar), Chris Wicklein (guitar), Chris York (drums)

Florida Death Metal act KILLING ADDICTION first emerged in the late 80's issuing the 'Legacies Of Terror' demo in 1990.

Singles/EPs:
Necrosphere, Seraphic Decay (1991) (7"
single)

Albums:
OMEGA FACTOR, JL America (1993)
Omega Factor / Equating The Trinity /
Nothing Remains / Dehumanized /
Altered At Birth / Necrosphere / Global
Frenzy / Impaled

KILLING CULTURE
(Los Angeles, CA, USA)
Line-Up: Marcus Peyton (vocals), Scott
Sergeant (guitar), Paul Poljiz (bass), Pat
Magrath (drums)

Brutal   headbangers   KILLING
CULTURE's debut album was produced
by ANTHRAX guitarist Scott Ian. The
band toured Germany in April 1997 as
part of the 'Full Of Hate' touring bill
alongside OBITUARY, ENTOMBED and
CROWBAR.

Albums:
KILLING CULTURE, Concrete Edel
0089532 CTR (1996)
Twins In Human / Resurrection 2000 /
Live / And Hate / Lockfist / World
Attraction / The Line / With Strife / Life
By Attrition / Verse 19 / Rhetoric God /
Slave Of One / Ironside

KILLJOY (USA)

Solo project from Killjoy of
NECROPHAGIA.

Albums:
COMPELLED BY FEAR, New
Renaissance (1989)
Body Count / Enemy Within (Cycle Of
Insanity) / Faith Against Faith / Infected /
Demise Of Humanity / Status Nine /
Frozen Refuge / Fall From Grace /
Compelled By Fear
BAD NEWS DAY, (199-)
Hazing / Plankowner / Gainesville / 2AM
/ New Scene / Eating Paste / A Little
Pain / Every Poor Sucker / Suicide /
Valve Days (Open Pool) / The One Who
Reaps The Rewards / Permanent Press
/ Leaving City / Gingerale

KONKHRA (HOLLAND)
Line-Up: Anders Lundemark (vocals /
guitar), Kim Mathieson (guitar), Thomas
Christiansen (bass), Johnny Nielsen
(drums)

KONKHRA, who like to label themselves
as "Death n' Roll", were founded in
Copenhagen during 1988 and initially
featured ex-FURIOUS TRAUMA bassist
Lars Schmidt. The band got around to
recording their debut demo tape in early
1990 with a second attempt the following
year.
KONKHRA signed to local label Progress
Records and issued the 'Stranded' EP.
This official debut, limited to only 3,000
copies, featured sleeve artwork by noted
Chicago tattoo artist Guy Aitchison. The
release was capitalized on by support
slots to acts such as FEAR FACTORY
and BRUTAL TRUTH.
With the release of their first full length
album in 1993's 'Sexual Affective
Disorder', KONKHRA put in an American
tour supported by label mates
MEATLOCKER and a January 1994
European trek with SUFFOCATION.
The third album, 'Spit Or Swallow', was
produced by DISMEMBER drummer Fred
Estby and was to push KONKHRA to the
status of being Progress Records best
selling act.
In support of the record the band toured
Europe in 1995 on a bill alongside
DEICIDE and SUFFOCATION. However,
Scandinavian   dates   alongside
IMMOLATION and CANNIBAL CORPSE
had KONKHRA succumbing to internal
pressures and splitting in two. Following
the tour both Neilsen and Mathiesen quit.
KONKHRA duly regrouped adding
American ex-TESTAMENT, MACHINE
HEAD and ATTITUDE ADJUSTMENT
drummer Chris Kontos.
Lundemark meantime also put his efforts
into side project DEAMON liaising with
ENTOMBED members guitarist Ulf
Cederland and drummer Nicke
Andersson.
In 1997 KONKHRA started work on a new
album 'Weed Out The Weak' as they
were brought up to strength with the
addition of ex-CANCER, OBITUARY and
DISINCARNATE guitarist JAMES
MURPHY.
Incidentally, KONKHRA's 'Homegrowth'
video featured a cover of
TERRORISER's 'The Dead Shall Rise'
and guest contributions from members of
NAPALM DEATH.
The 'Come Down Cold' album sees
Kontos replaced by Per M. Jensen.
Although Murphy contributes guitar once
again for live work, starting out on a
European support to NAPALM DEATH,
Lars Mayland filled in on guitar.

Singles/EPs:
Time Will Destroy / Day-Break / Stranded / Lustration Of The Need / Spread Around / Deathwish, Progress PRL002 (1992) ('Stranded' EP)
Facelift / Drowning (Dead Dreaming / Warzone / Basic Facts Of Life, Progress PCD18 (1995)

Albums:
SEXUAL AFFECTIVE DISORDER, Progress PRL CD7913009 (1993)
Center Of The Flesh / Seasonal Affective Disorder / The Dying Art / Visually Intact / Evilution (Exordium Expired) / Lucid Dreams / Blindfolded / Thoughts Abandoned / Chaos To Climb / Empty Frames
SPIT OR SWALLOW, Progress PCD19 (1995)
Centuries / Spit Or Swallow / Life Eraser / Hail The Body, Burden The Spirit / Hooked / Facelift / Scorn Of The Earth / Subconscience / Necrosphere / Hold Another Level
LIVE ERASER, Progress PCD31 (1996)
Hooked / Warzone / Basic Facts Of Life / S.A.D. / The Dying Art / Centuries / Drowning (Dead Dreaming) / Facelift / Subconconscience / Life Eraser / Spit Or Swallow
WEED OUT THE WEAK, Diehard PCD 44 (1997)
Heavensent / Time Will Heal / Crown Of The Empire / Kinshasa Highway / Through My Veins / The Reckoning / Misery / Melting / Inhuman / Pain And Sorrow (Segue) / My Belief
COME DOWN COLD, (2000)
Godgiven / White / Lost To The World / Divide And Conquer / Truly Defiled / Gold / Sight For Sore Eyes / Back In The Day / Convene The Freaks / Blessed / Life Is Fragile / Procreation

KOROVA (AUSTRIA)
Line-Up: Christof Niederwiesr (vocals / guitar / keyboards), Georg Razeburger (guitar), Michael Kröll (bass), Moritz Neuner (drums)

Albums:
A KISS IN THE CHARNEL FIELD, Napalm NPR009 (1995)
Intro: Der Weltenbrand / Das Kreuz und der Meltzenapfel / After The Fruits Of Ephemeral Pulchritide / Lachrydeus Mittelgard (Slahan Fontagr Inn Awebi) / Entlebt in tristem Morgenblut / Latin Dreams In Turpentine / Intro: Im Teich Erlischt Ein Bächlein / Awakening From

Perpetual Contemplation (Yellow Mahogony Tomb I) / Nordsciltim In The Filth Where All Cull Perambulates Pain / Salomeh, Des Teufels Braut / A Kiss In The Charnel Field
DEAD LIKE AN ANGEL, (1998)
Europa In Flammen / Strangulation Alpha / Our Reality Dissolves / Trip To The Bleeding Planets / Dead Like An Angel / Echoworld Caravans / Der Schlafmann Kommt / Tantra-Nova-Hyper Cannibalism

KOROZY (BULGARIA)
Line-Up: Possessor (vocals / guitar), Vampira (bass), Inscriptor (keyboards), Trolon (drums)

Albums:
LONG ROAD TO THE LAND OF BLACK, (1999)
Road To The Land Of Black / Dying Memories / Welcome To The Black Palace / Birth Of The Witch / The Blessing Of The Kehajota Witch / Soul Belongs To Evil / The Anger Of Servant

KRABATHOR (CZECH REPUBLIC)
Line-Up: Christopher (vocals / guitar), Bruno (bass), Skull (drums)

KRABATHOR date to 1984. The band issued a glut of demos in the mid 80's including 1988's 'Breath Of Death', 'Total Destruction' and 'Brutal Death' before the project was put on ice as members served their national service for two years.
April of 1991 had KRABATHOR back in action with the demo session 'Feelings Of Dethronisation', the band's first with English lyrics. Signing to Czech label Monitor Records KRABATHOR's debut went on to sell some 16,000 copies backed by a video for the track 'Pacifistic Death'.
In an effort to break Western markets the group signed to German label Morbid Records for the limited edition mini-album 'The Rise Of Brutality'.
KRABATHOR's third effort 'Lies' shifted over 15,000 copies enabling a tour of Europe which saw the band on the road with IMPALED NAZARENE in October 1995. The Spring of 1996 had the band gigging with CANNIBAL CORPSE, IMMOLATION, GRAVE and ROTTING CHRIST. The band also broke the ice in America performing at the infamous Milwaukee Metalfest. Returning to Europe KRABATHOR resumed activities with shows backing DEICIDE,

ENTOMBED, NIGHTFALL, NAPALM DEATH and SINISTER. Headline dates saw support from South Africans GROINCHURN and Germans SANITY DAWN.

The KRABATHOR duo of Bruno and Skull founded side project HYPNOS in 2000 releasing an eponymous album. Skull kept himself doubly busy by uniting with frontman Christopher in a project titled MARTYR in union with the notorious American Deathster Paul Speckman of MASTER and ABOMINATION fame for the 'Murder: The End Of The Game' album.

Singles/EPs:
The Rise Of Brutality EP, Morbid (1995)
Breath Of Death / Bestial War / Apocrypha / Orthodox / Slavery, Morbid MR 035 (1997) ('Mortal Memories' EP)

Albums:
ONLY OUR DEATH IS WELCOME..., Monitor-MDD (1992)
Royal Crown / Psychedelic / Eternal / Convict To Contempt / Before The Carnage / Pacifistic Death / Preparing Your End / Killing My Wrath / Worried Childhood / Madness Of The Dark Shadow
COOL MORTIFICATION, Monitor (1993)
Faces Under The Ice / In The Blazing River / Evil Coroners Of The Mind / The Loop / Without The Following Dawn / Forget The Gods / Absence Of Life / Temporary Reign Of Insignificancy / Absence Of Life (Absence Of Mind mix)
LIES, Morbid MR019 (1995)
The Truth About Lies / Unnecessary / Short Report On The Ritual Carnage / Tears, Hope And Hate / Pain Of Bleeding Hearts / Rebirth Of Blasphemy / Imperator (Strikes Again) / Stonedream / Believe
ORTHODOX, Morbid SPV 084 12852 (1998)
Orthodox / Liquid / Shit Comes Brown / To Red Ones / Tales Of Your History / Touch The Sun / Body As A Cover / Parasites / About Death
UNFORTUNATELY DEAD, System Shock (2000)
They Are Unfortunately Dead / The Eagles You Can Have / Mirror Of Your Steps / Different Fate / Surviving On Arrogance / To Be Unknown / Living On The Threat Of One Finger / The Evil Men Can Do / Death Through The Centuries

KREATOR (GERMANY)
Line-Up: Mille Petrozza (guitar / vocals), Jörg Tritze (guitar), Rob (bass), Ventor (drums)

Essen based trio formed in 1982 as TORMENTOR, and, having adopted the new monicker of KREATOR, the German outfit were to become much favoured by European Thrash fans in the mid 80s.

KREATOR toured Europe and America consistently, improving with each album release and keen to augment their live sound would spend time searching for a second guitarist. Wulf from SODOM joined for a brief period in 1986 and KREATOR were found sharing the billing with RAGE and DESTRUCTION that year, after which guitarist Jorg Tritze was added to the line-up.

In 1987 KREATOR toured Britain opening for CELTIC FROST and America as support to DIRTY ROTTEN IMBECILES backed by a promotion video for 'Toxic Trace' that gained the band valuable MTV exposure. It ensured sales of the band's third album, 'Terrible Certainty', were racked up ever more and set the tone for the subsequent 'Into The Light' and 'Extreme Aggression' albums.

The latter album was produced by leading American based Thrash knob twiddler Randy Burns and, amongst all new KREATOR originals, featured a cover version of the RAVEN track 'Lambs To The Slaughter'.

Just prior to their 1989 American tour playing alongside SUICIDAL TENDENCIES Tritze was ousted in favour of SODOM's Frank Blackfire. This line-up would record 1990's 'Coma Of Souls' in Los Angeles; once again with Randy Burns at the production helm.

A rather bizarre incident occurred later the same year when KREATOR pulled out of their London Electric Ballroom show complaining that they would have to play with a decibel meter in attendance! Still, no such problems prevented the group from completing a successful South American tour in 1992 performing in Chile, Brazil and Argentina.

Having left Noise after a lengthy relationship of nearly ten years, KREATOR signed to G.U.N. Records in late 1994 with the first fruits of the new deal coming in the form of 1995's 'Cause For Conflict'. And the group also introduced a new line-up of Petrozza, BLACKFIRE bassist Christian Giesler and ex-WHIPLASH drummer Joe

Cangelosi. However, by the end of the year both Godszik and Cangelosi were to depart. The band filled the gap with guitarist Tommy Vetterli and drummer Jürgen Reil.

More recently, in addition to a brace of new records in 1996 and 1997, KREATOR contributed a version of JUDAS PRIEST's 'Grinder' to the 'Legends Of Metal Volume II' tribute album in 1996.

A tribute album to KREATOR emerged in 2000 titled 'Raise The Flag Of Hate'. Contributors included PAZUZU, ANGEL CORPSE, ACHERON, MYSTIFER and BLACK WITCHERY.

Singles/EPs:
Flag Of Hate / Take Their Lives / Awakening Of The Gods, Noise 0047 (1986) (12" single)
After The Attack, Noise (1986)
Behind The Mirror / Gangland, Noise 0084 (1987) (12" single)
Impossible To Cure / Lambs To The Slaughter / Terrible Certainty (Live) / Riot Of Violence (Live) / Awakening Of The Gods (Live), Noise NO118-4 (1988) ('Out Of The Dark... Into The Light' EP)
People Of The Lie, Noise (1990)
Lost / Hate Inside Your Head, G.U.N. GUN 072 BMG 74321 30960-2 (1995) (Promotion release)
Isolation / Men Without God, G.U.N. GUN 079 BMG 74321 33082-2 (1995) (Promotion release)

Albums:
ENDLESS PAIN, Noise NO025 (1985)
Endless Pain / Total Death / Storm Of The Beast / Tormentor / Son Of Evil / Flag Of Hate / Cry War / Bone Breaker / Living In Fear / Dying Victims
PLEASURE TO KILL, Noise NO037 (1986)
Intro (Choir Of The Damned) / Ripping Corpse / Death Is Your Saviour / Pleasure To Kill / Riot Of Violence / The Pestilence / Carrion / Command Of The Blade / Under The Guillotine / Flag Of Hate / Take Their Lives / Awakening Of The Gods
TERRIBLE CERTAINTY, Noise NO100 (1987)
Toxic Trace / No Escape / One Of Us / Behind The Mirror / Blind Faith / Storming With Menace / Terrible Certainty
INTO THE LIGHT, Noise NO200-2 (1988)
Impossible To Cure / Lambs To The Slaughter / Terrible Certainty / Riot Of

Violence / Awakening Of The Gods / Flag Of Hate (Live) / Love Or Hate Us (Live) / Behind The Mirror
EXTREME AGGRESSION, Noise NO129 (1989)
Extreme Aggression / No Reason To Exist / Love Us Or Hate Us / Stream Of Consciousness / Some Pain Will Last / Betrayer / Don't Trust / Bringer Of Torture / Fatal Energy
COMA OF SOULS, Noise N1058 (1990)
When The Sun Burns Red / Coma Of Souls / People Of The Lie / World Beyond / Terror Zone / Agents Of Brutality / Material World / Paranoia / Twisted Urges / Hidden Dictator / Mental Slavery
RENEWAL, Noise NO193 (1994)
Winter Martyrium / Renewal / Reflection / Brainseed / Karmic Wheel / Realiätskontrolle / Zero To None / Europe After The Rain / Depression Unrest
CAUSE FOR CONFLICT, G.U.N. GUN 071 BMG 74321 30002-2 (1995)
Prevail / Catholics Despot / Progressive Proletarians / Crisis Of Disorder / Hate Inside Your Head / Bomb Threat / Men Without God / Lost/ Dogmatic / Sculpture Of Regret / Celestial Deliverance / Isolation
SCENARIOS OF VIOLENCE, Noise N0222-2 (1996)
Suicide In Swamps / Renewal / Extreme Aggression / Brainseed / Terrorzone / Ripping Corpse / Tormentor/ Some Pain Will Last / Toxic Trace / People Of The Lie / Depression Unrest / Coma Of Souls / Europe After The Rain / Limits Of Liberty / Terrible Certainty / Karmic Wheel
OUTCAST, G.U.N. GUN BMG 74321 45262-2 (1997)
Leave This World Behind / Phobia / Forever / Black Sunrise / Nonconformist / Enemy Unseen / Outcast / Stronger Than Before / Ruin Of Life / Whatever It May Take / Alive Again / Against The Rest / A Better Tomorrow
PAST LIFE TRAUMA: 1985-1992, Noise (2000)
Betrayer / Pleasure To Kill / When The Sun Burns Red / Endless Pain / Winter Martyrium / Flag Of Hate / Extreme Aggression / After The Attack / Trauma / Reaper Of The Lie / Renewal / Terrible Certainty / Love Us Or Hate Us / Total Death / Europe After The Rain / Under The Guillotine / Terror Zone / Tormentor

KRISIUN (BRAZIL)
Line-up: Alex Carmago (vocals / bass), Moyses Kolesne (guitar / keyboards), Max Kolesne (drums)

Sao Paulo Death Metal merchants KRISIUN first offered their 1991 demo 'Evil Age'. A further tape 'Curse Of The Evil One' backed it up the following year leading to the band's first official product the 'Unmerciful Order' EP. Other releases included shared EPs with Germans HARMONY DIES and VIOLENT HATE. Signing to Germany's G.U.N. Records KRISIUN debuted proper with 1996's 'Black Force Domain'.

Switching to Century Media Records KRISIUN's 2000 album 'Conquerors Of Armageddon' was produced by MORBID ANGEL's Eric Rutan.

Albums:
UNMERCIFUL ORDER, (1993)
They Call Me Death / Unmerciful Order / Crosses Towards Hell / Agonize The Ending / Summons Of Irreligious / Meaning Of Terror / Infected Core / Insurrected Path (Depth Classic) / Rises From The Black
BLACK FORCE DOMAIN, G.U.N. GUN147 (1997)
Black Force Domain / Messiah Of The Double Cross / Hunter Of Souls / Blind Possession / Evil Mastermind / Infamous Glory / Respected To Perish Below / Meanest Evil / Obsession By Evil Force / Sacrifice Of The Unborn
APOCALYPTIC REVELATION, G.U.N. (1998)
Creations Scourge / Kings Of Killing / Apocalyptic Victory / Aborticide (In The Crypts Of Holiness) / March Of The Black Hordes / Vengeances Revelation / Rites Of Defamation / Meaning Of Terror / Rises From Black
CONQUERORS OF ARMEGEDDON, Century Media (2000)
Intro - Ravager / Abyssal Gates / Soul Devourer / Messiah's Abomination / Cursed Scrolls / Conquerors Of Armageddon / Hatred Inherit / Iron Stakes / Endless Madness Descends

KRIXHJÄLTERS (SWEDEN)
Line-Up: Pontus Lindqvist (vocals / bass), Pelle Ström (guitar), Rasmus Ekmann (guitar), Stefan Källfors (drums)

Initially a side project of AGONY guitarist Pelle Ström, after two singles and a brace of albums KRIXJHÄLTERS changed their name to the easily pronounceable OMNITRON and, later, COMECON. Both vocalist Pontus Lindqvist and guitarist Rasmus Ekmann remained with the group in the transformation from OMNITRON to COMECON.

Singles/EPs:
Hjälter Skelter, C.B.R. CBR 107 (1988)
A Krixmas Carol / No Rest / Putrefiction / Next Focus / Requiem, Aeternum, Dona Eis Domine, C.B.R. CBR 116 (1990)
Albums:
KRIXHJÄLTERS, Rosa Honung FAS 14 (1984)
EVILUTION, Chicken Brain CBRCD 108 (1989)

LAKE OF TEARS
(SWEDEN)
Line-Up: Daniel Brennare (vocals / guitar), Jonas Eriksson (guitar), Mikael Larsson (bass), Johan Ouidhuls (drums)

LAKE OF TEARS have created their own niche in the European Gothic Rock scene with their blend of psychedelic Dark Metal. The 1994 debut album was produced by CEMETARY's Matthias Lodmalm and ENTOMBED's Tomas Skogsberg, the latter also adding guitar and keyboard touches.
The band toured hard throughout 1996, opening for such acts as TIAMAT, EDGE OF SANITY and RAGE, but guitarist Jonas Eriksson had departed by the 1997 album and his duties were handled by guesting musicians in the form of guitarist Magnus Sahlgren and keyboard player/ guitarist Ronny Lahti. The track lifted for the single 'Lady Rosenred' featured a lead guest vocal by Jennie Tebler.

Singles/EPs:
Lady Rosenred / Devil's Diner / A Crimson Cosmos, Black Mark BMCD 106 (1997)

Albums:
GREATER ART, Black Mark BMCD 49 (1994)
Under The Crescent / Eyes Of The Sky / Upon The Highest Mountain / As Daylight Yields / Greater Art / Evil Inside / Netherworld / Tears
HEADSTONES, Black Mark BMCD 72 (1995)
A Foreign Road / Raven Land / Dreamdemons / Sweetwater / Life's But A Dream / Headstones / Twilight / Burn Fire Burn / The Path Of The Gods (Upon The Highest Mountain Part II)
A CRIMSON COSMOS, Black Mark BMCD 97 (1997)
Boogie Bubble / Cosmic Weed / When My Sun Comes Down / Devil's Diner / The Four Strings Of Mourning / To Die Is To Wake / Lady Rosenred / Raistlin And The Rose / A Crimson Cosmos
FOREVER AUTUMN, Black Mark BMCD 132 (2000)
So Fell Autumn Rain / Hold On Tight / Forever Autumn / Pagan Wish / Otherwheres / The Homecoming / Come Night I Reign / Demon You - Lily Anne / To Blossom Blue

LAMENT (MEXICO)
Line-Up: Marco Perez (vocals), Iram (bass), Abel Gomez Torres (vocals / drums)

Christian Mexico City based Death Metal act LAMENT, previously entitled BEHEADED, were founded during 1993. Unfortunately the bands original drummer Arturo Guzman would die before the act landed a deal. Signing to Steve Rowe of MORTIFICATION's label Rowe Productions LAMENT debuted with the Jeff Scheetz produced 'Tears Of A Leper'. Although Scheetz would also contribute with lead guitar LAMENT would stand out from the crowd by employing the bass guitar as a prominent lead instrument.
Following this release vocalist Marco Perez quit the band. Drummer Abel Gomez Torres took over the lead vocal role for the 1998 album 'Through The Reflection' recorded for Finnish Christian Metal label Little Rose Productions.

Albums:
TEARS OF A LEPER, Rowe Productions (1997)
Sacrifice Of Righteousness / From Pain To Hope / The Mystery Of Iniquity / Rivers Of Loneliness / Legal / Terminating Existence / Absolute Predominance / Tears Of A Leper / A Cry Of Anguish / Chaos Of Darkness
THROUGH THE REFLECTION, Little Rose Productions (1998)
Through The Reflection / Come Near / 1250 Dead Without Reason / A Dream At Sunset / The Wind Of My Heart / A Cry Near The Forest / Roars Of Wind / Tears… Instruments For Reflection

LAST DAYS OF HUMANITY
(HOLLAND)
Line-Up: Bart (vocals), William (guitar), Anne (guitar), Erwin (bass), Rutger (drums)

Grindcore act founded during the early 90's as a trio of vocalist / guitarist Hans, bass player Dennis and drummer Erwin. It would be only the latter that saw it through until the present day line up through an ever fluid roll call.
The 2000 band comprised of Erwin, now a bass player, alongside guitarists William and Anne, vocalist Bart and drummer Rutger.

Singles/EPs:
Ulcerated Offal / Carnal Trash / Infected

Excremental Slush / Defleshed By Flies, (1996) ('Defleshed By Flies' 7" split single with RAKITIS)
Split, (199-) (7" split single with C.O.O.)
Pathological Dreams, (199-) (7" split single with VULGAR DEGENERATE)

Albums:
HYMNS OF INDIGESTIBLE SUPPURATION, (199-)
Maggot Feast On A Swollen Fetus / 48th Cut / Rectal Bowel Inquisition / Intoxicated / The Taste Of Festering Vomit / Consuming Purulent Sputum / From Flesh To Liquid Mess / Reeking Mush Beneath Each Cavity / Orgasmic Abortion / Catering From The Womb / Acute Palatable Haemorrhage / Perforated Festering Scrotum / Stirred Intestines / Wet Remains / Purulent Odour In Stoma / Defecating Anal Sludge / Rancid Tumour Execration / Wide Open Wounds On A Disfigured Corpse / Hymns Of Indigestible Suppuration / Ulcerated Offal / Defleshed By Flies / Bowel Exhibition / Raped In The Back Of A Van
THE SOUND OF RANCID JUICES SLOSHING AROUND YOUR COFFIN, Bones Brigade CDBB001 (1998)
Born To Murder The World / Necrotic Eruption / Entangled In Septic Gore / Slithered Limbs / Cannibalistic Remains / Hacked Into Red Mush / Putrid Mass Of Burnt Excrement / The Smell Of The Dead / Rancid Cottered Rectum / Bloodsplattered Chainsawslaughter / Submassive Obliteration / Septic Convulsion / The Sound Of Rancid Juices / Liquidized Disgorgement / Putrefying Immortality / Carnal Tumour / Consumed In Gore / Drowned In Septic Guts / Cadaver Breath / Excremental Carnage / Malignant Haemorrhage / Mucupurulent Fleshfeast / Pro-Rectal Fermentation / A Reeking Pile Of Septic Brainfluid / Disembowelment Of Scattered Gastric Pieces / Festering Fungus Infection
LAST DAYS OF HUMANITY, Gowap (1998) (Split album with MURDER CORPORATION)

LEPROSY FART (SWITZERLAND)
Line-Up: Simon Steinemann (vocals), Roger Sommer (guitar), Heiko Muuss (guitar), Simon Bischoff (bass), Adrian Slemeniak (drums)

A tactlessly named Death Metal band from Switzerland, LEPROSY FART also betrayed more than a few Doom influences in their music.

Formed in Winterthur during 1994 by guitarist Roger Sommer and original vocalist Roger Fritschi, the group also consisted of drummer Daniel Schürch and bassist Simon Bischoff early on before Schürch was replaced by Adrian Slemeniak.

Singles/EPs:
Intro / Leprosy / I Can't Find My Way / R.I.P. / To The End Of Life, Leprosy Fart (1996) ('Leprosy Fart' EP)

LEUKEMIA (SWEDEN)
Line-Up: Jojje (vocals / guitar), Kekko (guitar / bass), Tarb (guitar)

LEUKEMIA's 1991 demo was titled 'Innocence Is Bliss' whilst the group's second album, 'Grey Flannel Souled', was produced by Tomas Skosberg and EDGE OF SANITY's Dan Swano.
The band are now known as LAME.

Albums:
SUCK MY HEAVEN, Black Mark BMCD 29 (1993)
Into The Morgue / I Nearly Forgot / Ucarved Miseria / Wandering / Sick Inside / You Es Of Ey / Everything Fall Apart / Memorized / Different But Same
GREY FLANNEL SOULED, Step One SOR 008 (1994)

LIERS IN WAIT (SWEDEN)
Line-Up: Christoffer Jonsson (vocals), Kristian Wahlin (guitar), Matthias Gustafson (bass), Hans Nilsson (drums)

Featuring the guitar talents of ex-GROTESQUE man Kristian Wahlin. LIERS IN WAIT utilized the services of THERION vocalist Christoffer Jonsson to record the album. Drummer Hans Nilsson later joined LUCIFERON.
Both Wahlin and Nilsson founded DIABOLIQUE for a 1998 album.

Albums:
SPIRITUALLY UNCONTROLLED ART, Dolores DOL007 (1991)
Overlord / Bleeding Shrines Of Stone / Maleficent Dreamvoid / Liers In Wait / Gateways

LIVIDITY (USA)
Line-Up: Dave Kibler (vocals), Matt Bishop (guitar), Mike Smith (bass), Dave Hoffman (drums)

LIVIDITY started life as a solo venture of

Dave Kibler during 1993. A three track demo emerged after which vocalist and drummer Tommy Davis was inducted for a further 1995 nine track session 'Ritual Of Mortal Impalement'. Some of these songs would also be featured on a split demo tape in collaboration with MORGUE FETUS.

In mid 1995 LIVIDITY was brought up to full strength with the addition of guitarist Matt Bishop and bassist Aaron Heath. This line-up would issue the 'Rejoice In Morbidity' tape for Polish label Immortal Records. However, shortly before recording new tracks for the 1997 album 'Fetish For The Sick' Heath was supplanted by Mike Smith. Further ructions before the close of the year saw Nick Null taking command of the drum stool as Davis made his exit.

A notorious live album 'Show Us Your Tits' crept out in 1999 leading in turn to the millennium released 'The Age Of Clitoral Decay', both on United Guttural Records.

The German Death Metal aficionados Cudgel Agency would also pair off LIVIDITY with Teutonic act PROFANITY for a split 7" single in 2000.

Tragedy would strike LIVIDITY with the premature death of Null. The drummer suffered a heart attack. Former GORGASM man Derek Hoffman would step into the breach as replacement.

Singles/EPs:
Split, Cudgel Agency (2000) (7" split single with PROFANITY)

Albums:
FETISH FOR THE SICK, Ablated ABLTD001 (1997)
Laceration Of An Unclean Cunt / Feasting On Mankind / Immortal Impact / Randomly Raped Rectum / Graveyard Delicacy / Pussy Lover / Brains For Lubrication / Devour Humanity / My Cock It Bleeds / Process Of Disembowelment / Rectal Wench
SHOW US YOUR TITS - LIVE, United Guttural (1999)
Rectal Wench / Feasting On Mankind / Devour Humanity / Lacerations Of An Unclean Twat / Graveyard Delicacy / Stench Of Virginity / Process Of Disembowelment / Pussy Lover / Orifice Reconstruction / Immortal Impact / Randomly Raped Rectum / My Cock It Bleeds / Brains For Lubrication / Fetal Scabs / Tortured Flesh - Rectal Wench / Fetal Scabs / Orifice Reconstruction

THE AGE OF CLITORAL DECAY, United Guttural (2000)
Oozing Vaginal Discharge / The Urge To Splurge / Chamber Of Bone / Anal Action Wife / Stench Of Virginity / Food / Dismembering Her Lifeless Corpse / Bloody Pit Of Horror / Sodomy Ritual

LIVING DEATH (GERMANY)
Line-Up: Thorsten Bergmann (vocals), Reiner Kelch (guitar), Frank Fricke (guitar), Dieter Kelch (bass), Andreas Oberhoff (drums)

An Extreme Thrash Metal act that attracted a sizable European cult following despite being dismissed by many critics, LIVING DEATH were formed by the Kelch brothers (guitarist Reiner and bassist Dieter) and guitarist Frank Fricke. The group's debut album, 'Vengeance Of Hell', was produced by Alex Thubeauville.

The 'Vengeance Of Hell' album is, naturally, very prehistoric in sound compared to what the group later achieved, so whilst Metal fans either loved its rawness or dismissed it as the worst record they'd ever heard, LIVING DEATH slowly but surely progressed. The Kelch brothers more than most, both later appeared anonymously as part of the MEKONG DELTA project albums.

Releasing the band's second album, 'Metal Revolution' in 1986 the group would eventually be signed to Aaarg Records, although the 'Back To The Weapons' EP was severely censored by the European record industry for its cover art depicting scenes of extreme violence. Copies without a rather large white circular sticker (which, if removed cause severe damage to the sleeve) covering the offending image are extremely hard to find.

By 1988 the band had truncated their title from LIVING DEATH to L.D. and issued the 'World's Neuroses' album. Shortly after its release the Kelch brothers quit and ex-VIOLENT FORCE vocalist Lemmy joined the band.

LIVING DEATH adopted a name change to SACRED CHAOS in January 1989. By 1990 Fricke had created LAOS for a solitary album in collusion with ex-AVENGER, RAGE and MEKONG DELTA drummer Jörg Michael.

Ultimately, LIVING DEATH drummer Atomic Steif joined SODOM in 1994.

Watch Out / You And Me / Heavy Metal Hurricane / Night Light, Earthshaker ESM 4007 (1985)
Nuclear Greetings / Bloody Dance / The Way (Your Soul Must Go) / Child Of Illusion, Aargg AAARRG 2 (1986) ('Back To The Weapons' EP)
Eisbein (Mit Sauerkraut) / Horrible Infanticide / Vengeance, Aaarrg AAARRG 9 (1987)
Killing Machine (Live) / Grippin' A Heart (Live) / Road Of Destiny (Live) / Screaming From A Chamber (Live), Aaarrg AAARRG 12 (1988)

Albums:
VENGEANCE OF HELL, Mausoleum SKULL 8360 (1984)
You And Me / Living Death / Nightlight / My Victim / Labyrinth / Heavy Metal Hurricane / Hellpike / Riding A Virgin / Vengeance Of Hell
METAL REVOLUTION, Earthshaker ES 4012 (1986)
Killing Machine / Grippin' A Heart / Rulers Must Come / Screaming From A Chamber / Intro / Shadow Of The Dawn / Panic And Hysteria / Road Of Destiny / Deep In Hell
PROTECTED FROM REALITY, Aaarrg AAARRG 5 (1987)
Horrible Infanticide (Part One) / Manilla Terror / Nature's Death / Wood Of Necrophiliacs / Vengeance / Horrible Infanticide (Part Two) / Intruder / The galley / War of independence / Eisbein (Mit Sauerkraut)
WORLD'S NEUROSES, Aaarrg AAARRG 15 (1988)
Last Birthday / Die Young / Schizophrenia / On The 17th Floor / Down / World's Neuroses / Bastard At The Bus Stop / Sacred Chao / Tuesday
KILLING IN ACTION, Intercord IRS 986.944 (1991)
Killing In Action / Hang 'Em High / Dire Weak Up / Hearteater / Polymorphic / World Wearness / Die For (For What We Lie For) / Stand Up / Tribute Of Gutter / Daily Life
LIVING DEATH, Aaarrg ARG 28-051-2 (1995)
Nuclear Greetings / Bloody Dance / The Way (Your Soul Must Go) / Child Of Illusion / Horrible Infanticide (Part One) / Manila Terror / Natures Death / Wood Of Necrophiliac / Vengeance (Horrible Infanticide Part Two) / Intruder/ The Galley / War Of Independence / Last Birthday / Die Young / Schizophrenia / On The 17th Floor / Down / Worlds

Neuroses / Bastard (At The Busstop) / The Testament Of Mr. George / Sacred Chao / Tuesday / Killing Machine / Grippin' A Heart / Road Of Destiny / Screamin' From The Chamble
METAL REVOLUTION, ABS Classics 100 (1996) (Digitally remastered re-issue)
Killing Machine / Grippin' A Heart / Rulers Must Come / Screaming From A Chamber / Intro / Shadow Of The Dawn / Panic And Hysteria / Road Of Destiny / Deep In Hell

LIVING SACRIFICE
(Little Rock, AR, USA)
Line-Up: Bruce Fitzhugh (vocals / guitar), Rocky Gray (guitar), Arthur Green (bass), Matt Putman (percussion), Lance Garvin (drums)

Noted Christian Death Metal band. Vocalist and bass player DJ fronted LIVING SACRIFICE for the first trio of albums before leaving. Guitarist Bruce Fitshugh took over the lead vocal position. Stylistically LIVING SACRIFICE opened as a straight down the line Thrash act for their eponymous 1991 debut but would develop into a full flown Death Metal machine complete with guttural vocals by the follow up 'Non Existent'. Tracks from this album would be radically remixed by CIRCLE OF DUST for a compilation 'Metamorphosis'. LIVING SACRIFICE underwent a further period of flux in 1998 when the Truby brothers guitarist Jason and bassist Chris decamped. The band briefly pulled in bass player Jay before finding former ESOCHARIS man Arthur Green as permanent replacement. LIVING SACRIFICE also added another ex-ESOCHARIS member Matt Putman on percussion in 2000.
Guitarist Rocky Gray and drummer Lance Garvin also operate the side project SOUL EMBRACED.
Clenched Fist Records issued a LIVING SACRIFICE tribute album during 2001 featuring such acts as MORDECAI, DIRGE, CRIMSON THORN, SOUL EMBRACED, KEKAL, NAILED PROMISE, SOTERIOS and MINDRAGE.

Albums:
LIVING SACRIFICE, R.E.X. 7901420219 (1991)
Violence / Internal Unrest / Second Death- Obstruction / Walls Of Separation / Phargximas / No Grave Concern /

Dealing With Ignorance / The Prodigal / Anorexia Spiritual
NON EXISTENT, R.E.X. 7901422475 (1992)
Emerge - Enthroned / Non Existent / Haven Of Blasphemy / ...To Nothing / Void Expression / Atonement - Distorted / Chemical Straight Jacket / Without Distinction
INHABIT, R.E.X. 41002-2 (1994)
In The Shadow / Not Beneath / Sorrow Banished / Unseen / Inhabit / Breathing Murder / Mind Distant / Darkened / Indwelling / Departure (Dead Silence)
REBORN, Tooth And Nail TND 1083-554 (1997)
Reborn Empowered / Truth Solution / Threatened / Awakening / 180 / No Longer / Something More / Sellout / Spirit Fall / Presence Of God / Reject / Liar
THE HAMMERING PROCESS, Solid State (2000)
Flatline / Bloodwork / Not My Own / Local Vengeance Killing / Altered Life / Hand Of The Dead / Burn The End / Hidden / Perfect / Conditional

LOBOTOMY (SWEDEN)
Line-Up: Max Collin (vocals), Etienne Belmar (guitar), Lars Jelleryd (guitar), Patric Carsena (bass), Daniel Strachal (drums)

LOBOTOMY, originally titled RAPTURE, had their debut demo, 'When Sunlight Draws Near', was released in 1990.
The band's ensuing 1993 demo, 'Nailed In Misery', was released as a cassette single on the Italian Obscure Plasma

label. Later, American label Thrash Corner put the 'Nailed In Misery' sessions together with a previous 1992 demo ('Against The Gods') to make a 1995 CD release titled after the 1992 effort.

Singles/EPs:
Flowertrip Part One / In Bloodstained Green / Turmoil, Rising Realm RRR001 (1993)
Porno For The Wicked / Invite The Needle / Sunblind / Divination / Bloodangel (Frenzy Sell Out mix), No Fashion (1999) ('Muerte - Holy Shit' EP)

Albums:
LOBOTOMY, Chaos CD04 (1995)
The Hate That Breathes / Just My Dark Thoughts / Soulshifter / Be Gone / Turmoil / Against The Gods / Nailed / Darkened Times / Misery End / In Bloodstained Greed
NAILED IN MISERY - AGAINST THE GODS, Thrash Corner THCROO7CD (1995)
KILL, No Fashion NFR 023 (1997)
Rise And Hate / Frozen / Swerve / Awaken / Cells Divide / Mindtool / On Red Ground / Kill / Serial Dream
HOLY SHIT, No Fashion (2001)

LOCK UP (SWEDEN / UK / USA)
Line-Up: Peter Tägtren (vocals), Jesse Pintado (guitar), Shane Embury (bass), Nick Barker (drums)

A multi-national collaboration between NAPALM DEATH's Shane Embury and DIMMU BORGIR and ex-CRADLE OF

LOCK UP

FILTH drummer Nick Barker together with Peter Tägtren of Sweden's HYPOCRISY and Embury's American NAPALM DEATH band mate guitarist Jesse Pintado.

The resulting debut album, which featured many songs originally destined for Pintado's side outfit TERRORIZER, was highly successful, even breaking the national charts in Germany and receiving many magazine 'Album of the month' awards.

The album was produced by ex-SABBAT guitarist Andy Sneap.

LOCK UP undertook a European tour in 2000 with ex-AT THE GATES singer Tomas Lindberg substituting for Tägtgren. The band were supported by DECAPITATED and CORPORATION 187.

Barker also figured anonymously in the notorious 'Mexican' Death Metal project BRUJERIA. Centred upon FEAR FACTORY's Dino Cazares and FAITH NO MORE's Jim Gould-Barker aided on the 2000 'Brujerizmo' album.

Albums:
PLEASURES PAVE SEWERS, Nuclear Blast (1999)
After Life In Purgatory / Submission / Triple Six Suck Angels / Delirium / Pretenders Of The Throne / Slow Bleed Gorgon - Pleasure Pave Sewers / Ego Pawn / The Dreams Are Sacrificed / Tragic Faith / Darkness Of Ignorance / Salvation Thru Destruction / Leech Eclipse / Fever Landscapes

LORDES WERRE (USA)
Line-Up: Steve Caroll (vocals), Ben Meyer (guitar), James Gaber (bass), Ben Elliot (drums)

Founded in 1993 by the Elliot siblings vocalist and guitarist Rob and bassist / drummer Ben. LORDES WERRE, a blasphemous Thrash influenced Death Metal outfit, issued the opening demo 'The Dark Ascension' in 1994 following this with the EP 'Canticles Of Armageddon'. Later recruits to the fold were bassist James "Hellstorm" Gaber and the veteran NASTY SAVAGE guitarist Ben Meyer.

Disturbingly Rob Elliott would be imprisoned for an alleged vandalizing of a church and more worryingly attempted rape. One track laid down before Elliot was jailed would be issued on the Necropolis compilation album 'Thrashing Holocaust'.

With the debut album recorded all but for the vocals LORDES WERRE pulled in the services of Steve Caroll, guitarist in Chicago's CIANIDE, as lead vocalist for the resulting 'Demon Crusades'.

Singles/EPs:
Chaotic Entirety / Stellar Gateway / Chant Of Making / Grandel / When The Stars Turn Black, (1996) ('Canticles Of Armageddon' EP)

Albums:
DEMON CRUSADES, R.I.P. (1999)

LOST CENTURY (GERMANY)
Line-Up: Andreas Lohse (vocals), Martin Bayer (guitar), Jens Schäfer (guitar), Rudi Görg (bass), Jason Kubke (drums)

Including ex-APOSTASY vocalist Andreas Lohse and former members of RESEARCH. LOST CENTURY's first demo of 1990 'Miserality' featured original guitarist Phillip who left prior to the second demo of 1992 entitled 'A Truth Beyond'. Guitar duties for this tape were handled by Stefan.

Stefan quit before recording of the debut album began and, after its release, the group toured Germany opening for POLTERGEIST and CORONER.

Lohse founded THOUGHTSPHERE releasing the 2000 album 'Vague Horizons'.

Albums:
NATURAL PROCESS OF PROGRESSION, DMP 021-93 (1993)
The End / Submit To Stagnation / Cling To The Unreal / Delivering The Sentence, Part I: Birth, Part II: Murder, Part III: Conviction And Death / Trivial (Towards Destination)
COMPLEX MICROCOSM - MOVEMENT IN NINE RITUALS, T&T-Noise TT11-2 (1994)
Descending / Silent Inside / Like The One Above / Fallen Star / Second Coming / Wind In The Willows / Life Itself / Traverse The Veil / Complex Microcosm
POETIC ATMOSPHERE OF SEASONS, T&T TT 0018-2 (1995)
Seal Of Thorns / Autumn's Gift / Unicorn / Breathing Underwater: Death / Last Days Of Spring / Winter Twilight / Kryogenic / Summer's Dishonest Apologies / Search / Owe Me Awe

LOST DREAMS (AUSTRIA)
Line-Up: Maggo Wenzel (vocals), Andreas Maierhofer (guitar), Herbert Sopracolle (guitar), Auer Tom (bass), Phillip Hörtnagl (keyboards), Marco Eller (drums)

Austrian Death Black act LOST DREAMS have had a confused history stretching back to the mid 90's. Originally guitarist Andreas Maierhofer handled lead vocals until Böhm Martin took over in 1996. However, by mid 1997 Martin had been supplanted by Maggo Wenzel and in addition LOST DREAMS pulled in female singer Tanja Falschunger. The keyboard position also changed as Haideggar Alexander made way for Babette Kach.
1999 had a switch on the drum stool with Stephan Zangerle having a brief term before Marco Eller landed the job. 2000 saw bassist Boris Hoerhager losing out to Auer Tom.

Albums:
REFLECTIONS OF DARKNESS, Lost Dreams (1999)
Reflections Of Darkness / Obsessed / Always Beside You / Burning Eyes / The Funeral Of God / Believe In Evil (Live)

LOST SOUL (POLAND)

Albums:
SCREAM OF THE MOURNING STAR, Relapse (2001)
My Kingdom / Divine Satisfaction / Tabernaculum Miser / The Highest Pleasure / Malediction / Entrance To Nothingness / We Want God / Nameless / An Eternal Sleep / Unclean

LOUDBLAST (FRANCE)
Line-Up: Stephane Buriez (guitar / vocals), Nicolas LeClerc (guitar), Francois Jamin (bass), Thierry Pinck (drums)

Lille based Death Metal band LOUDBLAST formed in 1986 with Buriez, Lecclerq, Jamin and drummer Joris Terrier. The group debuted with the split LP 'Licensed To Thrash' on New Wave Records.
The success of this debut record enabled LOUDBLAST to tour Europe with the likes of HOLY MOSES, TANKARD and SODOM. Having recorded a demo entitled 'Bazooka Rehearsal' in September 1988 (which were sold on a mail order basis), LOUDBLAST signed to Jungle Hop Records and released their first full blown album, 'Sensorial Treatment', at the close of 1989. A further release, 'Total Virulence', followed; after which Terrier quit, his place being taken by ex-AGGRESSOR drummer Thierry Pinck.
1991's 'Disincarnate' was produced by noted Death Metal producer Scott Burns at Tampa's Morrisound studios in Florida and up in its release the group toured as support to CANNIBAL CORPSE in France during mid 1991 before performing at the 'Monsters Of Death' festival the same year alongside MORGOTH, MASSACRE and IMMOLATION.
Following a tour with DEATH in Europe during 1992 the band parted ways with Pinck and adopted a quick replacement in Herve Coquerel. LOUDBLAST's 1993 album 'Sublime Dementia' was once again produced by Burns in Florida.
The 1994 mini album 'Cross The Threshold' includes a cover version of SLAYER's 'Mandatory Suicide'.

Albums:
LICENSED TO THRASH, New Wave (1986) (Split LP)
Scared To Death / Let The Blood Run Red / Elm Street / Black Death
SENSORIAL TREATMENT, Jungle Hop JH 117 (1989)
Fatal Attraction / From Beyond / Visions Of Your Fate / Agony / Trepanning / Rebirth / Infinite Pleasure / Malignant Growth / Pouss Mouse
TOTAL VIRULENCE, Jungle Hop (1990)
DISINCARNATE, Major (1991)
Steering For Paradise / After Thy Thought / Dusk To Dawn / Outlet For Conscience / Disquieting Beliefs / Horror Within / Arrive Into Death Soon / Wrapped In Roses / Shaped Images Of Discarnate Spirits
SUBLIME DEMENTIA, Noise NO207 (1993)
Presumption / Wisdom... (Farther On) / Turn The Scales / About Solitude / Subject To Spirit / Fire And Ice / In Perpetual Motion / Fancies / Sublime Dementia / My Last Journey
CROSS THE TRESHOLD, Noise N0223-3 (1994)
Malignant Growth / No Tears To Share / Mandatory Suicide / Cross The Threshold / Subject To Spirit / Sublime Dementia
THE TIMEKEEPER: LIVE 1995, WMD CD122 126 (1995)
Intro / Presumption / Wisdom... Farther On / Subject To Spirit / Cross The Threshold / Steering For Paradise /

Shaped Images Of Discarnate Spirits / Fancies / About Solitude / Outlet For Conscience / Fire And Ice / No Tears To Share / Sublime Dementia / Wrapped In Roses / This Dazzling Abyss / Malignant Growth / My Last Journey
FRAGMENTS, XIII Bis (2000)
Man's Own / Flesh / Frozen Tears / Taste Me / Into The Keep / Labyrinth / Vices / Worthy Of Angels / Pleasure Focus / Ecstatic Trance / I Against I / Carpe Diem

LOUDHELL (SWEDEN)
Line-Up: Daniel Holmgren (vocals / guitar), Björn Hansen (guitar), Fredrik Lind (bass), Björn Stenmark (drums)

Singles/EPs:
End Of Discussion / Heroin-A / Walk Away / Aerie Collapse / Xs Cumosity, Loudhell LHCDS 395 (1995)

LOUD PIPES (SWEDEN)
Line-Up: Nandor Condor (vocals), Freddy Eugene (guitar), Carl Leen (bass), Peter Starwind (drums)

UNLEASHED guitarist Fredrik Lindgren ('Freddy Eugene') is also a member of Punk outfit LOUD PIPES.
MERCILESS, UNANIMATED, REGURGITATE and FACE DOWN drummer Peter Stärjvind ("Peter Starwind") is also a member of LOUD PIPES. MERCILESS bassist Fredrik Karlen (Carl Leen) is also a member.
Lindgren created Stoner Metal act TERRA FIRMA in 1999.

Albums:
THE DOWNHILL BLUES, Osmose KRON-H 10 CD (1997)
You Got That Right Punk / Clean Your Head / Land Of The Free / Morphine Trip / Downhill Blues / Charged With Murder / Take Me Back / Kill 'Em / Stressed To Death / Stupid, Stupid / Don't You Ever / Evil Juice / Keep On Lying / Crime In Progress / You Got That Right Punk (Part II)

LUBRICANT (FINLAND)
Line-Up: Sami Paldanius (vocals), Sami Viitassari (guitar), Tero Järvensivu (bass), Aki Ala-Kokko (drums)

The Finnish Hardcore Death Metal band LUBRICANT formed in 1991. In November of the same year they released their first demo ('Swallow The Symmatric Swab') which sold 700 copies and prompted interest from Morbid Records.
Ultimately, LUBRICANT were signed by the label and the EP, 'Nookleptia' was released in 1994. The group later supported acts like SENTENCED, AT THE GATES and ENSLAVED.

Singles/EPs:
Monohemerous Joy / Thrombose / Declaration Of Galloping Consumption / Laceration Of Vasocontrictive Emotion / Explusive Gastroscopia / Semistarvation, Morbid MR 008 (1993) ('Nookleptia' EP)

LUCIFERION (SWEDEN)
Line-Up: Wojtek Lisiski (vocals / guitar), Mikael Nicklasson (guitar), Peter Wiener (drums)

LUCIFERION's guitarist Micke Nicklasson and drummer Peter Andersson are both ex-SARCAZM, whilst vocalist Wojtek Lisicki previously sang with HIGHLANDER. Nicklasson also sings lead vocal for LIERS IN WAIT.
Following the recording of the group's debut 'Demonication (The Manifest)' drummer Peter Wiener quit to be superseded by ex-LIERS IN WAIT drummer Hasse Nilsson. The album featured a version of SODOM's 'Blasphemer'.
LUCIFERION also covered METALLICA's 'Fight Fire With Fire' for the Black Sun Records tribute album 'Metal Militia'. Nilsson would join his erstwhile colleague guitarist Kristian Wahlin founding DIABOLIQUE.

Albums:
DEMONICATION (THE MANIFEST), Listenable POSH007 (1994)
Intro / On The Wings Of The Emperor / Graced By Fire / Rebel Souls / Satan's Gift / The Manifest / Risus De Lucifer (Suffering Of Christ) / Tears Of The Damned / Blasphemer / The Voyager.

LUNATIC INVASION (GERMANY)
Line-Up: Ramlow (vocals / keyboards), Wulfert (guitar / keyboards), Hellbach (bass), Majewski (drums)

An atmospheric Doom / Death Metal group from Germany, LUNATIC INVASION also have a rather Gothic touch.

Albums:
TOTENTANZ, Invasion IR 015 (1995)

242

Totentanz / Haut / Deads Paradise / Sturm / Asche Zu Asche / Fallen Angel / Gathering Of Bones / Dance Macabre / Prozession / The Haunted Palace / Dark Prayers / Blut Gott

IN THE EPITHELIAL TISSUE OF THE INTESTINE, Millennium (2000) (Split album with FLESH GRINDER)

LYMPHATIC PHLEGM (BRAZIL)
Line-Up: Andre Luiz (vocals), Rodrigo Alcântara (guitar / bass)

Splatter-Gore Grinders LYMPHATIC PHLEGM were founded as the duo of vocalist Andre Luiz and guitarist / bassist Rodrigo Alcântara during 1996. From their inception the band has relied on a drum machine.
In 2000 LYMPHATIC PHLEGM shared a split album with FLESH GRINDER. LYMPHATIC PHLEGM would contribute to the IMPETIGO homage album 'Wizards Of Gore'.

Albums:
BLOODSPLATTERED PATHOLOGICAL DISFUNCTIONS,
Putrid Nausea Productions (199-)
Intro: The Pathology Begins… / Prostatic Affection Consequent To Blenorrhagical Urethritis / Congenital Tumour Constituted By Embryonic Tissues And Foetal Residues / Emphysema Cadaverosum (Fermented Cadaveric Dissolution) / Suppurated Inflammatory Intumescentia Of The Ophthalmic Conjunctive / C.H.S. - Chronic Hyperglicemy Syndrome (Diabetes Melittus) / Vulva Fermentation / Degenerative Affection Of The Semitendious Muscular Tract / Surgical Suppression Of The Extremities By Abnormalities On The Basic Mechanisms Of Sanguine Coagulation / Inflammatory Fermentation Of The Castric Tissue / Pneumo - Engurgitation Consequent To The Embolism Of A Peripheral Branch Of The Pulmonary Arteries / Mephetic Emanation Of Malignant Omphalitis / Abnormal Multiplication Of The Diaphragmatic Tissue Cells / Spontaneous And Spasmodic Contraction Of The Muscle Membranous Ligaments Of The Esophagous / Affection Characterized By Inflammation Of The Bronquioles And Corresponding Pulmonary Lobules / Infectious Pyelonephritis By Pathogenic Bacteriologie Proliferation On The Renal Parenchyma / Sub - Acute Inguinal Lymphogranulomatous Ganglionar Maceration
MALIGNANT CANCEROUS TUMOUR

MACABRE
(Chicago, IL, USA)
Line-Up: Corporate
Death (vocals / guitar),
Nefarious (bass),
Dennis The Menace
(drums)

Chicago's MACABRE are noted for their extreme music based around an almost obsessive theme of serial murderers. Frontman C.D. ('Corporate Death') actually owns several paintings by the renowned serial killer John Wayne Gacy given to him personally by the now executed murderer. C.C. even attended the trial of Jeffrey Dahmer for inspiration. 2000's 'Dahmer' album, produced by Neil Kernon, is a concept based around the twisted life of the cannibalistic necrophile mass murderer Jeffrey Dahmer.

Singles/EPs:
Grim Reality, Decomposed (1987)
Shit List, Gore (1988)
Nightstalker, (1992)
Fishtales / Behind The Wall Of Sleep / Slaughter Thy Poser / Freeze Dried Man, (1995) ('Behind The Walls Of Sleep' EP)

Albums:
GRIM REALITY, Vinyl Solution SOL 18 (1989)
GLOOM, Vinyl Solution (1990)
Embalmer / Trampled To Death / Holidays Of Horror / Fritz Haarmann The Butcher / Evil Ole Soul / Harvey Glatmann / David Brom Took An Axe / Cremator / I Need To Kill / Ultra Violent / Rat Man / Hey Laurie Dann / Patrick Purdy Killed Five And Wounded Thirty / Exhumer / Funeral Home
SINISTER SLAUGHTER, Nuclear Blast NB 070CD (1992)
Night Stalker / The Ted Bundy Song / Sniper In The Sky / Montreal Massacre / Zodiac / What The Hell Did You Do? / The Boston Strangler / Mary Bell / Reprise / Killing Spree (Postal Killer) / Is It Soup Yet? / White Hen Decapitator / Howard Unrah (What Have You Done Now?) / Gacy's Lot / There Was A Young Man Who Blew Up A Plane / Vampire Of Dusseldorf / Shotgun Peterson / What's That Smell? / Edward Kemper Had A Terrible Temper / What The Heck Richard Speck (8 Nurses You Wrecked) / Albert Was Worse Than Any Fish In The Sea
UNABOMBER, Decomposed (1999)
The Unabomber / Ambassador Hotel / The Brain / David Brom Took An Axe / Dr. Holmes He Stripped Their Bones / Ed Gein / Serial Killer
DAHMER, Hammerheart (2000)
Dog Guts / Hitchhiker / In The Army Now / Grandmother's House / Blood Bank / Exposure / Ambassador Hotel / Cup Of Coffee / Bath House / Jeffrey Dahmer And The Chocolate Factory / Apartment 213 / Drill Bit Lobotomy / Jeffrey Dahmer Blues / McDahmers / Into The Toilet With You / Coming To Chicago / Scrub A Dub Dub / Konerak / Temple Of Bones / Trial / Do The Dahmer / Baptized / Christopher Scarver / Dahmer's Dead / The Brain

MACABRE END (SWEDEN)
Line-Up: Per Boder (vocals), Jonas Stålhammer (guitar), Ola Sjöberg (guitar), Thomas Johansson (bass), Niklas Nilsson (drums)

MACABRE END later changed their name to GOD MACABRE releasing an album in 1994. Guitarist Jonas Stålhammer also doubles as vocalist for UTUMNO.

Singles/EPs:
Consumed By Darkness / Ceased To Be / Spawn Of Flies, Corpse Grinder CGR001 (1991)

MACERATION (DENMARK)
Line-Up: Jonas Holmberg (vocals), Lars Bangholt (guitar), Jakob Schultz (bass), Stefan L. Nielsen (drums)

Death Metal act MACERATION were formed by Bangholt and Schultz in Esberj during 1990. Nielsen is ex-AGONISE. Schultz also had links with INVOCATOR, whilst the 'A Serenade Of Agony' album featured a guest showing from the legendary Death Metal figure Dan Swanö of EDGE OF SANITY singing under the guise of Day Disyraah.

Albums:
A SERENADE OF AGONY, Progress Red PRLCD 7913004 (1993)
Intro - Silent Lay The Gentle Lamb / A Serenade Of Agony / Transmogrified / Pain And Pleasure Incarnate / The Watcher / The Mind Rampant / Reincarnation - Time Flies / The Forgotten

MACHEZATO (SPAIN)

Line-Up: Carlos Cadaver (vocals), Dopi Dr. Beltan (guitar), Rober (guitar), Chinin El Mescalinas (bass), Marcos (drums)

Initially a Noisecore unit Spain's MACHETAZO would evolve down a path to Goregrind with later releases. The band debuted a year after their formation with the 1995 demo '46 Cabezas Aplastados Por Un Yunque Oxidado' which featured renditions of A.C. and GUT songs. The tape provoked such an impact on the underground scene it would be re released by Ironia Productions.

MACHEZATO's sophomore effort, the 1998 'Realmente Distruto Comiendo Cadaveres' - this time paying homage to CARCASS and EXTREME NOISE TERROR with covers, would also see a re-release - this time on 10" vinyl format issued by Fudgeworthy Records.

In 1999 MACHEZATO not only abandoned all pretences of Noisecore but indeed most of its membership. At one stage the band was down to a solo endeavour of drummer / guitarist / bassist Dopi Dr. Beltan. Adopting a Grind direction MACHEZATO cut a shared 7" single in collusion with Japanese band CORRUPTED. MACHEZATO's efforts being an original 'Potro De Tortura' and a cover of ST. VITUS's 'Bitter Truth'.

Eventually former member and bass player Chinin El Mescalinas returned for the debut album 'Carne De Cementerio' recorded for the American Razorback concern. In keeping with tradition further covers were included with S.O.B. and ABCESS tracks. Guest vocals were handled by DEFACE man Carlos Cadaver.

Until now MACHEZATO had been employing the temporary services of OBSESION COMPULSIVA band members to flesh out their own act. However, a live drummer was found with ICON man Marcos, second guitarist Rober and Carlos Cadaver committed fulltime too.

2001 saw a further split single with BODIES LAY BROKEN for the Discos Al Pacino label. One of MACHEZATO's tracks '(El Increible) Prpucio Septico' translating as 'The Incredible Septic Cock'!

Future split singles were planned with IMPALED and DENAK.

Singles/EPs:

Potro De Tortura / Bitter Truth, Frigidity (2000) (Split 7" single with CORRUPTED)

La Mascara Del Demonio / (El Increible) Prepucio Septico / La Venganza De Los Muertos Sin Ojas, Discos Al Pacino (2001) (Split 7" single with BODIES LAY BROKEN)

Albums:

REALMENTE DISTRUTO COMIENDO CADAVERES, Fudgeworthy (1999) (10" vinyl release)

CARNE DE CEMENTERIO, Razorback (2000)
El Enjambre Asesino / (Todos Somos) Alimento De Los Gusanos / La Cara Mazada A Golpes / Humillado Y Descuartizado Por Mongolicosi / Torso / P.U.S. (Purulento Urologo Sarnoso) / Suicide Fuck / Obecede A Tu Demonio Interior / Pudrete Como Un Cerdo / Masticasesos / Las Ninos No Deberian Jugar Con Cosas Muertos / El Ataque De King Ghidorh / Delusion Of Terror / Maruta / Los Cuertos Del Munon Garjrenso II

MALAMOR (NY, USA)

Line-Up: Jason Kolts (vocals), Ben Kolts (guitar), Sean Kennedy (guitar), Dave Markle (bass), Shawn Mann (drums)

New York Death Metal band MALAMOR (taken to mean "All love is evil") originated in 1993 with an initial line up roster of guitarists Ben Kolts and Sean Kennedy, bass player Carl Carlew and drummer Kevin Sharp. Vocals were handled by Ben Kolt's sibling Jason. By the following year there was a clean sweep in the rhythm section with new recruits being bass player Dave Markle and drummer Shawn Mann. The band made their presence felt with the 1995 demo tape 'Condemn The Rising'. SUFFOCATION's Frank Mullen added guest lead vocals to MALAMOR's debut album 'Dead To The World'.

MALAMOR would contribute a version of 'Suicide Machine' to a Dwell Records DEATH tribute compilation and more surprisingly added their take of LED ZEPPELIN's 'Out On The Tiles' to another homage affair.

Albums:

DEAD TO THE WORLD, Pulverizer (199-)

MALEDICTION (UK)

Line-Up: Shaun Stephenson (guitars), Rich Mumford (guitars), Darren O'Hara (guitars), Mark Fox (bass), Alisdair Dunn (drums)

Harrogate thrashers that excited considerable underground interest with their single released on the French Thrash label. MALEDICTION released a demo 'Framework of condition' in 1992 featuring a live recording of a gig supporting BOLT-THROWER.

Singles/EPs:
System Fear, Thrash (1991)
Mould Of An Industrial Horizon, (1991)
Dark Effluvium, (1995)

Albums:
THE TEARS THAT PRECEDE BIRTH, (1993)
CHRONICLES OF DISSECTION, Soundphaze GWBCD 001 (1993)
Mould Of An Industrial Horizon / Weeping Tears Of Covetousness / Infestation / Framework Of Contortion / Longterm Result / System Fear / Doctrines Eternal Circles

MALEFACTOR (BRAZIL)

Line-Up: Vladimir Mendes Senna (vocals), Danilo Coimbra (guitar), Wallace Guerra (guitar), Roberto Souza (bass), Luciano Gonzag Veiga Dias (keyboards), Alexandre Deminco Lemos (drums)

Guitarist Jafet Amoedo decamped in mid 2000 to be replaced by erstwhile MYSTIFIER and GRIDLOCK man Martin Mendonca.

Albums:
CELEBRATE THY WAR, Megahard (1999)
THE DARKEST THRONE, Demise (2001)

MALEVOLENCE (PORTUGAL)

Line-Up: Carlos Cariano (vocals / guitar), Frederico Saraiva (guitar), Aires Pereira (bass), Paulo Pereira (keyboards), Gustavo Costa (drums)

A Portuguese Black Death Metal band that has supported both SINISTER and CRADLE OF FILTH. MALEVOLENCE debuted with the demo 'Pleasure Of Molestation'.
1999's 'Martyralized' was recorded in Sweden with an all new line-up centred upon surviving founder member vocalist Carlos Cariano.

Albums:
DOMINIUM, Danger (199-)
Desespero / Dominium Of Hate / The Burning Picture / Under Inhuman Torch / Enchanted Mask / Swallowed In Black / My Eyes (Throne Of Tears) / Sweet Bloody Vision / Erotica / Ceremonial Gallery
MARTYRALIZED, Maquiavel Music Entertainment (1999)
The Brotherhood Of Christ / Diabolical Eve (Chronicles Of Master Lusitania) / Hunters Of The Red Moon / Les Salls Obscures De Rode Noire XVIII / Thy Extremist Operetta / Insubordination / A Shining Onslaught Of Tyranny / Oceans Of Fire / Martyralized

MALEVOLENCE (NEW ZEALAND)

Auckland Death Metal act previously entitled BLACKMASS led by vocalist / guitarist Daryl. The 1996 album was a self-financed affair.

Albums:
ALMOST LIKE SOMETHING COMPLETELY SINISTER, (1996)
Too Slow To Die / Vengeance / I'm The One / Vampires Kiss / Blut Und Liebe / Suburban Execution / The Cage (Of The Insane) / Riding On The Bus

MALEVOLENT CREATION
(Buffalo, NY, USA)

Line-Up: Brett Hoffman (vocals), Phil Fasciana (guitar), Jeff Juszkiewicz (guitar), Jason Blachowicz (bass), Mark Simpson (drums)

Brutal uncompromising Death Metal act centred on guitarist Phil Fasciana created in 1987. Guitarist Jeff Juszkiewics parted ways with the band in 1991.
Swede Peter Tägtren had also been a member of MALEVOLENT CREATION and MELTDOWN but would return to Sweden to found HYPOCRISY, initially titled SEDITIOUS.
In order to complete a planned American tour with DEVASTATION and DEMOLITION HAMMER the band temporarily pulled in the services of MONSTROSITY guitarist Jon Rubin.
For 1992's 'Retribution' the band utilized the services of ex-SOLSTICE members guitarist Rob Barrett and drummer Alex

MALEVOLENT CREATION
Photo : Martin Wickler

Marquez. In 1994 both Fasciana and Barrett had ensconced themselves in the studio with drummer 'Crazy' Larry Hawke kicking off a side project named HATEPLOW.

By 1995 MALEVOLENT CREATION had parted ways with both their label Roadrunner Records and vocalist Brett Hoffman who busied himself guesting for Swiss act SILENT DEATH. Demos were recorded with bassist Jason Blachowicz handling lead vocals.

The 1996 album 'Joe Black', which comprised of rare tracks, demos and a take on SLAYER's 'Raining Blood', was a limited edition release.

The 1997 line-up, which included drummer Derick Roddy (following the tragic death of Crazy Larry in May of that year in a fire whilst attempting to save his pet dog), saw the band, now with Barrett concentrating fulltime on HATEPLOW, trimmed to a quartet with only Blaschowicz and Fasciana remaining from their origins. Roddy would also session for AURORA BOREALIS and later NILE.

Hoffman returned for 1998's 'Fine Art Of Murder'. MALEVOLENT CREATION now comprised of Hoffman, Fasciana, Barrett, bassist Gordon Sims and ex-SUFFOCATION / R.I.P. drummer Dave Culross.

In 2000 MALEVOLENT CREATION

drummer Dave Culross aided INCANTION laying down session drums for their 'Infernal Storm' album. The same year found Culross in collusion with Fasciana and Barrett for their HATEPLOW project album 'The Only Law Is Survival'.

In a display of brotherhood HATEPLOW would support MALEVOLENT CREATION on their February 2001 headlining shows across Europe. Returning from Europe Hoffman was arrested upon entry into the United States and imprisoned for parole violation dating back to 1995. The incarceration of their vocalist forced MALEVOLENT CREATION to withdraw from a projected series of American dates planned with MONSTROSITY.

Albums:
THE TEN COMMANDMENTS,
Roadrunner RC 93611 (1991)
Memorial Arrangements / Premature Burial / Remnants Of Withered Decay / Multiple Stab Wounds / Impaled Existence / Thou Shalt Kill! / Sacrificial Annihilation / Decadence Within / Injected Sufferage / Malevolent Creation
RETRIBUTION, Roadrunner RC 91811 (1992)
Eve Of The Apocalypse / Systematic Execution / Slaughter Of The Innocence / Coronation Of Our Domain / No Flesh Shall Be Spared / The Coldest Survive / Monster / Mindlock / Iced
STILLBORN, Roadrunner RR 90422 (1993)
Dominated Resurgency / The Way Of All Flesh / Dominion Of Terror / Geared For Gain / Stillborn / Ordain The Hierarchy / Carnivorous Misgivings / Genetic Affliction / Ethnic Cleansing / Disciple Of Abhorrence
ETERNAL, Pavement ZYX IRC 128-2 (1995)
No Salvation / Blood Brothers / Infernal Desire / Living In Fear / Unearthly/ Enslaved / Alliance For War / They Breed / To Kill / Hideous Reprisal / Eternal / Tasteful Agony
JOE BLACK, Pavement (1996)
Joe Black / Self Important Freak / Sadistic Perversity / No Salvation / To Kill / Tasteful Agony / Genetic Affliction / Raining Blood / Remnants For A Withered Decay / Impaled Existence
IN COLD BLOOD, Pavement PM 32258CD (1997)
Nocturnal Overlord / Prophecy / Compulsive / Narcotic Genocide / Violated / Leech / In Cold Blood / Visions

Of Malice / Seven / Preyed Upon / Millions / Condemned / Seizure
THE FINE ART OF MURDER, Pavement ZYX IRC 127-2 (1998)
To Die Is At Hand / Manic Demise / Instinct Evolved / Dissect The Eradicated / Mass Graves / The Fine Art Of Murder / Bone Exposed / Purge / Fracture / Rictus Surreal / Scorn / Day Of Lamentation / Scattered Flesh
MANIFESTATION, Pavement (2000)
In Cold Blood / Condemned / Nocturnal Overlord / Fine Art Of Murder / Scorn / Blood Brothers / Impaled Existence / Living In Fear / Manic Demise / To Die Is At Hand / Infernal Desire / Bone Exposed / Alliance Or War / Mass Graves / Joe Black / Self Important Freak / Multiple Stab Wounds / Eve Of The Apocalypse / Slaughter Of Innocence / Monster
ENVENOMED, Pavement 32361 (2000)
Homicidal Rant / Night Of The Long Knives / Kill Zone / Halved / Serial Dementia / Bloodline Severed / Pursuit Revised / Conflict / Viral Release / The Deviant's March / Envenomed

MALIGNANCY (Yonkers, NY, USA)
Line-Up: Danny Nelson (vocals), Ron Kachnic (guitar), Desmond Tolhurst (bass), Roger Beaujard (drums)

Although founded in 1992 by vocalist Danny Nelson MALIGNANCY is best known as the side project of MORTICIAN men guitarists Roger Beaujard and Desmond Tolhurst. The Yonkers act came together when Nelson united with guitarist Javier Velez and drummer Kevin Chamberlain as CARCINOGEN.
Chamberlain soon made his exit as an all new line-up, now billed MALIGNANCY, saw the recruitment of second guitarist Larry Remlin, bass player Frank Madiao and drummer John Marzan. However Remlin would break ranks swiftly as did his fleeting replacement Tom Dorney. The 'Eaten Out From Within' demo bore a MALIGNANCY line-up of Nelson, Velez, Madiao and Marzan.
Once again the band fractured with just Nelson remaining. Undaunted he built around himself a fresh cadre of drummer Roger Beaujard, guitarist Ron Kachnic and bassist Desmond Tolhurst for a 1997 demo session 'Ignorance Is Bliss'. This tape secured a deal with United Guttural Records who promptly tested the market with a 1998 promotional CD.
MALIGNANCY toured in Europe during 2000 appearing at the Czech Republic

'Brutal Assault' festival prior to December dates in America with GOATWHORE and MORTICIAN. Tolhurst would depart following these dates necessitating guitarist Lance taking over this role.
The 2001 release 'Ignorance Is Bliss' on Primitive Recordings comprises of early demo tracks. A split EP is planned in alliance with Czech band INTERVALLE BIZARRE.

Albums:
MALIGNANCY PROMO, United Guttural (1998)
Profitable Extinction / Oral Excrement / Intestinal Sodomy / Cerebral Tissue Extraction / Rotten Seed / Ignorance Is Bliss / Your Life Is Shit / Post Fetal Depression
INTRAUTERINE CANNIBALISM, United Guttural (1999)
Rotten Seed / Intrauterine Cannibalism / Intestinal Sodomy / Internal Corruption / Profitable Extinction / Ignorance Is Bliss / Your Life Is Shit / Oral Excrement / Waterlogged Corpse / Cerebral Tissue Extraction / Fried Afterbirth / Post Fetal Depression / Bag
MOTIVATED BY HUNGER, Primitive Recordings (2000)
Motivated By Hunger / Vaginal Incisors / Separated Anxiety / Atmosphere Of Decay / Cystic Fibrosis / Intrauterine Cannibalism (Live)
IGNORANCE IS BLISS, Primitive Recordings (2001)
Skinned Alive / Cervical Erosion / Gory Fetish / Rotten Seed / Ignorance Is Bliss / Your Life Is Shit / Post Fetal Depression / Profitable Extinction / Oral Excrement / Intestinal Sodomy / Cerebral Tissue Extraction

MALIGNANT TUMOUR
(CZECH REPUBLIC)
Line-Up: Bilos (vocals / bass), Richard (guitar), Marek (drums)

The industrious Grindcore merchants MALIGNANT TUMOUR would share cassette releases with GRIDE, CEREBRAL TURBULANCY and SQUASH BOWELS. Demos included 'Symphonies For Pathologist', 'Crash Syndrome' and 'Analyze Of Pathological Conceptions'.
MALIGNANT TUMOUR's 1996 shared single with MASTIC SCUM 'Sick Sins Syndrome' includes AGATHOCLES and REGURGITATE cover versions.
Guitarist Richard also operates in Doom

Metal band LOVE HISTORY.
The 1997 shared album 'Eat The Flesh…
And Vomica', released in union with
Polish act SQUASH BOWELS, included
two AGATHOCLES cover versions 'No
Use… (Hatred)' and 'Go Fucking Nihilist'
along with a rendition of DEAD
INFECTION's 'Maggots In Your Flesh'.
The 1998 'Rock Stars - Money Wars'
shared EP with Polish act DEAD
INFECTION included a further
AGATHOCLES cover 'Lay Off Me'.

Singles/EPs:
Split, (199-) (7" split single with
IMMURED)
Split, (199-) (7" split single with
DECOMPOSED)
Dysecteria Bacillaris / Acute
Haemmorrhagical Necrosis Of Pancreas
/ Lymphogranuloma Veneres / Chronical
Myeloid Leukemia / Herpos Labialis /
Climax-Menopause-Polyuria, Epidemie
(1996) ('Swarms Of Virulency' 7" split
single with INGROWING)
Endocarditis Streptoccia Acuta /
Affections Of Outlet Urinary Way / A
Start At Least / Lyssa / Grind Gut
Wrenching / Desensitized, Epidemie
(1996) ('Sick Sins Syndrome' 7" split
single with MASTIC SCUM)
Split, (199-) (7" split single with
WARSORE)
Split, (199-) (7" split single with
AGATHOCLES)
Split, (199-) (7" split single with
VOMITO)
Hungry Urinary Urn, (199-) (4 way split
7" single with C.S.S.O., NEGLIGENT
COLLATERAL COLLAPSE and CUM)
Nature Warning / Human Extinction /
This Filth Stinks / Lay Off Me /
Government Shitheads / Hope Against A
System / Mendacious T-Levision /
Violence Against Fascistic Cunts, Morbid
(1998) ('Rock Stars - Money Wars' 7"
split single with DEAD INFECTION)

Albums:
EAT THE FLESH… AND VOMICA,
Obscene Productions (1997) (Split
album with SQUASH BOWELS)
Maggots In Your Flesh / Epiphilitis /
Acute Haemorrhagical Necrosis Of
Pancreas /Subacute Endocarditis /
Decubitis / Mors Praenatalis / Pephigus
Vulgaris / Disease Of Oral Cavities / No
Use… (Hatred) / Pertussis / Diptheria /
Idiopathic Colitis Ulcerosa /
Mucormycosis Of Gastrointestinal Tract /
Parasitical Cysts / Dysenteria Bacillaris /
Embryopathia / Purulent Attack / Reason
To Hate / Necrotic Urocystitis With
Ammoniacal Fermentation / Putrefaction
Decomposition / Impetigo Contagiosa /
Intravascular Disseminated Coagulate /
Ingrowing Of The Alien Things In The
Body / Pulmonary Collapse / Go Fucking
Nihilist / Waterhouse-Fridrichsen
Syndrome

MANGLED (HOLLAND)

MANGLED emerged in 1989 led by the
trio of Pepijn Howen, Wilko Reynders and
Erwin Hermsen. By 1991 Harald Gielen
and Paul Dunn had completed the line-up
for recording of the inaugural 1992 three
track demo tape 'Cadaverous'.
A sophomore promotional cassette
'Perish' was issued the following year
attracting the attention of the Wild Rags
label who promptly re-issued the session
on CD format.
However, 1995 would see the departure
of Dunn and also later of Reynders. The
latter's place was taken by Floris De
Jonge for recording of the '…In
Emptiness' album. MANGLED would also
be brought back up to strength with the
addition of INHUMANE man Loek
Peeters.
Promoting the 'Ancient Times' album, a
concept work based on the depravities of
the Roman empire released on former
member Wilko Reynders label Fadeless,
MANGLED toured Europe in alliance with
Italians Natron and Sweden's
CENTINEX. November 1999 saw a
further burst of live activity sharing billing
with VOMITORY, DAWN OF DECAY and
DERANGED.
MANGLED would cut their version of
'Visions From The Dark Side' for a 2000
MORBID ANGEL tribute album. The band
would later see inclusion on a CANNIBAL
CORPSE homage compilation released
by Dwell Records with 'A Skull Full Of
Maggots'.
Hermsen would act as producer for
INHUME's 2000 album 'Decomposing
From Inside'.

Singles/EPs:
Perish, Wild Rags (1995)

Albums:
IN EMPTINESS, Wild Rags (1997)
ANCIENT TIMES, Fadeless (1998)
Raise My Fist In The Face Of God / Eve
Of Mourning / In Ancient Times I: De
Christianis / Bathe In Blood / Era: Odium

/ Goatrider / The Sleeping Paradise / In Ancient Times II: Erotica / In Ancient Times III: Bellum Gallicum / Mangled **MOST PAINFUL WAYS**, Hammerheart (2001)
Hate / Blood Fed Orgasm / Evilterrestrial / Mortifying Body Parts / Warfare Embowelment / Revelation Of Soulside Pain / Hellrose Place / Formaldehyde / Scream And Bleed / Spontaneous Human Combustion

MANGLED TORSOS (GERMANY)
Line-Up: Olli (vocals / guitar), Frank (bass), Patrick (drums)

Formed in the summer of 1990, MANGLED TORSOS describe themselves as a very aggressive, fun Grindcore project and explained that the choice of band name highlighted this philosophy to the max.
1992 saw the recording of the group's first demo, 'Incalculate Of Your Subconscious', after which Frank replaced MANGLED TORSOS' original bassist.
In the spring of '93 the 2 track EP 'Anatomia Reformata' appeared as a limited edition of a mere 360 copies. Morbid Records promptly stepped in to sign the group.
In addition to the two albums released since 1994, the band have supported the likes of DEAD, AGATHOCLES, MIASMA, BLOOD and PYOGENESIS.

Singles/EPs:
Anatomia Reformata EP, (1993)

Albums:
DRAWINGS OF THE DEAD, Morbid MR 013 CD (1994)
Intro / Unsuspecting Sacrifice / Lost Emotions / Drawings Of The Dead / Morphea / Deranged Body Love / Malignant Tumor / Dehumanization / Dissemble
GODLESS, (1995)

MANIFEST TO DESTROY
(Kansas City, MO, USA)
Line-Up: Doug Cole (vocals / guitar), Mike Henderson (guitar), Theresa Cole (bass), Johnnie Reed (drums)

Missouri based MANIFEST TO DESTROY are a Christian Death Metal band. The act had Ryan Sales on drums from 1998 until 1999 when his position was taken by Johnnie Reed.

Adam Knapp was lead vocalist until late 2000 when guitarist Doug Cole took over singing duties.

MANOS (GERMANY)
Line-Up: Mike Andre (vocals / guitar), Andreas Löhne (bass), Carsten Rothweiler (drums)

MANOS were formed originally under the title of LÖENENHERZ in 1984 with original drummer Ingo Zach. In 1988 the band changed titles to MANOS, recruiting drummer Carsten Trothweiler around the same period. The following year the group issued the 'Kranker Tannenbaum' demo, followed by a further tape entitled 'Faust'.
MANOS played support shows with BIOHAZARD, MASTER, INCUBUS and PROTECTOR and signed to Poserslaughter Records in 1991.
The group would add new bassist Mario Loebelt for the debut album.

Singles/EPs:
Manos EP, Poserslaughter (1992)

Albums:
LA BUMM DIE FETTE, Poserslaughter PSR-WIMP 012 (1993)
Sentence Of Death / Kranker Tannenbaum / Hol Mir 'Ne Bockwurst / Hau Auf Die Sau / Hip Hop / Roland K. / Costa Brava / Komm In Den Garten / Einer Geht Noch Rein / Der Fuchs Schleicht / Drehrumbum / Lilo / Das Letze Lied / Putzfrau
TERRIBLE REALITY, Poserslaughter PSR-WIMP 015 (1995)
From The Cradle To The Grave / Metal Attack / Suicidal Confusion / Hell - Phantom / We Mosh / Terrible Reality / Insidious Attack / Blutige Luscht / Voice Of Satan / Acid War / Ulehule / Dirty Vision / Fuck Yourself / Hypocritical World / Ballade Von Den Sechsen / Evasion
AT MANIA OF DEATH, Morbid MR041 (1998)
At Mania Of Death / Against / Pestilence / Trade In The Blood / Mirror Of Truth / Execution / Rage After Death / Teacher's Pants / Empire Of Carrion / Lulle / Fate And Death
LIVING BURIAL, Morbid (2000)
Incest Ain't Correct / Living Burial / Nervelied / Detractor / Bad Chicken Attack / Enchanted Land / Witching Excess / Terror Spreads Terror / Uprising Of The Dead / Insularity / Lionheart

MARDUK (SWEDEN)
Line-Up: Joakim Grave (vocals), Morgan Håkansson (guitar), Roger B. War (bass), Fredrik Andersson (drums)

An extreme Scandinavian Death Metal band initially called GOD switching names to that of the Sumerian illegitimate God MARDUK in 1990. Founder member guitarist Morgan Håkansson was previously a member of ABHOR and Punk Rock act MOSES.

The first demo featured ex-LUCKY SEVEN vocalist Andreas Axelsson. Other musicians included guitarist Joakim Göthberg and bassist Rickard Kalm. MARDUK's less than tactfully titled 'Fuck Me Jesus' EP - actually their first demo pressed onto vinyl - was graced with a sleeve depicting a naked woman inserting a cross between her legs from behind and was subsequently banned across Europe.

By the time the group's debut album arrived in 1992 MARDUK's line-up had shifted to Håkansson, Axelsson, Göthberg, guitarist Magnus Andersson and Bogge Svensson of Viking Metallers ALLEGIANCE on bass.

Prior to the ensuing 'Those Of The Unlight' album, Göthberg assumed the lead vocal role as Axelsson had left to join EDGE OF SANITY. Andersson also left to concentrate on his various project bands; such as ALLEGIANCE, OVERFLASH and CARDINAL SIN. Göthberg joined Andersson as the drummer in CARDINAL SIN before founding DARKIFIED.

With third album 'Opus Nocturne' emerging in 1994, the group would tour Europe the same year supporting IMMORTAL on their 'Sons Of Northern Darkness' tour. MARDUK's roster at this juncture comprising of Håkansson, ex-CHAINED bassist Roger 'B. War' Svensson, vocalist Joakim Av Gravf and A CANOUROUS QUINTET drummer Fredrik Andersson.

In 1996 the 'Heaven Shall Burn... When We Are Gathered' album was issued and MARDUK also released the 'Glorification' EP, which featured the band's cover versions of tracks by PILEDRIVER, VENOM, DESTRUCTION and BATHORY.

At this point in time MARDUK's line-up consisted of Håkansson (also an active member of ABRUPTUM by now), vocalist Legion, guitarist Kim Osara, 'B. War' and Andersson.

For their 1996 European tour MARDUK drafted in their producer and HYPOCRISY and ABYSS guitarist Peter Tägtgren as a stand in member, although plans were laid to convene ex-NECROPHOBIC and DARK FUNERAL member David 'Blackmoon' Parland into the fold.

Various members of MARDUK collaborated with Swedish Punk act WOLFPACK to create MOMENT MANIACS. The recordings resulted in the 1999 'Two Fuckin' Pieces' album.

2000 saw the issue of an MCD 'Obedience' featuring MARDUK's rendition of CELTIC FROST's 'Into The Crypt Of Rays'. MARDUK members also contributed to the 2000 album 'The Howling' by DEVILS WHOREHOUSE.

Singles/EPs:
Here's No Fucking Silence EP, Slaughter (1992)
Fuck Me Jesus / Departure From The Mortals / The Black / Within The Abyss / Shut Up And Suffer, Osmose Productions OPCD 015 (1993) ('Fuck Me Jesus' EP)
Glorification Of The Black God (Remixed Version) / Total Desaster / Sex With Satan / Sodomise The Dead / The Return Of The Darkness And Evil, Osmose Productions OPMCD 043 (1996) ('Glorification' EP)
Obedience / Funeral Bitch / Into The Crypt Of Rays, Regain (2000) ('Obedience' EP)

Albums:
DARK ENDLESS, No Fashion Necropolis CDS17 (1992)
Still Fucking Dead (Here's No Peace) / The Sun Turns Black as Night / Within The Abyss / The Funeral Seemed To Be Endless / Departure From The Mortals / The Black... / Dark Endless / Holy Inquisition
THOSE OF THE UNLIGHT, Osmose Productions OPCD015 (1993)
Darkness Breeds Immortality / Those Of The Unlight / Wolves / On Darkened Wings / Burn My Coffin / A Sculpture Of The Night / Echoes From The Past / Stone Stands On It's Silent Vigil
OPUS NOCTURNE, Osmose Productions OPCD028 (1994)
Intro / The Appearance Of Spirits Of Darkness / Sulphar Souls / From Subterranean Throne Profound / Autumnal Reaper / Materialized In Stone / Untrodden Paths (Wolves Part II) / Opus Nocturne / Deme Quaden Thyrane

/ The Sun Has Failed
HEAVEN SHALL BURN... WHEN WE ARE GATHERED, Osmose Productions OPCD 040 (1997)
Summon The Darkness / Beyond The Grace Of God / Infernal Eternal / Glorification Of The Black God / Darkness It Shall Be / The Black Tormentor Of Satan / Dracul Va Domni Din Nov In Transylvania / Legion
LIVE IN GERMANIA, Osmose Productions (1997)
Beyond The Grace Of God / Sulphar Souls / The Black / Darkness It Shall Be / Materialized In Stone / Infernal Eternal / On Darkened Wings / Wolves / Untrodden Paths (Wolves Part II) / Dracul Va Domni / Legion / Total Desaster
NIGHTWING, Osmose Productions (1998)
Preludium / Bloodtide (XXX) / Of Hell's Fire / Slay The Nazarene / Nightwing / Dreams Of Blood And Iron / Dracole Wayda / Kaziklu Bey - The Lord Impaler / Deme Quaden Thyrane / Anno Domini 1476
PANZER DIVISION MARDUK, Osmose Productions (1999)
Panzer Division Marduk / Baptism By Fire / Christraping Black Metal / Scorched Earth / Beast Of Prey / Blooddawn / 502 / Fistfucking God's Planet
INFERNAL ETERNAL, Blooddawn BLOOD 007 (2000)
Panzer Division Marduk / Burn My Coffin / Baptism By Fire / The Sun Turns Black As Night / Of Hells Fire / 502 / Materialized In Stone / Beast Of Pray / Those Of The Unlight / Sulphar Souls / Dreams Of Blood And Iron / Fistfucking God's Planet / On Darkened Wings (Live) / Into The Crypt Of Rays (Live) / Still Fucking Dead (Live) / Slay The Nazarene (Live) / Departure From The Mortals (Live) / Legion (Live) / Video

MARTYR (CANADA)
Line-Up: Francois Mongrain (vocals / bass), Daniel Mongrain (guitar), Pier-Luc Lampron (guitar), Patrice Hamelin (drums)

Technical Quebec Death Metal. MARTYR opened proceedings with the 1995 demo session 'Ostrogoth'. The 1997 album 'Hopeless Hopes' was a self financed affair. Following recording drummer Francois Richard made way for Patrice Hamelin.
In 1998 MARTYR put in a showing at the infamous Milwaukee Metalfest. Guitarist Daniel Mongrain, whilst retaining his ties

to MARTYR, would join GORGUTS in the Autumn of 1999 appearing on their 'From Wisdom To Hate' album.
MARTYR's second album 'Warp Zone', featuring GORGUTS vocalist Luc LeMay as guest, arrived in 2000.

Albums:
HOPELESS HOPES, Martyr (1997)
Hopeless Hopes / Prototype / Elementals / Non Confrmis / Ostrogoth / The Blinds Reflection / Inner Peace / Ars Nova / Nipsky
WARP ZONE, (2000)

MARTYR (CZECH REPULIC / USA)
Line-Up: Paul Speckman (guitar), Christopher, Skull (drums)

MARTYR are a studio project from Skull and Christopher of Czech's KRABATHOR and renowned MASTER / ABOMINATION man Paul Speckman.

Albums:
MURDER X: THE END OF THE GAME, System Shock (2000)
Make Sure You've Spoke / From When The Sadness Closes / The End Of The Game / Quiet Cruelty / Kill With Me / All About Life / Crooked Teeth / Never Without Sin / When Jesus Lands In Detroit / Face To Face

MASSACRA (FRANCE)
Line-Up: Fred Death (vocals / guitar), Jean Marc Trisani (guitar), Pascal Jorgensen (bass), Chris Palengat (drums)

A French Metal band with a five album strong back catalogue, original drummer Chris Palengat was replaced in time by Matthias Limmer.
Early MASSACARA works pursue regular Death Metal themes of violence and gore although 1994's 'Sick' sees the band delving into questions of humanity and moral justice.
Whilst various members of MASSACRA formed an Industrial side project titled ZERO TOLERANCE in 1996 (releasing the 'Zero For All' album on Active Records), founding member Fred Death sadly lived up to his surname and died in April 1997 of skin cancer.

Albums:
FINAL HOLOCAUST, Shark (1990)
Apocalyptic Warriors / Researchers Of Torture / Sentenced For Life/ War Of

Attrition/ Trained To Kill/ Nearer To Death/ Final Holocaust/ Eternal Hate/ The Day Of Massacara
ENJOY THE VIOLENCE, Shark 018 (1991)
Enjoy The Violence / Ultimate Antichrist / Gods Of Hate / Atrocious Crimes / Revealing Cruelty / Full Of Hatred / Seas Of Blood / Near Death Experience / Sublime Extermination / Agonizing World
SIGNS OF THE DECLINE, Shark Vertigo 512897-2 (1992)
Evidence Of Abominations / Defying Man's Creation / Baptized In Decadence / Mortify Their Flesh / Traumatic Paralyzed Mind / Excruciating Commands / World Dies Screaming / Signs Of Decline / Civilization In Regression / Full Frontal Assault
SICK, Phonogram 518 676-2 (1994)
Twisted Mind / Madness Remains / Ordinary People / Closed Minded / Harmless Numbers / Lack Of Talk / Broken Youth / Can't Stand / My Reality/ Suckers / Piece Of Real
HUMANIZE DHUMAN, Rough Trade RTD 311.4003.2 (1995)
Need For Greed / Feel Unreal / My Only Friend / Mad To Be Normal / How Free Are You / Humanize Human / Dejected / Zero Tolerance / Pay For My Tears

MASSACRE (FL, USA)

Line-Up: Kam Lee (vocals), Rick Rozz (guitar), Pete Sison (bass), Syrus Peters (drums)

Death Metal act MASSACRE were created by DEATH refugees vocalist Kam Lee, guitarist Rick Rozz, bassist Terry Butler and drummer Bill Andrews. After MASSACRE's formation the band was put on hold whilst Rozz, Butler and Andrews sessioned on DEATH's 'Leprosy' album, MASSACRE getting back into gear following completion of DEATH commitments.
The band's first European tour, now with second guitarist Steve Swanson, saw Texan's DEVASTATION and German act MORGOTH supporting. The 1992 EP 'Inhuman Conditions' features a version of VENOM's 'Warhead' that include singer Cronos on vocals.
MASSACRE toured Europe in 1993 on a package bill with GRAVE and DEMOLITION HAMMER. Upon their return the band folded with Rozz creating MINDSWEEP.
For 1996's 'Promise' reformation album MASSACRE drafted in two new members

bassist Pete Sison and drummer Syrus Peters.
By 2000 Lee had created two acts, KAULDRON and SOUL SKINNER.

Singles/EPs:
Provoked / Accurser, Earache (1989) (Free 7" with 'From Beyond' LP)
Inhuman Conditions / Plains Of Insanity / Provoked / Accurser / Warhead, Earache MOSH 060T (1992)

Albums:
FROM BEYOND, Earache MOSH 027 (1989)
Dawn Of Eternity / Cryptic Realms / Biohazard / Chamber Of Ages / From Beyond / Defeat Remains / Succubus / Symbolic Immortality / Corpsegrinder
PROMISE, Earache MOSH96 (1996)
Nothing / Forever Torn / Black Soil Nest / Promise / Bitter End / Bloodletting / Unnameable / Where Dwells Sadness / Suffering / Inner Demon

MASTER (Chicago, IL, USA)

Line-Up: Paul Speckmann (vocals / bass), Chris Mittelbrun (guitar), Bill Scmidt (drums)

MASTER is but one of the outlets, alongside solo work and DEATHSTRIKE, utilized by Death Metal genius Paul Speckmann. As a vocalist Speckmann is able to pour more genuine venomous rage into his vocals than perhaps any other.
MASTER's second album features drummer Aaron Nickeas and guest guitar by CYNIC / DEATH man Paul Masvidal, original guitarist Chris Mittelbrun having left for pastures new in SINDROME, a later incarnation of fellow Chicago act DEVESTATION.
Speckmann released an eponymous solo album almost simultaneously with MASTER's second outing. 2000 found the man united with Skull and Christopher from the Czech Republic's KRABATHOR for the MARTYR project and the resulting 'Murder: The End Of The Game' album.

Albums:
MASTER, Nuclear Blast NB 040 (1990)
Pledge Of Alliance / Unknown Soldier / Mangled Dehumanization / Pay To Die / Funeral Bitch / Master / Children Of The Grave / Terrorizer / The Truth / Pledge Of Alliance (Original mix) / Re-Entry And Destruction / Terrorizer (Original mix)
AND ON THE 7TH DAY GOD

CREATED MASTER, Nuclear Blast NB 054CD (1992)
What Kind Of God / Latitudinarian / Heathen / Used / Demon / Constant Quarrel / Judgement Of Will / America The Pitiful / Whose Left To Decide / Submerged In Sin

MASTIC SCUM (AUSTRIA)

Singles/EPs:
Tilt EP, (199-)
Split, (199-) (7" split single with BLOCKHEADS)
Political Shit / A Load Of Koky / The Human Scum / Rock Out With Your Cock Out, Epidemie (1996) ('Riot' 7" split single with MALGNANT TUMOUR)

Albums:
FAKE, (199-)
ZERO, Noise Variations (1999)
Inhume / Filthkick / I Need A Spliff / Demand The Change / Overdose / L.O.W. / Deaf, Dumb & Blind / Emotive Synergy / Blood Effusion / Arouse Suspicion / Kill The Mute / What In The World? / Lust For Life / Deep Shit / Fuck Authority / Suckass / Exhume

MAZE OF TORMENT (SWEDEN)
Line-Up: Pehr Larsson (vocals / bass), Peter Karlsson (guitar), Kjell Enblom (drums)

Originally titled TORMENT upon the band's formation in 1994 by former HARMONY members drummer Kjell Enblom and guitarist Peter Karlsson. The duo were soon joined by VINTERLAND guitarist Pehr Larsson.
The trio, still operating under the name HARMONY, recorded a demo which came to the attention of Deviation Records based in Scotland. The band then switched titles to TORMENT for a three track demo. Upon signing to Corrosion Records the band title became MAZE OF TORMENT for the 1996 album 'The Force' produced by EDGE OF SANITY's Dan Swäno.
MAZE OF TORMENT added bass player Thomas Nyqvist shortly after the album's release.
MAZE OF TORMENT's 2000 album 'Death Strikes' was produced by Tomas Skogsberg.

Albums:
THE FORCE, Corrosion CR 6-503-2 (1996)

Shapeless In The Dark / Dream Of Blood / Souls Been Left To Die / The Force / Brave The Blizzard / Battle Of The Dead / The Last Candle / Land Unknown
FASTER DISASTER, Iron Fist Productions (1999)
The Reality / Five Inch / Dead Soul / Horror Visions / Ancient Treasure / Faster Disaster / The Devil's Kill / Hide The Light / Bite The Dust
DEATH STRIKES, Necropolis NR056CD (2000)
Death Strikes / Sodomizing Death Spell / Intense Slaughter / This Is Death / Aggressive Bloodhunt / The Infernal Force / The Sadist / Angels From Hell / The Evil Beneath The Flames

MEATHOOK SEED (UK / USA)
Line-Up: Christophe Lamouret (vocals), Mitch Harris (guitar), Shane Embury (bass), Ian Tracey (drums)

MEATHOOK SEED are an amalgam of NAPALM DEATH men guitarist Mitch Harris and bassist Shane Embury, OUT vocalist Christophe Lamouret and drummer Ian Tracey. The 2000 album title is a twist on 'B.I.B.L.E.'.

Albums:
EMBEDDED, Earache (1993)
Famine Sector / A Furred Grave / My Infinity / Day Of Conceiving / Cling To An Image / A Jilted Remnant / Forgive / Focal Point Blur / Embedded / Visible Shallow Self / Sea Of Tranquility
BASIC INSTRUCTIONS BEFORE LEAVING EARTH, Dreamcatcher (2000)

THE MEATSHITS (CA, USA)
Line-Up: Robert Deathrage (vocals), Leyla Shelton, Doug Carranza, Aaron Copelan, Vince Castillo, Andy Garcia

An infamous name on the American underground circuit. The band, founded in 1987 previously known as CHEMICAL DEPENDENCY and led by Robert Deathrage a.k.a. M.C. Cuntkiller, are renowned for their sickening mixture of hardcore pornography and brutal Death soaked Grindcore. THE MEATSHITS issued a barrage of offensive demo cassettes and were one of the very first bands to utilize sampling. Titles included 'Frectate Fumes', 'Meet The Shits', 'Menstrual Samples', 'Bowel Rot', Regurgitated Semen', 'Let There Be Shit', 'Fuck Frenzy' and 'Genital Infection'.
A slew of split singles followed over the

years as THE MEATSHITS struck up vinyl alliances with ANAL MASSAKER, DEAD, ANAL CUNT, BUTT AUGER CRAP, CATATONIC EXISTENCE, PSYCHO, Japans C.S.S.O and NECROPHILIACS.

<u>Singles/EPs:</u>
Crack Slave / Eternal Misery / Time For Sex / Test Tube Butt Baby / Lust For Death / Nose Candy / Bible Belt / Porno Palace / Rotting Fuckhole / Bullshit Lottery / Feverish Fucking / Oriental Orgasms / No Holes Barred / Body Heat / Drunk And Horny / The Golden Shower Girls / Censor Shit / Gallons Of Cum / Let There Be Shit / Acid Rain Meltdown, Wicked Sick 4 (1991) (7" split single with ANAL CUNT)
Live Split, Regurgitated Semen RSR002 (1992) (Double 7" split single with W.B.I.)
Final Exit / Fuck Attack / Fuck The Wet Spot / Vaginal Fallout / Get Naked Cunt / Pussy Fart / Love Song / Butt Pus / Lip Service / Pulsating Vaginal Infection / Bobbing For Stools / Brown Sugar / Anal Majesty / Vulgar Display / Church Approval / Sex For Profit (Not For Fun) / Ninety Proof Holy Water / Masterpiece Of Defecation / Legacy Of Shit / Cancerous Foreskin / A.I.D.S. Victim / Fuck Frenzy (Thrash version) / Regurgitated Semen / Regurgitated Semen (Part II / The Meat Shits, Regurgitated Semen RSR003 (1992) (7" single)
Proud To Be An Asshole / Greek Sex / Drive It Home / Tongue Probe / Harmony Excretion / Ice Slut / Orgasm Plasma / Face Hole / Fuck Fart / Meat Sauce / Dildo Girls / Wall To Wall Fucking / Negative Feedback / Fuck-Suck Action / Semen Sealed Asshole / Fuck Rush / No Solution / Maggot Puke / French Fuck / Sex Smells, Axction ACT 15 (1992) (7" split single with PSYCHO)
Split, (1992) (7" split single with BUTT AUGER CRAP)
Split, (1992) (7" split single with DISSENSION)
Make Me Cum, Psycho Mania PMR005 (1993) (7" single)
Moan Of Orgasm / Make Me Cum / Hugs And Drugs / Midnight Snack / Bizarre Fetish / Fingered / Working Girl / Mutated Testicle / Fear Of Sex / Torn Hymen / Cold Cunt / Anal Worship / Half Eaten Pussy / Bought The Farm / Skid Row Graduate / Stagnant Pussy Fumes / Blood In Your Stools / Slap Happy Pappy / Human Extinction / Am I Shit? /

Alcoholic Aphrodisiac / Hypersexual Nymphomaniac / Stinking In The Earth / Sexual Death Sentence / Latex Euphoria / Dis-Pleasure / Spray Of Secretion / Vaginal Hell / Sexual Wasteland / Erotic Oblivion / Talk Dirty To Me / Introduction To Anal Sex
Sexual Abuse / Psychotic Interlude / Public Execution / The Meat Shits Part VI / In Pain / Incubator Of Death / You Wish You Were Me / Going Mental / This Is The End, Gutted GR008 (1993) ('Sexual Abuse' 7" single)
For Those About To Shit We Salute You, (199-) (7" single)
Split, (199-) (7" split single with ANAL MASSAKER)
Mindfuck Delirium, (199-) (7" single)
Get Ready To Deep Throat / Leaving In Pieces / Dripping In Sweat / Cum Spurting / Vaginal Leprosy / Slippery When Erect / Genital Hospital / Sex Novelty / Another Day Of Death, Regurgitated Semen RSR007 (199-) ('Another Day Of Death' 7" split single with NECROPHILIACS)
Mind Control / Lucky Stuff / Waterworks / Sushi Girls / Potty Pals / Hypocrite Shit / Another Orgasm / Fighting Words / Fucked From Behind / Concentration Of Hate / Back To The Seventies / Backfired / Eve Of Your Death / Hate Dance, Morbid Granny M666001MC (1994) ('Rape Bait'. 7" split single with CATATONIC EXISTENCE)
Bowel Rot, (1994) (7" single)
Intro / Sexual Abuse / Hatred Speaks / Fucked Up Part II / Mental Skip / Incubator Of Death / I Spy (Masturbation) / You Should Have Thanked Me / Pink In Your Face / Stay Hard And Fuck / Dirty Old Farts / Mr. Stinky / Go Fuck Yourself / Anal Rampage / Vacuum Cunt / Piece Of Fuck / Barbaric Bitch Beater / Emotion Sickness / Death Of All Fours / Fucked Up Part III / Outro, Hellion (1995) ('Take This And Eat It' 7" EP)
Punishment (Tomb Of The Guardian Angel) / Seven Year Jock Itch / Semen Splurge / Lick Up The Blood / …Of Hate / Back To The Seventies / Backfire / Eye Of Your Death / G.G. Is Now Death / Burn In Her Lies / Mistake Fuck, Morbid Single Productions 004 (1995) (7" split single with C.S.S.O.)
Homosexual Slaughter (Demon Wind Re-mix) / Barbaric Bitch Beater (Scissors Re-mix) / Homosexist (M.R.R.) / Another Brutal Fucked Up Song / Floats On The Water (Shit) / Perversion Spree / San Francisco Gay Massacre /

Bursting Fluids (On Her Face) / Faggot (Freak) / Outro (I Hate Their Kind), Gulli GR007 (1995) ('Sewer In My Mind' 7" split single with DEAD)

Albums:
ECSTACY OF DEATH, (199-)
Depravity / There Is No God / Children Of Rape / Menstrual Bloodlust / First Blow Job / Perverted Vengeance / I Shit On Your Grave / The Devil Made Me Do It / Bulimic Excretion / Orgasmic Euphoria / Finger Fuck Surprise / Poor Feminine Hygiene / Bow To The Penis God / In You I Cum / Act Of Love / Anal Quickie - Act Of Hate / Cock Rock Faggots / Septic Jesus / Orgasm Of Cardiac Arrest / Bloodbath Cleansing / Forced Into Submission / Meat Rabbit / Revenge On A World Full Of Cunts / Eat My Fuck / Hairless But Hard / Isolated And Gang Raped / Sex Life / Cocaine Cunt Numb / Violent Outburst Of Sodomy / Elvis Is Still Dead / Manipulation Of Mankind / Fag Killer / Three Way Fuck / Would You Please Die / Surgically Removed Vagina / Runaway Sex Slave / Hermaphrodite Horror / Forbidden Fruit / Fornication / Mental Midget / Ignorance Is Bliss / She Never Says No / Ejaculation Evacuation / Don't Have A Nice Day / Disposal Of Human Garbage / Cum On Your Fucking Face / Excrement Infection Of The Male Urethra / A.C. (Anal Cunt) / Intelligence Refused / She Likes It Hard / Strenuous Fuck / F.B.M. / Bathe In Holy Excrement
VICIOUS ACTS OF MACHISMO, (199-)
THE SECOND DEGREE OF TORTURE, (199-)
FUCK FRENZY, (199-)
SINS OF THE FLESH, (199-)
IF YOU WANT SHIT YOU GOT IT, (199-)

MEDIA IN MORTE (AUSTRIA)
Line-Up: Martin Rajek (vocals / guitar), Stefan Dietrich (bass), Andreas Reinalter (drums)

Austrian Death Metal act created in 1988. MEDIA IN MORTE's first demo was issued in 1990 followed by a second effort titled 'Not Immortal' in 1991.

Albums:
REMEMBER THE FUTURE, Inline 55 C-8787-002 (1994)
American Death / Who Needs A Reich? / Not Immortal / Generated Disease / The Master Race / Deprivation Of Liberty /

Into The Dark Ages / Fools / The Die Is Cast / A Temporary Grave / The Whole Shocking / Truth / Remember The Future

MEGAMOSH (GERMANY)
Line-Up: Beck (vocals), Steve (guitar), Matzer (guitar), Ussi (bass), Johnny (drums)

MEGAMOSH, founded as a quartet in 1987, supported PROTECTOR and WEHRMACHT on German tours in 1989 promoting their 'Fight The Epidemic Prince' EP.
MEGAMOSH pulled in second guitarist Steve in 1991 for a string of dates in Holland. Following release of the second album 'A Different Kind Of Meat' the band have guested for EXUMER, SODOM, CORONER and PESTILENCE amongst others.

Singles/EPs:
Fight The Epidemic Prince EP, (1989)

Albums:
CALL TO ACCOUNT, (1990)
A DIFFERENT KIND OF MEAT, Prophecy 22772 (1992)
I Am Trapped / Organ Dealer / Euphoria (Apoplexy II) / Killerflies / Struck By Blindness / Different / No More Mother / You Forced Me / No Cure In Sight / Set Me Free / When You Know You're Lost

MEGASLAUGHTER (SWEDEN)
Line-up: Emil Ilic (vocals), Kenneth Arnestedt (guitar), Alex Räfling (bass), Putte Räfling (drums)

MEGASLAUGHTER, formed in 1987, were initially known as DINLOYD. Their first demo as MEGASLAUGHTER, 'Death Remains' surfaced in 1989 and garnered the band a deal with French label Thrash Records.
After one album MEGASLAUGHTER split in 1992, with vocalist Emil Lilic resurfacing in 1997 fronting MURDER CORPORATION, a project band assembled by members of DERANGED that released the 'Blood Revolution 2050' album.

Albums:
CALLS FROM THE BEYOND, Thrash THR010 (1991)

MELISSA (RUSSIA)
Line-Up: Nick Touzov (vocals / guitar), Paul Ginkin (guitar), Sergey Olkhovsky

(bass), Paul Droban (drums)

Adventurous Death Metal act from Obninsk near Moscow. MELISSA debuted as a quartet of guitarists Nick Touzov and Paul Ginkin, bass player Sergey Olkhovsky and drummer Paul Droban. Following the acts first album 'In Mourning' MELISSA splintered down to the remaining guitar duo of Touzov and Ginkin.

Alexander H. was pulled in for session drums on the sophomore outing in 1998 'In Peace?'. In recent years MELISSA have employed a variety of musicians for live work including bassist / keyboard player Sergey Bondarenko, guitarist Alex O., drummer Roman Tchinnikov and even saxophonist Alexander Mamonov and violinist Sergey Pasov.

Albums:
IN MOURNING, Metalagen (1995)
Hate / Dark Deeds / Beyond / Vampire / Suicide / Distraught With Grief / Narcotherapy / Evil Beauty / All 4 1 / Exhausted
IN PEACE?, Matek (1998)
Down And Fall / Innocent Peace / This Time / Doncha Feel The Sky? / Pizza Song / Mindrape / Scars / Burning / Knife In A Back

MENTAL DEGENERATION UNIT
(FRANCE)

A rare attempt at Death Metal humour. The MENTAL DEGENERATION UNIT album 'Trous Du Cul' includes expected ANAL CUNT cover versions alongside renditions of VILLAGE PEOPLE songs.

Albums:
TROUS DU CUL, Troudac (1999)
Carmageddon / Come Here / Cherie! Ou T'as Range Mon Epee? Faut Que J'Aille Courir Dans La Foret / Poivrorotti / Anal M.D.U. Cunt / Hu-La-Up!… / I Am A Cannibal / J'Ai Note Une Influence Steve Vai Dans Le Solo Du Milieu / Stop Complaining / Love Story / La Tounga / Viva Ebola / Obao San (Live At Woodstock) / 357 Danone / European Community / Se Branler Sur Un Toit / Oh! Zarma / In The Navy / Anus Dilatus / Reconstruction Sonore De La Naissance De Troudball King / Douce Odeur D'Une Chatte Morte / M.D.U. Man / Impaled Jerusalem / Entretien D'Hedoniste Aux Pensee Permissive / I Think About Your Lord / Frozen Anus Mix

MENTAL HOME (RUSSIA)
Line-Up: Sergey Dmitriev (vocals / guitar), Denis Samusev (bass), Michael Smirnoff (keyboards), Igor Dmietriev (drums)

Moscow Death Metal act formed in November of 1993. The original MENTAL HOME line-up comprised of the two Dmitriev siblings, vocalist / guitarist Sergey and drummer and keyboard player Igor. Also involved was lead guitarist Roman Povarov and bass player Denis Samusev. Taking an atmospheric Doomladen Death Metal approach the quartet released their inaugural demo session 'Funeral Service' in January of 1994.

Shortly after, the MENTAL HOME returned to the studio and in July of the same year 'Mirrorland' was issued by the domestic Metal Agen concern, soon selling out of its initial 5,000 run.

A setback occurred when Povarov injured his hand in an accident. The guitarist shifted over to keyboards to accommodate his disability and MENTAL HOME drafted Sergey Kalachov for the 'Vale' outing. This album would see a release through Morbid Noizz. Quite spectacularly the album actually sold out after a few months and hit the number one position in the Russian Metal charts. Despite this upward turn in the bands fortunes Povarov departed. Michael 'Maiden' Smirnoff took not only the vacant keyboard position but also became MENTAL HOME's business manager.

In March of 1997 the band retired to the studio completing the 'Black Art' album by June. With MENTAL HOME's profile riding high the first brace of albums were also reissued.

The bands progress had not gone unnoticed outside of Russia and American based The End Records engineered a deal with the band to release 'Vale' and 'Black Art'.

Albums:
FUNERAL SERVICE, (1994)
MIRROR LAND, (1995)
VALE, The End TE001 (1998)
Stranger Dove / Southern Calm Waters / Aevin's Cave / The Euphoria / The Vale / My Necklace / Christmas Mercy / Their Finest Voyage
BLACK ART, The End TE006 (1998)
Under The Wing / The Plague Omen / Into The Realms Of Marena / Silent Remembrance / In The Shades Of

Inspiration / Pagan Freedom / Winter Art / On A Hand Of The Universe / Tides Of Time
UPON THE SHORES OF INNER SEAS, The End (2000)
Downstairs / Late To Revise / Eternal Moan / Bliss / Against My Will / Breakdown / Stained / Amidst The Waves '99

MENTAL HORROR (BRAZIL)
Line-Up: Claudio Cardoso (vocals / bass), Adriano Martini (guitar), Robles Dresch (drums)

Albums:
EXTREME EVOLUTIVE TRAUMA, Death Vomit (2000)
Intro Of Vengeance / Burning Alive / Genocidal Inquisition / Black Spiritual Void / Rising For Chaos / Screams Of Tiamat / Fragellum Forms / Anguish Seas / Tortured (Bleeding For The Plague) / Profane Spawn / Proclaiming Vengeance

MERCENARY (DENMARK)
Line-Up: Kral (vocals / bass), Nikalai Brinkmann (guitar), Rasmus Jacobsen (drums)

Founded in 1991 as a Thrash act MERCENARY would soon develop distinct Death Metal leanings by the time of their 1993 demo entitled 'Domicile'. MERCENARY, fronted by Kral (real name Hans Henrik Andersen) would lose his sibling guitarist Jonne along the way but recorded further tracks for a limited demo recording 'Gummizild' produced by Bo Summer of ILLDISPOSED. One of these tracks would also surface on the compilation album 'Fuck You We're From Denmark - Vol. 3'.
MERCENARY's next move was to hook up with INVOCATOR man Jacob Hansen as producer for recording of a 1996 EP 'Supremacy'.
Guitarist Nikalau Brinkman is ex-CROSSBONES whilst drummer Rasmus Jacobsen is an erstwhile member of HUMANATICUM.

Singles/EPs:
Supremacy, (1996)

MERCILESS (SWEDEN)
Line-Up: Roger Peterrson (vocals), Erik Wallin (guitar), Fredrik Karlen (bass), Stefan Karlsson (drums)

MERCILESS formed with original vocalist Kalle in 1986. The group released two demos, 'Behind The Black Door' and 'Realm Of The Dark'. As drummer Stefan Karlsson joined Punk act DIA PSALMA was superseded by Peter Stjärvind in 1991. MERCILESS released a promo split single with COMECON the same year.
Various members of the band pursue careers in other acts. Stärjvind is also a member of UNANIMATED, FACEDOWN and LOUD PIPES. Bassist Fredrik Karlen is also in LOUD PIPES rebilling himself Carl Leen.
In their time the group has opened for SEPULTURA, ENTOMBED and SODOM.

Albums:
THE AWAKENING, Deathlike Silence ANTIMOSH 001 (1991)
Pure Hate / Souls Of The Dead / The Awakening / Dreadful Fate / Realm Of The Dark / Dying World / Bestial Death / Denied Birth
THE TREASURES WITHIN, Active ATV 26 (1992)
The Treasures Within / Mind Possession / Darkened Clouds / The Book Of Lies / Perish / Shadows Of Fire / Life Aflame / Act Of Horror / Branded By Sunlight / Dying World
UNBOUND, No Fashion NFR 007 (1994)
Unbound / The Land I Used To Walk / Feebleminded / Back To North / Silent Truth / Lost Eternally / Nuclear Attack / Forbidden Pleasure

MERCYLESS (FRANCE)
Line-Up: Max Otero (vocals), Stephane Viard (guitar), Rade Radojcic (bass), Gerald Guenzi (drums)

French act MERCYLESS debuted with two demos; 1988's 'Immortal Harmonies' and 1989's 'Visions Of The Past'. A following demo, 'Vanishing Nausea', enabled MERCYLESS to contribute the track 'Without Christ' for their first single on Jungle Records.
The group has also contributed a track to the 'Total Virulence' compilation album.

Singles/EPs:
Without Christ, Jungle (1991)

Albums:
ABJECT OFFERINGS, Vinyl Solution TERRA 331 (1992)
Nyarlathotep - Abject Offerings / A Message For All Those Who Died /

Substance Of Purity / Flesh Divine / Without Christ / Unformed Tumours / Burned At The Stake / Selected Resurrection
COLOURED FUNERAL, Century Media CD 77054 (1993)
Spiral Of Flowers / Mirrors Of Melancholy / Travel Through A Strange Emotion / Forgotten Fragments / Contemplations / Agrazabeth / Serenades... (Into Your Limb) / Naked Forms / Beyond God
SURE TO BE SURE, System Shock (2000)

MERLIN (RUSSIA)
Line-Up: Mary Abaza (vocals / bass), Alex Ioffe (guitar), Arteom Nazarov (guitar), Nick Byckolff (drums)

Female fronted Death Metal formation MERLIN convened in 1992 as a trio of Mary Abaza on bass and lead vocals, guitarist Alex Ioffe and drummer Nick Byckolff. Demos 'Welcome To Hell' and 'Prisoner Of Death' preceded the debut cassette album 'Deathroteque'.
MERLIN would sign to the Canadian GWN label for an international release of sophomore outing 'They Must Die' in 1998. Hobgoblin Records would issue the album domestically.
Second guitarist Arteom 'Bolt' Nazarov, ex-ANAL PUS, would augment MERLIN the same year.

DEATHROTEQUE, (199-) (Cassette release)
They Must Die / Holder Of The War / Don't Try / I'm Glad / I Gotta Fall / That's My Time / Black Revenge / Die / Waiting For Death / Leave Me Alone
THEY MUST DIE, GWN (1998)
Unburied / I Want Blood / They'll Never See / They Must Die / Entering The Gates Of Paradise / Don't Waste My Time / Let The Blood Spill / Sixth Victim / R.I.P.

MESHUGGAH (SWEDEN)
Line-Up: Jens Kidman (vocals), Fredric Thordendal (guitar), Peter Nordin (bass), Nicolas Lundgren (drums)

An experimental Death-Thrash band named after the Yiddish term for 'Crazy', MESHUGGAH formed in Umea during 1987 and released a six song demo in 1990.
Quite oddly, the quartet has often suffered quite a few delays to their schedule thanks to a catalogue of injuries to band members. Guitarist Fredrik Thorendahl has cut the top off a finger and drummer Tomas Haake trapped his hand in a lathe machine. And when MESHUGGAH toured Europe in 1995 supporting American outfit MACHINE HEAD guitarist Martin Hagstrom actually stepped in for the headliner's guitarist Rob Flynn after the American had suffered a hand injury.
Nicolas Lundgren was to replace founder member Haake. More recently, Fredric Thorendahl assembled a side project modestly titled FREDRIK THORENDAHL'S MUSICAL DEFECTS, recording an album in 1997.

Singles/EPs:
Cadaverous Mastication / Sovereigns Morbidity / The Depth Of Nature, Garageland BF 634 (1989) ('Psykadelisk Testbild' EP)
Humiltitive / Sickening / Ritual / Gods Of Rapture / Aztec Two-Step, Nuclear Blast NB102-2 (1994) ('None' EP)
Selfcaged / Vanished / Suffer In Truth / Inside What's Within Behind, Nuclear Blast (1995)
Sane / Future Breed Machine (Live) / Future Breed Machine (Mayhem version) / Futile Bread Machine (Campfire version) / Quant's Quantastical Quantasm (Ambient techno by Quant of DOT) / Friend's Breaking and Entering (Ambient techno by Friend of DOT) / Terminal Illusions (Video), Nuclear Blast (1997) ('The True Human Design' EP)

Albums:
CONTRADICTIONS COLLAPSE, Nuclear Blast NB049 (1991)
Paralyzing Ignorance / Erroneous Manipulation / Abnegating Necessity / Internal Evidence / Qualms Of Reality / We'll Never See The Day / Greed / Choirs Of Devastation / Cadaverous Mastication
DESTROY ERASE IMPROVE, Nuclear Blast NB121 (1995)
Future Breed Machine / Beneath / Soul Burn / Transfixion / Vanished / Acrid Placidity / Inside What's Within Behind / Terminal Illusions / Suffer In Truth / Sublevels
CHAOSPHERE, Nuclear Blast (1998)
Concatenation / New Millennium Cyanide Christ? / Corridor of Chameleons / Neurotica / The Mouth Licking What You've Bled / Sane / The Exquisite Machinery of Torture / Elastic

MESSIAH (SWITZERLAND)
Line-Up: Andy Kaina (vocals), R.B. Brogi (guitar), Patrick Hersche (bass)

Founded in 1984 by guitarist R. B. Brogi, MESSIAH built up impressive sales of their first two albums. 'Extreme Cold Weather' sold in excess of 12,000 units alone, prompting a deal with Noise Records.

MESSIAH's line-up changed in 1993 with the departure of vocalist Andy Kaina and bassist Patrick Hersche. The bass position was filled by Oliver Koll and a new vocalist was found in ex-THERION man Christofer Johnsson.

Singles/EPs:
Birth Of A Second Individual / Psychomorphia / Right For Unright / M.A.N.I.A.C., Noise N0244-3 (1994) ('Psychomorphia' EP)
The Ballad Of Jesus, Noise NO244-3 (1994)

Albums:
HYMN TO ABRAMELIN, Chainsaw Murder (1986)
Hymn To Abramelin / Messiah / Anarchus / Space Invaders / Thrashing Madness / Future Aggressor / Empire Of The Damned / Total Maniac / The Dentist
EXTREME COLD WEATHER, Chainsaw Murder 004 (1988)
Extreme Cold Weather / Enjoy Yourself / Johannes Paul Der Letzte (Dedicated In Hate To Pope John Paul II) / Mother Theresa (Dedicated In Love To Mother Theresa) / Hyper Bores / Radezky March: We Hate To Be In The Army Now / Nero / Hymn To Abramelin (Live) / Messiah (Live) / Space Invaders (Live) / Thrashing Madness (Live) / Golden Dawn (Live) / The Last Inferno (Live) / Resurrection (Live) / Ole Perversus (Live)
CHOIR OF HORRORS, Noise NO183-2 (1991)
Choir Of Horrors / Akasha Chronicle / Weeping Willows / Lycantropus Erectus / Münchhausen Syndrom / Cautio Criminalis / Northern Commans / Weena
ROTTEN PERISH, Noise CD084 04552 (1992)
Prelude: Act Of Fate / For Those Who Will Fail / Living With A Confidence / Raped Bodies / Lines Of Thought Of A Convicted Man / Conviction / Condemned Cell / Dreams Of Eschaton / Anorexia Nervosa / Deformed Creatures / Alzheimer's Disease / Ascension Of A

Divine Ordinance
UNDERGROUND, Noise NO244-2 (1994)
Battle In The Ancient North / Revelation Of Fire / Underground / Epitaph / The Way Of The Strong / Living In A Lie / Screams Of Frustration / The Ballad Of Jesus / Dark Lust / One Thousand Pallid Deaths / The End

MIDVINTER (SWEDEN)
Line-Up: Kheeroth (vocals), Damien (guitar / bass), Zathanel (drums)

The debut album by Death Metallers MIDVINTER was produced by KING DIAMOND guitarist Andy La Rocque. The band, founded by a union of erstwhile FOGBOUND and APOLLGON members, first tested the waters with the 'Midvinternatt' demo. MIDVINTER's initial line up comprised of vocalist Björn, guitarist Damien and drummer Krille. Following the demo an alliance was struck with BEWITCHED and NAGLFAR personnel Adde and Stolle although this version of MIDVINTER did not gel and the band folded. Unfortunately Björn, according to band sources, was subsequently admitted to a mental hospital.

MIDVINTER was resurrected in 1996 with new members ex-SETHERIAL vocalist Kheeroth and ex-SETHERIAL and member of SORHIN Zathanel on drums. Guest musicians on the album included DISSECTION's Jon Nodtveidt and former AT THE GATES and OXIPLEGATZ guitarist Alf Svensson.

Zathanel would later renew his SETHERIAL links founding BLACKWINDS for a 1999 EP in collaboration with his former band colleagues vocalist / guitarist Lord Kraath and drummer Lord Alastor Mysteriis.

Albums:
AT THE SIGHT OF THE APOCALYPSE DRAGON, Black Diamond (1997)
Dod Fodd / All Things To End Are Made / Moonbound / Hope Rides On Devils Wings / Dreamslave / Noctiluca In Aeturnum- Of Nights Primeval / Ett Liv Fornekat / De Vises Hymn

MINAS TIRITH (NORWAY)
Line-Up: Frode (vocals), Stian (guitar), Gottskalk (bass)

Avant garde act founded in 1989 with Black persuasions combined with elements of Jazz, Doom and Death Metal. MINAS TIRITH bassist Gottskalk also has connections with TULUS and OLD MAN'S CHILD.

Singles/EPs:
Mythology, AR (1993)

Albums:
THE ART OF BECOMING, Art 196 (1996) The Living Dead / The Colour Of Nothing / Sympathy From The Devil / The Art Of Becoming / In The Night I Walk / X = 666 / In Union We Die / A Child Is Born In Babylon / Holy Brother
DEMONS ARE FOREVER, Facefront (1999)

MINDCOLLAPSE (SWEDEN)

Albums:
VAMPIRES DAWN, Vod VODCD007 (2001)

MINISTRY OF TERROR (HOLLAND)
Line-Up: Hans Mertens (vocals), Remco Hulst (guitar), Henri Satler (guitar), Elzo Nijboer (bass), Tjerk De Boer (drums)

MINISTRY OF TERROR, comprising ex-GOD DETHRONED members, first made an impression with their 1993 demo 'As Chaos Reigns'.

Albums:
FALL OF LIFE, Foundations 2000 (1995) Move On To Hate / Agony / Darkened / Lost / Human Nature / Fall Of Life / As Chaos Reigns / Hollow / Tears Of Humiliation / Relentless

MISERY (AUSTRALIA)
Line-Up: Damon Robinson (vocals / bass), L. Kannanhinij (guitar), Scott Edgar (guitar), Anthony Dwyer (drums)

A Queensland Death Metal group with strong similarities to MORBID ANGEL. The band date back as far as 1988 issuing two demos 'Sorting Of The Insects' in 1992 and 'Astern Diabolous' in 1993.

Singles/EPs:
Seeds Of Doubt / Torn / Venganza Del / Innocent Torture, Valve (1994) ('Insidious' EP)
Dark Inspiration, Subcide Productions (1995) (7" single)

Albums:
A NECESSARY EVIL, Velvet Urge (1993) Lifeless / Inverted Prophet / Born Dead / H.I.V. / Septic Octopus / I Endure / Sound Cancer / Body Farm / Sorting Of The Insects / Misery
REVEL IN BLASPHEMY, Warhead WHCD 18-2 (1997) Godspeak / Act Of War / Plague Of Humanity / Dark Inspirations / Infinite Hate / Morbid Dreams / All That Is Evil / A Song Before Dying / Remembrance / Altered States / Revel In Blasphemy
CURSES, Venomous (2000) Sweet Oblivion / Intent To Kill / Immortal / Swine / Blood For Blood / There Is No God / Consumate The Virgin / Two Faced / Zealot / Shitmouth / Eyes Wide Shut / The Chosen Fool

MISFORTUNE (SWEDEN)
Line-Up: Daniel Saidi (vocals), Peter Rudhberg (guitar), Martin Unoson (guitar), Henrik Viklund (bass)

MISFORTUNE guitarists Peter Rudhberg and Martin Unoson both perform in MURDER MARKET featuring on the 'Undusted' album. Vocalist Daniel Saidi has side projects EBLIS and SAIDI.

Singles/EPs:
The Prophecy / Midnightenlightened / Pain Unbearable, Blackened (1999)

Albums:
FORSAKEN, Blackend (2000) Forsaken / Scenary Of Despair / Rape Of Bewildered Dreams / In Matus / Burn! / Through Chaos Fulfilled / A Real Of The Unblessed / Apostates Of Hate

THE MOANING (SWEDEN)
Line-Up: Mikael Grankvist (guitar), Patrick Tornkvist (guitar), Niklas Svensson (bass), Andreas Nilzon (drums)

Guitarist Mikael Grankvist is also a SATARIEL member. Fellow six stringer Patrick Tornkvist is with THE EVERDAWN. Bassist Niklas Svensson operates with THE EVERDAWN and GATES OF ISHTAR.

Albums:
BLOOD FROM STONE, No Fashion (1997) Blood From Stone / Still Born / Of Darkness I Breed / Dying Internal Embers / A Dark Decade's Rising /

Dreams In Black / Mirror Of The Soul / Dark Reflections

MOANING WIND (SWEDEN)

Line-Up: Johan Carlsson (vocals / bass), Tomas Bergstrand (guitar), Magnus Eronen (guitar), Martin Bjöörn (bass)

Karlstad Death Metal act. MOANING WIND had their track 'All My Gates Are Closed' included on a Belgian compilation issued by Shiver Records.

Albums:
VISIONS IN FIRE, Corrosion CR 6-505-2 (1996)
Hunted / Longing Away / Lost Forever / The Epoch That Died / Dark Side… Black Sun / A Fallen Arrow / Torn By The Wind / Awakened Spirit / Silence / Visions In Fire

MONOLITH (UK)

Singles/EPs:
Sleep With The Dead, Cacophonous CHTONIC 701 (1995)

Albums:
TALES OF THE MACABRE, Vinyl Solution SOL036CD (1993)
Morbid Curiosity / Sleep With The Dead / Misery / Undead Burial / Devoured From Within / Locked In Horror / Catalogue Of Carnage / Maceration

MONSTER X (USA)

Singles/EPs:
Split, (199-) (7" split single with SPAZZ)
Split, (199-) (7" split single with HUMAN GREED)

MONSTROSITY (FL, USA)

Line-Up: George 'Corpsegrinder' Fisher (vocals), Jon Rubin (guitar), Kelly Conlan (bass), Lee Harrison (drums)

Brutal Death Metal band that, despite an ever fluid line-up, remain centred upon drummer Lee Harrison. CYNIC guitarist Jason Gobel guests on MONSTROSITY's 'Imperial Doom' album and also filled in for live shows.
MONSTROSITY guitarist Jon Rubin stood in for MALEVOLENT CREATION on a temporary basis for their 1991 American tour. MONSTROSITY bassist Rob Barrett was busted on a drugs charge and was as such unable to travel outside America. Touring in Europe saw the band utilizing the services of Mark

Van Erp until the permanent recruitment of Kelly Conlan.
For the 1997 'Millennium' album MONSTROSITY drafted in guitarist Jason Morgan. Lead vocals were recorded by Fisher but after his defection to CANNIBAL CORPSE the band pulled in former EULOGY man Jason Avery for live work.
Morgan departed following recording of 1999's 'In Dark Purity' to join MORBID ANGEL / HATE ETERNAL guitarist Erik Rutan's ALAS project. In came ex-ETERNAL guitarist Tony Norman and a guesting Jay Fernandez of BRUTALITY. Morgan created WYNJARA for an eponymous 2000 album in alliance with ex-MALEVOLENT CREATION guitarist J.P. Soars.

Albums:
IMPERIAL DOOM, Nuclear Blast NB055 (1991)
Imperial Doom / Definitive Inquisition / Ceremonial Void / Immense Malignancy / Vicious Mental Thirst / Burden Of Evil / Horror Infinity / Final Cremation / Darkest Dream
MILLENNIUM, Nuclear Blast NB208-2 (1997)
Fatal Millennium / Devious Instinct / Manic / Dream Messiah / Fragments Of Resolution / Manipulation Strain / Slaves And Masters / Mirrors Of Reason / Stormwinds / Seize Of Change
IN DARK PURITY, Olympic (1999)
The Hunt / Destroying Divinity / Shapeless Domination / The Angels Venom / All Souls Consumed / Dust To Dust / Suffering To The Conquered / The Eye Of Judgement / Perpetual War / Embraced By Apathy / Hymns Of Tragedy / In Dark Purity / The Pillars Of Drear / Angel Of Death

MORBID ANGEL (Tampa, FL, USA)

Line-Up: David Vincent (vocals / bass), Trey Azagthoth (guitar), Erik Rutan (guitar), Pete Sandoval (drums)

Florida Black Death metal act MORBID ANGEL, founded in 1984, broke down the barriers between extreme music and commercial success but seemingly blew their chances of entering the big league with a series of remarks attributed to main man Trey Azagthoth (real name George Emmanuel III) being allegedly fascist in nature. The world's rock media erupted in an outcry against these supposed Nazi leanings. Nevertheless, despite the

MORBID ANGEL
Photo : Martin Wickler

controversy and the band's denials, MORBID ANGEL had racked up combined sales of over 1,000,000 albums sold by 1998.

At one time MORBID ANGEL featured a rhythm section of bassist Sterling Von Scarborough and drummer Mike Browning, both previously with INCUBUS. Coincidentally INCUBUS was also to donate guitarist Gino Marino to MORBID ANGEL in 1992. Browning eventually ended up after his MORBID ANGEL stint in NOCTURNUS (and much later AFTER DEATH) whilst Von Scarborough was to resurrect INCUBUS after his post MORBID ANGEL act USURPER.

What was to be the band's debut album 'Abominations of Desolation', recorded in 1986, was shelved due to the band's ever fluctuating line-up. MORBID ANGEL's commercial debut the 'Thy Kingdom Come' single featured drummer Wayne Hartshill.

Scarborough was supplanted by ex-TERRORIZER man David Vincent. The bassist had been an acquaintance of the band for some time having produced the 'Abominations Of Desolation' sessions. With this more solid unit MORBID ANGEL's sales began to accelerate as did their worldwide recognition.

In 1991, just upfront of a lengthy American tour, MORBID ANGEL's planned debut album 'Abominations Of Desolation' finally saw a release through Earache Records. The album had been bootlegged relentlessly upon the band's ascendancy into the upper echelons of the Thrash ranks.

Guitarist Richard Brunelle drifted away in mid 1992. MORBID ANGEL filled his shoes briefly with former INCUBUS man Gino Marino but before long Brunelle was back.

1993 saw MORBID ANGEL of such a stature that their 'Covenant' album was produced by Flemming Rasmussen and signed to the massive Warner Bros. corporation in America. With tour support now guaranteed the band criss crossed America opening for BLACK SABBATH and MOTÖRHEAD.

Brunelle departed for good in 1994 and the band closed the gap with ex-RIPPING CORPSE guitarist Eric Rutan.

MORBID ANGEL undertook an enormous touring schedule throughout 1995 and into 1996. Dates began in their home state of Florida for an American tour before extensively covering Europe until February 1996 saw the band back in America prior top a return trip to Europe. These shows yielded the live album 'Entangled In Chaos'.

The band seemingly suffered a double hammer blow in 1997 not only with the departure of Vincent, so often the band's mouthpiece, but also the collapse of their deal with Earache Records. However, Azagthoth picked up the pieces and renegotiated a revised deal with their former label and pulled in ex-MERCILESS ONSLAUGHT / CEREMONY / INTERSINE man Steve Tucker to plug the gap left by Vincent.

In 1998 Vincent found himself playing bass in the S&M inspired GENITORTURERS, but then he is the husband of frontwoman Geni after all!

Although Rutan appeared as main songwriter and contributor to the 'Formulas Fatal To The Flesh' album MORBID ANGEL pulled in guitarist Richard Burnelle for live work as Rutan decamped to concentrate on his other two acts ALAS and HATE ETERNAL. However, rehearsals for the tour to promote the record did not go well and with Burnelle being dispensed with Rutan got the call for assistance. Following the 'Formulas Fatal To The Flesh' tour Rutan decamped yet again and produced the 'Conquerors Of Armageddon' album for Brazilian Black Metallers KRISIUN in 2000.

Rutan returned to the fold later in 2000 for the 'Gateways To Annihilation' album, a record that kicks off with an intro of a genuine swamp frog chorus!

MORBID ANGEL toured Europe in December 2000 headlining an almighty Death Metal package that included ENSLAVED, THE CROWN, BEHEMOTH, HYPNOS and DYING FETUS.

Singles/EPs:
Thy Kingdom Come / Abominations Of Desolation / Blasphemy Of The Holy Ghost, Morbid Angel (1988)
God Of Emptiness / Sworn To The Black / Sworn To The Black (Laibach remix) / God Of Emptiness (Laibach remix), Earache MOSH 112T (1994)

Albums:
ALTARS OF MADNESS, Earache MOSH 11 (1989)
Visions From The Darkside / Chapel Of Ghouls / Maze Of Torment / Damnation / Bleed For The Devil

BLESSED ARE THE SICK, Earache MOSH 31 (1991)
Intro / Fall From Grace / Brainstorm / Rebel Lands / Doomsday Celebration / Day Of Suffering / Blessed Are The Sick / Leading The Rats / Thy Kingdom Come / Unholy Blasphemies / Abominations / Desolate Ways / The Ancient Ones / In Remembrance

ABOMINATIONS, Earache MOSH 048 (1991)
The Invocation / Chapel Of Ghouls / Unholy Blasphemies / Angel Of Disease / Azaghoth / The Gate / Lord Of Fevers And Plagues / Hell Spawn / Abominations / Demon Seed / Welcome To Hell

COVENANT, Earache MOSH 081 (1993)
Rapture / Pain Divine / World Of Shit / Vengeance Is Mine / Lion's Den / Blood On My Hands / Angel Of Disease / Sworn To Black / Nar Mattaru / God Of Emptiness

ENTANGLED IN CHAOS - LIVE, Earache MOSH167 (1996)
Immortal Rites / Blasphemy Of The Holy Ghost / Sworn To The Black / Lord Of All Fevers And Plagues / Blessed Are The Sick / Day Of Suffering / Chapel Of Ghouls / Maze Of Torment / Rapture / Blood On My Hands / Dominate

FORMULAS FATAL TO THE FLESH, Earache MOSH180 (1998)
Heaving Earth / Prayer Of Hatred / Bil Ur-Sag / Nothing Is Not / Chambers Of Dis / Disturbance In The Great Slumber / Umulamahri / Hellspawn: The Rebirth / Covenant Of Death / Hymn To A Gas Giant / Invocation Of The Continual One / Ascent Through The Spheres / Hymnos Rituales De Guerra / Trooper

GATEWAYS TO ANNIHILATION, Earache (2000)
Kawazu / Summoning Redemption / Ageless / Still I Am / He Who Sleeps / To The Victor The Spoils / At One With Nothing / Opening Of The Gates / Secured Limitations / Awakening / I / God Of The Forsaken

MORBID SYMPHONY (UK)
Line-Up: Steve Sanders (vocals), Gary Lloyd (guitar), Keith Hill (drums)

Following the single release MORBID SYMPHONY produced a further demo, 'The Obscure Depths Of Light', in 1995.

Single/EPs:
Morbid Symphony Vs. Skin Flick Productions, Dark Earth (1995)

MORDANCY (HOLLAND)
Line-Up: Stefan (vocals), Martin (guitar), Peter (guitar), Silvio (bass), Thomas (drums)

Remscheid act MORDANCY date back to 1987. Their second demo 'Different Ways' scored the band a deal with D&S Records. The 'Scars' album resulted from the deal.

Singles/EPs:
The Progressive Downfall EP, (1995)

Albums:
SCARS, D&S Records DSR CD012 (1993)
Dark Age Of Reason / Utopia Within Reach / Lies / To Sleep (Perchance To Scream) / Scars / Law And Order / In God We Rust / Advanced Humanity / Colour Life By Numbers

MORDOR (POLAND)
Line-Up: Pawel Zielinski (vocals), Pawel Medera (guitar), Jacek Woszczyna (guitar), Bartek Kuzniak (bass), Darek Boral (keyboards), Gerard Niemczyk (drums)

A melodic Death Metal band from Poland.

Albums:
PRAYER TO..., Arctic Serenades SERE009 (1995)
False Prayer / Why Me? / There's Nothing Left / Ice Bound / Nothing Makes Any Sense / Wild-Storm Song / The First One Will Be The Last One / Two Real Stories

THE EARTH, P.R.M.A. AMS009R (1998)
The Earth / Cienie / Higher And Higher / The Rain / The Colours Of The Night / Flowers / The Last Of The Mohicans / No More Suffer / Visions Of Life

MORGOTH (GERMANY)
Line-Up: Marc Grewe (vocals), Harry Busse (guitar), Carsten Otterbach (guitar), Sebastian (bass), Rudiger Hennecke (drums)

Initially heavily influenced by American Death Metal acts, Germany's MORGOTH cut their teeth whilst still teenagers with their 1988 six song demo 'Pits of Utumno' followed by a 1989 tape entitled 'Resurrection Absurd'. The latter demo was pressed up for MORGOTH's first EP. Before the release of the 'Cursed' album the group undertook a mammoth tour with OBITUARY and DEMOLITION

HAMMER in the autumn of 1990. Earlier in the year the first two EPs were combined as one album. In America alone this record sold more than 10,000 copies resulting in a 60 date tour with KREATOR.

1991's 'Cursed' album was mixed by Randy Burns and provided MORGOTH with further success, 1994's 'Odium' increasing the group's pulling power and coinciding with a German tour alongside UNLEASHED and TIAMAT.

Amazingly, on the brink of a massive breakthrough, the group split due to personal difficulties between band members. Grewe founded POWER OF EXPRESSION with ex-URGE members releasing an eponymous tribute to B'LAST the same year.

Having been offered the chance to play in Mexico during 1994 MORGOTH reformed and would go on to record a brand new album, 'Feel Sorry For The Fanatic', in 1996. The style was rather different and more modern in approach than previous triumphs.

A latter day member was former JESTER'S MARCH and HOUSE OF SPIRITS bass player Martin Hirsch. Post-MORGOTH guitarist Carsten Otterbach would enter the realms of artist management handling the affairs of such heavyweights as DIMMU BORGIR, IN FLAMES and ICED EARTH.

Singles/EPs:
Dictated Deliverance / Travel / The Afterthought / Selected Killings / Lies Of Distrust, Century Media 9708-1 (1990) ('Resurrection Absurd' EP)
Burnt Identity / Female Infanticide / White Gallery / Pits Of Utumno / Eternal Sanctity, Century Media 609711 (1990) ('The Eternal Fall' EP)

Albums:
ETERNAL FALL, Century Media 9708-2 (1990) ('The Eternal Fall' & 'Resurrection Absurd' EPs combined)
Burnt Identity / Female Infanticide / White Gallery / Pits Of Utumno / Eternal Sanctity / Dictated Deliverance / Travel / The Afterthoughts / Selected Killing / Lies Of Distrust
CURSED, Century Media 7719-2 (1991)
Cursed / Body Count / Exit To Temptation / Unred Imagination / Isolated / Sold Baptism / Suffer Life / Opportunity Is Gone / Darkness
ODIUM, Century Media CD9749 (1994)
Resistance / The Art Of Sinking /

Submission / Under The Surface / Drowning Sun / War Inside / Golden Age / Odium
FEEL SORRY FOR THE FANATIC, Century Media 77119-2 (1996)
The Fantastic Decade / Last Laugh / Cash... / ... And It's Amazing Consequences / Curiosity / Forgotten Days / Souls On A Pleasuretrip / Graceland / Watch The Fortune Wheel / A New Start

MORGUE (GERMANY)
Line-Up: Volker Binias (vocals), Ralph Rietmann (guitar), Torsten Bartscherer (guitar / keyboards), Malte von Ramin (bass), Heiko Steinfurth (drums)

Formed in the autumn of 1991 in Castrop-Rauxel, Death Metal outfit MORGUE recorded their first demo in 1992 and would offer a self-financed, demo CD in 1994.

Albums:
DREAMSCAPES, Dreamscape (1994)
(...) / Hate In My Eyes / Glass Tears / Final Chapter / And Only Silence Will Remain / A Jester's Dream / (...)

MORGUL (NORWAY)
Line-Up: Jack D. Ripper (vocals / guitar / bass), Hex (drums)

A notoriously disturbing duo. MORGUL came together in late 1990 revealing their presence with the demos 'Vargavinter' and 'In Gowns Flowing Wide'. The 'Parody Of The Mass' album was produced by Mikael Hedlund of HYPOCRISY.

Albums:
LOST IN SHADOWS GREY, Napalm NPR028CD (1997)
PARODY OF THE MASS, Napalm (1998)
Black Hearts Domain / Healing The Blind / Torn / Ballad Of Revolt / Adoration Of The Profane / Author Of Pain / The End
THE HORROR GRANDEUR, Century Media (1999)
The Horror Grandeur / Ragged Little Dolls / The Murdering Mind / A Third Face / Elegantly Decayed / Cassandra's Nightmare / The Ghost
SKETCH OF SUPPOSED MURDERS, Century Media 77323-2 (2001)
Violent Perfect Illusions / The Dog And The Monster / Dead For A While / Machine / Of Murder And Misfortune / Truth, Liars And Dead Flesh / Stealth /

Once Again / She

MORPHEUS (SWEDEN)
Line-Up: David Brink (vocals), Stefan Ekström (guitar), Sebastian Ramstedt (guitar), Johan De Daux (bass), Markus Rüden (drums)

MORPHEUS were formed by ex-CARBONISED members drummer Markus Rüden and guitarist Stephan Ekström, together with ex-members of EXHUMED. The single features guitarist Janne Rudberg, who left prior to the album to form EXCRUCIATE.

Singles/EPs:
In The Arms Of Morpheus, Opinionate OP003 (1991)

Albums:
SON OF HYPNOS, Step One STEP005 (1995)
Depths Of Silence / Through The Halls Of Darkness / God Against All / The Third Reich 3797 A.C. / Of Memories Made (The God Of Dreams) / Memento Mori / Among Others / Inflame The Mass / Wonderland / Dreams

MORTAL DECAY (NJ, USA)
Line-Up: John Hartman (vocals), Anthony Divgenze (guitar), Joe Gordon (guitar), Ron Steinhauer (bass), Anthony Ipri (drums)

MORTAL DECAY issued the demos 'Dawn Of Misery', 'Grisly Aftermath' and 'Brutalizing Creations' upfront of their debut album.

Albums:
SICKENING EROTIC FANATICISM, Pulverizer (1997)
Decomposed With Nitric Acid / Sickening Erotic Fanaticism / Revived Half Dead / Mediating Through Mayhem / Apparitions / Opening The Graves / Colombian Necktie / Soaking In Entrails / Consume The Rancid Gore / Rejoice In Moribund

MORTALITY (GERMANY)
Line-Up: Darm (guitar), Martin Mayrhofer (guitar), Dr. Pohl (bass), Schmaus (drums)

Munich based Death Metal band MORTALITY released the demo 'Prophet's Dream' in 1989 before playing shows with the likes of ATROPHY and SACRED REICH. A second demo 'Dr.

Schnabel' followed in 1992.
The group Submitted the track 'They Will Never Stop' to the G.U.N. Records compilation album 'Crossing All Over' in 1993 prior to a third demo 'Moonface Was Here'.
A deal was struck with G.U.N. Records and MORTALITY performed more shows opening for SUN and DANZIG.

Albums:
ELEPHANT MAN, Polly 001-2 (1995)
The Drake / Elephant Man / They Will Never Stop / Remembrance / Prophet's Dream (Part 1) / Two Bulls On Motorbikes / Journey On A Ghostship / B.D.V.Z.Z. / Brown Plague / Moonface Was Here... / Prophet's Dream (Part 2)

MORTAL TERROR (GERMANY)
Line-Up: Stefan Kunth (vocals), Jens Hertig (guitar), Dirk Wieland (guitar), Lutz Prößdorf (bass), Marcus Farmer (drums)

Death Metallers MORTAL TERROR took the familiar path of releasing various demos before a record deal transpired. These tapes comprised 1989's 'United Nations', 1991's 'The Functional Autonomy Of Motives' and 'The Cognitive Triad' in 1992.
The group signed to D&S in 1994, issuing 'The Evolving Self' debut the following year. The second record, 'Posthuman', emerged the same year and featured a cover version of 'Sweet Dreams' by the EURYTHMICS in a Death Metal style!

Albums:
THE EVOLVING SELF, D&S Records (1995)
Progressive Jesus / Living In A Casket / Level Of Permissiveness / God Is Plutonium / Scarred / The Cognitive Triad / World In My Hand / Goal Neurosis / Seconds
POSTHUMAN, D&S Records DS 036 (1995)
Natural Evil / Rhythm Of Death / The Tower / Need Of Addiction / Social Suicide / Silence Is Silence / Belief / Word Burns Flesh / They Crawl / Uniform Choice / Sweet Dreams / Selbsjustiz

MORTA SKULD
(Milwaukee, WI, USA)
Line-Up: Dave Gregor (vocals / guitar), Jason O'Connel (guitar), Jason Hellman (bass), Kent Truckenbrod (drums)

Deathsters MORTA SKULD were created in 1990 issuing their first demo tape 'Gory Departure' shortly after. MORTA SKULD's sophomore release was a 1991 three track demo tape 'Prolong The Agony' that featured VIOGRESSION drummer Jeff Jaeger. Tracks were 'Through The Eyes Of Death', 'Of Evil' and 'Feast From Within'.

The band signed to Deaf Records - a subsidiary of Yorkshire label Peaceville, found a permanent drummer in Kent Truckenbrod after the tape's completion in time for 1993's debut 'Dying Remains'. Touring commenced in promotion of the record with valuable supports to OBITUARY, DEATH, DEICIDE and NAPALM DEATH.

The second album saw MORTA SKULD out on the road opening for FEAR FACTORY and CANNIBAL CORPSE. The band kept up this work ethic for 1995's 'For All Eternity' guesting for TESTAMENT and MORBID ANGEL. However, the departure of longterm guitarist Jason O'Connell saw MORTA SKULD pull in ex-REALM man Takis Kinis for 1997's 'Surface' album.

MORTA SKULD rounded off the millennium by cutting two tracks for tribute albums - OZZY OSBOURNE's 'Believer' and MERCYFUL FATE's 'Desecration Of Souls'.

Singles/EPs:
Sacrificial Rite, Peaceville Collectors CC4 (1993) (Split single with VITAL REMAINS)

Albums:
DYING REMAINS, Peaceville DEAF 11 (1992)
Lifeless / Without Sin / Devoured Fears / Dying Remains / Useless To Mankind / Rotting Ways / Withering Seclusion / Hatred Creation / Scarred / Consuming Existence / Presumed Dead
AS HUMANITY FADES, Peaceville DEAF 64 (1994)
Unknown Emotions / A Century Of Ruins / Humanity's Lost / Awakening Destiny / Paradise Of The Masses / No World Escapes / Different Breeds / Sanctuary Denied / Relics / The Sorrow Fields
FOR ALL ETERNITY, Peaceville CDVILE 57 (1995)
Bitter / For All eternity / Vicious Circle / Justify / Tears / Germ Farm / Second Thought / Crawl Inside / Burning Daylight
SURFACE, System Shock (1997)
The Killing Machine / Save Yourself / The Anger In Disguise / Time Will Never Forget / Surface / Lords Of Discipline / If I Survive / In Nothing We Trust

MORTICIAN (USA)
Line-Up: Will Rahmer (vocals / bass), Roger Beaujard (guitar), Desmond Tolhurst (guitar)

Gore Death Metallers founded by ex-INCANTATION frontman, horror movie

MORTICIAN

fan and daytime florist (!) Will Rahmer. The band was named after the character of an undertaker from the movie 'Phantasm'. MORTICIAN's early drummer Matt Cicero died and since then the band has employed a drum machine in the studio and pulled in session drummers as and when needed for touring. MORTICIAN's 1995 album 'House By The Cemetery' included a version of CELTIC FROST's 'Procreation Of The Wicked'.

The band were unable to tour to promote early releases as both Rahmer and guitarist Roger Beaujard were both on police probation, one for possession of drugs and an unlicensed firearm and one for assault.

Road work in 1997 saw FUNERAL PYRE man Vick Novak inducted as drummer. MORTICIAN added guitarist Desmond Tolhurst, from Beaujard's side project MALIGNANCY, for the 'Zombie Apocalypse' album.

The 1999 release 'Chainsaw Dismemberment's cover (depicting a woman with limbs hacked off) was banned by many record stores. For touring purposes the band pulled in former DEHUMANISE drummer George Torrez.

Beaujard and Tolhurst's project group MALIGNANCY issued the 'Intrauterine Cannibalism' album. For the 2001 MORTICIAN album 'Domain Of Death' the band included two cover versions, namely takes on PUNGENT STENCH's 'Pulsating Protoplasma' and DISASTROUS MURMUR's 'Extra Uterine Pregnancy'.

Rahmer's day job has found the man immortalized in the ANAL CUNT song 'Morbid Florist'.

Singles/EPs:
Brutally Mutilated, Seraphic Decay (1990)

Albums:
MORTAL MASSACRE, (1993)
Mortal Massacre / Drilling For Brains / Redrum / Mortician / Brutally Mutilated / Necrocannibal
HOUSE BY THE CEMETARY, Relapse (1995)
Defiler Of The Dead / Barbaric Cruelties / World Domination / Driller Killer / House By The Cemetery / Procreation Of The Wicked / Scum / Gateway To Beyond / Flesheaters / Noturam Demondo
HACKED UP FOR BARBECUE,

Relapse (1996)
Bloodcraving / Embalmed Alive / Cremated / 3 On A Meathook / Brutally Mutilated / Deranged Insanity / Cannibal Feast / Blown To Pieces / Fog Of Death / Brutal Disfigurement / Apocalyptic Devastation / Inquisition / Hacked Up For Barbecue / Abolition / Necrocannibal / Ripped In Half / Morbid Butchery / Decapitated / Drilling For Brains / Eaten Alive By Maggots / Witches Coven / Worms / Annihilation / Mortician
ZOMBIE APOCALYPSE, Relapse (1998)
Devoured Alive / Incinerated / Zombie Apocalypse / Slaughterhouse / Hell On Earth / F.O.D. (Fuck Of Death) / Horrified / Charred Corpses / Dissected / Blood Harvest
CHAINSAW DISMEMBERMENT, Relapse (1999)
Stab / Fleshripper / Drowned In Your Blood / Mass Mutilation / Mauled Beyond Recognition / Rabid / Bloodshed / Decayed / Final Bloodbath / Island Of The Dead / Brutalized / Slaughtered / The Crazies / Silent Night, Bloody Night / Chainsaw Dismemberment / Psychotic Rage / Funeral Feast / Wolfen /Dark Sanity / Camp Blood / Tormented / Slaughterhouse (Part II) / Barbarian / Rats / Mater Tenebrarum / Splattered / Obliteration / Lords Of The Dead (Mortician Part II)
DOMAIN OF DEATH, Relapse (2001)
Brood Of Evil / Maimed And Mutilated / Bonecrusher / The Hatchet Murders / Extinction Of Mankind / Domain Of Death / Cannibalized / Pulsating Protoplasma / Martin (The Vampire) / Telepathic Terror / Mutilation Of The Human Race / Wasteland Of Death / Dr. Gore / Extra Uterine Pregnancy / Tenebrae / Devastation / Necromonicon Exmortis

MORTIFICATION (AUSTRALIA)
Line-Up: Steve Rowe (vocals / bass), Michael Carlisle (guitar), Jayson Sherlock (drums)

MORTIFICATION made their mark on the international scene by being one of a handful of Christian extreme Metal bands. Their evangelistic message was as uncompromising as their music which gave no concessions when pitted against more familiar acts of the genre.

Melbourne frontman Steve Rowe cut his teeth with the more mainstream Metal act LIGHTFORCE created in 1987. American label Pure Metal released their debut 1989 album 'Mystical Thieves' as LIGHTFORCE guested for STRYPER on

269

their Australian tour the same year.

In 1990 Rowe founded MORTIFICATION with guitarist Michael Carlisle and drummer Jayson Sherlock soon signing a deal with American label Intense. MORTIFICATION's sense of industry saw the rapid release of 'Break The Curse', 'Scrolls Of Megilloth' plus the live video 'Grind Planets' and a set up to German label Nuclear Blast for Europe.

MORTIFICATION toured America in 1992 with former VENGEANCE RISING drummer Johnny Vasquez. Album sales increased with 'Post Momentary Affliction' surpassing the 30,000 sales mark in Europe alone.

MORTIFICATION switched drummers once more in 1994 bringing in Phil Gibson for their sixth album 'Bloodworld'. This feat coincided with Rose's first novel 'Minstrel'.

1995 found MORTIFICATION splintering but with American tour commitments Rose employed Canadian musicians Jason Campbell on guitar and drummer Bill Price. The band added ex-DELIVERANCE guitarist George Ochoa to record the 'EnVision EvAngelene' record.

Rowe was diagnosed with leukemia in 1996 but this has hardly affected the band's work ethic. Indeed it was later announced that Rowe's cancer had been 'miraculously' cured.

For 1998's 'Triumph Of Mercy' album on new label Metal Blade Rowe was joined by guitarist Lincoln Bowen and drummer Keith Bannister. Interestingly MORTIFICATION's first drummer Jayson Sherlock provided the artwork for the album.

In March of 2000 Bannister left being replaced by the 15 year old Adam Zaffarese for MORTIFICATION's world tour. Carlisle would found side project CYBERGRIND releasing the 'Transcend' album the same year.

Singles/EPs:
Noah Sat Down And Listened To Mortification EP, (1996)
Live Without Fear EP, (1996)

Albums:
MORTIFICATION, Intense FLD 8501(1991)
Until The End / Brutal Warfare / Bathed In Blood / Satan's Doom / Turn / No Return / Break The Curse / New Awakening / Destroyer Beholds / Journey Of Reconciliation / Majestic Infiltrations Of Order
BREAK THE CURSE, Intense (1991)
Blood Sacrifice / Brutal Warfare / Impulsation / Turn / New Beginning / Illusion Of Life / Your Last Breath / Journey Of Reconciliation / The Majestic Infiltration Of Order / Butchered Mutilation
SCROLLS OF MEGILLOTH, Intense (1992)
Nocturnal / Terminate Damnation / Eternal Lamentation / Raise The Chalice / Lymphosarcoma / Scrolls Of The Megilloth / Death Requiem / Necromanicide / Inflamed / Ancient Prophecy
POST MOMENTARY AFFLICTION, Nuclear Blast NB082 (1993)
Allusions From The Valley Of Darkness / From The Valley Of Shadows / Human Condition / Distarnish Priest / Black Lion Of The Mind / Grind Planetarium / Pride Sanitorium (Reprise) / Overseer / This Momentary Affliction / Flight Of Victory / Impulsation / Liquid Assets / Vital Fluids / The Sea Of Forgetfullness
LIVE PLANETARIUM, Intense 9468 (1994)
Grind Planetarium / Distarnish Priest / Brutal Warfare / Destroyer Beholds / Inflamed / Scrolls Of The Megilloth / Symbiosis / Time Crusaders / Black Snake / From The Valley Of Shadows / Human Condition / Majestic Infiltration Of Order / This Momentary Affliction
BLOODWORLD, Intense 9488 (1994)
Clan Of The Light / Blood World / Starlight / Your Life / Monks Of The High Lord / Symbiosis / Love Song / Live By The Sword / JGSH / Dark Allusion
PRIMITIVE RHYTHM MACHINE, (1995)
Primitive Rhythm Machine / Mephibosheth / Seen It All / The True Essence Of Power / Toxic Shock / 40:31 / Gut wrench / Confused Belief / Providence / Killing Evil
BEST OF 5 YEARS, (1995)
New Beginnings / Blood Sacrifice / The Majestic Infiltration Of Order / Nocturnal / Scrolls Of Megilloth / Distarnish Priest / Grind Planetarium / Brutal Warfare / Time Crusaders / Blood World / Your Life / Primitive Rhythm Machine / Mephibosheth
ENVISION EVANGELENE, Nuclear Blast NB 6159 (1996)
EnVision EvAngelene / Northern Storm / Peace In Our Galaxy / Jehovah Nissi / Buried In Obscurity / Chapel Of Hope / Noah Was A Knower / Crusade For The King
TRIUMPH OF MERCY, Metal Blade MB 14192 (1998)

At War With War / Triumph Of Mercy / Welcome To The Palodrome / From Your Side / Influence / Drain Dweller / Raw Is The Stonewood Temple / Unified Truth / Visited By An Angel
HAMMER OF GOD, Metal Blade MB 14258 (1999)
Metal Crusade / Martyrs / Lock Up The Night / In The Woods / Pearl / Hammer Of God / Liberal Mediocrity / Extreme Conditions / Ride The Light / DWAM / Medley / God Rulz / At War With War / Visited By An Angel / Unified Truth / Metal Crusade
10 YEARS LIVE NOT DEAD, Metal Blade MB 14304 (2000)
Dead Man Walking / Buried Into Obscurity / Medley / Martyrs / Peace In The Galaxy / Hammer Of God / Influence / Steve Thanks / Mephibosheth / Chapel Of Hope / Liberal Mediocrity / God Rulz / King Of Kings

MOURNING (HOLLAND)
Line-Up: Marc (vocals / bass), Rene (guitar), Pim (guitar), Andre Van Der Ree (drums)

Death Metal act MOURNING, from Gouda, date to 1989. The band initially recorded a proposed split album with ETERNAL SOLSTICE in 1990, but this was not released as planned. However, three tracks were culled from these sessions for a demo.
With guitarist Pim having quit at the close of 1991, the original split album was finally released in 1992 and original drummer Misha Hak quit just before MOURNING signed a deal with Foundation 2000 Records. Hak later contributed drums to ETERNAL SOLSTICE's debut full length album 'The Wish Is Father To The Thought'.
By coincidence ETERNAL SOLSTICE added Hak's replacement in MOURNING, Andre Van Der Ree, to their line-up in 1994.

Albums:
MOURNING, Midian Creations (1992) (Split CD with ETERNAL SOLSTICE)
GREETINGS FROM HELL, Foundations 2000 FDN 2006 (1993)
Intro - Arma Satani / Sweet Dreams / Demon's Dance / Territorial / Denial Of Your Destiny / Only War And Hell / What? / Deranged Or Dead /

MOURNING SIGN (SWEDEN)
Line-Up: Robert Pörschke (vocals), Petri Aho (guitar), Kari Kainulainen (guitar), Thomas Gardh (bass), Henrik Persson (drums)

Swedish Death Metal band MOURNING SIGN fired bassist Thomas Gardh after the debut album was released. His replacement turned out to be Petri Aho.

Singles/EPs:
Redeem / Desert Sun / Godsend / No Paradise, Godhead GOD015CD (1995) ('Alienor' EP)

Albums:
MOURNING SIGN, Godhead GOD016 (1995)
I'll See To That / Dreaming Blind / Ashes Of My Relics / Sleepless / Like Father Like Son / Absorb My Eyes / En To Pan / Seems Endless / Misbegotten
MULTIVERSE, Godhead GOD022 (1996)
Just Another Jesus / I'll Be Dancing / Subtle Climax / Repent/ The Piper / Get Real / Seed Of Revival / My Turn To Sleep / Temptress / Neerg / New Life

MUCUPURULENT (GERMANY)
Line-Up: Timo Reichert (vocals / guitar), Sera Scarvo (guitar), Ralph Glaser (drums)

The Gore obsessed MUCUPURULENT debuted with the 'Bizarre Tales Of The Abnormal' demo. A shared cassette with P.O.O. (PISSED OFF ORGASMS) led to a split single in union with CABAL.

Singles/EPs:
Oral Sex Masturbation / Stainless Spoon / Votzenkrebs / Pussy Berserker, Bizarre Leprous (1998) ('Remind The Bizarre' 7" split single with CABAL)

Albums:
SICKO BABY, Sub Zero (1997)
Lacerated Tits / Cybersex Deliria / Scrotal Hernia / Oral Sex Masturbation / Mangled To The Gore / Pussy Berserker / Suborbital Ejaculation / Abhorrent Dissection / Splattering Nirvana / Vaginal Cancer / Gay's Erection / Cumshot Messiah / Stainless Spoon / Corroded Testicles / Splatter Whore / Fistfucked Baby / Spermsoaked Bitch Consumer / Pierced By A Driller / Extra Uterine Pregnancy / Urethal Discharge / Outro
HORNY AS HELL, Sub Zero (1999)

Punishment / Cum In My Face / Horny As Hell / Bondage Fingers / The Guzzler / Zombie Squad 69 / Goatfuck / Little Pink Examine Room / Vulva Shut / Rip Bunny Master / Hellshelter Babe **DEVILISH, DIRTY AND LIVE**, Fleshfeast (2000) (Split album with INFECTED PUSSY)

MURDER CORPORATION
(SWEDEN)
Line-up: Jens Johansson (vocals), Johan Axelsson (guitar), Dan Bengtsson (bass), Rikard Wermén (drums)

MURDER CORPORATION are made up by guitarist Johan Axelsson, bassist Dan Bengtsson and drummer Rikard Werman from DERANGED and fronted by ex-MEGASLAUGHTER vocalist Emil Lilic.

Albums:
BLOOD REVOLUTION 2050, Qabalah-Repulse QAB 003 (1996)
Bulls Eye 8 Straight In The Head / Cyber Genocide / Blood Revolution 2050 / Point Blanc Rage / I'm In Hell
SANTA IS SATAN, Psychic Scream (199-) (Split CD with GRINDBUTTO)
WHOLE LOTTA MURDER GOIN' ON, Psychic Scream (199-)
Murder In Mind / Forcefed / Procreate Insanity / Violated / Self-Inflicted Virus / Wallow In Greed / Hostage Situation / Highest Power / Self-Teached Judges / Castration Crucifixtion / Retract The Hostile / Forced Into Regression / Buried Alive / Cat Scratch Fever / Chaos Killed The World / Headshot .357 / Held In Bondage / Legalize Murder
TAGGED AND BAGGED, Psychic Scream (2000)

MURDER SQUAD (SWEDEN)

MURDER SQUAD is a side project of ENTOMBED's Uffe Cederland and Peter Stjärnvind with DISMEMBER's Matti Karki and Richard Cabeza.

Albums:
UNSANE, INSANE, MENTALLY DERANGED, (2001)

JAMES MURPHY (USA)

Solo albums by journeyman Death Metal guitarist. Murphy's credits include AGENT STEEL, DEATH's 'Spiritual Healing' and OBITUARY's 'Cause Of Death' in 1990, sessions with British Deathsters CANCER, DISINCARTE during 1993 and

two albums with TESTAMENT 'Low' and 'Live At The Fillmore'.
Murphy's debut solo effort in 1996 'Convergence' has guests Chuck Billy of TESTAMENT, STRAPPING YOUNG LAD's Devin Townsend and NAJI'S KITCHEN's Eddii Ellis.
The 1999 album 'Feeding The Machine' sees valuable guest contributions from GEEZER vocalist Clark Brown, ARTENSION's Vitalij Kuprij, Chuck Billy once again and BAD ENGLISH / JOURNEY / OZZY OSBOURNE drummer Deen Castronova.
1999 found Murphy recording with Danes KONKHRA. By 2000 Murphy was once again a member of TESTAMENT and had also resurrected DISINCARNATE.

Albums:
CONVERGENCE, (1996)
Since Forgotten / Convergance / The Lost One / Vision / Touching The Earth / Red Alert / Deeper Within / Shadows Fall / Tempus Omnia Revelat
FEEDING THE MACHINE, Diehard EFA CD10839 (1999)
Feeding The Machine / Contagion / No One Can Tell You / Epoch / Deconstruct / Odyssey / Through Your Eyes (Distant Mirrors) / Race With Devil On Spanish Highway / Visitors / In Lingua Morta

MUTANT (SWEDEN)
Line-Up: Peter Lake (guitar), Henrik Ohlsson (drums)

Black Metal formed by members of THEORY IN PRACTICE.

Albums:
EDEN BURNT TO ASHES, Mutant (1998)
Demon World / Beyond Bet Durrabia / Eden Burnt To ashes / Dark Spheres / Abduct To Mutate
THE AEONIC MAJESTY, Listenable (2000)
The Majestic Twelve / Demonworlds / Premonitions Erupt / Beyond Bet Durrabia / The Aeonic Majesty / Immemorial Lunacy / Dark Spheres / Eden Burnt To Ashes / Abduct To Mutate

MY DARKEST HATE

Albums:
MASSIVE BRUTALITY, Vile Music (2001)

MYRKSKOG (SWEDEN)

Line-Up: Master V (vocals / bass), Savant M (guitar), Destructhor (guitar), Anders Eek (drums)

A highly individual approach to the genre makes MYRSKOG a unique proposition. The band, founded in the early 90's, include former SUFFERING members and has had a fluid line up leading to the 1995 demo 'Apocalyptic Psychotasia'. MYRKSKOG's Destructhor (real name Thor Anders Myhren) also features on the 2000 ZYKLON album, the side project of EMPEROR's Samoth and Trym. Drummer Anders Eek has credits with ODIUM, FUNERAL and THE FLESH. Drums on the 'Deathmachine' album were handled by Sechtdaemon. Drummer Bjørn Thomas has also featured in the ranks of MYRKSKOG. Session keyboards were handled by Custer (real name Per Arvid). Frontman Master V also operates as live keyboard player for LIMBONIC ART.

Singles/EPs:
A Poignant Scenario Of Death / Death Beauty Lust Ecstasy / A Macabre Death Fare To The Devil, (199-) ('Apocalptic Psychotasia - The Murder Tapes' EP)

Albums:
DEATH MACHINE, Candlelight (2000) Discipline Misanthropy / The Hate Syndicate / A Poignant Scenario Of Horror / Sinthetic Lifeworm / Syndrome 9 / Morphinemangle Torture / Deathfare To The Devil / Death Machine / Pilar Deconstruction (Syndrome 9 Remix)

MYSTERIIS (BRAZIL)

Extreme Death Metal.

Albums:
ABOUT THE CHRISTIAN DESPAIR, (199-)
Ave Mysteriis (Baphomet Signs) / Song For Anu / Feeling The Ancient Hordes Of The Abyss / Blasphemy Calls / The Valley Of Triumphant / Nocturnal Celebration / Diabolical Cosmos Dimensions / Sobre O Desespero Cristao
FUCKING IN THE NAME OF GOD, (2000)

MYTHIC (OH, USA)

Line-Up: Dana Duffey (vocals / guitar), Mary Bielich (bass), Terry Heggen (drums)

MYTHIC - Photo: Danielle Duffey

Although MYTHIC's career was fleeting they certainly left their mark on the Metal scene. Far from being a typical girl Rock group MYTHIC employed the trademark guttural growls of Dana Duffey with guitars tuned way down making them probably the most well known of all female Death-Doom Metal acts.

In early 1991, guitarist Dana Duffey contacted the all female Death Metal band DERKETA after seeing them in an underground fanzine to see if they were interested in adding a fourth member. At that time, the Pittsburgh based DERKETA had actually broken up, unbeknownst to Dana who was living in Toledo, OH at the time. Dana decided to visit Pittsburgh, PA to meet with the remaining members of DERKETA, former WORMHOLE and MASTER MECHANIC bassist Mary Bielich and drummer Terri Heggen. All seemed to go well so Dana relocated to Pittsburgh and the trio began writing music. It was decided that Dana would also be the vocalist and main lyricist for the band. The name MYTHIC was chosen and the band was officially born.

Within a month a three song rehearsal tape was recorded on a 4 track recorder to spread the word throughout the underground scene. The tracks being 'The Destroyer', 'Scarred For Life' and 'Grande Grimoire'. MYTHIC than played several shows on the East coast including in Rhode Island, Cleveland, Detroit, and Pittsburgh. Later that same year they recorded an official demo entitled 'The Immortal Realm' which was recorded live. Tracks were: 'Thy Future Forecast', 'The Destroyer', 'The Oracle', 'Taste of the Grave', 'Grande Grimoire' and 'Lament Configuration'. This six song tape received heavy promotion, proving MYTHIC to be substantially more than an all girl novelty. Within a year of forming they were offered a MCD from Relapse Records. Again, MYTHIC were eager to record and entered the studio immediately. The three song release entitled Mourning In The Winter Solstice was released in 1992 on MCD, 7" record (both

273

traditional black and limited blue vinyl) and cassette. Soon after this release, MYTHIC parted ways with Terri Heggen and a session drummer was used for what would be the final performance at the legendary Milwaukee Metalfest VI.

After the festival, MYTHIC strangely disbanded. Dana promptly formed Black Metal band DARK MOON and later her more prominent act DEMONIC CHRIST. Bielich went on to join the Doom band NOVEMBERS DOOM, Brian Griffin of BROKEN HOPE's side project EM SINFONIA and by 2001 was a member of PENANCE.

Singles/EPs:
Winter Solstice / Lament Configuration / Spawn Of Absu, Relapse (1992)
('Mourning In The Winter Solstice' EP)

NAILBOMB
(BRAZIL / UK)
Line-Up: Max Cavalera,
Alex Newport

Explosive and uncompromising high-profile mix of then SEPULTURA vocalist Max Cavalera and FUDGE TUNNEL's Alex Newport.

Albums:
POINT BLANK, Roadrunner RR 9055-2 (1994) 62 UK
Wasting Away / Vai Toma No Cu / 24 Hour Bullshit / Guerillas / Blind And Lost / Sum Of Your Achievements / Cockroaches / For Fuck's Sake / World Of Shit / Exploitation / Religious Cancer / Shit Panata / Sick Life
PROUD TO COMMIT COMMERCIAL SUICIDE, Roadrunner RR 8910-2 (1995)
Wasting Away / Guerillas / Cockroaches / Vai Toma No Cu / Sum Of Your Achievements / Religious Cancer / Police Truck / Exploitation / World Of Shit / Blind And Lost / Sick Life / While You Sleep, I Destroy Your World / Zero Tolerance

NAKED WHIPPER (GERMANY)
Line-Up: Dominus A.S. (vocals / bass), Michael (guitar), Oliver (guitar), Markus (drums)

"Sado-grind" Metallers NAKED WHIPPER follow the path of deliberate intent to shock. Mainman Dominus A.S. left BLOOD in 1993 to concentrate on NAKED WHIPPER, which until then had been a side project.
NAKED WHIPPER were augmented in the studio by MALAPHAR musicians Markus and Oliver. The first fruits of this liaison was a three track demo featuring 'Hyperincest', 'Anal Queen' and 'Pagan Pussy Gore Intruder'. This cassette was eventually pressed as a limited edition of 500 7" singles.
The album contains such sensitive odes as 'The Ultimate Molester' and 'Perverse Delights'.

Singles/EPs:
Hyperincest / Anal Queen / Pagan Pussy Gore Intruder, United Forces (1993)

Albums:
PAIN STREAKS, MMI MMI017CD (1995)
Pagan Pussy Gore Intruder / The Ultimate Molester / Whore Of Damnation / Perverse Delight / Nunrider / Anal Queen / Painstreaks / Naked Whipper / Hyperincest / Nuclear Solutions - Creation Of A New Demonic Age / Nunrider (Live) / The Ultimate Molester (Live) / Whore Of Damnation (Live) / Perverse Delight (Live) / Pagan Pussy Gore Intruder (Live) / Impure (Live) / Hyperincest (Live) / Naked Whipper (Live) / Painstreaks (Live) / Anal Queen (Live) / Nuclear Solutions - Creation Of A New Demonic Age (Live)

NAPALM DEATH (UK)
Line-Up: Barney Greenaway (vocals), Jesse Pintado (guitar), Mitch Harris (guitar), Shane Embury (bass), Danny Herrera (drums)

An Extreme Grindcore Metal band that defined the genre, often taking it to its absolute limits. NAPALM DEATH came together in 1981 as a Punk act, contributing a track to the third 'Bullshit Detector' album, but started to veer more towards Thrash when DOOM / EXTREME NOIZE TERROR drummer Micky Harris joined in 1986. Bassist Jim Whitley contributed to DOOM's first recordings for the 'A Vile Peace' compilation album around this period.
By the time of their debut 28 track album 'Scum' no original band members had survived the line-up turmoil. Original member Frank Healey joined SACRILIGE B.C. whilst guitarist Justin Broadrick departed to HEAD OF DAVID (later forming GODFLESH) following recording of their initial demos and were replaced by guitarist Bill Steer of 'Phoenix Militia' fanzine and vocalist Lee Dorrian.
Whitely quit shortly after the album release, having his position filled for a series of dates supporting DIRTY ROTTEN IMBECILES on a what was to be a temporary basis by UNSEEN TERROR's Shane Embury who was later to join fulltime.
NAPALM DEATH's debut certainly made an impression, pushing Rock music to extremes and beyond. The band also contributed tracks to two compilation albums at this time; namely 'North Atlantic Noize Attack' and 'Pathological'.
With the exception of Dorrian all members of the band had ongoing side projects at the time of 'Scum'. Steer formed the brutal CARCASS and secured a deal with Earache Records (to later quit to concentrate on his this project fulltime), bassist Shane was drumming for UNSEEN TERROR whilst Harris plied his non-NAPALM extra-curricular activities

with both EXTREME NOIZE TERROR and UNSEEN TERROR.

Still, second album 'From Enslavement To Obliteration' comprised a staggering 54 tracks, many being mere seconds long and, in July 1989, NAPALM DEATH undertook their first successful tour of Japan.

Eventually vocalist Lee Dorrian departed to form the successful CATHEDRAL and former BENEDICTION man Barney Greenaway stepped into his shoes. Steer also quit to concentrate on CARCASS and had his position filled by ex-TERRORIZER guitarist Jesse Pintado. The band soon added a second guitarist in ex RIGHTEOUS PIGS man Mitch Harris and the group set to work once more.

Initial copies of the 1990 album 'Harmony Corruption' came with a free live album - recorded at London's ICA - and early 1991 saw the American leg of the 'Grindcrusher' tour with NAPALM DEATH, NOCTURNUS and GODFLESH.

As NAPALM DEATH were due to tour America once more in the summer of 1991 drummer Mickey Harris quit to form SCORN. This was not before he had been arrested in a case of mistaken identity for the robbery of a jewellers in Derby!

Harris' replacement was American Danny Herrarra, who joined in time for the dates which saw NAPALM DEATH on a bill with SICK OF IT ALL, SEPULTURA and SACRED REICH as well as the band's first shows in Russia.

1992's 'Utopia Banished' album once more saw NAPALM DEATH undertaking extensive roadwork in Europe with OBITUARY and DISMEMBER and in America alongside CARCASS, CATHEDRAL and BRUTAL TRUTH. Further shows followed in Holland, opening for FAITH NO MORE prior to inaugural South African shows.

Returning from the political turmoil of South Africa, NAPALM DEATH released their version of the DEAD KENNEDY's classic 'Nazi Punks Fuck Off' as a single, donating all proceeds to the anti-racism campaign. The single went on to sell over 10,000 copies and the year was rounded off by a headline Canadian tour.

1994 saw the release of 'Fear, Emptiness, Despair' and a British tour with label mates ENTOMBED. Initial reaction to the album was lukewarm, with media attention mainly focused on ENTOMBED rather than NAPALM DEATH. The band fared better in

America, touring alongside OBITUARY.

The band scored a notable success with the inclusion of the track 'Plague Rages' on the soundtrack album to the film 'Mortal Kombat' which broke the American Billboard top five. Further evidence of a return to form came with the well received 'Greed Killing' mini-album.

In 1996 Embury teamed up with Dan Lilker of BRUTAL TRUTH to record the MALFORMED EARTH BORN album 'Defiance Of The Ugly By The Merely Repulsive'. Embury also forged an alliance with SICK OF IT ALL vocalist Lou Koller in BLOOD FROM THE SOUL and the 'To Spite The Gland That Breeds' album.

Confusion surrounded the band in early 1997 as it was announced that Greenaway had departed, one of the reasons being the Aston Villa supporting, AOR loving vocalist's well known fear of flying. The band quickly announced their new frontman to be Phil Vane of EXTREME NOISE TERROR and, quite paradoxically, within days EXTREME NOISE TERROR put out a press statement concerning their new vocalist - Barney Greenaway!

Vane made his mark on a split EP with COALESCE, but upon it's release it became apparent that Greenaway and NAPALM DEATH had patched up their differences and were back together as recording began for the 'Inside The Torn Apart' album.

NAPALM DEATH conducted a lengthy European tour as support to MACHINE HEAD during April and May of 1997. In an attempt to keep themselves in the press, the band issued a split EP with German act FATALITY, a band who won a competition to cover a NAPLALM DEATH track to win a space on the release!

NAPALM DEATH toured South America to wind up roadwork for the year, but only after Embury had suffered a head injury requiring stitches he suffered whilst moshing at an ENTOMBED gig in Nottingham!

Whilst on tour, the band's video, shot for the track 'Breed To Breathe' came under such severe criticism from several European TV stations drastic editing was required. The video featured live footage shot at the notorious New York CBGB's club interspersed with documentary footage of various scenes of brutality.

It's worth noting that, amongst all their accomplishments, NAPALM DEATH have a place in the record books for having recorded the shortest single ever (with a running time of a mere one second) on a record given away free with the Earache Records 'Grindcrusher' compilation album.

In addition to his work in NAPALM DEATH Barney Greenaway is known for his alternative career as a journalist. Having contributed to a number of titles, including 'Raw' and Germany's 'Rock Hard', Barney was found to be penning a computer games column in the late 90s version of 'Kerrang!'

The band signed to new label Dreamcatcher during 1999 following a festival appearance at Germany's legendary Wacken Open Air show. First recordings from this new liaison was the 'Leaders Not Followers' EP which comprised of covers by the likes of DEATH (an obscure demo track that never made it as an official release), RAWPOWER, Chilean Hardcore act PENTAGRAM, EXCEL, Canada's SLAUGHTER and REPULSION as well as a re-recording of their live favourite 'Nazi Punks Fuck Off'.

Both Embury and Pintado also made a mark later the same year with the their LOCK UP project, a new unit created with Peter Tägtgren of Swedes HYPOCRISY and ex-CRADLE OF FILTH / DIMMU BORGIR drummer Nick Barker. The resulting album 'Pleasures Pave Sewers' proved extremely successful charting in Germany.

Both Embury and Harris also embroiled themselves in a further side project LITTLE GIANT DRUG with vocalist / guitarist Simon Orme and drummer Simon Hornblower to issue the 2000 album 'Prismcast'.

NAPALM DEATH toured Europe in early 2000 with guests KONKHRA. Later European gigs, with NASUM as openers, found Harris performing onstage sitting down, the guitarist having broken his foot falling downstairs in a video shoot.

Singles/EPs:
Repeat At Length, Earache (1988) (7" single flexidisc)
Rise Above / Missing Link- Mentally Murdered / Walls Of Confinement / Cause And Effect - No Manual Effort, Earache MOSH 14 (1989) ('Mentally Murdered' EP)
Suffer The Children / Siege Of Power, Earache MOSH 24 (1990) (7" single)
Suffer The Children / Siege Of Power / Harmony Corruption, Earache MOSHT 24 (1990) (12" single)

Mass Appeal / Pride Assassin, Earache MOSH 046 (1991) (7" single)
Mass Appeal / Pride Assassin / Unchallenged Hate / Social Sterility, Earache MOSHT 046 (1991) (12" single)
World Keeps Turning / A Means To An End / Insanity Excursion, Earache MOSH 065 T (1992)
Nazi Punks Fuck Off / Aryanisms / Nazi Punks Fuck Off (Live) / Contemptuous, Earache MOSH092 (1994)
Food Chains / Upward And Uninterested, Earache MOSH 168 CD (1997) ('In Tongues We Speak' split EP with COALESCE)
Breed To Breathe / All Intensive Purposes / Stranger Now / Bled Dry / Time Will Come, Earache MOSH 185CD (1997) (Includes 'Suffer The Children' by FATALITY)

Albums:
SCUM, Earache MOSH 3 (1987)
Multinational Corporations / Instinct Of Survival / The Kill / Scum / Caught In A Dream / Polluted Minds / Sacrificed / Stage Of Power / Control / Born On Your Knees / Human garbage / You suffer / Life? / Prison Without Walls / Negative Approach / Success? / Deceiver / C.S. / Parasites / Pseudo Youth / Divine Death / As The Machine Rolls On / Common Enemy / Moral Crusade / Stigmatized / M.A.D. / Dragnet
FROM ENSLAVEMENT TO OBLITERATION, Earache MOSH 8 (1988)
Evolved As One / It's A Man's World / Lurid Fairytale / Private Death / Impressions / Unchallenged Hate / Uncertainty Blurs The Vision / Cock Rock Alienation / Retreat To Nowhere / Think For A Minute / Display To Me... / From Enslavement To Obliteration / Blind To The Truth / Social Sterility / Emotional Suffocation / Practice What You Preach / Inconceivable / Worlds Apart / Obstinate Direction / Mentally Murdered / Sometimes / Make Way
HARMONY CORRUPTION, Earache MOSH 19 (1990) 67 UK
Vision Conquest / If The Truth Be Known / Inner Incineration / Malicious Intent / Unfit Earth / Circle Of Hypocrisy / The Chains That Bind Us / Mind Snare / Extremity Retained / Suffer The Children
LIVE AT THE ICA LONDON, Earache MOSH 19L (1990) (Free with 'Harmony Corruption')
Rise Above / Success? / From Enslavement To Obliteration / Control / Walls Of Confinement / Instinct Of

Survival / Siege Of Power / Avalanche Master Song / You Suffer? / Deceiver **DEATH BY MANIPULATION**, Earache MOSH 51CDL (1991)
Mass Appeal Madness / Pride Assassin / Unchallenged Hate / Social Sterility / Suffer The Children / Siege Of Power / Harmony Corruption / Rise Above / The Missing Link / Mentally Murdered / Walls Of Confinement / Cause And Effect / No Mental Effort
UTOPIA BANISHED, Earache MOSH053 (1992) 58 UK
Discordance / I Abstain / Dementia Access / Christening Of The Blind / The World Keeps Turning / Idiosyncratic Aryanisms / Cause And Effect / Judicial Slime / Distorting The Medium / Got time To Kill / Upward And Uninterested / Exile / Awake To A Life Of Misery / Contemptuous
THE PEEL SESSIONS, Strange Fruit SFRCD 120 (1993)
The Kill / Prison Without Walls / Dead Part One / Deceiver / Lurid Fairytale / In Extremis / Blind To The Trash / Negative Approach / Common Enemy / Obstinate Direction / Life? / You Suffer
FEAR EMPTINESS DESPAIR, Earache MOSH 109 (1994)
Twist The Knife (Slowly) / Hung / Remain Nameless / Plague Rages / More Than Meets The Eye / Primed Time / State Of Mind / Armageddon X7 / Retching On The Dirt / Fasting On Deception / Throwaway
GREED KILLING, Earache MOSH 146 (1995)
Greed Killing / My Own Worst Enemy / Self Betrayal / Finer Truths, White Lies / Antibody / All Links Severed / Plague Rages (Live)
DIATRIBES, Earache MOSH 141 (1996)
Greed Killing / Glimpse Into Genocide / Ripe For The Breaking / Cursed To Crawl / Cold Forgiveness / My Own Worst Enemy / Just Rewards / Dogma / Take The Strain / Diatribes / Placate, Sedate, Eradicate / Corrosive Elements
INSIDE THE TORN APART, Earache MOSH 171 (1997)
Breed To Breathe / Birth In Regress / Section / Reflect On Conflict / Down In The Zero / Inside The Torn Apart / If Symptoms Persist / Prelude / Indispose / Purist Realist / Low Point / The Lifeless Alarm
ENEMY OF THE MUSIC BUSINESS, Dreamcatcher (2000)
Taste The Poison / Next On The List / Constitutional Hell / Vermin / Volume Of Neglect / Thanks For Nothing / Can't Play, Won't Pay / Blunt Against The Cutting

Edge / Cure For The Common Complaint / A Necessary Evil / CD (Conservative Shithead Part 2) / Mechanics Of Deceit / (The Public Gets) What The Public Doesn't Want / Fracture In The Equation

NASUM (SWEDEN)
Line-Up: Mieszko Talarczyk (vocals / guitars), Anders Jakobsen (guitar), Jesper Liverod (bass), Rickard Alriksson (drums).

NASUM members Rickard Alriksson and Anders Jakobsen are also members of Gore Metal band NECRONY. The pair got Grindcore side project NASUM into gear during late 1992 shortly after receiving an offer from the notorious German label Poserslaughter to cut a shared 7" split single with Australians BLOOD DUSTER. The Swedes contributed their tracks only to find the released single 'Blind World' in union with Belgian veterans AGATHOCLES.
NASUM made a dent in musical history with their donation of 9 tracks lasting a mere blistering three and a half minutes for the Swedish compilation album 'Really Fast Volume 9'.
The duo, then joined by guitarist / bassist Mieszko Talarczyk, laid down further songs for a 4-way split album on Talarczyk's own Grindwork Productions label in alliance with fellow Swedes RETALIATION and Japanese bands C.S.S.O. and VIVISECTION. Other songs from these sessions would be included on a split 7" single shared with Americans PSYCHO.
NASUM worked with EDGE OF SANITY's Dan Swanö to record the 'Industrislaven' release, again for Poserslaughter. This record, listed as an album below, features 18 songs but lasts a mere 16 minutes! In order to promote the album NASUM's inaugural gigs were arranged, including a Berlin show with DEAD and MANOS. However, Alriksson bowed out of these shows and NASUM enrolled SUFFER / SERPENT drummer Per Karlsson for the tour. Alriksson would eventually leave the band and after a brief period with FLESHREVELS man Jallo Lehto on the kit, NASUM pared down to a duo once more with Jakobsen assuming drum duties. With this line-up NASUM recorded tracks for a split release 'Black Illusions' in collaboration with ABSTAIN.
NASUM's reputation had by now attracted international interest and the group signed to American Death Metal

specialists Relapse Records for the 1998 album 'Inhale-Exhale'. Initial copies came with a free 7" EP of cover versions comprising DROPDEAD's 'Bullshit Tradition', S.O.B.'s 'Device', 'REFUSED's 'The Real' and 'Rio De San Atlanta, Manitoba' originally by PROPAGHANDI. The same year saw NASUM paired off with Portland's WARHATE for a further split 7" single.

NASUM boosted the band's strength back up to trio status with the enrollment of BURST's Jesper Liverod on bass in September of 1999. In this incarnation NASUM put in their first American gig at the sprawling Milwaukee Metalfest and managed a slew of further gigs as part of the 'Contamination 99' American tour together with MORGION, EXHUMED, TODAY IS THE DAY and SOILENT GREEN.

In 1999 Jakobsen and Talarczyk created project act KRIGSHOT with guitarist Jallo to release the 'Maktmissbrukare' album. Talarczyk would also act as co-producer for the debut WITHIN REACH album.

NASUM's 2000 album 'Human 2.0' was once more released by Relapse although a later Japanese release on Ritual Records, re-dubbed 'Human 2.01', saw the addition of extra tracks.

NASUM toured Europe in the autumn of 2000 as support to NAPALM DEATH prior to a string of Scandinavian dates alongside THE HAUNTED.

NASUM would be featured on two tribute albums in 2001 with a version of 'Visions Of War' for a DISCHARGE homage and a take of 'Tools Of The Trade' for the Death Vomit Records 'Requiems Of Revulsion' CARCASS tribute.

Singles/ EPs:
Blind World, Poserslaughter (1993) (7" split single with AGATHOCLES)
Smile When You're Dead, Ax/ction 026 (1995) (7" split single with PSYCHO)
World In Turmoil, Blurred (1996) Black Illusions, Yellow Dog (1998) (7" split single with ABSTAIN)
Bullshit Tradition / Device / The Real / Rio De San Atlanta, Manitoba, Relapse (1998) (Free 7" EP with 'Inhale-Exhale' album)
And You Were Blind To What Lay Beyond The Horizon / Stolen Pride / Silent / Losing Faith, Relapse (2000) (7" split single with WARHATE)
Split, (2001) (7" split single with ASTERISK)

Albums:
INDUSTRISLAVEN, Poserslaughter WIMP014 (1995)
Löpande-Bands Principen / Cut To Fit / Fantasibilder / Distortion & Disinformation / Brinn/ Krigets Skörd / Mer Rens / Ditt Öde / Ingenting Att Ha! / Revolution / Den Mörka Tiden / Forcefed Opinion / Domehagen / Dolt Under Ytan / I Helvetet / Skithus / Söndermald
INHALE - EXHALE, Relapse (1998)
This Is… / The Masked Face / Digging In / Time To Act! / Disdain And Contempt / I See Lies / Inhale-Exhume / Too Naked To Distort / There's No Escape / The Rest Is Over / Disappointed / Lagg Om! / You're Obsolete / Tested / Shapeshifter / Feed Them, Kill Them, Skin Them / When Science Fails / Closing In / The World That You Made / The System Has Failed Again / For What Cause? / Fullmatad / Screwed / Shaping The End / The New Firing Squad / No Sign Of Improvement / My Philosophy / I'm Not Silent / The Breathing Furnace / Information Is Free / Burning Inside / A Request For Guidance / Grey / Worldcraft / It's Never Too Late / Du Ar Bevakad / Blinded / Can De Lach
HUMAN 2.0, Relapse RR 6427 (2000)
Mass Hypnosis / A Welcome Breeze Of Stinking Air / Fatal Search / Shadows / Corrosion / Multinational Murderers Network / Parting Is Such Sweet Sorrow / The Black Swarm / Sixteen / Alarm / Detonator / Gargoyles And Grotesques / Nar Dagarna… / Resistance / The Idiot Parade / Den Svarta Fanan / We're Nothing But Pawns / Defragmentation / Sick System / The Professional League / Old And Tired? / Words To Die For / Riot / The Meaningless Trial / Sometimes Dead Is Better

NATRON (ITALY)
Line-Up: Domenico Mele (guitar), Lorenzo Signorile (bass), Max Marzocca (drums)

Technically minded ultra-fast Death Metal band NATRON have been active on the underground scene since 1992. Two demos heralded their arrival in the shape of 1994's 'Force' and 1997's 'A Taste Of Blood'.

NATRON's 1998 album 'Hung, Drawn & Quartered' was produced by guitarist Tommy Talamanca of SADIST.

Albums:
HUNG, DRAWN & QUARTERED, Headfucker HF01 (1998)

Elmer The Exhumer / Enthroned In Repulsion / Leechlord / Flesh Of A Sick Virgin / The Stake Crawlers / Undead Awaken / Heretics Consume The Deceased / Morgue Feast
NEGATIVE PREVAILS, Holy (1999)
By The Dawn Of The 13th / Pyheritic / I Bleed Black / Posed To Slaughter / Blood Streams / A Religious Sickopathetic / Bewitched By The Engraved / Cosmic Autopsies / Message In A … Coffin / Negative Prevails: Outro

NAUSEA (USA)

Singles/EPs:
Psychological Conflict, Baphomet (1991)
Cybergod, Allied (199-) (7" single
Lie Cycle, Graven Image (199-) (7" single)

Albums:
CRIMES AGAINST HUMANITY, Wild Rags (1992)
NAUSEA, Headache (199-) (Split album with TERRORIZER)
EXTINCTION THE SECOND COMING, Profane Existence (199-)
Tech-No-Logic-Kill / Inherit The Wasteland / Johnny Got His Gun / Self Destruct / Butchers / Sacrifice / Godless / Clutches / Extinction / Battered / Blackened Dove / Void / Cybergod / Body Of Christ / Here Today / Lie Cycle / Fallout / Right To Live / Blood And Circus

NECROFEAST (HOLLAND)
Line-Up: Dagon (vocals), Centurion (all instruments)

Dutch Metal band NECROFEAST, founded by ex-NIDHUG man Centurion, formed in 1995 and their first output was a two track demo featuring the songs 'Doomed Christ' and 'The Blessing'.
The group's 1996 debut album features a cover of BATHORY's 'The Return Of Darkness And Evil'. NECROFEAST signed to Spanish label The Drama And Sin for the 2000 'Soulwinds' effort. The album included a take on the COUNTESS track 'Bloed In de Sneeuw'. NECROFEAST's Krieger (also known as 'Centurion') also operates with FLUISTERWOUD, Polish act MORDEAOTH and WELTER.

Albums:
NECROFEAST, Creation Necromantical Mystical Productions (1996)

Hymn Of The Hordes / Time For Revenge / The Return Of Darkness And Evil / The Blessing / Doomed Christ / Northern Wrath / Outro
SOULWINDS, The Drama And Sin DAS004 (2000)
Slag Om Germania / Soulwinds In The Battle Sky / Runendans / Roep Oan De Raaf / A Sacrifice In Ingoi / Hymn - Spirit Of Death / Secrets Of The Shadowdancer / The Halls Of Glory Of Walhalla / Bloed In De Sneeuw / Ceumige Strijd Tegn Al Light En Leben

NECROMANICIDE (MALAYSIA)
Line-Up: Andre (vocals / guitar), Nick Lee (guitar), Adrian (bass), Jeret Christopher (drums)

NECROMANICIDE offered the unusual proposition of not only being a Christian Grindcore Thrash Metal band but also one based in a predominantly Muslim country.
The band debuted with tracks on the compilation album 'The Underground Scene' in 1995 issued by Japanese label Pony Canyon Records and sharing space with Singapore bands STOMPING GROUND and OPPOSITION PARTY.

Albums:
HATE REGIME, Pony Canyon (1998)

NECROMASS (ITALY)
Line-Up: Ain Soph Aur (vocals / bass), J.C. Kerioth (guitar), Nachzerehmara (guitar), Black Wizard (drums)

NECROMASS guitarist Marco M also operates as a member of HANDFUL OF HATE.

Singles/EPs:
Connected Body Pentagram, **Carnefication** (1992) (7" single)
His Eyes, CNF (1993) (7" single)
Bhoma, Miscarriage (1995) (7" single)

Albums:
MYSTERIA MYSTICA ZOFIRIANA, Unisound (1994)
Night (Madness… Knowledge… Evil) / Necrobarathrum / Mysteria Mystica Zorifiana 666 / Exterior Circle / Sodomatic Orgy Of Hate / Black Mass Intuition (Atto 1: Introibo Ad Attare, Atto 2: Silver Reign) / Sadomasochist Tallow Doll / Into An Image Of Left
ABYSS CALLS LIFE, Dracma (1996)
(An Animal) Forever / Vibrations Of

Burning Splendour / Into The Warmth Of Darkness / Bloodstorm Collide / Impure / Abyss Calls Life / A Serpent Is Screaming In The Abyss / Before To Obsess
CHRYSALIS' GOLD, Necromass (1998)

NECROMICON (SWEDEN)

Line-Up: Daniel (vocals), Nicklas (guitar), Stefan (guitar), Patrick (bass), Roger (keyboards), Robert (drums)

NECROMICON opened proceedings with the February 1994 demo 'When The Sun Turns Black' although the band had formed a year earlier. Following this inaugural tape bass player Hendrick took over guitar duties and Jonas filled the four string position. A further demo 'Through The Gates Of Grief' was cut before Hendrick's departure. Jonas moved over to guitar whilst Patrick joined on bass. NECROMICON also augmented their sound with the inclusion of keyboard player Roger.

After a string of live gigs Jonas was sacked. After the release of debut album 'Realm Of Silence' new guitarist Stefan joined the band.

NECROMICON member Baron De Samedi (Jonas?) would later join GATES OF ISHTAR before founding BATTLELUST.

Albums:
REALM OF SILENCE, Impure Creations (1996)
The Spawn Of Dracula / Gates Of Grief / Ages Unfold / Through The Darkness / In Blackened Robes / The Hateful One / Dreams Of The Ancients / Realm Of Silence
SIGHTVEILER, Hammerheart (1998)
Introduction / Gone Below / Homecomings / The Uprising / Veiled In Crimson / Endless Agony / In Desperation / Leaving Now / Ever After
PECCATA MUNDI, Hammerheart (2000)
Peccata Mundi / Heavens Of Hate... Fields Of Fire / The Find Of Alone / Voluptuous Womb / Awaiting The Long Sleep / Firebreeze / Lost Equilibrium / Suicide Caravan / Black Horsemen

NECRONY (SWEDEN)

Line-Up: Rickard Alriksson (vocals / drums), Anders Jacobson (guitar)

Örebo Gore-mongers with lyrics that read more like a perverted mortician's notebook than a Rock song, NECRONY's debut recordings were issued as the 1991 demo 'Severe Malignant Pustule'.

A single followed the same year in the shape of 'Mucu-Purulent Miscarriage' prior to the debut album which bizarrely consists entirely of cover versions by the likes of BOLT-THROWER, CARCASS, CARNAGE and NAPALM DEATH.

EDGE OF SANITY's Dan Swanö guested.

Both Alriksson and Jacobsen are also members of NASUM. Jacobsen also operates in ROUTE NINE with Swanö.

Singles/EPs:
Mucu-Purulent Miscarriage / Multiocular Merphea-Sakroblaster, Poserslaughter PSR 001 (1991)

Albums:
PATHOLOGICAL PERFORMANCES, Poserslaughter PSR WIMP001 (1993)
Rigor Mortis Sets In / Dextrous Embryectomy / Submassive Necrosis Disgorgement / Gynopathological Excav-Eater / Accumulation Of Exudate / Ocular Obliteration / Pro-Rectal Carnage / Excavated, Eviscerated And Emaciated / Effervescing Discharge Of Putrescent Corpulence / The Squirming Worms / Acute Pyencephalus And Cerebral Decomposure / Funeral Ferocity
NECRONYCISM: DISTORTING THE ORIGINALS, Poserslaughter PSR WIMP009 (1995)
Fermenting Innards / Swarming Vulgar Mass Of Infected Virulence / Die In Pain / Mucupurulence Excretor / Dis-Organ-ised / Bodily / Deceiver / The Day Man Lost

NECROPHAGIA (OH, USA)

Line-Up: Killjoy (vocals), Larry Madison (guitar), Bill James (bass), Joe Blazer (drums)

Renowned Death Metal act NECROPHAGIA bowed in with the 1986 demo 'Death Is Fun'. NECROPHAGIA split in 1989 with vocalist KILLJOY forming a new band that bore his name signing a deal with Ann Boleyn's New Renaissance for the 'Compelled By Fear' album.

Killjoy reformed the band in the late 90's with a fresh line up of bass player Dustin Havnen, drummer Wayne Fabra and guitarist Anton Crowley. News rapidly spread throughout the Metal world that 'Anton Crowley' was none other than PANTERA vocalist Phil Anselmo.

Killjoy was involved in the 2000 all star Black Metal project EIBON. With a solitary track on the 'Moonfog 2000' compilation album EIBON consisted of Killjoy, MAYHEM's Maniac, SATYRICON's Satyr Wongraven, DARKTHRONE's Fenriz and PANTERA's Phil Anselmo.

The same year found Killjoy fronting VIKING CROWN (with 'Crowley' again) and yet another extreme Metal banding of well known names THE RAVENOUS. Included in the latter project was STORMTROOPERS OF DEATH bassist Dan Lilker and AUTOPSY and ABCESS guitarist Chris Reifert.

Singles/EPs:
And You Will Live In Terror / They Dwell Beneath / It Lives In The Woods / Black Blood Vomitorium, Red Stream (1999) ('Black Blood Vomitorium' EP)

Albums:
SEASON OF THE DEAD, New Renaissance NRCD15 (1987)
Season Of The Dead / Forbidden Pleasure / Bleeding Torment / Insane For Blood / Reincarnation / Ancient Slumber / Mental Decay / Abomination / Terminal Vision / Painful Discharge / Beyond And Back
READY FOR DEATH, New Renaissance (1990)
DEATH IS FUN, Red Stream (199-)
Abomination / Young Burial / Black Apparition / Chainsaw Lust / Death Is Fun / Intense Mutilation / Autopsy On The Living Dead / Witchcraft / Power Through Darkness
HOLOCAUSTO DE LA MORTE, The Plague (1999)
Blood Freak / Embalmed Yet I Breathe / The Cross Burns Black / Deep Inside, I Plant The Devil's Seed / Burning Moon Sickness / Cadaverous Screams Of My Deceased Lover / Children Of The Vortex / Hymns Of Divine Genocide
A LEGACY OF HORROR, GORE AND SICKNESS, (199-)
World Funeral / Lust Of The Naked Dead / Hemorage / Ready For Death / Ancient Slumber / Black Apparition / Blood Thirst / Mental Death / Communion Of Death / Return To Life / Witchcraft / Autopsy On The Living Dead / Death Is Fun / Communion Of Death / Insane For Blood / Rise From The Crypt / Kill / Chainsaw Lust / Demonic Possession

NECROPHILIACS (USA)

Singles/EPs:
Split, (199-) (7" split single with INCISIVE)
Split, (199-) (7" split single with THE MEATSHITS)

Albums:
PRIMITIVE AND UNCIVILIZED, (199-)
HARDCORE PSYCHOS, Perverted Taste (1995)

NECROPHOBIC (SWEDEN)
Line-Up: Anders Strokirk (vocals / bass), Dave Parland (guitar), Tobbe Sidegard (keyboards), Joakim Sterner (drums)

Death Metal act created in 1989. NECROPHOBIC once included ex-DARK FUNERAL guitarist Dave Parland in the ranks.

The band's initial demo, 'Slow Asphyxiation', sold a commendable 700 copies, prompting a 1991 three track tape entitled 'Unholy Prophecies', recorded at the ever popular Sunlight studios.

NECROPHOBIC's first commercial release came with an EP titled 'The Call' on U.S. label Wild Rags Records that featured ex-CREMATORY vocalist Stefan Harrvik. A track also followed on a compilation album on Witchhunt Records. In late 1995 keyboard player Tobbe Sidegard joined fellow Swedes THERION and Parland quit in 1996 to concentrate on his solo outfit BLACKMOON.

1997's 'Darkside' album witnessed a fresh NECROPHOBIC line-up comprised Tobbe Sidegard on vocals and bass, drummer Joakim Sterner and new guitarist Martin Halfdahn.

Singles/EPs:
Shadows Of The Moon / The Ancient Gate / Father Of Creation, Wild Rags WRR-NEC (199-)
Spawned By Evil / Die By The Sword / Nightmare / Enter The Eternal Fire, Black Mark BMCD 60 (1996) ('Spawned By Evil' EP)

Albums:
THE NOCTURNAL SILENCE, Black Mark BMCD 40 (1993)
Awakening / Before The Dawn / Unholy Prophecies / The Nocturnal Silence / Shadows Of The Moon / The Ancients Gate / Sacrificial Rites / Father Of Creation / Where Sinners Burn

DARKSIDE, Black Mark BMCD 96 (1996)
Black Moon Rising / Spawned By Evil / Bloodthirst / Venasectio / Darkside The Call / Descension / Mailing The Holy One / Nifelhel / Christian Slaughter
THE THIRD ANTICHRIST, Black Mark BMCD 146 (2000)
Rise Of The Infernal / The Third Of Arrivals / Frozen Empire / Into Armageddon / Eye Of The Storm / The Unhallowed / Isaz / The Throne Of Souls possessed / He Who Rideth In Rage / Demonic / One Last Step Into The Great Mist

NECROPOLIS (UK)

Line-Up: Sven Olaffsen (vocals), Billy Liesegang (guitar), Trev Thoms (guitar), Keith More (guitar), Algy Ward (bass), Steve Clark (drums)

The debut album from Black Metallers NECROPOLIS is not all it seems. Drummer Steve Clark, previously with FASTWAY and mentor of Jazz Rock act NETWORK, assembled this band allegedly in an attempt to show the younger genre of Death Metal bands just how this kind of music should be performed. An odd contrast of styles were to make up NECROPOLIS with ex-NINA HAGEN and JOHN WETTON guitarist Billy Liesegang, additional guitars from ASIA and ARENA man KEITH MORE, former TANK, DAMNED and ATOMGOD bassist Algy Ward and erstwhile HAWKWIND guitarist Trev Thoms.
The album, recorded in 1993, includes a guest session from ex-MOTÖRHEAD and FASTWAY guitarist FAST EDDIE CLARKE.
Following recording of 'End Of The Line' Clark and Ward resumed activity with NETWORK for the 'Refusal To Comply' album.

Albums:
END OF THE LINE, Neat Metal NM021 (1997)
Victim / Samaritan / A Taste For Killing / Shadowman / 145 Speed Overload / The Bitterness I Taste

NECROSE (BRAZIL)

Albums:
CHORDS OF CHAOS, Lofty Storm Productions (1998) (4-way split album with EXHUMED, EAR BLEEDING DISORDER and EXCRETED ALIVE)
Diesel And Extinction / Pornocracy /

Crush The Power Part II / I Don't Care / Love Your Hate / Claudia / Sport Assassin / 13th Floor Fatality / Predestinate Death / Football Hysteria Motherfucker / The Dictator / Blueshit - A Blues Hit? / Arbor Insomnia / Preconception (Nothing Particular) / Life's A Joke / In It For The Money / M.T.V. / Sweet Earache / Don't Spread The Holocaust / Sinister End

NECROSIS (Rhode Island, NY, USA)

Albums:
ACTA SANCTORUM, Black Mark BMCD 45 (1995)

NEMBRIONIC (HOLLAND)

Line-Up: Bor (vocals / guitar), Dennis (guitar), Jamil (bass), Noel Rule (drums)

Rooted in the Dutch Grindcore scene NEMBRIONIC HAMMERDEATH founded in 1988. Following an EP, 'Themes Of An Occult Theory', in 1993 and a split debut album with CONSOLATION entitled 'Tempter' for the Dutch Displeased label the band evolved into simply NEMBRIONIC.
As NEMBRIONIC the band recharged their career with the 1995 opus 'Psycho One Hundred'.
In 1997 a new release 'Bloodcult' was issued, a mini-album version of their previous 'Themes' 7" EP including three brand new numbers and an unreleased track from the archives. A further full album 'Incomplete' arrived in 1998.

Albums:
PSYCHO ONE HUNDRED, Displeased D00032 (1995)
Kill Them / Coffin On Coffin / Strength Through Hate / Strength Through Pain / Warzone / Modo Grosso / Death To The Harmless / 15 Minutes / In Ebony / Strength Through Power / Psycho 100 / Bulldozer
BLOODCULT, Displeased D0052 (1997)
Warfare Noise / Corroded / Bloodcult / Yog Sotoh / Approach To Coincidence / Against God / Confrontation With Terror
INCOMPLETE, Displeased (1998)
Riotkill / Dawn Of Rage / Hawkeye / Assassinate / Incomplete / Corroded / Warfare / Beastmachine / In Harmony With Blood / Black Heart / Murdered Streaking / Murdered Mooning / Fleshman / Fleshman II / Riotkill - Roadkill

NEMBRIONIC HAMMERDEATH
(HOLLAND)
Line-Up: Bor (vocals / guitar), Dennis (guitar), Jamil (bass), Noel Rule (drums)

A Dutch Grindcore act founded in 1988. Two years later the band drafted former FRIED FULL RUBBER drummer Noel Rule and CONSOLATION guitarist Dennis. It was to be 1991 before the first NEMBRIONIC HAMMERDEATH demo - 'Lyrics Of Your Last Will' - appeared.
The group would then contribute the track 'In Your Own Hell' to the compilation album 'And Justice For None', promoting these releases with support shows to NOCTURNUS, CONFESSOR, CONSOLATION, GRAVE and ALTAR.
An EP, 'Themes Of An Occult Theory', in 1993 pre-empted shows with PESTILENCE before the group shared their debut album with CONSOLATION on the split release 'Tempter' for the Dutch Displeased label. More than 30 shows were put in to promote the album touring alongside AT THE GATES and CONSOLATION throughout Europe.
For their next release, the 'Psycho One Hundred' album, the band evolved into simply NEMBRIONIC.

Singles/EPs:
Approach To Coincidence / Bow For The Overlord / Yog Sototh Against God, Displeased 000021 (1993) ('Themes Of An Occult Theory' EP)

Albums:
TEMPTER, Displeased (1993) (Split album with CONSOLATION)
Millionth Beast / Tempter / My Commitment / Yog Sathoth / Approach To Coincidence / In Your Own Hell / Towards The Unholy: I) Thundermarch , II) Waterside, III) Towards, IV) Token, V) Unholy, VI) Endless, VII) Purge
PSYCHO 100, Displeased D00032 (1995)
Kill Them / Coffin On Coffin / Strength Through Hate / Strength Through Pain / Warzone / Modo Grosso / Death To The Harmless / 15 Minutes / In Ebony / Strength Through Power / Psycho 100 / Bulldozer

NEOLITHIC (POLAND)
Line-Up: Piotr Wtulich (vocals / guitar), Miroslaw Szymanczak (guitar), Michal Sarnowski (bass), Robert Bielak (keyboards/violin), Janusz Jastrzebowski (drums)

Atmospheric Death Metal outfit NEOLITHIC were created in November 1991 and debuted with the 'The Personal Fragment Of Life' demo. This recording was later re-released in CD format by Adipocere Records.
Both bassist Michael Sarnowski and keyboard player Robert Bielek were to lose their positions as NEOLITHIC welcomed in replacements Tomasz Wlodarski and Michal Stefaniak.

Albums:
THE PERSONAL FRAGMENT OF LIFE, Adipocere AR 028 (1995)
Intro / Wickedness Of The Objects / Nightly Friends / Unupdate Museum (In Memory Of Bruno Schulz) / Undesirable Return / Landscape
FOR DESTROY THE LAMENT, Adipocere AR 033 (1996)
For Destroy / The Lament / Oddity / Gardens Of Phantasms / Szacunek Dla Zmarlego / Last Fix / Chattles / Choreografia / Stained-Glass Window

NEPHENCY (SWEDEN)
Line-Up: Martin Hallin (vocals / guitar), Adrian Kanebäck (guitar), Matthias Fredriksson (bass), Kim Arnell (drums)

Albums:
WHERE DEATH BECOMES ART, Black Diamond BDP 004 (1998)
Enchanted Bliss / Chain Of Command / Worshipped By The Mass / Imperial Dementia / Desolated / Tournament In Torment / Cursed / Hatred And Fantasies / The Meeting

NERGAL (SWITZERLAND)
Line-Up: Mike Burger (vocals / guitar), Gisela Imhof (bass), Nick (drums)

NERGAL began life as a Death Metal band dubbed P.S.F. in 1989. The original trio comprised frontman Mike Burger, bassist Beat Oswald and drummer Nick. Oswald exited and P.S.F. pulled in Peter Sarbuck for a demo 'Grotesque Ecstasy'. A name switch to NERGAL also witnessed a change to a Black Metal stance and the recruitment of former DAMNATORY and BERKAHAL bassist Gisela Imhof. The band's debut came with a split 7" single sharing vinyl with previous P.S.F. material.
NERGAL signed to the Colombian label Warmaster for a split album with Poles BUNDESWEHRA in 1993.

Rites Of Beltane, Wild Rags (1992)
(Split 7" single with P.S.F.)

Albums:
NECROSPELL, Warmaster (1993) (Split
EP with BUNDESWEHRA)
Necrospell / Rites Of Beltane /
Summoning The Watchers (Of The Four
Quarters) / Fountain (In Eternal Falls)

NIGHT IN GALES (GERMANY)
Line-Up: Christian Müller (vocals), Frank
Basten (guitar), Jens Basten (guitar),
Tobias Bruchmann (bass), Christian
Bass (drums)

Delivering modern, Scandinavian style
Death Metal this German outfit released
an EP 'Sylphlike' in 1995. NIGHT IN
GALES was forged the same year
staking their claim with a six track demo
CD 'Sylphlike' resulting in a deal with
Nuclear Blast Records.
The band's debut was produced by
Wolfgang Stach.
The 2000 album was produced by Harris
Johns and featured a raucous cover of
the ALANNAH MYLES hit 'Black Velvet'.
Johns would also handle production for
2001's 'Necrodynamic' although the band
had switched to pastures new with
Massacre Records. For the first time
NIGHT IN GALES saw a domestic
Russian release with the album being
issued there by Art Music.
NIGHT IN GALES toured Japan in April of
2001 alongside DEW SECENTED and
DEFLESHED.

Singles/EPs:
Bleed Afresh / Sylphlike / Avoid Secret
Vanity / Mindspawn / When The Lightning
Starts / Flowing Spring, Night In Gales
(1995) ('Sylphlike' EP)

Albums:
RAZOR, (1996)
TOWARDS THE TWILIGHT, Nuclear
Blast (1997)
Towards A Twilight Kiss / Of Beauty's
Embrace / Razor / From Ebony Skies /
Autumn Water / Slavesrun / Through
Ashen Meadows / Avoid Secret Vanity /
Tragedians
THUNDERBEAST, Nuclear Blast (1998)
Intruder / Darkzone Anthem / Perihelion /
Crystalthorns Call / Feverfeast /
Thunderbeast / I Am The Dungeon God /
Blackfleshed / The Distortion / Stormchild
/ Heroes Of Starfall / From Ebony Skies

NAILWORK, Nuclear Blast (2000)
Nailwork / Blades In Laughter /
Wormsong / All Scissors Smile / How To
Eat A Scythe / Black Velvet / Filthfinger /
The Tenmiletongue / Hearselights /
Down The Throat / Quicksilver Spine
NECRODYNAMIC, Massacre MAS
CD0273 (2001)

NIHILIST (SWEDEN)
Line-Up: Lars-Göran Petrov (vocals),
Alex Hellid (guitar), Uffe Cederland
(guitar), Johnny Hedlund (bass), Nicke
Andersson (drums)

NIHILIST mark the genesis of
ENTOMBED. Adding ex-CARBONISED
bassist Lars Rosenberg NIHILIST
metamorphosed into ENTOMBED while
bassist Johnny Hedlund teamed up with
UNLEASHED.
The debut single was originally the demo
'Drowned', whilst the second single
turned out to be an unofficial bootleg.
Post-ENTOMBED drummer Nicke
Andersson would become Nicke Royale
for his role in THE HELLACOPTERS.

Singles/EPs:
Severe Burns / When Life Has Ceased,
Bloody Rude Defect BRD001 (1989)
Radiation Sickness / Face Of Evil /
Morbid Devourment, Bootleg (1991)

NIKUDOREI (JAPAN)

Grindcore act NIKUDOREI's '2000' album
was graced with cover artwork depicting
a male member being sliced open. Nice.

Albums:
GENITAL TORTURE, HG Facts (2000)

NILE (NC, USA)
Line-Up: Karl Sanders (vocals / guitar),
Dallas Toller Wade (guitar), Chief Spires
(bass), Pete Hamourra (drums)

North Carolina Death Metal that are
justifiably being touted as the next major
league contenders. NILE are nothing if
not ambitious, infusing all of their work
with strong ancient Egyptian and eastern
themes.
A series of demos led the initial trio of
frontman Karl Sanders, bassist Chief
Spires and drummer Pete Hamourra to a
deal with Visceral Productions. However,
this label was to collapse before anything
could be arranged and NILE were soon
snapped up by Relapse Records, the

NILE

band augmenting their sound with the addition of second guitarist Dallas Toller Wade.

NILE toured America in 2000 supported by INCANTATION and IMPALED. Unfortunately Hamourra damaged his arm to such a degree he was unable to perform on the 'Black Seeds Of Vengeance' album. Derrick Roddy of MALEVOLENT CREATION and AURORA BOREALIS stepped in for the studio duties whilst Tony Laureno took over the mantle for live work.

When released 'Black Seeds Of Vengeance' would break NILE from the cult underground into the Death Metal mainstream putting the focus on the band as longterm contenders. The album, which had taken over a year to compose and arrange, featured a vast array of instrumentation as diverse as tablas, African choirs, Tibetan doom drums, gongs and sitars.

The 2000 Hammerheart release 'In The Beginning' combines the two early mini-albums 95's 'Festivals Of Atonement' and 97's 'Ramses Bringer Of War'.

Following European touring in early 2001 longstanding bassist Chief Spires decamped.

Singles/EPs:
The Howling Of The Jinn / Ramses Bringer Of War / Die Rache Krieg Lied Der Assyriche, (1997) ('Ramses Bringer

Of War' EP)

Albums:
FESTIVALS OF ATONEMENT, Relapse (1995)
Divine Intent / The Black Hand Of Set / Wrought / Immortality Through Art / Godless-Extinct
AMONGST THE CATACOMBS OF NEPHREN-KA, Relapse RR 6983 (1998)
Smashing The Antiu / Barra Edinazzu / Kudurru Maglu / Serpent Headed Mask / Ramses Bringer Of War / Stones Of Sorrow / Die Rache Krieg Lied Der Assyriche / The Howling Of The Jinn / Pestilence And Iniquity / Opening Of The Mouth / Beneath Eternal Oceans Of Sand
IN THE BEGINNING, Hammerheart (2000)
Divine Intent / The Black Hand Of Set / Wrought / Immortality Through Art / Godless-Extinct / The Howling Of The Jinn / Ramses Bringer Of War / Die Rache Krieg Lied Der Assyriche
BLACK SEEDS OF VENGEANCE, Relapse (2000)
Invocation Of The Gate Of Aat-Ankh-Es-En-Amenti / Black Seeds Of Vengeance / Defiling The Gates Of Ishtar / The Black Flame / Libation Unto The Shades Who Lurk In The Shadows Of The Temple Of Anhur / Masturbating The War God / Multitude Of Foes / Chapter For Transforming Into A Snake / Nas Akhu

Khan She En Asbiu / To Dream Of Ur / The Nameless City Of The Accursed / Khetti Satha Shemsu

NINNGHIZHIDDA (GERMANY)
Line-Up: Mephistopholes (vocals / guitar), Baalberith (guitar), Ash Saan (keyboards), Lightning Bolt (drums)

A blasphemous German Death Metal combo previously signed to the now defunct Invasion label.
NINNGHIZHIDDA, who debuted with the demo 'The Horned Serpent', recorded their opening 'Blasphemy' album with a line-up of vocalist / guitarist Mephistopholes (Patrick Kalla), guitarist Baalberith (Renè Bogdanski), keyboard player Dr. Faustus and drummer Kerberos.
Later additions to NINNGHIZHIDDA included vocalist / bassist Zagan in the spring of 1998 and also Ventor. However, Zagan, Ventor and Dr. Faustus would all break away from the band prior to their signature with Dutch label Displeased for a second album.
The band's line-up for the 2001 'Demigod' opus stood at frontman Mephistopholes, guitarist Baalberith, keyboard player Ash Saan (Sascha George) and drummer Lightning Bolt (Markus Aust - also known as Tsatthoggua).

Albums:
BLASPHEMY, Invasion (1998)
Moonlight Serenade / Of Demons And Witches (Part I) / Baphomet (In The Name Of...) / Reach The Jewels Gleam / Of Demons And Witches (Part II) / Dressed In Mourning / The Horned Serpent / Crucify The Lambs Of Christ / Deny Thy Philosophy / Nailed Upon A Cross / Ode To Thy Horned Majesty
DEMIGOD, Displeased (2001)

NOCTES (SWEDEN)
Line-Up: Jöhan Lonn (vocals), Holger Thorsin (guitar), Pasi Lundegard (guitar), Asa Rosenberg (bass), Carl Leijon (keyboards), Hugo Thorsin (drums)

NOCTES previously operated under the name of CONCEALED. A continuing series of line up changes afflicted CONCEALED to such a degree that band opted for a name change to NOCTES. The band's debut album was recorded at the renowned Sunlight studios in late 1996. Following recording of 'Pandemonic Requiem' frontman Jöhan

Lonn relinquished bass duties to new member Asa Rosenberg.

Albums:
PANDEMONIC REQUIEM, No Fashion NFR025 (1998)
Twilight Elysium / Reverie / Attila / Purgatory Temptations / Hokmah Nisthara / Butterfly / In Silence / Winterdawn / Lamia / Orphean Horizons / Outra
VEXILLA REGIS PRODEURT INFERNI, (199-)
Mirrorland / Frozen To Sleep / Demonica / A Demon From Within / Vexilla Regis Prodeurt Inferni / The Lost Garden / Darkside Whispers / The Dream Dominion / Persephone / Carnifax / De Profundis Clamavi

NOCTUARY (USA)

Born out of the early 90's extreme Metal band SUMMONED. NOCTUARY's 2000 album 'When Fires Breed Blood' included session lead guitar from EVIL DEAD and DEATH veteran Albert Gonzales, vocals from James Reyes and drums from Rob Alaniz. The mini-album release on Largactyl Records is a CD pressing of NOCTUARY's 1996 demo 'Where All Agony Prevails'.
Former NOCTUARY man Daren Winn would join RAVENS OVER GOMORRAH.

Albums:
FOR SALVATION..., Lost Disciple LDR004 (1999)
Funeral Ceremony / For Salvation... / Forever Shrouded Within This World / Sorrow In Wilder Darkness / Eternal Nightmare / The Once Forgotten Past / Lost In Illusions / Consumed By Fear / Black Bleeding Soul / Cast Into The Brooding Shadow / Journey To The Lost Kingdom
WHERE ALL AGONY PREVAILS, Largactyl LR001 (2000)
Funeral Ceremony / Where All Agony Prevails / Black Angels Return / Eternal Nightmare / His Majesty Of The Shadows / Nocturnal Sanctuary
WHEN FIRES BREED BLOOD, Lost Disciple LDR010 (2000)
Chapter I - "The Fires Burning Cold": Clouds Donning The Black Sky, ... And Hate Embraced The Night / Chapter II - "A Call To Arms": Legions March Into Unearthly Realms / Chapter III - "The Battles": Vengeance Before Valour, A Tears Descent From Heaven / Chapter

IV - "A Victory Celebration": At journeys End / Chapter V - "The Rebirth"

NOCTURNAL BREED (NORWAY)
Line-Up: Ben Hellion (guitar), Archon (guitar), Andy Michaels (drums)

Although Scandinavia threw up a confusion of side project acts in the late 90s put together by various Black Metal musicians made good, NOCTURNAL BREED boast more pedigree than most. A distinctly retro old style Death Metal offering performed by members of DIMMU BORGIR, LORD KAOS, SATYRICON, COVENANT and GEHENNA. NOCTURNAL BREED debuted in 1998 with the 'Aggressor' album.
NOCTURNAL BREED had in fact been operating much earlier than this with a pre-DIMMU BORGIR founding member Erkjetter Silenoz on guitar going under the stage name of Ed Dominator.
Guitarist Archon also has credits with MALEFICUM and his own project ARCHON.

Albums:
AGGRESSOR, Hammerheart (1998)
Rape The Angels / Frantic Aggressor / Maggot Master / Nocturnal Breed /

Death - Evil Dead / Metal Storm Rebels / Dead Dominions / Alcoholic Rites / Revelation 666 / Blaster / Locomotive Death
TRIUMPH OF THE BLASPHEMER, (199-)
Triumph Of The Blasphemer / Screaming For A Leather Bitch / I'm Alive / Frantic Aggressor / Evil Dead
NO RETREAT - NO SURRENDER, (199-)
The Artillery Command / Thrash The redeemer / Warhorse / Killernecro / No Retreat - No Surrender / Beyond Control / Sodomite / Fists Of Fury / Under The Blade / Roadkill Maze / Possessed / Armageddon Nights / Insane Tyrant

NOCTURNUS (FL, USA)
Line-Up: Mike Browning (vocals / drums), Mike Davis (guitar), Sean McNennerey (guitar), Jeff Estes (bass), Louis Panzer (keyboards)

For their debut 'The Key' NOCTURNUS plied a unique combination when it came to plying their particular brand of death metal, unafraid to add the keyboards of Louis Panzer and with lead vocals being handled by ex-MORBID ANGEL / INCUBUS drummer Mike Browning. MASSACRE's Kam Lee adds backing

NOCTURNUS
Photo : Martin Wickler

vocals.

Bassist Jeff Estes made way for James Sullivan for touring which included dates BOLT-THROWER and NAPALM DEATH. 1992's 'Thresholds' saw the band adopt a more conformist approach by adding former TORTURED SOUL vocalist Dan Izzo to the line up. Browning quit to work with ACHERON. In a further change Sullivan lost his place and NOCTURNUS utilized the talents of Chris Anderson in the studio although a more permanent position went to ex-FALLEN IDOLS man Emo Mowery. NOCTURNUS toured Europe together with CONFESSOR in 1992.

NOCTURNUS resurfaced in 2000 with a fresh vocalist Emo and a new album 'Ethereal Tomb'.

Singles/EPs:
Possess The Priest, Morbid Sounds DEAD 02EP (1994)

Albums:
THE KEY, Earache MOSH 23 (1990)
Lake Of Fire / Standing In Blood / Visions From Beyond The Grave / Neolithic / BC-AD (Before Christ- After Death) / Andromeda Strain / Droid Sector / Destroying The Manger / Empire Of The Sands
THRESHOLDS, Earache MOSH55 (1992)
Climate Controller / Tribal Vodoun / Nocturne In B.M. / Arctic Crypt / Aquatic / Subterranean Infiltrator / After Reality / Gridzone
ETHEREAL TOMB, Season Of Mist (2000)
Orbital Decay / Apostle Of Evil / Edge Of Darkness / The Killing / Séance For The Trident / Paranormal State / The Science Of Horror / Outland

NOIZ (GERMANY)

Albums:
SEEDS OF THE LIVING, (199-)
Leaving Despair's Empire / Stranger / Believer's Shelter / Charity / Pathway / Radical / Save / Final Day / Crown Of Thorns / God's Love / Baptism And New Life

NOMAD (POLAND)
Line-Up: Bleyzabel (vocals), Christian (vocals), Patrick (guitar), Nameless (guitar), Hermann (bass), Rodzyn (drums)

Created in 1994 by former PUTREFACTION members vocalist Bleyzabel and bassist Hermann. NOMAD released the 1996 'Disorder' demo followed by the 1997 effort 'The Tail Of Substance' promoting this release by touring alongside CHRIST AGONY and LUX OCCULTA.

NOMAD signed to the Novum Nox Mortis label for the album 'The Devilish Whirl'. However, despite promotional CDs being issued to the media the label collapsed before the record's commercial release.

Albums:
THE DEVILISH WHIRL, (1999)

NO RETURN (FRANCE)
Line-Up: Tanguay (vocals), Alain Clement (guitar), Laurent Janaut (bass), Didier Le Baron (drums)

NO RETURN went under the title of EVIL POWER from their formation in 1984 before changing titles to NO RETURN in 1988.

The debut album 'Psychological Torment', featuring original vocalist Phil, was produced by CORONER's Marquis Marky. Following it's release, NO RETURN toured supporting SACRED REICH, DARK ANGEL, SODOM and EXHORDER.

A new frontman in Tanguay was found in time for the second album 'Contamination Rises' recorded in Florida and produced by Tom Morris.

Albums:
PSYCHOLOGICAL TORMENT,
Semetary WMD 772089 (1991)
Mutants' March / Reign Of The Damned / Vision Of Decadence / Tragic Giving / Radical Disease / Degeneration Of The Last Decade / Nightly Aggression / Electro Mania / Religion / Psychological Breakdown
CONTAMINATION RISES, FNAC Music 592043 (1991)
Damnation / Memories / Raving Lunatics / Uncontrolled Situation / Trash World / Sacred Bones / World Of Impurities / Civil War / Perversion / Sorrow / Mass Grave / Revolt Of The Hanged
SEASONS OF SOUL, Semetary WMD 121131 (1995)
Damnation Nr. 2 / Paralyzed Conflicts / No Respect, News Reel / Worrying, Law Of Silence / While Poverty Reigns / Circle Of Hypocrisy / Soul's Virginity / Psychological Revenge / Injustice System / Wisdom / Loaded Gun Nr. 13 /

Just One Step (Psychic Sketch)

NUCLEAR ASSAULT
(New York, NY, USA)
Line-Up: John Connelly (vocals / guitar), Anthony Bramante (guitar), Dan Lilker (bass), Glenn Evans (drums)

With the mid-eighties thrash explosion, New York's NUCLEAR ASSAULT leapt to the fore due to the prime motivating force of ex-ANTHRAX bassist Dan Lilker. Although the gangly mop-topped bassist had severed ties with ANTHRAX in 1983, due to disagreements with then vocalist Neal Turbin, it took two and a half years to assemble his next project NUCLEAR ASSAULT. In the interim, Lilker had involved himself with the spoof Metal of STORMTROOPERS OF DEATH alongside ANTHRAX guitarist Scott Ian and METHOD OF DESTRUCTION vocalist Billy Milano.
NUCLEAR ASSAULT's line up for the inaugural 'Brain Death' EP was Lilker, vocalist John Connelly, guitarist Anthony Bramante and ex-HARTER ATTACK / TT QUICK drummer Glenn Evans.
Despite NUCLEAR ASSAULT's rapidly growing profile on the crossover scene, Evans found time to invest in a new label, Arena Records. The first release on Arena was the 'Salt In The Wound' single by his previous outfit HARTER ATTACK.
1987's mini-album 'The Plague', a collection of old and new material including the infamous 'Buttfuck' (a song lyrically aimed at MÖTLEY CRÜE vocalist VINCE NEIL), was originally to be titled 'Cross Of Iron' and to have had a cross as the sleeve artwork. However, the American record company Combat cited possible objections that may have come from religious organizations. NUCLEAR ASSAULT's first foray into Europe came the same year, with dates alongside AGENT STEEL.
A return to Europe in 1988 as guests to SLAYER gave NUCLEAR ASSAULT access to far greater crowds and, fuelled by their reaction, the band returned for further dates as headliners, support being granted by ACID REIGN and RE-ANIMATOR. Further gigs saw the band opening for SEPULTURA in South America.
The band set about another American tour in 1992, bolstering their live sound by including former TT QUICK guitarist Dave DiPietro and ex-PROPHET guitarist Scott Metaxas. As Lilker announced details of his new act BRUTAL TRUTH the same year and an immediate signing with Earache Records, the demise of NUCLEAR ASSAULT became inevitable. A last effort under the banner NUCLEAR ASSAULT came with 1993's 'Something Wicked' with the band comprising now of Connelly, DiPietro, Metaxas and Evans.

Singles/EPs:
Brain Death / Final Flight / Demolition, Combat 88561 8119-1 (1986)
Fight To Be Free / Equal Rights / Stand Up, Under One Flag 12 FLAG 105 (1989)
Fight To Be Free / Equal Rights / Stand Up / Brain Death / Final Flight / Demolition, Under One Flag CD12 FLAG 105 (1989)
Good Times, Bad Times / Hang The Pope (Live) / Lesbians / My America / Happy Days, Under One Flag 12 FLAG 107 (1989)
Critical Mass, Relativity (1989) (USA promotion)
Trail Of Tears, Relativity (1989) (USA promotion)

Albums:
GAME OVER, Under One Flag FLAG 5 (1986)
Live, Suffer, Die / Sin / Cold Steel / Betrayal / Radiation Sickness / Hang The Pope / After The Holocaust / Stranded In Hell / Nuclear War / My America / Vengeance / Brain Death
THE PLAGUE, Under One Flag MFLAG 13 (1987)
Game Over / Nightmares / Buttfuck / Justice / The Plague / Cross Of Iron
SURVIVE, Under One Flag FLAG21 (1988)
Rise From The Ashes / Brainwashed / F / Survive / Fight To Be Free / Got Another Quarter / Great Depression / Wired / Equal Right / P.S.A. / Technology / Good Times, Bad Times
HANDLE WITH CARE, Under One Flag FLAG 35 (1989)
New Song / Critical Mass / Inherited Hell / Surgery / Emergency / Funky Noise / F (Wake Up) / When Freedom Dies / Search And Seizure / Torture Tactics / Mother's Day / Trail Of Tears
OUT OF ORDER, Under One Flag FLAG 64 (1991)
Sign In Blood / Fashion Junkie / Too Young To Die / Preaching To The Deaf / Resurrection / Stop Wait Think / Doctor Butcher / Quocustodiat / Hypocrisy / Save The Planet / Ballroom Blitz

LIVE AT HAMMERSMITH ODEON,
Roadracer RO 91672 (1992)
Intro - The New Song / Critical Mass /
Game Over / Nightmares / B.F. / Survive
/ Torture Tactics / Trail Of Tears /
Mothers Day / My America / Hang The
Pope / Lesbians / Fucking Noise / Good
Timkes, Bad Times

SOMETHING WICKED, Alter Ego
ALTGOCD 003 (1993)
Something Wicked / Another Violent End
/ Behind Glass Walls / Chaos / Forge /
No Time / To Serve Men / Madness
Descends / Poetic Justice / Art / Other
End

ASSAULT AND BATTERY, Receiver
RRCD 244 (1997)
Happy Days / Enter Darkness / Leaders
/ Hang The Pope / Radiation Sickness /
Hypocrisy / Behind Glass Walls / No
Time / Hour Shower / Sadam /
Preaching To The Deaf / Hang The Pope
/ Ping / Torture Tactics / Fight To Be Free
(Live) / Trail Of Tears (Live) / Ping Again
(Live) / Butt Fuck (Live)

NUCLEAR DEATH (AZ, USA)

Albums:
BRIDE OF INSECT, Wild Rags (1990)

NUNSLAUGHTER (Pittsburgh, USA)
Line-Up: Don Of The Dead (vocals /
bass), Megiddo (guitar), Insidious (bass),
Jim Sadist (drums)

A notorious name in Death and Black
Metal circles. NUNSLAUGHTER, not
noted for their subtlety, date back to the
late 80's with an initial incarnation of
bassist Don Of The Dead, guitarist Jer
The Butcher, vocalist Gregoroth and
drummer Behemoth Bill. This line-up cut
the opening 'Ritual Of Darkness'
cassette. Both Butcher and Behemoth
would exit signalling a prelude to a
turbulent career for the band as
membership ebbed and flowed with each
successive release. NUNSLAUGHTER's
second demo 'The Rotting Christ' saw the
inclusion of guitarist Rick Rancid and
drummer John Sicko.
1991 saw the departure of both Sicko and
Gregoroth and the emergence of new
drummer Vlad The Impaler as Don Of
The Dead took over lead vocal duties for
the provocative demo 'Impale The Soul
Of Christ On The Inverted Cross Of
Death'.
In 1993 the inaugural demo 'Ritual Of
Darkness' was bootlegged in Brazil on a

7" single. Meantime NUNSLAUGHTER
laid down a fourth demo 'Guts Of Christ'
with predictably another skinsman Mark
Perversion.
By 1995 NUNSLAUGHTER reconvened
the original founding trio of Don,
Gregoroth and Butcher. Along with
drummer Jim Sadist another session
'Face Of Evil' was issued. The line-up did
not stay the course though and soon new
faces included bass player Chris 213 and
guitarist Blood for a split 7" single with
BLOODSTICK in 1997. This would herald
a NUNSLAUGHTER tradition as further
shared singles quickly surfaced shared
with CRUCIFER, DECAPITATOR and
female act DERKETA.
Later members include guitarist Megiddo
and bassist Insidious. European touring
in 2000 witnessed the temporary
enlistment of SOULLESS guitarist Wayne
Richards.

Singles/EPs:
Burn In Hell / Hell's Unholy Fire / Death
By The Dead / Killed By The Cross / I
Am Deaths, (1990) ('Killed By The
Cross' 7" single)
Inri / Power Of Darkness / Sacrifice,
(1997) (Split 7" single with
BLOODSTICK)
Emperor In Hell / Demon's Gate / Bring
Me The Head Of God, (1998) (Split 7"
single with DECAPITATOR)
If The Dead Could Speak / Devil Meat /
Black Beast, (1998) (Split 7" single with
CRUCIFER)
Church Bizarre / Midnight Mass / It Is I /
Poisoned Priest, (1998) ('Blood Devil' 7"
single)
Black Horn Of The Ram / The Devil /
Murder By The Stake, Evil Dreams
(1999) (split 7" single with DERKETA)

Albums:
HELL'S UNHOLY FIRE, Revenge
Productions (2000)
Burn In Hell / Killed By The Cross /
Death By The Dead / Perversion Of
Gore / The Dead Plague / Cataclysm /
Burning Away / Nun Slaughter /
Blasphemy / Seas Of Blood / Altar Of
The Dead / Satanic / Blood For Blood /
Impale The Soul Of Christ On The
Inverted Cross Of Death / I Am Death /
Hells Unholy Fire

NYCTOPHOBIC (GERMANY)
Line-Up: Christian Zimmermann
(vocals), Markus Burgert (guitar), Markus
Zoen (bass), Tom Will (drums)

A brutal Grindcore act founded in 1992 by drummer Tom Will and bassist Markus Zorn. Other early recruits were guitarist Christopher and vocalist Stephan with second guitarist Martin Hub added in June of 1994. Shortly after NYCTOPHOBIC dispensed with Stephan and drafted singer Alex Schulze for a 1995 demo. Tracks from these sessions formed part of their split single 'Four Ways To Misery' on M.M.I. records. This was quickly followed by a further 7" EP 'Negligenced Respect' prior to a split EP with the undisputed kings of the format Belgian fellow Grindsters AGATHOCLES. Both Christopher and Schulze decamped in December of 1995 and NYCTOPHOBIC enlisted singer Christian Zimmermann and guitarist Markus Bugert for the full length album 'War Criminal Views'.

In 1997 NYCTOPHOBIC toured Europe with American acts EXHUMED and HEMDALE. A further split 7" venture with ENTRAILS MASSACRE was released the same year.

NYCOTOPHOBIC are unfortunately blessed with a vocalist whose style makes it rather difficult to understand a word he's singing! We are assured, however, that the group's lyrics can often be very political in nature!

Singles/EPs:
Live In Mannheim, Lull Rex (1994)
(Split EP with AGATHOCLES)
Four Ways To Misery EP, M.M.I. (1994)
Negligenced Respect, M.M.I. (1994)
Inner Manipulation, T&M T&M001
(1997) (Split EP with ENTRAILS MASSACRE)
Sterility, Revenge Productions (1998)
(7" split single with EXHUMED)

Albums:
WAR CRIMINAL VIEWS, Morbid MR 029 (1996)
Earthrise / Horrid Truth / Inner Manipulation / Access Denied / Jehova's Liars / Fundamentals / Rapid Eye Movement / Suffer Life / War Criminal Views / The Pain Of A Conquered Being / Racial Heirarchy / The Remaining Silence / War Seeds / Responsibilities / Denial / Destructive Ignorance / Theatric Symbolization Of Life
SPLIT, E.N.D. (1999) (Split album with MESRINE and TRAUMATISM)
INSECTS, Morbid (2000)
They / Taught To Fear / Hate / Walls Of Seclusion / Unconsciously Dead / Co(g)-Existence / Never To Be Led / Ill-Justice / World Turns Red / Waste Of Time / Restless / Swallow - Spit It Out / Needless Compromises / X 15. Pride Breeds Rage / Insects / Co(g)-Existence

OATHEAN
(SOUTH KOREA)

OATHEAN were previously titled ODIN upon their formation in 1993.

Albums:
THE EYES OF TREMENDOUS SORROW, (1998)
Intro / The Last Elegy For My Sad Soul / Transparent Blue Light - So Too Much Tearful... / In Fear With Shiver / Frigid Space / The Eyes Of Tremendous Sorrow / The Rotten Egg Smell On My Belly / Punishment Of Being Alone - It's Cruel Strength Breaks Me Away

OBERON (SWEDEN)
Line-Up: Oberon, Randi Wedvich (vocals), Roger Egseth (drums)

Although essentially a solo project of Oberon, additional musicians on the album include vocalist Randi Wedvich and drummer Roger Egseth. OBERON first came to attention with the demo 'Through Time And Space'. A second tape 'Lily White' followed in 1995.

Albums:
OBERON, Prophecy Productions PRO 004 (1997)
Stay / The Nightingale / Out From A Deep Green Emerald Sea / L.I.T.L.O.T.W. / Lily White

OBITUARY (Brandon, FL, USA)
Line-Up: John Tardy (vocals), Trevor Peres (guitar), Allen West (guitar), Daniel Tucker (bass), Donald Tardy (drums)

Hailing from the same Florida town as NASTY SAVAGE, Brandon's OBITUARY ply unadulterated brutal Death-Gore Metal.
Starting out in 1985 as school band XECUTIONER. With a line-up of guitarist Trevor Peres, with the Tardy brothers, vocalist John and drummer Donald rounding things out - the band issued a self-financed single under the original name, the 1,000 run 'Metal Up Your Ass'/ 'Psychopathic Minds' on their own Xecution Records. Further recordings came in the form of a two song demo 'Find The Arise' and 'Like The Dead' which eventually surfaced on the 'Raging Death' Godly Records compilation.
Adopting the new title of OBITUARY, so as to avoid confusion with Boston's EXECUTIONER, the band initiated recording of a full length album for Godly Records, but were to sign the tapes over to Roadrunner prior to completion.
Bassist Daniel Tucker was officially listed as a missing person in Florida after disappearing on May 1, 1989. Tucker was later found alive in September having seemingly suffered injury and partial amnesia in a car crash. After recovering he chose not to pursue a 'heavy Metal lifestyle'.
Allen West quit in 1990 just as the group had added Frank Watkins to fill the vacancy left by Tucker's decision not to rejoin. West (who joined SIX FEET UNDER and LOWBROW) was replaced by ex-AGENT STEEL / HALLOWS EVE / DEATH guitarist JAMES MURPHY in time to record the 'Cause Of Death' album which included a cover of Swiss Avant-garde merchants CELTIC FROST's 'Circle Of The Tyrants'.
The following year Murphy departed to join British deathsters CANCER and West was reinstated as the band set out touring America opening for SACRED REICH.
OBITUARY slotted in a short European co-headline tour towards the end of 1994 sharing the billing with Brazilians SEPULTURA, support coming from ROLLINS BAND and VOODOO CULT.
Toured Europe in 1995 headlining over EYEHATEGOD and PITCHSHIFTER.
In late 1997 Roadrunner chose to re-issue the first two albums in re-mastered form with the addition of bonus tracks.
Peres created a side project titled CATASTROPHIC in 2000.

Albums:
SLOWLY WE ROT, Roadracer RO 9489-2 (1989)
Internal Bleeding / Godly Beings / Till Death / Slowly We Rot / Immortal Visions / Gates To Hell / Words Of Evil / Suffocation / Intoxicated / Deadly Intentions / Blood Soaked / Stinkpuss
CAUSE OF DEATH, Roadracer RO 9370-2 (1990)
Infected / Body Bag / Chopped In Half / Circle Of The Tyrants / Dying / Find The Arise / Cause Of Death / Memories Remain / Turned Inside Out
THE END COMPLETE, Roadrunner RC 92012 (1992) 52 UK
I'm In Pain / Back To One / Dead silence / In The End Of Life / Sickness / Corrosive / Killing Time / The End Complete / Rotting Ways

WORLD DEMISE, Roadrunner RR 89952 (1994) 65 UK
Don't Care / World Demise / Buried In / Redefine / Paralyzing / Lost / Solid State / Splattered / Final Thoughts / Boiling Point / Set In Stone / Kill For Me
SLOWLY WE ROT, Roadrunner RR8768-2 (1997) (Remastered, re-issue with bonus tracks)
Internal Bleeding / Godly Beings / 'Til Death / Slowly We Rot / Immortal Visions / Gates To Hell / Words Of Evil / Suffocation / Intoxicated / Deadly Intentions / Bloodsoaked / Stinkupuss / Find The Arise (Demo Version) / Like The Dead (Demo Version)
CAUSE OF DEATH, Roadrunner RR 8767-2 (1997) (Remastered, re-issue with bonus tracks)
Infected / Body Bag / Chopped In Half / Circle Of The Tyrants / Dying / Find The Arise / Cause Of Death / Memories Remain / Turned Inside Out / Infected (Demo Version) / Memories Remain (Demo Version) / Chopped In Half (Demo Version)
BACK FROM THE DEAD, Roadrunner RR 8831-2 (1997)
Threatening Skies / By The Light / Inverted / Platonic Disease / Download / Rewind / Feed On The Weak / Lockdown / Pressure Point / Back From The Dead / Bullituary
DEAD LIVE, Roadrunner RR 8755 (1998)
Download / Chopped In Half / Turned Inside Out / Threatening Skies / By The Light / Dying / Cause Of Death / I'm In Pain / Rewind / 'Til Death / Kill For Me / Don't Care / Platonic Disease / Back From The Dead / Final Thoughts / Slowly We Rot

OBLIGATORISK TORTYR
(SWEDEN)

Albums:
OBLIGATORISK TORTYR, Osmose Productions OPCD 107 (2001)
Ingen Atervando / Spolmask / Du Ar Sa Svag / Stenkross / Smart Bryter Kriget Ut / Min Fiende / Din Fradsaves Grav / Maskin / Obligatorisk Tortyr / Tryckkokare / My Hatred / Icke-Humanitar / Destructionspatrull 666 / Varlden Ar Vacker / Avloppsbrunn / Helmantlad / Torstar Efter Rov / My Prey / 3 + 3 / Du Ger Mig Inte Nat / Doda Vardlen / Krossa Livet / Total War / Aldrig-Inget / Slattermaskin

OBNOXIOUS (GERMANY)
Line-Up: Harald Heuser (vocals), Marco Pfiefer (guitar), Günter Lahmne (bass), Markus Weil (drums)

Albums:
TWILIGHT OF AUTUMN PAST, Compudisc MH 1000 (1994)
Intro / Life In A Second / Methylhydroxypropylcellulose / The Counterbalance / Autumn / Euthanasia / Prophet With Profit / Beyond The Twilight

OBSCENITY (GERMANY)
Line-Up: Oli (vocals), Henne (guitar), Jens (guitar), Thimo (bass), Sascha (drums)

OBSCENITY, founded in 1989, recorded a demo entitled 'Age Of Brutality' in 1991 before the arrival of the debut album on West Virginia Records in 1993. A further demo, 'Amputated Soul', gained the band a deal with D&S Records.
Original guitarist Dirk was to be replaced by Jens, whilst the bass player's position was eventually filled on a permanent basis by Thimo.
OBSCENITY toured in Europe supporting the likes of CANNIBAL CORPSE, BENEDICTION, DEATH and SINISTER. The band parted ways with D&S Records in January of 1996 to sign with the Morbid label.

Albums:
SUFFOCATED TRUTH, West Virginia WVR 084-57262 (1993)
Forgotten Past / Utter Disgust / Depression / Ruthless Greed / Fatal Porosity / Life Beyond / Age Of Brutality / Corrupted Minds/ Infestical Plague
PERVERSION MANKIND, D&S Records DSRCE 021 (1995)
Realm Of The Dead / Lost Identity / Amputated Souls / Perversion Mankind / Removal Of Poverty / Para-Dies / Embryonic Execution / Genutopia / The Revenge / Mental Death / Prophecy II
THE 3RD CHAPTER, Morbid MR 030 CD (1996)
Intro / Disgrace Over You / Nuclear Holocaust / Sensation Mongering / Disengaged / I'm Your God / Abducted And Gutted / Still Alive / Tarot / Schattenspiele
HUMAN BARBECUE, Morbid MR 039 (1998)
Eaten From Inside / Human Barbecue / Eternal Life / Infanticide / Soulripper / Lycanthropy / Utter Disgust / Dress Of

Skin / Life Beyond / Obscenity / Raining Blood
INTENSE, Morbid (2000)

OBSCURATION (FRANCE)

Albums:
THE FIFTH SEASON, Obscuration (1997)

OBSECRATION (GREECE)
Line-Up: Kostas Dead (vocals), Manolis (guitar), John (guitar), Spiros Ruthren (bass), Alexandros (drums)

Formed in 1991 rooted in the Death Metal acts PARAKMI, MORBID ILLUSION and CURSE. The duo of vocalist Kostas Dead and drummer Jim first forged an alliance in 1989 with the band PARAKMI. This unit would evolve into MORBID ILLUSION with the inclusion of INSANITY bassist Nectarios and guitarist John from NECROMANCY.
In 1990 another name change occurred this time to CURSE as new faces bassist Billy and guitarist Apostolis were welcomed. In 1991 the final name switch came as CURSE became OBSECRATION with Billy switching instruments to bass as Nectarios returned to take over the guitarist's role for the debut demo 'Petrified Remains'. However, the group lost Nectarios in July as he departed to fulfill his national service obligations. In September OBSECRATION plugged the gap by enlisting ex-AVATAR members guitarist Nick and bassist Sotiris for their first gig. Predictably the line-up fractured once again with Billy joining EPIDEMIC and both Nick and Sotiris leaving.
1992 witnessed further changes with the return of Billy and Sotiris as well as new guitarist John for the second demo session 'The Morning Of The Ghoul'. Further live work ensued utilizing the services of erstwhile BLOOD COVERED drummer Angelos to promote the band's first commercial release the 'Oblivious' EP on Molon Lave Records. By March the bass position was temporarily in the care of Spiros from SEPTIC FLESH prior to Leftiris assuming the role.
OBSECRATION cut their full length debut album 'The Inheritors Of Pain', produced by Magus Wampyr Daoloth of NECROMANTIA, for the Dutch Hammerheart label with unsurprisingly a revised line-up comprising Kostas Dead, guitarists Spiros N. and Billy, bassist

Spiros Ruthren and drummer Paul OBSECRATION's line-up ebbed and flowed thereafter with John rejoining replacing Spiros N. before he and brother Paul bailed out. By 2000 former LEPROSY members guitarist Manolis and drummer Alexandros were involved. Kostas would become a founder member of TERRA TENEBRAE but would depart prior to recording of their 'Subconscious' album.

Singles/EPs:
Oblivious, Molon Lave (1993)

Albums:
THE INHERITORS OF PAIN, Hammerheart (1995)
The Inheritors Of Pain Part I / Horror In The Gothic Genie's Game / For The King Of This World / … The Usurper From Darkness / Suffering Under The Unnamable Shade / The Serenity Of The Crystal Sentiments / Offsprings Of The Black Dimensions / The Inheritors Of Pain Part II
OCEANUM OBLIVIONE, Invasion INV015 (2000)

OBTAINED ENSLAVEMENT
(NORWAY)
Line-Up: Pest (vocals / bass), Døden (guitar), Heks (guitar), Torquemada (drums)

A Black Metal band with Grindcore influences founded during 1989. OBTAINED ENSLAVEMENT started life as a trio of vocalist Pest (Thomas Kronenes), guitarist Døden (Ove Saebo) and drummer Torquemada. Three years later second guitarist Heks (Heine Salbu) was added for the demo 'Out Of The Crypts'.
OBTAINED ENSLAVEMENT issued their debut 1994 album 'Centuries Of Sorrow' on Likstøy Music. The record was picked up by the Effigy label the following year for wider distribution. During the interim between albums Pest would session for the notorious Black Metal institution GORGOROTH appearing on the 1996 album 'Antichrist True Norwegian Black Metal'.
Sophomore effort 'Witchcraft' saw the inclusion of bassist Tortur although his position was short-lived. T. Reaper of MALIGNENT ETERNAL and GORGOROTH took the place for the band's Napalm Records debut 'Soulblight'. Keyboards were handled by

Morrigan of AETURNUS.

Albums
CENTURIES OF SORROW, Effigy EFFI
002 (1995)
Desecration Of My Soul / As I Slowly
Fade / Dark Holiness / Symbolic /
Unblessed / Haze Of Knowledge /
Centuries Of Sorrow / Pure... Sorrow
WITCHCRAFT, Wounded Love WLR 013
(1997)
Mono: Prelude Funebre / Di: Velts Of
Wintersorrow / Tri: From Times In
Kingdoms / Tetra: Witchcraft / Penta:
Warlock / Hexa: Torned Winds From A
Past Star / Hepta: Carnal Lust / Octa:
The Seven Witches / Nona: O'Noccurne
SOULBLIGHT, Napalm (1998)
A Black Odyssey / The Dark Night Of
The Souls / Soulblight / Nightbreed /
Voice From A Starless Domain / The
Goddess' Lake / Charge
**THE SHEPHERD AND THE HOUNDS
OF HELL**, Napalm (2000)
Scrolls Of The Shadowland / Ride The
Whore / Lucifer's Lament / Millenium
Beast (Awaiting The Feast) / Stepping
Over Angels / The Shepherd And The
Hounds Of Hell / Utopia Obtained

OCTOBER TIDE (SWEDEN)

Line-Up: Jonas Renske (vocals / drums),
Fredrik Norrman (guitar / bass)

OCTOBER TIDE are the outfit created by
KATATONIA's vocalist Jonas Renske,
also known under his stage name of 'Lord
Seth'.
Renske involved himself in the BLOOD
BATH Black Metal supergroup in 2000
alongside his KATATONIA band mate
guitarist Blackheim, OPETH's Mikael
Akerfeldt and EDGE OF SANITY's Dan
Swanö.
OCTOBER TIDE's 1999 album 'Grey
Dawn' found Renske in collaboration with
Morten of A CANOUROUS QUINTET.

Albums:
RAIN WITHOUT END, Vic VIC003 (1997)
12 Days Of Rain / Ephemeral / All Painted
Cold / Sightless / Losing Tomorrow / Blue
Gallery / Infinite Submission
GREY DAWN, Avantgarde (1999)
Grey Dawn / October Insight /
Sweetness Dies / Heart Of The Dead /
Floating / Lost In The Dark - And The
Gone / Into Deep Sleep / Dear Sun

ODIOUS (GERMANY)

Line-Up: Markus Föckler (vocals),
Dietmar Kalmann (guitar), Andreas
Weiss (guitar), Christian Storck (bass),
Thorsten Reichert (drums)

Formed in Landstuhl during 1990, Death
Metal band ODIOUS released their first
demo in 1993 and followed it up in 1995
with a demo CD

Singles/EPs:
28000 Wishes / Falling Apart / Only
Sometimes / Too Proud To Forgive,
Odious (1995) ('Fallen Apart' EP)

OFFENSE (SPAIN)

Line-Up: Mariano (vocals / bass), Javi
(guitar), Loren (guitar), Wensho (drums)

Spanish Death / Doom band OFFENSE
were formed in 1990 by the trio of Javi,
Loren and Wensho. They were soon
joined by bassist Fede and vocalist
Murgui and this line-up recorded the
demos 'Basic' and 'The Cry'. 'Basic' went
on to sell more than 1,200 copies.
Tragically, Fede perished in a cycling
accident on the 14th December 1990 and
this event not only prevented OFFENSE
from rehearsing but led to the departure
of Murgui.
Once over the grief of losing their
bandmate OFFENSE recruited vocalist /
bassist Mariano and the group later
signed to Abstract Emotions and issued
the 7" 'Shining Down' EP in 1995.
An album was to follow

Singles/EPs:
Shining Down EP, Abstract Emotions
(1995)

Albums:
ASIDE, Abstract Emotions AE 003 (1995)
Seating On Distress / Why? / The Defect
/ Law Of Life / Shining Down / Aside /
Basic

OLD GRANDAD

(San Francisco, CA, USA)
Line-Up: Erik Moggridge (vocals / guitar),
Max Barnett (bass), Will Carroll (drums)

A noted Stoner infused Death Metal band
founded by erstwhile EPIDEMIC guitarist
Erik Moggridge, bass player Max Barnett
and former BROOD, WARFARE D.C. and
MACHINE HEAD drummer Will Carroll.
OLD GRANDAD folded in 2000.

Albums:
VOL. 666, Hectic (1997)
Blatant Drug Song / Urine Angel / No
Hell To Fear / Emerald City / Feeling
Fine / Medieval Weaponry Control & You
/ Forty Two / Cheech And Chong I /
Don't Call Me A Deadhead / 114 / Sick
Sense / Bovine / Crawl All The Way /
Cheech And Chong II
OGD EP / SAN FRAN666CO
BOOTLEG, Hectic (1998)
I'm Frying On Acid / Fear / All Calls In
Daze / The Other Red Meat / The Highs
That Bind / Blatant Drug Song (Live) /
Medieval Weaponry Control & You (Live)
/ Urine Angel (Live) / Bovine (Live) / No
Hell To Fear (Live) / Don't Call Me A
Deadhead (Live)
THE LAST UPPER, MIA Records (1999)
This One's For The Children / Your Guts
On Rye / Rise / Brakedown / 6th Street
Paradise / Woman Hurt In Bizarre
Exorcism / Animuircus / Relatively Far
From The Equator / The Long Burn /
Bleed At The Knees / Daily City
Crackhouse / Zero Sky

OLEMUS (AUSTRIA)
Line-Up: Robert Bognar (vocals / guitar),
Eugen Baumann (guitar), Roland Kössler
(drums)

A hybrid of Death Metal and Symphonic
sounds OLEMUS from Linz was founded
in 1993 with the average age of the band
being an incredible 14 years old.
OLEMUS started out as a trio of frontman
Robert Bogner, guitarist Simon Öller and
drummer Roland 'Kanzla' Kössler. Within
two years OLEMUS had issued their
inaugural demo 'Learning To Die'
capitalizing on this with a further effort
entitled 'Blind'.
The band cut their first album 'Bitter
Tears' for the N.S.M. concern and would
release the 'Psycho-Path' EP shortly after
as Eugen Baumann was added on guitar.
Female vocals were supplied courtesy of
Tanja Hofer and Simone Hauzender.

Singles/EPs:
Soul Perish / Psycho Path / Alone / Cold,
(1998) ('Psycho-Path' EP)

Albums:
BITTER TEARS, N.S.M. (1997)
Innocent And Wretched / Bitter Tears /
Dreaming / Forever Gone / Scarred For
Life / Scourge Of Seclusion / Slave Of
Arrogance / Bastards / Ole-Mus
FOREVER, (2000)

PASSION FALL, CCP 100215-2 (2001)

ON THORNS I LAY (GREECE)
Line-Up: Steven (vocals), Chris (guitar /
keyboards), Jim (bass), Fotis (drums)

Previously known as PHLEBOTOMY
(and originally a trio with Steven handling
drums as well as lead vocals) during this
time they released the demo 'Beyond The
Chaos' in March 1992 and the limited
edition EP 'Dawn Of Grief'.
The band adopted the new title of ON
THORNS I LAY at the same time they
added drummer Fotis in February 1992.
And, in early 1994, the group recorded
the 'Voluptuous' demo, inciting interest
from Holy Records. A deal would follow.
The sophomore effort 'Orama' was a
concept album based on the legend of
Atlantis.

Albums:
SOUNDS OF BEAUTIFUL
EXPERIENCE, Holy HOLY12CD (1995)
Voluptuous Simplicity Of The Line / All Is
Silent / A Sparrow Dances / Cleopatra /
A Dreamer Can Touch The Sky / Rainy
Days / Sunrise Of A New Age / One
Thousand Times / TAXIDI NOSTALGIAS
ORAMA, Holy HOLY29CD (1997)
Atlantis I / The Songs Of The Sea /
Oceans / In Heaven's Island / Atlantis II /
Atlantis III / If I Could Fly / Aura / The
Blue Dream
CRYSTAL TEARS, Holy (1999)
Crystal Tears / My Angel / Obsession /
Crystal Tears II / Ophelia / Eden / Enigma
/ Midnight Falling / All Is Silent / Feelings
FUTURE NARCOTIC, Holy (2000)
Infinity / Future Narcotic / The Threat Of
Seduction / Feel Her Lust / Love Can Be
A Wave / Ethereal Blue / Heaven's
Passenger / Desire / Back To That
Enigma / The K Song

OPETH (SWEDEN)
Line-Up: Mikael Åkerfelt (vocals / guitar),
Peter Lindgren (guitar), Martin Mendez
(bass), Martin Lopez (drums)

Another in the long list of albums
produced by EDGE OF SANITY's Dan
Swanö. Vocalist / guitarist Mikael Åkerfelt
and drummer Anders Nordin are ex-
ERUPTION. Starting life influenced by
the rawer Black Thrash acts, OPETH
have steadily matured into more
melancholic landscapes with each
successive release.
The late 80's act ERUPTION had

featured Åkerfeldt, Nordin, guitarist Nick Döring and bassist Stephan Claesberg. When singer David Isberg's previous band OPET had floundered when the main mass of members split off to create CROWLEY, the two parties combined to reforge the act subtly retitled OPETH. Second guitarist Andreas Dimeo was recruited for OPETH's debut gig supporting THERION. However, shortly after both Dimeo and Döring decamped quickly after. The former CRIMSON CAT duo of Kim Pettersson and Johan De Farfalla plugged the gap for a second show but the pair would also drift off and more significantly Isberg left for pastures new in LIERS IN WAIT.

Åkerfeldt took the lead vocal role as he rebuilt the band with Nordin and bassist Stephan Guteklint. Securing a deal with the British Candlelight Records label the debut album 'Orchid' was cut using previous member De Farfalla on session bass. Gigs followed including a British show alongside VED BUENS ENDE, HECATE ENTHRONED and IMPALED NAZARENE.

OPETH's second album was promoted with a support slot to MORBID ANGEL in the UK and to CRADLE OF FILTH in Europe. Following these dates both Nordin and De Farfalla made their exit Akerfeldt teamed up with Swanö, KATATONIA's Blackheim and Jonas Renske to create side project BLOOD BATH in 2000.

Albums:
ORCHID, Candlelight CANDLE 010CD (1995)
In Mist She Was Standing / Under The Weeping Moon / Silhouette / Forest Of October / The Twilight Is My Robe / Requiem / The Apostle In Triumph
MORNING RISE, Candlelight CANDLE 015 (1996)
Advert / The Night And The Silent Winter / Nectar / Black Rose Immortal / To Bid You Farewell
MY ARMS, YOUR HEARSE, Candlelight CANDLE 025CD (1998)
Prologue / April Ethereal / When / Madrigal / The Amen Corner / Demon Of The Fall / Credence / Karma / Epilogue
STILL LIFE, Peaceville (1999)
The Moon / Godhands Lament / Benighted / Moonlapse Vertigo / Face Of Melinda / Serenity Painted Death / White Cluster
BLACKWATER PARK, Peaceville (2001)
The Leper Affinity / Bleak / Harvest / The Drapery Falls / Dirge For November /

Funeral Portrait / Patterns In The Sky / Blackwater Park

OPPRESSOR (CZECH REPUBLIC)
Line-Up: Tim King (vocals / bass / keyboards), Adam Zadel (guitar), Jim Stopper (guitar), Tom Schofield (drums)

A Death Metal act from the Czech Republic.

Albums:
AGONY, Die Hard RRS 958 (1996)
Gone / Suffersystem / In Exile / Passage / Valley Of Thorns / Redefine / Sea Of Tears / I Am Darkness / Carnal Voyage

OPPROBRIUM
(New Orleans, LA, USA)
Line-Up: Francis M. Howard (guitar), Luiz Carlos (guitar), Moyses M. Howard (drums)

New Orleans Death Metal band OPPROBRIUM, led by the Howard brothers Francis and Moyses, were formerly known as INCUBUS releasing two albums 'Serpent Temptation' and 'Beyond The Unknown'. The name switch was forced onto the band due to the presence of the Californian act of the same name.
The 2000 album 'Discerning Forces' was recorded in Rio De Janeiro and produced by Harris Johns.

Albums:
DISCERNING FORCES, Nuclear Blast (2000)
Digitrap / Discerning Forces / Ancient Rebellion / Dark Entanglement / Drowning / Escapism / Merciless Torture / Moments Of Despair / Blood Conflict / Awakening To The Filth

OPTHALAMIA (SWEDEN)
Line-Up: Legion (vocals), It (guitar), Night (bass), Winter (drums)

Formed by It (real name Tony Särkää) in 1989 under the name of LEVIATHAN, It was later to create ABRUPTUM and VONDUR.
OPTHALAMIA's debut album had guest lead vocals from Shadow, in reality DISSECTION vocalist Jon Nödtveidt. Bass was supplied by Mourning (real name Robert Ivarsson).
OPTHALAMIA drummer Winter (real name Benny Larsson) is also a member of EDGE OF SANITY and PAN-THY-

MONIUM. Bassist Night (real name Emil Nödtveidt) now plays with SWORDMASTER.

OPTHALAMIA vocalist All - who also fronts VONDUR - replaced Legion (real name Erik Hagstedt) who quit to front MARDUK.

With the apparent disappearance of It and the jailing for murder of Shadow it seemed OPTHALAMIA's career was over but the band re-emerged in 1998 for the 'Dominion' album, a concept affair based on Shakespeare's 'Macbeth'!

The other 1998 release 'A Long Journey' is in fact a re-recording of the debut album with extra tracks including a VENOM cover.

Albums:
A JOURNEY IN DARKNESS,
Avantgarde AV003 (1994)
A Cry From The Halls Of Blood - Empire Of Lost Dreams / Enter The Darkest Thoughts Of The Chosen - Agonys Silent Paradise / Journey In Darkness - Entering The Forest / Shores Of Kaa-Ta-Nu - The Eternal Walk Pt II / A Lonely Soul - Hymn To A Dream / Little Child Of Light - Degradation Of Holyness / Castle Of No Repair - Lies From A Blackened Heart / This Is The Pain Called Sorrow - To The Memory Of Me / I Summon Thee Oh Father - Death Embrace Me
VIA DOLOROSA, Avantgarde AV013 (1995)
Intro - Under Ophthalamian Skies / To The Benighted / Black As Sin, Pale As Death / Autumn Whispers / After A Releasing Death / Castle Of No Repair (Part II) / Slowly Passing The Frostlands / A Winterlands Tear / Via Dolorosa / My Springnights Sacrifice / Ophthalamia / The Eternal Walk (Part III) / Nightfall Of Mother Earth / Summer Distress / Outro - Message To Those After Me / Death Embrace Me (Part II) / A Lonely Ceremony / The Eternal Walk / Deathcrush
TO ELISHA, Necropolis NR013 (1997)
A Cry From The Halls Of Blood - Empire Of Lost Dreams (1991 demo) / A Lonely Ceremony - The Eternal Walk (1990 rehearsal) / Journey In Darkness - Entering The Forest (Rehearsal) / Castle Of No Repair - From A Blackened Heart (1991 demo) / Shores Of Kaa Tu Nu - The Eternal Walk Part II (1991 demo) / Nightfall Of Mother Earth - Summer Distress (1994 rehearsal) / Enter The Darkest Thoughts Of The Chosen - Agony's Silent Paradise (1992 version) / Deathcrush (Rehearsal) / Sacxrifice

(Rehearsal) / I Summon Thee Father - Death Embrace Me (1991 demo)
DOMINION, No Fashion NFR024 (1998)
A LONG JOURNEY, Necropolis (1998)

ORDER FROM CHAOS (USA)
Line-Up: Pete Helmkamp (vocals / bass), Chuck Keller (guitar)

ORDER FROM CHAOS debuted in 1988 with the 'Inhumanities' and 'Crushed Infamy' demos. Following the debut single 'Will To Power' on the Putrefaction label a further demo 'Alienus Sum' was issued.

The 1994 'Plateau Of Invincibility' album included two VENOM cover versions.

Chuck Keller founded VULPECULA whilst Pete Helmkamp created ANGEL CORPSE.

Singles/EPs:
Will To Power, Putrefaction (1990) (7" single)
Jericho Trumpet, Gestapo (1994) (7" single)
Into Distant Fears (Live), Eternal Darkness (1994) (7" single)
Pain Lengthens Time (Live), (1994) (7" single)
B / Nucteremon / Dead Of The Night - Senile Decay / Stillbirth Machine (Live) / Plateau Of Invincibility (Live), Shivadarshana (1994) ('Plateau Of Invincibility' EP)
The Edge Of Forever / Webs Of Perdition / Imperium / De Stella Nova, Ground Zero (1996) ('And I Saw Eternity' EP)

Albums:
STILLBIRTH MACHINE, (1991)
The Edge Forever / Power Elite / Iconoclasm Conquest / Forsake Me This Mortal Coil / Stillbirth Machine / Blood And Thunder / As The Body Falls Away
DAWNBRINGER, Shivadarshana (1994)
STILLBIRTH MACHINE / CRUSHED INFAMY, Osmose Productions (1998)
AN ENDING IN FIRE, Osmose Productions (1998)
Dawn Bringer Invictus / Tenebrae / The Sign Draconis / Plateau Of Invincibility / The Angry Red Planet / There Lies Your Lord, Father Of Victories / Nucleosynthesis / De Stella Nova / An Ending In Fire

ORIGIN (USA)
Line-Up: Mark Manning (vocals), Paul Ryan (guitar), Jeremy Turner (guitar),

Clint Appelhanz (bass), John Longstreth (drums)

Founded in the summer of 1997 by guitarists Paul Ryan and Jeremy Taylor later adding erstwhile guitarist Clint Appelhanz on bass, Mark Manning on vocals and drummer George Fluke.
Opened for SUFFOCATION in early 1998 prior to recording the inaugural demo 'A Coming Into Existence'. Reaction to this release led to ORIGIN's inclusion as opening act on the monolithic 'Death Across America' nationwide tour with NILE, GORGUTS, CRYPTOPSY and OPPRESSOR.
Line-up ructions led to the inclusion of former ANGELCORPSE drummer John Longstreth in February of 1999. Appelhanz too would be replaced, this time by CEPHALIC CARNAGE veteran Doug Williams.
Touring to break in the new unit would lead to a deal with Death Metal connoisseurs Relapse Records. However, in early 2001 Manning departed to be replaced by former ILL OMEN man Jim Lee.

ORPHANAGE (HOLLAND)
Line-Up: Lex Vogelaar (vocals / guitar), Rosan Van Der Aa (vocals), George Oosthoek (vocals), Eric Hoogendoorn (bass), Guus Eikens (keyboards), Erwin Poldermann (drums)

Dutch outfit ORPHANAGE's driving force is guitarist/vocalist Lex Vogelaaar - a former member of TARGET - and he initially recorded a trial demo with keyboard player Guus Eikens titled 'Morph', which led to the formation of ORPHANAGE.
This initial recording also utilized the services of CELESTIAL SEASON vocalists Jason Kohnen and Stefan Ruiters, together with PARALYSIS drummer Stephan Van Haestregt.
As the project evolved into a permanent band ORPHANAGE added bassist Eric Hoogendoorn and vocalist Martine Van Loon, although at the time she was still fronting THE GATHERING. In 1994 this line-up recorded the demo 'Druid', a tape that also featured the talents of THE GATHERING keyboardist Frank Boeijen.
Enrolling yet another vocalist in George Oosthek, ORPHANAGE contributed two tracks to the DFSA Records compilation album 'Paradise Of The Underground' prior to the departure of Van Haestregt.
A temporary replacement was found in

GOREFEST's Ed Warby.
Drummer Erwin Polderman was recruited in time for the debut album 'Oblivion'. Vocalist Rosan Van Der Aa was eventually replaced by Martine Van Loon. Following the groundbreaking 1996 album 'By Time Alone' (a heady mix of Metal and Gregorian choirs) ORPHANAGE issued the 'At The Mountains Of Madness' EP co-produced by former VENGEANCE man Oscar Holleman. ORPHANAGE also put in a showing at the Dynamo festival in 1997.
In 1996 both Hoogendoorn and Poldermann founded a side project SILICON HEAD together with PLEURISY guitarist Axel Becker. SILICON HEAD's debut album 'Bash' was produced by Vogelaar.

Singles/EPs:
At The Mountains Of Madness (Video mix) / Five Crystals (Oscar mix) / The Crumbling Of My Denial (Live) / Sea Of Dreams (Live), Displeased DSFA 1008 (1997)

Albums:
OBLIVION, Displeased DSFA 1001 (1995)
Chameleon / Weltschmerz / The Case Of Charles Dexter Ward / In The Garden Of Eden / Journey Into The Unknown / Druid / Veils of Blood / Sea Of Dreams / The Collector / Victim Of Fear
BY TIME ALONE, Displeased DSFA 1004 P (1996)
At The Mountains Of Madness / Five Crystals / The Dark Side / Deceiver / Cliffs Of Moher / By Time Alone / Ancient Rhymes / Odyssey / Requiem / Leafless / Deliverance
INSIDE, Nuclear Blast NB 510-2 (2000)
Grip / Twisted Games / Inside / The Stain / Pain / Deal With The Real / Behold / Weakness Of Flesh / Kick / Drag You Down / From The Cradle To The Grave

OSSUARY INSANE
(Eagan, MN, USA)
Line-Up: Cantor Celebrant (vocals / guitar / bass), Der Prophet (guitar), Das Rage (drums)

Albums:
DEMONIZE THE FLESH, Galdre (1998)
Fallen To The Pits / Inverted In Darkness / Summoned To Death / Imprecari / The Olde Ragged Cross / Von Pagen Blut / Blaspheme Unto Rebirth / Excruciate With Flames / From Beneath The Blood

Remix / Summoned To Death Remix /
Blaspheme Unto Rebirth Remix

OVERDOSE (BRAZIL)
Line-Up: B.Z. (vocals), Sergio Cichovicz
(guitar), Claudio David (guitar), Eddie
Weber (bass), Andre Marcio (drums)

Bela Horizonte's OVERDOSE
internationally are known for sharing their
debut album 'Seculo XX' with Brazil's
biggest Rock export SEPULTURA.
Following this OVERDOSE secured a
placing on the 'Metal Massacre 9'
compilation album.
A string of Brazilian release albums
followed prior to 1994's 'Progress Of
Decadence' being released in America on
Fierce Recordings and Europe on Music
For Nations. OVERDOSE spent the year
touring America on a package bill with
SKREW and SPUD MONSTERS prior to
European dates including the Dynamo
festival.
OVERDOSE were back in America
touring with CROWBAR to promote
1996's 'Scars'. The band's 1993 'Circus
Of Death' album was issued in America
during 1999 by Pavement Records.

Albums:
SECULO XX, Cogumelo (1985) (Slip LP
with SEPULTURA)
CONSCIENCE, Cogumelo (1987)
YOU'RE REALLY BIG, Cogumelo (1989)
ADDICTED TO REALITY, Cogumelo
(1991)
CIRCUS OF DEATH, Cogumelo (1993)
The Zombie Factory / Children Of War /
Dead Clouds / Profit / The Healer /
Violence / A Good Day To Die /
Powerwish / Beyond My Bad Dreams
PROGRESS OF DECADENCE, Under
One Flag CDFLAG 83 (1994)
Rio, Samba E Porrada No Morra / Street
Law / Straight To The Point / Progress
Of Decadence / Capitalist Way / Deep In
Your Mind / Noise From Brazil / Al
Uquisarrera / Farela / No Truce / Faithful
Death / Stupid Generation / Zombie
Factory
SCARS, Music For Nations CDMFN 213
(1996)
The Front / My Rage / Manipulated
Reality / How To Pray / Scars / Still
Primitive / Just Another Day / School /
Last Words / Postcard From Hell / Who's
Guilty??? / Out Of Control - A Fairy Tale
/ Nu Dos Otro E Refresco

OVERFLASH (SWEDEN)
Line-Up: Devo (vocals / guitar / bass),
Dan Swanö (drums)

A Death Metal project from CARDINAL
SIN's Magnus 'Devo' Andersson (also a
former member of MARDUK), the album
involved the ever busy EDGE OF
SANITY vocalist Dan Swanö filling a
drumming role.

Albums:
THRESHOLD TO REALITY, MNW
ZONE MNWCD 257 (1993)
Total Devastation / Enter Life Between /
Land Beyond / Future Warrior / Nuclear
Winter / Life Converter / Infinity (Journey
I) / Strange Environment (Journey II) /
The Evolution / Threshold To Reality

OXIPLEGATZ (SWEDEN)

A one man undertaking by ex-AT THE
GATES man Alf Svensson, contributing
vocalists to the project included Uno
Bjurling (vocalist with Svensson's Punk
outfit ORAL), Håkan Bjurgvist and Sara
Svensson.
Alf Svensson had originally formed
GROTESQUE with Tomas Lindberg,
Kristian Wahlin and Thomas Eriksson.
The quartet released an EP entitled
'Incantation' before splitting due to
personal differences.
While Wahlin proceeded to form LIERS
IN WAIT, Svensson and Lindberg put AT
THE GATES together, although Alf
Svensson would ultimately choose to
leave the group in order to pursue his
other musical avenues.
The 1997 release, 'Worlds And Worlds',
includes a track entitled 'Graveyard
Dream' that was originally written in 1990
for GROTESQUE.

Albums:
FAIRYTALES, Fairytale FTCD 001
(1995)
Starseed / Fairytale / Northern Stars /
His Time Has Come / I See It Now… /
Dark Millenium (There Shall Never Be
Another Dawn) / Conclusion / Lust For
Life / Numb / Departure / Vision / Adrift /
Oh No…
WORLDS AND WORLDS, Adipocere
FTCD003 (1997)
Battle Of Species / First Contact -
Conflict / Aftermath / Quest / Graveyard
Dream / Usurpers / The End Is Nigh /
Abandon Earth / Journey
SIDEREAL JOURNEY, (1999)

A Black Hole Is Swallowing The Sun /
They Learned Of Its Existence / For
Persistence / Bringer Of Obliteration /
Into Nowhere / For Persistence / So It's
Our Final Hour / The Light From The
Perishing Sun / Ahead - The Universe! /
No Longer Will we Be The Meek Ones /
How Could We Ever Know / Head For
That Star / As One Surveys This Ocean /
The Londrive A Silent Vibration / Several
Planet In Orbit / Enemies!? / Once More
Proven- We Are Not Alone / Lightspeed
Flung Into Hyperspace / No Clue To
Where This Jump Is Taking Them /
Breathless / Turning Up The Power,
Accelerating Again / This Time Passage
Was Violent / Rings, Spread Like
Rippled Water / They Stare Unblinking /
Eternal Night / How Many Worlds /
These Beings Failed And Perished /
Ahead Once More / This Journey Has
Taken Us / The Moon Was Land In Orbit
/ Can This Be What We Hore For /
Teraform - Alter The Environment / And
So One Day The Sleepers Awaken

PAGANIZER (SWEDEN)

PAGANIZER's demo 'Stormfire' would later be pressed onto CD as a shared album with Singapore act ABATTOIR. Vocalist / guitarist Rogga would aid BLODSRIT on drums.
PAGANIZER evolved into CARVE.

Albums:
STORMFIRE, (199-) (Split album with ABBATOIR)
DEADBANGER, Psychic Scream (1999)
Branded By Evil / The Mask Of Evil / Deadbanger / Heads Of The Hydra / Storms To Come / Time To Burn / Sinners Burn / Into The Catacombs / Phantoms / Metal Crusade
STILLBORN REVELATIONS, Psychic Scream (2001)

PAGAN RITES (SWEDEN)

Line-Up: Unholy Pope (vocals), Fiend (guitar), Black Agony (guitar), Lord Of The Deeps (bass), Sexual Goatlicker (drums).

Vocalist 'Unholy Pope' (real name Thomas Karlsson and an ex-AUTOPSY TORMENT member) and bassist 'Black Agony' (real name Adrian Letelier) joined TRISTITIA after the single release.
PAGAN RITES were still a going concern in 2000 but surviving through constant line up ructions. The band, now fronted by Karlsson now billing himself Devil Lee Rot, pulled in guitarist Angerboder of THE ANCIENTS REBIRTH and NIFELHEIM bassist Tyrant.
Drummer Sexual Goatlicker would decamp with haste necessitating the recruitment of another NIFELHEIM man Hellbutcher.

Singles/EPs:
Flames Of The Third Antichrist / Sodomy In Heaven, Stemra STEMA002 (1993)

Albums:
PAGAN RITES, Warmaster WAR008 (1996)
Frost / Lord Of Fire / Crucified In Flames / Pagan Rites / Unholy Ancient War / Metal King / Images Of The Moon / Return To The Lake Of Fire / Hail Victory! / Heathen Land / Domain Of The Frozen Souls / Land Beyond Our Dreams / Pagan Metal / Winter Grief / Once Upon A Time / Under The Church / Blood Of My Enemies

PAIN (SWEDEN)
Line-Up: Peter Tägtgren

The solo project from HYPOCRISY vocalist / guitarist Peter Tägtgren, PAIN's album is based more along electronic Metal sounds than straight ahead Rock. Nevertheless, Tägtgren produced, engineered and composed the material all on his own.

Albums:
PAIN, Nuclear Blast NB 235-2 (1996)
On Your Knees (Again) / Rope Around My Neck / Learn How To Die / Don't Let Me Down / Breathe / Greed / Choke On Your Lies / The Last Drops Of My Life
REBIRTH, Stockholm 542 139-2 (1999)
Supersonic Bitch / End Of The Line / Breathing In, Breathing Out / Delusions / Suicide Machine / Parallel To Ecstasy / On And On / 12:42 / Crashed / Dark Fields Of Pain / She Whipped / End Of The Line (Uncut Video)

PAINKILLER (UK)
Line-Up: Bill Laswell (bass), Mick Harris (drums), John Zorn (Saxophone)

A Side project of NAPALM DEATH drummer Mick Harris, PAINKILLER's album boasts guest appearances from Justin Broadrick and C.C. Green of GODFLESH.

Albums:
BURIED SECRETS, Earache (1992)
Tortured Souls / One Sided Pessary / Trailmarker / Blackhole Dub / Buried Secrets / The Ladder / Executioner / Black Chamber / Skinned / The Toll

PANDEMIA (CZECH REPUBLIC)
Line-Up: Michal (vocals), Alex (guitar), Jarda (bass), Tom (drums)

Death Metal act created in 1995 by erstwhile SUFFERING personnel vocalist Matthew, guitarist Alex and bass player Jarda. The band's original drummer was ejected in favour of incomer Pavel as the group title evolved into PANDEMIA. The 1995 'Dust On The Eyes' demo gave an indicator of what was to come but Matthew would decamp in favour of new frontman Michal after these recordings. A second cassette 'Dance In Vicious Circle' was issued in January of 1997 leading to a domestic tour alongside KRABATHOR and Polish veterans VADER. With the close of these gigs new drummer Tom was enrolled as PANDEMIA's second demo scored a commercial release courtesy of Anti Nazi Productions. The year ultimately ended on a high note as PANDEMIA guested for DIMMU BORGIR, KRABATHOR, KRISIUN and KREATOR in Prague.

1998 witnessed a valuable high profile support to DEATH in Prague. The second demo proved its staying power by gaining yet another re-release, this time by Lithuanian label Soundless Records as a split collaboration with South Africans GROINCHURN. As 1998 closed PANDEMIA cut new tracks in the studio for a third demo and also spread the word branching out with live gigs in continental Europe.

The third demo would also find a commercial release as Greek label Adenon Productions put the session out with extra tracks, one of which was a DEATH cover version 'Infernal Death'. American concern Lost Disciple Records would take the band up for the debut album 'Spreading The Message'. Promoting the album PANDEMIA put in performances in Poland, Belgium, Spain and Portugal. Gigs into 2000 saw a full blown European tour billed in alliance with REBAELLIUN, VADER, FLESHCRAWL and VITAL REMAINS.

In early 2001 drummer Marthus split away from the band and former incumbent Pavel re-took the position.

Albums:
SPREADING THE MESSAGE, Lost Disciple (1999)
Intro / Stiffness / Majestic Suffering / Free Strokes / Intro / The Tones Are Weaker / Slavemind / Leaves In The Storm / Spreading The Message / Presentiment Of The Souls / Created Again / Outro

PAN.THY.MONIUM (SWEDEN)
Line-Up: Derelict (vocals), Aag (guitar), Mourning (guitar), Day Dissyraah (bass), Winter (drums)

PAN.THY.MONIUM is one of many project ventures pursued by EDGE OF SANITY vocalist Dan Swanö. With PAN.THY.MONIUM Swanö played guitar under the disguise of 'Aag'. EDGE OF SANITY drummer Benny Larsson also contributed, going under the pseudonym of 'Winter' (Larsson drums for OPTHALMIA under the same guise), whilst vocalist 'Derelict' is in reality DARKIFIED frontman Robert Karlsson.

During 1997 guitarist Mourning left to join ASHES, appearing on their debut 'Death Has Made It's Call' album the same year. Ironically, Robert Karlsson later became a permanent frontman for EDGE OF SANITY for their 'Cryptic' album, ousting Swanö.

Singles/EPs:
The Battle Of Geeheeb / Thee-Pherenth / Behrial / In Remembrance, Relapse CD 6936-2 (1993) ('Khaoohs And Kon-Fus-Ion' EP)
I / II / III / Vvoiiccheeces / IV, Avantgarde AV008 (1994) ('Dream II' EP)

Albums:
DAWN OF DREAMS, Osmose Productions OPCD006 (1992)
KHAOOHS, Osmose Productions OPCD014 (1993)
I Manens Sken Dog En Skugga / Under Ytan / Jag & Vem / Lava / Lömska Försat / I Vindens Väld / Klieveage / Ekkhoeece III / Khaoohs I / Utsikt / Khaoohs II

PANTOKRATUR (GERMANY)
Line-Up: Eddy Kloß (vocals / bass), Hansi Makowski (guitar), Chreddy Riepert (guitar), Karin Groß (keyboards), Arthur Gramsch (drums)

A Gothic Death Metal band with a great deal of Thrash influence and a penchant for abstract philosophy. The band was created in 1989, a demo 'Faces Of Fate' following in 1991. Line up changes, including the recruitment of Karin Groß on keyboards, ensued upfront of the 'Act' EP.

Singles/EPs:
Trip To The Other Side / Act / Sarcastic Lies / Flight Of Life, Pantokratur (1993) ('Act' EP)

PANZERCHRIST (DENMARK)
Line-Up: Lasse Hoile (vocals), Jes Christiansen (guitar), Finn Henriksen (guitar), Nikolaj Brink (bass), Michael Enevoldsen (drums)

A brutal Death Metal / Grindcore quintet from Aarhus. PANZERCHRIST include ex-ILLDISPOSED drummer Michael Enevoldsen in the line-up. Later line-ups had female bassist Karina Bundgaard taking the place of Nikolaj Brink. The band name was inspired by the DARKTHRONE album 'Panzerfaust'.

A six track 1995 demo led to a record

deal. Guitarist Jens Christensen was added to the group prior to recording of the '6 Seconds To Kill' album. However, the band would split with only Enevoldsen and frontman Lasse Hoile surviving. New recruits for the 'Outpost Fort Europa' record were guitarists Rasmus Nørland and Kim Jensen and bassist Karin B. Nielsen.

ILLDISPOSED man Bo Summer joined the band for 2000's 'Soul Collector'. The album, sung in German, entirely comprised songs devoted to second world war German panzers!

An ex-PANZERCHRIST guitarist F. Conquer would go on to the infamous 122 STAB WOUNDS and join Norwegian Black Metal band A WINTER WITHIN during 2000.

Albums:
6 SECONDS TO KILL, Voices Of Wonder SE003CD (1996)
OUTPOST FORT EUROPA, Serious Entertainment (1999)
SOUL COLLECTOR, Mighty Music (2000)
Das Leben Will Gewonnen Sein / Y2Krieg / Der Panzertöter / Panzergrenadier / Schwarz Ist Unser Panzer (Ich Hatt Einen Kamaraden) / Unsere Höchste Ehre / Kalt Wie Der Finsternis / Zum Gegenstoss

PARAMAECIUM (AUSTRALIA)

PARAMAECIUM are a Christian orientated Death Metal band centred upon the talents of vocalist and bassist Andrew Tompkins. The third album 'A Time To Mourn' received worthy reviews internationally and included guitarist Ian Arkley of British act ASHEN MORTALITY and female vocals from Tracy Bourne.

Albums:
EXHUMED OF THE EARTH, (199-)
The Birth And Massacre Of The Innocents / Injudical / The Killers / Untombed / The Voyage Of The Severed / Haemorrhage Of The Hatred / Removal Of The Grave
WITHIN THE ANCIENT FOREST, (199-)
In Exordium / Song Of The Ancient / I Am Not Alive / The Grave, My Soul / Gone Is My Former Resolve / Of My Darkest Hour / Darkness Dies
A TIME TO MOURN, (199-)
A Moment / I'm Not To Blame / My Thoughts / Betrayed Again / Enter In Time / Live For The Day / Ever The Walls / Unceasing

PARRACIDE (GERMANY)
Line-Up: Dirk Widmann (vocals), Patrick Hagmann (guitar), Oliver Irgang (guitar), Mario Bayer (bass), Michael Zeissl (keyboards), Marc Werner (drums)

A German, Gothic Death Metal act.

Albums:
PARRACIDE / EVEREVE, Parracide-Evereve (1995) (Split album with EVEREVE)
Depression / Lost / Absorbed Mind / TB / Endpoint

PARUSIE (SWITZERLAND)
Line-Up: Danny (vocals), Dave (guitar), Marcel (guitar), Rolf (bass), Adi (drums)

The Swiss Death Metal act PARUSIE released their debut album in 1995.

Albums:
...IN SILENCE, Parusie (1995)
Intro / On The Street / Deadline 105 / Pushed Of In Silence / Execution By The Cord / Aggression / Perfect Kill / Psychical Pain / Fatal Mistake

PATHOLOGIST (CZECH REPUBLIC)
Line-Up: Martin 'Cyklo' Cvilink (vocals), Daniel Hary 'Harok' (guitar / bass), Stanislav 'Stanley' Mazur (drums)

PATHOLOGIST are essentially the Czech answer to the better known Grindcore acts obsessed with medical themes.

Albums:
PUTREFACTIVE AND CADAVEROUS ODES ABOUT NECROTICISM, M.A.B. MAB 002 (1992)
Putrefactive And Cadaverous Odes About Necroticism / Malignant Introduction / Open The Dissection Ward / Reek With Suppuration / Cadaveric Metamorphoses / Genital Pathological Perversity / Tumorous Defects And Diseases / Anatomical Necropsy / Progression Of Putrefaction (Part II) / Decomposition Of Corpses / Carcass Dismemberment / Vomitory Corporal Dysfunction / Rotten Outroduction
GRINDING OPUS OF FORENSIC MEDICAL PROBLEMS, M.A.B. MAB 008 (1995)
Paroxysmal Prelude / Cannibalistic Disfigurement / Putrescence / Cadavers In Medical Jurisprudence / Uterogestation To Abortion / Exhumed Dead Body / Infectious Agonizing

Parasitism / Gynaecological Sickness / Secretion Of Ejaculate

PERISHED (NORWAY)

Line-Up: Bathyr (vocals), Ymon (guitar), Ihizahg (guitar), Bruthor (bass), Knut Erik Jensen (keyboards), Jehmod (drums)

Death Metal band PERISHED were created in 1991. Demo tapes 'In Hoc Signo Vinces' and 'Through The Black Mist' followed upfront of a 1996 EP for Solistitium Records.
The debut album 'Kark' sees sessions from Tom Arild Johansen and Knut Erik Jensen.
PERISHED drummer Jehmod would join BLACKTHORN.

Singles/EPs:
Kald Som Aldri For / Gjennom Skjoerende Lys, Solistitium SOL008 (1997)

Albums:
KARK, Solistitium SOL022 (1998)
Introduksjon / Imens Vi Verter… / Stier Til Visdoms Krefter / På Nattens Vintervinger / Iskalde Strømmer / … Og Spjuta Fauk / Befri De Trolske Toner / Renheten Og Gjenkomsien

PESSIMIST (USA)

Line-Up: Ralph Runyan (vocals / bass), Kelly McLachlin (guitar), Bill Hayden (guitar), John Gordon (drums)

Self-styled 'Dungeon Metal' act PESSIMIST trace their history as far back as 1989 when guitarist Kelly McLachlin, a veteran of RESISTANCE, DEATH FORCE and Grindcore act DEMOLITION cut the 'Tunnel Vision' demo. McLachlin had previous to founding PESSIMIST been involved with the Tampa, Florida act CAULDRON which featured a pre-ICED EARTH Matt Barlow.
PESSIMIST laid down a second demo session 'Dark Reality' during 1993 but were assailed by constant line-up changes. Rob Kline was pulled in on second guitar as the promotion release 'Let The Demons Rest' secured a deal with Lost Disciple Records.
PESSIMIST operated toward the close of the millennium with temporary members bass player Eric Little and drummer Dave Roffeld. With this line up the band would contribute a version of 'Phantasm' to a POSSESSED tribute album.
Latter day PESSIMIST recruits include

former FEAR OF GOD men guitarist Bill Hayden and drummer John Gordon with frontman Ralph 'Reaper' Runyan, previously a member of New Jersey's CORRUPTURE.
Dave Brenzeal of TROKKAR and CAULDRON would later take the drum stool.

Singles/EPs:
Absence Of Light, Wild Rags (1995)

Albums:
CULT OF THE INITIATED, Lost Disciple (1998)
The Stench Of Decay / Let The Demons Rest / Cult Of The Initiated / Drunk With The Blood Of The Saints / Dungeonlorde / Pyrosexual / Innocence Defiled / Unholy Union
BLOOD FOR THE GODS, Lost Disciple (1999)
Century Of Lies / Unspeakable Terror / Psychological Autopsy / Demonic Embrace / Mers Rea / Whore Of The Undead / Unborn (Father) / Tunnel Rats / Wretched Of The Earth

PESTILENCE (HOLLAND)

Line-Up: Patrick Mameli (vocals / guitar), Patrick Uterwyck (guitar), Tony Choy (bass), Marco Foddis (drums)

A popular Death Grindcore Metal outfit that have seen considerable album sales in Europe in spite of an ever fluctuating line-up, PESTILENCE were conceived in spring 1986 and were originally a trio of guitarist Randy Meinhard, drummer Marco Foddis and vocalist / guitarist Patrick Mameli. As a three piece PESTILENCE released their first demo 'Dysentry'.
The group later added vocalist / bassist Martin Van Drunen, who assumed vocal duties from Mameli, and cut another demo entitled 'The Pennance'. The debut album, 'Malleus Malificarum', was produced by Kalle Trapp.
In January 1989 PESTILENCE underwent a major line-up reshuffle with Foddis and Meinhard quitting. Meinhard, replaced by former THERIAC man Patrick Uterwijk, joined SACROSANCT and later SUBMISSION. Van Drunen concentrated from this point purely on vocals and the band drafted in the aptly named Bass on bass guitar.
In early 1993 the band recruited new bassist Jereon Thesseling. Vocalist Van Drunen quit following 'Consuming

Impulse' to join ASPHYX, SUBMISSION and later BOLT-THROWER.

For 'Testimony Of The Ancients' PESTILENCE employed the services of Florida's CYNIC bassist Tony Choy and Dutchman Jeroen Thesseling joined PESTILENCE as a permanent bassist in late 1993. The same year saw the release of the band's last album 'Spheres'. Following European dates with CYNIC the band folded.

Albums:
MALLEUS MALIFICARUM, Roadrunner RR95191 (1988)
Malleus Malificarum / Antromorphia / Parricide / Subordinate To The Domination / Extreme Unction / Commandment / Chemotherapy / Bacterial Surgery / Cycle Of Existence / Orculum Infame / Systematic Instruction
CONSUMING IMPULSE, Roadrunner RR 9421 (1989)
Dehydrated / Process Of Suffocation / Suspended Animation / The Trauma / Chronic Infection / Out Of The Body / Echoes Of Death / Deify Thy Master / Proliferous Souls / Reduced To Ashes
TESTIMONY OF THE ANCIENTS, Roadracer RO 9285 (1991)
The Secrecies Of Horror / Bitterness / Twisted Truth / Darkening / Lost Souls / Blood / Land Of Tears / Free Us From Temptation / Prophetic Revelations / Impure / Testimony / Soulless / Presence Of The Dead / Mindwarp / Stigmatized / In Sorrow
SPHERES, Roadrunner RR9081 (1993)
Mind Reflections / Multiple Beings / The Level Of Perception / Aurian Eyes / Soul Search / Personal Energy / Voices From Within / Spheres / Changing Perspective / Phileas / Demise Of Time
MIND REFLECTIONS – THE BEST OF PESTILENCE, Roadrunner RR 8996 (1995)
Out Of The Body / Twisted Truth / The Process Of Suffocation / Parricide / Mind Reflections / Dehydrated / Land Of Tears / Hatred Within / The Secrecies Of Horror / Subordinate To The Domination / Dehydrated (Live) / Chemotherapy (Live) / Presence Of The Dead (Live) / Testimony (Live) / Chronic Infection (Live) / Out Of The Body (Live)

PHLEBOTOMY (GREECE)

PHLEBOTOMY later adopted the new title ON THORNS I LAY, recording an album for Holy Records to follow up the

'Dawn Of Grief' record issued in 1994.

Albums:
DAWN OF GRIEF, Holy (1994)

PHLEBOTOMISED (HOLLAND)
Line-Up: Dennis Geestman (vocals), Tom Palms (guitar), Jordy Middelbosch (guitar), Patrick Van Der Zee (bass), Maarten Post (violin), Ben Quak (keyboards), Lawrence Payne (drums)

A Dutch Death Metal act, PHLEBOTOMIZED debuted with the demo 'Devoted to God' before issuing a pair of EPs and a full blown album in the mid 90's.
The band was originally titled BACTERIAL DISEASE upon their formation in 1989, adopting PHLEBOTOMIZED the following year, shifting musical direction from a Hardcore sound to more of a Death Metal feel in the process.

Singles/EPs:
In Memory Of Our Departed Ones (1914-1918) / Mustardgas / Preach Eternal Gospels / Tragic Entanglement / Atraxia, MM 010 (1993) ('Preach Eternal Gospels' EP)
In Search Of Tranquility EP, (1994)

Albums:
IMMENSE, INTENSE, SUSPENSE, Massacre CD052 (1995)
Immense, Intense, Suspense / Barricade / Desecration Of Alleged Christian History / Dubbed Forswearer / In Search Of Tranquility / Subtle Disbalanced Liquidity / Devoted To God / Mellow Are The Reverberations / Gone...
SKYCONTACT, Cyber Music CYCD 20 (1997)
Stole Show Soul / Achin' / Sometimes / I Lost My Cookies In The Disco / I Hope You Know (In 4 Parts): A Cry In July / Never Lose Hope / Imagine This / Out To You

PHLEGETHON (FINLAND)
Line-Up: Jussi Nyblom (vocals / bass), Teemu Hannonen (guitar), Juha Tykkyläinen (guitar), Lasse Pyykkö (drums)

A Finnish Doom / Death Metal band.

Albums:
FRESCO LUNGS, Witchunt WIHU 9208 (1992)

Stone Me / Without Tea Waters / 0-520 / Encapsulation Of The Ark Of The Covenant / Ornaments / The Golden Face

PHOBIA (Orange County, CA, USA)
Line-Up: Shane McLachlan (vocals), Steve Burda (guitar), Bruce Reeves (bass), Matt Mills (drums)

Dreadlocked Grindcore act with Thrash tendencies. Founded in 1990 PHOBIA soon issued the opening 'What Went Wrong?' demo. 1994 saw a West Coast tour alongside Hardcore acts LACK OF INTEREST and CAPITALIST CASUAL-TIES.
In 1999 PHOBIA would tour Europe and the UK releasing a split 7" with Japanese band CORRUPTED.

Singles/EPs:
Live Split, Misanthropic (1993) (12" split single with PLUTOCRACY)
Enslaved, Slap A Ham SLAP029 (1997) (12" single)
Split, (1999) (7" split single with CORRUPTED)

Albums:
ALL THAT REMAINS, Relapse (1990)
RETURN TO DESOLATION, Relapse (1994)
MEANS OF EXISTENCE, Slap A Ham SLAP047 (1998)
Rape Theft Murder / Taxes At Work / Stink Head / Morally Content / Blood Sport / Discommunicate / Piece Of Mind / Means Of Existence / Snail / Scars / Another Social Disease / State And Enemy / Systematically Imprisoned / Suffer For Arrogance / Infant Suffering / Cheap Life / Ruined
DESTROYING THE MASSES, Pessimiser (1999)

PIG DESTROYER (Boston, MA, USA)

PIG DESTROYER's '38 Counts Of Battery' album included CARCASS cover versions 'Exhume To Consume', 'Regurgitation Of Giblets' and 'Genital Grinder' along with a take on THE MELVINS' 'Oven'.

Albums:
38 COUNTS OF BATTERY, Relapse (2001)
Deflower / Tentacle / Yellow Line Transfer / Under The Fingernails / Elfin / Unwitting Valentine / Oven / Three Second

Apocalypse / Treblinka / Fingers In The Throat / My Fellow Vermin / Endgame / One Funeral Too Many / Higher Forms Of Pornography / Honeymoon / Alcatraz Metaphors / Flesh Upon Gear / Pixie / Genital Grinder - Regurgitation Of Giblets / Exhume To Consume / Burning Of Sodom / Delusional Supremacy / Alcatraz Metaphors / Treblinka / Seven And Thirteen / Scouring The Wreckage / Torquemada / Frailty In Numbers / Suicide Through Decay / Dark Satellite / Seven And Thirteen / Flag Burner / Delusional Supremacy / Martyr To The Plague / Ruination / Synthetic Utopia / Monolith / Frailty In Numbers

PILE OF EGGS (Parma, OH, USA)

Albums:
THE EGG FILES, Eggscab (1999)
Intro / Laughing At You A.K.A. (Cows Tripping) / Oooo Waa Chic-E Chic-E / Powerful Karate Chop / Why Is She So Stupid? / I'm A Fucking Grub / Bullshit Artist / The Sounds Of Crazy Alien Creatures Destroying The World / Oooowwa / A Juice-E Bowl Of Lips / Gargling Staples / Running To The Toilet Seat / Borg / Let's Dig Up G.G.'s Grave / Back n' Forth Jam / We Don't Belong In Society / Dude Man / Screaming Makes Me Feel Better / Stink / The Outro

POINT BLANK (GERMANY)
Line-Up: Olli (vocals), Hendrik (guitar), Christoph (guitar), Henne (bass), Andreas (drums)

Formed in Oldenburg during May 1994, OBSCENITY members Olli and Henne helped out in the studio due to line-up problems affecting this Death Metal outfit. By all accounts, the group is still looking for a permanent bassist and vocalist.

Singles/EPs:
Darkness / War / You Are My Slave / Lack Of Truth, Point Blank 3310PB (1996) ('Point Blank' EP)

POLLUTED INHERITANCE
(HOLLAND)
Line-Up: Ronald Camonier (vocals / guitar), Erwin Wesdorp (guitar), Menno de Fouw (bass), Friso Van Wijk (drums)

A Death / Thrash band, POLLUTED INHERITANCE's debut album was produced by ex-HOLY MOSES man Andy Classen.

Albums:

ECOCIDE, West Virginia WVR SPV 084-57312 (1992)

Faces / Dissolved / Eaten / Memories Of Sadness / Substance Of Existence / Fear / Stillborn / After Life / Rottings / Look Inside

BETRAYED, Displeased DSFA 1002 (1996)

Intro / Forgotten Cause / Mental Connection / Elimination / Betrayed / Emptiness / Drowning (In Faith) / Indulge / Never To Be Free / Need Me / My Voice

POSSESSED

(San Francisco, CA, USA)

Line-Up: Jeff Beccara (vocals / bass), Larry LaLonde (guitar), Mike Tarrao (guitar), Mike Sus (drums)

One of the instigators of the Bay Area Thrash scene. Founded as teenagers during 1983 POSSESSED were originally fronted by singer Barry Fisk. Tragedy struck the band early in their career though when Fisk committed suicide.

With Jeff Beccara replacing Fisk the band, including guitarists Mike Tarrao and Brian Montana with drummer Mike Sus, cut a 1984 demo which excited the interest of Metal Blade Records. The label gave an inclusion to POSSESSED's 'Swing Of The Axe' to their 'Best Of Metal Massacre' compilation but did not sign the band up for an album.

This honour fell to Combat Records although not before Montana was fired, apparently for disagreeing with the bands image of leather, studs and inverted crosses. Larry LaLonde took his place for the debut 'Seven Churches'.

POSSESSED toured Europe with VOIVOD in 1986. The 'Beyond The Gates' album, produced by Carl Canedy of THE RODS, came wrapped in a lavish fold out sleeve, a rare extravagance for a Thrash act.

The follow up mini album 'The Eyes Of Horror' was produced by none other than guitar guru JOE SATRIANI and found the group mellowing out slightly.

POSSESSED fractured leaving Tarrao to carry on the name. LaLonde would join BLIND ILLUSION then create the offbeat but commercially successful PRIMUS. Beccara suffered the misfortune of being shot by two drug addicts and was paralyzed from the waist down.

POSSESSED resurfaced in 1992 comprising Tarrao, guitarist Mark Strausberg, bassist Bob Yost and drummer Walter Ryan. The band supported MACHINE HEAD the same year and cut a three song demo. POSSESSED's last incarnation came in 1993. Former POSSESSED guitarist Mike Hollman joined hardcore merchants PRO-PAIN in 1994.

Ryan joined MACHINE HEAD. Torrao later forged IKONOCLAST.

Although their career was short the band's music is now held in high regard in particular by today's Black Metal legions.

Albums:

SEVEN CHURCHES, Roadrunner RR 9757 (1985)

Exorcist / Burning In Hell / Seven Churches / Holy Hell / Fallen Angel / Pentagram / Evil Warriors / Satan's Curse / Twisted Minds / Death Metal

BEYOND THE GATES, Under One Flag FLAG 3 (1986)

Heretic / Tribulation / March To Die / Phantasm / No Will To Live / Beyond The Gates / Beast Of The Apocalypse / Séance / Restless Dead / Dog Fight

THE EYES OF HORROR, Under One Flag FLAG 16 (1987)

Confessions / My Belief / The Eyes Of Horror / Swing Of The Axe / Storm In My Mind

POSSESSION (Olathe, KS, USA)

Singles/EPs:

Seers Vision / Sounds Of Sorrow / Have No Fear, (1993) ('The Unnamable Suffering' EP)

Albums:

ETERNALLY HAUNT, Possession (1995)

SCOURGE AND FIRE, (1996)

POSTMORTEM (GERMANY)

Line-Up: Matthias Reutz (vocals), Marcus Marth (guitar), Dirk Olesch (guitar), Tilo Voigtlaender (bass), Marco Thaele (drums)

A Death Metal band from Berlin, POSTMORTEM released their first demo, 'Secret Lunacy', in 1991. A second tape, 'Last Aid To Die', appeared the following year before the band signed to the Frankfurt based Husky Records in 1993. The group sold more than 4,000 copies of their debut album 'Screams Of Blackness' before Dirk Olesch left the group.

POSTMORTEM's follow up album, 'The Age Of Mass Murder', was issued in

March 1997.
The group has so far played with acts like MORBID ANGEL, HATE SQUAD, CEMETARY, ATROCITY, IN FLAMES, CREMATORY and PYOGENESIS.
The 'Der Totmacher' EP includes a twisted cover version of 'Anna', the song made famous by German Electronic Pop band TRIO.

Singles/EPs:
Pink Giant / Der Totmacher / Autumn Rose / Postmortem / Anna, Morbid MR031 CD (1996) ('Der Totmacher' EP)

Albums:
SCREAMS OF BLACKNESS, Husky (1993)
God Et Sins / Suicide / Reincarnation / Dreamland / Buried Alive / Lunacy / Bad Times / Shadows Of Memory / Assvibrator / Deathcontrol / Destroy The World / Treibjagd / Gutes Gefuehl
THE AGE OF MASS MURDER, Morbid 033 CD (1997)
Hi / And / Welcome / In / Our / World / Of / Violence / And / Serial / Crime! / Listen To... / The Baby!!! / Albert 'Cannibal' Fish / To Henry Lee Lucas (From Otis) / Co-Ed Killer / The Manson Cult / Der Totmacher / Green River / Your Innocence / The Age Of Massmurder / Rosa Riese / The Son Of Sam / Are We Not Men? / 25 Cromwell Street

POWER OF EXPRESSION
(GERMANY)
Line-Up: Marc Grewe (vocals), Fabian Richter (guitar), André 'Earl' Meyer (guitar), Christian Desbonnets (bass), Micha Rode (drums)

Some members of this German outfit were previously in URGE and idolized the Hardcore band B'LAST. So much so, that POWER OF EXPRESSION's debut album was a complete reworking of B'LAST's 'Power Of Expression' album with MORGOTH vocalist Marc Grewe fronting alongside additional guest vocalists in CITIZENS ARREST and TASTE OF FEAR singer Daryl Kahan and PITBULL's Mickey Jewicz.
In December 1995 the group supported VOI VOD in Germany and followed that slot with similar roles opening up for BOLT THROWER and SENTENCED in January 1996.

Singles/EPs:
Water / Is There Justice? / My Disease / Find It / Water (Long Version), Century Media (1996) ('Water' EP)

Albums:
THE POWER OF EXPRESSION, Lost & Found LF 107/ CD (1994)
Time To Think / Surf And Destroy / Fuckin' With My Head / EIB / Our Explanation / The Future / Break It Down / Time Awaits / It's Alive / I Don't Need / Look Into Myself / Nightmare
X-TERRITORIAL, Century Media 77120-2 (1996)
Water / Nothing Changes / Where Is Justice? / We Are All Twisted / Black Crowes On Speed (Push You Down) / Lie To Me / Recess / Check Your Head / Commander Ozone / Senses

PRIMIGENIUM (SPAIN)

Albums:
AS ETERNAL AS THE NIGHT, Wild Rags (1996)
ART OF WAR, Full Moon Productions (1997)
Ridden Into Battle - Prologue / Embrace Me Darkness / Black Sword Of Vengeance / Shall The Forest Open For Us / ...And Jesus Wept? / Anachronism / Pact Of Solitude / Enemy / Dragon's Tears - Epilogue

PRIMORDIAL (IRELAND)
Line-Up: Alan 'Naihmass Nemtheanga' Averill (vocals), Ciaran Mac Uiliam (guitar / keyboards), Pol Mac Amhlaidh (bass), D. Mac Amhlaidh (drums)

Pagan Death Metallers PRIMORDIAL, who came to the fore with their 'Dark Romanticism' demo, are heavily reliant on Celtic imagery and influences. The split single with Sweden's KATATONIA features the band's 1993 demo 'To Enter Pagan'.

Singles/EPs:
To Enter Pagan, Misanthropy (1996) (Split EP with KATATONIA)
The Calling /Among The Lazarae / The Burning Season / And The Sun Set On Life Forever, Hammerheart (1999) ('The Burning Season' EP)

Albums:
IMRAMA, Cacophonous NIHIL 08 (1995)
Fuil Arsa / Infernal Summer / Here I Am King / The Darkest Flame / The Fires... /

Mealltach / Let The Sun Set On Life Forever / To The Ends Of The Earth / Beneath A Bronze Sky / Awaiting The Dawn...
JOURNEY'S END, (199-)
Graven Idol / Dark Song /Autumn's Ablaze / Journey's End / Solitary Mourner / Bitter Harvest / On Aistear Deirneach
SPIRIT THE EARTH AFLAME, Hammerheart (2000)
Spirit The Earth Aflame / Gods To The Godless / The Soul Must Sleep / The Burning Season / Glorious Dawn / The Cruel Sea / Children Of The Harvest / To Enter Pagan

PROBOSCIS (SWEDEN)
Line-Up: Magnus Liljendahl (vocals), Joacim Carlsson (guitar), Andreas Eriksson (bass), Linus Bladh (drums)

Vällingby's PROBOSCIS are an eclectic outfit, ranging in musical styles from Death Metal to Funk to Hardcore. Formed in 1991 by ex-AFFLICTED vocalist Magnus Liljendahl (vocals) and Joacim Carlsson (guitar) together with erstwhile THE MOOR drummer Linus Bladh. After the release of the single 'Fall In Line' Carlsson left to join FACEDOWN. His replacement was former URA KAIPA and CREMATORY man Mikael Lindevall. The band also changed drummers, adding Björn Viitanen.
PROBOSCIS have also, in their time, contributed a cover of VENOM's 'Seven Gates Of Hell' to the 1993 Primitive Art Records tribute album 'Promoters Of The Third World War'.

Singles/EPs:
Fall In Line / Nothing Personal / Organized Madness / C.S. Theme / Avalanche, Amigo CSP CSP001 (1995)

Albums:
STALEMATE, Diehard (1997)
Losing Streak / Devaluate / Burned / Enemy / Now And Then / Sulaco / Stalemate / Hollywood Ending / Ashes / Living Lie

PROFANITY (GERMANY)
Line-Up: Tom (vocals / guitar), Martl (bass), Armin (drums)

Bobingen Death Metal act PROFANITY began life with distinct Black overtones but would shed these predilections with successive releases. The opening shot in 1994 came with 'The Transitory' demo

followed up by 1995's 'Into The Unforeseen'. Undergoing a line-up shift PROFANITY would then induct the rhythm section of bassist Martl and drummer Armin into the ranks. However, Martl would depart and in came four stringer Daniel for recording of the debut album 'Shadows To Fall'.
PROFANITY got out on the road promoting this release putting in gigs with KRABATHOR and CANNIBAL CORPSE as well as having a valuable slot at the 'Fuck The Commerce' festivals.
Signing to the German Death Metal specialists Cudgel Agency PROFANITY cut two tracks, including a cover of POSSESSED's 'The Exorcist', for a split 7" single with Americans LIVIDITY. December of 1998 found Daniel being enticed away to join melodic Rockers REACTOR and the resulting vacancy was once again filled by Martl.

Singles/EPs:
Drowned In Dusk / The Exorcist, Cudgel Agency (1997) (Split 7" single with LIVIDITY)

Albums:
SHADOWS TO FALL, (1997)
Soulburn - The Weeping Willow / Shallow Ruins / Fall Of The Shadows / Like A Razorblade / Darkened Water Sky / Into The Unforeseen / Bloodflow / An Age Of Growing Tragedy
SLAUGHTERING THOUGHT, Cudgel Agency CUD005 (2000)
Intro / During The Long Hours Of Darkness / Drowned In Dusk / Soultornado - Hate Burn Inside / The Springs Within / Giants Of Void Vortex / Soulitude / Strangulated With Thoughts / When Colour Becomes Pallor

PROPHECY OF DOOM (UK)

Singles/EPs:
Until The Again, (1995)

Albums:
ACKNOWLEDGE THE CONFUSION MASTER, Deaf (1990) (Split album with AXEGRINDER)
Prophetic Believers Prepare / Insanity Reigns Supreme / Hybrid Thought / Earth Reality Victim / Rhetorical Fusion / Prophetic Believers Act / Rancid Oracle / Calculated Mindrape / Acknowledge The Confusion Master
PEEL SESSIONS, Strange Fruit (1991)
Insanity Reigns / Supreme / Earth Reality

Victim / Rancid Oracle / Hybrid Thought

PROTECTOR (GERMANY)

Line-Up: Martin Missy (vocals), Hansi Muller (guitar), Ede Belichmeier (bass), Michael Hasse (drums)

Death Thrashers PROTECTOR emanate from Wolfsburg and date to their formation in 1986 by guitarist Hansi Muller and drummer Michael Hasse. Having added vocalist Martin Missy and bassist Ede Belichmeier in March 1987, the group recorded their first two song demo. This tape led to a deal with Atom H Records and the first mini-album, 'Misanthropy', the same year.

1988's 'Golem' featured SODOM's Angel Ripper on the track 'Space Cake' and PROTECTOR toured Germany to support the album guesting for American act WEHRMACHT.

Unfortunately, vocalist Missy quit and was replaced by Olli Wiebel but Missy rejoined in time to record 'Urm The Mad'. The group released another mini-album, 'Leviathan's Desire', in 1990 and toured Germany once more, this time as support to NAPALM DEATH. However, line-up problems hit the band prior to recording 'A Shedding Of Skin'. Belichmeier quit - having his position filled by bassist Matze Grün - and Muller also departed leaving Wiebel to record guitar parts as PROTECTOR became a trio.

Tragedy struck in February 1992 when Hasse died as a direct result of his drug addiction. Although PROTECTOR would eventually find a new drummer in Marco Pappe and toured alongside D.V.S. and CRUSHER.

PROTECTOR split after recording 'The Heritage' in 1994.

Albums:
MISANTHROPY, Atom H (1987)
Misanthropy / Holy Inquisition / Agoraphobia / The Mercenary / Kain And Abel / Holocaust
GOLEM, Atom H H007 (1988)
Delirium Tremens / Apocalyptic Revelations / Golem / Germanophobe / Protector Of Death / Operation Plagma Extrema / Meglomania / Only The Strong Survive / Omnipresent Aggression / Space Cake
URM THE MAD, Atom H (1989)
Capitacism / Sliced, Hooked And Grinded / Nothing Has Changed / The Most Repugnant Antagonist Of Life / Quasimodo / Urm The Mad / Decadence

/ Atrocities / Molotov Cocktail
LEVIATHAN'S DESIRE, Atom H (1990)
Intro / Humanized Leviathan / Subordinate / Mortal Passion / Kain And Abel
A SHEDDING OF SKIN, Major C&C CC016 038-3 (199-)
Intro / Mortuary Nightmare / A Shedding Of Skin / Face Fear / Retribution In Darkness / Doomed To Failure / Thy Will Be Done / Whom Gods Will Destroy / Necropolis / Tantalus / Death Comes Soon / Unleashed Terror / Toward Destruction
THE HERITAGE, Major C&CCC020 046-2 (1994)
Mental Malaria / Scars Bleed Life Long / The Heritage / Lost Properties / Convicts On The Streets / Projective Unconsciousness / Paralizer / Chronology / Palpitation / Outro
LOST IN ETERNITY, Major CC030 057-2 (1995)
Misanthropy / Protector Of Death / Tantalus / Mental Malaria / A Shedding Of Skin / Lost Properties / The Mercenary / Golem / Kain And Abel / Doomed To Failure / The Heritage / Humanized Leviathan / Germanophobe / Holocaust / Convicts On The Street / Palpitation

PSYCHO (USA)

Singles/EPs:
Split, Axction ACT 14 (1991) (7" split single with ANAL CUNT)
Threshold Of Pain, Axction (1995) (7" split single with ROT)
Fuergo Y Azufre, Axction (1996) (7" split single with NASUM)
Split, (199-) (7" split single with THE MEATSHITS)
Split, (199-) (7" split single with COLD OUT)
Split, (199-) (7" split single with SATANS WARRIORS)

Albums:
MASS CONSUMPTION, Thrash (1992)
SHRUNKEN, Axction (1994)

PUNGENT STENCH (AUSTRIA)

Line-Up: Martin Shirenc (vocals / guitar), Jacek Perkowski (bass), Alex Wank (drums)

Vienna's PUNGENT STENCH deal in deliberately sick and overgrossed song content and imagery designed to shock. Having debuted with the 1988 demo 'Mucus Secretion', a split EP with

DISHARMONIC ORCHESTRA followed in 1989. The group toured with MASTER and ABOMINATION during 1990 in order to promote their debut album, 'For God Your Soul... For Me Your Flesh'.

In late 1991 copies of the 'Been Caught Buttering' album were confiscated by British customs due to concern about the sleeve photograph depicting a sawn in half decapitated head. However, the album was eventually passed as the photograph had been on display in various art galleries previously.

Naturally, PUNGENT STENCH lapped up the controversy and toured hard, capitalizing on the shock value they created. Dates included gigs in Israel and American shows with BRUTAL TRUTH and INCANTATION.

The 'Dirty Rhymes And Psychotronic Beats' album is worth noting as it features a cover of THE MENTORS' legendary 'Four 'F' Club'.

Drummer Alex Wank later formed the Industrial group SPINE. Shirenc created HOLLENTHON and forged KREUZWEGOST with Silenius of SUMMONING.

Premier American Death Metal outfit MORTICIAN would cover 'Pulsating Protoplasma' on their 2001 album 'Domain Of Death'.

Singles/EPs:
Pulsating Protoplasma / Dead Body Love / Miscarriage / In The Vault / Rip You Without Care / Festered Offals / Pungent Stench, Nuclear Blast NB 019 (1989) (Split EP with DISHARMONIC ORCHESTRA)
Extreme Deformity / Mucous Secretion / Molecular Disembowelment, Nuclear Blast (1989)
Blood, Pus And Gastric Juice, Nuclear Blast (1990) (Split EP with BENEDICTION)
Praise The Names Of The Musical Assassins / Viva La Muerte / Why Can The Bodies Fly / Blood, Pus And Gastric Juice (Groove Version) / Horny Little Piggy Bank / Four 'F' Club / Blood. Pus And Gastric Juice (Tekkno House Mix), Nuclear Blast NB 078 (1993) ('Dirty Rhymes And Psychotronic Beats' EP)

Albums:
FOR GOD YOUR SOUL... FOR ME YOUR FLESH, Nuclear Blast NB 029-2 (1990)
Intro / Extreme Deformity / Hypnos / For God Your Soul, For Me Your Flesh / Just Let Me Rot / Pungent Stench / Bonesawer / Embalmed In Sulphuric Acid / Blood, Pus And Gastric Juice / Suspended / Animation / A Small Lunch
BEEN CAUGHT BUTTERING, Nuclear Blast NB052-2 (1992)
Shrunken And Mummified Bitch / Happy Re-Birthday / Games Of Humiliation / S.M.A.S.H. / Brainpan Blues / And Only Hunger Remains / Sputter Supper / Sick Bizarre Defaced Creation / Splatterday Night Fever
CLUB MONDO BIZARRE FOR MEMBERS ONLY, Nuclear Blast NB079-2 (1994)
True Life / Klyster Boogie / Choked Just For A Joke / Hydrocephalus / I'm A Family Man / Treatments Of Pain / In Search Of The Perfect Torture / Practice Suicide / Fuck Bizarre / Rape-Pagar Con La Misma Moneda
PRAISE THE NAMES OF THE MUSICAL ASSASSINS, Nuclear Blast (1997)

PUNISHED EARTH (BELGIUM)

Albums:
FRANKENSTEIN, Uxicon (2000)
Awakening Of The Flesh / Under Authority / Watery Mouth At First Sight / Run Amok / Decade Of Misanthropy / Final State / Religious Suppression / The Whale / New World Order / Maniac With A Screwdriver / In The Name Of Democracy / Superficial World / Desperate Wishes (Breakdown) / Pedofile In The Neighbourhood / Punished Earth / Weak Is The Flesh

PUNISHMENT (SWEDEN)
Line-Up: Daniel Westerberg (vocals), Micke Lövqvist (guitar), Pelle Öberg (bass), Mikael Öberg (drums)

Hardcore Metallers PUNISHMENT were known in a previous twin guitar incarnation as INFANTICIDE.

Singles/EPs:
Life / Muscle Man / Lust For Pleasure / Erased Jealousy, Punishment DEMOCD 1 (1995)

PURGATORY (GERMANY)

A Death Metal / Grindcore act, PURGATORY formed in 1989 and released two EPs and three demos before the debut album arrived in 1996. The group have supported NAPALM

DEATH, CANNIBAL CORPSE, SAMAEL, ENTOMBED, KRABATHOR and EMINENZ in their short time together. PURGATORY supported AMON AMARTH for a tour of Germany in December 2000.

Singles/EPs:
Psycopathia Sexualis EP, Perverted Taste (1995)
Sadistic Spell EP, Perverted Taste (1995)

Albums:
DAMAGE DONE BY WORMS, Perverted Taste PT015 (1996)
Orgy Of Sickness Dreams / Deep Under The Light / Sodomizing Time / Robes Of Skin / Psychopathia Sexualis Pt II / Necrocannibalistical Insanity / Brought Of Incest / Irresolute Subjection / Final Breath / Frozen Braincells / Paroxysm Of Mortal Lust / Sadistical Spell / Necronomical Necrosy
BESTIAL, Perverted Taste PT022 (1998)
My Blood / Ulcer Of Hate / Immolation Of The Weak / The Bestial / Back From The Shadowlands / Your Soul Will Never Rest / Malignant Spawn / Enslaved By Madness / Tormented Flesh / Burned
BLESSED WITH FLAMES OF HATE, Perverted Taste (2000)
Damned And Betrayed / Visions Beyond Light / The Daimonian / March Of The Eminent Beast / Pharynx Of Evil / Captured Souls / Blessed With Flames / In Blasphemy / … And Blood Flows / The Rack

PURULENT SPERMCANAL (CZECH REPUBLIC)

Singles/EPs:
Split, (199-) (7" split single with VISCERA)

Albums:
PUAKA BALAVA, Leviathan (1997)
Violent Sexual Orgy / Incest Party / Massacre In The Oriental Porno / Masturbation In The Mortuary / Sadistic Emotion / Cannibalistic Festivals Of Murder / Victim Of Homosexual / Bloody Penis / Dying With Vaginal Bleed / Brutal Fuck / Sexual Deviation / Dessert From Human Meat / Perverse Orgasm / Jesus Anal / The Final: Pathological Report About Genital Torture
LEGALIZE OF CANNIBALISM, Leviathan (1998)

PUS (FINLAND)

Albums:
CASES OF DEATH, (2000)
Blood Trickling Stumps / 20 Sadistic Intrusions / Phases Of Decay / Rusty Scissors Stabbing At The Chest / Coat Hanger Twisting Your Throat / Mass Graves For Kids / Sodomized

PUTREFY (IRELAND)

Albums:
PUTREFY, Isolated ISO 003 (1995) (Split album with ALTERED VISION)

PUTRID OFFAL (FRANCE)

Singles/EPs:
Split, (199-) (7" split single with AGATHOCLES)

Albums:
PREMATURE NECROPSY, (199-) (split album with EXULCERATION)

PYOGENESIS (GERMANY)
Line-Up: Flo Schwarz (vocals / guitar), Tim Ellermann (guitar), Roman Schönsee (bass), Wolle (drums)

PYOGENESIS have evolved from their inception in 1990 as a basic Thrash outfit into one of the more creative extreme Metal bands. Their first demo led to a deal with a Colombian record company on which label two EPs were released. Not satisfied with this arrangement, PYOGENESIS signed to French Black Metal label Osmose to release the 'Ignis Creatio' album, but found themselves lumped in with the predominantly Satanic acts on Osmose and original drummer Pit was asked to leave following the album's release and was replaced by Wolle.
PYOGENESIS opened for ANATHEMA on their February 1994 European tour. Bassist Joe Proell was superseded by ex-DYSTROPHY Roman Schönsee in early 1995.
PYOGENESIS made a clean break from their Metal roots in 1996, crossing over to more of an Indie Pop stance signaled by their 'Love Nation Sugarhead' mini-album. The record featured SKYCLAD vocalist Martin Walkyier on the track 'Female Drugthing'.
The group toured Europe as support to Americans SOCIAL DISTORTION in early 1997.
Schönsee created THE DREAMSIDE

then THE BLOODLINE for the 2000 album 'Opium Hearts'. Members of PYOGENESIS also operate the extreme Grindcore act GUT.

<u>Singles/EPs:</u>
Through The Flames / In The End / Down / Lost In Revery, Nuclear Blast NB 106-2 (1993) ('Waves Of Erotasia' EP)
Still Burn In Fire / Like Tears (In The Dust) / On Soulwings / Underneath Orion's Sword / Ignis Creatio, Osmose Productions OP CD013 (1993) ('Ignis Creatio' EP)
Silver Experience / Love Nation Sugarhead / Female Drugthing / So Called Sensation / The Zentury / Clones, Nuclear Blast NB 27361 62052 (1996) ('Love Nation Sugar Head' EP)

<u>Albums:</u>
SWEET X RATED NOTHINGS, Nuclear Blast NB113-2 (1994)
Intro / Fade Away / Sweet X Rated Nothings / It's On Me / I'll Search / Skykiss / These Roads / Golden Sins / Masquerade / Through The Flames / Extasis / Coming Home
TWINALEBLOOD, Nuclear Blast NB136 (1995)
Undead / Twinaleblood / Weeping Sun / Every Single Day / Abstract Life / Empty Space / Sinfeast / Those Churning Seas / Snakehole / Addiction Hole / God Complex / Supavenus / Bar Infernale / I'm Coming
UNPOP, Nuclear Blast (1996)
Blue Smiley's Plan / Get Up / Love Nation Sugarhead / Alternative Girl / Rhapsodie In E / Junkie On A Cloud / To Me / Cheapo Speakers / All The Pills / Silver Experience / My Style / Ton-Recycling / XXL Ego King / Lower All Your High Standards / Sehnsucht

PYREXIA (USA)
Line-Up: Darryl Wagner (vocals), Tony Caravella (guitar), Guy Marchais (guitar), Chris Basile (bass), Mike Andrekio (drums)

A Deathcore unit with blasphemous overtones. Guitarist Guy Marchais would later join INTERNAL BLEEDING and CATASTROPHIC.

<u>Singles/EPs:</u>
Hatred And Disgust / Bludgeoned By Deformity / The Enshrined, (199-) ('Hatred And Disgust' EP)

<u>Albums:</u>
SERMON OF MOCKERY, Drowned (1993)
Sermon Of Mockery / Resurrection / Abominat / The Uncreation / God / Demigod / Inhumanity / Lithurgy Of Impurity

 QUORTHORN
(SWEDEN)

Quorthorn is the enigmatic mentor and driving force behind cult outfit BATHORY. Quorthon's second album, a double album affair, saw the man exploring distinctly poppier territory.

<u>Singles/EPs:</u>
Not More And Never Again / Feather / Boy in The Bubble, Black Mark BMCD 666-9 (1994) (Promotion release)

<u>Albums:</u>
ALBUM, Black Mark BMCD 666-9 (1994)
No More And Never Again / Oh No No / Boy / Major Snooze / Too Little Much Too Late / Crack In My Mirror / Rain / Feather / Relief / Head Over Heels
PURITY OF ESSENCE, Black Mark BMCD 666-13 (1997)
Rock n' Roll / I've Had It Coming My Way / When Our Day Is Through / One Of Those Days / Cherrybutt And Firefly / Television / Hit My Head / Hump For Fun / Outta Space / Fade Away / I Want Out/ Daddy's Girl / Coming Down In Pieces / Roller Coaster / It's Ok / All In All I Know / No Life At All / An Inch Above The Ground / The Notforgettin' / Deep / Label On The Wind / Just The Same / You Just Got To Live

RAISE HELL
(SWEDEN)
Line-Up: Jonas Nilsson
(vocals / guitar), Torstein
Wickberg (guitar), Niklas
Sjostrom (bass), Dennis
Ekdahl (drums)

RAISE HELL
Photo : Martin Wickler

Much lauded Death Metal combo founded in 1995 as IN COLD BLOOD by vocalist / guitarist Jonas Hilsson, bass player Niklas Sjöström and guitarist Torstein Wickberg. The following year drummer Dennis Ekdahl completed the rankings. The band, very much rooted in the Black Metal scene, were all still in their mid teens by the time the band was finalized, leading to jibes about them being "the Death Metal HANSON".
In the summer of 1997 IN COLD BLOOD issued their only demo 'Nailed'. A record company bidding war erupted, which included the Earache label, after which Germany's Nuclear Blast emerged as the victors. However, at this point an American Hardcore act of same title was discovered hence the name switch to RAISE HELL.
By the time debut 'Holy Target' arrived RAISE HELL's average band member age was just 18. The record displayed a remarkable maturity for an act so young blending Death and Thrash Metal with unashamed anti-Christian lyrics. The group got straight into gear touring

Europe to promote the album alongside DISMEMBER, AGATHODAIMON, NIGHT IN GALES and CHILDREN OF BODOM. The 2000 album 'Not Dead Yet' found RAISE HELL maneuvering away from their Black Metal roots.
Ekdahl also drums for SINS OF OMISSION.

Albums:
HOLY TARGET, Nuclear Blast (1998)
The March Of Devil's Soldiers / Raise The Dead / Beautiful As Fire / Holy Target / Legions Of Creeps / The Red Ripper / Black Visions / Mattered Out / Superior Powers
NOT DEAD YET, Nuclear Blast NB 443-2 (2000)
Dance With The Devil / Babes / Back Attack / Devilyn / Not Dead Yet / No Puls / User Of Poison / He Is Coming / Soulcollector

RAMP (PORTUGAL)
Line-up: Rudi Darte (vocals), Ricardo, Antonio, Miguel, Paulo

Started in the early 90's by musicians with a common love of American Thrash Metal, Portuguese outfit RAMP scored a deal with Polygram Records and soon elevated themselves to the position of biggest homegrown act in their native land.
RAMP debuted with a six track EP which in turn led to the debut full length album 'Thoughts'. The band have opened for SEPULTURA, PARADISE LOST, NAPALM DEATH and FEAR FACTORY.

Albums:
THOUGHTS, Polygram (199-)
INTERSECTION, Uniao Lisboa (1995)

RAMPAGE (Augusta, GA, USA)
Line-Up: Lord Vic Naughty (vocals / guitar), Earwhig Ringworm (guitar), Tom Coffinsmasher (bass), Paul Bearer (drums)

Georgia's schizophrenic Death Metal band RAMPAGE have proved an elusive beast to categorize. Many albums are deliberately humorous whilst increasingly latter day albums are deadly serious affairs, in particular the overtly Black Metal 'Bellum Infinitium' concept outing.
The band's first attempt at a formation was as far back as 1989 with Lord Vic Naughty on bass, Paul Bearer on guitar and Sexxxual Rush (real name Ben) on

vocals. This unit soon disbanded and it would not be until 1995 when Lord Vic and Bearer, the latter now on drums, reunited. In 1997 the mini-album 'Misogyny - Thy Name Is Woman' was issued followed shortly after by the full length 'This End Up'. Although a less tongue in cheek affair 'This End Up' would still obviously mimic POSSESSED's infamous logo and include an irreverent take on 'Jailhouse Rock'.

In 1998 RAMPAGE undertook the 'Gore To Your Door' tour in alliance with GORTICIAN. For these shows Lord Vic pulled in guitarist X Re, bassist Sven Hemlock and drummer Aldo Eniwan. Predictably the band would break up while on the road with roadies taking over musical duties in order to fulfill the dates. Lord Vic would combine RAMPAGE with FESTERING SORE for a split EP including original 'Doom Metal' along side takes on VENOM's 'Leave Me In Hell' and IMMORTAL's 'Unsilent Storms In The North Abyss'. An admittedly 'fake' live album 'Cummin' Atcha Live', with suitably pornographic cover photograph, followed before recording of the ambitious 'Bellum Infinitium'. Despite being a weighty affair the album would include versions of the KISS classic 'War Machine' and DARKTHRONE's 'In The Shadow Of The Horns'.

Besides RAMPAGE Lord Vic has scored production credits with MEGIDDO, FESTERING SORE and EYES OF LIGEIA. The man also operates the spoof Metal Rap band THE GUYS WHO WEAR BLACK TOO MUCH in collaboration with GORTICIAN's High C.

Further split albums are planned for 2001 including unions projected with MEGIDDO, CHERNOBOG and ENBILULUGUGAL although reportedly RAMPAGE is now purely a Lord Vic solo venture.

Singles/EPs:
Doom Metal / Leave Me In Hell / Unsilent Storms In The North Abyss, Unsung Heroes (1999) (Split EP with FESTERING SORE)

Albums:
MISOGYNY - THY NAME IS WOMAN, Unsung Heroes (1998)
The Wigglesnake Blues / Kill Ya Tonite / Deadrot / The Round Mound Of Rebound / Cocksucker / Deathcrush / Bloody Leg (The Wifebeatah Mix)

THIS END UP, Unsung Heroes (1998)
Bloody Leg / Burn In Hell / Ticket To Hell / Satanic Symphonies / Satanic Death / Heavens Gate / The Sceptre / Rampage / The Gates Of The Abyss / Six Bells At Midnight / Eye Of The Hellstorm / Jailhouse Rock '98 (The Emperor Mix) / Witches Sabbath XXX
CUMMIN' ATCHA LIVE, Unsung Heroes (1999)
Bloody Leg / Born In Hell (On The Bayou) / Deadrot / Satanic Death / The Gates Of The Abyss / Cocksucker / Buried Alive-Money For Nothin' / Six Bells At Midnight / Rampage / Ticket To Hell / The Round Mound Of Rebound / Twisted Minds / Storm Over Avalon / Wanderlust
BELLUM INFITIUM, Unsung Heroes (2000)
Up From The Depths - Rainbow Skies / Sisters Of Death / Storm Over Avalon / The Wakening - Soulsword / Excalibur / Nemesis / The Vow / The Final Day - Into The Great Beyond - Orbis Tertius / War Machine / In The Shadows Of The Horns

THE RAVENOUS (USA)

Line-Up: Killjoy (vocals), Chris Reifert (guitar), Dan Lilker (bass),

Something of an extreme Metal supergroup. Contributing are former ANTHRAX, NUCLEAR ASSAULT and BRUTAL TRUTH and present day S.O.D. and HEMLOCK bassist Dan Lilker, NECROPHAGIA's Killjoy on vocals and Chris Reifert of ABCESS and AUTOPSY. Clint Bower and Danny Coralles also aid in the studio.

Albums:
ASSEMBLED IN BLASPHEMY, Hammerheart (2000)
Shrieks Of The Mutilated / Dead, Cut Up, And Ready To Fuck / Orgy In Dog's Blood / Feasting From The Womb / Keep My Grave Open / Assembled In Blasphemy / Perverted Before God / Hallucinations Of A Deranged Mind / Ageless Existence / Anointing The Worms

REBAELLIUN (BRAZIL)

Line-Up: Marcello Marzari (vocals / bass), Ronaldo Lima (guitar), Fabiano Penna (guitar), Sandro M. (drums)

Death Metal band led by guitarist Fabiano Penna founded as BLESSED in 1996. REBAELLIUN have opened for MYSTIC CIRCLE and LIMBONIC ART.

317

In 2000 REBAELLIUN formed part of the 'No Mercy' Festivals across Europe together with VADER, FLESHCRAWL and VITAL REMAINS.

Albums:
BURN THE PROMISED LAND, (1999)
At War / And The Immortals Shall Rise / Killing For The Domain / Spawning The Rebellion / Flagellation's Of Christ (The Revenge Of King Beelzebuth) / Hell's Decree / The Legacy Of Eternal Wrath / Burn The Promised Land / Triumph Of The Unholy Ones

RECIPIENTS OF DEATH (CA, USA)
Line-Up: Dead Rich G. (vocals / bass/guitar), Zac Taylor (guitar), Albert Gomez (guitar), Chris Broguiere (drums)

For the second album guitarists Albert Gomez and Zac Taylor were substituted by John Lisi.

Albums:
RECIPIENTS OF DEATH, Wild Rags WRE 905CD (1988)
Raping Death / Seizure / Necropolis (City Of The Dead) / Carnage / Gunned Town / The Aftermath / Fleshburn
FINAL FLIGHT, Wild Rags (1990)
Final Flight / Behind Closed Doors / Recrimination / F.O.A.D. (intro), Democratic Lie

REDEEM (Tuckerton, NJ, USA)
Line-Up: Keith Lenox (vocals), Luke Washack (guitar), Athur Hunt (guitar), Dominick Renaldo (bass), Joshua Godbolt (drums)

Albums:
A DIADEM OF BEAUTY, (199-)
Persecution Stands To Uplift / Dead As Heart / The Growth Of Separation / Ballad Of Remembrance / Tearing At The Walls Of His Temple / Seeing The Light (Unknown Prophecy) / New Fire From Within / The Dayspring From On High / Memories Change To Forgiveness

RED HARVEST (NORWAY)
Line-Up: Jimmy Bergsten (vocals / guitar), Jan F. Nygard (guitar), Thomas Brandt (bass), Cato Bekkevold (drums)

Oslo's RED HARVEST kicked off their career with distinct Thrash Metal leanings but had introduced Industrial elements with each successive release. The band debuted with the demos 'Occultia' and

'Psychotica'. The band's sixth album 'Cold Dark Matter' features DARKTHRONE's Fenriz as guest musician.
By 1995 RED HARVEST guitarist Jan F. Nygard had departed and the group had added guitarist Ketil Eggum and keyboard player Lars R. Sorensen.
Drummer Cato Bekkevold also has credits with DEMONIC.
RED HARVEST supported MAYHEM on their September 2000 European dates.
RED HARVEST's 1999 album 'New Rage World Music' would be re-issued in 2001 by Nocturnal Art Productions with a bonus live version of 'Absolut Dunkel:Heit' recorded in Vienna and studio tracks which included a guesting Maniac from MAYHEM on vocals. Relapse Records would also pick up the 'Cold Dark Matter' album re-issuing it adding the original 'New Rage World Music' tracks.

Singles/EPs:
The Harder They Fall / Enlighten The Child / Dream Awake / Tears, Voices Of Wonder VOW046 (1995) ('The Maztür Nation' EP)

Albums:
NO MINDS LAND, Black Mark BMCD 19 (1991)
The Cure / Righteous Majority / Acid / No Next Generation / Machines Way / (Live And Pay) The Holy Way / Crackman / Face The Fact
THERE'S BEAUTY IN THE PURITY OF SADNESS, Voices Of Wonder VOW039 (1994)
Wounds / Naked / Resist / Mindblazt / Mastodome / Shivers / (?) / Mother Of All / Alpha Beta Gamma L.E.A.K. / Sadness / The Art Of Radiation
HYBREED, Voices Of Wonder VOW052 (1996)
Maztür Nation / The Lone Walk / Mutant / After All... / Ozrham / On Sacred Ground / The Harder They Fall / Underwater / Monumental / In Deep / The Burning Wheel
NEW RAGE WORLD MUSIC, Voices Of Wonder VOW072 (1999)
Ad Noctum / Move Or Be Moved (Preview) / Swallow The Sun / Pity The Bastard / Concrete Steel Vs. The Brain (PTB Remix)
COLD DARK MATTER, Nocturnal Art Productions ECLIPSE014 (2000)
Omnipotent / Last Call / Absolut Dunkelheit / Cold Dark Matter / Junk-O-

Rama / Fix Hammer Fix / The Itching Scull / Death In Cyborg Era / Move Or Be Moved
COLD DARK MATTER, Relapse RLP6479 (2000)
Omnipotent / Last Call / Absolut Dunkelheit / Cold Dark Matter / Junk-O-Rama / Fix Hammer Fix / The Itching Scull / Death In Cyborg Era / Move Or Be Moved / Ad Noctum / Move Or Be Moved (Preview) / Swallow The Sun / Pity The Bastard
NEW RAGE WORLD MUSIC, Nocturnal Art Productions ECLIPSE019 (2001)
Ad Noctum / Move Or Be Moved (Preview) / Swallow The Sun / Pity The Bastard / Concrete Steel Vs. The Brain (PTB Remix) / Final Scorn /Absolut Dunkel:Heit (Live) / The Supreme Truth / Terrorsonic Zodiac

REGNANT (CHILE)

Albums:
TRANSVISCERAL, (199-)

REGREDIOR (LITHUANIA)
Line-Up: Marius (vocals), Rytis (guitar), Tomas (bass), Linas (drums)

Death Metallers debuted with the demo tape 'Born In A Coffin'. REGREDIOR split after the 'Forbidden Tears' effort with vocalist Marius joining GHOSTSTORM.

Singles/EPs:
Touched By Thanat, (1995)

Albums:
FORBIDDEN TEARS, Shiver SHR 010 (1995)
Reflection Of The Shadows Age / Hungry Ghost / Forbidden Tears / Touched By Thanat / Return To The Kingdom Of Mandragora

REGURGITATE (SWEDEN)
Line-Up: Rikard Jansson (vocals), Urban Skytt (guitar), Joppe Hanson (bass), Peter Stjarnvind (drums)

Extreme Grindcore act that relish in the most sickening subject matters. The band was created as a trio of vocalist Rikard Jansson, guitarist Mats Nordrup (also drummer with GENERAL SURGERY and CREMATORY) and drummer Peter Stjarnvind. The latter has an enviable list of credits with acts such as UNANIMATED, FACE DOWN, MERCILESS and LOUD PIPES.

Debuted with the 1994 cassette 'Concrete Human Torture' which found REGURGITATE in a rather more politically inclined mode than the full on Gore that was to come. For recording of the split album with Germany's DEAD for the infamous Poserslaughter label Nordrup took up drum duties as Stjarnvind's other acts became his priority. CREMATORY guitarist Urban Skytt laid down guitars. However, Nordrup would make his exit and the band regrouped with Stjarnvind back on drums, Skytt joining full time and another former CREMATORY man bassist Joppe Hanson completing the roster. This quartet cut the 'Effortless Regurgitation Of Bright Red Blood' album. Issued in 1999 the album includes an AGATHOCLES cover version.
The album covers are not for the faint hearted. The 2000 album 'Carnivorous Erection' had its release delayed due to furor caused by the album artwork which featured a rather vicious penis with bared teeth!
Drummer Peter 'Flinta' Stjarnwind is presently a member of ENTOMBED and LOUD PIPES.

Singles/EPs:
Split, (199-) (7" split single with VAGINAL MASSAKER)
Brainscrambler / Regurgitated Giblets / Internal Bleeding / Methylated Bile / Liquid Excrements / Carnal Cacophony / Vomit Breath / Suicide, Glued Stamp (199-) (7" split single with PSYCHOTIC NOISE)
Split, Obsession (1994) (7" split single with GRUDGE)
Split, Noise Variations (1996) (7" split single with INTESTINAL INFECTION)

Albums:
REGURGITATE, Poserslaughter (1994) (Split album with DEAD)
Cannibalistic Miscarriage / Praedilctio For Mennohagia / Organic Convulsions / Expelling Pyorrhoea / Purulent Vulvectomy / Morbid Reality / Terror Reign / Fear!? / Desensitized / Generic Words
EFFORTLESS REGURGITATION OF BRIGHT RED BLOOD, Relapse (1999)
Intro: The Act Of Intestinal Regurgitation / Disgorging Foetus / Confluent Macular Drug Eruption / Bullous Impetigo / Fleshfeast / Anorectal Ulceration / Vulva Fermentation / Multicystic Kidney / Mucupurulent Offal Grinder / Total

Dismemberment Of A Female Corpse / Carnal Cacophony / Vomit Breath / Complete Rectal Prolapse / Testiculat Trauma / Genital Cancer / Malignant Tumor / Diffuse Systemic Scerosis / Owner Of A Necrotic Intestine / Newborn Regurgitation / Torsion Of The Testicle / Worm Eaten Rectum / Chronic Lymphatic Leukemie / Meatal Ulcer / Purulent Discharge From The Urethra / Vaginal Obstriction / Cloudy, Grayish Vomitus / Fleshmangler / Splattered Brains / Bulging Vaginal Septum / Acute Urinary Infection / Severe Necroses Of The Face / Bleeding Peptic Ulcer / Face Mutilation / Extensive Ulcerate Tumor / Tumescent Foetal Fluids To Expurgate / Carbonized Bowels / Effortless Regurgitation Of Bright Red Blood **CARNIVOROUS ERECTION**, Relapse RLP6465 (2000)
You're About To Fuckin' Die / Domination Through Mutilation / Escort Service Of The Dead / Obscene Body Slayings / Fecal Freak / Humiliated In Your Own Blood / Just Another Stillborn / Parade Of The Decapitated Midgets / Ruptured Remains In A Doggybag / Copious Head Carnage / Carnivorous Erection / Relentless Pursuit Of Human Flesh / Dismantle The Afterbirth / Choked In Shit / Funeral Genocide / Rancid Head Of Splatter / Rage Against Humanity / To Boil A Corpse / Bloody Pile Of Human Waste / Drenched In Cattleblood / Carbonated Death / Skull Of Shit And Sludge / Desperate Need For Violation / 37 Stabwounds / Vomified (Regurgitated To The Core) / Headless She Died / Breath Like Rotten Meat / I Wanna Kill / Claw Hammer Castration / Festering Embryonic Vomit / Smeared With Bloodmixed Semen / The Pulsating Feast / Stinking Genital Warts / Pyronecrobestiality / Self Disembowelment / Savage Gorewhore / The Combustion And Consumption Of Pyorrheic Waste

REGURGITATION (USA)
Line-Up: Ben Deskns (vocals / guitar), Tony Tipton (guitar), Brian Baxter (vocals / bass), Dan Baker (drums)

REGURGITATION, assembled in 1994 by vocalist / guitarist Ben Deskns and guitarist Tony Tipton, underwent constant line up fluctuations during their early years. Nevertheless, a 1996 demo 'Conceived Through Vomit' emerged before the band was judged stable with the drafting of vocalist / bassist Brian

Baxter and drummer Dan Baker.

Albums:
TALES OF NECROPHILIA, Ablated ABLTD002 (1999)
Out Of The Womb / Repulsive Genital Disfigurement / Seed Of The Sanguinary / Acid Enema / Fermenting Vaginal Excrements / Menstrual Cykill / Cadaveric Impregnation / Fetal Suffocation

REIGN (UK)
Line-Up: John Cook (vocals / bass), Mick Sturrie (guitar), Ronnie McClean (drums)

REIGN debuted with the well received demo 'The Silent Nation'. REIGN gained valuable exposure on the British 'Underground Titans' tour alongside GOMORRAH, INCARCERATED and DECOMPOSED. Toured Europe with MORTIFICATION in 1994.

Albums:
EMBRACE, Mausoleum 904016-2 (1995)
Ad Extremum / Forlorn Existence / Wings Of Sorrow / Erosion / A Sombre Tale / Obscured / Infinity Within / Never Forever / Lacuna / Colour Circus
EXIT CLAUSE, Mausoleum 71278-60015-2 (1995)
Freakshow / In Isolation / Alles Im Arsch / Dei Gratia / Abolition (My Release) / Violate / Chemical Rebirth / Exit Clause

REINCARNATION (SPAIN)

Singles/EPs:
Seeds Of Hate, (1995)

REPULSION (MI, USA)

Highly influential Death Metal band cited by many of today's protagonists of the genre as a direct influence. In 1994 ex-REPULSION bassist Scott Carlson joined British Doomsters CATHEDRAL for live work.
NAPALM DEATH paid homage to REPULSION by covering 'Maggots In Your Coffin' on their 2000 'Leaders Not Followers' album.

Singles/EPs:
Repulsion, (199-) (7" single)
Excrutiation, (199-) (7" single)

Albums:
HORRIFIED, Necrosis NECRO 2CD (1989)

Stench Of Burning Death / Acid Bath / Radiation Sickness / Splattered Cadavers / Festering Boils / Eaten Alive / Slaughter Of The Innocent / Pestilent Decay / Decomposed

RESURRECTED (GERMANY)
Line-Up: Carsten Scholz (vocals), Thomas Granzow (guitar), Stefan Bays (bass), Michael Scholz (drums)

Black tinged Death Metal act RESURRECTED was formed by the Scholz brothers vocalist Carsten and drummer Michael in 1993 together with guitarist Thomas Mayer. This latter member would be replaced by Thomas Granzow before the close of the year.
In 1994 RESURRECTED opened proceedings with the demo 'Darkside Of Reality'. Two further cassettes ensued ; 'Sinner Of An Unable God' and 1996's 'The Lament Of Configuration'.
A deal was struck with Underground Productions for the release of the 7" single 'Bloodline' in 1997 before Eaststar Records offered RESURRECTED an album deal. However, soon after the release of the 'Raping Whores' opus the two parties severed links as RESURRECTED signed to Death Metal specialists Perverted Taste.
Promotion for the second album 'Faireless To The Flesh', which included a rendition of DEICIDE's 'Sacrificial Suicide', saw European touring alongside FLESHGRIND and labelmates COERCION. The band also put in a showing at the 16th annual Milwaukee Metalfest.
RESURRECTED had their debut album re-issued on the Perverted Taste label and for the American market United Guttural Records released second effort 'Faireless To The Flesh' although the latter version was minus the cover track 'Sacrificial Suicide'.
A third album, 'Butchered In Excrement' produced by Olaf Oebels, emerged in 2001.

Singles/EPs:
Bloodline, Underground Productions (1997) (7" single)

Albums:
RAPING WHORES, Eaststar (1998)
…As Heaven Declines / Rotten And Worthless / Hook Handed Demon / Damned By Temptation / Suffer My Insanity / Blessed By The Priest / Pray

The Lord… / Impiety Breed / Nailed On Cross (Let Him Fester) / Wide Open Cunt
FAIRELESS TO THE FLESH, Perverted Taste PT027 (2000)
Intro / Two Faces, One More Fist / React With Hate / Premature Ejaculation / Unceremonious Promiscuous / Raping Whores / Christcunt / Denomination / Embellish / Virgin Immaculate / Sacrificial Suicide
BUTCHERED IN EXCREMENT, Perverted Taste (2001)

RESURRECTURIS (ITALY)
Line-Up: Jerry Di Tullio (vocals), Carlo Strappa (guitar), Janos Muri (guitar), Gianluca Bassi (bass), Omar Moretti (drums)

Powerful Metal act with Death Metal tendencies RESURRECTURIS arrived with the 1995 demo 'No Flesh Shall Be Spared'. A further effort 'Evil Confounding Evil' led to a record deal with the Dutch Diamond label.
RESSURECTURIS utilized the female vocals of guitarist Carlo Strappa's sister Gloria on the 'Nocturnal' album.

Albums:
NOCTURNAL, Diamond (1999)
Nocturnal / Freeze Frame / Il Male Contro Il Male / Fear No Evil / Dark Moods / Born Defeated / No Cheating Allowed / Isole / Abisso Notturno / Flashes (Then The End) / Midnight Letter

RETALIATION (SWEDEN)
Line-Up: Henke Forrs (vocals / bass), Andreas Carlsson (vocals / guitar), Jonas Albrektsson (guitar), Jocke Petersson (drums)

Stark, uncompromising Death-Grind Metal band RETALIATION came together in 1993. Founded by former NEFARIOUS man Henke Forrs ("Dedicated rape and string terrors") and guitarist Andreas Carlsson ("Sonic Torture and pain") RETALIATION at first employed a drum machine for their opening 1993 demo 'Acrid Genital Spew'. By the following year RETALIATION had pulled in second guitarist Jonas Albrektsson ("666 string holocaust and genocide") and drummer Jocke Petersson ("Assault and battery discharges") for the sophomore cassette session 'Devastating Doctrine Dismemberment'.
RETALIATION's debut commercial release came courtesy of the German

Death Metal aficionados Regurgitated Semen Records and a split 7" single with GUT entitled 'The Misanthrope'.

It was during 1994 that RETALIATION performed their first, and to date only, gig on a billing with THY PRIMORDIAL and DAWN.

RETALIATION then featured on the now renowned 3" 4-way split CD 'Grindwork' ranking alongside fellow Swedes NASUM and Japanese acts VIVISECTION and C.S.S.O. Italian label Headfucker then picked up the band for a split 7" single 'Pray For War' in allegiance with American Deathsters EXHUMED. In keeping with the band's no holds barred style the single sleeve artwork featured a photograph of a firing squad victim. The same label would issue RETALIATION's debut album 'The Execution'.

In 2000 RETALIATION shared a further split 7" single, this time with Australian band THE KILL for the American Mortville label. The single included a cover version SKITSYSTEM's 'Jag Värar'.

Singles/EPs:
Intro / Nailgun Rectal Entry / The Undertaker / Lowlife / Disfigured Stillborn Intercourse / The Misanthrope / Dethrone The Dictator / Corrupted / Outro, Regurgitated Semen (1994) ('The Misanthrope' 7" split single with GUT)
Grindwork, Grindwork Productions (1995) (4-way 7" split single with C.S.S.O., VIVISECTION and NASUM)
Retribution / Like Cancer On Society / Strife / Born Of Chaos / Distrust / Pray For War / Fierce / Path Of The Derelict / The Anti-Filanthrope / 9mm / Killing The World, Headfucker (1996) ('Pray For War' 7" split single with EXHUMED)
Blindside / Slaves Of Faith / Jag Värar / Black Malice (Holocaust remix), Mortville (2000) ('Suicidal Disease' 7" split single with THE KILL)

Albums:
THE EXECUTION, Headfucker (1999)
Genocide Angels / All In Your Head / Suicidal Disease / Anorectic Epileptic / No One Knows My Grave / Sick Of Complacence / Black Malice / Inferior / Given A Reason / Near / Crushing Defeat / War! War! War! / Like Weeds / Another Dead Hero / Ignorance / Last Stop / The Rest Of Me / Return To Zero / The Harsh Bitter Truth / Time To Pray / Unjustified Existence / Sans Mercy - Outro

RHADAMANTYS (HOLLAND)

Line-Up: Nico Nielen (vocals), Ard Van Bers (guitar), Nico Vooys (bass), Gerrit Koekebakker (guitar/keyboards), Johan Koelwijn (drums)

RHADAMANTYS were created in 1990 from the amalgamation of GOD'S ACRE and JUDGEMENT. The original line-up featured Ard Van Bers on guitar and lead vocals. For a brief interlude Van Bers joined DONOR but soon returned to RHADAMANTYS in order to record the first two track demo 'Inquiring Minds'.

In 1992 second guitarist Jaco Voorsaat was added and by the end of the year Van Bers concentrated solely on guitar as the band enlisted ex-MUTILATED BONES vocalist Nico 'Nuke' Nielan. The band's sound was further enhanced by the addition of former CREEPMIME drummer Gerrit Koekebakker on guitar and keyboards.

Albums:
LABYRINTH OF THOUGHTS, Displeased (1995)
Saxum Tanali / Source Of Your Intelligence / Cryptical Evidence / Inner Crisis / Unknown Works In Collision / Pile On The Agony

RIGHTEOUS PIGS (NV, USA)

Line-Up: Joe Caper (vocals), Mitch Harris (guitar), Steven Chiatovich (bass), Scott Leonard (drums)

RIGHTEOUS PIGS 'Live And Learn' album sees Scott Leonard behind the drumstool but by the second album Alan Strong had taken his position.

Guitarist Mitch Harris left the band to team up with British grind kings NAPALM DEATH.

Singles/EPs:
Turmoil, Nuclear Blast (1990)

Albums:
LIVE AND LEARN, Nuclear Blast NB12 (1989)
Stone Cold Bitch / I Hope You Die In A Hotel Fire / Just Friends / Malevolent Supplication / Stool Softener / Flee Jurisdiction / Joint Effort / Sickened By Your Own Existence / Fly The Friendly Skies / Dormant Catastrophe / Celibate Tease / Misconduct / Hidden Zit / Destined To Rot / Minor Consumption / Incontinent
STRESS RELATED, Nuclear Blast NB035 (1990)

Eulogy / Boundaries Unknown / Open
Wound / Turmoil / Stress Related /
Overdose / Sickened By His Own
Existence / Fly The Friendly Skies /
Crack Under Pressure / Ruinous Dump /
Incarcerated / Manson Klan

RIGOR MORTIS (SPAIN)

Albums:
VETEAL INFIERNO, Ariola (1983)
Mujer De La Calle / Vete Al Infierno /
Muerete Mas / Suicido / Lucifer / Hey
Amigo / La Ciudad / Rigidez Mortal / Tan
Solo Quiero / Soy Rockero

RIGOR MORTIS (NY, USA)
Line-Up: Robert Vigna (guitar), Thomas
Wilkinson (guitar),

Two erstwhile RIGOR MORTIS members
guitarists Robert Vigna and Thomas
Wilkinson would later found
IMMOLATION.

Singles/EPs:
Holocaust / Warriors Of Doom, Seraphic
Decay (1990)

RIPPING CORPSE (NJ, USA)

RIPPING CORPSE was the pre-MORBID
ANGEL home for guitarist Erik Rutan.
The man makes guest appearances on
the Japanese Speed Metal band RITUAL
CARNAGE's albums.
RIPPING CORPSE members Shaune,
Scott and Brandon founded DIMMAK
together with erstwhile TORTURE
KRYPT bassist Dennis for the 1999
album 'Enter The Dragon'.

Albums:
SPLATTERED REMAINS, CCG
Underground CCG006 (1990)
DREAMING WITH THE DEAD, Under
One Flag FLAG 57 (1991)
Sweetness / Dreaming With The Dead /
Anti God / Glorious Depravity / Beyond
Humanity / Feeling Pleasure Through
Pain / Through The Skin To The Soul /
Rift Of Hate / Deeper Demons /
Sickness Of Will / Chugging Pus /
Seduction Of The innocent

RITUAL CARNAGE (USA / JAPAN)
Line-Up: Damian Montgomery (vocals /
bass), Masami Yamada (guitar), Wataru
Yamada (guitar), Naoya Hamaii (drums)

Tokyo Speed Death Metal crew RITUAL

CARNAGE, founded in 1994 and fronted
by Florida native 'Nasty' Damian
Montgomery. RITUAL CARNAGE has
been wrought by internal dissention with
an ever flowing stream of ex-members
but has steadfastly managed to retain
loyal support. Within the genre RITUAL
CARNAGE are recognized as one of the
elite of the scene.
Montgomery was previously bass player
with PAGAN FAITH in Florida before he
was transferred to Tokyo on a tour of duty
with the U.S. Air Force. In Japan
Montgomery joined Hardcore outfit S.I.C.
This tenure lasted until 1988 with
Montgomery returning to America.
In 1993 Montgomery, training to be a
tattooist, relocated back to Japan and the
following year teamed up with the band
SCRAP TAMBOURINE. This led in turn to
his formation of RITUAL CARNAGE
where initially he was joined by SECTION
8 drummer Alex Amedy and bassist Bill
Jokela. The line up soon morphed with
BLOODSHOWER members guitarist Ken
and drummer Shinjiro Sawada
complementing Montgomery on a 1996
demo session. These two recruits would
decamp soon after in order to
concentrate on BLOODSHOWER.
Undeterred Montgomery reassembled
RITUAL CARNAGE with Amedy making a
return to the drum stool and bassist Hideo
Ideno. This version of the band undertook
one gig during 1997. Former CRACKED
BRAIN guitarist Eddie joined the fold in
August for two support gigs to
MORTICIAN in Tokyo.
The band recorded their 'The Highest
Law' album at Morrisound Studios in
Florida. The album sees guest
appearances from MORBID ANGEL /
RIPPING CORPSE guitarist Erik Rutan
and CANNIBAL CORPSE's
'Corpsgrinder' Fisher. These recordings
secured a deal for a European release
with the French concern Osmose
Productions.
RITUAL CARNAGE yet again underwent
a transformation with ex-CRACKED
BRAIN drummer Naoya Hamaii
supplanting Amedy and Shige Kamazawa
taking over guitar as Montgomery
adopted the role of lead vocalist. This
would be short-lived though as in June of
1998 Idemo broke ranks and
Montgomery added bass guitar to his
duties. In this incarnation RITUAL
CARNAGE undertook European touring
with Osmose labelmates IMPALED
NAZARENE and DRILLER KILLER. In
March of the following year the band

would also accompany IMPALED NAZARENE on their Japanese dates. The live activity to promote 'The Highest Law' did not end there though as RITUAL CARNAGE journeyed back to Europe for further gigs with BENEDICTION and IMMORTAL as well as guesting for Swedish Black Metal premier league act MARDUK on their tour of Japan in June. The solidity displayed by the band came to an end with the close of gigging as Kamazawa departed. In his stead the band enrolled DISGUST guitarist Nakabayashi for recording of a sophomore album 'Every Nerve Alive'. The album reaped controversy in Malaysia where its no holds barred lyric sheet was deemed offensive and removed before distribution. Promotion included dates in the Eastern European countries in alliance with Czechs KRABATHOR before Nakabayashi too took leave.

In December of 1999 the TYRANT veteran Hidenori Tanaki filled the six string vacancy. RITUAL CARNAGE would cut tracks for tribute albums on Dwell Records namely VENOM's 'Welcome To Hell' and KREATOR's 'Impossible To Cure'. Predictably RITUAL CARNAGE was assailed once again by line-up fluctuations as Tanaki split away on acrimonious terms. The band responded by augmenting the band with two new guitarists, the Yamada brothers Masami and Wataru, both of KING'S EVIL. The renewed band guested for VADER's September Japanese tour and later for DISMEMBER.

The band laid down further songs for tribute albums with two MOTORHEAD tracks 'One Track Mind' and 'Mean Machine' for a homage by German label Remedy. Montgomery would also contribute vocal parts to SIGH's 'Scenario IV - Dead Dreams' album.

It seems Eddie Van Koide is now the occupier of the RITUAL CARNAGE lead guitarist slot. 2001 gigs had the band doing the rounds of Japan with GOD DETHRONED and KRABATHOR.

Albums:
THE HIGHEST LAW, Osmose Productions OPCD 073 (1998)
Servant Of The Black / The Unjust (Must Die) / Succumb To The Beast / The Highest Law / Master / Domain Of Death / Chaos And Mayhem / Damnator / Metal Forces / Attack / Onslaught- Death Metal
EVERY NERVE ALIVE, Osmose Productions (2000)

Awaiting The Kill / 8th Great Hell / Death, Judgement, Fate / Burning Red, Burn 'Til Death / End Of An Ace / World Wide War / Scars Of Battle / Every Nerve Alive / The Wrath / Escape From The Light / Far East Aggressors / Hit The Lights / F.O.A.D. / No Compromise / End's Demise

ROSICRUCIAN (SWEDEN)
Line-Up: Lars Linden (guitar / vocals), Magnus Söderman (Guitar), Johan Wiegal (keyboards), Fredrik Jacobsnon (bass), Patrik Marchente (drums)

Previously known as ATROCITY with vocalist Glyn Grimwade. Adopted the title ROSICRUCIAN in 1989 when the first demo 'Initiation Into Nothingness' was recorded. The band added second guitarist Lars Linden after the release of their second demo in 1990.

Grimwade opted to leave after the 'Silence' album and was duly replaced by ex-MEZZROW frontman Ulf Petersson. Finding themselves without a drummer the drums on the second album 'No cause for celebration' were handled by Johnny Bergman of MR. HANGPIKE. ROSICRUCIAN finally located a permanent drummer in Andreas Wallström in late 1994.

Linden, Söderman and Jacobsen later formed SLAPDASH releasing the 'Bound' album in 1996. The following year Söderman involved himself in the ZEALION project band.

Albums:
SILENCE, Black Mark BMCD 25 (1993)
Column Of Grey / Way Of All Flesh / Within The Silence / Esoteric Traditions / Autocratic Faith / Nothing But Something Remains / Aren't You Bored Enough / Back In The Habit / Defy The Opposition / Do You Know Who You're Crucifying
NO CAUSE FOR CELEBRATION, Black Mark BMCD 57 (1994)
Much About Nothing / Classic Guitar / Parts Of Me / No Cause For Celebration / Stench Of Life / Stagnation Of Emotions / Words Without Meaning / The Opening Of Glory End / Naked Face Down / A Moment Of War / Jazz Blues

ROT (BRAZIL)

Grindcore band ROT would tour Germany during 1994 alongside their compatriots ABUSO SENORO and Germans ENTRAILS MASSACRE. In 1998 all three bands featured on a live

video.
The 1999 split single with NO PREJUDICE comprises of live tracks.

Singles/EPs:
Split, (199-) (7" split single with PSYCHO)
Anger Against Conformity / Hidden From Yourself / Very Important People / The Pest (11/90) / The Extreme Vanity / Removing The Mask, Grinding Madness (1993) (7" split single with MINDFART)
Face The Facts / Education / Our Freedom - A Lie / Drowned In Restrictions, Elephant (1994) (7" split single with AGATHOCLES)
Split, Regurgitated Semen (1995) (7" split single with ENTRAILS MASSACRE)
Drowned In Restrictions, (199-)
Almighty God, (199-)
Fatality?, (199-)
Split, (199-) (7" split single with TWISTED TRUTH)
Strong Asociality / No Longer A Threat / Technological Error / Russian Roulette / Seeding The Absurd, Absurd (1999) (7" split single with NO PREJUDICE)

Albums:
UNCERTAIN FUTURE, (1996) (Split album with INTESTINAL DISEASE)
Painful Existence / Uncertain Future / Living To Deceive / Slave Of Majority / Destroy Everything / Rejecting The Media / Our Freedom - A Lie / The Actor / World Abruption / Subversive Not Alternative / Fatality? / Technologic Error / Restricted / Still Not For Me / Violent Acts / Where's My Happiness / Smiling Faces / The Hunger / Almighty God / Putting Down The Structure
CRUEL FACE OF LIFE, (199-)
SPLIT, (199-) (Split album with SUBLIME CADAVERIC DECOMPOSITION)
Cynical Excuse / Little Rockstars / Pull The Trigger / Punk As Fuck / Another Boring Day / Surfer Boy / Despise Their Judgement / Socially Conform / As A Whole
SOCIOPATHIC BEHAVIOUR, (199-)
Feasting His Death / What A Joke / Unjustifiable Fruit / Life Is Not So Kind / No Fear To Sin / Being Different / Strong Asociality / Clones / Happiness Get Away / Seeding The Absurd / Learn Some Respect / Russian Roulette / Infibulation / Humanity Has Begun / Filled With Hatred / All Around Me / Murder Days / Downtrodden / Happening In The Scene / Nothing To Hope / Abstract / Wonderful Tomorrow /

Catching The Fish Hook / Thank You Anyway / Stinks Like Shit / Dream After Dream / From Creation To Collapse / Nightmare Factory / Symptoms Of A New Age / Common Sense / Amazing Lunacy / No Longer A Threat / Social Gear

ROT (HOLLAND)
Line-Up: Steven (vocals), Nydoom (guitar), Snouck (guitar), Jurjaan (drums)

ROT is in fact an amalgam of some of the more notorious characters on the Dutch Death Metal scene apparently so named after they deemed their first attempt at a rehearsal as 'Rotten'. Both guitarist Nydoom and Snouck are members of KILL2CHILL, vocalist Steven is from CATAFALQUE whilst drummer Jurjaan operates in SKUNKMILK.
Nydoom also has his own illustrious solo project BLOWN TO BITS having issued a split album with ANAL PENETRATION.

ROTTEN SOUND (FINLAND)

Grind merchants ROTTEN SOUND's 'Still Psycho' album included a cover version of CARCASS's 'Reek Of Putrefaction'.

Albums:
STILL PSYCHO, Necropolis NR062 MCD (2000)

ROTTING (CANADA)
Line-Up: Korey Arnold (vocals), Rob McAuley (guitar), Jason Balzer (bass), Keith Devry (drums)

Ontario Death Metal band ROTTING began life in 1992 soon releasing the opening 'Christ Crusher' demo. A second tape, 'Drown In Rotting Flesh', was offered in 1995. For maximum horrific effect the 1998 debut album 'Crushed' was graced with a photographic sleeve depicting a recently decapitated corpse.

Albums:
CRUSHED, United Guttural (1998)
Sexually Tortured / Christian Castration / Laid To Rest / Evil I / Blood / Guts / Soulburn / In Vain / Let Them Bleed / Unholy Penetration
THE ORIGINAL CHRIST CRUSHER, (2000)

ROTTING FLESH (BRAZIL)

Singles/EPs:
Infactious Monstrosities, (199-)

Albums:
**SUBMANDIBLE LIMPHATIC
MUSCLES**, Lofty Storm LSR002 (1996)
Suppurated Inflammation Of Fecal
Excretor / Unincinerated Inner-
Crematorium Furnaces /
Phlebothrombosis (Intensive
Bloodsoaked On Arterial Ducts) / Blood
Carnage (Human Flesh Exposed) /
Encephalic Diffuse Enema / Consumed
By Neo-Cannibalistic Worms / Thoraco-
Abdominal Traumatism / Embryonic
Fecundation (Maceration Part II) /
Bizarre Anti-Putrefaction Embalming /
Mucouteral Maceration / Truculent
(Cortuse Cut) Disembowel /
Manifestation Of Chronic Disease /
Consumed By Neo-Cannibalistic Worms
/ Decomposition Of Fetid Limbs /
Intestinal Virulency / Mucouteral
Maceration / Cerebral Haemorrhage /
Malignant Pulmonary Cancer

ROUTE NINE (SWEDEN)

Line-Up: Dan Swanö (vocals / guitar /
bass / keyboards), Anders Jacobsson
(drums)

ROUTE NINE is a side project of
NECRONY and EDGE OF SANITY
members. Swanö is a noted producer on
the Swedish metal scene as well as being
a member of PAN-THY-MONIUM,
UNICORN and NIGHTINGALE.

Singles/EPs:
**Before I Close My Eyes Forever (Part
1)** / Before I Close My Eyes Forever (Part
2), Inorganic ORGAN001 (1995)

RU DEAD? (GERMANY)

Line-Up: Chris (vocals), Gero (guitar), Uli
H. (guitar), Mad (bass), Rüdiger (drums)

Guitarist Uli H is ex-POISON. RU DEAD?
came together in 1989 releasing the five
track 'Simply Dead' demo the following
year. Promotion included live dates with
NAPALM DEATH, PROTECTOR and
ASPHYX.
More demos followed in 1991 and 1992.
Tracks were lifted from the latter for a 7"
EP on Morbid Records titled 'Hypnos'.
However, guitarist Gero departed to join
FLESHCRAWL and RU DEAD? split.
In 1994 Gero quit FLESHCRAWL to

reform RU DEAD? with previous
members in a revised look featuring Gero
on vocals and new recruit Almir taking
over his guitar duties. The group released
a four track CD in 1995.

Singles/EPs:
Hypnos, Morbid (1992)
When Your Heart Turns Black / And
The Moon Whispers / Horrid Tomorrow /
Doomworld, Schädel 001 (1995)
('Nothing Will Be Forgiven' EP)

RUDRA (SINGAPORE)

Line-Up: Kathi (vocals / bass), Alvin
(guitar), Bala (guitar), Shiva (drums)

Named after the Hindu God of destruction
and created as RUDHRA in 1992 as a
Death Black Metal trio of vocalist / bassist
Kathi, guitarist Bala and drummer Shiva.
The band would feature on numerous
compilation albums including 'Battle Of
The Bands', 'Made In Singapore' and
'The Birth Of Death', RUDHRA issued
their own demo 'The Past' in 1994.
The band would fold in 1996 but Kathi
and Shiva pulled the act back together
newly billed as RUDRA by the end of the
year with new guitarist Alvin. MANIFEST
guitarist Burhan would fill in on a
temporary basis until the resumption of
duties from Bala.

Albums:
RUDRA, Candlelight (1998)
Obeisance / Bliss Divine / Black /
Mahamaya / The Ancient One / Atman /
War Legion / For The Dying / Sin No
War (demo) / Ananda (Demo)
METAL LEGION, Candlelight (1998)

RUINATION (LITHUANIA)

Line-Up: Donatas Abrutis (vocals), Ainius
Staneika (guitar), Saulius Vinslovas
(guitar), Andrius Kraskauskas (bass),
Vytautas Diskevicius (keyboards),
Vytenis Beinortas (drums)

Vilnius act RUINATION started life in a
Death / Doom mode but soon switched to
a more concentrated Black attack after
supporting DEICIDE in their home town.
After signing with Spanish label Goldtrack
the band cut their debut album 'Visionary
Breed' with producer Peter Tägtgren of
HYPOCRISY in Sweden. Support gigs to
promote the album included Lithuanian
guest slots to both HYPOCRISY and
APOCALYPTICA.
Tägtgren would also produce the

sophomore 'Xura' album.

Albums:
VISIONARY BREED, Goldtrack (1998)
My Soul's Enchantment / Back Of
Dreams / Loss Of Hopes / End Of
Prayer / Autumn's Blaze / Never / Listen
To The Wind / The Key / My Life, My
Cross / I Found The Feelings / A Lover /
From Your Eyes / Dead Loss Spring .
Just A Joke / Me Kosdykumos
XURA, (1999)
Eject II / Souls On Fire / Trust Again /
Long Way / World In Stain / Xura (The
Lord Of Pleasures Unattached) / For
Ever Descending / Dreamfield / Don't
Take My Name In Vain

RUNEMAGICK (SWEDEN)

Line-Up: Nicklas Rudolfsson (vocals /
guitar), Fredrik Johnsson (guitar), Peter
Palmdahl (bass), Jonas Blum (drums)

Side project of the ever industrious
Nicklas Rudolfsson of SWORDMASTER,
SACRAMENTUM and DEATHWITCH.
RUNEMAGICK came together in 1990
originally with the 'Fullmoon Sodomy'
demo. Early live gigs found
DISSECTION's Johan Norman and
DECAMERON's Alex Losbäck in the fold.
RUNEMAGICK was put on hold in 1993
as Rudolfsson's time was allotted to other
acts.
In 1997, with a gap in his schedule,
Rudolfsson resurrected RUNEMAGICK
pulling in ex DISSECTION bassist Peter
Palmdahl, guitarist Fredrick Johnsson
and drummer Jonas Blum.
Blum is also skinsman for GRIEF OF
EMERALD featuring on their 'Malformed
Seed' album.

Albums:
THE SUPREME FORCE OF ETERNITY,
Century Media 7935-2 (1998)
At The Horizons End / The Black Wall /
When Death Is The Key / For You, My
Death / Curse Of The Dark Rune /
Nocturnal Creation / The Supreme Force
/ Sign Of Eternity (Part II)
ENTER THE REALM OF DEATH,
Century Media (1999)
Hymn Of Darkness / Enter The Realms
Of Death / Longing For Hades / Dwellers
Beyond Obscurity / Abyss Of Desolation
/ Beyond (The Horizon's End) / Dethrone
The Flesh / The Portal Of Doom /
Dreamvoid Serpent / The Call Of Tombs
/ Lightworld Damnation / Dark
Necroshades

RESURRECTION IN BLOOD, Century
Media (2000)
Resurrection Of The Dark Lord / Reborn
In Necromancy / Death Collector / Dark
Dead Earth / Lord Of The Grave / Choir
Of Hades / Resurrection In Blood / Hail
Death / Dominion Of The Necrogods /
Demonstrosity / The Gates Of Hades /
Return Of The Reaper / Celebration Of
Death

RUPTURE (AUSTRALIA)

Line-Up: Gus Chambers (vocals),
Stumble Fuck (guitar), Zombo (bass),
Dick Diamond (drums)

Perth based highly controversial
Grindcore / Punk / Metal band.
RUPTURE go all out in a deliberate
attempt to shock. The Australian censor
board would ban the sleeve artwork to
RUPTURE's 'Filthy Habit' EP. The 'Lust
And Hate' album suffered a similar fate.
Despite a stream of releases and a
burgeoning reputation many believed the
band had gone over the edge of
acceptability with their 1999 album. Not
only was the title unsavoury enough but
lyrics such as "Kill the homosexuals" left
critics dumbfounded.

Singles/EPs:
Baser Apes, Slap A Ham 019 (199-)
Righteous Fuck, Off The Disk 012
(1991)
Split, Yeah Mate (1991) (7" split single
with THE SCROUNGERS)
Gatecrash The Orgy, (199-) (6" single)
Freudsteins House, Regurgitated
Semen RSR019 (1993)
Split, (1997) (7" split single with
BRUTAL TRUTH)
Split, (199-) (7" split single with
SLAVESTATE)
Split, Regurgitated Semen RSR023
(199-) (7" split single with
FLÄCHENBRAND)

Albums:
KILL FOR FUN, Ecocentric 102 (1991)
(Split album with BELCHING BEET)
BRUTAL BADLANDS, HG Fact HG107
(199-)
LUST AND HATE, (199-)
RIGHTEOUS APES, (199-)
CUNT OF GOD, Rhetoric (1999)
Toilet Paper Bible / The 69th Floor / (I
Wanna Have A) Smack Overdose /
Fuckwasp / Negation Or Sedation? /
Exterminants 51-230769 / Keep My
Grave Open / Trillyon Sign / Astral

Robots / Amen Semen / Lucifer In The
Sky With Diamonds / Satan's Slut /
Emergency 666 / Mentally Decapitated /
Psi War / Tattooed Christian / The
Religion That Hath No Name / The Cunt
Of God / Stare At The Sun / Martyr Hari
Death Bop / Poof Biff

SABBATIC FEAST
(Lafayette, LA, USA)
Line-Up: Levi Fuselier (vocals), Josh Clement (guitar), Sean Anders (guitar), Chad Segura (bass), Xul Myron (drums)

Louisiana's SABBATIC FEAST, founded in 1995, include former NECROLUST members drummer Xul Myron (real name Bryan Schultz) and guitarist Sean Anders. Schultz was also previously with MYSTIC FIX.

Albums:
REOPEN THE WOMB, (199-)
Prophecy Of The Dead / And Still They Scream... / The Angel Is Bleeding / Killing Christ / Evil Sex Acts / Shadows Linger
SCALING THE VORTEX, L.F.T.B. LFTB 1313 (1999)
Survival Game / White Collar Crimes / Bodies Never Found / Population Control (Kill Everything...) / Vultures / Shit The Flesh / Harvesting Scabs / Dream Of A Violent Breed / Unborn Virus / Convulse In The Cryptic Fluid / Dance With The Goat / Saints Of Genocide / 6th Oracle Of The 6th Light Of The 6th Lokas

SACRAMENTUM (SWEDEN)
Line-Up: Nissé Karlen (vocals), Anders Brolycke (guitar), Johan Norrrman (guitar), Freddy Andersson (bass), Niklas Rudolfsson (drums)

A Death Metal five-piece, SACRAMENTUM's vocalist Nissé Karlen was previously with RUNEMAGICK.
Karlen formed the group as TUMULUS and recorded a demo in 1993 entitled 'Sedes Imporium'. In 1994 the group released their self-produced promo EP, 'Finis Maloum' later released by Adipocere Records.
However, after the departure of bassist Freddy Andersson, Nissé doubled up on bass whilst former DECAMORAN and DISSECTION guitarist Johan Norrman also played in the group for a period before he quit and was replaced by Anders Brolycke.
The SACRAMENTUM album, 'Far Away From The Sun', was produced by EDGE OF SANITY mainman Dan Swanö.

Singles/EPs:
Moonfog / Travel With The Northern Winds / Devide Et Impera / Pagan Fire / Finis Malorum (Outro), Northern

Production EVIL001 (1994) ('Finis Malorum' EP)

Albums:
FAR WAY FROM THE SUN, Adipocere AR034 (1994)
Fog's Kiss / Far Away From The Sun / Blood Shall Be Spilled / When Night Surrounds Me / Cries From A Restless Soul / Obsolete Tears / Beyond All Horizons / The Vision And The Voice / Outro - Darkness Falls For Me / Far Away From The Sun (Part Two)
THE COMING OF CHAOS, Century Media 77178-2 (1997)
Dreamdeath / ... As Obsidian / Awaken Chaos / Burning Lust / Abyss Of Time / Portal Of Blood / Black Destiny / To The Sound Of Storms / The Coming Of Chaos
THY BLACK DESTINY, (199-)
Iron Winds / The Manifestation / Shun The Light / Demoneaeon / Overlord / Death Obsession / Spiritual Winter / Raptures Paradise - Peccata Mortali / Weave Of Illusion / Thy Black Destiny

SACRED CHAO (GERMANY)
Line-Up: Thorsten Bergmann (vocals), Fred (guitar), Lemmie (bass), Atomic Steif (drums)

SACRED CHAO was ex-LIVING DEATH vocalist Thorsten Bergmann's next project after his departure from the notorious Thrashers.
SACRED CHAO also featured ex-VIOLENT FORCE members drummer Atomic Steif and bassist Lemmie in the group. Steif later teamed up with SODOM.

Singles/EPs:
Cry For More / Life Means Nothing / Dirty Dreams / Leave You Right Now, Aaarrg AAARRG 20 (1989) ('Sacred Chao' EP)

SACRED SIN (PORTUGAL)
Line-Up: José Costa (vocals / bass), Rui Dias (guitar), Antonio Pica (guitar), Carlos A.C. (keyboards), Eduardo 'Dico' (drums)

Death Metallers SACRED SIN were created by erstwhile members of NECROPHILIAC, MASSACRE and SILENT SCREAM. The band toured Portugal in summer of 1993 promoting their 7" EP 'The Shades Behind'. The full length album 'Darkside' led to festival appearances. Other shows would include supports to MANOWAR, TIAMAT, NAPALM DEATH and SENTENCED.

A second pressing of 'Darkside' included a live EP and SACRED SIN's work ethic paid off when they inked a deal with major label BMG.

The 'Eye M God' album was to provide SACRED SIN, now with ex-DISAFFECTED man Quim Aries on drums, with a European tour support to MALEVOLENT CREATION.

SACRED SIN would cut cover tracks for two tribute albums in 2001, namely VENOM and TARANTULA songs.

Singles/EPs:
The Shades Behind, Slime (1992)

Albums:
DARKSIDE, Musica Alternavata MA001 (1993)
Darkside / In The Veins Of Rotting Flesh / Ode To My Crucifying Lord / Deliverance / The Chapel Of The Lost Souls / Requiem... For Mankind / Gravestone Without Name / Suffocate In Torment / Life - A Process Revealed / Terminal Collapse / A Monastery In Darkness / The Shades Behind
EYE M GOD, Dinamite DT 95012 (1995)
Intro / Evocation Of The Depraved / Inductive Compulsion / Eye M God / Death-Bearing Machine / The Nighthag (Nocturnal Queen) / One With God / Guilt Has No Past / A Human Jigsaw / Link To Nothingness / Dead Mind Breed / The Endless Path Of Hecate
ANGUISH... I HARVEST, (199-)
Ghoul Plagued Darkness / Thirteenth Moon / Lead Of Insects / Firethrone / Profane / (Hope) Still Searching / Aghast / Astral / Feathers Black / The Shining Trapezoid
TRANSLUCID DREAM MIRROR, Demolition DEMCD 111 (2000)
Translucid Dream Mirror / Un Clef De Grands Miseres / Ravish The Soul / Sukunft Kenntnis / Gift Of Second Sight / Malificai Genii / Extra Natural Mediator / Mel Lacrimae In Tenebrae / Transmutation / By The Wyvern We Flowed / Prelude To Phenomena / Unbridled Hate / The Shadow Gate

SACRILEGE (SWEDEN)

Line-Up: Michael Andersson (vocals), Daniel Svensson (vocals / drums), Daniel Dinsdale (guitar), Richard Bergholtz (guitar), Daniel Kvist (bass)

SACRILEGE vocalist Michael Andersson would depart prior to recording of the second album 'The Fifth Season'

necessitating drummer Daniel Svensson to take the role.

Svensson joined premier Death Metal band IN FLAMES as drummer during 1998.

Albums:
LOST IN THE BEAUTY YOU SLAY, Black Sun (1996)
Frozen Thoughts / Beyond The Gates Of Pain / Without Delight / Crying Statues Of Paleness And Ice / Fettered In Shackles Of Light / Lost In The Beauty You Slay / Silence In A Beloved Scream / Torment Of Life / Initio Silentium Noctis
THE FIFTH SEASON, Black Sun BS013 (1997)
Summon The Masses And Walk Through Fire / Sweet Moment Of Triumph / Nine Eyes Of Twilight / Feed The Cold / Fifth Season / Moaning Idiot Heart / Dim With Shame / Seduction Nocturne / In Winter Enticed / Sorc

SACROSANCT (HOLLAND)

Line-Up: Michel Lucarelli (vocals), Randy Meinhard (guitar), Michel Cerrone (guitar), Christian Colli (bass), Marco Foddis (drums)

Meinhard and Foddis were both previously with PESTILENCE. SACROSANCT toured Germany in 1992 as support to DARK ANGEL following which Michael Lucarelli and Gerrit Knol departed, although this didn't prevent the group from contributing the song 'Shining Through' to the 'Stop War' compilation album.

The 'Tragic Intense' album featured ex-PHARAO musicians vocalist Collin Kock and guitarist Mike Kock and was produced by then TORCHURE vocalist S.L. Coe.

SACROSANCT's 1992 line up comprised of the Kock brothers, Meinhard, Colli and drummer Haico Van Atticum.

In 1994 both Meinhard and Colli joined SUBMISSION, the short lived band assembled by ex-PESTILENCE and ASPHYX vocalist Martin Van Drunen.

Guitarist Michel Cerrone created IMPERIUM for a 1993 album.

Albums:
TRUTH IS - WHAT IS, No Remorse NRR 1009 (1990)
Dimension Of Violence / Execrated (They Will Be) / Skin To Skin / The Sickened Thrill / Terminal Suicide / Disputed Death / Catalepsy / Truth Is -

What Is / The Die Is Cast / Injured
RECESSES FOR THE DEPRAVED 1MF
(1991)
Illusive Supremacy / Like Preached
Directions / Astrayed Thoughts / Mortal
Remains / Hidden Crimes Untold / Enter
The Sanctum / With Malice Pretense /
The Silence Of Being
TRAGIC INTENSE, 1MF 377.003-2
(1993)
From Deep Below / Godforesaken /
Shining Through / Fainted / At Least
Pain Lasts / The Gathering Of The
Tribes / The Breed Within

SADIST (ITALY)
Line-Up: Andy (vocals / bass), Tommy
Talamanca (guitar), Peso (drums)

Previously known as NECRODEATH and
formed in 1991, under the original
monicker the Italians released the 'Into
The Macabre' record before switching to
the SADIST handle and promptly coming
up with the 'Black Screams' 7" single for
Italian label Obscure Plasma.
The single sold around 2,500 copies, but
following its release original vocalist
Fabio quit and thus bassist Andy took
over singing duties.
After touring through Italy, Portugal and
France SADIST signed to Nosferatu
Records and recorded the 'Above The
Light' debut album before a parting of the
ways occurred with Andy and SADIST
drafted in vocalist Zanna and bassist
Chicco. Both appeared on the 'Tribe'
album prior to SADIST reuniting with
Andy.
'Tribe' was recorded in England at the
Rhythm Studio.
Guitarist Tommy Talamanca produced the
debut album from extreme Death Metal
band NATRON in 1998.

Singles/EPs:
Black Screams, Obscure Plasma (1991)

Albums:
ABOVE THE LIGHT, Nosferatu
NOSF001 (1993)
Nadir / Breathin' Cancer / Enslaver Of
Lies / Sometimes They Come Back /
Hell In Myself / Desert Divinities / Sadist
/ Happiness n' Sorrow
TRIBE, Rising Sun CD34435 (1996)
Escogido / India / From Bellatrix To
Betelgeuse / Den Siste Kamp / Tribe /
Spiral Of The Winter Ghosts / The Ninth
Wave / The Reign Of Asmat
CRUST, Displeased D00056 (1997)

Perversion Lust Orgasm / The Path /
Fools And Dolts / Holy … / Ovariotomy /
Instinct / Obsession – Compulsion / …
Crust / I Rape You / Christmas Beat

SADISTIC INTENT
(Los Angeles, CA, USA)
Line-Up: Bay Cortez (vocals / bass), Rick
Cortez (guitar), Vincent Cervera (guitar),
Emilio Marquez (drums)

SADISTIC INTENT have a lineage
stretching back as far as 1987. The band,
originally led by vocalist Enrique Chavez,
signed to the Wild Rags label for the 1990
EP 'Impending Doom'. Following tours of
America and Mexico the band would
break free from Wild Rags on rather
acrimonious terms issuing the limited
edition self financed 7" single 'A Calm
Before The Storm'.
Line up troubles afflicted the band for the
next few years before a newly resettled
line up cut the 'Resurrection' mini album
in 1994. A further demo session 'Ancient
Black Earth' ensued the following year
which was pressed up as a limited edition
run CD in 1996. The same year
SADISTIC INTENT were included on the
CELTIC FROST tribute album 'In Memory
Of' with their version of 'Return To The
Eve'. Live action saw the band
undertaking tours of America and Mexico
as well as putting in a showing at the
legendary Milwaukee Metalfest.
In 1998 SADISTIC INTENT shared space
on a shared 7" single with Germany's
UNGOD. 1999 found the band on another
homage album, this time honouring
POSSESSED with the novel addition of
erstwhile POSSESSED singer Jeff
Becerra on guesting vocals. A further
tribute affair had SADISTIC INTENT
donating to a SLAYER collection.

Singles/EPs:
Lurking Terror / Existence / Morbid
Faith / Impending Doom, Wild Rags
(1990) ('Impending Doom' EP)
Second Coming / Dark Predictions,
Sadistic Intent (1991) ('A Calm Before
The Storm' 7" single)
Ancient Black Earth EP, Dark Realm
(1996)

Albums:
RESURRECTION, Dark Realm (1994)
Resurrection / Asphyxiation / Conflict
Within / Dark Predictions / Condemned
In Misery / A Mass For Tortured Souls
THE SECOND COMING OF

DARKNESS, Necropolis (2000)

SADISTIC NOISE (GREECE)

SADNESS (SWITZERLAND)
Line-Up: Steff (vocals / guitar), Chiva (guitar / keyboards), Erik (bass), Gradel (drums)

Following the first SADNESS demo, merely titled 'Y', in 1990 bassist Erik departed to join ALASTIS. His place was taken by Andy and a further demo, 'Eodipus', was released.
SADNESS signed to the Polish label Mystic Records for the 'Evangelion' album and toured Poland alongside BEHEMOTH, ASGARD, COLD PASSION and LIMBONIC ART.
'Danteferno' was produced by former CELTIC FROST bass player Martin E. Ain.
In 1997 Chiva debuted his side project act CHIVA with the 'Oracle Morte' album.

SADUS (Antioch, CA, USA)
Line-Up: Darren Travis (vocals / guitar), Rob Moore (guitar), Steve DiGeorgio (bass), Jon Allen (drums)

SADUS came together as a quartet in 1984 of vocalist Darren Travis, guitarist Rob Moore, bassist Steve DiGeorgio and drummer Jon Allen although it was to be two years until the first fruits of this liaison came into being with the 1986 'D.T.P' demotape. These sessions led directly to the inclusion of two tracks on the 1987 'Raging Death' compilation album.
Quick to capitalize on this achievement SADUS stuck their hands in their pockets to self-finance the debut album pulling in METAL CHURCH guitarist John Marshall as producer.
The pace of progress was quickened as a deal with label Roadrunner Records was secured resulting in a further album 'Swallowed In Black' and touring with the likes of SEPULTURA and OBITUARY.
SADUS was put on ice for 1991 as DiGeorgio opted to assist DEATH for their 'Human' album. With this added exposure Roadrunner re-released the 'Illusions' debut retitled 'Chemical exposure' as SADUS regrouped for a summer American tour opening for MORBID ANGEL.
Although a further album for Roadrunner, 1992's 'A Vision Of Misery', resulted in a European headline tour SADUS found themselves labelless upon their return. Further setbacks occurred when DiGeorgio was enticed back to DEATH for the 'Individual Thought Patterns' album and a subsequent year long bout of touring. DiGeorgio was to return for club shows with SADUS but before any momentum could be gained Moore bailed out.
SADUS continued as a trio crafting the Scott Burns produced 'Elements Of Anger' in 1997. The in demand DiGeorgio along with drummer Jon Allen also operated a side project DRAGONHEART with ex-VICIOUS RUMOURS and present day TESTAMENT guitarist Steve Smyth and his fellow TESTAMENT six stringer Eric Peterson. DiGeorgio teamed up with ICED EARTH in late 2000.

Deceptive Perceptions / Under The Knife / Echoes Of Forever
CHRONICLES OF CHAOS, Mascot M 7025-2 (1997)
Certain Death / Undead / Sadus Attack / Torture / Hands Of Fate / Illusions / Man Infestation / Good Rid'nz / Powers Of Hate / Arise / Oracle Of Obmission / Through The Eyes Of Greed / Valley Of Dry Bones / Slave To Misery / Facelift / Deceptive Perceptions / Echoes Of Forever
ELEMENTS OF ANGER, Mascot M 7026-2 (1997)
Aggression / Crutch / Words Of War / Safety In Numbers / Mask / Fuel / Power Of One / Stronger Than Life / Unreality / In The End

SAD WHISPERINGS (HOLLAND)

Line-Up: J.A. Van Leeuwen, E.R. Veniga, M. Schrikkema, W.W.B. Wolda

A melodic Doom / Death Metal act.

Albums:
SENSITIVE TO AUTUMN, Foundations 2000 SDN 2007 (1993)
The Tombstone / Vale Of Tears / Free As The Wind / Fear Glanced Eyes / Tears On My Pillow / Timeless Grief / The Last Day Of April / Leaving Me Behind / Sparks In The Dust / Sensitive To Autumn

SAMAEL (SWITZERLAND)

Line-up: Vorphalack (Vocals / guitar), Masmisiem (bass), Xytraguptor (drums)

Proud to be recognized as one of the gloomiest bands in Europe. Over a series of finely crafted albums SAMAEL have built up an enviable reputation for quality Metal with a unique touch. SAMAEL heralded their arrival with the 1987 demo recording titled 'Into The Infernal Storm Of Evil'.

Swiss act SAMAEL's 1989's 'Medieval Prophecy' mini-album featured a cover of HELLHAMMER's 'The Third Of The Storm'. SAMAEL's next release in 1990 was the demo tape 'From Dark To Black'. The 'Rebellion' mini-album boasted a cover of ALICE COOPER's 'I Love The Dead'.

The group added keyboard player Rudolphe H. for live dates in 1995 with SENTENCED and for the recording of 1996's 'Passage' all drum parts were programmed and Xytraguptor (later simply 'Xytra') assumed a new role as keyboard player. A second guitarist, Khaos from French Death Metallers GORGON, was also brought in for recording and live dates. SAMAEL's relationship to SENTENCED was strengthened as Vorphalack added backing vocals to the Finn's 'Down' outing.

SAMAEL
Photo : Martin Wickler

SAMAEL
Photo : Martin Wickler

333

SAMAEL's 'Worship Him' album went on to sell over 10,000 copies in Europe. The follow up 'Blood Ritual' was produced by GRIP INC.'s Waldemar Sorychta.

For 'Ceremony Of Opposites', produced by Sorychta once again, SAMAEL added keyboard player Rudolphe H.

SAMAEL's 1996 album 'Passage' would be re-released two years later with ambient classical remixes of all tracks by Xystra. 1999's 'Eternal' was widely acknowledged to be a classic of the genre.

Singles/EPs:
Medieval Prophecy, Necrosound (1989)
Rebellion / After The Sepulture / Into The Pentagram / I Love The Dead / Static Journey, Century Media 77099-2 (1995) ('Rebellion' EP)

Albums:
WORSHIP HIM, Osmose Productions OPCD001 (1991)
Sleep Of Death / Worship Him / Knowledge Of the Ancient Kingdom / Morbid Metal / Rite Of Cthulhu / The Black Face / Into The Pentagram / Messengers Of The Light / Last Benediction / The Dark
BLOOD RITUAL, Century Media CM97372 (1992)
Epilogue / Beyond The Nothingness / Poison Infiltration / After The Sepulture / Macabre Operetta / Blood Ritual / Since The Creation / With The Gleam Of Torches / Total Consecration / Bestial Devotion / Until The Chaos
SAMAEL 1987-1992, Century Media 77085-2 (1993)
Epilogue/ Beyond The Nothingness / Poison Infiltration / After The Sepulture / Macabre Operetta / Blood Ritual / Since The Creation / With The Gleam Of Torches / Total Consecration / Bestial Devotion / ...Until The Chaos / Sleep Of Death / Worship Him / Knowledge Of The Ancient Kingdom / Morbid Metal / Rite Of Cthulhu / The Black Face / Into The Pentagram / Messengers Of The Light / Last Benediction / The Dark
CEREMONY OF OPPOSITES, Century Media CD 77064-2 (1994)
Black Trip / Celebration Of The Fourth / Son Of Earth / 'Til We Meet Again / Mask Of The Red Death / Baphomet's Throne / Flagellation / Crown / To Our Martyrs / Ceremony Of Opposites
PASSAGE, Century Media 77127-2 (1996)
Rain / Shining Kingdom / Angel's Decay

/ My Saviour / Jupiterian Vibe / The Ones / Liquid Souls / Moonskin / Born Under Saturn / Chosen Race / A Man In Your Head
EXODUS, Century Media 77210-2 (1998)
Exodus / Tribes Of Cain / Son Of Earth / Winter Solstice / Ceremony Of The Opposites / From Malkuth To Kether
PASSAGE / XYSTRA, Century Media (1998)
Rain / Shining Kingdom / Angel's Decay / My Saviour / Jupiterian Vibe / The Ones / Liquid Souls / Moonskin / Born Under Saturn / Chosen Race / A Man In Your Head / Regen / Glanzednes Königreich / Des Engels Untergang / Jupiterianische Schwingungen / Die Volter Kamen / Der Stamm Kains / Mondhaut / Mein Retter / Wintersonnenwerde / Ein Mensch Im Kopf
ETERNAL, Century Media (1999)
Year Zero / Ailleurs / Together / Ways / The Cross / Us / Supra Karma / I / Nautilus And Zeppelin / Infra Galaxia / Berg / Radiant Star

SANATORIUM (SLOVAKIA)
Line-Up: Martin Belobrad (vocals / bass), Onecque (guitar), Dzordz (drums)

SANATORIUM are not only the leading Death Metal force in Slovakia but their frontman Martin Belobrad is the prime motivator behind Erebos Productions as well as acting as tour promoter for international Metal acts touring the country.

SANATORIUM arrived with a 1995 demo cassette 'Subculture' followed by 'Autumn Shadows'. This second tape would be re-issued by Czech label View Beyond on a 7" single. A third demo 'Necrologue' emerged in 1998.

SANATORIUM's 2001 album saw a guest vocal performance from Miroslav of GOREOPSY.

Singles/EPs:
Autumn Shadows, View Beyond (1999)

Albums:
ARRIVAL OF THE FORGOTTEN ONES, Erebos Productions ERE011 (1999)
Throne Of The Undead / Necrologue Written In Forest / Race Of The Dimension Unknown / Diseases Awareness Of Reality / Cemetary Of Memories / Guardians Of Deceitful Dawn / Evolution Of Decay / Autumn Shadows / Red Moon / Minulost

SANCTUS (Los Angeles, CA, USA)
Line-Up: Jason McCrarey (vocals), Royce Hsu (guitar), Mike O' Meara (guitar), Brent Gobson (bass), Adrian Ross (keyboards), Michael Chi (drums)

California act SANCTUS were created in 1998 under the name of PANTHEON, issuing a demo under this name. Scoring a deal with Metal Blade Records the band duly adopted the new title of SANCTUS.

Albums:
AEON SKY, Metal Blade (2000)
Emyreal / If We Fall… / Odyssey / November / Tired Of The Pain / Thought I Saw Your Wings / Thy Desolation / Remnants

SANITY'S DAWN (GERMANY)
Line-Up: Max Kielhauser (vocals / guitar), Andreas Schorn (bass), Sven Horl (drums)

A Death Metal band from near Hannover, SANITY'S DAWN released the 'Preachers Of Blood' demo before commercially released material.

Singles/EPs:
Mortal Consumption EP, (1993) (Cassette release)

Albums:
LOOKING FOR SANITY, (1991)
ARTERIA MORBUS, (1995) (Cassette release)
CRYPTIC MENU, Tank 2402 (1997)
Intro / Ballgames With A Torn Off Head / Mutilation / Blinddarm / Torture / In My Fridge / Notturno / Clump Of Flesh / Maggots In The Anal Tract / Kranker Blick
MANGLED IN THE MEATGRINDER, (199-)
Burp / Mangled In The Meatgrinder / Gargling With Rancid Pus / I Eat Shit / Schleimhartsepsis / Suppurative Pustules / Fleisch / Koerperfresser / Nice To Eat You / Morgue / Cancer Comes Cadaverous / I Need You For Barbecue / Sweet Scent Of Suet Soup / Delicious Burst Ulcers By Maximum Microwave Power / Intestines Pierced Alive / Ich Will Kuehe

SARCASM (SWEDEN)
Line-Up: Heval Bozarslan (vocals), Fredrik Wallenberg (guitar), Dave Janney (bass), Henrik Forslund (drums)

SARCASM was one of Sweden's more illustrious and elusive Death Metal names. Founded in October of 1990 by vocalist Heval Bozarslan and guitarist Fredrik Wallenberg. This duo was soon joined by bass player Dave Janney and drummer Henrik Forslund to complete the line up for the 1992 'In Hate' demo.
Within months another tape surfaced suitably entitled 'Dark'. By late 1993 Forslund switched instruments over to guitar and SARCASM drafted Oscar Karlsson on the skins. Now a quintet the group released a third promotional cassette 'A Touch Of The Burning Red Sunset'.
SARCASM would undergo line-up turbulence as Wallenberg departed to be supplanted by Anders Erikkson for the recording of the debut album 'Burial Dimensions'. However, the ructions within the band would stall its release and SARCASM duly split.
Despite achieving no commercial release SARCASM's reputation remained and in 1999 the American Breath Of Night label would issue the demos on CD format titled 'A Touch Of The Burning Red Sunset'.
SARCASM would reform with reformed with Bozarslan, Janney and Eriksson joined by Simon Winroth.

Albums:
A TOUCH OF THE BURNING RED SUNSET, Breath Of Night BON3CD (1999)
Dark / Upon The Mountains Of Glory / Through The Tears Of God / Never After / You Bleed (I Enjoy) / Nail Her Up / Pile Of Bodies / In Hate… / A Touch Of The Burning Red Sunset

SARCAZM (SWEDEN)
Line-Up: Krister Albertsson (vocals / guitar), Niclas Engelin (guitar), Beppe Kurdali (bass), Peter Andersson (drums)

SARCAZM's guitarist Niclas Engelin was formerly with IDIOTS RULE and, in addition to the 'Breathe, Shit, Exist' album, SARCAZM also contributed their version of 'Motorbreath' to the METALLICA tribute album 'Metal Militia'. Ex-SARCAZM vocalist Micke Nicklasson and drummer Peter Andersson wound up later forming LUCIFERION. Guitarist Niclas Engelin created GARDENIAN debuting with the 1997 record 'Two Feet Stand'.

Albums:
BREATHE, SHIT, EXIST, Deathside
DS10394 (1994)
Pure Hate / Covered Again / My Inner
Rots / Breathe, Shit, Exist

SARCOFAGO (BRAZIL)
Line-Up: Wagner Lamounier (vocals /
guitar), Gerald Minelli (bass), M. Joker
(drums)

A veteran act on the South American
Death Metal scene. The Satanically
inspired SAROFAGO employ Death
Metal with distinct Punk leanings allied to
blasphemous lyrics.
Rather alarmingly guests on the 'Rotting'
album included Oswaldo Pussy Ripper
and Eugenio Dead Zone. Adverts for the
album announced "Formed by Wagner
Antichrist who left SEPULTURA because
they were too commercial!"
SARCOFAGO debuted with the 1986
demo 'Satanic Lust' leaving no
pretensions as to which musical direction
the band was headed. The equally to the
point demos 'The Black Vomit' and
'Christ's Death' ensued upfront of the first
full length album 'I.N.R.I.'.
For 1991's 'The Laws Of Scourge' the
band comprised vocalist / guitarist
Wagner 'Antichrist' Lamounier, guitarist
Fabio Jhosko, bass player Gerald
'Incubus' Minelli and drummer Lucio
Olliver. OVERDOSE mainman Claudio
David would provide backing vocals.

Albums:
I.N.R.I., Cogumelo (1987)
Satanic Lust / Desecration Of Virgin /
Nightmare / I.N.R.I. / Christ's Death /
Satanas / Ready To Fuck / Deathrash /
The Last Slaughter / Recrucify / The
Black Vomit
ROTTING, Cogumelo (1989)
The Lust / Alcoholic Coma / Tracy /
Rotting / Sex, Drinks And Metal /
Nightmare
THE LOST TAPES OF COGUMELO,
Cogumelo (1990)
THE LAWS OF SCOURGE, Under One
Flag CDFLAG 66 (1991)
The Laws Of Scourge / Piercings /
Midnight Queen / Screeches From The
Silence / Prelude To A Suicide / The
Black Vomit / Secrets Of A Window /
Little Julie / Crush, Kill, Destroy
HATE, Cogumelo (1995)
DECADE OF DECAY, Cogumelo (1996)
THE WORST, Cogumelo (1997)
The End (Intro) / The Worst / Army Of

The Damned / God Bless The Whores /
Plunged In Blood / Satanic Lust / The
Necrophiliac / Shave Your Head /
Purification Process

SARCOPHAGUS (De Kalb, IL, USA)
Line-Up: Andrew Jay Harris (vocals /
guitar), Daniel Guenther (guitar), Marcus
Matthew Kolar (bass), Duane Timlin
(drums)

Blasphemous Death Metal band
SARCOPHAGUS are in fact yet another
outlet for the creative forces of Andrew
Jay Harris, more commonly known as
Akhenaten of JUDAS ISCARIOT and
WELTMACHT alongside Lord Imperial of
KRIEG. Harris also owns Breath Of Night
Records and has issued the one off
JESUS FUCKING CHRIST single
'Unalive At Golgotha'.
Debuted with the demo 'Cursed Are The
Dead' in 1991. At this point the band
comprised of Harris, bassist Marcus
Matthew Kolar, vocalist Frank Drago,
guitarist Michael Matejka and drummer
Paul Bruneau. A stream of demos
followed including 'Sarcophagus' in 1993
(bootlegged on a 7" single the following
year), 'Der Ubermensch' and 'Apathy' in
1995. By 1994 though SARCOPHAGUS
was down to a duo of Harris and Kolar.
A projected album on the Interment label
to be titled 'Thirteen Songs' was
announced but never released. 1997 saw
SARCOPHAGUS up to full band strength
with the enlistment of guitarist Daniel
Guenther and FOREST OF IMPALED
drummer Duane Timlin.
One of Harris' side concerns
WELTMACHT also includes Timlin under
the pseudonym of Cryptic Winter.
Akhenaten would relocate to Germany for
later JUDAS ISCARIOT releases and
would also become live bass player for
the infamous Czech Black Metal act
MANIAC BUTCHER.

Albums:
DEADNOISE, (1994)
Banned From The Altar / From The
Cross / Masquerade / Mental Atrocities /
Black / The Absence
**FOR WE... WHO ARE CONSUMED BY
DARKNESS**, Pulverizer PRCD001
(1996)
Godless / Our Black Autumn / Die
Totenmaske / Fuck Pig / Agony's Tale /
Wrath / Damned Below Judas / Si
Piangiamo Or Dunque Uniti / Breath Of
Night

**SARCOPHAGUS- DEADNOISE-
UBERMENSCH**, Pulverizer (1996)
Sarcophagus / Human Machines /
Morbid Dreams / Banned From The Altar
/ From The Cross / Masquerade / Mental
Atrocities / Black / The Absence / Die
Totenmaske / Fuck Pig / Si Piangiamo
Or Dunque Uniti / Ubermensch
**REQUIEM TO THE DEATH OF
PASSION**, Nightfall (1997)
From The Ruin Of Paradise / The Dark
Lord Of Impurity / Requiem To The
Death Of Passion / In Silent Death / Of
Fire Surrounding All The Heavens /
Bastard Sons Of Ignorance / Infernal
Supremacy / The Pagan Battlefield

SATANIC SLAUGHTER (SWEDEN)
Line-Up: Toxine (vocals), Ztephan Dark
(vocals / guitar), Patrick Jensen (guitar),
Richard (guitar), Goat (bass), Mique
(drums)

SATANIC SLAUGHTER are one of
Scandinavia's older Black Death Metal
acts having formed in 1985. Previous to
this date the band went under the
politically incorrect name of EVIL CUNT.
Of the original line-up only guitarist
Ztephan Dark remains. Original bassist
Goat became a pyromaniac and now
resides in a mental hospital!
SATANIC SLAUGHTER released their
demo 'One Night In Hell' during 1988.
Vocalist Moto was replaced by Andy. In
December of the following year the band
was put on ice as Dark was imprisoned,
convicted of assault. The man would later
join MORBIDITY, CRUZIFIED ANGEL
and MORGUE.
The band got back together in 1992 with
members of SÉANCE, including vocalist
Toxine, drummer Mique and guitarists
Patrick Jensen and Richard were
involved.
However, in 1997 SATANIC
SLAUGHTER collapsed yet again, this
time due to time honoured musical
differences. Dark resolved himself to pick
up the pieces with all the other ex-
members creating the high profile act
WITCHERY. Jensen also became a
member of THE HAUNTED.
In 1999 SATANIC SLAUGHTER brought
in former TRIUMPHATOR drummer
Martin Axenroth to replace previous
incumbent Robert Eng. The 2000 line-up
comprised Dark, Axenroth, guitarist
Christian Ljungberg, vocalist Andreas
Deblén and bassist Filip Carlsson.

Albums:
SATANIC SLAUGHTER, Necropolis
NR004 (1995)
Immortal Death / Forever I Burn / Dark
Ritual / Into The Catacombs / Breath Of
The Serpent That Rules The Cold World
/ On Black Wings / Nocturnal Presence /
Legion Of Hades / Divine Exorcism / I'll
Await My Lord / Embraced By Darkness
/ Domine Lucipheros
LAND OF THE UNHOLY SOULS,
Necropolis NR014 (1997)
Intro / Hatred Of God / Servant Of Satan
/ Satanic Queen / Demons Feast /
Forever I Burn / Legion Of Hades /
Breath Of The Serpent That Rules The
Cold World / Immortal Death / Land Of
The Unholy Souls / One Night In Hell /
Dark Ritual / Forever I Burn
AFTERLIFE KINGDOM, Loud n' Proud
LNP012 (2000)
The Arrival - Afterlife Kingdom /
Nocturnal Crimson Nightmare / When
Darkness Prevails / Divine Repulsion /
Through The Dark Profound / Autumn /
Ad Noctum / Flag Of Hate

SATARIEL (SWEDEN)
Line-Up: Par Johansson (vocals), Mikael
Grankvist (guitar), Magnus Alakangas
(guitar / keyboards), Mikael Degerman
(bass), Robert Sundelin (drums)

SATARIEL was a 1993 union of erstwhile
members of defunct outfits BEHEADED
and DAWN OF DARKNESS namely
vocalist Pär Johansson on vocals,
guitarist Maguns Alakangas and bassist
Mikael Degerman. A later recruit was
guitarist Mikael Grankvist for the debut
demo 'This Heavens Fall'. SATARIEL
added Mats Ömalm after this recording
but his exit followed swiftly after.
1995 also saw the departure of Grankvist.
Further changes apparent on the second
session 'Hellfuck' included the addition of
guitarist Fredrik Andersson and drummer
Andreas Nilzon. By 1996 Nilzon was out
of the picture and Robert Sundelin took
the drum stool position. However,
SATARIEL was put on ice for a lengthy
period when both Sundelin and
Degerman undertook their military
service.
When SATARIEL reformed Grankvist too
was back in the fold for the debut album
'Lady Lust Lilith' on Pulverized Records.
SATARIEL guitarist Mikael Grankvist also
operates in THE MOANING. Drummer
Robert Sundelin is a member of
NECROMONICON.

Between 1993 and 1995 Johansson also put time into his side project BELSEMAR releasing the demos 'De Svarta Gudarnas Sömn' and 'Epistles Of Pain'. Not to be confused with the theatric Russian band of the same name that issued the album 'The Queen Of The Elves Land'.

Albums:
LADY LUST LILITH, Pulverized (1998)
Devils Dozen XIII / The Well Of The Artist / Four Moons Till Rising / The Span Of The Shadows / Lady Lust Lilith / The Great Necropolis - Baphomet Erected / Behind What's I / They're Sheep To Be Slain / A Vision Of An Ending / Greeting Immortality
PHOBOS AND DAIMOS, Hammerheart (2001)

SATURNUS (DENMARK)
Line-Up: A.G. Jensen (vocals), Kim Larsen (guitar), Brian Hansen (bass), Anders Ro Nielsen (keyboards), Jesper Saltoft (drums / keyboards)

A Danish Doom / Death band initially titled ASSESINO. The band can trace it's history back to the 1991 union of vocalist Thomas A.G. Jenson, guitarists Kim Sindahl and Christian Brenner, bass player Brian Hansen and drummer Pouli Choir as ASSESINO.
The band actually split but reunited with fresh recruit Jesper Saltoft. A period of flux ensued with Sindahl decamping and guitarist Michael Andersen and keyboard player Anders Ro Nielsen being drafted. At this stage the unit opted for the new title of SATURNUS.
1994 saw the inclusion of guitarist Kim Larsen and the following year the exit of Andersen. A support gig to Britain's doom mongers MY DYING BRIDE made a weighty impression on the band who acknowledge their shift in style to a gloomy, melancholic style from this juncture.
SATURNUS cut their debut album 'Paradise Belongs To You' for the Euphonious label which included new drummer Morten Skrubbeltrang. Promoting the album SATURNUS ambitiously employed an 8 piece choir for live gigs.
After a mini-album 'For The Loveless Lonely Nights' a switch in drummers had Peter Poulsen joining in time for the Flemming Rasmussen produced 'Martyre' album.

SATURNUS suffered further internal strife in 1999 with new enlistees being drummer Morten Plenge, guitarist Tais Pedersen and bassist Peter Heede. Both Larsen and Nielsen sessioned on BLAZING ETERNITY's debut album of 2000.

Albums:
PARADISE BELONGS TO YOU, Euphonious PHONI 005 (1996)
Paradise Belongs To You / Christ Goodbye / As We Dance The Path Of Fire And Solace / Pilgrimage Of Sorrow / The Fall Of Nakkiel (Nakkiel Has Fallen) / Astral Dawn / I Love Thee / The Underworld / Lament For This Treacherous World
FOR THE LOVELESS LONELY NIGHT, Euphonious (1998)
Starres / For Your Demons / Thou Art Free / Christ Goodbye (Live) / Rise Of Nakkiel (Live) / Consecration
MARTYRE, Euphonious (2000)
Inflame Thy Heart / Empty Handed / Noir / A Poem (Written In Moonlight) / Softly On The Path You Fade / Thou Art Free / Drown My Sorrow / Lost My War / Loss (In Memorium) / Thus My Heart Weepeth For Thee / In Your Shining Eyes

SCATTERED REMNANTS
(Fitchburg, MA, USA)
Line-Up: Jason Hendershaw (vocals), Rob Settergren (guitar), Jamie Harman (guitar), Dan Egan (bass), Steve Gonsalves (drums)

SCATTERED REMNANTS, created in 1992, arrived on the scene with the 1994 promotional tape 'Procreating Mass Carnage'. The following year a CD EP 'Inherent Perversion' followed and shortly after the initial demo would be re-released on CD format.
However, SCATTERED REMNANTS rhythm section of bassist Ron Miles and drummer Eric Roy had decamped previously and the band were dealt another blow when guitarist Jay Sarate quit too. The latter's position was taken by Jamie Harman.
Signing to the Repulse label the band drafted former EXHUMED bassist Dan Egan and utilized the services of session drummer Steve Gonsalves to record the 1998 'Destined To Fail' album.

Singles/EPs:
Inherent Perversion, (1995)
Procreating Mass Carnage, (1997)

Albums:
DESTINED TO FAIL, Repulse RPS
035CD (1998)
Destined To Fail /Lamentation Of
Tortured Souls / Draped In Sorrow / At
The Right Of Nothingness / As Whores /
Angelic Redemption / Virtuous
Abandonment / Vaginal Vomit

SCHEITAN (SWEDEN)
Line-Up: Pierre Törnvist (vocals / guitar /
bass), Oskar Karlsson (drums)

A Black Metal project formed by THE
EVERDAWN vocalist Pierre Törnkvist
and THE EVERDAWN and GATES OF
ISHTAR drummer Oskar Karlsson, both
had originally recorded only one track to
find a suitable label for the project but, in
the end, an entire conceptual record was
cut for Invasion Records.
Törnkvist, a former member of
DECORTICATION, also opted to reform
side band THE EVERDAWN. Törnkvist
also operates in THE MOANING.

Albums:
TRAVELLING IN ANCIENT TIMES,
Invasion I.R. 024 (1996)
October Journey / Autumn Departure /
Riding The Icewinds / December At
Fullmoon / In Battle With Angels /
Leaving The Mortals / Devastating
Heaven / Portals Of Might
BEZERK 2000, (1998)
Raincoat / Exitways / Soulside / Sad To
Say / V / Terror / Bombraid Over
Wastelands / Bezerk 2000 / The Scheitan
NEMESIS, Century Media (1999)
Fury Flow / Psyched / Black Rain /
Marionette / Forgive Me / A Silent Hum /
Ways / My Isle / Emergency

SCHIZO (ITALY)
Line-Up: Vittorio Blanco (vocals / guitar),
Alberto Penzin (bass), Pat Pappalardo
(drums)

SCHIZO date back to 1985. The band
actually split following the release of
'Mainframe Collapse' in 1989 but
reformed to release the 'Wounds (In The
Clay)' demo in 1992.

Albums:
MAINFRAME COLLAPSE, Crime (1989)
Violence At The Morgue / Threshold Of
Pain / Make Her Bleed / Slowly /
Epileptic Void / Removal Part I & II /
Psycho Terror / Sick Of It All / Manifold
Hallucinations / Behind The Curtain /

Main Frame Collapse / Delayed Death
SOUNDS OF COMING DARKNESS, AV
Arts AVRCD008 (1994)

SCORN (UK)
Line-Up: Mick Harris (vocals / drums),
Justin Broadrick (guitar), Nik Bullen
(bass)

Ex-DOOM drummer Mick Harris quit
NAPALM DEATH in 1991 to team up with
EXTREME NOIZE TERROR before
forming SCORN. Justin Broadrick and
Nik Bullen were both active members of
GODFLESH. Whilst touring Europe
supporting the likes of CADAVER,
CANCER and PITCH SHIFTER to
promote the debut 'Vae Solis' album
Broadrick was replaced by CANDIRU
guitarist Pat McCahan.
In October 1992 SCORN made recording
history by releasing the longest duration
single ever with the EP 'Deliverance'
clocking in at 40 minutes.
The 1993 album 'Colossus' features
guitarist Neil, later of SAND.
Following the release of the third album
'Evanescence' - which featured OLD
guitarist Jimmy Plotkin - SCORN
appeared at the Norwegian Quartz
festival before touring Europe once more
alongside GOD and PITCH SHIFTER.
Nik Bullen departed following the 'Ellipsis'
remix album, leaving SCORN as a solo
project for Harris.
An album launch party in October 1995
for the 'Gyral' album was noted for the
non-appearance of SCORN who had
broken down on the motorway!
Harris joined Eraldo Bernocchi in radically
overhauling the works of Croatian act
TRANSMISIA for the 1997 release 'Frigid
Prose'.
In 1999 Harris created experimental side
project OCOSI releasing the album '(In)'.

Singles/EPs:
Lick Forever Dog / On Ice
(Disembodied In Dub) / Heavy Bones
(Ambient Freaks Mix) / Heavy Blood
(The Blood Fire Dub), Earache MOSH
61 (1992)
Deliverance / Deliverable Through Dub /
Delivered / To High Heaven / Black Sun
Rising, Earache MOSH 78 (1992)
White Irises Blind / White Irises Blind
(Minimal Mix) / Black Ash Dub / Drained
/ Host Of Scorpions, Earache MOSH 93
(1993)
Silver Rain Fell / Silver Rain Fell
(Meatbeat Manifesto remix), Earache

MOSH 122T (1994)
Days Passed, Atomic ATOM 1 (1994)
(with DUBWAR & ULTRAVIOLENCE)

Albums:
VAE SOLIS, Earache MOSH 54 (1992)
Spasm / Suck And Eat You / Hit / Walls
Of My Heart / Lick Forever Dog /
Thoughts Of Escape / Deep In - Eaten
Over And Over / On Ice / Heavy Blood /
Scum After Death (Dub) / Fleshpile /
Orgy Of Holiness / Still Life
COLOSSUS, Earache MOSH 91 (1993)
Endless / Crimson Seed / Blackout / The
Sky Is Loaded / Nothing Hunger /
Beyond / Little Angel / White Irises Blind /
Scorpions / Nights Ash Black / Sunstroke
EVANESCENCE, Earache MOSH 113
(1994)
Silver Rain Fell / Light Trap / Falling /
Automata / Days Passed / Dreamspace /
Exodus / Night Tide / The End / Slumber
ELLIPSIS, Earache SCORN CD1 (1995)
Silver Rain Fell (Meat Beat Manifesto
Mix) / Exodus (Scorn Mix) / Dreamspace
(Coil - 'Shadow Vs Executioner' Mix) /
Night Ash Black (Bill Laswell - 'Slow
Black Underground River' Mix) / Night
Tide (Scanner - 'Flaneur Electronique'
Mix) / Falling (Autechre - 'FR13' Mix) /
The End (P.C.M. - 'Nightmare' Mix) /
Automata (Germ Mix) / Light Trap (Scorn
Mix)
GYRAL, Earache SCORN CD2 (1995)
Six Hours One Week / Time Went Slow /
Far In Out / Stairway / Forever Turning /
Black Box / Hush / Trondheim - Gavle
LOGGHI BAROGGHI, Earache MOSH
158 (1996)
Look At That / Do The Geek / The Next
Days / Spongie / Out Of / It's On / Logghi
Barogghi / Black Box II / Nut / A Mission /
Pithering Twat / Fumble / Weakener / Go

SCROTUM GRINDER
(Tampa, FL, USA)

Florida Grind act with strong Hardcore
persuasions. SCROTUM GRINDER
feature both male and female lead
vocals.

Singles/EPs:
Scrotum Grinder EP, Burrito 7 (199-)
Split, Burrito 10 (199-) (7" split single with
COMBAT WOUNDED VETERAN)

SCULPTURE

Albums:
SPIRITUAL MATRIX, (199-)

A Contemplation Of David / Sodom / No
Liberation / Spiritual Matrix / No Respect
/ Scorning / Dawn Of Eternity / Grinding
Sacrifice / Death Is Death / Twilight Traps

SCUM (FINLAND)
Line-Up: P.T. Askola (vocals), Jani
Riikonen (guitar), Jussi Haakana (guitar /
keyboards), Micky Jaatinen (bass), Tony
Peiju (drums)

A Nordic Death Metal quintet.

Albums:
MOTHER NATURE, Black Mark BMCD
46 (1994)
Creation Of Flesh / Voyage Into The
Depth Of Insanity / Sickness Prevails /
Mother Nature / Macabre Moors Of
Morgoth / Shadow Hunting / House Of
The Rising Sun / Final Vision / Message
**PURPLE DREAMS AND MAGIC
POEMS**, Black Mark BM CD 82 (1995)
Dance Of The White Demons / Circus Of
The Freaks / Narcotic Dreams / In The
Crest Of The Northern Wave / Flames
Of The Silver Sea / White Dragon /
Conception / Oriental Fantasy / Valley Of
Dark Dreams

SEANCE (SWEDEN)
Line-Up: Johan (vocals), Patrick Jensen
(guitar), Tony (guitar), Bino (bass), Mique
(drums)

SEANCE came into being from an
amalgamation of two Linköping acts
ORCHRIST (who released the 1989
demo 'Necromonicon') and TOTAL
DEATH in 1990, the band name SEANCE
coming from an ORCHRIST song title.
December 1990 saw the first SEANCE
gig, with the Swedes playing alongside
MERCILESS and TOXAEMIA.
The group's first demo, 'Levitised Spirit',
was released in 1991 and gained the
band a deal with Black Mark Records.
After their release of the 'Forever Laid To
Rest' album bassist Bino (real name
Christian Karlsson) lost his place to ex-
MORGUE man Rickard Limfeldt.
When SEANCE dissolved various
members founded trad Metal act
WITCHERY. As well as WITCHERY
drummer Mique, vocalist Toxine and
guitarists Patrick Jensen and Richard
also performed in SATANIC
SLAUGHTER.
Jensen formed THE HAUNTED with
former AT THE GATES personnel.

Albums:
FOREVER LAID TO REST, Black Mark
BMCD 17 (1992)
Who Will Not Be Dead / Reincarnage /
Blessing Of Death / Sin / Haunted /
Forever Laid To Rest / Necromonicon /
Wind Of Gehenna / Inferna Cabballa
SALT RUBBED EYES, Black Mark
BMCD 44 (1994)
Soulerosion / 13th Moon / Saltrubbed
Eyes / Controlled Bleeding / Angelmeat
(Part II) / Til Death Do Us Join / Sanctum
/ Skinless / Hidden Under Scars

SEIRIM (GERMANY)
Line-Up: Joerg Weinhold (vocals),
Soeren (guitar), David (bass), Dreier
(drums)

Originally titled DECOMPOSITION upon
their formation by the trio of guitarist
Soeren, bassist David and drummer
Dreier. Later recruits vocalist Joerg
Weinhold and guitarist Torsten were
pulled in for the 'Demon' demo, By the
close of 1993 the title DECOMPOSITION
was dispensed with as the band became
SEIRIM. One of their first ventures was
the issue of a live cassette sharing space
with BASILISK prior to another
promotional cassette 'Of Dark One' in
1995.
In 1996 SEIRIM would join forces with
PURGATORY for a split 7" on Perverted
Taste Records.

Singles/EPs:
Split, Perverted Taste (1996) (Split 7"
single with PURGATORY)

Albums:
EMPIRE OF THE DEAD, Cudgel Agency
CUD003 (1999)
Intro: Empire Of The Dead / Children Of
The Night / Cold Light Of The Moon /
Reincarnation For My Soul / Magic
Sword / Time Of Endless Might /
Command Of Death / ...Of The Dark
One - Outro

SELEFICE (GREECE)
Line-Up: Miltos Jalagiannis (vocals /
guitar), Petros Milhopoulos (guitar /
keyboards), Dimitris Vrahidis (bass),
Vaggelis Kalergis (drums)

A melodic Death Metal act.

Albums:
WHERE IS THE HEAVEN, Molon Lave
(1991)

'Utopia' Intro / I Was Born In Darkness /
Die / The Duty Of Lie / The Prayer /
Nothing But Freedom / I Will Die By Evil
Ways / Where Is The Heaven / (Outro)
Years Of Emptyness

SEMPITERNAL DEATHREIGN
(HOLLAND)

Albums:
SPOOKY GLOOM, Foundations 2000
DQL/C 8099 (1993)

SENTENCED (FINLAND)
Line-Up: Ville Laihiala (vocals / bass),
Miika Tenkula (guitar), Sami Lopakka
(guitar), Sami Kukkohovi (bass), Vesa
Ranta (drums)

An Oulu based Death Metal band that
leaned more towards the classic
NWoBHM sound as each album
progressed until later works centred upon
a Doom-Death direction. Indeed, the
band's classic British Rock influences
were so evident the 1994 EP even went
so far as to cover IRON MAIDEN's 'The
Trooper'.
SENTENCED was created during 1989
by the trio of guitarists Miika Tenkalu and
Sami Lopakka along with drummer Vesa
Ranta. In this incarnation the band cut
their inaugural demo sessions the
following year dubbed 'When Death Joins
Us'. After recording SENTENCED's
numbers were brought up to full strength
with the addition of vocalist / bassist
Taneli Jarwa as they scored a deal with
the French Thrash label for the 1991
debut album 'Shadows Of The Past'. This
effort garnered the band praiseworthy
media coverage internationally prompting
a fresh deal with the domestic Spinefarm
label. 1993's sophomore outing 'North
From Here' would see the band adding a
greater degree of melody to their work
whilst retaining the technical edge.
'The Trooper' EP, for new label Century
Media, kept the faithful happy until the
arrival of 'Amok'. This album succeeding
in selling of 30'000 units.
SENTENCED toured Europe with
TIAMAT and SAMAEL as Century Media
re-released the bands first brace of
albums to a wider audience.
Ever eager to experiment the 1995 EP
'Love And Death' included a version of
BILLY IDOL's 'White Wedding'.
Jarwa often toured as bassist for
IMPALED NAZARENE when the
SENTENCED schedule allowed. Jarwa

had departed following the 'Love And Death' EP.

Jarwa's place was filled by former BREED man Ville Laihiala for the 1996 Waldemar Sorychta produced 'Down' album. Backing vocals came courtesy of Vorphalack of SAMAEL. The bands new lead vocalist brought another new dimension the SENTENCED sound as Laihiala opted for a clean vocal style more suited the more recent, doomier outings. Global touring had SENTENCED hitting their stride with dates in Europe, America and Japan. SENTENCED also formed part of the billing for the December 1996 'Dark Winter Nights' touring festival alongside DEPRESSIVE AGE, LACRIMOSA, THE GATHERING and DREAMS OF SANITY.

The 1998 opus 'Frozen', which found bassist Sami Kukkohovi of BREED and MYTHOS added to the roster, would once again be produced by Sorychta.

The 2000 'Crimson' album would lend recognition to SENTENCED's status as it reached the coveted no. 1 position in the Finnish album charts. Later in the same year the album would be re-launched on picture disc vinyl format.

Meantime erstwhile frontman Jarwa resurfaced fronting THE BLACK LEAGUE the same year.

In February of 2001 Century Media repackaged the 'Amok' and 'Love & Death' records on a single CD re-release. Laihiala was also to be revealed as in collaboration with Jesper Stromblad of IN FLAMES on an extra-curricular band project.

Singles/EPs:
The Trooper / Desert By Night / In Memoriam / Awaiting The Winter Frost, Spinefarm SPI 015 (1993) ('The Trooper' EP)
The Way I Wanna Go / Obsession / Dreamlands / White Wedding / Love And Death, Century Media 77101-2 (1995) ('Love And Death' EP)

Albums:
SHADOWS OF THE PAST, Thrash THR015-NR340 (1992)
When The Moment Of Death Arrives Rot To Dead / Disengagement / Rotting Ways To Misery / The Truth / Suffocated Beginning Of Life / Beyond The Distant Valleys / Under The Suffer / Descending Curtain of Death
NORTH FROM HERE, Spinefarm SPI13CD (1993)

My Sky Is Darker Than Thine / Wings / Fields Of Blood / Harvester Of Hate / Capture Of Fire / Awaiting The Winter Frost / Beyond The Wall Of Sleep / Northern Lights / Epic
AMOK, Century Media CD77076-2 (1994)
The War Ain't Over! / Phoenix / New Age Messiah / Forever Lost / Funeral Spring / Nepenthe / Dance On The Graves (Lil 'Siztah') / Moon Magick / The Golden Stream Of Lapland
DOWN, Century Media 77146-2 (1996)
Intro - The Gate / Noose / Shadegrown / Bleed / Keep My Grave Open / Crumbling Down (Give Up Hope) / Sun Won't Shine / Ode To The End / 0132 / Warrior Of Life (Reaper Reedemer) / I'll Throw The First Rock
STORY - GREATEST KILLS, Spinefarm SPI44CD (1997)
Noose / Nepenthe / Sun Won't Shine / Dance On The Graves / The Way I Wanna Go / White Wedding / My Sky Is Darker Than Thine / The Trooper / Desert By Night / In Memorium / Awaiting The Winter Frost / The Truth
CRIMSON, Century Media 77346-2 (2000) **1 FINLAND**
Bleed In My Arms / Home In Despair / Fragile / No More Beating As One / Broken / Killing Me, Killing You / Dead Moon Rising / The River / One More Day / With Bitterness And Joy / My Slowing Heart
AMOK / LOVE & DEATH, Century Media (2001)
The War Ain't Over! / Phenix / New Age Messiah / Forever Lost / Funeral Spring / Nepenthe / Dance On The Graves (Lil 'Siztah') / Moon Magick / The Golden Stream Of Lapland / The Way I Wanna Go / Obsession / Dreamlands / White Wedding / Love And Death

SEPSISM (Pacoima, CA, USA)
Line-Up: Fernando Avila (vocals), Leon Morrison (guitar), Armando Madrigal (bass), Phillip Hernandez (drums)

California's SEPSISM, although created in 1990, have taken 9 years to issue their debut album due to a series of ongoing line up fluctuations. The band's only surviving founder members are vocalist Fernando Avila and drummer Phillip Hernandez.

Guitarist Leon Morrison joined the ranks in 1993 and SEPSISM was boosted to a twin guitar act with the inclusion of Danny Halstead the following year. Halstead would appear on the 'Severe Carnal

Butchery' demo but broke ranks shortly after.

A 1996 demo session 'Necrotic Flesh Rot' led to an album deal with Repulse Records and the enlistment of bassist Armando 'Mondo' Madrigal.

By 2000 Madrigal was out of the picture and in his stead came Danny Bourlier. This latest recruits tenure was predictably brief though.

Guitarist Salvador Altamirano was pulled in for European dates in April / May of 2000. However, with the dates completed Altamirano too would part ways with SEPSISM.

Albums:

PURULENT DECOMPOSITION,
Repulse RPS038CD (1999)
Surgical Atrocity / Pathological Disfigurement / Necrotic Flesh Rot / Shredded In Cannibalistic Violence / Dissection / Internal Fermentation / Uterocasket / Brutally Butchered / Murdering At Random / Venenoen La Sangre / Punctured Internal Organs / Born Into Oblivion

SEPTIC CEREMONY (AUSTRIA)
Line-Up: Roland (vocals / guitar), Thomas (guitar), Michael (keyboards), Thomas (bass), Gerald (drums)

SEPTIC CEREMONY were previously known as LEVIATHAN.

Albums:

DIABOLOS REBELLION, CCP 100 189-2 (1998)
Septic Silence / Screams In A Faithless Time / Tears About… / Apocalyptical Visions / The Symphonie Of The Diabolos Rebellion / In Breathless Sleep

SEPTIC FLESH (GREECE)
Line-Up: Spiros (vocals / bass), Chis Antoniou (guitar), Sotiris (guitar), Kostas (drums)

SEPTIC FLESH describe themselves as "Dreamy Emotional Death" and the band first made their mark with the track 'Melting Brains', which appeared on numerous compilation albums.

In early 1991 this was capitalized on by the 5 track demo 'Forgotten Path'. The tape sold well, shifting 800 copies. Their debut vinyl came in the form of the mini album 'Temple Of The Lost Race', which surfaced in early 1992.

A further demo, this time highlighting their talents on the solitary track 'Morpheus - The Dream Lord' secured a deal with Holy Records. In early 1993 Spiros would deputize for OBSECRATION.

Sotiris teamed up with Gunnar Theys of ANCIENT RITES and the industrious Magus Wampyr Daoloth of NECROMANTIA to forge the DANSE MACABRE project but bowed out before completion.

SEPTIC FLESH's 1998 release 'A Fallen Temple' found the band re-recording their debut effort and adding new songs.

Toured Europe as headliner in the spring of 1999 with support from MISANTHROPE and NATRON.

Antoniou issued a self titled side project album CHAOSTAR in 2000. All the members of SEPTIC FLESH contributed. The 2000 release 'Forgotten Paths' is a collection of early demos.

Spiros also involves himself in the THOU ART LORD side concern.

Albums:

TEMPLE OF THE LOST RACE, (1992)
Erebus / Another Reality / Temple Of The Lost Race / Setting Of The Two Suns
MYSTIC PLACES OF DAWN, Holy HOLY05 (1994)
Mystic Places Of Dawn / Crescent Moon / Return To Carthage / The Underwater Garden / Pale Beauty Of The Past / Chasing The Chimera / Behind The Iron Mask / (Morpheus) The Dream Lord / Mythos- Part One: Elegy, Part Two: Time Unbounded
ESOPTRON, Holy HOLY13 (1995)
Breaking Of The Inner Seal / Esoptron / Burning Phoenix / Astral Sea / Rain / Ice Castle / Celebration / Succubus Priestess / So Clean, So Empty / The Eyes Of The Set / Narcissism
OPHIDIAN WHEEL, Holy (1997)
The Future Belongs To The Brave / The Ophidian Wheel / Phallic Litanies / Razor Blades Of Guilt / Tarturus / On The Topmost Step Of The Earth / Microcosmos / Geometry In Static / Sharmanic Kite / Heaven Below / Enchantment
A FALLEN TEMPLE, Holy (1998)
Brotherhood Of The Fallen Knights / The Eldest Cosmonaut / Marble Smiling Face / Underworld Act I / Temple Of The Last Race / The Crypt / Setting Of The Two Suns / Erebus / Underworld Act II / The Eldest Cosmonaut (Dark version)
REVOLUTION DNA, Holy (1999)
Science / Chaostar / Radioactive / Little Music Box / Revolution / Nephilim Sons / DNA / Telescope / Last Ship To Nowhere

/ Dictatorship Of The Mediocre / Android / Arctic Circle / Age Of A New Messiah **FORGOTTEN PATHS (THE EARLY DAYS)**, Black Lotus BLRCD 017 (2000) Intro / Power Of The Dark / Melting Brains / Unholy Ritual / Curse Of Death / Forgotten Path / Outro / Power Of The Dark (Live) / Forgotten Path (Live) / Melting Brains (Live)

SEPTIC GRAVE (SWEDEN)
Line-Up: Daniel Engman (vocals), Fredrik Hjärström (guitar), Robert Lindmark (bass), Jörgen Björnström (drums)

SEPTIC GRAVE bass player Robert Lindmark would join PROPHANITY during 1996.

Singles/EPs:
Caput Mortam, Midnight Sun MSR3 (1995)

SEPULTURA (BRAZIL)
Line-Up: Max Cavalera (vocals / guitar), Andreas Kisser (guitar), Paulo Jr. (bass), Igor Cavalera (drums)

SEPULTURA rank as the undisputed leaders of Brazilian bands on the international Rock scene. Created in Bela Horizonte during 1983 SEPULTURA's initial albums were timed perfectly to benefit from the Thrash explosion of the early 80's. Although the act's early albums were far from sensational the fact that the band more than looked the part allied to their professed influences of British Punk and American Metal stood them in good stead until the breakthrough 'Arise' album.

The band took on typical Death Metal noms de guerre for the early part of their career, Max Cavalera being known as "Max Possessed", Jairo T. calling himself "Tormentor", Igor Cavalera as "Igor Skull Crusher" and Paulo D. known as "Destructor". Jairo was superseded following 'Morbid Visions' by erstwhile PRESILENCE man Andreas Kisser.

Jairo would at first announce he no longer had any interest in Metal but emerged in 1990 as a member of Thrashers THE MYST for the 'Phantasmagoria' album. The band had other SEPULTURA connections with vocalist Korg (previously with CHAKAL) credited for the lyrics to SEPULTURA's 'To The Wall' and bassist Marcello Diaz being a SEPULTURA roadie.

Kisser had risen through the ranks of local amateur Metal bands such as SPHINX, an outfit that took on covers by acts such as SLAYER and JUDAS PRIEST before injecting original material and retitling themselves PESTILENCE.

Although 1989's 'Beneath The Remains' signalled the first move away from the standard Thrash fare for the band it was to be 'Arise', with cover artwork from noted Sci-Fi artist Michael Whelan, that took SEPULTURA into new realms of creativity. The band had extricated itself from the familiar run of the mill Thrash acts to create a quite unique album. By now the act's raucous live shows were also beginning to build a solid fanbase. SEPULTURA had become national heroes in Brazil putting in a worthy performance at the 1990 'Rock In Rio' festival sharing the same stage with major league international acts.

1993's 'Chaos A.D.' saw SEPULTURA stripping down their sound to Punk basics, the band's lyrical stance now becoming far more openly political. America too was now coming under the SEPULTURA spell and 'Chaos A.D.' broke the Billboard charts.

Demos for the 'Roots' album were recorded by FUDGE TUNNEL's Alex Newport. SEPULTURA then took the brave step of recording tracks deep in the Brazilian jungle with the Xavante Indians. The resulting album took the band's aesthetic into totally new areas of operation as they offered the Rock world an album of unrelenting Metal infused with their own cultural heritage and ethnicity. 'Roots' proved to be their biggest seller to date going top 5 in Britain.

1997's filler album 'Blood Rooted' gave fans more than the usual interim product in anticipation of the new look SEPULTURA and SOULFLY albums. Featured were a barrage of live tracks and also the cut 'Mine' with FAITH NO MORE's Mike Patton on lead vocals plus 'Lookaway' with KORN's Jonathon Davis and Patton once more. Other rare cuts included the band's cover of CELTIC FROST's 'Procreation (Of The Wicked)', DEAD KENNEDY's 'Drug Me' and BLACK SABBATH's 'Symptom Of The Universe'.

With the media attention firmly focused on SOULFLY for a lengthy period the spotlight was pointed firmly back into the SEPULTURA camp when it was announced that Cavalera's position had finally been filled. The new recruit was the black goliath Derrick Green, formerly of ALPHA JERK, OVERFIEND and OUTFACE.

The Howard Benson produced 'Against' continued the tradition of tribalism with the inclusion of the Japanese Kodo drummers on the track 'Kamaitachi'. A reworking of the track, retitled 'Diary Of A Drug Fiend' with vocals from FAITH NO MORE's Mike Patton, was at the last minute removed from the album for fear of a sales backlash due to it's lyrical content. The finished album did include though a rare appearance outside of METALLICA for Jason Newstead appearing as guitarist and guest vocalist for the track 'Hatred Aside'.

The band tested the waters with American shows billed as TROOPS OF DOOM. SEPULTURA proper got to grips with promoting the 'Against' album properly with an American support tour opening for SLAYER.

The single from the album 'Choke' featured versions of BAD BRAINS tracks 'Gene Machine' and 'Don't Bother Me'. The also band contributed a track to the 1999 BAD BRAINS tribute album 'Never Give In'. Green meantime turned up as a guest on INTEGRITY 2000's self titled album of the same year.

In April of 2000 Swedish label Black Sun released a SEPULTURA tribute 'Sepulchral Feast' which included honours paid by artists such as SACRAMENTUM, SWORDMASTER, DEATHWITCH, GARDENIAN, CHILDREN OF BODOM, LORD BELIAL, DEFLESHED, THE CROWN and IMPIOUS.

SEPULTURA returned in 2001 with the Steve Evetts produced 'Nation' album. Recorded in Brazil the record saw such diverse guest performances from JELLO BIAFRA on 'Politricks', Reggae artist Dr. Israel, the noted Finnish cello quartet APOCALYPTICA on the mellow 'Valtio' and HATEBREED's Jamey Jasta.

Singles/EPs:
Under Siege (Regnum Irae) / Orgasmatron / Troops Of Doom (New version), Roadracer RO 2424-6 (1991)
Arise / Troops Of Doom (Live) / Inner Self (live), Roadrunner RR 2406-6 (1992)
Territory / Policia, Roadrunner RR 2382-7 (1993) 66 UK
Refuse - Resist / Inhuman Nature / Propaganda, Roadrunner RR 2377-8 (1994) 51 UK
Slave New World / Desperate Cry,

Roadrunner RR 2374-2 (1994) 46 UK (CD single)
Slave New World / Crucifacados Pelo System / Drug Me / Orgasmatron (Live), Roadrunner RR 2374-8 (1994) (12" single)
Roots Bloody Roots / Symptom Of The Universe, Roadrunner RR 2320-7 (1996) 19 UK
Roots Bloody Roots / Procreation (Of The Wicked) / Refuse - Resist (Live) / Territory (Live), Roadrunner RR 2320-2 (1996) (CD single)
Roots Bloody Roots / Propaganda (Live) / Beneath The Remains (Live) / Escape To The Void (Live), Roadrunner RR 2320-5 (1996) (CD single)
Ratamahatta / Mass Hypnosis (Live), Roadrunner RR 2314-7 (1996) (7" single) 23 UK
Ratamahatta / War / Slave New World (Live) / Amen - Inner Self (Live), Roadrunner RR 2314-2 (1996) (CD single)
Ratamahatta / War / Roots Bloody Roots (Demo) / Dusted (Demo), Roadrunner RR 2314-5 (CD single)
Attitude / Dead Embryonic Cells, Roadrunner RR 2299-7 (1996) (7" single) 46 UK
Attitude / Lookaway (Master Vibe mix) / Mine, Roadrunner RR 2299-2 (1996) (CD single)
Attitude / Kaiowas (Tribal Jam) / Clenched Fist (Live) / Boitech Is Godzilla (Live), Roadrunner RR 2299-5 (1996) (CD single)
Choke / Gene Machine / Don't Bother Me / Against (Demo), Roadrunner (1998)

Albums:
BESTIAL DEVASTATION, Cogumelo (1984) (Split LP with OVERDOSE)
Bestial Devastation / Antichrist / Necromamcer / Warriors Of Death
MORBID VISIONS, Cogumelo (1985)
Morbid Visions / Mayhem / Troops Of Doom / War / Crucifixion / Show Me The Wrath / Funeral Rites / Empire Of The Damned / The Curse
SCHIZOPHRENIA, Roadrunner (1987)
Intro / From The Past Comes The Storms/ To The Wall / Escape From The Void / Inquisition Symphony / Screams Behind The Shadows / Septic Schizo / The Abyss / RIP (Rest In Peace) / Troops Of Doom
BENEATH THE REMAINS, Roadrunner (1989)
Beneath The Remains / Mass Hypnosis / Inner Self / Lobotomy / Sarcastic Existence / Slaves Of Pain / Primitive Future / Hungry / Stronger Than Hate

ARISE, Roadracer RO 9328-2 (1991) 40 UK
Arise / Dead Embryonic Cells / Desperate Cry / Murder/ Subtraction / Altered State / Under Siege (Regnum Irae) / Meaningless Movements / Infected Voice
CHAOS A.D., Roadrunner (1993) 11 UK, 32 USA
Refuse- Resist / Territory / Slave New World / Amen / Kaiowas / Propaganda / Biotech Is Godzilla / Nomad / We Are Not As Others / Manifest / The Hunt / Clenched Fist / Policia / Inhuman Nature
ROOTS, Roadrunner RR 8900-2 (1995) 4 UK, 27 USA
Roots Bloody Roots / Attitude / Cut-Throat / Ratamahatta / Breed Apart / Straighthate / Spit / Lookaway / Dusted / Born Stubborn / Jasco / Itsari / Ambush / Endangered Species / Dictatorshit / Chaos B.C / Symptom Of The Universe / Kaiowas (Live)
BLOOD ROOTED, Roadrunner RR 8821-2 (1997)
Procreation (Of The Wicked) / Inhuman Nature / Policia / War / Crucificados Pelo Sistema / Symptom Of The Universe / Mine / Lookaway (Master Vibe Mix) / Dusted (Demo version) / Roots Bloody Roots (Demo version) / Drug Me / Refuse-Resist (Live) / Slave New World (Live) / Propaganda (Live) / Beneath The Remains - Escape To The Void (Live) / Kaiowas (Live) / Clenched Fist (Live) / Biotech Is Godzilla (Live)
AGAINST, Roadrunner (1998)
Boycott / Choke / Old Earth / Floaters In Mud / Boycott / Rumors / Tribus / Common Bonds / F.O.E. / Rezu /Kamaitachi / Unconscious / Drowned Out / Hatred Aside / T3rcrmillenium
NATION, Roadrunner (2001)
Sepulnation / Order Wars B / Revolt / One Man Army / Vox Populi / The Ways Of Faith / Uma Cura / Who Must Die / Saga / Tribe Of Nation / Polotricks / Human Cause / Reject / Water / Valtio

SERPENT (SWEDEN)
Line-Up: Piotr Wawrzeniuk (vocals), Johan Lundell (guitar), Lars Rosenberg (bass), Per Karlsson (drums)

SERPENT date back to 1993 when the band were formed as a side project by then ENTOMBED bassist Lars Rosenberg and CONCRETE SLEEP / THERION's bassist Andreas Wahl. The band soon enlisted THERION drummer Piotr Wawrzeniuk on vocals and drums before completing the line-up with guitarist Johan Lundell.

Wahl departed in 1994 and was replaced by Ulf Samuelsson of SUFFER. Drummer Per Karlsson, another former SUFFER compatriot, joined SERPENT following recording of the debut album.
Unsatisfied with the reception to the debut album, SERPENT split from Radiation Records before undergoing an even more traumatic event when Rosenberg left the fold. Ironically, his swift replacement was none other than Wahl. This line up soon got back into action by donating a fresh recording, a song titled 'The Fog', to a couple of compilation albums prompting a deal with Heathendoom Music.
Karlsson joined T.A.R. in January of 1997.

Albums:
IN THE GARDEN OF SERPENT, Radiation RAD006 (1996)
Fly With The Flow / Save From Ourselves / The Order / Stoned The Dawn / Magic / Lost Dreams / Frozen Cosmos / In Memorium / Drown / Corpse City
AUTUMN RIDE, Heathendoom HDMCD005 (1997)
Prologue / Dimension Zero / The Shot / Chasing The Dragon / Autumn Ride / The Fog / Mars's Boogie / Live Through This

SERPENT OBSCENE (SWEDEN)
Line-Up: Erik Tormentor (vocals), Nicklas Eriksson (guitar), Johan Thorngren (guitar), Jonas Eriksson (drums)

Albums:
SERPENT OBSCENE, Necropolis (2000)
Devastation / Serpent Prophecy / Sadistic Abuse / Rapid Fire / Pestilent Seed (The Plague) / Evil Rites / Morbid Horror / Violent Torture / Act Of Aggression

SERPENT RISE (BRAZIL)

Albums:
SERPENT RISE, Sound Riot (1999)
Travelling Free... / Kharma / Betrayer God / Reflex In The Last Mirror / Mistress Of My Paradise / During The Eternity / ...In The Cosmic Sea

SEVERE TORTURE (HOLLAND)
Line-Up: Dennis (vocals), Thijs (guitar), Patrick Boley (bass), Seth Van Der Loo (drums)

Beginning life in 1997 SEVERE TORTURE comprised CENTURIAN

members drummer Seth Van Der Loo and bassist Patrick Boley alongside vocalist Erik and guitarists Thijs and Jelle. This version of the band cut the 1998 'Baptized' demo before Eric quit to team up with SINISTER.

Undaunted SEVERE TORTURE enrolled Dennis as a replacement but following a support gig to IMMOLATION guitarist Jelle departed. The band resolved to persevere as a four piece for an appearance at the Tilburg 'No Mercy' festival and touring into Eastern Europe with Polish act DAMNATION.

A two track vinyl promotional single was issued on Damnation Records upfront of their debut album 'Feasting On Blood'.

Albums:
FEASTING ON BLOOD, Hammerheart (2000)
Feces For Jesus / Blood / Decomposing Bitch / Baptised In Virginal Liquid / Twist The Cross / Butchering Of The Soul / Rest In Flames / Severe Torture / Pray For Nothing / Vomiting Christ

SEXORCIST (HOLLAND)

Singles/EPs:
Split, Sicktone (199-) (split 7" single with EXTREME SMOKE 57)
Sexorcist, Wild Rags (1993)

Albums:
THE WHOLE STORY, (199-)
Welcome To Your Death / Their Last Travel / Bitch / Sickness Of Snuff / Incest / Pathology Of Crowling / Suck / Faggot / Animal Revenge / Mourning / Suffer / Disabuse Of Social Welfare / Suicidal Thoughts / Blow A Bullet / Suffer / Mourning / Dreamraper / Deathmetal / Deathmetal / Exulceration / Dreamraper / Sex Slave / Suck Me / Shithead / Attitude Of A Dickhead / Toilet Love / Frogmatize / Dissect / Smoke From A Dildo / Anal Torture / Smoke From A Dildo / Gasping Tits / Rot Away / Fist Fuckin' Metal / The Curse Of Lord Dildo / Sexual Mutilation / Bestial Lust / Possessed By Cunts / Penetrate My Nose / Piss On My Head / Mark Anaal / The Rape Of A Rabbit / Stream Of Cadavers / Extremely Rotten Cunts / A.I.D.S. / Die By A Dildo / Bondage / Beware Of My Dick / Smegma For Breakfast / Spanish Superfly / Two Little Nuts / Pulsating Sperm / Pussy Miaow / Fuck Bloody Gore

SHADOWDANCES (LITHUANIA)
Line-Up: Juodas (vocals / drums), Raima (guitar), Lokys (guitar), Tadas (bass), Bakas (keyboards)

The Death Metal band SHADOWDANCES was originally formed as BLOODY ALTAR in 1991, but had initially struggled to find a real identity. As CONSCIOUS ROT the Lithuanians released the 'Paranoia In The Evening' demo and toured with REGREDIOR and DISSECTION.

In 1994 drummer Joudas took up the vocalist role for 'The Soil', the group's latest demo, before, having adopted the SHADOWDANCES moniker, a signing to Abstract Emotions took place.

Singles/EPs:
Monody (Sing With Me) / Sasha D'Ark / Meltin Nite / Silent / Till Windows Lights / (I Dance With The Ghost), Abstract Emotions AE005 (1996) ('Burning Shadows' EP)

SHREDDED CORPSE
(Jacksonville, AR, USA)
Line-Up: Rocky Gray (vocals / guitar / keyboards), David Sroczynski (drums)

Arkansas Death Metal duo SHREDDED CORPSE date back to 1991. A string of unsavoury demos ensued including 'Vomit', 'Death Brings Erection' and 'Ejaculate On The Soul'. In 1992 guitarist Joseph Bates worked with the band.

Both vocalist Rocky Gray and drummer David Sroczynski would found side project SEMINAL DEATH in 1995. The first commercially available SHREDDED CORPSE outing came with the 1996 'Exhumed And Molested' album issued on the Wild Rags imprint. Two tracks from this album would also feature on the 'Frozen Dawn III' compilation album.

The 'Human Obliteration' CD is a collection of early demos.

Sroczynski and Bates would create INNER WAR for a projected 2001 album.

Albums:
EXHUMED AND MOLESTED, Wild Rags (1996)
Cadaveric Desecration / Nailed Open Hole / Dead Inside Myself / Slaughter And Masurbate / Death Brings Erection / World Holocaust / Erase My Existence / Mind War
HUMAN OBLITERATION, Frozen Dawn (1999)

SICKENING GORE (SWITZERLAND)

Line-Up: Matt Burr (vocals / guitar), Alex Burr (guitar), Danny Büsch (bass), Chris Huwiler (drums)

Previously known as REACTOR, releasing the 'The Tribunal Above' demo in 1991, this Swiss group changed titles to SICKENING GORE in 1992, adding vocalist Nenad Dukic.

The band toured supporting the likes of HOLY MOSES, BENEDICTION and AUTOPSY, although following signing to Germany's Massacre Records Dukic quit, leaving guitarist Matt Burr to handle vocal duties.

Further support slots followed with SAMAEL, ASPHYX and ATROCITY prior to recording debut album 'Destructive Reality'.

Albums:
DESTRUCTIVE REALITY, Massacre CD025 (1994)
Ancestral Hate / Blood For Tears / Obscene Existence / Massacre Of Innocents / Free Of Conscience / Covered In Blood / Psychopathic Butchery / Suppression Of Being

SICKNESS (Margate, FL, USA)

South Florida Death Metal act led by guitarist Sergio Cesario. SICKNESS debuted in 1994 with the 'Torture Of Existence' demo. The 1996 album 'Ornaments Of Mutilation' was produced by MALEVOLENT CREATION / SUFFOCATION drummer Dave Culross. SICKNESS have also contributed cover versions to METALLICA and SLAYER tribute albums.

Albums:
ORNAMENTS OF MUTILATION, (1996)
Anatomy Of Murder / Cold Bitch / Necrosick / Burn The Soul / Putrid Incest / Postmortal Ceremony / Deceased / I Am Christ
PLAGUE, Delusions Of Grandeur (1999)

SIGH (JAPAN)

Line-Up: Mirai, Shinichi, Satoshi (drums)

Extreme Japanese act SIGH founded in 1989 are noted for having their first album release issued on Euronymous' Deathlike Silence label prior to the Black Metal mentor's untimely death at the hands of Count Grisnackh.

SIGH issued two demos in 1990

'Tragedies', with drummer Kazuki, and 'Desolation' leading to a single release with German label Wild Rags and their first album 'Scorn Defeat' for the aforementioned Norwegian label Deathlike Silence.

Following the murder of Euronymous SIGH contributed a track to a VENOM tribute album and committed recordings to a split EP with KAWIR, including the VENOM cover 'Schizo', before being signed by British label Cacophonous. A cassette release entitled 'A Tribute To Venom' was also issued comprising seven live VENOM cover versions.

The 2000 album 'Scenario IV: Dread Dreams' has SIGH utilizing English language lyrics from various singers including DECEASED's King Fowley, NECROPHAGIA's Killjoy and RITUAL CARNAGE's Damien Montgomery.

Mirai and Shinichi also have a side band CUTTHROAT with members of ABIGAIL.

Singles/EPs:
The Knell / Desolation / Taste Defeat, Wild Rags (1992) ('Requiem For The Fools' EP)
Suicidigonic / Schizo, (1994) (Spilt EP with KAWIR)

Albums:
SCORN DEFEAT, Deathlike Silence Anti-Mosh 007 (1993)
A Victory Of Dakini / The Knell / At My Funeral / Bundali / Ready For The Final War / Weakness Within / Taste Defeat
INFIDEL ART, Cacophonous (1995)
Isuna / The Zombie Terror / Desolation / The Last Elegy / Suicidogenic / Beyond Centuries
GHASTLY FUNERAL THEATRE, Cacophonous (1997)
Intro - Souhki / Shingontachkawa / Domain Seman / Imiuta / Shikigami / Outro - Higeki
HAIL HORROR HAIL, Cacophonous (1997)
Hail Horror Hail / 42 49 / 12 Souls / Burial / The Dead Sing / Invitation To Die / Pathetic / Curse Of Isanagi / Seal Of Eternity
SCENARIO IV: DREAD DREAMS, Cacophonous NIHIL34CD (1999)
Diabolic Suicide / Infernal Cries / Black Curse / Iconoclasm In The Fourth Desert / In The Mind Of A Lunatic / Severed Ways / Imprisoned / Waltz: Dead Dreams / Divine Graveyard

SILENT DEATH (SWITZERLAND)
Line-Up: Bret Hoffmann (vocals), Oli Stübi (guitar), Beat Mühlemann (bass), Orlando Maccarone (drums)

SILENT DEATH date to 1990, releasing debut demo 'Infinite Answer' the following year and supported CANNIBAL CORPSE and MESSIAH on their 1992 European tour.
Whilst recording the first album the band effectively split, with three of their number departing. Remaining members Oli Stübi and Orlando Maccarone added temporary musicians to fulfill live dates. The band eventually utilized the services of MALEVOLENT CREATION vocalist Bret Hoffmann for the 'Stone cold' mini-album.

Singles/EPs:
Horrified Realization / Eradication / Undesirable Demise / Blind Rage / Betrayal, Massacre CD044 (1994) ('Stone Cold' EP)

SINERGY (USA / FINLAND)
Line-Up: Kimberley Goss (vocals), Alexi Laiho (guitar), Roope Latvala (guitar), Marco Hietala (bass), Erna Siikavarta (keyboards), Tommi Lillman (drums)

Metal band founded by former CRADLE OF FILTH and DIMMU BORGIR keyboard player Kimberley Goss. Bass was in the hands of Sharlee D'Angelo, a veteran of MERCYFUL FATE, WITCHERY and ARCH ENEMY. The band's original drummer was Ronny Milianowicz whilst guitars came courtesy of THY SERPENT, IMPALED NAZARENE and CHILDREN OF BODOM man Alex Laiho. SINERGY debuted live supporting METALIUM and PRIMAL FEAR in Europe during 1999.
SINERGY adopted a fresh line-up for the second album 'To Hell And Back'. Joining Goss were TAROT bassist Marco Hietala, TO DIE FOR drummer Tommi Lillmann and WALTARI guitarist Roope Latvala. The album included a twisted cover of the BLONDIE hit 'Hanging On The Telephone'.
As Laiho's commitments to the increasingly successful CHILDREN OF BODOM for live work SINERGY pulled in second guitarist Peter Huss.
Milianowicz created DIONYSUS in 2000 with LORD BYRON and LUCA TURILLI vocalist Olaf Hayer and NATION members Johnny Öhlin and bassist

Magnus Norberg.
SINERGY contributed a somewhat out of character rendition of 'Gimme, Gimme, Gimme' to a 2001 Death Metal ABBA tribute album.

Albums:
BEWARE THE HEAVENS, Nuclear Blast (1999)
Venomous Vixens / The Fourth World / Born Unto Fire And Passion / The Warrior Princess / Beware The Heavens / Razor Blade Salvation / Swarmed / Pulsation / Virtual Future
TO HELL AND BACK, Nuclear Blast NB 503-2 (2000) 27 GERMANY
The Bitch Is Back / Midnight Madness / Lead Us To War / Laid To Rest / Gallowmere / Return To The Fourth World / Last Escape / Wake Up In Hell / Hanging On The Telephone

SINISTER (HOLLAND)
Line-Up: Mike (vocals), Ron (guitar), Andre (guitar), Aad Kloosterwaard (drums)

SINISTER formed in 1988 as a trio of Mike, Ron and Aad adding bassist Corzas in early 1989. This line up released the 'Perpetual Damnation' demo. Sales of the tape were strong and SINISTER toured supporting ENTOMBED and DISHARMONIC ORCHESTRA.
Corzas left in May 1991 and bass duties were handed over to SEMPITERNAL DEATHREIGN's Frank Faase. Another line up shuffle saw Ron moving over to bass as SINISTER added second guitarist Andre.
Their second demo had secured enough interest to land a deal with Nuclear Blast. The band had also released three singles, one a split EP with MONASTERY, and appeared on a compilation album in the interim. In 1991 SINISTER toured as support to ATROCITY. More touring opened up 1992 as SINISTER gained a valuable support slot to MORGOTH.
A deal was struck with Nuclear Blast Records with debut album 'Cross The Styx' being produced by ATROCITY's Alexander Krull. The band toured to promote 'Cross The Styx' by opening for DEICIDE, ENTOMBED, CANNIBAL CORPSE and ATROCITY among others.
SINISTER's second album, 'Diabolical Summoning', was produced by Colin Richardson, with a third album appearing

349

in 1995 entitled 'Hate'. In 1998 the band enlisted former SEVERE TORTURE man Erik.

Mike and Aad Kloosterwaard founded HOUWITZER in 1999 for the 'Death But Not Buried' album. Kloosterwaard is also a member of the reformed THANATOS.

Singles/EPs:

Sinister, Sicktone 3 (1991) (Split 7" with MONASTERY)

Putrefying Remains / Spiritual Immolation, Witchhunt 9103 (1991)

Compulsory Resignation, Seraphic Decay 019 (1992)

Bastard Saints / Reborn From Hatred / Rebel's Dome / Cross The Styx / Epoch Of Denial, Nuclear Blast NB183 (1996) ('Bastard Saints' EP)

Albums:

CROSS THE STYX, Nuclear Blast NB 061-2(1992)
Carnificinia Scelesta / Perennial Mourning / Sacramental Carnage / Doomed / Spiritual Immolation / Cross The Styx / Compulsory Resignation / Corridors To The Abyss / Putrefying Remains / Epoch Of Denial / Perpetual Damnation / Outro

DIABOLICAL SUMMONING, Nuclear Blast NB081 (1993)
Sadistic Intent / Magnified Wrath / Diabolical Summoning / Sense Of Demise / Leviathan / Desecrated Flesh / Tribes Of The Moon / Mystical Illusions

HATE, Nuclear Blast NB 131-2 (1995)
Awaiting The Absu / Embodiment Of Chaos / Art Of The Damned / Unseen Darkness / 18th Century Hellfire / To Mega Therion / The Cursed Mayhem / The Bloodfeast

AGGRESSIVE MEASURES, Nuclear Blast (1998)
The Upcoming / Aggressive Measures / Beyond The Superstition / Into The Forgotten / Enslave The Weak / Fake Redemption / Chained In Reality / Emerged With Hate / Blood Follows The Blood

SINS OF OMMISSION (SWEDEN)
Line-Up: Toni Kocmut (vocals / guitar), Martin Persson (guitar), Thomas Fallgren (bass), Dennis Ekdahl (drums)

SINS OF OMMISSION, founded by ex-members of acts such as BESERK, METEPSYCHOSIS and MOURNFUL, initially comprised singer Toni Kocmut, guitarists Martin Persson and Johan Paulsson, bass player Thomas Fällgren and drummer Dennis Ekdahl.

In 1997 Paulsson made his exit and his position was covered by RAISE HELL's Jonas Nilsson.

SINS OF OMMISSION added former A CANOUROUS QUINTET vocalist Martin Hansen as Kocmut reverted to simply guitar.

Drummer Dennis Ekdahl also performs with RAISE HELL whilst both Persson and Kocmut session on albums by THYRFING.

Albums:

THE CREATION, Black Sun (1999)

SIRRAH (POLAND)
Line-Up: Tomasz Zyzyk (vocals), Roger Trela (guitar), Matt (guitar), Kryzstof Majecki (bass), Chris P. (keyboards), Magdelena Brudzinska (viola), Michael Bereznicki (drums)

One of the few Rock bands to break out of Poland and into the Western scene, SIRRAH ('Harris' backwards, but also an old English phrase for contempt), were created in 1992 and initially recorded their debut album for Polish label Melissa Records during 1994.

SIRRAH at this point comprised guitarist Maciej Pasinski, guitarist Radek Bajsarowicz, vocalist Tomasz Zyzyk, keyboard player Krzysztof Passowicz and female violinist Magdalena Brudzinkska.

Two years later the band signed to another, larger domestic label Metal Mind and also to Music For Nations in England and, dissatisfied with their first attempt and also having undergone a line-up change, opted to entirely re-record their first album again.

In the meantime a cassette of the original version of 'Acme' had found it's way to Germany's Nuclear Blast Records, who issued the title track as part of their 'Beauty In Darkness' compilation CD.

Now with extensive European coverage, SIRRAH's prominence rose with gigs in Poland opening for ROTTING CHRIST, SAMAEL, MOONSPELL and even DEEP PURPLE.

SIRRAH employ the use of female vocalist Gosia Lyko for live work.

The band's second album 'Will Tomorrow Come?' saw Bajsarowicz replaced by Roger Trela.

Albums:

ACME, Melissa (1994)

ACME, Music For Nations (1996)
Acme / Passover / On The Verge / AU Tomb / Iridium / Pillbox Impressions / Panacea / Bitter Seas / In The Final Moment

WILL TOMORROW COME?, Music For Nations CDMFN 225 (1997)
To Bring Order / ...For The Sake Of Nothing / Patron / Lash / Will Tomorrow Come? / High Treason / Sepsis / Rhea / Madcap / Floor's Embrace

SIX FEET UNDER (USA)
Line-Up: Chris Barnes (vocals), Allen West (guitar), Terry Butler (bass), Greg Gall (drums)

Initially created as a side project by CANNIBAL CORPSE frontman Chris Barnes, OBITUARY guitarist Allen West and erstwhile MASSACRE / DEATH bassist Terry Butler.

The debut album predictably kept up the gore factor of the various band members

previous acts and consistent touring pushed the release past the 35,000 sales mark.

SIX FEET UNDER evolved into a fully fledged band when Barnes was ejected from his previous host.

The live mini-album 'Alive And Dead' comprised cuts recorded during the previous bout of touring, two fresh studio recordings plus a version of JUDAS PRIEST's 'Grinder'. The release plugged a gap between bouts of studio recording whilst West was committed to the latest OBITUARY album.

By 2000 West had created his own act LOWBROW with NASTY SAVAGE men Ben Meyer and Curt Beeson and DEATH bassist Scott Carino.

SIX FEET UNDER's 'Graveyard Classics' album was a compilation of cover versions of artists such as AC/DC, BLACK SABBATH, SEX PISTOLS, DEAD KENNEDYS, EXODUS, SAVATAGE, VENOM and JIMI HENDRIX. John Bush of ANTHRAX / ARMORED SAINT guests on vocals for a version of the SCORPIONS 'Blackout'.

SIX FEET UNDER
Photo : Martin Wickler

Albums:
HAUNTED, Metal Blade 986-2 (1995)
The Enemy Inside / Silent Violence / Lycanthropy / Still Alive / Beneath A Black Sky / Human Target / Remains Of

351

You / Suffering In Ecstasy / Tomorrows Victim / Torn To The Bone / Haunted
ALIVE AND DEAD, Metal Blade (1996)
Insect / Drowning / Grinder / Suffering In Ecstasy / Human Target / Lycanthropy / Beneath A Black Sky
WARPATH, Metal Blade 3984-14128-2 (1997)
War Is Coming / Nonexistence / A Journey Into Darkness / Animal Instinct / Death Or Glory / Burning Blood / Manipulation / 4:20 / Revenge Of The Zombie / As I Die / Night Visions / Caged And Disgraced
GRAVEYARD CLASSICS, Metal Blade (2000)

SKINLESS (New York, NY, USA)

SKINLESS issued the 'Swollen Heaps' promotional tape upfront of their debut album 'Progression Towards Evil'. The band, centred upon guitarist Noah Carpenter, has been wrought by ongoing line up fluctuations since its inception in 1992.
Bob Bealac was added in early 1997 and Joe Keyser in November of the same year. SKINLESS would support MORTICIAN on an American tour following release of the 'Progression Towards Evil' debut.

Singles/EPs:
Split, Cudgel (2001) (split 7" with MALEDICTIVE PIGS)

Albums:
PROGRESSION TOWARDS EVIL, United Guttural (1998)
Confines Of Human Flesh / Extermination Of My Filthy Species / Tampon Lollipops / Milk And Innards / Cuntamination / Scum Cookie / Bobbing For Heads / Fetus Goulash / Crispy Kids
FORESHADOWING OUR DEMISE, Relapse (2001)
Foreshadowing Our Demise / Smothered / The Optimist / Salvage What's Left / Tug Of War Intestines / Affirmation Of Hatred / Enslavement / Merrie Melody / Pool Of Stool

SKOURGE (USA)

Albums:
END OF VIEW, Stagnant Blood (1998)
Burned And Buried / Fist Of The Northstar / Dry Heave / End Of You / Bloodclot Soup / Blind Date / T.S.S. / Chaos Unleashed / Ascend To Doomsday / 24 Seconds / Imminent Disbelief / Drinking Song

SKRUPEL (GERMANY)
Line-Up: Igor (vocals), Stefan (guitar), Sven (bass), Micha (drums)

SKRUPEL are a Grindcore act laden with Hardcore influences. The band arrived in 1995 with an inaugural line-up featuring two vocalists Weidex and Igor, guitarist Ronald, bassist Sven and drummer Micha. A demo 'The Image Of God (With

SKINLESS

A Gasmask)' arrived the same year followed by a 7" single on the Regurgitated Semen label. The band switched to the Thought Crime label for their next outing, the 7" '...No Lies' EP. However, in 1997 both Weidex and Ronald quit. SKRUPEL shared a split 7" single with STALKER during 1998 with new guitarist Stefan.

Singles/EPs:
Intro / Cellarjail / Unreal / A Volley Of Stupidity / Real Animal / Endlosschleife / Arbeitszwang, Regurgitated Semen RSR018 (1996)
Santa Racist / Auschwitz / What We Listen To / Raucherbein / Commercial Presentation / Warthog / Hin & Her / Mine, Thought Crime (1997) ('...No Lies' 7" single)
Anschliessen / Of The Same Cohere / Phobia / We, Thought Crime (1998) (7" split single with STALKER)

SKULL CRUSHER (AUSTRIA)
Line-Up: Andreas Ibitz (vocals / bass), Christian Bokovac (guitar), Robert Windisch (guitar), Wolfgang Rathgeb (drums)

A very brutal Death Metal band that recorded their debut album in a Slovenian studio in order to keep the costs down! SKULL CRUSHER have supported the likes of MASSACRA, TIAMAT and SENTENCED.
Originally a self-financed release 'The Darkside Of Humanity' was re-released the following year by AFM Records.

Albums:
THE DARKSIDE OF HUMANITY, Skull Crusher SCCDX1 (1996)
Into Day Rat / Damned To Death / Human Bastards / Insanity, World's Brutality / World's Ignorance / Agony, Blood, War / Darkside Of Humanity / No Right To Live

SKYFIRE (SWEDEN)
Line-Up: Andreas Hedlund, Martin Hanner, Jönas Sjogren, Tobias Björk

The inaugural SKYFIRE demo 'Within Reach' saw a guesting Mattias Holmgren, drummer with NAGLFAR and EMBRACING, as lead vocalist. Still without a permanent singer the band enlisted MORNALAND's Henrik Wenngren for their second effort 'The Final Story'.
SKYFIRE's 2001 debut album 'Timeless

Departure' was produced by Tommy Tägtpren.
Albums:
TIMELESS DEPARTURE, Hammerheart (2001)
Intro / Fragments Of Time / The Universe Unveils / By God Forsaken / From Here To Death / Breed Through Me, Bleed For Me / Dimensions Unseen / Skyfire / Timeless Departure

SKYFORGER (LATVIA)
Line-Up: Rihard (vocals / guitar), Peter (vocals / guitar), Edgar (vocals / bass), Imant (vocals / drums)

SKYFORGER, named after a mythological God, was created by erstwhile GRINDMASTER DEAD members guitarist Peter, bassist Edgar and drummer Imant. Fourth member Rihard was enrolled later to complete the line up. SKYFORGER's 2000 album 'Latvian Riflemen' is a historical concept album relating the story of Latvian recruits in the Russian army during the first world war.
SKYFORGER blend Metal with traditional Folk instruments.

Albums:
KAUJA PIE SAULES, Mascot (1998)
Zviegtin Zviedza Kara Zirgi / Kauja Pie Saules 1236 / Sewchu Ozols / Viestarda Ciinja Pie Mezhotnes / Kurshi / Kaleejs Kala Debesiis / Kam Puushati Kara Taures / Kauja Garozas Silaa 1287 / Sveetais Ugunskrusts
LATVIAN RIFLEMEN, Mascot M70482 (2000)
Latvian Riflemen / Battle Of Plakani, Battle Of Veisi / The March Of 1916 / Death Island / Six Days Of Madness / Colonel Briedis / In The Tirelis Swamp / Be Like A Man / In Life's Darkest Hour

SLEEPING GODS (GERMANY)
Line-Up: Anja Henning (vocals), Tim Siebrecht (vocals / guitar / bass), Anja Henning (vocals), Markus Stephan (guitar), Lars Pristl (drums)

A Gothic / Death Metal band, SLEEPING GODS were formed in Kassel in 1993 and would record their debut two years later. Guest bass on the debut album was supplied by producer Andy Classen of HOLY MOSES fame.

Albums:
ABOVE AND BEYOND, AFM 34326-422

(1995)
Scene Of Emptiness / The Die Is Cast /
Blood Is Thicker Than Water / Vivianes
Lamentation / Through The Timeless /
Extreme Unction / Sleeping Goddess /
Threats Of Providence
REGENERATED, AFM CD 37584-422
(1997)
The Wingless / Regenerated / Dead
Calls / Just A Blue Blackness / None To
Soon / Vastness / Some Far Beyond /
Dreaming / Reflection Of Soul

SOAR THROAT (UK)

Singles/EPs:
Abraham's Ear, Ecocentric 109 (199-)
Death To Capitalist Hardcore, Meantime
(199-)
**Nevermind The Napalm...Here's
Sorethroat**, Manic Ears (199-)

Albums:
DISGRACE TO THE CORPSE OF SID,
Earache (198-)
AND WE DON'T CARE, Weasel (1990)
UNHINDERED BY TALENT, Meantime
(199-)

SODOM (GERMANY)
Line-Up: Tom Angelripper (vocals / bass),
Frank Blackfire (guitar), Chris Witchunter
(drums)

Lambasted throughout much of their
career the legacy of German Thrash outfit
SODOM has witnessed a renaissance of
appreciation for their brutal almost
primitive Death Metal attack. SODOM
debuted as a trio consisting of
Angelripper, Witchunter and Agressor
with the demo 'Witching Metal' in 1983.
In 1984 a second demo, 'Victims Of
Death', included the original tracks
boosted with the addition of four new
songs. The demo began to receive a
great deal of positive press, although
Agressor would choose to opt out. He
was eventually replaced by Grave
Violator and the new line-up debuted for
the first time at the 'Black Metal Night' in
Frankfurt.
After a further show with DESTRUCTION
and IRON ANGEL, SPV signed the band
and would swiftly release SODOM's
debut EP entitled 'In The Sign Of Evil'.
Grave Violator left at the end of 1985 and
the debut, full blown 'Obsessed By
Cruelty' album featured an additional
guitarist in Ahathoor on the track 'After
The Deluge'. Immediately after the record

was released Destructor quit to join
KREATOR. Blackfire replaced him.
During a lull in 1986 Witchhunter travelled
to Sweden to rehearse with BATHORY
for a proposed European tour with
CELTIC FROST and DESTRUCTION.
The tour was shelved and the drummer
returned to SODOM.
SODOM toured Europe as co-headliners
with WHIPLASH in 1987, promoting the
Harris Johns produced 'Persecution
Mania' album, but Blackfire also quit the
band to join KREATOR on an American
tour on the eve of the 'Agent Orange' tour
with SEPULTURA in 1989. The band
found a temporary replacement to fulfill
the dates in MEKONG DELTA's Uwe
Baltrusch. Still, the latest album, 'Agent
Orange', sold strongly shifting in excess
of 90,000 units in Europe. In January
1990 SODOM recruited new guitarist
Michael Hoffman (ex-ASSASSIN) and the
ensuing 'Better Off Dead' produced by
Harris Johns, included a cover of the
THIN LIZZY classic 'Cold Sweat'. For the
1994 album 'Get What You Deserve'
album SODOM drafted in a new drummer
in the shape of ex-LIVING DEATH /
VIOLENT FORCE / SACRED CHAO man
Atomic Steif.
Angelripper issued a solo album of
drinking songs 'Ein Schöner Tag' in 1995
whilst SODOM were put on ice for a
while. Back with the main band, the man
formed a new line-up comprised guitarist
Bornemann and his ex-CROWS /
RANDALICA colleague, drummer Bobby
Schottkowski in order to record the new
studio album 'Til Death Do Us Unite' for
new label G.U.N. Records.
''Til Death Do Us Unite' featured a
drastically reworked version of PAUL
SIMON tune 'Hazy Shade Of Winter' (as
made popular by THE BANGLES). The
original version of the album also sported
a wonderful cover photograph
juxtaposing a pregnant woman with a
male beer belly. Sadly this clever image
was banned.
SODOM continued their resurgence with
the Harris Johns produced 'Code Red' on
fresh label Drakkar. The millennium
seems likely to herald a SODOM tribute
album.

Singles/EPs:
Outbreak Of Evil / Sepulcharal Voice /
Blasphemer / Witching Metal / Burst
Command Til War, Steamhammer SPV
60-2120 (1984) ('In The Sign Of Evil' EP)
Sodomy And Lust / The Conqueror /

My Atonement, Steamhammer SH 0061 (1987) ('Expurse Of Sodomy' EP)
Ausgebombt / Don't Walk Away (Live) / Incest (Live), Steamhammer S1 7604 (1989)
The Saw Is The Law / Tarred And Feathered / The Kids Wanna Rock, Steamhammer 050 76305 (1991)
Aber Bitte Mit Sahne / Sodomised / Abuse / Skinned Alive, Steamhammer CDS 055-76723R (1993)
Get What You Deserve / Jabba The Hut / Delight In Slaying / Die Stumme Ursel / Eat Me, Steamhammer SPV GET 1 (1993) (Promotion release)

Albums:
OBSESSED BY CRUELTY, Steamhammer SPV 08-2121 (1986)
Deathlike Silence / Brandish The Sceptre / Proselytism Real / Equinox / After The Deluge / Obsessed By Cruelty / Fall Of Majesty Town / Nuctemeron / Pretenders To The Throne / Witchhammer / Volcanic Slut
PERSECUTION MANIA, Steamhammer 076-75092 (1988)
Nuclear Winter / Electrocution / Iron Fist / Persecution Mania / Enchanted Land / Procession To Golgotha / Christ Passion / Conjugation / Bomberhagel
MORTAL WAY OF LIFE (LIVE), Steamhammer SPV DO 807575 (1988)
Persecution Mania / Outbreak Of Evil / Conqueror / Iron Fist / Obsessed By Cruelty / Nuclear Winter Electrocution / Blasphemer / Enchanted Land / Sodomy And Lust / Christ Passion / Bombenhagel / My Atonement
AGENT ORANGE, Steamhammer 076-75972 (1989)
Agent Orange / Tired And Red / Incest / Remember The Fallen / Magic Dragon / Exhibition Bout / Ausgebombt / Baptism Of Fire
BETTER OFF DEAD, Steamhammer 08 76261 (1991)
An Eye For An Eye / Shellfire Defense / The Saw Is The Law / Turn Your Head Around / Capture The Flag / Bloodtrails / Never Healing Wound / Better Off Dead / Resurrection / Stalnorgel
TAPPING THE VEIN, Steamhammer 076-76542 (1993)
Body Parts / Skinned Alive / One Step Over The Line / Deadline / Bullet In The Head / The Crippler / Wachturm / Tapping The Vein / Back To War / Hunting Season / Reincarnation
GET WHAT YOU DESERVE, Steamhammer SPV CD 084-76762 (1994)

Get What You Deserve / Jabba The Hut / Jesus Screamer / Delight In Slaying / Die Stumme Ursel / Freaks Of Nature / Eat Me / Unbury The Hatched / Into Perdition / Sodomised / Fellows In Misery / Moby Dick / Silence Is Consent / Erwachet / Gomorrah / Angel Dust
MAROONED LIVE, Steamhammer 084-76852 (1994)
Intro / Outbreak Of Evil / Jabba The Hut / Agent Orange / Jesus Screamer / Ausgebombt / Tarred And Feathered / Abuse / Remember The Fallen / An Eye For An Eye / Tired And Red / Eat Me / Die Stumme Ursel / Sodomised / Gomorrah / One Step Over The Line / Freaks Of Nature / Aber Bitte Mit Sahne / Silence Is Consent / Wachturm Erwachet / Stalinhagel / Fratricide / Gone To Glory
MASQUERADE IN BLOOD, Steamhammer SPV 085-76962 (1995)
Masquerade In Blood / Gathering Of Minds / Fields Of Honour / Braindead / Verrecke! / Shadow Of Damnation / Peacemaker's Law / Murder In My Eyes / Unwanted Youth / Mantelmann / Scum / Hydrophobia / Let's Break The Law
TEN BLACK YEARS – BEST OF, Steamhammer SPV DCD 086-18342 (1996)
Tired And Red / The Saw Is The Law / Agent Orange / Wachturm / Erwachet / Ausgebombt / Sodomy And Lust / Remember The Fallen / Nuclear Winter / Outbreak Of Evil / Resurrection / Bombenhagel / Masquerade In Blood / Bullet In The Head / Stalinorgel / Shellshock / Angel Dust / Hunting Season / Abuse / 1000 Days Of Sodom / Gomorrah / Unwanted Youth / Tarred & Feathered / Iron Fist / Jabba The Hut / Silence Is Consent / Incest / Shellfire Defense / Gone To Glory / Fraticide / Verrrecke! / One Step Over the Line / My Atonement / Sodomized / Aber Bitte Mit… / Die Stumme Ursel / Mantelmann
'TIL DEATH DO US UNITE, G.U.N. GUN 199 BMG 74321 39034-2 (1997)
Frozen Screams / Fuck The Police / Gisela / That's What An Unknown Killer Diarised / Hanging Judge / No Way Out / Polytoximaniac / 'Til Death Do Us Unite / Hazy Shade Of Winter / Suicidal Justice / Wander In The Valley / Sow The Seeds Of Discord / Master Of Disguise / Schwerter Zu Pflugscharen / Hey, Hey, Rock n' Roll Star
CODE RED, Drakkar 74321 67384 2 (1999)
Intro / Code Red / What Hell Can Create / Tombstone / Liquidation / Spiritual

Demise / Warlike Conspiracy / Cowardice / The Vice Of Killing / Visual Buggery / Book Burning / The Wolf And The Lamb / Addicted To Abstinence

SOILS OF FATE (SWEDEN)

Line-Up: Henke Crantz (vocals / bass), Mange Lindvall (guitar), Jocke (drums)

Ultraspeed Death Metal act SOILS OF FATE date back to 1995 and the union of vocalist / bassist Henke Crantz and guitarist Mange Lindvall. This duo issued the 1997 demo 'Pain... Has A Face' before adding second guitarist Trevor Kolbjer.

This newest recruit lasted a year before bailing out. SOILD OF FATE, finally with a drummer named Jocke, issued a three track promotional CD entitled 'Blood Serology' on their own Empty Veins Music imprint. Upon the release of the debut album 'Sandstorm' Jocke too made his exit.

Singles/EPs:
Bloated On Reality / Flowing Under Skin / Stripped Humanity, Empty Vein Music (1998) ('Blood Serolgy' EP)

Albums:
SANDSTORM, Retribute (2001)

SOILWORK (SWEDEN)

Line-Up: Bjorn Strid (vocals), Peter Vicious (guitar), Ludvig Svartz (guitar), Ola Flink (bass), Carlos Del Olmo (keyboards), Jimmy Persson (drums)

SOILWORK blend a heady mixture of Thrash and Death Metal. Frontman Bjorn Strid goes under the name of 'Speed' whilst guitarist 'Peter Vicious' real name is Peter Wichers. The 1998 album 'Steel Bath Suicide' was produced by Fredrik Fredman'.

SOILWORK have also previously employed drummer Henry Ranta and guitarist Ola Flenning.

Albums:
STEEL BATH SUICIDE, Listenable POSH012 (1998)
Entering The Angel Diabolique / Sadistic Lullaby / My Need / Skin After Skin / Wings Of Domain / Steelbath Suicide / In A Close Encounter / Centro De Predomino / Razorlives / Demon In Veins / The Aardvaarl Trail
THE CHAINHEART MACHINE, Listenable (1999)

The Chainheart Machine / Bulletbeast / Millionflame / Generation Speedkill / Neon Rebels / Possessing The Angels / Spirits Of Future Sin / Machine Gun Majesty / Room No. 99
A PREDATOR'S POSTCARD, Nuclear Blast (2001)
Bastard Chain / Like The Average Stalker / Needlefeast / Neurotica Rampage / The Analyst / Grand Failure Anthem / Structure Divine / Shadowchild / Final Fatal Force / A Predator's portrait

SOILWORK
Photo : David Falk

SOLID (BELGIUM)

Line-Up: Jim (vocals), 'Dompi' Dominick (guitar), Kris (bass), Frederik (drums)

A Death Metal band from Belgium, SOLID featured former members of the Hardcore band SPIRIT OF YOUTH. Having worked with original vocalist Sid on the 'Sales Of Mankind' album, the singer quit during the recording of the 'Darkside Moments' album. SOLID replaced Sid with Jim, previously a member of the German group SHAFT.
As an aside, every member of SOLID is a vegan.

Singles/EPs:
Sadness Of Mankind EP, DIY (1996)
Albums:
DARKSIDE MOMENTS, Die Hard PCD-37 (1996)

Unwanted Desire / Final Decrease / Darkside Moments / Blood Runs Black / Infection / The Cross / Dawn / Ready To Explode / Solid / Blindness / The Damned

SOLITARY CONFINEMENT
(GERMANY)
Line-Up: Lohm (vocals), Micha (guitar), Christian (guitar), Frank (bass), Mungo (drums)

Formed in 1987, SOLITARY CONFINEMENT delivered a brutal combination of Death Metal and Hardcore.

Singles/EPs:
Polluted Earth EP, Solitary Confinement (1992) (7" single)

Albums:
EINZELHAFT, Autonomy APRO 025 (1996)
Parasit / Acid / Don / Religious Shit / Der Held / Selbstkastei / Asche / Red Button / Push Away / Sense Of Death / Qual / Cry Out / Geballter / Solitary Confinement

SOLITUDE (Delaware, USA)
Line-Up: Keith Saulsbury (vocals / guitar), Dan Martinez (guitar), Rodney Cope (bass), Mike Hostler (drums)

Delaware's SOLITUDE, forged in 1985, made an impact on the tape trading scene with their 'Focus Of Terror' demo in 1987 and the following year's 'Sickness' recording. A final demo 'Fall Of Creation' led directly to a deal with Red Light Records and a license with a subsequent England's Music For Nations label.
SOLITUDE have toured alongside CELTIC FROST, DEATH ANGEL and SACRED REICH.

Albums:
FROM WITHIN, Bulletproof CDVEST 18 (1994)
Twisted / No Future / Tipping The Balance / Alter The Red / Mind Pollution / From Within / The Afterlife / A Loss Of Blood / The Empty / Poisoned Population / In This Life / Side Winder

SORCERY (SWEDEN)

Satanic Death Metal. SORCERY guitarist Peter Lake would later surface as a member of THEORY IN PRACTICE and RIVENDELL. Bass player Daniel Bryntse's later labarinthyne activities included WITHERING BEAUTY, WINDWALKER, MORRAMON and Doom Metal band FORLORN.
The SORCERY 'Bloodchilling Tales' album was re-released in 1999 by No Colours Records.

Singles/EPs:
Rivers Of The Dead / The Rite Of Sacrifice, Thrash (1990) (7" single)

Albums:
BLOODCHILLING TALES, Underground UGR003 (1991)
Bloodchilling Tales / Legacy Of Blood / The Rite Of Sacrifice / Death / Dragons Of The Burning Twilight / Rivers Of The Dead / Immortality Given / Descend To The Ashes / Lucifer's Legions / By These Words

SOUL EROSION

Albums:
FURIOUS MIND DEGENERATION, Shock Wave (2001)

SOULFLY (BRAZIL / USA)
Line-Up: Max Cavalera (vocals / guitar), Lucio Bandeira (guitar), Marcello D. Rap (bass), Roy Mayorga (drums)

High profile extreme Nu-Metal band centred upon the larger than life character of ex-SEPULTURA frontman Max Cavalera. Joining him was former THORN / CRISIS drummer Roy Mayorga. As SOULFLY were announced as part of the prestigious Ozzfest '98 European touring package Bandeira was forced to, at first, temporaly bow out having touring commitments with his previous act. Stepping into the breach was American Logan Mader who sensationally had only just quit the successful MACHINE HEAD amidst a bitter war of words.
As SOULFLY limbered up for the Ozzfest with a batch of American dates Mader's position within the band was made permanent. However, the guitarist was out by the end of the year due to friction between Cavalera and the guitarist over his side project MYSTRISS. The final straw came when Mader neglected to turn up for a soundcheck at a support gig to BLACK SABBATH. Mader was replaced by Mike Doling, previously with American Punk act SNOT.
Both Cavalera and Doling contributed to

the 'Strait Up' album, a tribute to SNOT frontman Lynn Strait who was killed in December 1999.

With the dawn of 2000 SOULFLY announced that Mayorga had been replaced by ex-FLESHHOLD drummer Joe Nunez as the band, still including bass player Marcelo D. Rapp, set about touring in America as headliners of the second stage at the Ozz Fest dates.

Mader and Mayorga founded PALE DEMONS alongside ex-OZZY OSBOURNE / SUICIDAL TENDENCIES bassist Robert Trujillo and ex-LIFE OF AGONY / UGLY KID JOE singer Whitfield Crane. Mayorga was then shortly after announced as the new drummer for OZZY OSBOURNE joining a recalled Trujillo.

SOULFLY's 2000 album 'Primitive' boasted an array of guests including SLAYER's Tom Araya, SLIPKNOT's Corey Taylor, DEFTONES Chino Moreno and WILL HAVEN's Grady Avenell. Rapper CUTTHROAT LOGIC also appears as does SEAN LENNON on the track 'Son Song'.

SOULFLY toured Russia, Europe and Britain in late 2000 with support act GLASSJAW.

Singles/EPs:
Tribe (Fuck Shit Up mix) / Tribe (Tribal Terrorism mix) / Quilombo (Zumbi dub mix), Roadrunner (1999)
Back To The Primitive / Terrorist (Total Deconstruction mix) / Back To The Primitive (Dub Shit Up mix) / Back To The Primitive (CD ROM video), Roadrunner (2000)

Albums:
SOULFLY, Roadrunner 8748 (1998) 14 FRANCE, 79 USA
Eye For An Eye / No Hope=No Fear / Bleed / Tribe / Bumba / First Commandment / Bumbklaat / Soulfly / Umbabauma / Quilombo / Fire / The Song Remains Insane / No / Prejudice / Karmageddon / Ain't No Feeble Bastard / Cangaceiro
SOULFLY REMIXES & LIVE, Roadrunner (1999) (Free CD with 'Soulfly' re-release)
Tribe (Fuck Shit Up mix) / Quilombo (Extreme Ragga dub mix) / Umbabaraumba (World Cup mix) / No Hope - No fear (Live) / Bleed (Live) / Bumba (Live) / Quilombo (Live) / The Song Remains Insane (Live) / Eye For An Eye (Live) / Tribe (Tribal terrorism

mix) / Umbabaurumba (Brazil '70 mix) / Quilombo (Zumbi dub mix)
PRIMITIVE, Roadrunner (2000)
Back To The Primitive / Pain / Bring It / Jumpdafuckup / Mulambo / Son Song / Boom / Terrorist / The Prophet / Soulfly II / In Memory Of... / Flyhigh

SOULGRIND (FINLAND)
Line-Up: Jussi Heikkinen, Ceasar T. Launonen (vocals), Luopio (keyboards), Agathon Frosteus (drums)

The extra-curricular project of TENEBRAE's Jussi Heikkinen. The man works constantly in collaboration with other Death Metal musicians on the albums issued under the SOULGRIND banner. For example, 'Ladit AD 1999: Bihttpotp' was recorded with DEMENTIA's Roope Latvala, Juke Eräkangas, Sauli Kivilahti, Henrick Laine and Kirsi Reunenen (female vocals).

For the 1998 'Whitsongs' release Heikkinen employed drummer Agathon Frosteus of THY SERPENT, BARATHRUM, NOMICON and GLOOMY GRIM, keyboard player Luopio of THY SERPENT whilst vocalist Ceasar T. Launonen is a NOMICON, WALHALLA and GLOOMY GRIM member. The album also sees contributions from female vocalist Whisper, also of GLOOMY GRIM.

Besides SOULGRIND Heikkinen is an active participant in GLOOMY GRIM, WALHALLA and FIRE TRANCE 666.

The 1999 'Kalma' album sees guest guitar from one Warhammer Newborn.

Singles/EPs:
Santa Sangra EP, MMI (1993)
Black Orchid / In My Darkest Sabbath / Anal Christ Pose, MMI (1995)

Albums:
LA MATANZA, EL HIMMO PAGANO, MMI M.M.I. 011 CD (1994)
Summoning / Kuoto / Santa Sangre / La Matanza, El Himmo Pagano / Black Abyss, Deep Enterium / Dark Misty Trail / Inner Chain Of Perversions / The Pit/ Virginity, A Sanctum Of The Red / Ainomonus (Outro)
LUST AND DEATH IN TUONELA A.D. 1999: BLACK INDUSTRIALHOLOCAUST THROUGH THE PANDEMONIUM OF THE BIZARRE, MMI M.M.I. 020 (1995)
Introitus Nostrodamus 1999 / Black Orchid / Darkseed Lust / As Shadows

Whisper The Shine / Shamanic Ecstasy / Spin Of Life / The Pandemonium Of The Bizarre / Immortal Desire / Industrial Holocaust (Inferia) / The End Of All
WHITSONGS, Icarus (1998)
Yermi / The Girl And The Boyar's Sun / Oterma And Katerma / Tumma / Revenge / Maids Of Hiss / Bwe Cross / The Dark One / Tuoni's Eyes / The Song Of Mantsi / Thalempe / The Serf's Son / Tuuri
KALMA, Holy HOLY048CD (1999)
Kalma / Goatride / Secrecy Supreme / Remembrance Through Deep Red Masquerade / Cage / Across The Field Of Thought / Seed (A Sermon In Stone) / Black Lust / Harsh Mother Time / Pagan Pride

SOULLESS (Cleveland, OH, USA)
Line-Up: Jim Lippucci (vocals), Wayne Richards (guitar), Jim Corrick (guitar), Tony Daprano (bass), Chris Dorn (drums)

SOULLESS evolved out of Cleveland Thrashers BLOODSICK during 1997. BLOODSICK was founded upon former DECREPIT drummer Chris Dorn, ex-DECIMATION vocalist Jim Lippucci, guitarists Brian Sekula and Todd Thozeski and bassist Chris Pello.
Sekula's exit saw the enlistment of erstwhile APT. 213 guitarist Jerry Kessler and when both Pello and Thozeski quit the numbers were made up with Kessler's former APT. 213 colleague Tony Daprano on bass and second guitarist Wayne Richards. With such a radical facelift the band opted for the revised title of SOULLESS.
Following recording of the debut album 'The Darkening Of Days' Kessler bowed out to be supplanted by former HOLY GHOST, DAHMER and ALL THAT IS EVIL man Jim Corrick. Richards meantime would deputize for the notorious NUNSLAUGHTER as live guitarist for their 2000 European shows.
SOULLESS have put in showings on a veritable slew of tribute albums having cut renditions of OZZY OSBOURNE's 'The Ultimate Sin', JUDAS PRIEST's 'Hell Bent For Leather', W.A.S.P.'s 'Tormentor' and METALLICA's 'Motorbreath'.

Albums:
THE DARKENING OF DAYS, (2000)
Devilish / Abandoned To Bleed / Turn / Blissfully Damned / Crumble Beneath / Down Hell's Path / Emptiness Domain /Hellbent / Lost / The Darkening Of Days

SOUL REAPER (SWEDEN)
Line-Up: Christoffer Hjertén (vocals), Johan Norman (guitar), Stefan Karlsson (guitar), Mikael Lang (bass), Tobias Kjellgren (drums)

Originally titled REAPER and forged by two erstwhile members of DISSECTION drummer Tobias Kjellgren and guitarist Johan Norman. Original second guitarist Mattias Eliasson would relinquish his post to Christoffer Hermansson for recording of the 'Written In Blood' album. Hermansson in turn exited in favour of Stefan Karlsson.

Albums:
WRITTEN IN BLOOD, Nuclear Blast NB 403-2 (2000)
Darken The Sign / Written In Blood / Satanized / Seal Of Degradation / Ungodly / Subterranean Night / Labyrinth Of The Deathlord

SPAZZ (Redwood City, CA, USA)
Line-Up: Chris Dodge (vocals / bass), Dan Lactose (guitar), Max Ward (drums)

Crusting Grindcore act SPAZZ emerged with an eponymous single on frontman Chris Dodge's own Slap A Ham label. The follow up was a cassette 'Blasted In Bangkok' given away at the sophomore SPAZZ live gig. A whole barrage of split 7" singles would ensue.
SPAZZ issued a split single with BRUTAL TRUTH that included the track 'Nuge On A Stick', a track that comprised of a humourous but barbed attack on TED NUGENT's hunting activities. The 'Funky Ass Little Platter' single is in fact a band spoof. The record does exist but only as 1" diameter toy records. Only 14 copies were made.
A further split effort with BLACK ARMY JACKET had SPAZZ covering tracks from such Hardcore veterans as SICK OF IT ALL, STRAIGHT AHEAD and YOUTH OF TODAY.
In 1999 Dodge forged a union with drummer Matt Martin of Hardcore mongers CAPITALIST CASUALTIES to create the ANCIENT CHINESE SECRETS project resulting in an album 'Careat Emptor'.
SPAZZ folded in January of 2001. Dodge would put together an alliance with DISCORDANCE AXIS drummer Dave Witte billed simply as CHRIS DODGE - DAVE WIITE for a 2001 album 'East West Blast Fest'

Spazz, Slap A Ham 16 (199-)
All Urban Outfield / Weedeater / Bleed Dry / Closet / No Room /Ghost Dance, Bovine (199-) (7" split single with FLOOR)
Split, Sludge (199-) (7" split single with RUPTURE)
Split, Slap A Ham (199-) (7" split single with C.F.D.L.)
Spazz Vs. Mother Nature / Nuge On A Stick / Donger, Rhetoric (199-) (7" split single with BRUTAL TRUTH)
Split, 625 Productions (199-) (7" split single with CHARLES BRONSON)
Split, H.G. Fact (199-) (7" split single with TOAST)
Crop Circles / Gas X / Jean Claude Bland Dan In A Steel Cage Match With Steve Seagal For The Title Of Crowned King Of Hilfiger Apparel: WWF Style /War In The Head / Eldar Mutant Stomp, Reservoir (199-) (7" split single with MONSTER X)
Funky Ass Little Platter, Slap A Ham (199-)
Union Made Mayhem / Mervins, Theologian (199-) (7" split single with HIRAX)
Split, Slap A Ham (199-) (7" split single with JIMMY WALKER)
Where's Winky? / Mega Armageddon Death Part 4 / Lather Punx / Timojhen's Answering Machine / You Suffer / Pray To The Windgod / Billy Milano's Head / Camp Chestnut Part 2 (Project House) / Untitled / No Neck Joe, Clean Plate ('Tastin' Spoon' 5" picture disc)
Finn's Mom Yodelling In The Bathtub / Dorsal Finn / Huckleberry Finn / Finn Pickers Rin Tin Finn / And You Thought We Were Kidding, Satan's Pimp (199-) (5" split single with GOB)
Satan's Scrilla / SoCal Battle Royale / Gilman 90210 / Short Songs / Dommriden' / Hey Bob, What's Up?, Deep Six (199-) (7" split single with LACK OF INTEREST)
Bolleri Mosh / Ahm Solo / On Parade / Stabbed In The Back / Rat Pack, Dogprint Zine (199-) (7" split single with BLACK ARMY JACKET)
Split, Sacapuntas (199-) (7" split single with SLOBBER)
Split, Coalition (199-) (7" split single with OPSTAND)
Split, Edison (199-) (7" split single with 25 TA LIFE)

DWARF JESTER RISING, Selfless (199-)

SPAZZ, Sound Pollution (199-) (Split album with ROMANTIC GORILLA)
LA REVANCHA, Sound Pollution (199-) WWF Rematch At The Cow Palace (A Luta Continua) / 4 Times A Day / Desperate Throat Lock / Bobby's Jackpot / Dewey Decimal Stichcore / Swampfoot / C.L.A. / Camp Chestnut / No Shadow Kick / The One With The Goat's Got An Orgy Up The Sleeve / Bitter (The Execution Of A Chump) / Let's Kill Fuckin' Everybody / Sweet Home Alabama / Raising Hate, Fear And Flower Power Violence / Climate Beast / Urinal Cake / 8 Drunkard Genaii / Sesos / Daljeet's Detonation / Turnbuckle Treachery / Backpack Bonfire / Don't Quit Your Day Job / Musica De La Roca / Coil Of The Serpent Unwinds / Golden Egg Stance / M.A.D.
SPLIT, Deported (199-) (Split album with SUBVERSION)
SWEATIN' TO THE OLDIES, Slap A Ham (199-)
Gary's Free Time (There's Lots Of It) / Crocket / One Ghetto To The Nest / Return Of The Wall Of Death / Who Writes Your Rules (Half Off) / Mighty Morphin Power Violence / Thrice The Heiney / Kiss Of The Sasquatch / Hot Dog Water Popsicle In The Hand Of Eric Wood / Problems In The Homeland / I Hate The Kids (S.O.A.) / Spudboy / Smoking Don's Crack Hole / Dirt The Purity / Knuckle Scraper / Box II (Yates Goes To Africa) / Spazz Vs. Mother Nature / Nuge On A Stick / Donger / Gnome Servant / DJ Tinkle Fingers' Diplomatic Service / Hard Boiled / 4 Times A Day / All Urban Outfield / Lethal / Hot Dog Water Popsicle In The Hand Of Eric Wood / The Box / Droppin' Many Ravers / In The Name Of… / Might For Right / Loach / Mad At The World / Tripper / Uniform / Bore / Hard Boiled / All Urban Outfield / Weedeater / Bled Dry / Closet / No Room / Ghost Dance / Hug Yourself / Yougottamoldit / Lethal / Anemonie / Gas Pump / Enterslavement / Hard Boiled (Live) / Burning Tongue (Live) / Kiss Of The Saquatch (Live) / Hot Dog Water Popsicle In The Hand Of Eric Wood (Live) / Dan Lifting Banner (Live) / Gertie / Enterslavement / Uniform / No Thought / Pressure / Burnt / Our Scene (Go!) / Force Fed / Biter / Precision Fastening / Lost Cause
CRUSH KILL DESTROY, Slap A Ham 54 (2000)
Zodiak / Snowcone Ribplate / Cool Guy / Dwarf Goober Militia / Let's Fucking Go!!!

/ Complete And Utter Eradication Of All Generic Pop Punk (Extended version) / Sword Of The Lord / A Legend In Your Own Mind / Street Jam To The Second Power / Hort / Black n' Dekker Crusty Wrecker / Bobby Dee In The Hour Of Chaos / Gary Monardo's Record Vault Shirt / Not Even Phased / Campaign For Emo Destruction / Hardcore Before Mark McCoy Was Emo Semen / Sluta / Shovetheinternetupyourgapinganalcavity @dork.cm / Hoarder / Now 50% More Pants Shitting / Let The Neatings Commence / Chris Pooped At The Skatepark / Jeb For Ruler Of The (Formerly) Free World / Staayyyle / Crush Kill Destroy

SPIRITUAL BEGGERS (SWEDEN)
Line-Up: Christian Stöstrand (vocals / bass), Mike Amott (guitar), Ludwig Witt (drums)

The highly rated SPIRITUAL BEGGERS was originally formed as a side project by ex-CARNAGE and CARCASS guitarist Mike Amott to CARCASS with ex-AEON man Christian Stöstrand, but became a full time venture following Amott's split from CARCASS after the 'Heartworks' album.

Having released an early mini-album on Wrong Again, the fully fledged 'Another Way To Shine' was originally intended to be released by Swedish label Megarock Records. However, a decision had been taken to fold the label in order to relaunch themselves as a production company, so the album was eventually issued by Music For Nations in a licensing deal.

Music For Nations showed enough faith in the band to issue the third album, 'Mantra III', in January 1998. Produced by Fredrik Nordström, the band continued to defy all trends by offering a tirade of 70's influenced heavy riffs.

'Mantra III' found Stöstrand adopting the name 'Spice' and the inclusion of keyboard player Per Wiberg. Heavy touring saw support dates to FU MANCHU.

During 1999 SPIRITUAL BEGGARS contributed their version of 'Mr White' to the TROUBLE tribute album issued on Freedom Records.

Witt founded side project FIREBIRD in 2000 in alliance with CATHEDRAL's Leo Smee and ex-CARCASS guitarist Bill Steer.

Spice also operated in the 'Music For The World Beyond' 2000 album by THE MUSHROOM RIVER BAND.

Amott also operates the equally successful ARCH ENEMY.

Albums:
SPIRITUAL BEGGERS, Wrong Again (1994)
Yearly Dying / Pelekas / The Space Inbetween / If This Is All / Under Silence / Magnificent Obsession
ANOTHER WAY TO SHINE, Music For Nations CDMFN 198 (1996)
Magic Spell / Blind Mountain / Misty Valley / Picking From The Box / Nowhere To Go / Entering Into Peace / Sour Stains / Another Way To Shine / Past The Sound Of Whispers
MANTRA III, Music For Nations (1998)
Homage To The Betrayed / Monster Astronauts / Euphoria / Broken Morning / Lack Of Prozac / Superbossanova / Bad Karma / Send Me A Smile / Cosmic Romance / Inside Charmer / Sad Queen Boogie / Mushroom Tea Girl
AD ASTRA, Music For Nations (2000)
Left Brain Ambassadors / Wonderful World / Sedated / Angel Of Betrayal / Blessed / Per Aspera Ad Astra / Save Your Soul / Until The Morning / Escaping The Fools / On Dark Rivers / The Goddess / Mantra

SQUASH BOWELS (POLAND)
Line-Up: Mariosch (vocals), Lechu (guitar), Paluch (bass), Rogal (drums)

Bialystok Grindcore band SQUASH BOWELS made their presence felt with the demo tape 'Dead?!'. A split album with MALIGNANT TUMOUR led in turn to a shared cassette with INFECTED PUSSY. A further split tape was issued in alliance with SM SNIPER as well as another promotional tape 'International Devastation'.

The first pressing of SQUASH BOWELS 'Dreams Come True… In Death' album featured a photograph of a dead body on the cover. Probably not wishing to be accused of stereotyping the second issue saw a change - to a photo of a woman being attacked by an axe.

The 1996 7" single 'Something Nice' was graced, presumably by a display of Grindcore irony, with a cover photograph of a disembodied woman. Split single releases included collaborations with Japan's CATASEXUAL URGE MOTIVATION, Mexico's DISGORGE and Sweden's BIRDFLESH.

Noise Product / Surge Of Assurance / The Grind Core-Spondent / New Standards / A Suspect / More Our Colours, Obliteration (1996) ('Something Nice' 7" single)
Split, (199-) (7" split single with CATASEXUAL URGE MOTIVATION)
Split, (1998) (7" split single with DISGORGE)
Split, Bizarre Leprous (1999) (7" split single with COCK AND BALL TORTURE)
Split, (2000) (7" split single with BIRDFLESH)

Albums:
DREAMS COME TRUE... IN DEATH, Obscene Productions (1995) (Split album with MALIGNANT TUMOUR) Lustmord / Tested Creatures / Regulation People's Fear / Human Acceleration / Holy Lies / A Suspect / Infanticide / Pseudo Faces / Victims... / Right To Live / Life Like A Dream / More Our Colours / Deadly Sick / The Mass Sickening / Old Things / Dash Of Life

STENTORIAN (HOLLAND)
Line-Up: Arne Sunter (vocals), Jeffrey Brugman (guitar), Paul Hendriksen (guitar), Paul Noomen (bass), Martijn Peters (drums)

Arnhem's STENTORIAN appeared on two compilations albums during 1993; Displeased Records' 'Against All Gods' and DSFA Records 'Resurrection Of Reality'. The group later toured Holland opening for GOREFEST, THERION, EXHORDER and DEADHEAD.

Albums:
GENTLE PUSH TO PARADISE, Jaciberg JR CD001 (1996)
This Jericho Dance / Collapsed At The Crossing Path / Man From The Forest / July The 24th / Into The Deep / The Loss / Weltschmewrz / Romancing The Lost Love

STIGMATHEIST (HOLLAND)
Line-Up: Patrick Koning (vocals), Ewald Busschler (guitar), Wilfrid Spijker (guitar), Rob Hilgerink (bass), Rene Kroon (keyboards), William Vlierman (drums)

Albums:
STANDING FOR HER GRAVE, (1996)
IT ALL ENDS TODAY, Euphonious (2000)

To Become What It Becomes / Within The Pains Of Pleasure / Meaningless / Released Souls / It All Ends Today / Deaths Departure / Condemned Disbelief / Suffer My Punishment / The End

STORMLORD (ITALY)
Line-Up: Cristiano Borchi (vocals), Piereangelo Giglioni (guitar), Francesco Bucci (bass), Fabrizio Cariani (keyboards), David Folchitto (drums)

Founded as a Power Metal trio in 1991 STORMLORD debuted with the demo 'Black Knight' the following year. A deal with Metal Hearse Productions led to the inclusion of the track 'Cataclysm' on the compilation album 'Dawn Of Gods'.
By 1997 STORMLORD could boast seven members and cut the EP 'Under The Sign Of The Sword' and another appearance on volume two of 'Dawn Of Gods'. Touring in Italy found STORMLORD sharing stages with ATROCITY, OVERKILL and the infamous DEATH SS.
The band then trimmed down to 5 members with bassist Maffeitor Fabban making way for Francesco Bucci as a deal was signed with German label Last Episode for the 'Supreme Art Of War' album.
A European tour with MYSTIC CIRCLE and GRAVEWORM ensued prior to the recruitment of keyboard player Simore Scazzocchio.

Singles/EPs:
Under The Sign Of The Sword / Riding The Sunset / The Scarlet Kingdom, Metal Horse (1997)
Where My Spirit Forever Shall Be / Sir Lorial / War - The Supreme Art, (199-)

Albums:
SUPREME ART OF WAR, Last Episode (1999)
Where My Spirit Forever Shall Be / A Descent Into The Kingdom Of The Shades / Sir Lorial / Age Of The Dragon / War - The Supreme Art / Immortal Heroes / Of Steel And Ancient Might

STRONG DEFORMITY (HUNGARY)
Line-Up: Tamas Biro (vocals), Szabolcs Fodor (guitar), Zsolt Bertalan (guitar), Tibor Kovacs (bass), Balazs Bertalan (drums)

Created by the merging of two other Hungarian acts STRONG DEFORMITY debuted with a modern Metal album, 'Power Of Pain...', that showed no sign of compromise.

The band had been created in 1995 heralding their arrival with a track on the compilation album 'Demonstration II' issued by the Hungarian arm of 'Metal Hammer' magazine.

Following the release of the 1996 album STRONG DEFORMITY toured Austria and Hungary including support dates to NAPALM DEATH.

Albums:
POWER OF PAIN..., Core & More COM 002 (1996)
Evolution / Without Mercy / Strikes To The Face / Pain Of The World / Two Fists / Everything Burns Up / Who Will Survive? / The Power / Frontline / Abyss

STRONGHOLD (NORWAY)

A Christian Death-Doom act. STRONGHOLD member Erik also operates in IMPLACABLE.

Albums:
PRAYERS FROM A YEARNING HEART, Nordic Mission NMCD02 (199-)
Prayer Of The Yearning / Praise / Tears / Lament / In Strongest Arms

SUBLIME CADAVERIC DECOMPOSITION (FRANCE)
Line-Up: Yov, Seb, Tristan, Bruno

French Grindcore merchants SUBLIME CADAVERIC DECOMPOSITION have a tradition of split releases. The band were planning a limited edition split EP with LYMPHATIC PHLEGHM for 2001.

Albums:
SUBLIME CADAVERIC DECOMPOSITION, (1997) (Split album with INFECTED PUSSY)
SPLIT, Bones Brigade BB002 (1998) (Split album with ROT)
Scrotum Rules / Necropedozoophilien / 3-0 Scatogorophage - La Deuuxxx! - GôÖÄÄââllll / Lady Died / Female Sphincter Dilation / Emmoroidal Meat / Drink - Smoke - Fuck- Eat! (Just Do It) / Royal Spice Fucking (Porcine Power) / Dead Dick / Stomach Masturbation / Penis Autodissection / Grunter Screams / Grinding Oesophage Ejaculation / Siprinose Addiction / Marie And Schulz / Pigs And Love / Move Your Ears!!! / Bitch Boys (Bloody Dance Musique) /

Stop Salad Vivisection Now!!! / Outro

SUFFER (SWEDEN)
Line-Up: Joakim Öhman (vocals), Ulf Samuelsson (guitar), Patrik Andersson (bass), Per Karlsson (drums)

Deathsters SUFFER date to 1988, when the first line-up comprised of vocalist Joakim Öhman, bassist Patrik Andersson and drummer Conny Granqvist.

The group added guitarist Ronny Eide in 1990, but a line-up shuffle saw Granqvist depart in favour of ex-WORTOX and ALTAR drummer Per Karlsson.

Following the release of the 'Structures' album, SUFFER split. Andersson joined IN BETWEEN DAYS.

Guitarist Ulf Samuelsson joined the THERION offshoot band SERPENT for their 'In The Garden Of The Serpent' album. He was joined by a further SUFFER member drummer Per Karlsson in 1996. The following year Karlsson joined T.A.R.

Öhman attempted a resurrection of SUFFER, with erstwhile members of ABHOTH guitarist Jörgen Kristensen and drummer Mats Blyckert, but this has yet to bear fruit.

Singles/EPs:
On Sour Ground / My Grief, New Wave NWR EP039 (1993)
Impressive Turns / Infectious / Global Warning / Wrong Side Of Life, Napalm NPRCD 002 (1993) ('Global Warning' EP)
Human Flesh (Live) / Wrong Side Of Life (Live), Immortal Underground IUPEP001 (1993)

Albums:
STRUCTURES, Napalm NPRCD006 (1994)
Temporary Sane / Passionate Structures / Lie Within / Selected Genes / A Frenetic Mind / Imaginary Homecoming / The Killing Culture / Freedom Of Speech

SUFFOCATION (NY, USA)
Line-Up: Frank Mullen (vocals), Terrance Hobbs (guitar), Doug Cerrito (guitar), Josh Barohn (bass), Doug Bohn (drums)

Now regarded as one of the most influential original Death Metal combos SUFFOCATION were initially founded as SOCIAL DISEASE during 1986. The band debuted with a line up of vocalist Frank Mullen, guitarists Doug Cerrito and Terence Hobbs, bassist Josh Barohn and

363

drummer Mike Smith. This unit arrived with the 3 track demo tape 'Reincremation' during 1990.

SUFFOCATION's inaugural album release 'Human Waste' emerged in 1991, issued by Nuclear Blast Records in Europe and Relapse in America. However, the band would switch labels to Roadrunner turning round 'Effigy Of The Forgotten' in the same year.

Barohn joined gore mongers AUTOPSY prior to founding WELT, an act that changed names in 1996 to IRON LUNG releasing the 'Chasing Salvation' album on Diehard Records.

The 1992 opus 'Breeding The Spawn' saw Chris Richards take the four string position. In 1994 SUFFOCATION donated the track 'Infecting The Crypts' to the 'Live Death' compilation album

Following touring to promote SUFFOCATION's 1995 album 'Pierced From Within' drummer Doug Bohn decamped. His place was taken by MALEVOLENT CREATION man Dave Culross.

During 1998 guitarist Doug Cerrito joined HATE ETERNAL for their 'Conquering The Throne' album, the act founded by RIPPING CORPSE / MORBID ANGEL guitarist Erik Rutan. Culross would rejoin MALEVOLENT CREATION.

Highlighting the undoubted impact SUFFOCATION had upon the scene Greek label Repulsive Echo compiled a 2001 tribute album with an all international cast. SUFFOCATION were duly paid homage by their countrymates PROPHECY, DEVOURMENT, PUTRILAGE, SEVERED SAVIOR, INTERNAL BLEEDING and DETRIMENTAL as well as Canadians ROTTING, Australians MISCREANT, Finns DEEP RED, Spains WORMED, Japan's VOMIT REMNANTS, Greeks INVERACITY, Dutch bands PYAEMIA and DISAVOWAL, Germans HARMONY DIES and even BEHEADED from Malta.

Albums:
HUMAN WASTE, Nuclear Blast (1991)
Infecting The Crypts / Synthetically Revived / Mass Obliteration / Catatonia / Jesus Wept / Human Waste
EFFIGY OF THE FORGOTTEN, Roadrunner (1991)
Liege Of Inveracity / Effigy Of The Forgotten / Infecting The Crypts / Seeds Of The Suffering / Habitual Infamy / Reincremation / Mass Obliteration / Involuntary Slaughter / Jesus Wept
BREEDING THE SPAWN, Roadrunner

(1992)
Beginning Of Sorrow / Breeding The Spawn / Epitaph Of The Credulous / Marital Decimation / Prelude To Repulsion / Anomalistic Offerings / Ornaments Of Discrepancy / Ignorant Deprivation
PIERCED FROM WITHIN, Roadrunner (1995)
Pierced From Within / Thrones Of Blood / Depths Of Depravity / Suspended In Tribulation / Torn Into Enthrallment / The Invoking / Synthetically Revived / Brood Of Hatred / Breeding The Spawn
DESPISE THE SUN, Vulture entertainment (1997)
Funeral Inception / Devoid Of Truth / Despise The Sun / Bloodchurn / Catatonia (Grind mix)

SUMMON (USA)
Line-Up: Xaphan (vocals / guitar), Ankharu (guitar), Necromodeus (bass), Anbrusius (drums)

Michigan band SUMMON evolved from the hotly tipped MASOCHIST. When MASOCHIST founder member Tchort was ejected from the band (to found WIND OF THE BLACK MOUNTAINS) the remaining members reforged the act as SUMMON.

The debut SUMMON album 'Baptized By Fire', which includes drummer Astaroth, has a cover version of MAYHEM's perennial 'Deathcrush'.

Vocalist Xaphan (Sean) also has credits with LUCIFER'S HAMMER.

Albums:
BAPTIZED BY FIRE, Baphomet (199-)
Sons Of Wrath / Visions Of Apocalyptic Grace / Baptized By Fire / The Silence Of Chaos / Dark Descent Of Fallen Souls / Realm Of No Return / Bring Black Desire / Beyond The Gates Of Scora / Eve Of Anti Creation / Eternal Darkness
DARK DESCENT OF FALLEN SOULS, Grinding Peace (1996)
Intro / Dark Descent Of Fallen Souls / Enter Into Eternal Oath / Eve Of Anti-Creation / Beyond The Gates Of Storm / Necromantic Lust / Under The Midnight Shadows / The Silence Of Chaos / Tales Of Immortality / Sorrows Of Moonlight Night / Outro - Tranquil Deed

SUNDOWN (SWEDEN)
Line-Up: Mathias Lodmalm (vocals / guitar), Andreas Johansson (guitar), Johnny Hagel (bass), Christian Silver

(drums)

SUNDOWN were formed by ex-TIAMAT man Johnny Hagel and CEMETARY's Mathias Lodmalm. The band folded in 2000 with Lodmalm resurrecting CEMETARY under the guise of CEMETARY 1213.

Singles/EPs:
Aluminium / 19 / Synergy / Slither / Don't Like To Live Today, Century Media LC 6975 (1997) ('Design 19' rough mixes promo EP)

Albums:
DESIGN 19, Century Media CD 77161-2 (1997)

SUPPOSITORY (HOLLAND)

Dutch Grindsters SUPPOSITORY include erstwhile AGATHOCLES guitarist Matti in the ranks. Their 1999 album 'Raised By Hatred' was a joint effort in collaboration with Matti's former employers.

Albums:
RAISED BY HATRED, Obscene Productions (1999) (Split album with AGATHOCLES)
Same Old Bullshit / Doorway To Destruction / Raised By Hatred / Dehumanized / Life Denied / Face The Facts / Wake Up Call / Unrevealed / Clueless Victims Of Society / Déjà vu?

SUPURATION (FRANCE)
Line-Up: Fabrice Loez (vocals / guitar), Ludovic Loez (guitar), Laurent Bessault (bass), Thierry Berger (drums)

A French Death Doom Metal band with Gothic influences, SUPURATION released two albums (the second, 'Still In The Spheres', including a cover of TEARS FOR FEARS' 'Shout') before shortening the band name to SUP.
In 1995 a limited edition CD emerged (only 500 copies were pressed) entitled '9092' containing a number of tracks previously only released as singles or on compilation albums between 1990 and 1992
The group would tour with Swiss outfit CORONER in early 1996.

Albums:
THE CUBE, Reincarnate SUP 07 CD (1993)
Prelude / The Elevation / Soul's

Speculum / 1308. JP. 08 / The Cube / Through The Transparent / Partitions / Spherical Inner-Sides / The Accomplishment / 4TX. 31B / The Dim Light
STILL IN THE SPHERES, Reincarnate SUP 08 CD (1994)
The Crack / The Cleansing / Back From The Garden / Variation On Theme 4Tx.31B / Shout
9092, Pias (1995)
The Creeping Unknown / Isolated / In Remembrance Of A Coma / Sultry Obsession / 1308. JP. 08 / Sojourn In The Absurd / Empheral Paradise / Reveries Of A Bloated Cadaver / In Remembrance Of A Coma / 1308. JP. 08 / Half-Dead / Hypertrophy-Sordid & Outrageous Emanation / Sultry Obsession / Reveries Of A Bloated Cadaver
ANOMALY, Revelation REV 003 (1995)
Anomaly / Pain Injection / In Those Times / The Work / Ocean Of Faces / In The Deepest Silence / Dialogue (D-ÄN & T-ÖN) / D-ÄN'S Last Order / Reset / D-ÄN'SUP V 1.1
TRANSFER, Revelation REV 005 (1996)
Ocean Of Faces (D-Än Mix) / Ocean Of Faces (Acoustic Version) / Pain Injection (Limb Mix) / Ocean Of Faces (Cradle Mix) / The Work (Acoustic) / Pain Injection (Demo Version) / In Those Times (Demo Version) / The Work (Demo Version)

SWORDMASTER (SWEDEN)
Line-up: Andreas Bergh (vocals), Emil Nödtveidt (guitar), Kenneth Gagfner (bass), Tobias Kjellgren (drums)

SWORDMASTER date to 1993 and their foundation by guitarist Nightmare (real name Emil Nödtveidt). Nightmare also plays with OPTHALAMIA and is the brother of the imprisoned DISSECTION mentor Jon.
Following the mini-album release on Florida's Full Moon Productions, drummer Tobias Kjellgren joined DECAMERON. He would eventually rejoin DISSECTION for their December 1995 European tour. His temporary replacement in SWORDMASTER was another ex-DISSECTION member, Ole Öhman.
The 'Wrath Of Time' mini-album was re-released on vinyl format in 1996, limited to 1,000 copies and with two extra tracks; 'Metallic Devastation' and 'Claws Of Death (Conspiracy)'. The band signed to Osmose Productions the same year but would start to draw themselves away from Black Metal with each successive

release.
Presently the band are credited as vocalist Whiplasher, guitarists Nightmare and Beast Electric, bassist Thunderbolt and drummer Terror.

<u>Singles/EPs:</u>
Wraths Of Time / Upon Blood And Ashes / Conspiracy - Preview / Outro, Full Moon Productions FMP004 (1995) ('Wraths Of Time' EP)

<u>Albums:</u>
POST MORTEM TALES, Osmose Productions OPCD055 (1997)
Indeathstries - The Master's Possession / Crust To Dust / Postmortem Tales / Past Redemption / Claws Of Death / Blood Legacy / The Serpent Season / Metallic Devastation / Black Ace
DEATHRAIDER, Osmose Productions (1999)
Deathraider 2000 / Firefall To The Fireball / Necronaut Psychout / Iron Corpse / Stand For The Fire Demon
MORIBUND TRANSGORIA, Osmose Productions OPCD084 (1999)
Deathspawn Of The Eibound / Towards The Erotomech Eye / The Angel And The Masters / Metalmorphosis - The Secret Of Cain / Sulphar Skelethrone / Moribund Transgoria / Doom At Motordome / The Grotesque Xtravaganza

SXOXB (JAPAN)

SXOXB (or SABOTAGE ORGANIZED BARBARIANS) offer Thrashed Grindcore with Hardcore persuasions. The band have had the honour of not only sharing a split single with BRUTAL TRUTH but also pioneers NAPALM DEATH.

<u>Singles/EPs:</u>
The Peel Sessions EP, (199-)
Split, (199-) (7" split single with NAPALM DEATH)
Split, (199-) (7" split single with BRUTAL TRUTH)

<u>Albums:</u>
LEAVE ME ALONE - DON'T BE SWINDLE, (199-)
WHAT'S THE TRUTH, (199-)
GATE OF DOOM, (199-)
VICIOUS WORLD, (199-)

T.A.R. (SWEDEN)
Line-Up: Torbjörn (vocals), Stefan Sjöberg (guitar), Juan (guitar), Östen (bass), Per Karlsson (drums)

T.A.R. was created in November 1993 by vocalist Torbjörn under the original band name of VULTURE KING. The band also included guitarist Juan, American bassist Preston and drummer Tommi Sykes.

During 1994 Östen came in on bass and second guitarist Conny. Still under the name VULTURE KING the band cut a demo 'Breaking The Chains' followed by a sophomore effort 'Act II' with another new guitarist Stefan Sjöberg.

VULTURE KING gigged with bands such as FACE DOWN and DISMEMBER before going into the studio for a third demo tape, now billed as T.A.R., 'Are You Deaf?'. By this time Sykes ad decamped. Former SUFFER and SERPENT drummer Per Karlsson joined in January of 1997.

Strangely the band's debut album 'Fear Of Life' had English and Spanish lyrics.

Albums:
FEAR OF LIFE, T.A.R. Productions TPCD001 (1997)
Authority Lies / Jesus Is Dead / True Violence / Broken Dreams / Kiss Of Death / Living In Hell / Stained Shadows / If / Choice / In Control / Ten And A Half

TEARS OF DECAY (GERMANY)
Line-Up: Michael Eden (vocals), Steffan Parth (guitar), Henne Siemens (guitar), Joerg Pirch (bass), Dirk Bakker (drums)

Death Metal band TEARS OF DECAY evolved from a former band MISTRUST. The band would solidify its line up in 1998 when they found bass player Joerg Pirch at the Wacken festival. TEARS OF DECAY put in their inaugural gig alongside SANITY'S DAWN and ANSARCA in February 1999. A second album provisionally titled 'Saprophyt' is planned for 2001.

Albums:
REDEMPTION, Cudgel Agency CUD006 (2000)
Intro / The Area Behind The Curtain Of The World / Negative Determination Of Life And Everything / Redemption / Dark Angel / Homo Homini Deus Est

TENEBRE (SWEDEN)
Line-Up: Kalle Metz (vocals), Franco Bollo (guitar), Fredrik Täck (guitar), Richard Lion (bass), Andreas Albin (drums)

Self Styled 'Evil' Metal band created by former FLEGMA members vocalist Kalle Metz and bassist Richard Lion along with ex FUNHOUSE guitarist Fredrik Täck and drummer Joel during 1996.

The opening release 'XIII' saw FUNHOUSE guitarist Martin as session player but Lukas Sunesson took the role on a more permanent basis shortly after. TENEBRE rounded off the year contributing two tracks 'Halloween II' and 'Vampira' to a MISFITS tribute album.

TENEBRE's second record 'Grim Ride' only saw a limited European release. 1999 saw the departure of Joel and the recruitment of ex-EMBRACED man Andreas Albin on the drum stool. Another change saw Sunesson exiting (the band claimed he was 'fat'!) with Franco Bollo (a.k.a. Jan Gajdos of FUNHOUSE) assuming the role.

TENEBRE's 2000 album, the deliberately mis-spelled 'Mark Ov The Beast', includes a guest performance from Steve Sylvester from cult Italian band DEATH SS.

Singles/EPs:
Halloween, RHCDM2 (1997)
Cultleader, RHCDM3 (1997)
Tombola Voodoo Master / Terror, (1999)

Albums:
XIII, RHCD3 (1997)
Thirteen / I / Taste My Sin / A Cross On Your Door / Tenebre / Rites Of Passage II / Dead But Dreaming / Moth To The Flame / No Wrong / Thunrida / The Case Of Charles Dexter Ward / Buried And Forgotten / March Of The Dying Angel
GRIM RIDE, (1998)
Demon / No Time For Pain / The Call / Demonicus Ex Deo / Like A Needle / Soulbleed / When Razors Cry / Love 666 / Scarecrow / Without / Darkness Bound
MARK OV THE BEAST, Regain RR0010-009 (2000)
Harvester Of Souls / Tombola Voodoo Master / Mark Ov The Beast / I Am Your Ritual / God Speaks In Tongues / Putana Satana / Gone With The Wind / The Undertaker / Come To Season / Thy Darkness Come / Alignment

TERATOMA (SPAIN)
Line-Up: Tito (vocals), José David (guitar), Juanma (guitar), Sergi (drums)

TERATOMA ("Monstrous Tumour") was created in 1993 but would shortly after their formation adopt the new title of SUFFERING. With the inclusion of guitarist Juanma in 1996 the band reverted back to TERATOMA issuing the demo tape 'From Inside'.

Drummer Sergi would replace the exiting Rocque for the album 'The Terato-Genus Reborn'. The record includes a cover version of SODOM's 'Christ Passion'.

Albums:
THE TERATO-GENUS REBORN, Flesh Feast Productions (2000)
The Teratogenus Reborn / Pathogenous Morphology / Decrepit Carnage / Venial Conspiracy / Hollow Preacher / I Will Feed On You / Dimension / Visceral Hate / Christ Passion / Suffering

THANATOS (HOLLAND)
Line-Up: Stephen Gebédí (vocals / guitar), Mark Staffhorst (guitar), Erwin De Brouwer (bass), Remo Vonarnhem (drums)

Dutch Thrash band THANATOS tend to stand out from the crowd with some inventive songs. THANATOS actually lay claim to being Holland's first Death Metal act having formed in 1984 with a line up of Stephen Gebédí, guitarist Remco De Maaijer and drummer Marcel Van Arnhem. This version of the band released the 'Speed Kills' demo prior to folding in 1985.

Gebédí reformed THANATOS for another demo session entitled 'Rebirth'. Van Arnhem returned along with new bass player André Scherpenberg. Rob De Bruijn would take over the drum stool but departed soon after. Another new recruit in 1987 was former SECOND HELL guitarist Mark Staffhorst.

Scherpenberg quit to join VIGILANT necessitating KILLER FORCE guitarist Erwin De Brouwer to handle bass guitar. However, soon De Brouwer would shift to guitar as Ed Boeser of KILLING ELEVATOR maneuvered into the bassist's job.

The group issued a 1987 demo entitled 'The Day Before Tomorrow', notable for featuring the live track 'Progressive Destructor' and followed this with a 1989 tape 'Omnicoitor'. Following their album

for Shark Records 'Emerging From The Netherworlds' they released another demo in 1991 featuring five tracks before Shark came up with a second record in 1992. Despite having two albums in the stores THANATOS were far from happy with their label and were vocal in their vehemence. Naturally the two parties went their separate ways.

THANATOS split with Gebédê and De Brouwer created CHURCH OF INDULGENCE in allegiance with bassist Peter Van Wees and drummer Dirk Bruinenberg. This band ground to a halt as De Brouwer united with ex-THANATOS man Ed Boeser in the alternative Rock act SMALLTOWN and Van Wees joined INCOMING. Bruinenberg would ally himself with the high profile act ELEGY.

THANATOS returned in 1999 with ex-CREMATION guitarist Paul Baayens, SINISTER / HOUWITSER drummer Aad Kloosterwaard and HOUWITSER / JUDGEMENT DAY bassist Theo Van Eekelen in the ranks for the 'Angelic Encounters' album.

Albums:
EMERGING FROM THE NETHERWORLDS, Shark 015 (1990)
Dawn Of The Dead / Outward Of The Inward / Bodily Dismemberment / Infernal Deceit / The Day Before Tomorrow / War / Rebirth / Progressive Destructor / Imposters Infiltration / Omnicoitor / Dolor Satanae
REALMS OF ECSTASY, Shark 025 (1992)
Intro - And Jesus Wept / Tied Up Sliced Up / Realm Of Ecstasy / Mankind's Afterbirth / In Praise Of Lust / Perpetual Misery / Human Combustion / Reincarnation / Terminal Breath
ANGELIC ENCOUNTERS, Hammerheart (2000)
Angelic Encounters / In Utter Darkness / Sincere Chainsaw Salvation / Infuriated / The Howling / Gods Of War / The Devil's Concubine / Speed Kills / Thou Shalt Rot / Corpsegrinder

THERGOTHON (FINLAND)

Various members of THERGOTHON later formed THIS EMPTY FLOW, releasing a 1996 album 'Magenta Skycode'.

Albums:
STREAM FROM THE HEAVENS, Avantgarde Music AV001 (1995)

Everlasting / Yet The Watchers Guard / The Unknown Kadath In The Cold Waste / Elemental / Who Rides The Astral Wings / Crying Blood + Crimson Snow

THERION (SWEDEN)

Line-Up: Christofer Johnsson (guitar / vocals), Peter Hansson (guitar), Erik Gustafsson (bass), Oskar Forss (drums)

Cited by many as the most adventurous Metal band at present. THERION present a sound swathed with huge operatic choirs and oriental orchestral arrangements. Although starting life as a run of the mill Death Metal band THERION have with each successive release wrung every ounce of adventurism out of each record increasing their status in Europe along the way.

The roots of THERION lay in the late 80s Swedish band BLITSKRIEG, which featured bassist / vocalist Christofer Johnsson, guitarist Peter Hansson and drummer Oskar Fors.

Formed as MEGATHERION in 1988, with a line up of Johnsson on vocals and guitar, guitarist Hansson, ex-CREMATORY bassist Johan Hansson and drummer Mika Tovalainen, shortly after the band shortened the name to THERION and replaced their rhythm section with bassist Erik Gustafsson and drummer Oskar Forss.

Initial demos in 1989 were completed with the temporary services of vocalist Matti Karki, now of DISMEMBER. This line up, minus Karki, recorded THERION's first mini-album 'Time Shall Tell', which was initially released as a limited edition of 1,000. However, subsequent pressings have been made.

Bassist Oscar Gustaffson left following the 'Of Darkness' album. For the 'Symphony Masses' album (released through Megarock in 1993) only Johnsson remained, adding guitarist Magnus Barthelson, bassist Andreas Wahl and former CARBONIZED drummer Piotr Wawrzenuik.

Wahl and Wawrzeniuk, guitarist Johan Lundell and ENTOMBED bassist Lars Rosenberg forged a 1993 side project titled SERPENT. The industrious Wahl also operated another side band CONCRETE SLEEP.

The group toured Europe in 1995 as support to Canadians ANNIHILATOR and the group drafted in ENTOMBED / SERPENT bassist Lars Rosenberg on a temporary basis for the shows.

Having signed to German label Nuclear Blast, 1995's 'Lepaca Kliffoth' featured a cover of CELTIC FROST's 'Sorrows Of The Moon'. The album also saw vocalist Claudia Maria Mohri, who appeared on

THERION
Photo : Martin Wickler

369

CELTIC FROST's 'Into The Pandemonium' album, and baritone Hans Groning.

THERION toured South America during 1995 during which Rosenberg opted to leave ENTOMBED and join THERION on a permanent basis.

In November the group added ex-UNANIMATED guitarist Jonas Mellberg together with former NECROPHOBIC keyboard player Tobbe Sidegard. Wawrzenuik and Rosenberg also released the debut SERPENT product 'In The Garden Of The Serpent' to round off 1995.

As 1996 began THERION contributed a track to a Japanese IRON MAIDEN cover album on the Toys Factory label and entered a new stage of their career with the 'Theli' release, an ambitious amalgam of Metal and Middle Eastern influences all overlaid with choral vocals.

With the release of 'Theli' THERION undertook an extensive tour of Germany, supporting AMORPHIS. Further dates saw the band as part of the 'Out Of The Dark' festivals on a bill alongside MY DYING BRIDE and SENTENCED.

The 1997 album release, originally planned as an EP, featured versions of RUNNING WILD's 'Under Jolly Roger', JUDAS PRIEST's 'Here Come The Tears', SCORPIONS 'Fly To The Rainbow' and IRON MAIDEN's 'Children Of The Damned'. The band would indulge in yet more covers with the 1999 release 'Crowning Of Atlantis' with a guesting Ralf Scheepers of PRIMAL FEAR making his presence felt on the bands version of 'Crazy Nights', originally by Japanese Metal band LOUDNESS. Also included were takes of MANOWAR's 'Thor' and ACCEPT's 'Seawinds'.

In keeping with their left field character THERION contributed a version of 'Summer Night City' to a 2001 Death Metal ABBA tribute.

Singles/EPs:
Time Will Tell / Dark Eternity / Asphyxiate With Fear / A Suburb To Hell, House Of Kicks (1990)
The Beauty In Black / Arrival Of The Darkest Queen / Evocation Of Vovin / The Veil Of Golden Spheres, Nuclear Blast NB125-2 (1995)
Siren Of The Woods (Single Version) / Cults Of The Shadow (Edit Version), Nuclear Blast NB 178-2/27361 61782 (1996)

Albums:
OF DARKNESS, Deaf DEAF 6 (1991)
The Return / Asphyxiate With Fear / Morbid Reality / Meglamaniac / A Suburb To Hell / Genocidal Raids / Time Shall Tell / Dark Eternity
BEYOND SANCTORIUM, Active ATV 23 (1992)
Future Consciousness / Pandemonic Outbreak / Cthulu / Symphony Of The Dead / Beyond Sanctum / Enter The Depths Of Eternal Darkness / Illusions Of Life / The Way / Paths / Tyrants Of The Damned
SYMPHONY MASSES - HO DRAKON HO MEGAS, Megarock MRR 002 (1993)
Baal Reginon / Dark Princess Naamah / A Black Rose / Symphoni Drakonis Inferni / Dawn Of Perishness / The Eye Of Eclipse / The Ritualdance Of The Yezidis / Powerdance / Procreation Of Eternity / Ho Dracon Ho Megas
LEPACA KLIFFOTH, Nuclear Blast NB 127 (1995)
The Wings Of The Hydra / Melez / Arrival Of The Darkest Queen / The Beauty In Black / Riders Of Theli / Black / Darkness Eve / Sorrows Of The Moon / Let The New Day Begin / Lepaca Kliffoth / Evocation Of Vovin
THELI, Nuclear Blast NB179 (1996)
Preludium / To Mega Therion / Cults Of The Shadow / In The Desert Of Set / Interludium / Nightside Of Eden / Opus Eclipse / Invocation Of Naamah / The Siren Of The Woods / Grand Finale - Postludium
A'RAB ZARAQ LUCID DREAMING, Nuclear Blast NB 249-2 (1997)
In Remembrance / Black Fairy / Fly To The Rainbow / Under Jolly Roger / Symphony Of The Dead / Here Come The Tears / Enter The Transcental Sleep / The Quiet Desert / Down The Qliphothic / Tunnel / Up To Netzach - Floating Back / The Fall Into Eclipse
VOVIN, Nuclear Blast NB 27361 63172 (1998)
The Rise Of Sodom And Gomorrah / Birth Of Venus Illegitima / Wine Of Aluqah / Clavicula Mox / The Wild Hunt / Eye Of Shiva / Black Sun Draconian Trilogy / The Opening / Morning Star / Black Diamonds / Raven Of Dispersion
CROWNING OF ATLANTIS, Nuclear Blast (1999)
The Crowning Of Atlantis / Mark Of Cain / Clavicula Nox (Remix) / Crazy Nights / From The Dionysian Days / Thor / Seawinds / To Mega Therion (Live) / The Wings Of The Hydra (Live) / Black Sun (Live)

DEGGIAL, Nuclear Blast NB 442-2 (2000) **43 GERMANY**
Seven Secrets Of The Sphinx / Eternal Return / Enter Vril-Ye / Ship Of Luna / The Invincible / Deggial / Emerald Crown / The Flight Of The Lord Of Flies / Flesh Of The Gods / Via Nocturna Part I, II / O Fortuna

THORIUM (DENMARK / SWEDEN)
Line-Up: Michael H. Anderson (vocals), Morten Ryberg (guitar), Allan Tvelebakk (guitar), Jonas Lindblood (guitar), Jesper Frost (drums)

The Danish / Swedish collaboration THORIUM boasts no less than three guitarists with bass duties reportedly delegated out to whichever one is the most drunk at the time! The band produced an outstanding Black Death Metal record but fell foul of their record company Diehard who relinquished the band's contract due to apparent Nazi lyrics. The situation was a huge misunderstanding and Diehard resigned the group.
Vocalist Michael H. Anderson, guitarists Morten Ryberg and Allan Tvelebakk are all erstwhile members of WITHERING SURFACE. Ryberg, a veteran of cult act ARISE, also plays with INFERNAL TORMENT.
Jonas Lindblood (Linblad) has credits with TAETRE whilst drummer Jesper Frost is known from INIQUITY.

Albums:
OCEAN OF BLASPHEMY, Diehard RRS948 (1999)
Crest For War / Abomination Of God / Crypts Of Chaos / Impaled / Betrayed By God / Countless Ways To Die / Ocean Of Blasphemy / Desecrating The Graves / Dawn Of Flames / Lunatic Of God's Creation

THRENODY (HOLLAND)
Line-Up: Rene Scholte (vocals / guitar), Erik Van De Belt (guitar), Henry McIlveen (bass), John Suyker (drums)

Dutch quartet THRENODY, founded in 1988, first released a 1990 demo, 'Ode To The Lamented', featuring original drummer Mark Van Bel. A further demo titled 'Profonation' scored a big impact on the underground Metal scene.
Having released the 'As The Heavens Fall' in 1995 the self-titled 1997 album saw a break up in ranks with only

vocalist/guitarist Rene Scholte and bassist Henry McIlveen surviving. New members were guitarist Menno Gootje and former HIGHWAY CHILE, HELLOISE and VENGEANCE drummer Ernst Van Ee.
Van Ee was to depart and THRENODY drafted Richard Van Leuwen. After touring Van Leuwen also broke ranks to join FROZEN SUN.
For the 1997 eponymous album Van Ee was back on the drum stool on a session basis. The sticksman was to later issue a 2000 solo album credited to simply VAN EE.

Albums:
AS THE HEAVENS FALL, Massacre CD024 (1995)
Cries / Regrets / Dark Ages / Ode To The Lamented / As The Heavens Fall / Come For Me / Despair / The Elder / Supersession Of Breath / In Memorium
BEWILDERING THOUGHTS, Massacre MASS CD065 (1995)
Dare Restrain / Willful / Bewildering Thoughts / Solitude / Fin De Siecle / Silence / Black Nazareth / Profanation / Autumn / Farewell
THRENODY, Massacre MASS PC0121 (1997)
None/ This Day / Vengeance / Shallow / Dead Man Progress / Instinct Of Pride / Your Truth / To Let Die / Loss Of Dreams / Revelations / Redemption / Outro

THRONE OF AHAZ (SWEDEN)
Line-Up: Fredrik 'Beretorn' Jacobsson (vocals), Marcus 'Whortael' Norman (guitar), Kalle 'Taurtheim' Bondesson (bass), Johan Mortiz (drums)

Umea based Death Metallers THRONE OF AZAZ formed in 1991 and initially comprised the duo of vocalist Beretorn and bassist Taurtheim.
The group was offered a deal by No Fashion Records after the release of the demo 'At The Mountains Of The Northern Storms' in 1992.
Prior to recording of the first album commenced original guitarist Peter was sacked due to musical differences and replaced by Nicklas 'Whortael' Svensson. The group started work on the record in March 1993, but it was beset by problems and took almost a year to complete.
'Nifelheim' eventually emerged in early 1995, by which time 'Whortael' was superceded by Marcus 'Vargher' Norman. And, although he played on the album,

drummer Johan Mortiz did not become a full member of the band until after it's release.

THRONE OF AZAZ returned to the studio in September 1995 in order to put 'On Twilight Enthroned' together, a record that would ultimately comprise eight tracks of hellish Black Metal. It also included a cover of the BLACK SABBATH anthem 'Black Sabbath'.

The group now listed themselves as: Veretorn (vocals), Varghar (guitar / keyboards) and Taurtheim (bass). Moritz still plays drums.

However, 'Varghar' Norman joined both ANCIENT WISDOM and BEWITCHED.

Albums:
NIFELHEIM, No Fashion NFR008 (1995)
Northern Thrones / An Arctic Star Of Blackness / Where Ancient Lords Gather / The Dawn Of War / Nifelheim / The Calling Blaze / A Winter Chant / The Kings That Were...
ON TWILIGHT ENTHRONED, No Fashion NFR016 (1996)
Fenris/ The Forlorn / With Shadow Wings / On Twilight Enthroned / Where Veils of Grief Are Dancing Slow / Let Blood Paint The Ground / Blackthorn Crown / Black Sabbath

THRONE OF CHAOS (FINLAND)
Line-Up: Mr. Kiljunen (vocals / guitar), Mr. Harmaja (guitar), Mr. Nora (bass), Mr. Sjoblom (keyboards), Mr. Laitenen (drums)

Albums:
FATA MORGANA, (199-)
MENACE AND PRAYER, Spikefarm NUALA 007 (2000)
From Clarity To Insanity / The Scaffold Scenario / Cold Bits Of Fire / Bloodstained Prophecy / Menace And Prayer / Synthetia / Opus Void / Divinity

THY PRIMORDIAL (SWEDEN)
Line-Up: Isidor (vocals), N. Nilsson (guitar), J. Albrektsson (bass), Morth (drums)

THY PRIMORDIAL started life billed as CARCHAROTH. A name change to LUCIFER ensued before a further name switch to PRIMORDIAL. As PRIMORDIAL the band released a 1995 demo 'En Mörka Makters Alla'. Discovering the Irish act of the same name the Swedes opted finally for THY PRIMORDIAL.

A second demo 'Svart Gryning' ('Black Dawn') led to a 7" single release.

THY PRIMORDIAL's debut album was recorded for the American Gothic label and intended for a 1995 release. However, the release was shelved and the act signed to the Pulverised label for the 'Where Only The Seasons Mark The Path Of Time' effort. The album was produced by Tommy Tägtgren. Seeing THY PRIMORDIAL making strides on their own Gothic hastily issued the intended debut 'Under Iskall Trollmáne'.

The band is fronted by Isidor, otherwise known as Michael Andersson. Both Andersson and bass player J. Albrektssson are also members of INDUNGEON together with MITHOTYN / FALCONER personnel Karl Beckmann and Stefan Wienerhall.

Drummer Morth (real name Jocke Petersson) sessioned on UNMOORED's 'Kingdoms Of Grief' album.

Singles/EPs:
Thy Primordial, Paranoia Syndrome (1996)

Albums:
WHERE ONLY THE SEASONS MARK THE PATH OF TIME, Pulverised ASH 002CD (1997)
The Conquest / Av Ondskapens Natur / Svart Gryning / Forthcoming Centuries / Where Only The Seasons Mark The Path Of Time / Enrapture... Silence / Eristallikar Vinternatt / Hail Unto Thee... Who Travels Over The Heavens / Tronad Av Natten / Dödsskuggan
UNDER ISKALL TROLLMÁNE, Gothic GOTHIC003 (1998)
Mitt Sokandes Ritual / Den Ondes Klor / Under Iskall Trollmáne / Blodsgras / Fe Viskande Tradens Skog / Bortom Nattsvart Himmel / De Morka Maktes Alla / The Impression Of War / Morkets Faste
AT THE WORLD OF UNTRODDEN WONDER, Pulverised (1999)
For Fires To Burn / Once Of The Fortunes Throne / The Fatal Journey / At The World Of Untrodden Wonder / Departure - Away In Spirit / Amongst The Chosen Lost / The Burden Of Time / To Ruin And Decay / My Beloved Darkness / Revealed Throughout The Ages
THE HERESY OF AN AGE OF REASON, Pulverised (2000)
Ceased To Decay / Ex Opere Operatu / Disguised As Beings Of Light / The Heresy Of An Age Of Reason / Mere Are They... / Tyrannize / The Enigma And

The Fall / The Dead Live - Shining
Crown Of Light

THY SERPENT (FINLAND)
Line-Up: Luopio (vocals / bass /
keyboards), Azhemin (vocals /
keyboards), Sami Tenetz (guitar),
Agathon Frosteus (drums)

A Doom Death Metal band THY
SERPENT formed in 1992 as guitarist
Sami Tenetz began recording rehearsal
tapes followed by more professional
sounding demos, including 1994's
'Frozen Memory'.
With interest from Spinefarm Records
Tenetz opted to recruit band members to
a project he had worked on single
handedly up to that point. After a number
of changes a stable group of musicians
were found that enabled recording of
1996's 'Forest Of Witchery' meisterwerk
to be commenced.
Oddly, Spinefarm has gone on record to
state that THY SERPENT will never play
live. Nevertheless, the 1998 album saw
the inclusion of CHILDREN OF BODOM
guitarist Alexi Laiho into the ranks.
Drummer Agathon Frosteus also
operates with GLOOMY GRIM,
NOMICON, BARATHRUM and
SOULGRIND. Luopio would session for
SOULGRIND's 1998 record 'Whitsongs'
whilst keyboard player Azhemin would
contribute to the 1999 SOULGRIND
album 'Kalma'. Members of the band
involved themselves with BARATHRUM
for the 2000 side project act SHAPE OF
DESPAIR issuing the 'Shades of...'
album.

Singles/EPs:
Death EP, Spinefarm (2000)

Albums:
FOREST OF WITCHERY, Spinefarm SPI
36CD (1996)
Flowers Of Witchery Abloom / Of
Darkness And Light / Traveller Of
Unknown Plains / Only Dust Moves... /
Like A Funeral Veil Of Melancholy / Wine
From Tears
LORDS OF TWILIGHT, Spinefarm
(1997)
Prometheus Unbound / The Forest Of
Blåkulla / Ode To The Witches - Part IV /
In Blackened Dreams / As Mist
Descends From the Hills / Unknown /
Epic Torment / In Blackened Dreams /
Ode To The Witches - Part III
CHRISTCRUSHER, Nuclear Blast NB

327-2 (1998)
Chambers Of The Starwatchers / Curtain
Of Treachery / Thou Bade Nothingness /
Go Free The Wolves / Circles Of Pain /
Christcrusher / Crystalmoors / Calm
Blinking
DEATH, Spinefarm SPI102CD (2000)
Deathbearer / Wounds Of Death / Sleep
In Oblivion / Parasites

TIAMAT (SWEDEN)
Line-Up: Johan Edlund (vocals / guitar),
Magnus Sahlgrem (guitar), Johnny Hagel
(bass), Lars Skold (drums)

A Death Metal combo, masterminded by
Johan Edlund, that has evolved
chameleon like with each successive
release.
Less tastefully known in their formative
years as TREBLINKA (during which time
vocalist Johan Edlund also pursued his
side project GENERAL SURGERY), the
Swedish quartet adopted the title of the
Sumerian goddess of chaos and mythical
planet TIAMAT. The band has evolved
from a derivative Speed Metal / Death act
to a more substantial stance in offering
aggression with adventurous Progressive
variances.
As TREBLINKA the band consisted of
vocalist/guitarist Johan "Hellslaughter"
Hedlund, bassist Klas Wistedt, guitarist
Stefan Lagergren and drummer Andreas
Holmberg, but upon taking the TIAMAT
moniker the Swedish group would be
rocked with constant reshuffling of
personnel. For the 'A Winter Shadow'
single released in 1990 by CBR Records
the band personnel would be credited as
Hellslaughter, guitarist A.D. Lord, bass
player Juck and drummer Oakbeach.
TIAMAT toured Europe in 1991 with label
mates UNLEASHED although 1992's
Astral Sleep' album saw both Lagergren
and Holmberg depart for EXPULSION
and the record was recorded by
vocalist/guitarist Johan Edlund, guitarist
Thomas Petersson, bassist Jörgen
Thulberg and drummer Niklas Ekstrand.
The band's 1993 line up comprised of
Edlund, keyboard player Kenneth Roos
and drummer Ekstrand. Live gigs were
performed with Edlund, Roos and
guitarist Thomas Petersson.
Musical differences saw TIAMAT split
following a 1993 tour of Europe to promote
the 'Clouds' album with UNLEASHED and
MORGOTH. Petersen and Roos departed,
leaving Johan Edlund to carry on with a
new line-up that included ex SORCEROR
bassist Johnny Hagel.

'The Sleeping Beauty- Live In Israel' was recorded in Tel Aviv in June 1993. Later shows found the band touring alongside PARADISE LOST and VOODOO CULT.

The band toured as support to TYPE O NEGATIVE in Europe during 1994 and TIAMAT successfully headlined the 1995 Dynamo Festival in Holland and toured Britain as support to BLACK SABBATH. The same year a limited edition album, 'A Musical History Of Tiamat', would give fans further live material in the form of an extra CD.

1994's Space Rock charged 'Wildhoney' album found keyboards contributed by GRIP INC. guitarist Waldemar Sorychta and the single choice, 'Gaia', included a cover version of PINK FLOYD's 'When You're In' as one of the additional tracks. Predictably the line up fluxed yet again with Ekstrand and Petersson discharging themselves and drummer Lars Skold welcomed into the fold.

1997's 'A Deeper Kind Of Slumber' heralded another shift in TIAMAT's musical landscape as Edlund ventured into distinctly ambitious Progressive Rock territory. Naturally the ebb and flow of band members continued unabated too with CEMETARY's Anders Iwers enrolling on guitar as in a straight swap Johnny Hagel joined CEMETARY. However, Iwers would manoeuvre to bass when Petersson rejoined later. Iwers would also find extracurricular activities deputising for Italian act LACUNA COIL after both their guitarists pulled out of an October 1997 tour at short notice.

TIAMAT returned with the 2000 Gothic infused 'Skeleton Skeletron' outing. Petersson bailed out yet again. The band, complete once more with a yoyo-ing Petersson bouncing back, got to grips with a November European package tour alongside running mates ANATHEMA and TRISTANIA. The album cover of the seminal ROLLING STONES track 'Sympathy For The Devil' was initially projected as a single but 'Brighter Than The Sun' was picked instead.

<u>Singles/EPs:</u>

A Winter Shadow / Ancient Entity, CBR CBR-S-125 (1990) (7" single)

Gaia (Video Edit) / The Ar (Radio Cut) /When You're In / Whatever That Hurts (Video Edit) / The Ar (Ind. Mix) / Visionaire (Remixes Longform Version), Century Media 77089-2 (1994) (Tour Sampler EP)

Cold Seed / Only In My Tears It Lasts (The Cat mix) / Three Leary Biscuits Century Media CD 77 167-2 (1997)

Brighter Than The Sun (Radio edit) / Sympathy For The Devil / Children Of The Underworld / Brighter Than The Sun, Century Media (1999)

For Her Pleasure / Lucy (Demon mix) / Brighter Than The Sun (Bullsrun mix) / As Long As You Are Mine (Lodmalm mix),

TIAMAT

Century Media (2001)

Albums:
SUMERIAN CRY, Metalcore CORE 9 (1991)
Intro: Sumerian Cry Part I / In The Shrines Of The Kingly Dead / The Malicious Paradise / Necrophagous Shadows / Apotheosis Of Morbidity / Nocturnal Funeral / Altar Flame / Evilized / Where The Serpents Ever Dwell / Outro / Sumerian Cry Part II / The Sign Of The Pentagram
THE ASTRAL SLEEP, Century Media CM7722 (1992)
Neo Aeon / Lady Temptress / Mountain Of Doom / Dead Boys Choir / Sumerian Cry (Part III) / Ancient Entity / The Southernmost Voyage / Angels Far Beyond / I Am The King (Of Dreams) / A Winter Shadow / The Seal
CLOUDS, Century Media 84 9736-2 (1993)
In A Dream / Clouds / Smell Of Incense / A Caress Of Stars / The Sleeping Beauty / Forever Burning Flames / The Scapegoat / Undressed
THE SLEEPING BEAUTY-LIVE IN ISRAEL, Century Media 77065 (1994)
In A Dream / Ancient Entity / The Sleeping Beauty / Mountains Of Doom / Angels Far Beyond
WILDHONEY, Century Media CD770802 (1994)
Wildhoney / Whatever That Hurts / The Ar / 25th Floor / Gaia / Visionaire / Kaleidoscope / Do You Dream Of Me? / Planets / A Pocket Size Sun
A MUSICAL HISTORY OF TIAMAT, Century Media (1995)
Where The Serpents Ever Dwell / The Sign Of The Pentagram / Ancient Entity / Dead Boys Choir / The Southernmost Voyage / A Winter Shadow / Smell Of Insence / A Caress Of Stars / The Sleeping Beauty / When You're In / Visionaire / Do You Dream Of Me? / A Pocket Sized Sun / Whatever That Hurts (Live) / The Ar (Live) / In A Dream (Live) / 25th Floor (Live) / Gaia (Live) / Visionaire (Live) / Kaleidoscope (Live) / Do You Dream Of Me? (Live) / The Sleeping Beauty (Live) / A Pocket Sized Sun (Live)
A DEEPER KIND OF SLUMBER, Century Media 77180-2 (1997) **39 SWEDEN**
Cold Seed / Teonanacatl / Trillion Zillion Centipedes / The Desolate One / Atlantis As A Lover / Alteration X / Four Leary Biscuits / Only In My Tears It Lasts / The Whores Of Babylon / Kite/ Phantasma /

Mount Marilyn / A Deeper Kind Of Slumber
SKELETON SKELETRON, Century Media (2000)
Church Of Tiamat / Brighter Than The Sun / Dust Is Our Fare / To Have And Have Not / For Her Pleasure / Diyala / Sympathy For The Devil / Best Friend Money Can Buy / As Long As You're Mine / Lucy

TO DIE FOR (FINLAND)
Line-Up: Jape Perätalo (vocals), Joonas Koto (guitar), J.P. Sutela (guitar), Miikka Kuisma (bass), Tonmi Lillman (drums)

TO DIE FOR drummer Tonmi Lillman was also employed on the second SINERGY album 'To Hell And Back' in 2000. SINERGY's Kimberley Goss supplies backing vocals to the 'All Eternity' album.

Albums:
ALL ETERNITY, Nuclear Blast NB 482-2 (2000)
Farewell / Live In You / In The Heat Of The Night / Our Candle Melts Away / Dripping Down Red / Sea Of Sin / Loveless / One More Time / Mary-Ann (R.I.P.) / Together Complete / Rimed With Frost / Lacrimarum

TORCHURE (GERMANY)
Line-Up: Martin (vocals), Mario Staller (guitar), Malte Staller (guitar), Dr. Fressenius (bass), Patrick (keyboards), Stefan (drums)

Dating from 1985 TORCHURE released their first demo 'Signs Of Premonition' in 1988. Drummer Stefan was ex-SATYRE. Further tapes, 'Hellraiser' in 1990 and 'Traces' in 1991, followed.
Having debuted with the 'Beyond The Veil' album in 1992 TORCHURE toured through Europe with SEPULTURA and PESTILENCE to improve their stature within German Death Metal circles. However, fate befell the band when two members of the band were killed in an accident.
Twin guitarists Mario and Malte Staller were added for the second album, 'The Essence'. The record was produced by S.L. Coe of SCANNER.
Promoting the album TORCHURE undertook a 40 date European tour sharing billing with DISHARMONIC ORCHESTRA.

BEYOND THE VEIL, 1MF 77 002 2 41 (1992)
The Veil Of Sanity / In His Grip / Abysmal Malevolence / Resort To Mortality / Genocidal Confessions / Apathetic / Depressions / Beyond The Veil
THE ESSENCE, 1 MF 3770036-2 (1993)
Invisible Truth / Sense Of Death / Sinister Seduction / Voice Of Power / Terminus / No Rest In Peace / Between The Urges / The Essence / Cry Of Madness / 8 / Traces / Lost Souls

TORMENT (GERMANY)
Line-Up: Jörn 'Kannixx' Rüter (vocals / bass), Carsten 'Tumanixx' Overbeck (guitar), Rudi 'Daswirdnixx' Olhanson (drums)

Hamburg's TORMENT underwent various line-up changes from their inception in 1984 and released two self financed singles before signing to Steamhammer. The debut album includes a cover of MOTÖRHEAD's theme song 'Motorhead'.
TORMENT's 1999 album 'Not Dead Yet' sees another MOTÖRHEAD cover version with 'We Are The Road Crew' and a medley cover section of DEATH, VENOM and RAZOR songs.

Singles/EPs:
State Of Torment / Bestial Sex / Deaf Metal / Chainsaw Massacre / What Shall We Do With A Drunken Torment, Torment (1987)
Das Neue / Shop 'Til Ya Drop, Remedy RP 18 085 (1989)
Sie Kam Zu Mir Am Morgen, (1992) ('Blood in urine' coloured vinyl!!)

Albums:
EXPERIENCE A NEW DIMENSION OF FEAR, Steamhammer SPV 084-76332 (1991)
Intro / Acid Rain / Religious Insanity / Shop 'Till Ya Drop / Bestial Sex / Motörhead / Chainsaw Massacre / Drunken Torment / Cry For Justice / Slaves Of Technology / Das Neue / Crucifixion / Ballad Of Peter's Dog / State Of War / Liebe Freunde Von Torment
TORMENT, (1993) (Split LP with MINOTAUR & DESERT STORM)
SPERMATIZED, (1997)
We Still Die / I'm The Doctor / Laws Of The Street / What You Don't Know / Our Own Way / The Hammer / The Prophecy / Rollo Der Wikinger

NOT DEAD YET, Remedy (1999)

TOTENMOND (GERMANY)
Line-Up: Olaf Pazzer (vocals / guitar), Roberto (bass), Sven P. Genz (drums)

Founded in 1989 as a Punk band TOTENMOND ('Dead Moon') have toured Germany supporting ATROCITY. The band have also made appearances at the prestigious Wacken Open Air and Dynamo Festivals exciting audiences with their brand of Hardcore Metal.
TOTENMOND started life as a quartet but ousted their singer to enable guitarist Olaf to take the lead vocal role. The band debuted with a 1996 demo 'Die Schlacht'. November of 1997 saw TOTENMOND on tour in Europe with SPUDMONSTERS and CRISIS then further dates with ORPHANAGE and WITHIN TEMPTATION.

Albums:
LICHTBRINGER, Massacre (1996)
Die Schlacht / Ragnarök / Tod Ist Freude / Vaterland / Sagenwelt / Kellerstahl / Kreuzenagel / Necrophiler Sonntag
VÄTERCHEN FROST, Massacre MAS PC0145 (1997)
Mutterliebe / Väterchen Frost / Bora Cemeha / Konigtraum
FLEISCHWALD, Massacre MAS CD0157 (1998)
Kadavarnazion / Leichen Der Liebe / Tod Und Niedergang / Dekadenz '98 / Fleischwald / Das Saure Kraut / Treibjagd / Der Misanthrop / Das Beil Und Der Vater / Raubbau

TOTTENKORPS (CHILE)
Line-Up: Christian Ortiz (vocals / bass), Fernando Toro (guitar), Christian Soto (guitar), Sergio Aravena (drums)

Santiago Death Metal band with an epic style. TOTTENKORPS emerged with the adventurous 1990 demo 'The King Of Hell Reclaims His Throne'. A further 1993 cassette 'Our Almighty Lords' was pressed up onto CD format by Brazilian label Hellion the following year.
TOTTENKORPS underwent numerous line up ructions but by 1998 had settled down to comprise founder members vocalist Gerardo Valenzuela and guitarist Francisco T. made their exit.
TOTTENKORPS regrouped with the aid of guitarist Christian Soto to record the album 'Tharnheim: Ati-Lan-Nhi, Cyclopean Crypts Of Citadels'.

Albums:
**THARNHEIM: ATI-LAN-NHI,
CYCLOPEAN CRYPTS OF CITADELS**,
Repulse (2000)

TOXAEMIA (SWEDEN)
Line-Up: Stevo Bolgakov (vocals /
guitar), Linus Olsson (guitar), Pontus
Cervin (bass), Emil Norman (drums)

Singles/EPs:
Beyond The Realm / Another Lie,
Another Death / Who Dies / Expired
Christianity, Ceretic Decay SCAM011
(1990)

TOXODETH (CA, USA)

Albums:
MYSTERIES ABOUT LIFE AND DEATH,
Wild Rags WRE 903CD (1990)

TRAUMA (INDONESIA)
Line-Up: Nino Aspirantu (vocals), Dedy
Yuniarto (guitar), Wilman Tarfig (guitar),
Patrick Athena (bass), Donny Arief
(drums)

Jakarta based Death Metallers founded in
1992 by former HOMICIDE vocalist Nino
Aspirantu. Also involved were erstwhile
DELIRIUM TREMENS guitarist Hella
Tanissan, guitarist Dedy Yuniarto, bass
player Patrick Athena and drummer
Donny Arief. TRAUMA issued the 1997
demo 'Incomplete Damnation' and put in
a valuable appearance on the Indonesian
compilation 'Metallik Klinik Volume I'.
Progress was barred when Tanissan quit
to join TENGKORAK. However, his place
was filled by ex-DEATH VOMIT man
Wilman Tarfig for the debut album
'Extinction Of Mankind'.

Albums:
EXTINCTION OF MANKIND, Morbid
Noise Productions (1998)
Human Suffering / Tragedi Umat
Manusia / ... By Dissolution / Incomplete
Damnation / Stench Of Corpse / Rotten
Grave / Threnody / Bestial Murder / Final
Executions

TRAUMA (POLAND)

Albums:
COMEDY IS OVER, Pagan MOON002
(199-)
DAIMONIAN, Pagan MOON014 (1998)
Intro / Suicide / Dust (Kill Me) /
Contradictions / Possessed / Name /

Outro / The Dawn - No Way Out /
Hidden Instincts / Human Race / No
Hope / Escape Into The Shadow
SUFFOCATED IN SLUMBER, System
Shock (2001)
A Gruesome Display / Unable To React /
Suffocated In Slumber / A Deep Scar /
Swallow The Murder / Words Of Hate /
Tools Of Mutual Harm / Dust (Kill Me) /
...Bloodshot Eyes

TRAUMATISM (CANADA)
Line-Up: Patrick (vocals), Kevin (guitar),
Dany (bass), Stephane (drums)

Albums:
TRUCULENT, (1997)
Souffleuse Attitude / Serial Hacking /
Sida / Necrocoprophagus / Fuckops /
Psychopathic Orgasm / Braincrusher /
Vaginal Mutilation / Your Head Is Full Of
Shit / Suck Or Die / Human Race / Eat
Christ
GROSSLY UNFAIR, (2000)

TREBLINKA (SWEDEN)
Line-Up: Johan 'Hellslaughter' Edlund
(vocals / guitar), Stefan 'Emetic'
Lagergren (guitar), Klas 'Juck' Wistedt
(bass), Calle n'ajse' Fransson (drums)

The far from tastefully named
TREBLINKA founded in 1987 later
changed their name to ABOMINATION.
Vocalist Johan Edlund and bassist Klas
Wistedt formed TIAMAT. Guitarist Stefan
Lagergren and drummer Calle Fransson
formed EXPULSION.

Singles/EPs:
Severe Abomination / Earwigs In Your
Veins, Mould in Hell MHR-S 001 (1989)

TRISTITIA (SWEDEN)
Line-Up: Thomas Karlsson (vocals), Luis
Beethoven Galvez (guitar / bass /
keyboards), Bruno Nilsson (drums)

Labeled as 'Extreme dark Doom'
TRISTITIA evolved from a meeting in
August 1992 between the half Chilean /
half Swedish guitarist ("All true axes of
darkness, hatred and madness") Luis
Beethoven Galvez and vocalist ("Chants
of death") Thomas Karlsson.
Galvez was a former member of PAGAN
RITES along with Karlsson, although the
latter had also worked with AUTOPSY
TORMENT.
TRISITIA's first four track demo in 1993
featured 'Winds Of Sacrifice', 'Dancing

Souls', 'Burn The Witch' and 'The Other Side'.

A second demo followed in 1994, once more boasting four tracks (in this instance 'Reminiscences Of The Mourner', 'Envy The Dead', 'Ashes Of The Witch' and 'Mark My Words'. It was only at this point that the band added drummer Bruno Nilsson and signed with French label Holy Records.

Nilsson was not in the group for long as he was to depart in favour of ex-PAGAN RITES drummer Adrian Letelier.

Albums:
ONE WITH DARKNESS, Holy HOLY11CD (1995)
Sorrow / Kiss The Cross / One With Darkness / Winds Of Sacrifice / Burn The Witch / Hymn Of Lunacy / Ashes Of The Witch / Dancing Souls / Adagio 1809 / Reminiscences Of The Mourner / Dance Of The Selenites
CRUCIDICTION, Holy HOLY 21 CD (1996)
Ego Sum Resurrectio / Christianic Indulgence / Crucidiction / Wintergrief / Envy The Dead / Lioness' Roar / Mark My Words / Gardenia / Final Lament
THE LAST GRIEF, Holy (2000)
Once Upon A Dawn... / In The Light Of The Moon / Slaughtery / Evolic / Golden Goddess Of Fire / Tears And Tequila / Angelwitch's Palace / Memory's Garden / Instrumental Hollowcoast / MediEvil / Under The Cross / Darknia: The Last Grief

TUMOUR (HOLLAND)

One man sick Grindcore project of Rogier Kuzen.

Albums:
RANCID DEFORMITIES, Mangled Maggot Stew (199-)
Brains For Breakfast / Minced In My Meatgrinder / Penetrating A Drill Through Your Bones / Man Eating Morons / My God Is Gore / The Evil-Hand-Syndrome / Christian Concentration Camp / Maimed / Rancid Deformities / Crippled Baldy Bastard / Smashing A Poserwimps Decomposed Brains In 12. Brutally Fucked With An Awfully Big Chainsaw / Torture / Vomitorial - Splatter - Parties / Pulverized Impact / Deceased Imaginations / Carnivora / Eyeball Eruption / Strangled With Your Own Intestines / Cumulative Mass Of Crunchy Stiffs / Severed Stoma / Outro

INSTANT LOBOTOMIE, Mangled Maggot Stew (2000) (Split album with TWISTED TRUTH)
Dissected, Decomposed & Thrown On A Fire! / The Aroma From A Fresh Splattered Fetus / Shredding Slaughter! / Instant Lobotomie! / Removing Entrails / Necrophile-Cabines! / Bluber! / Juggling With Three Battered Heads! / Supper-Time! / Separate The Brain From The Corpse / Time For Extravagant Punishment, You're All Covered With Blood / Fascinating Blender Details! / Squashy... / Stomach Spasm! / The Last Body! / Sounds Of Sickness I! / Splatter-Outro-Shits! / Gory Re-Constructions! / Outro

TWISTED TRUTH
(CZECH REPUBLIC)

Albums:
TERROR ERROR, Mangled Maggot Stew (2000) (Split album with TUMOUR)
Intro / The Circle / Attack Of Aversione / Deformation Future / Look To My Eyes / Decline / Roy / Anti-Manual Hard Rock Song / Deciver / The Kill 11. Visible Exterminate / D. / Senility / Fear / Mass Suicide / Condition D / Retired Alkoholic Disorder / Unholy God / Blood / Empty Brain / Excellent, Good & Positive / Different / At The Own Reality

TYRANT (JAPAN)

TYRANT included RITUAL CARNAGE man Damian Montgomery in the ranks before recording of the 'Under The Dark Mystic Sky' debut.

Albums:
UNDER THE DARK MYSTIC SKY, Pulverised ASH 004 CD (1998)
Prologue To Tragedy / Grudge Of Dannoura / Ghost Waltz / The God Of Winter / Vice / Into The Hades / Under The Dark Mystic Sky / Mirage Beneath The Black Moon

ULTIMATUM
(Albuquerque, NM, USA)
Line-Up: Scott Waters (vocals), Robert Gutierrez (guitar), Steve Trujillo (guitar), Tom Michaels (bass), Sean Griego (drums)

One of the leading Christian Death Metal acts. ULTIMATUM was forged in 1992 with lead guitarist Robert Gutierrez also handling lead vocals. Both Gutierrez and initial drummer John Carroll were both erstwhile members of HOLY SACRIFICE whilst guitarist Steve Trujillo was a veteran of both HOLY SACRIFICE and ANGELIC FORCE.

ULTIMATUM first issued the 1993 demo 'Fatal Delay'. Drummer Mike Lynch joined up in 1994 but EXTRACTION's Rick Campbell would deputize for ULTIMATUM's inaugural gig supporting GODFEAR. For recording of a second demo session 'Symphonic Extremies' ULTIMATUM enlisted bassist Tom Michaels.

Lynch would be supplanted in 1996 by Sean Griego for recording of the 'Puppet Of Destruction' album released by Rowe Productions, the label headed by MORTIFICATION main man Steve Rowe. The band signed to German label Gutter Records, a subsidiary of Massacre, for the 2000 album 'The Mechanics Of Perilous Times'. The record included a cover version of VENGEANCE RISING's 'Burn'.

ULTIMATUM would contribute their version of 'Sins Of Omission' to the Dwell Records TESTAMENT tribute 'Jump In The Pit'. In 2001 the band put in an appearance at the annual STRYPER Expo in California.

Albums:
SYMPHONIC EXTREMITIES, Juke Box Media (1996)
Symphonic Extremities / The Killing Fields / E.N.D. (Erroneous Notion Of Death) / Black Light / Darkest Void / Ode To Noise / The Grip / Fatal Delay / Megaton / Blink / World Of Sin
PUPPET OF DESTRUCTION, Rowe Productions (1998)
Never / Mortal Stomp / Scorn / Puppet Of Destruction / Gutterbox / Repentance / World Of Sin / Crosshope / Conform To reality / Charged - Power
THE MECHANICS OF PERILOUS TIMES, Gutter (2000)

Temple Of The Spirit / Greed Regime Inc. / Perilous Times / Shroud Of Science / The Purging / Crash Course / Warlord's Sword / Burn / Mutul Mitlu / Violence And Bloodshed

ULTRAVIOLENCE (UK)
Line-Up: Johnny Violent (vocals),

ULTRAVIOLENCE toured Europe in 1998 alongside fellow Earache crew GENERATION X-ED in a double billing dubbed the 'Deathmatch Tour'. The single to accompany these dates, a cover of BLACK SABBATH's 'Paranoid', was a split affair between both artists.

Singles/EPs:
I, Destructor / Zeus / Treason, Earache MOSH102 (1993)
Heaven Is Oblivion / Disco Boyfriend, Earache MOSH 148 CD (1997)
Paranoid, Earache (1998) ('Deathmatch Tour '98' EP with GENERATION X-ED)

Albums:
LIFE OF DESTRUCTOR, Earache MOSH103 (1994)
I Am Destructor / Electric Chair / Joan / Hardcore Motherfucker / Digital Killing / Only Love / We Will Break / Hiroshima / Destructor's Fall / Death Of A Child
PSYCHO-DRAMA, Earache MOSH 142CD (1995)
Birth - Jessica / The Reject / Disco Boyfriend / Pimp / Psychodrama / Birth - Hitman / Stone Faced / Murder Academy / Hitman's Heart / Contract / Lovers / Suicide Pact / God's Mistake / Searching Hell / Heaven Is Oblivion

UNANIMATED (SWEDEN)
Line-Up: Micke Jansson (vocals), Jonas Melberg (guitar), Jonas Bohlin (guitar), Richard Cabeza (bass), Jocke Westman (keyboards), Peter Stjärnvind (drums)

UNANIMATED were created in 1989. The inaugural line-up of the group found guitarists Chris Alverez and Jonas Melklberg teamed with Richard Cabeza on lead vocals and bass and ex-MERCILESS drummer Peter Stjärvind. By the time of their first demo tape, 'Firestorm', UNANIMATED had replaced Alverez with Jonas Bohlin, whilst Cabeza left for a time to join DISMEMBER as the band drafted in Micke Jansson on lead vocals and Daniel Lofthagen on bass. Some versions of the first UNANIMATED album, 'In The Forest Of The Dreaming

Dead', possess a cover of VENOM's 'Buried Alive'.

For the band's second album, 'Ancient God Of Evil', (a record hyped by No Fashion as one that took Death Metal into a new dimension) bass parts were once more handled by Cabeza, although he was still a full time member of DISMEMBER.

UNANIMATED split, with Stjärvind joining FACE DOWN. The drummer also holds down credits with REGURGITATE, LOUD PIPES and latterly ENTOMBED.

Albums:
IN THE FOREST OF THE DREAMING DEAD, No Fashion NFR004 (1994)
At Dawn / Whispering Shadows / Blackness Of The Fallen Stars / Fire Storm / Storms From The Skies Of Grief / Through The Gates / Wind Of A Dismal Past/ Silence Ends / Moonlight Twilight / In The Forest Of The Dreaming Dead / Cold Northern Breeze
ANCIENT GOD OF EVIL, No Fashion NFR009 (1995)
Life Demise / Eye Of The Greyhound / Oceans Of Time / Dead Calm / Mirielle / The Depths Of A Black Sea / Ruins / Dying Emotions Domain / Die Alone

UNCANNY (SWEDEN)
Line-Up: Jens Törnroos (vocals), Mats Forsell (guitar), Fredrik Norrman (guitar), Christoffer Harborg (bass), Kenneth Englund (drums)

Death Metal outfit UNCANNY are, uncannily, like a heavier version of UNLEASHED.

Albums:
SPLENIUM FOR NYKTOPHOBIA, Unisound USR 008 (1994)
Elohim / Faces From The Tomb / Brain Access / Timeless / Screaming In Phobia / Enkelbiljetten / Indication Vitalis / Soul Incest / Strangskitten / Towards The Endless Throne / Lepra / The Final Conflict (The Pornoflute Part Two) / Splenium For Nyktophobia

UNDER BLACK CLOUDS
(GERMANY)
Line-Up: Andreas Greupner (vocals), Andre Andrejew (guitar), Christoph Dobberstein (bass), Simon Schmitt (keyboards), Rene Puhlmann (drums)

A Symphonic Death Metal duo. UNDER BLACK CLOUDS hired session musicians to record the albums listed below.

Albums:
DAWN, Invasion GTR-209 (1995)
Hope For The Near End / To Silence You / Into Another World / Mortal Words / The Mercilessness Of Time / The Reason Why... / Do You Have Confidence In Me? / Beyond The Summer Sun / In A Spare Moment
AS DARKNESS FALLS, Ars Metalli ARS 001 (1996)
Luna's Sisters / The Night Of Our Flight / As Blackness Comes / Signal To Noise / The Double Headstone / I Feel Good / Winter Solstice / I Feel Good! / Winter Solstice/ Death Of A Rose

UNDEROATH (FL, USA)
Line-Up: Dallas (vocals), Corey (guitar / vocals), Octavio (guitar), Matt (bass), Chris (keyboards), Aaron (drums)

Florida Death Metal strongly infused with a Christian ethic. The debut 1999 record 'Acts Of Depression' contains a secret hidden track, namely a narrative titled 'Spirit Of A Living God'.

UNDEROATH added keyboard player Chris and bassist Matt for the 2000 album 'Cries Of The Past'.

Albums:
ACT OF DEPRESSION, Takehold (1999)
Heart Of Stone / A Love So Pure / Burden In Your Hands / Innocence Stolen / Act Of Depression / Watch Me Die / Spirit Of A Living God
CRIES OF THE PAST, Takehold (2000)
The Last / Walking Away / Giving Up Hurts The Most / And I Dreamt Of You / Cries Of The Past

UNHALLOWED
(Oak Ridge, NJ, USA)
Line-Up: Bob Thompson (guitar), Jenn Corrao (bass), Moe Shahenkari (drums)

New Jersey brutal Metal band UNHALLOWED made their mark with the less than subtle 'Deathfist Of Sodomy' demo in 1996. Founded as a trio of guitarist Bob Thompson, bass player Jenn Corrao and drummer Moe Shahenkari, UNHALLOWED would draft INSATANITY's Jay Lipitz on guitar for a brief period. The 'Punchfucking Blasphemy' album would be recorded but put on hold as Lipitz departed.

UNHALLOWED pulled in vocalist Frank

Bleakly in early 2000 but he would soon leave to join fellow New Jersey Death act DRIPPING.

Albums:
PUNCHFUCKING BLASPHEMY,
Unhallowed (2000)
Encrusted / Shrunken Genitals / Mighty Meat Sword / Present The Excrement / Funeral Cross / Black Death Garden / Death Fist Of Sodomy / Eveing The Plague

UNHOLY GRAVE (JAPAN)
Line-Up: Takaho (vocals), Kajisa (guitar), Tadashi (guitar), Ume (bass), Debuzo (drums)

Singles/EPs:
Split, Riotous Assembly RIOT 017 (199-) (7" split single with DEPRESSOR)
Ethnocide, Riot City Japan 003 (199-)
Split, Riot City Japan (199-) (7" split single with REFORM CONTROL)
Split, (199-) (7" split single with MAD THRASHER)
Split, MCR Company MCR094 (199-) (7" split single with CHICKENSHIT)
Slaughtered Civilians / My Nightmare / Japan's Warcrime / Confession / Ei Skit Sota / Kim After Kim, MCR Company MCR099 (1996) ('Agonies' 7" split single with AGATHOCLES)
Split, (199-) (7" split single with ENTRAILS MASSACRE)
Split, (199-) (7" split single with VIOLENT HEADACHE)
Split, (199-) (7" split single with MY MINDS MINE)
Split, (199-) (7" split single with WARSORE)
Terror EP, (199-)
Morbid Reality EP, (199-)
Split, (1998) (7" split single with ARSEDESTROYER)
Xeroxed Person / Zillion Of Bodies / Life After Death / Land For Sacrifice / Mutilated Souls, Headfucker (1998) (7" split single with CAPTAIN 3 LEG)
Nein, AH 10360 (199-)
Torchered Alive, Farewell (199-) (10" single)
Racism, Def American (2000) (7" split single with CAPIALIST CASUALTIES)

Albums:
CRUCIFIED, Eclipse (1995)
Maniacal Damage / Human Mummification / Mental Disease / Atrocity- War Of Aggression / Worthless Prize / Korean Residents In Japan / Be

Born Poor / Forced Unfair Future / Blind - Death From Overwork / Euthanasia / The Unknown Ghost - Fugitives / Discrimination / Protestant? Catholic? / Shameless Bighead / Mass Imbeciles - Racism / Greedy Pig
INHUMANITY, (199-)
Undocumented Workers / Hizbullah / Mata Apara / Buried Terror / Single Mothers By Choice / Failure Teaches Success / Deprogramming / Boy Soldiers / C.T.B.T.-Undulation / Nono For Mururoa / Cult Of Terror / Don't Swallow Media's Story / Ugly Lust For Power / Contradiction / Nerve Gas Attack / Mind Devolution / Stop Terrorism / Awake / Invisible Bleeder / The Pus In Your Brain / Religion? Gods? / Lies Behind Their Smile / Under Suspicion Hell / The Killing Continues / Missing Children / Who Killed The Victims? / Inhuman Sexual Slavery / No Racial Superiority / The War Dead / Nanking Atrocity / Incomprehensible Law / Resign! History Distorter / Our Common Slogan
HATRED, (199-)
UNHOLY GRAVE, Grind Malaya (199-) (Split album with MASS SEPERATION)

UNLEASHED (SWEDEN)
Line-up: Johnny Hedlund (vocals / bass), Frederik Lindgren (guitar), Thoimas Olsson (guitar), Anders Schulktz (drums)

Featuring ex-NIHILIST guitarist Johnny Hedlund, UNLEASHED recorded demos in 1989 titled 'Revenge' and 'Utter Dark' that soon sold out, prompting a deal with Germany's Century Media Records. The group debuted with the 'Where No Life Dwells' album in 1991 and UNLEASHED toured Europe and America during the year as support to MORBID ANGEL.
Returning in 1992 with 'Shadows In The Deep' (featuring a cover of VENOM's 'Countess Bathory') UNLEASHED toured hard once more to promote the album, including a European headline tour with support acts TIAMAT and SAMAEL before American shows with CANNIBAL CORPSE.
The group's third album, 'Across The Open Sea', is notable for including a cover of JUDAS PRIEST's 'Breaking The Law'.
The group cut a live album during 1993, although the recordings were initially released as a bootleg prior to the band responding by issuing the 'Live in Vienna' album the following year.
In addition to his work in UNLEASHED

guitarist Fredrik Lindgren is also a member of Punk outfit LOUD PIPES billing himself 'Freddy Eugene'. Lindgren created Stoner Metal act TERRA FIRMA in 1999 with COUNT RAVEN vocalist Christian Linderson for an eponymous album.

UNLEASHED Photo: Martin Wickler

Singles/EPs:
The Utterdark Revenge / Unleashed / Where No Life Dwells, CBR (1991)
The Dark One / Where Life Ends, Century Media CM7 020 (1991)

Albums:
WHERE NO LIFE DWELLS, Century Media 84 9718 (1991)
Where No Life Dwells / Dead Forever / Before The Creation Of Time / For They Shall Be Slain / If They Had Eyes / The Dark One / Into Glory Ride / ...And The Laughter Has Died / Unleashed / Violent Exstacy / Where Life Ends
SHADOWS IN THE DEEP, Century Media 84-9732-2 (1992)
The Final Silence / The Immortals / A Life Beyond / Shadows In The Deep / Countess Bathory / Never Ending Hate / Onward Into Countless Battles / Crush The Skull / Bloodbath / Land Of Ice
ACROSS THE OPEN SEA, Century Media 77055-2 (1993)
To Asgaard We Fly / Open wide / I Am God / The One Insane / Across The Open Sea / In The Northern Lands /

Forever Goodbye (2045) / Execute Them All / Captured / Breaking The Law / The General
LIVE IN VIENNA '93, Century Media 77056-2 (1994)
The Final Silence / Bloodbath / Before The Creation Of Time / Shadows In The Deep / Never Ending Hate / If They Had Eyes / Open Wide / Onward Into Countless Battles / Where No Life Dwells / Dead Forever / Countess Bathory / The Immortals / Into Glory Ride / Breaking The Law
VICTORY, Century Media CD77090-2 (1995)
Victims Of War / Legal Rapes / Hail The New Age / Defender / In The Name Of God / Precious Land / Berserk / Scream Forth Aggression / Against The Wind / Revenge
EASTERN BLOOD - HAIL TO POLAND, Century Media CD 77118-2 (1996)
Execute Them All / The Immortals / Revenge / The Defender / In The Name Of God / Against The World / Victims Of War / Shadows In The Deep / Before The Creation Of Time / Berserk / Into Glory Ride / Dead Forever / If They Had Eyes/ For They Shall Be Slain / Unleashed / The Immortals / The Dark One / Into Glory Ride / Shadows In The Deep / Violent Exstasy / Before The Creation Of Time
WARRIOR, Century Media 77124-2 (1997)
Warmachine/ In Hellfire / Mediawhore / Down Under Ground / My Life For You / Death Metal Victory / Hero Of The Land / Löngt Nid / Born Deranged / I Have Returned / Ragnarök / Your Pain My Gain / The End

UNMOORED (SWEDEN)
Line-Up: Christian Älvestam (vocals / guitar), Rickard Larsson (guitar), Torbjorn Öhring (bass)

UNMOORED emerged with the 1995 demo 'Shadow Of The Obscure' issuing the later tape 'More To The Story Than Meets The Eye' prior to recording of the debut album 'Cimmerian'. Following this release drummer Niclas Wahlén decamped.
Still without a drummer the 2000 album 'Kingdoms Of Greed' would be sessioned by Jocke Petterson, better known as Morth from THY PRIMORDIAL and also a veteran of DAWN and CRANIUM. Members billed on the recording were frontman Christian 'Evil Spice' Älvestam,

guitarist Rickard 'Infernal Spice' Larsson and bassist Torbjorn 'Hellish Spice' Öhring.
Älvestamd and Petterson would also become members of Death Metal band SOLAR DAWN.

Albums:
CIMMERIAN, Pulverised ASH008 (1998)
Trendmade Bitch / Now And Forever / Down At Zero / Blood By Tragedy / Here Today, Gone Tomorrow / Warsong / Solution .45 / Final State
KINGDOMS OF GREED, Pulverised ASH012 (2000)
Feral Blaze / Tellurian Crown / Self Invoked / Torchbearer / Final State Part II (Last Entry) / Thrown Off The Scent / Milestone / In The Dark Midst Of Winter

UNPURE (SWEDEN)
Line-Up: Kolgrim (vocals / bass), Hräsvelg (guitar / drums)

Albums:
UNPURE, Napalm NPR011 (1995)
To The Ancients / Ashes With The Wind / Otherside Of The Sea / Call Of Doom Part I / Across With War / Arrival Of Chaos / A Forest Event: i) Behind The Mist, ii) The Eclipse / Lords Of War / Surrounded By Darkness / Outro
COLDLAND, Napalm NPR022 (1996)
Blacker Than Ever / Coldland / Full Of Hate / Cold Freezing Dark / Call Of Doom (Part II) / Horny Goats / Count Dracula / Frozen / All Dead / Valley Of Whirling Winds

USURPER (Atlanta, GA, USA)
Line-Up: Sterling Von Scarborough (vocals / bass), Danny Klein (guitar), Rich Fuscia (drums)

1993 act founded by former MORBID ANGEL and INCUBUS man Sterling Von Scarborough. USURPER only cut demos.

UTOPIE (GERMANY)

Rosenheim based Porn obsessed Goregrinders UTOPIE heralded their arrival with the tapes 'Psychopathologic Menstration Orgasm' and 'Phalluskult Usus'.

Albums:
INSTINCT FOR EXISTENCE, Bizarre Leprous Productions (1999)
My Blood Through Your Vein - My Words Through Your Mouth / Spat Out To Live /

He Put His Erected Phallus In Her Anal Canal And Said: "Hey Mom This Time I Trust You - I Don't Want Your Shit On My Cock!" / Short Erection 9 / Kill - Fuck - Mutilate / Phalluskult Usus / Suffocate And Perish In Separation Of Humanity / Stop Viagra - Smoke Pot 1/ Long Erection / Short Erection 10 / The Way To Be An Autocannibal / Psychopathologic Menstruationorgasm / Short Erection 11 / Our Life - Our Reality / You Are What I Eat

UTUMNO (SWEDEN)
Line-Up: Jonas Stålhammer (vocals), Staffan Johansson (guitar), Dennis Lindahl (guitar), Dan Öberg (bass), Johan Hallberg (drums)

Swedish Dark Death Metal outfit UTUMNO's vocalist Jonas Ståhlhammer is also guitarist in GOD MACABRE. UTUMNO's debut album was recorded at Sunlight Studios and produced by Tomas Skogsberg.
Drummer Johan Hallberg, under the pseudonym of 'Necro-Nudist', would join arch-infernal act CRANIUM.
Not to be confused with the Norwegian Black Metal UTUMNO that would become EMANCER.

Singles/EPs:
Saviour Reborn / In Misery I Dwell, Cenotaph CTR001 EP (1991)

Albums:
ACROSS THE HORIZON, Cenotaph CTR007CD (1994)
The Light Of Day / I Cross The Horizons / In Misery I Dwell / Saviour Reborn / Sunrise / Emotions Run Cold

VADER

VADER
(POLAND)
Line-Up: Piotr Wiwczarek
(vocals / guitar), Jackie
(bass), Docent (drums)

A Polish Thrash band with intense drumming and unashamed reliance on esoterica as a staple of their subject matter, VADER came together in 1986 with a line up of vocalist guitarist Peter, bassist Jackie and drummer Docent.

The band soon released their first demo tape, 'Necrolust', and this gained VADER a deal with Carnage Records. A deal was struck to subsequently distribute the 1990 demo 'Morbid Reich'. A 1991 demo featured the tracks 'The Final Massacre', 'Reign Carrion', 'Breath Of Centuries' and 'Vicious Circle'.

Upon the release of their debut album, 'The Ultimate Incantation', VADER toured Europe with BOLT-THROWER and GRAVE. Further dates in America followed with DEICIDE, SUFFOCATION and DISMEMBER.

'The Darkest Age - Live', which includes a cover of SLAYER's 'Hell Awaits', was recorded in front of a home crowd in Krakow. June 1995 found VADER out on the road in Europe once more touring alongside CRADLE OF FILTH, MALEVOLENT CREATION, OPPRESSOR, DISSECTION and SOLSTICE.

The 'Sothis' EP witnessed another cover, BLACK SABBATH's anthem 'Black Sabbath', as well as a complete rework of VADER's 1989 track 'The Wrath'.

Having added guitarist China to augment their live sound, VADER undertook a full European tour in the spring of 1996 as guests to CANNIBAL CORPSE.

Wiwczarek produced the debut album by fellow Poles DECAPITATED during 2000. VADER themselves headlined the European 'No Mercy' festivals alongside Americans VITAL REMAINS, Brazilians REBAELLIUN and Germany's FLESHCRAWL.

Docent has a project band titled MOON in union with CHRIST AGONY frontman Cezar releasing two albums to date.

Docent and Mauser assembled side project DIES IRAE in 2000 for the 'Immolated' album.

Singles/EPs:
Hymn To The Ancient Ones / Sothis / De Profundis / Vision And The Voice / The Wrath / R'Lyeh / Black Sabbath, Massive

MASS 001 MCD (1995) ('Sothis' EP)

Albums:
THE ULTIMATE INCANTATION, Earache (1992)
Creation / Dark Age / Vicious Circle / The Crucified Ones / Final Massacre / Testimony / Reign Carrion / Chaos / One Step To Salvation / Demon's Wind / Decapitated Saints / Breath Of Centuries
THE DARKEST AGE - LIVE '93, Arctic Serenades SERE 007 (1994)
Macbeth (intro) / Dark Age / Vicious Circle / Crucified Ones / Demon's Wind / Decapitated Saints / From Beyond (Intro) / Chaos / Reign-Carrion / Testimony / Breath Of Centuries / Omen (Outro) / Hell Awaits
DE PROFUNDIS, System Shock IRC 067 (1995)
Silent Empire / An Act Of Darkness / Blood Of Kingu / Incarnation / Sothis / Revolt / Of Moon, Blood, Dream And Me / Vision And The Voice / Reborn In Flames
FUTURE OF THE PAST, System Shock IRC 092 (1996)
Outbreak Of Evil / Flag Of Hate / Storm Of Stress / Death Metal / Fear Of Napalm / Merciless Death / Dethroned Emperor / Silent Scream / We Are The League / IFY / Black Sabbath
BLACK TO THE BLIND, Impact IR-C-104 (1997)
Heading For Internal Darkness / The Innermost Ambience / Carnal / Fractal Light / True Names / Beast Raping / Foetus God / The Red Passage / Distant Dream / Black To The Blind
LIVE IN JAPAN, System Shock IRC 132-2 (1999)
Damien / Sothis / Distant Dream / Black To The Blind / Silent Empire / Blood Of Kings / Carnal / Red Passage / Panzerstoss / Reborn In Flames / Fractal Light / From Beyond / Crucified Ones / Foetus God / Black Sabbath / Reign In Blood / Omen / Dark Age
LITANY, (2000)
Wings / The One Made Of Dreams / Xefer / Litany / Cold Demons / The Calling / North / Forward To Die!! / A World Of Hurt / The World Made Flesh / The Final Massacre
REIGN FOREVER WORLD, Metal Blade CD 076-103182 (2001)
Reign Forever World / Frozen Paths / Privilege Of The Gods / Total Disaster / Rapid Fire / Freezing Moon / North (Live) / Forwards To Die!! (Live) / Creatures Of Light And Darkness (Live) / Carnal (Live)

VAGINAL MASSAKER (GERMANY)

Singles/EPs:
Split, (199-) (7" split single with REGURGITATE)

Albums:
PERVERS, Galdre (1997)

VASTION (Lawrenceville, GA, USA)
Line-Up: Craig Nast (vocals), Rusty Adams (guitar), Bill Murff (bass), Jeff Adams (drums)

Created in 1994 Death act VASTION have released a string of demos. 1998's 'Horrid Sights Of Hate' was followed by the 1999 efforts 'Buried And Nameless' and 'Cold Stare Of The Dead'.

Albums:
CLOSED EYES TO NOTHING, Retribute (2000)
Closed Eyes To Nothing / Cease To Exist / Passage Of Pain / Buried And Nameless / Murder Is Not Enough / Horrid Sights / Ensuring Your Death / To Die Alone / Who Lies Who Dies / Cold Stares Of The Dead

VEHEMENCE (USA)
Line-Up: Nathan Gearhart (vocals), Bjorn Dannov (guitar), John Chavez (guitar), Mark Kozuback (bass), Andrew Schroeder (drums)

Death Metal combo forged in 1995 by former BLUDGEON vocalist Nathan Gearhart and guitarists Bjorn Dannov and Scott Wiegand. The bands rhythm section was completed by drafting in bassist Mark Kozuback and drummer Andrew Schroeder, both of REVOLUTION and Punk band MISTAKEN IDENTITY.
A demo emerged in 1998 but upfront of the debut album 'The Thoughts From Which I Hide' Wiegand made his exit. VEHEMENCE drafted BRIDES OF CHRIST and DEPRECATED man John Chavez as replacement.
VEHEMENCE formed part of the 'North American Extermination' tour in 2001 along with BRODEQUIN and Japanese act VOMIT REMNANTS.

Albums:
THE THOUGHTS FROM WHICH I HIDE, (2000)
I Take Your Life / Saying Goodbye / Whore Cunt Die / What You've Become /

No One Wins / Nameless Faces, Scattered Remnants / Devour The Rotten Flesh / Reconditioning The Flock

VEHEMENT (Chicago, IL, USA)
Line-Up: B.N.O. (vocals / bass), Guitarzan Mike (guitar), John Crazylegs (drums)

Technical Death Metal group founded by frontman B.N.O. (real name Peter James Beno Jr.). The singer / bassist had previous to VEHEMENT been a member of Punk band JOHNNY VOMIT and Death Metal units ZYKLON B and ETERNAL HATRED. It Was this latter band where he met drummer John 'Crazylegs' Conteras.
The pair split away from ETERNAL HATRED to form VEHEMENT with guitarist Guitarzan Mike. VEHEMENT debuted in 1998 with a track appearing on the Chicago compilation 'Culture Shock III'.

Albums:
UNBALANCED FOR MANKIND, Cellar (1999)
Immaculate Entrapment / Allergicide / Inhale The Mist / Forever Lost / Creation / Intergalactic Landmarks / Overrolled / Prepare For War / Procrehatred

VENGEANCE RISING
(Los Angeles, CA, USA)
Line-Up: Roger Martinez (vocals / guitar), Jamie Mitchell (guitar), Joe Monsorb'nik (bass), Jonny Vasquez (drums)

Although one of the leading lights of the Christian Death Metal scene for a lengthy period VENGEANCE RISING would become embroiled in bitter recriminations as vocalist Roger Martinez, now solo, has reportedly disowned his previous beliefs. Martinez, who is reported to be planning another anti-Christian VENGEANCE RISING album to be titled 'Realms Of Blasphemy' as well as an exposé treatise 'The Lixivium Letters', claims to have been duped into believing in and promoting God.
The band was created in 1985 by former SACRIFICE members along with guitarists Larry Farkas and Doug Thieme and drummer Glenn Mancaruso. Martinez, previously with PROPHET, was enrolled as singer the following year. The band was initially billed as VENGEANCE but another act of the same name was

discovered. The album sleeves, which featured a close up of a nailed crucified hand - actually that of Pastor Bob Beeman, for the Caesar Kalinowski produced debut 'Human Sacrifice' had to be reprinted with the new logo.

Following the 1990 Ron Goudie produced 'Once Dead' album promotional tour the band splintered. Only Martinez remained to carry on with the name as Farkas, Mancaruso and bassist Roger Dale Martin all quit. Martin founded Biker Blues band TRIPLE ACE whilst the others created DIE HAPPY.

Meantime Martinez enrolled guitarist Derek Sean and drummer Chris Hyde of DELIVERANCE for the 'Destruction Comes' opus.

For the 1992 'Released From The Earth' album Martinez employed guitarist Jamie Mitchell, bass player Joe Monsrb'nik and drummer Jonny Vasquez. Backing vocals came courtesy of MORTIFICATION's Steve Rowe, TORNIQUET men Victor Marcios and David Vasquez and Jimmy Brown of DELIVERENCE. Jonny Vasquez would then join MORTIFICATION for touring.

Touring upon the album release saw DELIVERANCE guitarist George Ochoa as live guitarist. Apparently upon completion of these dates, sometime between 1995 and 1997, Martinez became an atheist.

Undeterred by the scandal Christian Deathsters ULTIMATUM would cover 'Burn' for their third album 'The Mechanics Of Perilous Times'.

Needless to say VENGEANCE RISING remains a hot topic of debate on the Christian music scene to this day.

Albums:
HUMAN SACRIFICE, Intense (1989)
Human Sacrifice / Burn / Mulligan Stew / Receive Him / I Love Hating Evil / Fatal Delay / White Throne / Salvation / From The Dead / Ascension / He Is God / Fill This Place With Blood / Beheaded
ONCE DEAD, Intense (1990)
Warfare / Can't Get Out / Cut Into Pieces / Frontal Lobotomy / Herod's Violent Death / The Whipping Post / Arise / Space Truck'in / Out Of The Will / The Wrath To Come / Into The Abyss / Among The Dead / Interruption
DESTRUCTION COMES, Intense (1991)
You Can't Stop It / The Rising / Before The Time / The Sword / He Don't Own Nothing / Countless Corpses / Thanatos / You Will Bow / Hyde Under Pressure /

Raeqoul
RELEASED UPON THE EARTH, Intense (1992)
Help Me / The Damnation Of Judas And The Salvation Of The Thief / Released Upon The Earth / Human Dark Potential / Instruments Of Death / Lest You Be Judged / Out Of Bounds / Bishop Of Souls / Tion / You Will Be Hated
ANTHOLOGY, Intense (1993)

VERMIN (SWEDEN)
Line-Up: Jimmy Sjøqvist (vocals / guitar), Moses Shitch (guitar), Johan Svensson (bass), Mathias Adamsson (drums)

VERMIN, a Swedish Death Metal troupe, were founded in 1991 issuing a seven track eponymous demo the following year. Further promotional cassettes included 'Life Is Pain' and 'Scum Of The Earth'. The band debuted commercially with the inclusion of one of their tracks on the compilation album 'Requiem Morbid Symphonies Of Death' before Chaos records issued all the VERMIN demos to date collected onto one CD 'Obedience To Insanity'.

The second album 'Plunge Into Oblivion', which saw bassist Johan Svensson replaced by David Melin, included Fred Estby of DISMEMBER.

In early 1997 founder member and guitarist Moses Shtieh decamped. VERMIN underwent a necessary reshuffle shifting Melin to guitar and bringing in bassist Timmy Persson.

Not to be confused with the Australian Nu-Metal VERMIN.

Albums:
OBEDIENCE TO INSANITY, Chaos CHAOSCD 01 (1994)
In Darkness Dwells (Intro) / Enjoy ? / Cremation Sustained / Into Nothingness / Trapped / Psychic Tomb / Obedience To Insanity (Outro) / Life Is Pain / Corroded Conscience / Internal Emptiness / Lunatic Fanatics / Human Extermination / Among The Tombstones (Intro) / Pile Of Pus / Namtab / Rotting Mass Of Human Flesh / Insain Pain (Intro) / Autopsy For Pleasure / Fated (To Die)
PLUNGE INTO OBLIVION, Chaos CHAOSCD 03 (1995)
When Hell Becomes Reality / Slave / Screw / The Silence / Life - See My Sorrow / Enemy / Eternal Love / Denials / Hypochrist / Plunge Into Oblivion / How Many Million / Bitter Hate / San Quentin

MILLENNIUM RIDE, No Fashion
NFR030 (1998)
Hungerface / Circle Of Time / Upright
Infinity / Demon Soul / Bloodlust /
Everlasting / Black / Devil Trip / Broken /
Species

VICTIMS OF INTERNAL DECAY
(Albany, OR, USA)
Line-Up: Lance Thrill (vocals), Terry Geil
(guitar), Nick Wusz (guitar), Ron Farris
(bass), Pat Wombacher (drums)

Although an unashamed Death Metal
band, Oregon's VICTIMS OF INTERNAL
DECAY (V.O.I.D.- "Born and raised on
beef and trees") are unique in not only
pursuing a path of Grunge flavoured
extreme Metal, but in reputedly having a
lead guitarist with one leg!
The band heralded their arrival with the
1989 demo session 'Democrazy' with a
line up of vocalist Lance Thrill, guitarists
Jason Moser and Dave Bruce, bassist
Aaron Baird and drummer Pat
Wombacher. A second tape followed in
1990 entitled 'Terminal Happenings'
which saw Hans Jochimsen on guitar.
V.O.I.D.'s third demo, 1991's 'Dead Fish
White', had John Eddleman on bass.
The 1994 album witnessed the inclusion
of Ron Farris on bass with the
aforementioned monoped Terry Geil on
guitar. The eponymous album included a
version of GREEN RIVER's 'One More
Stitch'. The band's line up would shift
again for a 1996 promotional recording
'Resin 67 Session' with Jochimsen
replaced by Nick Wusz.
Due to Geil's alleged lack of limb the
band are known as "Death on nine legs"!

Albums:
VICTIMS OF INTERNAL DECAY, (1994)
Absolute Worship / Bathed In Sickness /
Bleed / One More Stitch / Jim's Lament /
Consummation / Under The Sun / In
Extremis / False Hate / Sterile Nature

VILE (CA, USA)
Line-Up: Juan Urtega (vocals), Colin
Davis (guitar), Aaron Strong (guitar), Jeff
Hughell (bass), Mike Hamilton (drums)

Shortly after recording VILE's 'Stench Of
The Deceased' album drummer Mike
Hamilton made his exit to join DEEDS OF
FLESH. A former VILE guitarist, Jim
Tkacz, had previously jumped ship to
DEEDS OF FLESH too.

Albums:
STENCH OF THE DECEASED, Vile
(1999)
Abort (The Fetus) / Cradle Of Deceit /
Surgery / Alive To Suffer / Stench... /
Terminal Existence / Severed /
Persecution

VIOLATION (GERMANY)
Line-Up: Wolfgang Dreiseital (vocals),
Alex Schödel (guitar), Larsen Beattie
(guitar), Martin Saalfrank (bass), Claudia
Reich (keyboards), Andreas Schmidt
(drums)

Albums:
BEYOND THE GRAVES, Last Episode
0073542 LEP (1998)
Dark Embrace / Genocide / Thuatra Dé
Danann / Carbonized / Bleeding Souls /
Invocation / Through The Gates Of Infinity
/ Bitterness / Fading Flames Of Life

VIOLENT FORCE (GERMANY)
Line-Up: Lemmie (vocals / guitar),
Stachel (guitar), Waldy (bass), Hille
(drums)

VIOLENT FORCE frontman Lemmie
would later join SACRED CHAO.
Drummer Hille departed to be replaced
by Atomic Steif. However, Steif was to
decamp to join SACRED CHAO also.
Steif later teamed up with SODOM.

Albums:
**MALEVOLENT ASSAULT OF
TOMORROW**, Roadrunner (1987)
Dead City / Soulbursting / Vengeance
And Venom / Malevolent Assault Of
Tomorrow / What About The Time After?
/ Sign Of Evil / Violent Force / The Night
/ Destructed Life / S.D.I.

VIOLENT HEADACHE (SPAIN)
Line-Up: Capo (vocals), Jordi (guitar),
Chico (bass), Tonyo (drums)

Extreme Barcelona act that blend both
male and female lead vocals into a genre-
defying mix of Death Metal, Thrash and
Grindcore. The band would issue the
demo 'Attack Of The Antijetcore
Argaraboys' prior to embarking on a
stream of shared single releases with
international acts. VIOLENT
HEADACHE's 2000 album 'Bombs Of
Crust' features over 50 tracks originally
recorded in 1995.
Singles/EPs:
Split, Psychomania (1991) (7" split

single with CRIPPLE BASTARDS)
Starbation, Anaconda (1992) (7" split single with AGATHOCLES)
Split, Pcum (1993) (7" split single with POSITI CAUSTICO)
Trituradora De Cadaveres, Nat (1997) (7" split single with CARCASS GRINDER)
Condemned Childhood, Blurred 11 (1997) (7" split single with EXCRETED ALIVE)
Bloody Progress, (199-) (7" split single with INTESTINAL DISEASE)
Split, (199-) (7" split single with PROYECTO TERROR)
Split, (199-) (7" split single with UNHOLY GRAVE)

Albums:
BOMBS OF CRUST, Six Weeks (2000)

VIRULENCE (USA)

Albums:
DORMANT STRAINS, JRB V006 (2000)
Meme Epidemics / Evolutionary Masquerade / Cortical Reproductive Abstractions / Branne Cvicene: Defensive Drilling

VISCERA (AUSTRALIA)

Grinding Deathcore act VISCERA display an unhealthy obsession for pornography. The band opened up with a split single shared with PURULENT SPERM CANAL. Demos included the delightful 'Is Your Vagina Normal?' and 'Finger Your Ring'. The band would later share singles with fellow Aussies DECOMPOSING SERENITY and American Grindsters VOMIT SPAWN.

Singles/EPs:
Split, (199-) (7" split single with PURULENT SPERM CANAL)
Skullfucked / Human Urinal / Frolick In Your Fuckhole / Toilet Tarts / Dick Cheesy Slurpy / Drowned In Smegma, Prolapse 02 (1998) (7" split single with DECOMPOSING SERENITY)
Split, No Weak Shit (1998) (7" split single with VOMIT SPAWN)

VISCERAL EVISCERATION
(GERMANY)
Line-Up: Hannes Wuggenig (vocals / guitar), Jürgen Hajek (guitar), Dominik Lirsch (bass), Stephan Sternad (drums)
Albums:
INCESSANT DESIRE FOR PALATABLE

FLESH, Napalm NPR004 (1994)
(I Am) Enamoured Of Dead Bodies / At The Epicurean Gynecologist / Muse Perverse / Knee Deep In Blood I Wade / Chewing Female Genital Parts / Tender Flesh... On The Bier / Gangling Menstrual Blood - Broth For Supper

VITAL REMAINS (RI, USA)
Line-Up: Jeff Gruslin (vocals), Paul Flynn (guitar), Tony Lazaro (guitar), Joe Lewis (bass), Ace Alonzo (drums)

An illustrious name in Death Metal circles. Although firmly in the Death Metal camp VITAL REMAINS infuse their whole being with blasphemous content. The band's first line up for recording of the demo 'Reduced To Ashes' in 1989 comprised vocalist Jeff Gruslin, guitarists Paul Flynn and Tony Lazaro, bass player Tom Supkow and drummer Chris Dupont. A further tape 'Excruciating Pain', with new drummer 'Ace' Alonzo, and a 7" single for French label Thrash 'Black Mass' bolstered the band's reputation and signaled a deal with British label Peaceville Records.
By the recording of 1997's 'Forever Underground' VITAL REMAINS had trimmed down to a trio of Lazaro, bassist Joseph Lewis and drummer David Suzuki.
VITAL REMAINS were included on the 1999 tribute to JUDAS PRIEST album 'Hell Bent For Metal' covering 'You've Got Another Thing Comin'.
Vocalist Jeff Gruslin was replaced by Thorns. However, in 2000 VITAL REMAINS sacked vocalist Thorns as the remaining band members cited alleged drug abuse. VITAL REMAINS rehired Gruslin in time for European dates as part of the 'No Mercy' festival package alongside Poland's VADER, Brazil's REBAELLIUN and Germany's FLESHCRAWL.
Late 2000 found Gruslin back on the scene as part of the prominent WOLFEN SOCIETY project which included erstwhile ACHERON man Vincent Crowley, INCANTATION's Kyle Severn and Lord Ahriman of DARK FUNERAL. The Dutch label Cyronics would re-issue the debut demo 'Reduced To Ashes' in CD format.

Singles/EPs:
Black Mass, Thrash (1991) (7" single)
Amulet Of The Conquering, Peaceville Collectors CC 4 (1993) (Split single with

MORTA SKULD)

Albums:
LET US PRAY, Peaceville CDVILE 58 (1992)
War In Paradise / Of Pure Unholiness / Ceremony Of The Seventh Circle / Uncultivated Grave / Malevolent Invocation / Isolated Magick / Cult Of The Dead / Frozen Terror / Amulet Of The Conquering
INTO COLD DARKNESS, Peaceville (1995)
Immortal Crusade / Under The Moons Fog / Crown Of The Black Hearts / Scrolls Of A Millenium Past / Into Cold Darkness / Descent Into Hell / Angels Of Blasphemy / Dethroned Emperor
FOREVER UNDERGROUND, Osmose Productions OPCD 050 (1997)
Forever Underground / Battle Ground / I am God / Farewell To The Messiah / Eastern Journey / Divine In Fire
DAWN OF THE APOCALYPSE, Osmose Productions (1999)
Intro / Black Magick Curse / Dawn Of The Apocalypse / Sanctity In Blasphemous Ruin / Came No Ray Of Light / Flag Of Victory / Behold The Throne Of Chaos / The Night Has A Thousand Eyes / Societe Des Luciferiens
REDUCED TO ASHES, Cyronics (2000)
Vital Remains / Smoldering Ritual / Morbid Death / Reduced To Ashes / More Brains / Slaughter Shack

VOIVOD (CANADA)

Line-Up: Denis 'Snake' Belanger (vocals / bass), Denis 'Piggy' D'Amour (guitar), Jean-Yves 'Blacky' Theriault (bass), Michael 'Away' Langevin (drums)

Jonquierer based avant-garde Thrash Metal 'Cyberpunk' act VOIVOD mixed Punk, extreme Metal and Sci-Fi in a unique combination that won them many fans during the mid 80's Thrash boom.
The French speaking VOIVOD were assembled in 1983 by frontman Snake ('Denis Belanger), guitarist Piggy (Denis D'Amour), bassist Blacky (Jean-Yves Theriault) and drummer Away (Michael Langevein). Initial VOIVOD gigs had the band including numerous cover versions in their set from the likes of JUDAS PRIEST, MOTÖRHEAD and VENOM.
The band's first forays into the recording studio resulted in the 1984 'To The Death' demo, quickly followed by a live tape 'Morgoth Invasion'.

From the band's official debut in 1984 with a track on one of the infamous 'Metal Massacre' compilations and the inaugural 'War And Pain' album VOIVOD immediately set themselves apart from the Thrash bandwagon.
VOIVOD were forced to pull out of their 'Dimension Hatross' world tour when Piggy was diagnosed with a brain tumour. They toured Europe with support from POSSESSED. 1989's 'Nothingface' features the band's take on PINK FLOYD's 'Astronomy Domine'.
VOIVOD's tenacity and reluctance to compromise was rewarded with a major label deal via MCA Records subsidiary Mechanic for 1991's 'Angel Rat', although Blacky had by this time been replaced by Pierre St Jean.
Snake backed out for 1995's 'Negatron' forcing Piggy and Away into a rethink on the band's future. Deciding to continue as a trio the band pulled in ex-LIQUID INDIAN / THUNDER CIRCUS vocalist / bassist Eric Forrest.
97's 'Phobos' included a cover version of KING CRIMSON's '21st Century Schizoid Man'. Touring to promote the album Forrest was severely injured during a road accident on tour in Germany during 1998.
The band's Montreal show in late 1999 reunited VOIVOD with Snake for one gig, the former frontman guesting with the band.
The 2000 live album 'Lives', recorded at the Dutch Dynamo Festival and the renowned New York CBGB's club, includes a cover of VENOM's 'In League With Satan'.

Singles/EPs:
Thrashing Rage / Slaughter In A Grave / Helldriver / To The Death, Noise N N0050PD (1986) ('Thrashing Rage' EP)
Cockroaches / Too Scared To Scream, Noise NPD 085 (1987) (12" picture disc)
Astronomy Domine (Radio edit) / The Unknown Knows, MCA Mechanic L33-17980 (1989) (Promotion release)
Into My Hypercube / Missing Sequences, MCA Mechanic CD45 18196 (1989) (Promotion release)
Clouds In My House (Remix) / The Prow (Remix) / Angel Rat / Panorama, MCA Mechanic CD45 2000 (1991) (Promotion release)
Fix My Heart / Fix My Heart (Radio edit), MCA MCASP 2822 (1993) (Promotion release)
Lost Machine / Jack Luminous, MCA MCASP 2684 (1993) (Promotion

release)
The Nile Song / Tribal Convictions
(Live), MCA MCASP 2926 (1994)
(Promotion release)
Nanoman / Erosion / Vortex,
Mausoleum MAJC 60018-2 (1996)
(Promotion release)

Albums:
WAR AND PAIN, Roadrunner RR 9825
(1984)
Voivod / Warriors Of Ice / Suck Your Bone
/ Iron Gang / War And Pain / Blower / Live
For Violence / Black City / Nuclear War
RRROOOAAARRR, Noise N0040 (1986)
Korgull The Exterminator / Fuck Off And
Die / Slaughter In A Grave / Ripping
Headaches / Horror / Thrashing Rage /
Helldriver / Build Your Weapons / To The
Death!
DIMENSION HATROSS, Noise N0106-1
(1988)
Prolog... Experiment / Tribal Convictions
/ Chaosmongers / Technocratic
Manipulators / Epilog... Macrosolutions
To Megaproblems / Brain Scan / Psychic
Vacuum / Cosmic Drama
NOTHINGFACE, Noise N 0142-2 (1989)
The Unknown Knows / Nothingface /
Astronomy Domine / Missing Sequences
/ X Ray Mirror / Inner Combustion / Pre-
Ignition / Into My Hypercube / Sub effect
ANGELRAT, MCA MCD 10293 (1991)
Shortwave Intro / Panorama / Clouds In
My House / The Prow / Best Regards /
Twin Dummy / Angel Rat / Golem / The
Outcast / Nuage Fractal / Freedoom /
None Of The Above
THE BEST OF VOIVOD, Noise NO 196-
2 (1992)
Voivod / Ripping Headaches / Korgull
The Exterminator / Tornado / Ravenous
Machine / Cockroaches / Tribal
Convictions / Psychic Vacuum /
Astronomy Domine / The Unknown
Knows / Panorama / The Prow
THE OUTER LIMITS, MCA MCD 10701
(1993)
Fix My Heart / Moonbeam Rider / Le
Pont Noir / The Nile Song / The Lost
Machine / Time Warp / Jack Luminous /
Wrong Way Street / We Are Not Alone
NEGATRON, Hypnotic HYP001CD
(1995)
Insect / Project X / Nanoman / Reality /
Negatron / Planet Hell / Meteor / Cosmic
Conspiracy / Bio TV / Drift / DNA (Don't
No Anything)
PHOBOS, Hypnotic HYPCD 1057
(1997)
Catalepsy I / Rise / Mercury / Phobos /
Bacteria / Temps Mort / The Tower /

Quantum / Neutrino / Forlorn / Catalepsy
II / M-Body / 21st Century Schizoid Man
KRONIK, Hypnotic HYP 1065 (1998)
Forlorn / Nanoman / Mercury / Vortex /
Drift / Erosion / Ion / Project X / Cosmic
Conspiracy / Astronomy Domine /
Nuclear War
LIVES, Century Media 77282 (2000)
Insect / Tribal Convictions / Nanoman /
Nuclear War / Planet Hell / Negatron /
Project X / Cosmic Conspiracy /
Ravenous Medicine / Voivod / In League
With Satan

VOMITING CORPSES (GERMANY)

During 1995 vocalist / bassist Michael
and drummer Heiner broke away creating
ANASARCA in alliance with members of
VAE SOLIS.

Albums:
**COMA: THE SPHERES OF
INFLUENCE**, Invasion IRO13CD (1995)
Kingdom Of The Blind / Dogmas Ignored
/ Banished From Remembrance / Ice
Age Of The Common Sense / Coma... /
Cold Blood / When Doves Cry / Si Vi
Pacem / Island Of Sorrow

VOMITO (BRAZIL)

Splatter Core merchants VOMITO
opened up proceedings with demo tapes
'Fetal Maceration' and 'Saprofagia'. A
split live cassette with CARNAL
TUMOUR followed. In 2000 VOMITO
shared a split album with Australian
Porngrinders   DECOMPOSING
SERENITY.

Albums:
ANATOMICAL PATHOLOGY, (1998)
VOMITO, Lofty Storm Productions (2000)
(Split album with DECOMPOSING
SERENITY)
Intro: Post-Traumatic Headache / Matar
Para Consumir / Necrophagous Gang
Bang / Genital Extirpation / Necrophile /
Sobrevivir / Sierra Eletrica / Fucking The
Virgin Cadaver / Psychopatic Quartering
/ O Fedorento Cheir Da Tua Merda
Vadia / Ellos Comem Su Carne / Gore
Mutilation / Hunting Humans / Gauderia

VOMITORIAL CORPULENCE
(AUSTRALIA)
Line-Up: Jason Mullinder (vocals), Paul
Munton (guitar), Paul Green (bass)
One of the very few Christian Grindcore
bands.

Albums:
SKINSTRIPPER, (2000)
Hammer Inflicted Brain Seizure And
Hemmorhaging Cranial Gestation /
Curse Or Blessing / Malignant
Cankerous Brain Feast And Tumorous
Cerebral Beverage Of The Cranium /
Blink / Numb / Stenching Putrefaction Of
Crepitated Decomposing Carcassile And
Eroded Internal Intestinal Tract And
Organs / Gorefiler Of The Flesh / Life? /
Defleshed / Cudgelate Mephistopheles
Brutally / Do It / One Question And One
Answer / Festering Insalubrious Bowel
Hemmoraging Of Gangrenous
Pustulosus And Abdominal Discharge Of
The Intestinal Tract / Holy Hypocrisy /
Cadaveric Necrotism Of
Neuropathological Catatoniar And ,
Pyrexia Malignant Growth Of The
Cerebrum / Hillbilly Heaven / Cerebral
Turbulency / Turn To Christ / HC4JC /
Excoriating Karrionic Cankerous
Emanation Of Sludge And Ulcerated
Flesh / Pathetic / Grotesque
Mucupurulent Disgorgement / Barnyard
Grind / Carrionic Hackticion /
Abolishment Of Belial and All
Impercating Creation / Death Comes
Quick / C.I.T.D.C. (Christ Is The Demon
Crusher)

VOMITORY (GERMANY)
Line-up: Lefty (vocals), Bio (guitar),
Steve Kocsis (guitar), Cheesy (bass),
Rainer (drums)

VOMITORY formed in late 1989 releasing
their debut single soon after. Added
bassist Cheesy in 1990 prior to releasing
the 'Witches And Demons' demo. Signed
to D&S Records in 1991. Guitarist Steve
Kocsis was enlisted prior to the second
album.
In spite of their name implying otherwise
VOMITORY actually play a distinct brand
of Death Thrash with Funk influences.

Singles/EPs:
Catastrophical Expectations, Vomitory
(1989)

Albums:
HOUR OF TRUTH, D&S Records (1991)
F.T.A. / Witches And Demons / The
Bringer Of Fate / Hour Of Truth / Pull
The Plug / Future Shock / Catastrophical
Expectations / Royal Rumble / Foolsway
BASCHILASOPHOCIC, D&S Records
CDR006 (1994)
Warchild / Free From Hair And Brain /

The Most Effective Vomitory /
Baschilasophocic / Sexjunks / A Little
Song About Dying / One Step To The
Abyss / Hour Of Death / Prophecy /
Pornos In The Parsonage / Tribute

VOMITORY (SWEDEN)
Line-up: Ronnie Olsson (vocals), Ulf
Dalgren (guitar), Urban Gustafsson
(guitar), Bengt Sund (bass), Tobias
Gustafsson (drums)

Between the single and album
VOMITORY released a 1994 demo tape
'Through Sepulcharal Shadows'.

Singles/EPs:
Moribund / Dark Grey Epoch, Witchhunt
9309 (1993)

Albums:
RAPED IN THEIR OWN BLOOD,
Fadeless (1997)
Nerve Gas Clouds / Raped In Their Own
Blood / Dark Grey Epoch / Pure Death /
Through Sepulchural Shadows / Inferno
/ Sad Forgotten Sinister Runes / Into
Winter Through Sorrow / Perdition /
Thorns
REDEMPTION, Fadeless (1999)
The Voyage / Forty Seconds Bloodbath /
Forever In Gloom / Embraced By Pain /
Redemption / Ashes Of Mourning Life /
Partly Dead
REVELATION NAUSEA, Metal Blade
(2000)

VOMIT REMNANTS (JAPAN)
Line-Up: Toshiyasu Kusayanagi (vocals),
Takahiro Kuwabara (guitar), Atsoyuki
Katou (guitar), Ryo Nagamazu (bass),
Keisuke Tsuboi (drums)

Uncompromising Death Metal from Tokyo
in a deliberately mimicked American
school style. VOMIT REMNANTS made
their mark with the demos 'In The Name
Of Vomit' in 1997 and 'Brutally Violated' a
year later. Both of these sessions would
feature FLESHMANGLER vocalist
Shinjiro who would leave the fold in 1999.
For the 'Supreme Entity' album, which
included a cover of SOIL OF FATE's
'Faces Of The Deceased', guitarist
Toshiyasu Kusayanagi switched to lead
vocals.
Touring saw an appearance at the 1999
Ohio 'Deathfest' and European shows in
alliance with FLESHLESS and
GODLESS TRUTH as the band drafted
second guitarist Atsuyuki Katou.

VOMIT REMNANTS toured America in April 2001 on their 'Extermination' dates billed alongside VEHEMENCE, BRODEQUIN and MORGUE. The band would also cut a version of 'Mass Obliteration' for a SUFFOCATION tribute album released by Repulsive Echo Records.

Albums:
SUPREME ENTITY, Macabre Mementos (1999)
Putrifying Dead Flesh / My Blessed Sickness / Decomposed Of Structure / Rotted Human Waste / Macabre Memories / Engorgement / Faces Of The Deceased / Murderous Thoughts Determined
INDEFENSIBLE VEHEMENCE, Supreme Musick (2001)

VOMIT SPAWN (USA)

Extreme Grindcore band founded in 1993. Issued the 1994 'Fetal Lust' promotional tape upfront of a further tape release 'Bootleg From A Keg Party', the latter including IMPETIGO, TERRORIZER and SLAYER cover versions. VOMIT SPAWN would issue a shared 7" single in collaboration with Australian gore mongers VISCERA.

Singles/EPs:
Split, No Weak Shit (1998) (7" split single with VISCERA)

VOMITURITION (FINLAND)
Line-Up: Keijo Bagge (vocals), Mika Aalto (guitar), Mikko Hannuksela (guitar), Harri Huhtalla (bass), Kai Hahto (drums)

VOMITURITION started life as a quartet. The debut mini album had Matti Kovero on bass and Keijo Bagge on second guitar. The second effort 'A Left Over' found Bagge concentrating on lead vocals and Harri Huhtalla on bass.

Albums:
HEAD TALES, Invasion I.R. 004CD (1994)
Inside The Depths Of Mind / Malignancy / Falling / Close Down Time / One's Belief / Ancient Psychotherapy / Olet Vitun Tyhmä (You're Fucking Stupid)
A LEFTOVER, Invasion IRO14CD (1995)
Sacred Tree The Pain / A Beast Revived / Depression / A Leftover / Head Tales / Insucceded / Expectations / Trifle / Improvement - Unimprovement /

Extinction / Abandonment / Malleus Maleficarum

VORACIOUS GANGRENE
(FRANCE)
Line-Up: Guillame (vocals), Jessy (guitar), Pat (guitar), Ben (bass), Stef (drums)

Albums:
HACKED TO DEATH, Voracious Gangrene VG01 (2000)
Hacked And Scattered / Random Gun Carnage / Reconciled By Death / Kill To Possess / Murder With No Valid Reason

VULPECULA (Kansas City, MI, USA)

Death Black Metal band VULPECULA comprises erstwhile ORDER FROM CHAOS and NEPENTHE members vocalist / bassist Chuck Keller and drummer Chris Overton.

Singles/EPs:
The Phoenix Of Creation, Eternal Darkness (1995)

Albums:
FON IMMORTALIS, Merciless (1997)
Astride The Darklands / Fons Immortalis / Down Among Them / Phoenix Of The Creation / The First Point Of Aries / Seven Legions Of Light

WADGE (CANADA)

Canuck Grind-Crustcore Metal band WADGE debuted with the 1993 demo 'Guise'. Split singles with ENEMY SOIL and PRAPARTION H led to an appearance on the 'Grind On The Mind' compilation. WADGE also make their presence felt on the 1997 compilation 'Noise Against The Machine' 7" single, the 1998 compilation cassette 'Carnival Pacino Grande' and a further 7" collection 'Cash, Gash & Trash' on Agitate Records.

Singles/EPs:
Split, Break It Out (1994) (7" split single with ENEMY SOIL)
Split, Regurgitated Semen RSR016 (1996) (7" split single with PRAPARATION H)
On A Mission, Regurgitated Semen RSR021 (1999) (10" single)
Split, Regurgitated Semen RSR026 (2000) (7" split single with SHIT ON COMMAND)

Albums:
WADGE, Regurgitated Semen RSR025 (2000) (Split album with BLOWER)

WAR (AUSTRIA / SWEDEN)
Line-Up: Peter Tägtren, Blackmoon (guitar), It, All, Mikael Hedlund

Deadly assemblage of VONDUR and OPTHALMIA members It and All together with HYPOCRISY and THE ABYSS men Peter Tägtgren and Mikael Hedlund with former DARK FUNERAL guitarist Blackmoon.

Albums:
TOTAL WAR, Necropolis NR019 (1998)
Satan / I Am Elite / Total War / The Sons Of War / Revenge / Reapers Of Stan / Satan's Millenium
WE ARE WAR, (1999)
War / We Are War / Soldiers Of Stan / Rapture 2 / Ave Satan / Kill God / 666 / Infernal / Hell / Execution / Bombenhagel

WARFARE (USA)
Line-Up: Rob Brannon (vocals / guitar), Rich Welzant (bass), Gary Forbes (drums)

A Christian Death Metal trio created in 1992.

WARHAMMER (GERMANY)
Line-Up: Volker Frerich (vocals), Marco Hoffmann (guitar), Rainer Filipiak (guitar), Frank Krynojewski (bass), Rolf Meyn (drums)

WARHAMMER are openly blatant about their appreciation to the cult legends HELLHAMMER. So much so in fact that their music is a deliberate homage to the Swiss forefathers. The band debuted with the demo session 'Towards The Chapter Of Chaos'.
WARHAMMER drafted second guitarist Rainer Filipiak for the 1999 'Deathchrist' outing.

Singles/EPs:
Riders / Blood And Honour / Alone / Warhammer, (199-) ('Riders' EP)

Albums:
THE WINTER OF OUR DISCONTENT, Voices Productions (1997)
Beyond Forgiveness / Damned For Extinction / The Shape Of The Enemy / Warzones / Drowned In Blackness / Devastation Of Silent Resistance / Under The Wings Of The Cross / Imposter Of All Times / The Void Inside The Darkness / The Winter Of Our Discontent / The Horror
DEATHCHRIST, Grind Syndicate Media (1999)
This Graveyard Earth / Mankinds Darkest Day / The Thorn Of Damnation / Deathchrist / The Capacity Of Tragic / Defy The Dark / The Demon's Breed / Among The Dead / The Tempter Of Destruction / The Realm Of Torment
THE DOOM MESSIAH, Nuclear Blast NB 603-2 (2000)
Remorseless Winter / Shadow Of The Decapitator / Cries Of The Forsaken / Hell Is Open… / Cruel Transcendency / The Doom Messiah / The Serpents Tantrum / Cruel And Dying World / In Pain We'll Burn / The Skullcrusher

WARPATH (GERMANY)
Line-Up: Dicker (vocals), Ozzy (guitar), Schröder (guitar), Maurer (bass), Krid (drums)

Hamburg's WARPATH first contributed two tracks to the West Virginia Records compilation album 'Cries Of The Unborn' prior to being offered a deal. The debut album, produced by Andy Classen of HOLY MOSES, features guest vocals from CRONOS mainman Conrad Lant

and Sabina Classen of HOLY MOSES.
In their time WARPATH toured alongside SODOM, FORBIDDEN and GOREFEST. The 1996 album 'Kill Your Enemy' includes a cover version of CRO-MAGS 'Sign Of Hard Times'.
Vocalist 'Dicker' (Dirk Weiss) created RICHTHOFEN in 1997 with ex-HOLY MOSES guitarist Andy Classen.

Albums:
WHEN WAR BEGINS... TRUTH DISSAPEARS, West Virginia 084-57162 (1994)
Resistance Is Useless / Die In Grief / Forest Of Anima / Last Vacation / Wardance / Absolution / You Are The Sickness / Those Crawling Insects / Tightrope Walk / The Ballad Of H / Hypocrite / Black Metal
AGAINST EVERYONE, Steamhammer SPV 084-76812 (1994)
Gate Crasher / In Rage / Against Everyone / Terminus / Give A Shit / I Hate / Night On Earth / Paranoia / Vote Of Censure / That's For Me / Mind Commits Murder / End Of Salvation
MASSIVE, Steamhammer SPV 085-76672 (1995)
Intro / Massive / Pain / Race War / Ambivalence / Save Me From The Wreckage / Fears Of The Past / Remember My Name / Always Near You / Thoughts Begin To Bite / Reason Enough To Die
KILL YOUR ENEMY, Steamhammer SPV 085-18252 (1996)
Kill Your Enemy / A Matter Of Fact / Die Maschine / Frustration Grows / Outburst Of Rage / The Struggle / Sign Of Hard Times / Stomp / Overrollin' / Kill Your Enemy Li

WELTER (HOLLAND)

A solo project of Herr Krieger, otherwise known as 'Centurion' of NECROFEAST. Krieger has credits with NIDHUG and also divides his duties with Polish act MEDEAOTH.
WELTER was originally planned as a two man project together with NIDHUG vocalist / bassist Idimmu titled YSORPEL. With Idimmu's exit Krieger renamed the project WELTER for the demo 'Als Her Licht Vervalt'.
The album 'The Elder Land' includes cover versions of BLACK ART and ABSURD songs.

Albums:
THE ELDER LAND, Berzerker (2000)
Van Kust Tot Heide / Ingvian Pride / Friescre Viking / The Law Of The North - Uitgedroogd Bloed / Infinite Fire Ablaze / Bij De Sabelking / Outro - Travel Over Land And Sea / Mourning Soul

WICKED INNOCENCE
(Salt Lake City, UH, USA)
Line-Up: Dallas Brown (vocals), Jason Martz (guitar), Dave Reeves (bass), Travis Jiron (drums)

Albums:
OMNIPOTENCE, Napalm (199-)
Thought / A Level Higher / Totality / Lines / The Greys / Omnipotence / Return To The Gates Of Rebirth / Epitaph
WORSHIP, Headfucker (199-)
Ragsdale Story / Empty Hand / Living Inside / Jealous And Self Conscious / Minus The Body / Remembering The Future / Before I Die / G.O.D. / Worship / Satan
OPIUM EMPIRE, SIS 0232000 (2001)
A Fire Will Burn / Breed / The Playground / Lack of Breath / Ancient Ones / Heighth / Territory of Wickedness / Kill the Rat / Cunnilingus / Opium Empire

WINDHAM HELL (Seattle, WA, USA)
Line-Up: Leland T. Windham (vocals / guitar / bass), Eric Friesen (guitar / bass / drums / keyboards)

One of the few Death Metal acts to stylistically stand head and shoulders above the pack. WINDHAM HELL, originally conceived as WYMONDHAM in 1986, fuse Death Metal with Baroque and neoclassical guitar work as well as infusing their work with a rich ambience.
As a one man project of guitarist Leland T. Windham WINDHAM HELL's first product emerged as the demo session 'Do Not Fear...Hell Is Here'. A second cassette 'Complete Awareness' surfaced in 1992 landing WINDHAM HELL a deal with Moribund Records.
Windham would be joined by another multi-instrumentalist Eric Friesen for later works.
WINDHAM HELL have, besides their CD output, released a shared tape in 1997 in collaboration with NOTHING.

Albums:
SOUTH FACING EPITAPH, Moribund (1994)
God Swallow / Paste Human /

Garmonbozia / Faces Of Carnage / Terror Soak / Human Foot / Tomorrow You're Going To Die / I Remember Drooling / Exsiccation / Wrapped In Plastique / Post

WINDOW OF SOULS, Moribund (1996)

Laceration Of The Soul / Inversion Soil / Clear Blue Plastique / Ionic Abyss / Excarnation / Crepusculum / Corporal Compendia / Ashes In The Green Chair / Sacremonte (Popocatepeti) / Spiritual Bleeding (Faces II) / The Rain / Darkness Deluge / The Last Of Summer

REFLECTIVE DEPTHS IMBIBE, Moribund (1999)

Postphoria / Nomis Syas Eid / Gathered Suicide / Aeolachrymation (Faces III) / Cold Granitic Bliss / Alpinia / Nocturnally Consumed / Deceased Eternity / Faded Epitaph Crescendo / Lower Levels Of The Skin / Sodflesh / Glacier Walk In Me / Wailing Souls: The Completion Of Awareness / Features Of Euphoria / Safterello Presto

WITCHERY (SWEDEN)

Line-Up: Toxine (vocals), Patrick Jensen (guitar), Ricard Corpse (guitar), Sharlee D'Angelo (bass), Mique (drums)

Trad Metal merchants WITCHERY were created in 1997 from the ashes of SÉANCE and SATANIC SLAUGHTER. Both vocalist Toxine and drummer Mique had also been members of TOTAL DEATH whilst Mique had also been involved in MORGUE together with guitarist Ricard Corpse.

WITCHERY came together when SATANIC SLAUGHTER vocalist Ztephan Dark fired his entire band just days before a scheduled album recording. Undaunted the quartet stuck together to found WITCHERY enlisting MERCYFUL FATE and ILLWILL bassist Sharlee D'Angelo. The latter's priority commitments to MERCYFUL FATE meant that recording of the debut WITCHERY album was delayed until the Autumn of 1997.

The band put in their debut show in April 1998 in Copenhagen although minus Ricard who was too ill to perform.

The 1999 mini album 'Restless And Dead' comprises originals plus various covers including ACCEPT's 'Restless And Wild', BLACK SABBATH's 'Neon Knights', W.A.S.P.'s 'I Wanna Be Somebody' and JUDAS PRIEST's 'Riding On The Wind'.

WITCHERY put in a showing at the renowned German Wacken Metal festival in 1999.

Guitarist Patrick Jensen, also operates with THE HAUNTED. Toxine and Corpse also busy themselves with INFERNAL. Mique has a side project entitled RHOCA GIL.

Latterly WITCHERY have cut versions of KING DIAMOND's 'The Shrine' and the SCORPIONS 'China White' for tribute albums.

Albums:

RESTLESS AND DEAD, Necropolis NR029 (1998)

The Reaper / Witchery / Midnight At The Graveyard / The Hangman / Awaiting The Exorcist / All Evil / House Of Raining Blood / Into Purgatory / Born In The Night / Restless And Dead

WITCHBURNER, Necropolis NR034 (1999)

Fast As A Shark / I Wanna Be Somebody / Riding On The Wind / Neon Knights / The Howling / The Executioner / Witchburner

DEAD, HOT AND READY, Necropolis (2000)

Demonication / A Paler Shade Of Death / The Guillotine / Resurrection / Full Moon / The Dead And The Dance Done / Dead, Hot And Ready / The Devil's Triangle / Call Of The Coven / On A Black Horse Thru Hell…

WITHERED BEAUTY (SWEDEN)

Line-Up: Daniel Bryntse (vocals / guitar), William Blackmon (guitar), Tobias Björklund (bass), Jonas Lindstro (drums)

A Swedish Death Black Metal band rooted in the Death Metal act CONSPIRACY of which founder members frontman Daniel Bryntse and guitarist Magnus Björk paid their dues. Bryntse was also earlier a member of STENCH.

A brace of mid 90's demos 'Screaming From The Forest' and 'Through Silent Skies' led to a deal with the German Nuclear Blast concern. The eponymous 1997 album being produced by HYPOCRISY's Peter Tägtgren.

Following the album Björk departed and guitarist William Blackmon filled the gap. Drummer Jonas Lindstrom was also employed to take over percussion, previously handled by Bryntse.

Bryntse spreads his talents far and wide appearing as bassist in SORCERY and as a member of WINDWALKER and Doom act FORLORN. As if all this activity was not enough he operates in Black

Metal act MORRAMON under the pseudonym of 'Vortex' and plays live with Punk band KALLT STAÄL.

Albums:
WITHERED BEAUTY, Nuclear Blast (1997)
Lies / Broken / Veil Of Nothing / The Worm / Through Silent Skies / Twilight Dreaming / Dying Alone / Failure / Joust / He Who Comes With The Dawn

WITHERED EARTH
(Rochester, NY, USA)
Line-Up: Adam Bonacci (vocals), Chris Burgio (guitar), Ron Cortese (guitar), Fred Decoste (bass), John Paradiso (drums)

WITHERED EARTH came into being in 1995 from a union of former DISGORGED members along with drummer John Paradiso of WITHIN.

Albums:
FORGOTTEN SUNRISE, (1999)
Forgotten Sunrise / The Nocturnium / Heaven Abandon / Dominion Under Angels Graves - The Astral Dread / Eternity Bleeds The Silence / There After The Fallen Praise / Growning / A Violent September Moon / Heaven's Abandon (Live) / Supernatural Terror Unearthed By Two Storms(Live)

WITHERING SURFACE (DENMARK)
Line-Up: Michael H. Anderson (vocals), Allan Tvedebrink (guitar), Heinz Schultz (guitar), Kaspar Boye-Larsen (bass), Jakob Grundel (drums)

WITHERING SURFACE were formed in Naesved during October 1994. National Danish radio voted their 1995 demo as the best demo recording of that year greatly boosting the band's profile.
The band's first commercially available recordings came with the inclusion of a track on the Serious Entertainment compilation album 'Extremity Rising Volume One'. Promoting this release WITHERING SURFACE undertook gigs with the likes of A CANOUROUS QUINTET, DAWN and INIQUITY.
The debut WITHERING SURFACE album boasts a guest appearance from IN FLAMES and HAMMERFALL man Jesper Strömblad and is produced by the DECAMERON duo of Fredrik Nordström and Alex Losbäck. Guitarist Morten Ryberg though was to lose his place to

Heinz Schultz.
Shows in Germany saw support dates to NIGHT IN GALES and PURGATORY.

Albums:
SCARLET SILHOUETTES, Euphonious PHONI 007 (1997)
Scarlet Silhouettes / Beautybeast / A Lily White Sign / … And She Blossomed / Majestic Mistress / Farewell / Behind The Other Side / Pityful Emblems / Your Shadow, My Shelter
THE NUDE BALLET, (199-)
Wither / Ode For You / Dreaming Purple / Will She Defy / Black As I / Whorebride / The Last One / Nude And Humble / Dancing With Fairies / Her Valley / The Ballet

WITHOUT GRIEF (SWEDEN)
Line-Up: Jonas Granvik (vocals), Tobias Ols (guitar), Daniel Thide (guitar), Bjorn Tauman (bass), Patrik Johannsson (drums)

WITHOUT GRIEF also employed bassist Ola Berg.

Albums:
DEFLOWER, Serious Entertainment SE008CD (1997)
Suicidal Stone / The Last Days / Deflower / Shallow Grave / The Failures Crown / Your Empty Eyes / Betrayer Of Compulsion / Vocalise
ABSORBING THE ASHES, Serious Entertainment (1999)
Kingdom Of Hatred / Lifeless / Ungodly / Instrumental / To The Evil / Blackborn Soul / Heaven Torn Apart / Only Darkness Lies Ahead

WITSCHSMELLER PURSUIVANT
(BELGIUM)
Line-Up: Lucifer Vecken (vocals), Roel Van Steeburger (guitar), Paul Evrard (guitar), Mike Mertens (bass), Luc Geenen (drums)

A Death Metal band whose title the band openly admit to having been inspired by the satirical TV series 'Blackadder'. Founded in 1994 by twin guitarists Lucifer Vecken and Paul Evrard together with bassist Mike Mertens. With the addition of ex-REDEFINED, SYSTEM SHIT and APOPLEXY guitarist Roel Van Steeburger the band maneuvered Vecken to the lead vocalist slot. WITSCHSMELLER PURSUIVANT's first candidate on the drum stool was Jakke

Merten but he would make way for former REDEFINED and DOMESTIC VIOLENCE man Luc Geenen. Geenen also operates as vocalist for MORBID VISIONS.

Albums:
MELISSA'S BIRTHDAY, (1998)
ENTER DELIRIUM, (2001)

WIZZARD (FINLAND)

Line-Up: Teemu Kautonen (vocals / bass), Dan (guitar), Grobi (drums)

WIZZARD mainman Teemu Kautonen is ex-DARKWOODS MY BETROTHED and NATTVINDENS GRAT. WIZZARD debuted with the demo 'I Am The King'. Although recorded in 1996 financial uncertainties with the band's German label resulted in a three year delay before the release of the debut album.

WIZZARD's early line up comprised of Kautonen, guitarist Hellboozer, second guitarist Demonos Sora of BARATHRUM and drummer Ville. After recording of the first record Wellu took over the drum position before Kautonen relocated to Germany establishing WIZZARD as an all new trio rounded off by THARGOS members guitarist Dan and drummer Grobi. By August of 1997 though the man was back in Finland laying down the sophomore 'Devilmusick' album for Spinefarm Records.

Line up for this release was Kautonen, guitarist Wilska Torquemada and drummer J. Crow. For live work another DARKWOODS MY BETROTHED man, drummer Tero, joined the fold. A package tour of Finland with BARATHRUM, HORNA and BABYLON WHORES was undertaken with JeeJee on second guitar and Torquemada switched to bass.

Further Finnish dates in April 1998 witnessed the departure of Tero and inclusion of erstwhile NIGHTWISH guitarist Samppa. With Pasi making up the numbers on drums a third album was recorded for Near Dark Productions but fiscal matters once more dogged the band and the album would be shelved. Fortunately for WIZZARD Massacre Records sub division Gutter Records licensed the album 'Songs Of Sin And Decadence' for 2000 release. WIZZARD's 2000 EP 'Tormentor' sees a cover of JUDAS PRIEST's 'Breaking The Law'. Kautonen relocated back to Germany and also resurrected his union with Dan and Grobi for a further

incarnation of WIZZARD.

Singles/EPs:
Songs Of Sin and Decadence / I Am The King / Breaking The Law / Get Slaughtered, Gutter (2000) ('Tormentor' EP)

Albums:
DEVILMUSICK, Spinefarm (1997)
Rock n' Roll (Devil's Music) / Feathers Burn, Leather Doesn't / One Way Ticket To Hell / Little Lyndsey / ...Down The Pit Of Doom / Iron, Speed, Metal / Dirty As Fuck / Satan's Blues (In A Minor) / Vultures Over Golgotha / Revenge Of The Witch
WIZZARD, Nasgûl's Eyrie Productions NEP016 (1999)
Black Leather And Cold Metal / Fenris Is Loose! / Demons Blood / The Lord Of Shadows / I Am The King / Get Your Kicks On Route 666 / Possessed By Inferno / Thou Daughter Of Fire / Pestilence / Saviours Of Metal / When The Sun Goes Down / My Unholy Witch / Leather, Booze And Rock n' Roll / Hot Lead / Sabbath
SONGS OF SIN AND DECADENCE, Gutter (2000)
Sins Of A Past Life / Temple Of Eternal Evil / A Midnight Rendezvous / The Fire Of Volcanus / Angel De La Barthe / Sundown Over Lavenham / Tormentor / Nacht Der Verdammten Seele / The Left Hand Of Eternity / Harbingers Of Metal

WOMBATTH (SWEDEN)

Line-Up: Tomas Lindfors (vocals), Tobbe Holmgren (guitar), Håkan Stevemark (guitar), Richard Lagberg (bass), Roger Enstadt (drums)

Singles/EPs:
Several Shapes / Corporal Punishment, Thrash THIN001 (1992)
Descent Into A Maelstrom / Laughter Through Thousand Winds / Lies After Cries Hope / Lavatory Suicide Remains, Napalm NPR 003 (1995) ('Lavatory' EP)

Albums:
INTERNAL CAUSTIC TORMENTS, Thrash CD-852102 (1993)

WORMED (SPAIN)

Line-Up: J. Oliver, Dani, Guillemoth, Phlegeton, Andy. C (drums)

Madrid Death Metal band WORMED date back to 1998. The self financed EP 'Floating Cadaver In The Monochrome', issued in 1999, was reissued by Colombian label Supreme Music. WORMED drummer Andy C. would loan himself to premier Spanish act AVULSED for their 2000 American dates.

In 2001 WORMED cut a version of 'Bloodchurn' for the Repulsive Echoes SUFFOCATION tribute album. Members of WORMED also operate the Grindcrust project band UNSANE CRISIS.

Singles/EPs:
Pulses In Rhombus Forms /
Ectoplasmic Iconosphere I / Ectoplasmic Iconosphere II / Floating Cadaver In The Monochrome, Wormed (1999) ('Floating Cadaver In The Monochrome' EP)

WOTAN (GERMANY)
Line-Up: Carsten Pusche (vocals), Robert Jonas (guitar), Brian Naunheim (guitar), Dirk Nuber (bass), Sascha Rankel (drums)

WOTAN take their name as signifying 'World Of Terror And Nausea'. A 1992 album produced by Paul Grau was shelved after recording and never released.

WOTAN have performed with the likes of ENTOMBED, GRAVE, ASPHYX, BENEDICTION and RAGE to name but a few.

Albums:
TRANQUILITY, D&S Records DSRCD 0017 (1997)
Assassinator / Face Of Truth / Burnt To Death / Bring It To An End / Wheel Of Pain / Idiocy Of Faith / Chained Man / Dark Dreams / Incarnation

WYNJARA (USA)

WYNJARA, named after an Aboriginal dialect, include former MONSTROSITY and ALAS guitarist Jason Morgan and MALEVOLENT CREATION and DIVINE EMPIRE six stringer J.P. Soars. The 2000 album includes a version of the SCORPIONS 'Animal Magnetism'.

Albums:
WYNJARA, Nocturnal Art Productions (2000)

XENOMORPH
(HOLLAND)
Line-Up: Death Xcelerator
(vocals), Coert Zwart
(guitar), C. Black (guitar),
Ciro Palma (drums)

XENOMORPH included in the ranks erstwhile DISSECT drummer Ciro Palma as well as ex-members of PUTREFY, EJACULATE and TERRAFORCE. The band's opening demos 'Carnificated Dreams' and 'Passion Dance' were released as the 'Acardiacus' album by Teutonic Existence Records. Palma would later join WITHIN TEMPTATION.

Albums:
ACARDIACUS, Teutonic Existence TER 008 (1997)
Acardiacus / Irrelevant Life / Abandoned (Body) / Carnificated Dreams / Moodswings / Wolf / A Trip To Catatonia / Collector Of Pain / The Frost Is All Over / Passion Dance
BANEFUL STEALTH DESIRE, System Shock (2001)

XYSMA (FINLAND)
Line-Up: Joanitor Mustaco (vocals), Thee Stranius (guitar), Mr. Lawny (guitar), Heavenly (bass), Marvelous S. Safe (drums)

Progressive Death Metal outfit from Finland. XYSMA debuted with the 1987 demo 'Swarming Of Maggots'. For the 1990 debut 'Yeah' the band credited themselves as vocalist Janitor, guitarist Olli Nurminen, bass player Vesa Litti and drummer Teppo Pulli.

Albums:
YEAH, Come Back (1990)
Why Am I I ? / On The Hill Of Desecration / Uranus Falls / Aspirations / Reflections Of Eternity / First Sunbeams Of The New Beginning / Above The Horizon / Importance Of The Dimensionless Mirage / Until I Reach The Unattainable / There's Only One Sun / Written Into The Sky / CCPT 2
ABOVE THE MIND OF MORBIDITY, Come Back (1993)
Foetal Mush / Paradise Of Steaming Cadavers / Entangled In Shreds / Mild Stench Of Rot / Dismemberment In Trance / Cranial Cradle
DELUXE, Spinefarm SPI 020 CD (1994)
I Feel Like Lou Reed / Hard Without Tenderness / Nice Pale / Need / Green

Gas Station Jacket / Le Mans 66 / So Divine / Getting Emotional / Head Off / So Divine (Reprise) / Viewmaster
LOTTO, Spinefarm SPI 029 CD (1995)
Shortest Route / We Just Came Inside / Do n' Do / New Gel In Town / Aquanaut / Shoes / One Hell Of A Man / The Tram / Millionaire / Bravado
ABOVE THE MIND OF MORBIDITY / YEAH, Come Back 84-140372 (199-)
Why Am I I ? / On The Hill Of Desecration / Uranus Falls / Aspirations / Reflections Of Eternity / First Sunbeams Of The New Beginning / Above The Horizon / Importance Of The Dimensionless Mirage / Until I Reach The Unattainable / There's Only One Sun / Written Into The Sky / Foetal Mush / Paradise Of Steaming Cadavers / Entangled In Shreds / Mild Stench Of Rot / Dismemberment In Trance / Cranial Cradle

ZAO (USA)
Line-Up: Cory Darst (vocals), Scott Melinger (guitar), Rob Horner (bass), Jesse Smith (drums)

ZAO's line up has proven to be almost as turbulent as the unique brand of music the band offers. Since their inception ZAO have sought to defy the critics mixing down tuned Death Metal with harsh tempo changes, acoustic passages and waves of feedback. All this overlaid with menacingly guttural and eerie whispered vocals extolling the band's Christian virtues.

The only core remaining member of the band is drummer Jesse Smith. ZAO's original incarnation seeing Smith joined by vocalist Eric Reeder, guitarist Roy Goudy and bassist Mic Cox. Second guitarist Ron Gray had joined up prior to signing to Tooth And Nail Records in September of 1996. Reeder would be supplanted by Shawn Jonas and Cox by Kevin Moran.

Prior to the release of 1998's 'Where Blood And Fire Bring Rest' ZAO split asunder as the entire band upped and left Smith. The undaunted drummer regrouped with a fresh new entity under the ZAO banner consisting of vocalist Daniel Weyrandt and guitarists Russ Cogdell and Brett Detar. A later recruit, Rob Horner on bass, brought the band back up to full strength.

ZAO's 1999 album 'Liberate Te Ex Infernis (Save Yourself From Hell)' proved to be a concept affair based upon five cycles of Dante's 'Inferno'. Both guitarists would drift away to create new acts with Cogdell founding LOS CAPITINOS and Detar JULIANA THEORY.

In December of 2000 Weyrandt opted out of ZAO to forge the Grindcore band THEY THAT KILL THEIR MASTERS.

ZAO would sign to the German label Century Media for the release of their eponymous Barry Poynter produced 2001 album. ZAO now stood at a quartet of Smith, Horner, guitarist Scott Melinger and former ENTRUST vocalist Cory Darst.

News emerged in the spring of 2001 that Smith was involved in a twin drummer collaboration billed as AMERICAN SPECTATOR in union with COALESCE members singer Sean Ingram and drummer James Dewees together with TFU personnel bassist Don Clark and guitarist Ryan Clark.

ZAO meantime toured America in March with support from BOYWUNDER and geared up for summer shows alongside LIVING SACRIFICE.

Singles/EPs:
Flight / Security, (1998) (Split EP with OUTCAST)
Skin Like Winter / Walk On By, Walk On Me (The Pianist's Prophecy), (1998) (Split EP with TRAINING FOR UTOPIA)
Repressed, (199-) (7" split single with THROUGH AND THROUGH)

Albums:
ALL ELSE FAILED, Tooth And Nail (1997)
Resistance / In Loving Kindness / Endure / Growing In Grace / Foresight / PS77 / Exchange / In These Times Of Silence / A Simple Reminder / All Else Failed
SPLINTER THROUGH THE BIRTH OF SEPERATION, Solid State (1997)
Times Of Separation / Surrounds Me / Exchange / Particle / Repressed / In Loving Kindness / Endure / The Children Cry For Help / Resistance / Song 1
WHERE BLOOD AND FIRE BRING REST, Solid State (1998)
Lies Of Serpents, A River Of Tears / To Think Of You Is To Treasure An Absent Memory / A Full Farewell / March / Ember / Ravage Ritual / Fifteen Rhema / For A Fair Desire / The Latter Rain / Violet
LIBERATE TE EX INFERIS (SAVE YOURSELF FROM HELL), Solid State (1999)
Intro / Savannah / Autopsy / If These Scars Could Speak / The Ghost Psalm / Desire The End / Dark Cold Soul / Skin Like Winter / Kathleen Barbra / Man In Cage Jack Wilson
ZAO, Century Media (2001)
5 Year Winter / Alive Is Dead / Tool To Scream / Witchhunter / Trash Can Hands / The Race Of Standing Still / F.J.L. / The End Of His World / The Dreams That Don't Come True / At Zero

Also available from

Rockdetector
A-Z of
BLACK METAL
Garry Sharpe-Young

Throughout the history of Rock no other genre has pushed the boundaries of aural extremity and social rebellion quite like Black Metal. Many of the bands in this book operate way beyond the parameters of the established Rock scene carving their own left hand path in the darkest depths of true underground music.

Over a decade Black Metal has spawned legions of bands making up a truly global rebellion. For the first time ever this ultimate authority documents detailed biographies, line-ups and full discographies with track listings of over 2,000 groups.

Included are in-depth treatises on the major artists such as CRADLE OF FILTH, DIMMU BORGIR, EMPEROR, MAYHEM, IMMOR-

TAL and MARDUK as well as spanning out to include sub-genres such as Viking Metal, the Black Ambient scene and even the ultimate irony of Christian Black Metal. Also chronicled are the originators such as VENOM, WITCHFYNDE, BATHORY and MERCYFUL FATE.

Paper covers, 416 pages, £14.99 in UK

Also available from British Steel

THE METAL COLLECTORS SERIES

WITCHFYNDE – THE BEST OF WITCHFYNDE
CDMETAL 1

Witchfynde were part of the New Wave Of British Heavy Metal (N.W.O.B.H.M.) of the early 80's that spawned the likes of Iron Maiden, Def Leppard and Judas Priest. Witchfynde still have a great significance on the later generations of Heavy Metal artists, Metallica and Paradise Lost regularly state the band as an influence. This CD includes 16 prime cuts that features the singles, "Give Em Hell", "In The Stars" and I'd Rather Go Wild as well as the best tracks from their rare LP's "Give Em Hell", "Stagefright" and "Cloak And Dagger". "Iron Page's" journalist Matthias Mader, an expert in the field has written the liner notes for this release on our Metal Series.
Tracklisting: Give 'Em Hell/ Unto The Ages Of The Ages / Ready To Roll / Leaving Nadir / Gettin' Heavy / Pay Now-Love Later / Stage Fright / Wake Up Screaming / Moon Magic / In The Stars / The Devil's Playground / I'd Rather Go Wild / Cloak And Dagger / Cry Wolf / Stay Away / Fra Diabolo

VARIOUS – HEAVY METAL RECORDS SINGLES COLLECTION VOL. 1
CDMETAL 3

This is a fifteen track round up of the first batch of singles released by Heavy Metal Records, the legendary Metal label of the early 80's. Again a highly collectable and expensive package when originally released, with rare and collectable tracks from, Buffalo, Dragster, Last Flight, Split Beaver, Satanic Rites and Handsome Beasts. This release appears on CD for the first time, with a full colour booklet that contains a full discography, detailed liner notes and pictures of each of the sleeves.
Tracklisting: HANDSOME BEASTS - All Riot Now / The Mark Of The Beast / Breaker / Crazy / One In A Crowd BUFFALO – Battle Torn Heroes / Women Of The Night DRAGSTER – Ambitions / Won't Bring You Back LAST FLIGHT – Dance To The Music / I'm Ready SPLIT BEAVER – Savage / Hound Of Hell SATANIC RITES – Live To Ride / Hit And Run

Also available from British Steel

THE METAL COLLECTORS SERIES

HERITAGE – REMORSE CODE
CDMETAL 4

First released by Rondelet Records in 1982 this was four piece Heritage's one and only LP and this is the first time it has ever appeared on CD. The single "Strange Place To Be" is featured on this release from one of the 'forgotten heroes' of the entire NWOBHM movement.

Tracklisting: Remorse Code / Attack Attack / Endless Flight / For Good Or Bad / Need You Today / Strange Place To Be / Slipping Away / Change Your Mood / Rudy And The Zips / A Fighting Chance / BONUS TRACKS: Misunderstood / Strange Place To Be (Single Version)

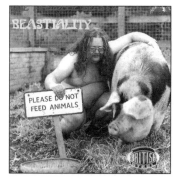

THE HANDSOME BEASTS - BEASTIALITY
CDMETAL 5

First time on CD for this legendary LP, originally issued as the first release by Wolverhampton based Heavy Metal Records. The original 9 track album has now been joined by four bonus cuts including the singles "All Riot Now" and "Sweeties" to give the definitive Handsome Beasts collection.

Tracklisting: Sweeties / David's Song / Breaker / One In A Crowd / Local Heroes / Another Day / Tearing Me Apart / High Speed / BONUS TRACKS: The Mark Of A Beast / All Riot Now / Sweeties (Single Version) / You're On Your Own

Also available from British Steel

THE METAL COLLECTORS SERIES

GASKIN – END OF THE WORLD / NO WAY OUT
CDMETAL 6

Gaskin were one of the most influential N.W.O.B.H.M. bands, to this day bands cite them as a major influence. In 1991 Lars Ulrich of Metallica included Gaskin on the "NWOBHM '79 Revisited" compilation he released. This double album on one CD features two extremely rare and collectable albums from the band. The original artwork is re-produced, with a full discography.
Tracklisting: END OF THE WORLD - Sweet Dream Maker / Victim Of The City / Despiser / Burning Alive / The Day Thou Gavest Lord Hath Ended / End Of The World / On My Way / Lonely Man / I'm No Fool / Handful of Reasons NO WAY OUT - Dirty Money / Free Man / Just Like A Movie Star / Say Your Last Word / Broken Up / Ready For Love / Come Back To Me / High Crime Zone / Queen Of Flames / No Way Out.

VARIOUS – N.W.O.B.H.M. RARITIES VOL. 2
CDMETAL 7

This album features 18 tracks from some of the finest N.W.O.B.H.M. acts of the early 80's, with nearly all of the tracks being released on CD for the first time. Included are the first two Samson singles, Stormtrooper, Xero, Paralex, The EF Band, Shiva and Janine. All the singles have a combined collectors value of over 300 (pounds). Pictures of each of the sleeves are included in the package.
Tracklisting: SAMSON – Telephone / Leavin' You STORMTROOPER – Pride Before A Fall / Still Comin' Home JANINE – Crazy On You / Candy XERO – Oh Baby / Hold On / Killer Frog PARALEX – White Lightning / Travelling Man / Black Widow SAMSON – Mr Rock 'n' Roll / Drivin' Music SHIVA – Rock Lives On / Sympathy EF BAND – Another Day Gone / Nightangel

Also available from British Steel

THE METAL COLLECTORS SERIES

VARIOUS – N.W.O.B.H.M. RARITIES VOL. 3
CDMETAL 14

Volume three of British Steel's series collecting together many ultra rare singles releases from the late 70's - early 80's new wave of British Heavy Metal movement, none of which have ever appeared on CD before. Vol.3 includes bands such as Twisted Ace, Soldier and Jaguar, plus the very first single by Girlschool.
Tracklisting: GIRLSCHOOL - Take It All Away / It Could Be Better TWISTED ACE - I Won't Surrender / Firebird SOLDIER Sheralee / Force JAGUAR - Back Street Woman / Chasing The Dragon DENIGH - No Way / Running STATIC Voice On The Line / Stealin' SEVENTH SON - Metal To The Moon / Sound And Fury WHITE LIGHTNING - This Poison Fountain / Hypocrite DRAGONSLAYER - I Want Your Life / Satan Is Free / Broken Head

VARIOUS - ROXCALIBUR
CDMETAL 15

This legendary 14 track compilation from the 1980's is released on CD for the first time ever. All cuts are unique to this album which gathered together some of the New Wave of British heavy metal scenes rising stars and includes contributions from Black Rose, Marauder, Battleaxe and Skitzofrenik.
Tracklisting: BLACK ROSE - No Point Runnin' / Ridin' High BRANDS HATCH - Brands Hatch / No Return BATTLEAXE - Burn This Town / Battleaxe SATAN - Oppression / The Executioner MARAUDER - Battlefield / Woman Of The Night UNTER DEN LINDEN - Wings Of Night / Man At The Bottom SKITZOFRENIK - Exodus / Keep Right On

THE METAL COLLECTORS SERIES

Available from all good record stores, plus mail-order with
VISA or MASTERCARD facilities.
Call 00 44 (0) 207 371 5844 for details.
E Mail jon@cherryred.co.uk
or
Write to the mail-order department at:
Cherry Red, Unit 17, Elysium Gate West, 126-128 New King's Road,
London SW6 4LZ.

CD Prices including postage:
£9.95 in the UK, £10.45 in Europe and £10.95 for the rest of the world.

CHERRY RED BOOKS

We are always looking for interesting books to publish.
They can be either new manuscripts or re-issues of deleted books.
If you have any good ideas then please
get in touch with us.

CHERRY RED BOOKS
a division of Cherry Red Records Ltd.
Unit 17, Elysium Gate West,
126-128 New King's Road
London sw6 4lz

E-mail: iain@cherryred.co.uk

Web: www.cherryred.co.uk